W9-BTO-092

HISTORY
OF
THE SCANDINAVIAN MISSION

This is a volume in the Arno Press
collection

SCANDINAVIANS IN AMERICA

Advisory Editor
Franklin D. Scott

Editorial Board
Arlow W. Andersen
H. Arnold Barton

See last pages of this volume for a
complete list of titles

BX
8617
. S3
. J4

History

OF THE

Scandinavian Mission

ANDREW JENSON

ARNO PRESS
A New York Times Company
New York • 1979

NOV 1 0 1986

472969

Publisher's Note: This book has been reproduced from the best available copy.

Editorial Supervision: Steven Bedney

————

Reprint Edition 1979 by Arno Press Inc.

SCANDINAVIANS IN AMERICA
ISBN for complete set: 0-405-11628-4
See last pages of this volume for titles.

Manufactured in the United States of America

————

Library of Congress Cataloging in Publication Data

Jenson, Andrew, 1850-1941.
    History of the Scandinavian mission.

    (Scandinavians in America)
    Reprint of the 1927 ed. published by the Deseret
News Press, Salt Lake City, Utah.
    1. Mormons and Mormonism in Scandinavia.
2. Missions--Scandinavia. 3. Scandinavia--
Church history. I. Title. II. Series.
BX8617.S3J4 1979   266'.93'48   78-15190
ISBN 0-405-11643-8

History

OF THE

Scandinavian Mission

BY

ANDREW JENSON
Assistant Church Historian

Author of "Church Chronology," "L.
D. S. Biographical Encyclopedia," "Joseph Smiths Levnetslob." "Kirkens Hi-
storie," "Jorden Rundt," etc. Formerly
editor of the "Historical Record," "Morgenstjernen," "Bikuben," etc. Special
correspondent of "The Deseret News" and
contributor of articles to a number of
other periodicals.

PRINTED BY THE DESERET NEWS PRESS
SALT LAKE CITY, UTAH
1927

ERASTUS SNOW
Founder of the Scandinavian Mission

PREFACE

WHEN the author of this volume filled his first mission for the Church to Europe in 1873-1875, he commenced to gather material for a history of the Scandinavian Mission from the original records kept in the different branches of the Aalborg Conference, Denmark, where he labored. On his second mission, in 1879-1881, when he filled the position of writer and translator for "Skandinaviens Stjerne" at the mission headquarters in Copenhagen, he gathered additional data from records kept in several of the other conferences and branches of the mission, and also gathered items from Church publications as well as from private journals and other sources. Then after his return home he culled data from the "Deseret News" and other periodicals, as well as from written Church documents, which enabled him to edit "Erindringer fra Missionen i Skandinavien" (Memoirs from the Scandinavian Mission), together with a number of biographies, etc., in the Danish-Norwegian language, which he published in four volumes of a periodical called "Morgenstjernen." While the work was progressing, he became intimately acquainted with the late Apostle Erastus Snow, the founder of the Scandinavian Mission, Elders John E. Forsgren, Peter O. Hansen, John Van Cott, Jesse N. Smith, Wm. W. Cluff, Canute Peterson, Chr. G. Larsen, Ola N. Liljenquist, Svend C. Larsen, and scores of others, who figured prominently in the early days of the mission. From them the author obtained much valuable information, which had never been written or printed before, but which is now incorporated in this volume. Finally he became associated with the Historian's Office, and on his historical tour through practically all the missionary fields of the Church in 1895-1897, he gathered all the old records he could find in these missions and shipped them to the Historian's Office, Salt Lake City, where they are now safely housed.

Next it became his privilege, as one of the assistant Church historians, to compile histories of all the Latter-day Saint missions, as well as of the Stakes of Zion, and, in pursuance of this labor, he compiled a voluminous history of the Scandinavian Mission in eighteen large manuscript volumes, covering a period of 78 years, from which material he has written this work now issued from the press.

In the onerous work of compilation, the author has been ably assisted by Elder J. M. Sjödahl, who has contributed most of the biographical notes contained in this book. The author is also indebted to Dr. John A. Widtsoe for valuable suggestions and encouragement, to Elders A. Wm. Lund and Hugo D. E. Peterson for efficient aid rendered in proof-reading, to Mrs. Mary F. Kelly Pye, who is an expert in research work, to Elder Adam L. Petersen, and to others.

No pains have been spared to make the work authentic and reliable in every particular. It has been a labor of love on the part of the author, who now takes pleasure in presenting the "History of the Scandinavian Mission" to the Latter-day Saints and their friends everywhere. It is the author's tribute to his race—the stalwart sons and daughters of the North—and he fondly hopes that, after he shall have passed to the Great Beyond, he may still live in the memory of his fellow-men as one who, during his sojourn in mortality, endeavored to the best of his ability to tell the story of a God-fearing people, whose devotion, integrity and noble characteristics may serve as an inspiration to future generations.

ANDREW JENSON.

TABLE OF CONTENTS
HISTORY OF THE SCANDINAVIAN MISSION

HISTORY OF THE DANISH-NORWEGIAN MISSION

HISTORY OF THE SWEDISH MISSION

HISTORY OF THE DANISH MISSION

HISTORY OF THE NORWEGIAN MISSION

ILLUSTRATIONS

History of the Scandinavian Mission

CHAPTER 1 (1850)

First mission of the Church—First missionaries called to continental Europe—Remarkable
journey across the Plains—Hospitality of
Saints of Kanesville, Iowa—Substantial assistance rendered the missionaries by Saints
in the States—Crossing the Atlantic—Generosity shown by the Saints in Great Britain—Arrival of Apostle Erastus Snow and fellow-missionaries in Copenhagen, Denmark.

When the gospel of Jesus Christ
in its fulness was restored to the
earth in the early part of the Nineteenth Century, through the instrumentality of the Prophet Joseph
Smith, the divine command was
given that it should be preached "to
every nation, and kindred, and tongue,
and people" (Rev. 14:6); or, as
Matthew records it, in the language
of the Savior, "This gospel of the
kingdom shall be preached in all the
world, for a witness unto all nations,
and then shall the end come" (Matt.
24:14). Even before the Church of
Jesus Christ of Latter-day Saints was
organized on the 6th of April, 1830,
Joseph Smith, jun., and Oliver Cowdery, while engaged in translating
the Book of Mormon, commenced to
preach the gospel in Harmony,
Pennsylvania, and also in Seneca and
Broome counties, New York, and in
other places. After the organization
of the Church and the ordination of
a number of brethren to the ministry,
the gospel was preached by the first
Elders in many of the States in the
Union, and also to a number of
Indian tribes. Oliver Cowdery,
Parley P. Pratt and three other
Elders proclaimed the gospel to the
people in western Missouri and to
the Delaware Indians "over the

boundary" early in 1831. This was
about nine months after the Church
was organized, and the field of labor
covered by these early missionaries
extended about 1200 miles west from
Fayette, New York.

Up to 1837 the preaching of the
gospel was confined to the United
States and the British provinces in
America, but in that year Apostles
Heber C. Kimball and Orson Hyde,
together with five other missionaries,
crossed the Atlantic Ocean and be-
gan missionary work in Great Britain.
Thousands were baptized in England,
Scotland, Wales and Ireland, and in
1840 the gathering to Nauvoo,
Illinois, commenced from the British
Isles.

So far, however, the preaching by
the Elders had been confined to
countries where the English language
is spoken, and no attempt had, as yet,
been made to comply with the
heavenly command to preach the
gospel to every "tongue." The first
attempt of that kind was made in
1843, when Addison Pratt and three
other Elders were called on a mission to the Pacific Islands. About
the time that Joseph, the Prophet,
sealed his testimony with his blood in
Carthage, Ill., the first branch of the
Church established among a non-Eng-
lish-speaking people was organized
on the island of Tubuai, in the South
Pacific Ocean. But it was not until
the Saints had passed through mobbings, persecutions and drivings in
Missouri, Ohio, and Illinois, and had
located permanently in the valley of
the Great Salt Lake, that missions.

1

where other tongues than English were spoken, received special attention. As soon as the pioneers of Utah had provided primitive log cabins and adobe huts for the convenience of their families, and had begun to produce from the earth the necessaries of life, the Twelve Apostles and the Seventies were reminded of their special calling to preach the gospel to all the nations of the earth. During the exodus from Nauvoo and the journeyings in the wilderness these officers had, like the rest of the people, been busily engaged in other labors; but now that a place of comparative peace and safety had been found "for the weary feet," vigorous missionary work was to be continued, and foreign countries, which up to that time had not heard the everlasting gospel in its purity, were remembered. By this time also, a few foreigners, speaking other languages than English, had become members of the Church, and some of them were quite anxious to carry the gospel message to their countrymen in the lands of their nativity. This, undoubtedly, had more or less influence on the First Presidency of the Church, whose special attention was thus drawn to several countries of continental Europe.

As early as 1842 a number of Norwegians in La Salle county, Ill., had become converts to "Mormonism" and some of them assisted in building the Nauvoo Temple; and as early as 1843 a few Danes, and at least one Swede, had become members of the Church in Boston, Mass. A young woman, Ellen Sanders Kimball, a native of Telemarken, Norway, crossed the Plains to Great Salt Lake Valley in 1847, being one of the three pioneer women of the original pioneer company under President Brigham Young. Hans Christian Hansen, a Dane, who had

embraced the gospel in Boston, was also one of the original company of pioneers, and John E. Forsgren, a native of Sweden, who likewise had received the gospel in Boston, Mass., served in the Mormon Battalion. These three Scandinavians, representing the three kingdoms, Denmark, Sweden and Norway, together with a few others, who had arrived in the Great Basin as early as 1849, were the first representatives of Scandinavia in the Rocky Mountains.

At a general conference of the Church, held in Salt Lake City, in October, 1849, a number of missionaries were called to distant lands and they became the first missionaries sent out from the "Valley" to preach the restored gospel in foreign countries. Apostle Franklin D. Richards and five other Elders were called to England; Apostle John Taylor and Elders Curtis E. Bolton and John Pack, to France; Apostle Lorenzo Snow and Elder Joseph Toronto, to Italy; Apostle Erastus Snow and Elder Peter O. Hansen, to Denmark, Elder John E. Forsgren, to Sweden under the direction of Apostle Erastus Snow, and Elders Addison Pratt, James S. Brown and Hiram Blackwell to the Society Islands. The missionaries thus called were set apart and received their instructions Oct. 7, 1849. The First Presidency set apart the Apostles to their respective missions and the Apostles then set apart the other brethren who had been called on missions. Predictions were made that great success would follow their administrations abroad. (Mill. Star, 12:133.)

It was already late in the season for crossing the mountains and plains, and, consequently, the Elders were compelled to make hasty preparations for their journey. After taking an affectionate leave of families and friends, the missionaries gathered at the mouth of Emigration

Canyon, Oct. 19, 1849, where President Brigham Young met with them and organized them for traveling, by appointing Shadrach Roundy captain of the company, and Jedediah M. Grant captain of the guard.*

The journey proved very toilsome and unpleasant at this inclement season of the year. John Taylor writes:

"Were it not for a mission of a public nature on which many of us were engaged, we should have felt great reluctance at leaving our comfortable homes and firesides to combat the chilling winds and pitiless storms of the Rocky Mountains and the desert plains. * * * The snows have fallen on our right and left, before and behind, but with the exception of a slight fall on the Sweetwater, and another on the day of our arrival at Fort Kearney, we have escaped unharmed."

On the 7th of December, 1849, the company arrived at old Fort Kearney, the present site of Nebraska City, Neb., on the Missouri River, in the midst of a fierce snow storm. Thence the missionaries crossed the Missouri River on the ice and a few days later they arrived at Kanesville, Iowa. The Saints living there were overjoyed at meeting friends from the Valley. The missionaries were hailed with songs, the firing of guns and other tokens of joy. From Kanesville the Elders took different routes to the several seaport towns, where they

embarked for England. The Saints in St. Louis (Missouri), New Orleans (Louisiana), Boston (Massachusetts) and many other places were kind to the missionaries and contributed liberally of their means to assist them on their journeys. By this timely aid the Elders were enabled to reach their respective fields of labor. Franklin D. Richards landed in Liverpool, March 29, 1850; Peter O. Hansen and others, April 8, 1850; Erastus Snow, April 16, 1850; Lorenzo Snow, April 6, 1850, and John E. Forsgren, April 19, 1850; while John Taylor, John Pack and Curtis E. Bolton did not arrive until May 27, 1850.

The brethren who were appointed to open up new missionary fields on continental Europe spent several weeks in England, visiting among the Saints and gathering means with which to commence operations in the different countries to which they had been called. At that time there were nearly thirty thousand Saints in Great Britain and some of these, being quite wealthy, contributed liberally of their means toward defraying the expenses of the Elders who soon afterwards opened the gospel door to the inhabitants of France, Switzerland, Italy, Germany, Denmark, Sweden and Norway.

Elder Peter O. Hansen became rather an exception to the general rule in opening up missions. Without waiting for his chief, Elder Erastus Snow, to get ready, after a short visit to Scotland he proceeded alone to his native land, Denmark, the Scottish Saints furnishing him clothes and means for his mission. He arrived in Copenhagen May 11, 1850, and quietly commenced missionary work among his relatives and others. Apparently he met with very little success. His own father would not receive him and most of his former friends turned a cold shoulder to-

---

*The company was composed of 35 men with twelve wagons, one carriage and 42 horses and mules. The personnel of the company were the following: Apostle John Taylor (called to France), Lorenzo Snow (to Italy), Erastus Snow (to Denmark), Franklin D. Richards (to England), Bishop Edward Hunter, Edwin D. Woolley and Joseph Heywood (going to the States on Church business), Jacob Gates, George B. Wallace, Joseph W. Young, Joseph W. Johnson, Job Smith, Hayden W. Church, John S. Higbee and Levi Stewart (going on missions to England), Curtis E. Bolton and John Pack (to France), Joseph Toronto (to Italy), Peter O. Hansen (to Denmark), John E. Forsgren (to Sweden), and Robert Pierce, George W. Hill, W. J. Stewart, Dr. Ezekiel Lee, Shadrach Roundy, Russell Homer Perrigrine Sessions, Abraham O. Smoot, Jedediah M. Grant, Charles Decker and Robert Graham (going to the States on business), Col. John Reece, merchant of New York, John H. Kincade, merchant of St. Louis, Mo., Antonio Duval (Mr. Kincade's driver), and Benjamin Homer returning to his home in the East.

wards him. A little pamphlet entitled "En Advarsel til Folket" (A Warning to the People), which he wrote and had printed, did not create

ERASTUS SNOW
Born Nov. 9, 1818, in St. Johnsbury, Vermont; died May 27, 1888, in Salt Lake City, Utah.

much of a stir among the people and none seemed to care anything about the message he brought to them from America, except a few honest and somewhat persecuted Baptists, who listened with some degree of interest to what he told them concerning the restoration of the gospel. In his communications to Apostle Erastus Snow, who was still in England, Elder Hansen was thus unable to give cheering news as to the prospects of making converts in Denmark.

Elder Erastus Snow spent several weeks in England and in Scotland, preaching the gospel and raising means among the English Saints to enable him to fill his mission to Denmark. After a pleasant visit with his brethren of the Twelve in London, Elder Snow left that city on the 8th of June, 1850, for Hull, accom-

panied by Elder George P. Dykes, whom Elder Snow had concluded to take with him to Denmark. Bro. Dykes had introduced the gospel into a Norwegian settlement in La Salle county, Ill., in 1842, and had in his intercourse with the Norwegians there acquired some knowledge of their language.

Arriving at Hull, Elders Snow and Dykes were joined by Elder John E. Forsgren, and on the 11th of June, 1850, these three Elders took passage on the steamer "Victoria" and arrived in Copenhagen, the capital of Denmark, Friday, June 14th, at 10 o'clock in the morning. Their baggage, books and papers passed the custom house without trouble, and Elder Peter O. Hansen, who met them at the landing, served as interpreter and conducted them to a hotel, where, after being shown into an upper room, the four missionaries offered up thanksgiving to God and dedicated themselves to his service.

PETER O. HANSEN
Born June 11, 1818, in Copenhagen, Denmark; died Aug. 9, 1894, in Manti, Utah.

CHAPTER 2 (1850)

The missionaries secure lodging in Copenhagen—Meeting with Peter C. Mönster, a Baptist minister—A visit with the American minister—Elder John E. Forsgren leaves for Sweden—First meeting held in Copenhagen—The first baptisms by divine authority in Denmark—Erastus Snow's first report—First confirmation meeting in Copenhagen—Interview with the "Kultus"-minister—A meeting hall rented—Organization of the first branch of the Church in Denmark.

Finding the hotel noisy and a favorite resort for such company as would be disagreeable to them, Erastus Snow and fellow-missionaries in Copenhagen resolved to seek a private boarding house, or rent a room in a more retired place. They spent most of the afternoon in rambling over the city and its environs, making observations, and, calling upon several families "to try their spirits and examine rooms," but found no place where the "ark seemed to rest."

The following night was a sleepless one to Brother Snow, though the other brethren rested. He had been very sick coming up the Cattegat, and his nerves were in a state of feverish excitement. The gaming at the billiard tables could be distinctly heard in the sleeping apartment occupied by the missionaries, and carriages to and from the hotel dashing over the pavement immediately under their window kept up a constant noise, until the dawn of day. Elder Snow walked the floor of his room part of the night and then threw himself upon his bed. He prayed earnestly that God would direct his footsteps to a peaceful home, where the Spirit of the Lord would delight to dwell.

The next morning (Saturday, June 15th), the brethren set out anew to find a suitable stopping place. Soon they acknowledged that the prayer of Erastus Snow had not been offered in vain, for when they called on a Mr. Lauritz B. Malling, who resided at No. 196 Bredgade (then also called Norgesgade), they were shown a commodious and pleasant upper room, looking into a beautiful back garden, which they rented. Into this room they immediately moved. They also engaged their board in the family, consisting of Mr. Malling, his kind-hearted wife, and a young lady of rank—a relative; there were no children in the household. Those people treated the Elders with the utmost kindness and took delight in hearing them sing and pray, although they understood no English. Soon, also, they became interested in the doctrines taught by the Elders and subsequently Mr. Malling and his wife became members of the Church.

On Sunday, June 16th, Elders Snow, Hansen, Forsgren and Dykes attended the meetings of Peter C. Mönster, a Baptist minister, who had suffered much persecution because of his religious belief, which differed materially from the established religion of the land—the Lutheran. This man received the Elders in a most friendly and cordial manner and promised to call on them at their lodging place the next day. In the afternoon Captain Simonsen, father of the young lady who resided with Mr. and Mrs. Malling, visited the family, dined and spent the evening with the brethren. This gentleman had been an officer in the service of the government for many years. He had also been a teacher of several languages and was sufficiently at home in English to carry on a conversation. The brethren obtained valuable information from him concerning the country and the manners and habits of the people.

The next day, Monday, June 17th, Mr. Peter C. Mönster called upon the Elders at their lodging, according to appointment. Concerning this visit Elder Snow journalizes as follows:

"Mr. Mönster's visit on Monday was very interesting. He related a short history of his life during the last eight years. He was about fifty years old; his countenance and bearing bespoke intelligence, meekness and sincerity, and he was the first man in recent years to preach baptism by immersion in Denmark. His persecutions had been similar to those of the Saints in America. He had often been brought before rulers and judges, had been fined, and six times imprisoned, three years in all—and yet he had continued to teach his faith, and some three hundred and fifty had been baptized into the Baptist church. Had he been a foreigner, he would have been expelled from the country, but being a native, they could only fine and imprison him. Yet the more he was persecuted, the more friends gathered to his standard, until now, by the late political revolution, his persecutors (the State priests) are restricted in their power, and he now enjoys comparative peace and quietness. Rigsdagen has not yet enacted the necessary laws for carrying into execution the liberal provisions of the constitution with regard to religion, and the old laws are still liable to be enforced, although they have become somewhat unpopular. * * I related to Mr. Mönster what the Lord had done for his people in America, the rise and progress of the Church—in short, their revelations and persecutions, etc. I told him the Lord had sent us to this land, not to undo any good that he had done, but that he and his people and all others, that would hear us, might receive more and obtain power to do a much greater work in the land. Our testimony produced a powerful effect on him. He received it with much tenderness, promised to investigate, and seek the Lord. We loaned him the Book of Mormon to read, also Bro. Hansen's Danish manuscript translation of it. * * After he had left us, we bowed before the Lord and prayed to our Father that he would pour out his spirit upon him and the honest-hearted of his followers, and raise up from their midst, friends and fellow-laborers with us in the work of God."

On Tuesday, June 18th, Elders Snow and Dykes visited the Hon. Walter Forward, U. S. Minister to Denmark, to whom Elder Snow had an introductory letter from Senator Cooper. Mr. Forward was a member of the bar from Pittsburgh, Pa., and had formerly been a member of President Harrison's cabinet. The brethren found him a frank and generous gentleman of the old school. He welcomed the missionaries cordially and made a good many inquiries about the "Mormon" people and their religion. Being acquainted with their general history, he expressed himself very liberally with regard to their unhallowed persecutions in America, and invited the brethren to continue their intercourse with him, promising to render them any aid which was in his power to give.

On Wednesday, June 19th, Elder John E. Forsgren took leave of his fellow-missionaries in Copenhagen, bound for Sweden, his native land, there to open up a missionary field among his countrymen. "He took leave of us," writes Elder Snow, "with our blessings upon his head, and full of the Holy Ghost, though his eyes were full of tears and his heart ready to burst. He goes by

JOHN ERIK FORSGREN

Born Nov. 7, 1816, at Gefle, Sweden; died Jan. 22, 1890, in Salt Lake City, Utah.

steamboat to Gefle, high up on the Swedish shore of the Baltic. In that vicinity he hopes to find his father from whom he has been absent for twenty years." In the afternoon of this day Elders Dykes and Hansen visited Mr. Mönster and imparted to him much more instruction with which he seemed elated and said that he wished to investigate the work thoroughly and store his mind with the evidence of its truth, that he might be able to lead his flock with him. Meantime the brethren had visited several other families, endeavoring to sow the seed of the gospel as best they could, Bro. Hansen acting as interpreter.

On Sunday, June 23rd, Elder Erastus Snow accompanied Mr. Mönster on a visit to Ishöi, a little town about ten English miles from Copenhagen, where there was a small branch of Mr. Mönster's Baptist church. Brother Snow was introduced to the people and then addressed them, aided by Mr. Mönster, who acted as interpreter. The Elders continued their labors quietly among the people, visiting a number of families, bearing testimony, answering questions, and they soon found themselves surrounded by a small circle of friends who were earnestly investigating the gospel.

On Sunday, July 21st, the Elders in Copenhagen held their first meeting in the house of Peter Beckström, who lived on Store Kongensgade. A spirit of investigation was manifested among those who attended the little meeting, especially among the followers of Mr. Mönster. During the following week, Mr. Mönster advised his disciples not to hold any more family meetings for fear of calling forth persecution and hatred, which, he said, might result in the American Elders being banished from the country; and he discour-

aged the zeal with which some of his members were investigating the doctrines taught by the Americans, as he called the missionaries from "the Valley.". But his warning came too late. The seed sown had commenced to take root, and by the 1st of August eight or ten of his flock had decided to be baptized. They told him of their intention, but he advised them in the strongest terms not to take a step of that kind. It appears that when Mr. Mönster found that his friends from America intended to organize a church of their own, independent of his, he felt grieved and disappointed, and he gradually withdrew his association from them. But, though Mr. Mönster never joined the Church, many of his flock, who became fully convinced that the message brought them from America was of God, received the truth with open hearts and applied for admission into the Church through the channel which God had appointed. Elder Snow urged no one to be baptized, but rather held them back, advising a more thorough investigation. Finally, however, the Lord warned him in a dream to do so no longer, and, consequently, he invited the believers to a little meeting on Sunday, August 11, 1850, at which Elder Peter O. Hansen read to them the Articles of Faith and several extracts of revelations which he had translated, and Brother Snow, through Elder Hansen as interpreter, gave them wise and kindly instruction and appointed the next day as the day for baptism.

Monday, August 12, 1850, will always be classed as one of the important days in the history of the Church of Jesus Christ of Latter-day Saints in the Scandinavian countries. In the evening of that memorable day, Apostle Erastus Snow baptized fifteen persons in the clear waters of Öresund, immediately outside of the ramparts of Copenhagen, as the first fruits of the preaching of the gospel of Christ in Denmark. Among those who were baptized on that oc-

ANNA BECKSTRÖM
The first woman baptized in Denmark, was born April, 1825, at Dalby, Skåne, Sweden; died Oct. 12, 1911, in Salt Lake City, Utah.

casion were the following: Ole Ulrick Christian Mönster and wife, Marie Christine; Hans Larsen and wife, Eline Dorthea; Andreas Christian Samuel Hansen and wife, Ane; Johan Bartholomæous Förster and wife, Henrietta; Andreas Ågren (Swedish), Anna Beckström (Swedish), wife of Peter Beckström; Johanne Andersen and Karen Marie Nielsen. Owing to the loss of the first record of the Copenhagen Branch, the names of the other three candidates cannot be obtained. The next day (Aug. 13th) Elder George P. Dykes baptized one more convert in the city of Copenhagen.

On Wednesday, Aug. 14th, in the evening, a meeting was held in Peter Beckström's house, at which occasion Apostle Erastus Snow and Elders Peter O. Hansen and George P. Dykes administered to some of those who

had been baptized, the ordinance of laying on of hands for the reception of the Holy Ghost. Among those confirmed were Andreas Ågren, Karen Marie Nielsen, Anna Beckström, Johanne Anderson and perhaps all the others who had been baptized on the 12th. This was the first time that this holy ordinance was administered in Denmark, and the new converts were filled with joy and happiness.

For some time after this, baptisms were frequent in the city of Copenhagen. Among others who were baptized on Saturday, August 17, 1850, were Christian Christiansen, Peter Beckström and Knud Hansen Brunn, all of whom subsequently became successful missionaries. Bro. Bruun was the first of the Lutheran denomination to receive the gospel in Denmark, as all those who had previously been baptized were Baptists. On this day Elder Erastus Snow wrote to the First Presidency of the Church his first report of the labors of himself and his fellow-missionaries in the Scandinavian Mission. Among other things he said:

"The Spirit of the Lord seemed to lead me to this city to commence my labors. From my first appointment, my mind rested upon Copenhagen as the best place in all Scandinavia to commence the work, and everything has since strengthened my conviction. It is the capital of Denmark, and was at one time the capital of the united kingdom of Denmark, Norway and Sweden. It is a beautiful city, strongly fortified, numbering about 140,000 inhabitants and is by far the largest and most influential town in the kingdom; from its central position on the east side of the island of Zealand [Sjælland], within sixteen miles of the Swedish shore, it affords an easy communication by steamboat to the principal places of Sweden, Norway and Denmark, and is the seat of learning for northern Europe, and I might add of priestcraft, infidelity and politics, and, in my opinion, it possesses more of the spirit of freedom than any other place in this part of the world. * * The government of Denmark, until recently, was an absolute monarchy. The king and his ministry both made and executed the laws and the Lutheran clergy had the superintendency and control of all the primary schools and public instruction of the country, with the exception of certain privileges granted to the Jews and to foreign mechanics who had been invited into the country, but no foreigner was permitted to proselyte from the Lutheran Evangelical Church, or preach against her doctrines, on pain of being expelled from the country. This mandate has been enforced against several foreign missionaries within the last ten or fifteen years, and would have been against us, in all probability, if we had come a little sooner. Mr. Peter C. Mönster, the Baptist reformer, introduced immersion, and now his followers number in Denmark about 360. At first he was fined, and afterwards imprisoned, and when he had served out one term in prison, he would preach until the priests would cause him to be arrested and imprisoned again, and so continued until he was imprisoned six times and three years in all. Meantime, French philosophy, infidelity and republican principles have been increasing in this city, and throughout the country, until, about the time of the late revolution in France, the death of the old king of Denmark afforded the Danish people an opportunity to reform their government. The heir to the throne was kept at bay until a constitution or 'Grundlov' was agreed upon, signed and proclaimed June 5, 1849. This secured to the people a 'Rigsdag,' or legislature, to be elected by the people and quite as much political freedom as is enjoyed in England. The press is sufficiently free and untrammelled for all purposes, for which we wish to use it, and while it protects and supports the Lutheran church as the state church, it secures to the citizens the right to dissent and organize other societies. * * Lutheranism is protected by similar laws in Norway and Sweden. Not long ago some Methodists were expelled from Sweden, and quite recently some Baptists, near Göteborg, were arrested and sentenced to leave the country. * * Last Monday, the 12th of August, we began to baptize; we baptized fifteen the first night and eleven more during the week, making twenty-six in all. The greater part of these are from Mr. Mönster's followers, and the best he had; and many more of them are believing, while the rest of them are full of wrath and indignation. * * Among those who are baptized are Germans, Swedes and Danes, all, however,

understand Danish, and they are well grounded in the work, and firm. We had with us one copy of Elder Orson Hyde's German work, which we kept moving among the Germans; and when we found any who could read English, we gave them English books, and to the Danes we read Bro. Hansen's translation of the Book of Mormon and Doctrine and Covenants, etc. We have operated only in private and in small family meetings, but we have now arrived at the time when we shall no longer seek retirement, but publicity. We hope soon to find a large public place, and we thank God that the seed has sprung up, and has deep root, so that if we are banished from the country, the work will spread.

"The Lord has visited the believers with many visions, and dreams, and manifestations of the Holy Spirit, and some have told us that they have seen us in vision before we came. They have drawn out of us by their faith, everything pertaining to the gathering, the redemption of the dead, etc., and drink it in as an ox drinketh up water. * *

"As far as my experience and observation extend, the Danes are a kind, hospitable people, especially the middle and lower classes; and a higher tone of morality pervades them than exists in the corresponding classes in England and America; and, if I mistake not my feelings, the Lord has many people among them.

"Brother John E. Forsgren accompanied us to this place and stopped a few days with us, and then we blessed him and sent him on his way. The Lord is with him; he is full of faith and the Holy Ghost. From here to the home of his childhood, where his relatives are, is about six hundred miles in a northeast direction up the Baltic."

On Sunday, Aug. 18, 1850, a small meeting was held in the home of Hans Larsen on Christianshavn (a part of the city of Copenhagen situated on the island of Amager), where a number of those recently baptized were confirmed members of the Church, and three children, daughters of Hans and Eline Dorthea Larsen, were blessed according to the pattern given by the Savior of the World eighteen hundred years previously. The names of the children were Petrine Christine, Marie Magdalene and Margrete Christine Larsen. These were the first children blessed by divine authority in Denmark.

On Sunday, August 25th, another meeting was held at the home of Hans Larsen on Christianshavn, on which occasion the Sacrament was administered for the first time in Denmark in this dispensation by divine authority. The first ordination of local brethren to the holy Priesthood also took place in this meeting, when Knud H. Bruun was ordained to the office of a Priest and Ole U. C. Mönster to that of a Teacher and appointed to watch over the Saints on Christianshavn. Bro. Bruun was on the eve of starting for the province of Jutland (Jylland) to fill a position there as a servant, and Elder Snow, considering the occasion opportune to introduce the gospel into that part of the country, ordained Bro. Bruun a Priest that he might have authority both to preach and baptize on his arrival in Jutland.

In the meantime baptisms became more frequent in Copenhagen and meetings were held often in the private houses of the Saints.

Early in the month of September the brethren visited the "Kultus" minister (the secretary or minister of church and education) and commenced a correspondence with him and also with the mayor of the city of Copenhagen, in regard to the object of the visit of the American Elders to Denmark, asking for permission to preach the gospel throughout the kingdom. These authorities requested a brief written synopsis of the faith, doctrines and organization of the Church of Jesus Christ of Latter-day Saints. This was immediately prepared and forwarded, together with a copy of the Book of Mormon in English. The "Kultus"

minister subsequently told the brethren that they might hold meetings in the city of Copenhagen, but remarked that they might possibly have trouble with the police on account of the evil reports which were already then circulating about the "Mormons."

On Sunday, Sept. 15, 1850, a meeting was held in a rented room in "Vingaardsstrædet," Copenhagen, on which occasion the first branch of the Church of Jesus Christ of Latter-day Saints was organized in Denmark, with Elder George P. Dykes as president, Johan B. Förster clerk, and Christian Christiansen treasurer. Lauritz B. Malling, Ole Svendsen and Andreas Ågren were appointed a committee to take charge of the financial affairs of the branch, and, among other things, it was enjoined upon these brethren to rent a suitable hall in which the Saints might hold public meetings. About fifty members were present at this meeting which approximately represented the membership in the Copenhagen Branch when it was first organized. Up to this time Elder Snow had not been prompted to rent any place for holding public meetings in Copenhagen, but had considered it best for him and his fellow-missionaries to confine themselves to private conversations with the people, and to the holding of small meetings in private houses. While they thus were making a host of friends they also had an opportunity of becoming acquainted with the laws of the land and the language, habits and customs of the people.

The committee appointed to secure a hall for holding meetings performed their task without delay and rented from Mr. Nehm a large and commodious hall in the rear building of a property then known as No. 85 (now 21), Lille Kongensgade.

near the heart of the city. Elder Snow paid fifty "rigsdaler" in advance for three months' rent. The converts were all laboring people and poor, but they furnished what was needed of seats and fixtures for the hall and began to make collections to pay rent.

On Wednesday, September 18th, Elder John E. Forsgren arrived in Copenhagen as an exile from Sweden. In the evening of that day the first meeting in the hall rented by the branch in Copenhagen was held. It was attended by the Saints and a few of their friends. Elder Forsgren gave a detailed account of his extraordinary experience and sufferings in the land to the north. In listening to his interesting, yet sad, story, the eyes of the Saints were moistened with tears and their hearts softened, for they began to realize that the same opposition and persecution, which followed the preaching of the gospel in the ancient days, would become an integral part of the experience which the advocates of the same principles would meet in the Nineteenth Century, even among the liberty-loving inhabitants of northern Europe.

CHAPTER 3 (1850)

Arrival of Elder John E. Forsgren at Gefle, Sweden—Mircaulous case of healing—First baptisms in Sweden—Elder Forsgren persecuted and arrested—Examined and tried by doctors and government officers—Banished from Sweden—Landing in Denmark and befriended by the American minister.

While the events recorded in the preceding chapter were occurring in Copenhagen, Elder John E. Forsgren, who on June 19, 1850, had taken leave of his fellow-missionaries, Erastus Snow, Peter O. Hansen and George P. Dykes in Copenhagen, Denmark, proceeded to Gefle, a seaport town of Sweden, situated at the mouth of the Gafvel River and on the Bay of Bothnia. Near this city he found his brother, Peter Adolph Forsgren, and sister, Christina Erika Forsgren, still living at the old homestead. His father, Johan Olaf Forsgren, was absent on a sea voyage to America. Elder Forsgren found his brother very sick with consumption and, by the physicians, declared past recovery. Upon making the object of his visit known among the neighbors, Elder Forsgren at once encountered opposition. The laws of the country prescribed penalties for any religious movement which the Lutheran priests regarded as inimical to the Lutheran creed, which was then, and is yet, the state religion of Sweden. The Lutheran priests, with the civil authorities on their side, were strict in enforcing the laws prohibiting religious liberty in the land, though many of the middle and lower classes, like many of the Danish people, were panting for more liberty. A number of the peasantry soon became interested in Elder Forsgren and his doctrines and listened attentively to what he had to say, but he was closely watched by the police, and, according to the Swedish laws and customs pertaining to travelers at that time, his passport was retained by "Landskansliet." This prevented him from going into any other town without permission, for at that time a traveler, native or foreign, who was found without a passport in Sweden was looked upon and treated almost as an escaped convict.

Under these circumstances Elder Forsgren fasted and prayed, asking the Lord to open the way before him, while he privately taught the gospel whenever he had an opportunity. He also translated into Swedish Orson Pratt's pamphlet entitled, "Remarkable Visions," but the printers refused to publish it. He therefore left the manuscript with some of the believers.

Among the converts to the truth of his teachings was· his brother, Peter A. Forsgren, who through faith and anointing with oil had been raised from his bed of sickness, and on the 26th day of July, 1850, he baptized

PETER ADOLPH FORSGREN

The first convert to "Mormonism" in Sweden, was born July 26, 1826, in Gefle, Gefleborgs län, Sweden, emigrated to Utah in 1852-53, and died as a Patriarch in the Church at Brigham City, Box Elder County, Utah, March 1, 1908.

him as the first fruit of preaching the gospel in its fulness in Sweden. This baptism took place about three weeks earlier than the first immersion by Erastus Snow in Copenhagen, Denmark. John E. Forsgren, consequently, performed the first baptism in the Scandinavian Mission.

Soon after Elder John E. Forsgren had baptized his brother, he also baptized his sister and two other persons in Gefle, after which he concluded to go to Stockholm, the capital of Sweden, in the hope of finding there more tolerance on the part of the officials and of the people, and, consequently, a better opening to introduce the gospel. Accordingly he called for his passport on

the 3rd of August, but he missed the steamer and was left at Gefle.

Almost immediately afterwards, he heard of a ship which was about to leave for New York with a company of emigrating farmers. He sought them at once, finding them lodging temporarily in a warehouse, waiting for the vessel to get ready. These emigrants were somewhat conversant with the Scriptures, and, being tired of the oppression and religious intolerance of their native country, had concluded to seek their fortunes in America. Elder Forsgren preached the gospel to them, and they received him gladly; wherefore he visited them frequently and instructed them concerning the principles of the restored gospel. On August 6th, they proposed a public meeting in a grove, a short distance out of town; and, after due deliberation, he decided to bear a public testimony and abide the consequences. It was under these circumstances that the first public Latterday Saint meeting was held in Sweden, on Tuesday, August 6, 1850. Elder Forsgren on that day went to the water and baptized seventeen persons belonging to the emigrant company. Everything passed off quietly and satisfactorily and the people, becoming interested, asked for a second meeting, which was held the following day.

On Wednesday, Aug. 7th, Elder Forsgren organized the newly baptized converts into a branch of the Church and ordained two of them to the office of Elders. He also ordained some Teachers among them, administered the Sacrament and instructed all the emigrants relative to their journey and their future proceedings. He gave the ordained Elders instructions how to baptize and confirm their traveling companions, should any of them desire to join the Church on the voyage, or afterwards.

At the appointed hour of the meeting, 6 o'clock p. m., the rumor of the first meeting had drawn a vast multitude both from the town and country to the place appointed. Among the number were some Lutheran priests and "stadsfiskalen" (city marshal) with members of the police force, ready to take Elder Forsgren into custody. They, however, took no steps to arrest him until he had finished his discourse, for the power of God rested upon him as well as upon the people. "Some wept, others rejoiced, and nearly all seemed to feel that surely a prophet had come among them." As soon as he was through speaking, the marshal and priests, full of indignation, and boiling over with rage, came forward and arrested him, amid terrible threats and denunciations. As he was marched into town, the vast multitude followed, and they were met by large crowds from the town and shipyards. As the officer in charge, by way of introducing his prisoner to the crowd, called him "dopparen" (the dipper), the multitude swung their hats and cried with deafening shouts: "Hurra for profeten" (Hurrah for the prophet).

The following day (August 8th) John E. Forsgren was brought before the chief officer of police at Gefle; next he was taken before the. chief officer of "landskansliet"; then before the chief priest and his associates, all of whom, in their turn, examined and questioned him, and made records of the proceedings. He answered them as the spirit gave him utterance, until they became confounded and perplexed and knew not what to do with him.

He was next ushered before "borgmästaren" (the city mayor) of Gefle, where all the before-mentioned dignitaries were assembled with the priests and police. Here he had another opportunity of bearing witness to the truth, for as they proceeded with their accusations of what he had said and done, he explained and bore testimony. Among other transgressions, which the marshal accused him of, was healing the sick. The chief priest sent for Elder Forsgren's brother to have him examined, as it was believed he was still sick. But when this brother came, he testified boldly that he was well and that he had been healed by the power of God, through the instrumentality of his brother. The doctor was ordered to examine Brother Forsgren's head, as they would fain have sent him to the asylum; but the doctor very significantly told them that he (John E. Forsgren) knew well what he was about. Everything increased their perplexitiy. Elder Forsgren was well dressed and bore passports from Washington, D. C. This, added to his bold indifference, made them feel dubious about imprisoning him. They finally concluded to send him to Stockholm with a full account of his doings in Gefle. The marshal suggested that for his bold, impudent demeanor he was worthy to go to Stockholm in irons; and the irons were produced for the purpose. But, after a little further consultation, he was dismissed with the following endorsement upon his pass, which was suggested by the chief priest:

"The bearer of this pass received it and had it signed August 3rd for his departure to Stockholm, but was unable to leave at that time. The North American consul, now present, rejects him, and leaves him without protection. The .bearer of the pass has, during the past few days, disturbed the general peace by illegal preaching in warehouses and in the open air before several hundred persons, and has even performed the act of baptizing several grown persons on the seashore. For these offenses he will leave Gefle before 8 o'clock tomorrow morning for the above mentioned place of destination without fail. —Gefle Landskansli, 8th Aug., 1850.*

When Elder Forsgren landed in Stockholm, he was again arrested, as the police officers had received from Gefle five or six pages of his sayings and doings there, and he was taken forthwith before the chief police officers of the kingdom for three successive days, where he again had an opportunity of expounding the principles of the gospel and bearing witness of its restoration to all in the court room.

During this time his fame spread through the city and notices appeared about him in the different newspapers. The officers of the law, after trying in vain to make him stop preaching, concluded to send him back to America. But as there was no vessel in the harbor by which they could ship him immediately, and the American minister would not permit them to imprison him, he was set free with a strict charge not to preach his doctrines. But the papers made known his whereabouts, and people from all quarters sought him; thus he received numerous invitations, visited many families in their private houses, and soon had a large circle of friends and acquaintances. In this manner he continued his labors for about a month, and many began to believe his testimony.

Finally, the authorities in Stockholm heard that several persons had decided to be baptized by Elder Forsgren, notwithstanding the heavy penalty fixed by law for such an offense. So Elder Forsgren was arrested on the night between the 9th and 10th of September, 1850, and taken on board an American vessel, which was ready to sail for New York. His passport was endorsed for that city and his passage paid. But, fortunately, the vessel on

which he had involuntarily embarked, had to touch at Elsinore (Helsingör), on the coast of Denmark, to pay the so-called "Öresundstold" (Danish toll), before she could pass from the Baltic into the sea of Cattegat. Elder Forsgren immediately took advantage of the opportunity of gaining his freedom, and as he, during the voyage from Stockholm, had won the friendship of the captain of the vessel, he had no difficulty in effecting a landing. Elated at the prospect of soon joining his fellow-missionaries in Copenhagen, about thirty miles distant from Elsinore, and as he was preparing to leave, he was arrested by the Danish police, at the instigation of the Swedish consul, who had received orders from his government to unite with the Danish police in having Forsgren re-shipped to New York, if he should attempt to land in Elsinore. As a cause for his arrest, the Danish authorities alleged that as he was without sufficient means he was a vagrant. Fortunately, however, Mr. Walter Forward, the American minister to Denmark, with whom Elder Erastus Snow had already formed a most friendly acquaintance, was visiting Elsinore at the time, and to him Elder Forsgren, as an American citizen, immediately applied for protection. Mr. Forward, in answer to the Danish authorities, said that he would be responsible for Mr. Forsgren, and assured them that there was no danger of his becoming a burden to the Danish government through lack of money, as he knew the prisoner had friends and means in Copenhagen. This stand on the part of Mr. Forward had the desired effect; Elder Forsgren was liberated and accompanied the minister to Copenhagen, where he arrived on the 18th of September, 1850, and received a hearty welcome from his beloved brethren in the priesthood, from whom he had been separated for three months. Thus ended the first attempt to introduce the gospel into Sweden.

It may be remarked in this connection, that the company of farmers, of whom Elder Forsgren had baptized seventeen, sailed for America soon after his arrest, and nothing authentic has ever been heard of them since, though Elder Forsgren claimed that some of them, subsequently, became identified with branches of the Church in the West.

CHAPTER 4 (1850)

The renting of Mr. Nehm's hall in Copenhagen—First ordinations to the Priesthood in Denmark—"En Sandheds Röst" published—Elder Erastus Snow visits England—Elder George P. Dykes raises up a branch of the Church at Aalborg—Cases of healing by the power of God—Opposition by the Lutheran clergy—Book of Mormon presented to King Frederik VII—Growth of the work in Denmark.

Meanwhile, in Copenhagen, the renting of Mr. Nehm's hall gave a fresh impetus to the work. For some time meetings were held regularly every Sunday from 10 a. m. to 12 m. and from 7 to 9 p. m., also on Wednesday evenings, commencing at 7:30 p. m. The hall being favorably located on one of the principal streets in the city of Copenhagen, the meetings were generally well attended; many persons were baptized. The new members enjoyed the spiritual gifts of the gospel to a considerable degree. Several manifestations of the power of God, especially in the healing of the sick, strengthened and comforted the believers and inspired them to renewed effort.

At the close of a general meeting held in Copenhagen the evening of Sunday, Sept. 22, 1850, Christian Christiansen was ordained a Teacher and Frederik Christian Sörensen and Johan A. Ahmanson were ordained Deacons under the hands of Apostles

Erastus Snow and the other American Elders. Elders Snow, Dykes, Forsgren and Hansen spent Tuesday, Sept. 24th, in prayer and council, and, agreeable to the admonitions of the Holy Ghost, it was decided that Elder Hansen should commence the revision and re-writing of the Book of Mormon and prepare the same for the press, while Elder Snow himself would make a visit to England for the purpose of attending conference there and endeavoring to procure necessary means wherewith to have the Book of Mormon printed in the Danish language. Elder Forsgren, in the meantime, was appointed to labor in and around Copenhagen, while Elder Dykes was commissioned to go to the city of Aalborg in the province of Jutland, Denmark. That night Elder Carl C. A. Chris-

CARL CHRISTIAN ANTHON CHRISTENSEN

This is the same C. C. A. Christensen who afterwards became prominent in the Scandinavian Mission as a missionary, and in Utah as a literary man and diligent Church worker. He died in Ephraim, Sanpete County, Utah, as a Patriarch, July 3, 1912.

tensen, a youth of eighteen years, came, persuaded by his mother, to the house of Peter Beckström, to hear what Brother Dykes had to say about religion. Elder Dykes, who lived with the Beckströms at that time, came home late and the conversation between the young man and Elder Dykes terminated after one hour's duration by the young man requesting baptism, which ordinance was performed by Elder Dykes two days later, Sept. 25, 1850.

After making all necessary arrangements, Elder Snow sailed from Copenhagen for England, Oct. 4, 1850. Immediately before leaving for England he issued from the press in Copenhagen his popular pamphlet entitled "En Sandheds Röst" (A Voice of Truth), in which the first principles of the gospel were explained and presented in a clear and logical style. Brother Snow wrote it originally in English and Bro. Peter O. Hansen translated it into the Danish language. With the exception of the little tract entitled "En Advarsel til Folket," written and published by Elder Hansen previous to Elder Snow's arrival in Copenhagen, "En Sandheds Röst" was the first publication of the Church published in the Scandinavian Mission. The first edition of this pamphlet, consisting of 2,000 copies, was printed by Mr. F. E. Bording, who continued to print for the Saints in Denmark until his death, which occurred Feb. 3, 1884, and his successor in business, or his heir, who was still running the same printing office as late as 1912, doing most of the printing for the Church, in Scandinavia.*

*Upwards of 200,000 copies of "En Sandheds Röst" have subsequently been published in Copenhagen, in the Danish and Swedish languages, and it is still one of the most popular pamphlets treating upon the principles of the gospel, which have been circulated by the Elders in Denmark, Sweden and Norway.

Agreeable to the appointment received at the council meeting Sept. 24, 1850, Elder George P. Dykes took passage on a steamer at Copenhagen bound for Aalborg, Elder John E. Forsgren succeeding him as president of the branch in Copenhagen.

During Elder Snow's absence in England, the Copenhagen Branch was divided into three districts, in each of which prayer meetings were held regularly. On the 13th of October Elder Forsgren ordained Christian Christiansen and Frederik C. Sorensen Priests, and Andreas Ågren and Johan B. Förster Teachers. Elder Forsgren also organized a branch council and many new converts were baptized.

Elder George P. Dykes arrived in Aalborg, Oct. 10, 1850. His means

GEORGE PARKER DYKES
Born Dec. 24, 1814, in St. Clair County, Illinois; died Feb. 25, 1888, at Zenos, Maricopa County, Arizona.

being very limited, he hired a small room in a side street and lived very economically. Thus he bought a dinner as a rule every day, but very rarely ate either breakfast or supper. "Under these gloomy circumstances," writes Elder Dykes, "I began to raise my warning voice to a very superstitious people, and soon I had enough to do, for the spirit that had for ages lulled the people to sleep under their ancient customs and dead ceremonies, was now awakened, and arose like the old lion from his slumbers and came forth in the powers of darkness which caused a trembling in the land such as has not been known for generations past. The people were astonished, their sleep was disturbed by night and their labors by day. There was something new in the land, it was the voice of God from on high—a message from that God whom they or their fathers had not known."

In Aalborg, as well as in Copenhagen, there were in 1850, quite a number of Baptists who seemed to be very sincere in their worship, and the success following the preaching of the gospel in the capital of Denmark was undoubtedly the main reason why the attention of the first Elders was drawn to the same class of people in the city of Aalborg. Among the leading Baptists in the vicinity of Aalborg was Hans Peter Jensen, the owner of a large mechanical establishment in Nörre Sundby. He was also "Forstander" or president of the Baptists in Aalborg and vicinity. This Mr. Jensen and other influential Baptists were endeavoring to adjust some differences of opinion existing among the members of that denomination concerning certain doctrinal points, when Elder Dykes, unexpectedly to them, arrived in Aalborg. Mr. Jensen became one of his first converts and he, together with his wife, Sarah Josephine Katrine Jensen, and six others were baptized Oct. 27, 1850, as the first fruits of the gospel in the province of North Jutland. The names of the other six were: Niels Christian Schou and

wife (Marie), Ole Christian Nielsen and wife (Else Katrine), and Hans Frederik Petersen and wife (Helene Mathilde). Some of these first converts in Aalborg subsequently became prominent and active in the Church, especially Hans Peter Jensen.

After his baptism, Brother Jensen, who had been a very active Baptist for eleven years, went to his co-religionists, to whom he felt himself attached by the most tender ties and affections, and endeavored to convert them to "Mormonism," showing them how the Baptists, in many respects had incorporated many erroneous doctrines into their creed. Some of them listened attentively to his testimony and explanations and were soon afterwards baptized, while others hardened their hearts against the principles of truth and were, from that time forward, the avowed enemies and opponents of Elder Dykes and his associates. Mr. Föltved succeeded Mr. Jensen as president of the Baptist organization in Aalborg.

The newly baptized members in Aalborg and Nörre Sundby were organized into a regular branch of the Church of Jesus Christ of Latter-day Saints, Nov. 25, 1850, with Hans Peter Jensen (who had been ordained a Priest the day before) as the president of the same. This was the first branch of the Church organized in North Jutland and the second in Denmark. The Aalborg Branch has had a continued existence ever since it was first organized, and is still one of the largest and best branches of the Church in the Scandinavian countries. Among the many converts who embraced the gospel in Aalborg was the late President Anthon H. Lund.

After an absence of twenty-six days, Elder Erastus Snow returned

2

to Copenhagen from England, Oct. 30, 1850, bringing with him sufficient means to have the Book of Mormon printed in the Danish language. On his return to Copenhagen, Elder Snow received a full-hearted welcome by the Saints in that city. He writes:

"Elder Dykes had gone to Aalborg, agreeable to his appointment, and, having opened his way through many adverse circumstances and much opposition, he had now begun to make many friends and enquirers after truth. Bro. Hansen had been diligent, but had proceeded very slowly with the Book of Mormon. Elder Forsgren had been blessed in his labors * * in Copenhagen and the meetings there were tolerably well attended. During my absence Elder Forsgren had also, pursuant to my instructions, ordained Bro. Christian Christiansen a Priest and some others, Teachers and Deacons. He has besides organized a branch council, established prayer meetings, etc., and the Saints were increasing in faith and the Holy Spirit, so that I had joy on my return. Several sick were also healed about this time, one or two of whom I will mention. A boy of four years of age, son of a Sister Andersen, had withered limbs and had never walked. He was anointed and blessed by Elder Forsgren in the name of Christ, and his limbs received strength and grew full and natural like those of other children. Another, Mrs. Thomsen, who was very low with childbed fever two weeks after her confinement, and had lost her child, was considered past recovery by her physicians. But a faithful Sister Andersen, who was her waiting nurse, talked with, and prayed for her, and told her and her husband of us. They sent for Elder Forsgren, who went to them, and they received his testimony with joy; and although the woman could not talk much, she was filled with faith at hearing his words, and he prayed for and laid hands upon her and her pain and fever left her straightway. She arose and dressed herself and walked and praised the Lord, and soon she and her husband and other friends were baptized unto the Lord. These and several other cases of healing and manifestations of the Holy Ghost made much excitement and stir among the people. Knowing the great power of priestcraft in the land and the hold Satan had upon the hearts of the people, I charged the Saints to keep these things from going abroad among the people and in every way used caution to prevent excitement. Nevertheless, excitement continued to increase as the work advanced. In the immediate vicinity of Mrs. Thomsen the people became exceedingly wrath, not only with her and those who believed, but even persecuted their prattling children who played in the yard. One of their neighbors who raged the most against the truth was seized by the devil and after fruitless attempts of the physician to restore him to his right mind, he was sent to the lunatic asylum. This was also charged to 'Mormonism.' About this time also the newspapers teemed with old English and American lies, translated and revamped, in which dirty work the Baptists made themselves conspicuous because we had baptized many of their members. The Bishop of Sjælland (the chief Bishop of Denmark) issued a pamphlet in which he detailed the usual catalogue of Trans-Atlantic lies and tried to crush the work of God with his influence. He thought it the duty of the government to protect the people against the dangerous sect. * * I replied to nothing that was published against us, but labored diligently to improve myself in the language and assist Bro. Hansen in translating the Book of Mormon. Meanwhile we continued the circulation of my "Voice of Truth," and to hold meetings among the Saints and in our hall; and to talk, pray, read and sing, and hear the Saints tell their dreams and manifestations of the Holy Spirit, truly cheering. We did not advertise our meetings, but still our hall soon became filled, especially in the evenings, and we had confirmations nearly every Sunday: the baptizing we did in a quiet way, mostly week evenings, to avoid excitement."

In this connection it is indeed pleasing to note that the Saints in Denmark, as well as in other parts of the world (where the gospel has been preached by Latter-day Saint Elders), were, from the beginning, blessed with the knowledge that these signs shall follow the believer. Many and marvelous are the cases which could be related in regard to the healing of the sick, the casting out of devils, the out-pouring of the gift of prophesy and other manifestations of God's mercy and power, which year after year marked the progress of the work of God in the Scandinavian Mission.

During the months of November and December, 1850, the Lutheran clergy commenced to hold evening meetings in their respective churches, something almost unheard of in that city up to that time. The priests expressed the hope that the people would have no excuse for attending the meetings of the "Mormons;" but as this did not have the desired effect, they next tried to stir up the university students to join the apprentices and the rough-neck element of the city and break up the meetings of the Saints. For a number of evenings the brethren at their meeting hall endeavored to bear with numerous insults and disturbances, and in vain did they appeal to the better feelings of their tormentors. The brethren also appealed to the mayor and chief of police for protection, but the police looked through their fingers at these proceedings of the mob and neglected to do their duty, as the "Kultus" minister had predicted would be the case, and while they gave the brethren fair promises, which they never fulfilled, they apparently encouraged the mob in their acts of violence. Under these circumstances, Elder Snow deemed it advisable to stop the evening meetings of the Saints, and notified the members of the branch accordingly. Thus when the time for holding the next meeting arrived, the members of the Church remained at home while the mob gathered in greater numbers than ever and uttered threats of violence, their particular object of hatred being Elder Forsgren. They surrounded the meeting hall, broke the door and made a terrible uproar, but they spent their fury upon the building and upon themselves, while the Saints were quietly praying in their own houses. Similar scenes

were repeated for some time as the evening upon which the Saints had been holding their meetings came around, and on each occasion several hundred men and boys would gather and set up a great howl; no women participated.

While this excitement ran its course Elder Snow and his missionary companions associated quietly with the Saints who gathered in small groups in solitary and peaceable places to pray and council with one another. After a time, the excitement died away to such an extent that meetings could again be held in the hall.

In the meantime the brethren had sent a deputation to His Majesty, King Frederik VII, presenting him with a copy of Elder Snow's "En Sandheds Röst" and also a copy of the Book of Mormon in English. The king gave the book to the queen dowager, who was religiously inclined. The book and the accompanying communication, according to a rumor, had such an effect upon the former queen that she was sick for several days afterwards.

On Sunday, Dec. 29th, two interesting meetings were held in Mr. Nehm's hall in Copenhagen. On this occasion Erastus Snow was for the first time sustained as president of the Scandinavian Mission by the unanimous vote of the Saints and Elder John E. Forsgren as the local president of the Copenhagen Branch.

At the close of the year 1850 there were about 135 members of the Church in Denmark, organized into two branches, one in Copenhagen and the other in Aalborg. Of the members about one hundred resided in Copenhagen and about thirty in Aalborg and vicinity. Twelve of the local brethren had been ordained to the lesser Priesthood, namely, ten in the Copenhagen and two in the

Aalborg Branch. The ordained officers in the Copenhagen Branch were the following: Priests: Knud H. Bruun, Christian Christiansen and Frederik Chr. Sörensen; Teachers: Ole U. C. Mönster, Andreas Ågren and Johan B. Förster; Deacons: Johan A. Ahmanson, Niels Olsen, Chr. J. Larsen and Andreas Chr. Samuel Hansen. In the Aalborg Branch the priesthood consisted of Priest Hans Peter Jensen and Teacher Niels Chr. Schou. There were also three or four members of the Church in Sweden, namely, those baptized by Elder John E. Forsgren in Gefle the previous summer.

At the close of the year 1850, Apostle Erastus Snow and Elders John E. Forsgren and Peter O. Hansen were located in Copenhagen, while Elder George P. Dykes was laboring in Aalborg and vicinity.

CHAPTER 5 (1851)

First ordinations to the Melchizedek Priesthood in Scandinavia—The Book of Mormon translated—Progress in Aalborg in the midst of persecution—Mobbing in Roskilde. First converts at Hirchholm—A Latter-day Saint hymn book published in Danish—Disturbances by mobs in Christianshavn—First missionaries called to Iceland.

New Year's Day, 1851, was observed as a day of fasting and prayer by the Elders and Saints generally in Copenhagen. The Saints met in their rented hall in Lille Kongensgade and enjoyed a goodly portion of the Holy Spirit. On that occasion the Melchizedek Priesthood was conferred upon a convert in Denmark for the first time, Brother Christian Christiansen, who had previously been appointed to succeed Elder John E. Forsgren as president of the Copenhagen Branch, being ordained an Elder by Apostle Erastus Snow. Andreas Ågren was ordained a Priest, Ole Svendsen a Teacher, and Hans Larsen a Deacon.

In the beginning of January, 1851, the first sheet of the Book of Mormon in the Danish language (16 pages) was issued from the press in Copenhagen; other sheets followed soon afterwards. As many of the

CHRISTIAN CHRISTIANSEN
Born Oct. 7, 1824, in Dölby, Saliing, Denmark; died Sept. 23, 1900, in Manti, Utah.

Saints were poor, it was deemed wise to let them have each sheet as it was issued from the press, thus enabling them to pay for the book by small installments. Though the book was received by some of the new converts to "Mormonism" with reservations, yet it was made the subject of diligent study and serious reflection, and by faith and prayers, as well as by the patient labors of the brethren in explaining its contents, it became the means of strengthening the faith of the Danish Saints.*

*Elder Peter O. Hansen had, while residing in Nauvoo, Illinois, translated a portion of the Book of Mormon into Danish with a view to completing the work at some future day in his native land, and, carrying out his original intentions, he finished the translation of the book after his arrival in Denmark; but as he had spent several years in foreign lands and to some extent forgotten his native language, it became necessary to submit his translation to a thorough revision. An educated Danish lady, who was a teacher of several languages, was engaged to assist in the work. This was begun immediately after Elder Snow's return to Denmark from England (October 30th, 1850), and occupied the time of the parties named for several months.

In January, 1851, Elder George P. Dykes, who had continued his labors with great success in the city of Aalborg and its environments, went to Hals, a small market town in Vendsyssel, where a few persons had joined the Church. The first of these converts were Lars Christian Larsen Domgaard and Niels Peter Larsen Domgaard, of Hals, who had been baptized in Aalborg by Brother Hans Peter Jensen. While visiting Hals, Elder Dykes encountered an infuriated mob who committed personal violence upon him and even threatened his life. In addition to that, the mobbers almost demolished the house in which he was found, tearing the tiles from the roof and breaking all the windows; but he finally escaped by the back way, through the aid of some women, without serious harm, and returned to Aalborg. Notwithstanding such acts of violence a number of converts were made, and soon a small branch of the Church was organized in Hals. From Aalborg, Elder Dykes extended his labors to a number of villages where well-attended meetings were held. The meetings in Aalborg were also well attended. But Elder Dykes became the target for opposition, both from the Baptists and Lutherans. Finally the mayor of Aalborg summoned him to appear before him, and the result was a most rigid examination of the doctrines taught by Elder Dykes. As the mayor could find no special charge on which to deal with him, according to law, that official contented himself with forbidding Elder Dykes to hold public meetings until the officials of the city could get instructions from higher authorities. The consequence of this order was that the hall which the Saints had rented for meeting purposes in Aalborg was closed for about three months, but during that time Elder Dykes found ample opportunity for promulgating the gospel by accepting invitations to visit the people in their houses.

In the meantime, Elder John E. Forsgren and Priest Andreas Ågren hired a hall and commenced preaching in Roskilde, a small city situated sixteen English miles west of Copenhagen, but after three meetings had been held there, the populace were incited by the Lutheran priests to drive the brethren away. A mob assembled one evening and commenced depredations upon the houses where the missionaries had been entertained; they also rushed Elder Forsgren through the streets, beating and abusing him in various ways until a late hour, when the police, which connived with the mob under the pretense of rescuing him, took him into custody. The next day Brothers Forsgren and Ågren were both sent away by order of the Borgmester (mayor), but at the request of the brethren the mayor admitted, and so entered upon his records, that there was no law authorizing his actions in the matter, but that he did it for the peace of the town. Several other attempts to secure places for preaching in the regions round about Copenhagen failed, and street preaching was not allowed. The brethren, however, were not so easily discouraged, for after their unpleasant experience in Roskilde, they commenced missionary work in Hirschholm, an estate situated about twelve miles north of Copenhagen. Here they also encountered much opposition and caused great excitement, but found friends who received their testimony and were baptized soon afterwards. A branch of the Church was the result of their labors.

One of the first converts to "Mormonism" in Hirschholm was Niels Jensen, a potter by trade, who afterwards became a well-known resident of the Second Ward in Salt Lake City, Utah, and a number of others who later distinguished themselves as faithful members of the Church in the Valleys of the Mountains. Among them was the late Anders W. Winberg, who subsequently fig-

ANDERS WILHELM WINBERG
Born April 13, 1830, near Lund, Sweden; died Aug. 8, 1909, in Salt Lake City, Utah.

ured as a successful local missionary in Denmark and Sweden, emigrated to Utah and afterwards filled a good mission to Scandinavia. For many years he presided over the Scandinavian meetings in Salt Lake City, and in 1876, with the consent of President Brigham Young, commenced the publication of "Bikuben," which is still being published as a Church organ for the Danish-Norwegian Saints in America.

At a Priesthood meeting held in Copenhagen, March 3, 1851, Christian J. Larsen, who was one of the early converts to the Church in Copenhagen, was ordained a Priest and his brother, Johannes Larsen, a Deacon. Elder Christian Christiansen and Priest Christian J. Larsen were then appointed to go to Jutland as missionaries, to assist Elder George P. Dykes. These two brethren left Copenhagen for their new field of labor March 12, 1851, and, traveling by way of Roskilde, Korssör and Aarhus, arrived in Aalborg on Sunday morning, March 16th. There they united their efforts with Elder Hans Peter Jensen of Nörre Sundby, Hans F. Petersen and others who had been baptized in Aalborg and vicinity, and by their energetic and faithful labors they became the instruments in the hands of the Lord to add many souls to the Church on both sides of the Limfjord, and soon a new branch of the Church was organized at Kjeldgaard, near Aalborg.

In the latter part of March, the first edition of a Latter-day Saint hymn book in the Danish-Norwegian language was published by Erastus Snow in Copenhagen. Most of the hymns used in this little volume were translations from the English Latter-day Saints' hymn book, and selections from Danish authors; some of these selections had previously been used by the new converts in their Baptist congregations. The translations were principally done by Elder Peter O. Hansen, and a special effort was made to have the translated hymns correspond in meter to the tunes sung by the Saints in Zion, the Apostle himself teaching the Saints to sing them. This first edition of the Danish Latter-day Saint hymn book contained only 28 hymns, but in addition to the hymns, extracts from some of the most important revelations translated from the Doctrine and Covenants, together with the Articles of Faith, were printed and bound in the same volume. In that form the little book gave the young Saints in Denmark, as well as the Elders, much joy and consolation. In October, 1851, a second edition of the hymn book was published, containing forty-five hymns. In the preface, Erastus Snow expressed a prophetic hope in connection with its future in the following words: "Thousands of Saints will also in Denmark be encouraged, comforted and strengthened by the use of these songs, and it is hoped that these few may be kindly accepted, until the Lord shall raise up gifted poets and give a greater abundance of the Songs of Zion." These sentiments have been most happily fulfilled, both as to the number of Saints and poets raised up since then. During the following seventy-five years about 50,000 copies of improved and enlarged editions of the Danish hymn book have been published in Denmark and sold in that country as well as in Norway and Sweden, not to speak of several editions of a very similar collection of hymns published in the Swedish language. The fifteenth Danish-Norwegian edition of the Latter-day Saint hymn book, published in 1906, contained 281 hymns, of which about forty are translations from English, a few selections from the hymn books of other denominations and the remainder originals. Many other poetical effusions in the Danish-Norwegian language have appeared in "Skandinaviens Stjerne" from time to time which have not yet found a place in the hymn-book, though perhaps entitled to as much appreciation as many of those used in the collection. On Monday, April 14, 1851, Elder George P. Dykes left Aalborg for Schlesvig, where he went by invitation of certain friends to open a new field of labor among German-speaking people. Elder Dykes had labored in Jutland six months and three days, and raised up a flourishing branch of the Church in the city of Aalborg, which, at the time of his departure, numbered about a hundred members, including one Elder, three Teachers and one Deacon. He had also published 1,000 tracts treating upon the doctrines of the gospel which he circulated gratis; also 1,000 copies of a leaflet containing scriptural references, and 800 copies of a chronological table published in order to show that the second coming of the Savior was nigh at hand. He had also circulated about 200 tracts which Brother Erastus Snow had sent him from Copenhagen. Bro. Dykes returned to Aalborg May 18, 1851.

In the meantime, Elder Erastus Snow and his fellow-missionaries labored successfully in the city of Copenhagen and vicinity. As many of the Saints in Copenhagen lived in that part of the city which is called Christianshavn, and which is mostly inhabited by the laboring classes, it was decided to rent a place

LATTER-DAY SAINT MEETING HALL IN CHRISTIANSHAVN, DENMARK
The meeting hall was in the second story of the house on the left.

there for holding meetings, and thus on the 25th of April, 1851, the Saints took possession of a hall situated on the corner of Dronningens Gade and Sankt Anna Gade, opposite one of the largest churches in the city, called "Vor Frelsers Kirke" (the Church of our Savior). In this hall good and spirited meetings were held for several years afterwards and many brethren, who later became prominent in the Church, here received their various degrees of the Priesthood and much valuable training for future usefulness.

Disturbances by mobs were soon transferred to the new hall on Christianshavn and that, too, with increased violence. Application for protection was ignored by the police authorities under the pretext that their duty was only to keep peace and order in the street, and not in the house. The brethren, therefore, soon came to the conclusion that if they wanted peace and protection, they would have to depend upon their own resources and strength and, consequently, prepared themselves for the next attack.

One evening the mob again appeared on the scene, while the hall was well filled with people. Apostle Snow placed two very strong brethren by the door, with instructions to get the disturbers out by force, if necessary, when he should give the signal.

Soon the rabble began their usual disorderly conduct, when Apostle Snow, filled with indignation, spoke with a voice like thunder, saying: "Now, brethren! if you will assist me, we will soon get these fellows out." Suiting his actions to the words he had uttered, he commenced to divest himself of his coat, in order to take a hand in the performance himself. This, however, did not become necessary, as fear seized upon the unruly element which quickly backed down towards the door where the brethren in attendance waited upon them and gave them forcible assistance down a long flight of stairs. The mobbers being thus ejected, the door was locked, and after that they tried in vain to open it from the outside. However, they broke the panels of the door and threw stones in through the windows. But as they were now in the street, they were finally dispersed by the police; and during the remainder of that evening a good meeting was held and peace was maintained in the hall. After that incident the mobs did not disturb the meetings in Christianshavn. In the other hall, in Lille Kongensgade, the disturbances had been so frequent and violent that the owner, Mr. Nehm, who had some special right as a tax-payer of real estate on one occasion called on the military to keep order, and thus one Sunday, two soldiers, with fixed bayonets on their guns, stood by the door inside the hall, while the Elders held their meeting and preached the gospel in peace.

Two natives of Iceland, Thorarinn Haflidason Thorason and Gudmund Gudmundson became converts to "Mormonism" in Copenhagen in the early part of 1851, (Gudmundson was baptized Feb. 15, 1851, by Peter O. Hansen). They were both young men who had spent some time in Denmark learning trades. Thus Thorason was a cabinet-maker and Gudmundson a jeweler. When these young men were ready to return to their native island in the spring of 1851, Elder Erastus Snow concluded to ordain them to the lesser Priesthood, so that they might have authority to preach the gospel to their countrymen. Hence, Brother Thorason was ordained a Priest by

Brother Snow at a Priesthood meeting held in Copenhagen, March 10, 1851, and at a fast meeting held April 18, 1851, Brother Gudmundson was ordained a Teacher by Erastus Snow. Soon afterwards these two brethren sailed for Iceland, after being instructed by Elder Snow and the other brethren in Copenhagen how to proceed with missionary labors after their arrival. Following the instructions received, they commenced immediately after their arrival in Iceland, to preach and to bear testimony to their countrymen. Several believed their testimony and Brother Thorason baptized a man, by the name of Benedikt Hanson, and his wife on Westmanöen.

"Having baptized these two persons," writes Elder John Thorgeirson, "they (Thorason and Gudmundson) were prohibited by legal authorities to preach, in consequence of which their operations were confined to instructions in private to those who would listen to them. These first missionaries to Iceland were not subject to mob violence in any way whatever, as nothing is more odious, in the eyes or to the minds of the Icelanders than lawlessness of any kind, but they were simply barred from addressing public gatherings by a decree of the court of justice, in accordance with the laws of the country." A further reason why Brother Thorason ceased active missionary work, according to the statement of his companion, was that his wife hardened her heart against the work and burned her husband's books.

Some time during the following December (1851) Brother Thorason was accidentally drowned while out in a boat fishing near the coast. This left Brother Gudmundson alone with the two baptized but unconfirmed members. He wrote a letter to

Copenhagen, reporting the death of his companion, and also stated that there were twenty-four persons on the island who desired baptism, but as he only held the office of Teacher he had no authority to administer that ordinance unto them.

When Elder Snow received this news he felt very sad, as he then remembered that when he ordained Brother Gudmundson to the office of a Teacher, the spirit of God whispered to him that he should ordain him an Elder, but he gave the inspiration no heed, as the young man seemed so lively and enthusiastic, while his companion, Brother Thorason, appeared to be more sedate and thoughtful. Elder Snow's great desire was now to find a suitable Elder whom he could send to Iceland. Brother Peter O. Hansen volunteered, but while endeavoring to obtain a passport from the proper officials in Copenhagen, the object of his intended visit to Iceland was discovered, and for that reason he was denied the necessary papers. Nearly two years passed, before the needed help could be sent to Iceland.

CHAPTER 6 (1851)

The Book of Mormon published in Danish—Erastus Snow's second visit to England—First missionaries on Bornholm—The gospel carried to southern Jutland and the island of Fyen—Persecutions in Aalborg—Saints abused and property destroyed—Elder Snow's report to President Brigham Young.

The last sheets of the Book of Mormon were received from the printers May 22, 1851, and immediately sent to the book-binders. Elders Snow and Hansen, who during the previous winter had been extremely busy translating and proof-reading the sacred volume, now felt themselves relieved from a great burden. The book was printed by Mr. F. E. Bording, who was paid 1,000 "rigsdaler" (about $500) for printing 3000 copies. Nearly 200 copies were for-

warded to subscribers in Copenhagen, Aalborg and other places as

F. E. BORDING
Died in Copenhagen, Feb. 3, 1884, 66 years
old.

they were issued from the press in
sheets.*

At a council meeting held in Christianshavn, May 21, 1851, President
Erastus Snow expressed his great joy
at the completion of the printing of
the Book of Mormon in the Danish
language, and as the work connected
with its revision and proof-reading
had proved a great mental strain on
all concerned, he decided to make a
trip to England, to attend a conference in London, and he advised
Brother Peter O. Hansen to take a
missionary tour to the southern part
of Jutland. Teacher L. J. Jpson and
Priest Andreas Agren were called to
commence missionary labors on the
island of Bornholm. About the same
time, two Swedish brethren, namely,
Nils Olson and Peter Beckström,
who had been ordained Priests, were
called to cross the Sound (Öresund)

*A second edition of the Danish Book of
Mormon (3000 copies) was published by Hector C. Haight in 1858, a third edition of 2000
copies by Niels Wilhelmsen in 1881, a fourth
edition of 2000 copies by Anton L. Skanchy
in 1902 and a fifth edition of 10,000 copies, by
Andrew Jenson in 1910.

to Sweden and quietly commence
missionary work in the province of
Skåne. As Sweden did not enjoy religious liberty, they were advised to
spread the printed work as much as
possible among their countrymen and
by a wise, prudent course to avoid
conflict with the Swedish police.
Elder George P. Dykes left Aalborg
for England, May 23, 1851.

Having appointed John E. Forsgren to take temporary charge of the
mission in the Scandinavian countries, Elder Erastus Snow sailed from
Copenhagen, May 24, 1851, for Wis-
mar, Germany, on his way to England. His main object in going to
England at this time was to obtain
more means to enable him to publish
other books and tracts, which were
needed for the Scandinavian Mission,
and also to obtain a much needed
rest.

Andreas Ågren and L. J. Ipson arrived on the island of Bornholm as
missionaries June 6, 1851. After
holding a few meetings on the island,
they both returned to Copenhagen,
giving an unfavorable report of the
prospects for preaching there. Their
failure, however, was partly due to
the unwise conduct of Brother Ipson,
who was excommunicated from the
Church, June 20, 1851. Brother
Ågren returned to Bornholm soon
afterwards, and two Sisters Bentsen,
natives of Bornholm, who had been
baptized in Copenhagen, also went
over to bear testimony to their friends
and relatives. The gospel seed soon
fell into congenial soil and on July
10, 1851, five persons (the first-
fruits of preaching the gospel on the
island of Bornholm) were baptized
by Brother Ågren. The next day he
baptized two more. In the latter
part of the month Elder Hans Peter
Jensen arrived as a missionary from
Copenhagen and confirmed the seven
persons who had been baptized by

Elder Ågren, and also baptized other converts*

In April, 1851, two brothers, Johannes and Lauritz Larsen, who had embraced the gospel in Copenhagen, returned to their native village, Greis, in the southern part of Jutland. Johannes had been ordained a Deacon. Both brothers were tailors by trade. While working at that vocation they were energetic in bearing testimony to the truth of the restored gospel wherever they had an opportunity to do so. Elder Peter O. Hansen and Priest William O. Andersen, who had been appointed on a special mission to Jutland, at the August conference held in Copenhagen, arrived in Fredericia, June 10, 1851. In that city they found a small branch of Baptists who had suffered great persecution because of their religion. On their arrival in Fredericia, Brothers Hansen and Andersen also called on Priest Knud H. Bruun, who served as a waiter in a hotel. The following Sunday (June 15th) the brethren held their first meeting in that city, in a large hall, hired in a hotel. Subsequently they visited Greis and other places and held a few small meetings. Elder Hansen baptized Kiersten Olesen at Greis, June 29, 1851, and Ebbe Jessen at Fredericia, July 5, 1851. These were the first converts to "Mormonism" in that part of the country. After ordaining Johannes Larsen to the office of a Priest, Elder Hansen returned to Copenhagen, where he arrived on the 7th of July. After his departure, Priest Wm. O. Andersen continued his labors in Fredericia and vicinity and also crossed over the sound (Lillebelt) to the island of Fyen, thus being the first "Mormon" to labor as a missionary on that

*The village of Arnager became the cradle of Mormonism on Bornholm, and Jens Nielsen, who died as a faithful member of the Church at Newton, Utah, some years ago, was the first man baptized on the island.

island. Elder Andersen encountered considerable opposition and some persecution. One case of that kind he described as follows:

"I appointed a meeting on a Sunday in Fredericia and had Brother Bruun write the address of the place of meeting on slips of paper which I distributed among the people. Sunday morning came, and I appeared at the appointed place with my Bible, but almost immediately I was confronted by a man who forbade me to hold the appointed meeting, saying that he was the owner of the premises and that the man who had given me permission to preach in the house was only a tenant. I told the people that had gathered what had happened, and as they were unwilling to separate, they followed me to the house of Brother Ebbe Jessen, which was soon surrounded by the multitude. Being requested by a post office official to speak to them, I endeavored to do so, but a policeman stepped up and told me that he was unable to protect me against the people, who were bent on doing me personal harm. Acting on the impulse of the moment, I threw a handful of my smaller tracts out over the multitude to divert their attention, and while the people were scrambling among themselves to catch them, or to pick them up, I improved the opportunity by slipping out through a door in the rear of the building, and by the assistance of a friendly blacksmith I hid in a small room on the top of a wardrobe. Here I remained while the angry mobbers sought for me; they even threatened to tear down the building, if the owner did not reveal my hiding place. At length the ruffians took their departure, and so did I, after the kind blacksmith had treated me to dinner. Acting upon the advice of my friends, I left Fredericia the next day for Copenhagen, where I attended the conference in August."

On Sunday, June 22, 1851, Elder Hans Peter Jensen and his brethren of the Priesthood in Aalborg concluded that they would perform the ordinance of baptism at a public place by the seaside (that is, in the open waters of the "Limfjord," near the city of Aalborg.) A great gathering of people, comprising both sexes of all ages, gathered at the appointed place to witness something that could not fail to arouse their highest curiosity. Before proceeding to baptize, Elders Christian J. Larsen and Hans Peter Jensen spoke to the people and warned them to flee from the "Church of the devil," intimating that the Lutheran priests represented that church. At these announcements the people became enraged and seized some of the brethren, whom they brought before a prominent clergyman of the city. They were followed thither by the mob, which next proceeded to the place where the Saints were holding their meetings and began an attack on the house; all the windows were broken, the doors torn down, and the members of the Church within reach grossly insulted. For a while it looked as if several of the Saints would lose their lives; but, strange to say, none was seriously hurt, though the mob seemed to be angry enough to commit almost any crime. Sister Mathilda Petersen, who had just become convalescent after confinement, and who occupied a room adjoining the hall, was compelled to leave the house. In the evening, the soldiers, of whom quite a number were quartered in the city at the time, were ordered out to quell the disturbance; but just before they arrived on the scene of the mobbing, a fearful storm accompanied by thunder and lightning, the like of which had scarcely been seen in Aalborg before, broke forth, and the mobbers, drenched to the skin, fled to their homes.

The six following nights mobbers repeated their depredations, and, not satisfied with having demolished the Saints' place of worship, hunted up all the members of the Church they could find in the city and vicinity and treated their private residences in much the same manner as they had the meeting hall. While **they** broke doors and windows, and

destroyed furniture and other property, they insulted the people in almost every conceivable way, sparing neither sex nor age.

The late Hans F. Petersen of Ephraim, Sanpete county, Utah, the man with whom Elder Dykes lived in the rooms adjoining the meeting hall, gives the following detailed account of these mobbings in his private journal:

"On Sunday, June 22 (1851) we held council meetings all day, and many of the Saints were present. About six o'clock in the evening most of the members went out to the fjord, at a point nearly a mile east of the town, to baptize three individuals who desired to join the Church. A large crowd of people followed us to the place selected for the baptisms; after we reached the spot, the crowd kept increasing, until hundreds of people had gathered, who soon gave vent to their evil designs by insulting the Saints, not only by applying to them vile and wicked epithets, but also by pushing and beating them in many different ways. Brother Christian J. Larsen and Hans Peter Jensen attempted to address the crowd and bear testimony to the word of God and the plan of salvation; but while they did so, the mob at intervals shouted, ridiculed and made the most hideous noises, only stopping now and then to listen to the speakers. Giving up the idea of baptizing the three candidates, we, at length, left the place, pushing our way through the immense crowd. Some of us were violently pulled along the road, and, while subjected to insults and blows, brought into town and up to the residence of the dean (Provsten), where we were asked to defend our case and prove what the speakers had said regarding the state church; that it was not the church of Christ. Nothing was accomplished by this interview with the priests, though the correctness of our statement was made pretty plain by the acts of the state church members who persecuted us.

"An hour or so later, an immense multitude gathered in the street (Slotsgaden) and outside of our meeting hall, partly as spectators and partly as a lawless mob, bent on further mischief; and they soon commenced their acts of violence. After using an abundance of foul language and crowding in and out through the rooms, several of the most desperate characters attacked a number of the brethren who were present, and whipped and ill-treated them unmercifully. Thus they trod on the neck of Brother Jens Thomsen, and I myself was subjected to severe beating, pushing and hair-pulling; in fact, I was terribly beaten about the whole body. While I was in their hands, my mother-in-law came running to rescue me, followed by my wife, who was still weak after a confinement. As the mob did not heed the pleadings of the women, my wife at last sent a well-directed blow into the face of one of the principal mobbers. This seemed to bring them somewhat to their senses, for the man who received the blow let go his hold on my person, which enabled me to tear loose from the rest and run into our sleeping apartment together with my wife and several of the Saints. Brother Thomsen also succeeded in getting loose and ran in great haste to us. We now locked the door and pressed hard against it on the inside until the mob broke it. My wife insisted that I should save myself by jumping out of the window; but it seemed inconsistent for me to run away and leave my wife and little infant to their fate. At last, however, I concluded that it was the best I could do under the circumstances, as it was evident that if I remained in the room I could neither defend myself nor my family. Therefore, committing my dear ones to the protection of God, I leaped through a window out into the street, and thence fled into a garden lying back of the house in which I lived. There I secreted myself under the gooseberry bushes, and while lying there I could hear quite distinctly what was going on in the house. My wife remained in the room for some time, unhurt by the mob; but at length, when a couple of rocks were thrown through the windows, she fled to the residence of Mr. Frandsen, a police officer.

"From my hiding place, I could hear the work of destruction going on, as the mob tore, splintered and broke windows, doors, tables, benches, kitchen utensils, etc. They continued their depredations until past 11 o'clock at night when a terrific storm accompanied by thunder and lightning, put a stop to their wicked doings. About the same time the troops were called out, but they did not arrive on the scene till the work of destruction was completed; a military guard was placed around the demolished building till daylight. After everything had become quiet, I climbed over the board fence, between 12 and 1 o'clock at night, and to my great joy and satisfaction, I found my wife and child safe at the house of Mr. Frandsen."

During the persecutions, the mob surrounded Elder Hans Peter Jensen's house in Nörre Sundby for several successive nights, broke windows and doors, tore off the tile from the roof of his buildings, and in other respects damaged his property. The last night of these attacks, Elder Jensen went out among the crowd, numbering between four and five hundred people, which had surrounded his premises and spoke to them. They all remained reasonably quiet and listened while he addressed them; but as soon as he was through, they raised a great howl and decided to cast him into a deep sand pit situated on the premises; with the assistance of a friend, however, he escaped this fate and got safely back into the house. The hostile attitude of the mob at last assumed such a character that it became necessary for Brother Jensen to leave his home, in order to save his life, which was threatened repeatedly. In the dead hours of night he traveled on foot (running part of the way) twenty miles in five hours, to the town of Hals, where he again found himself surrounded by a mob led by several persons who recognized him. By using a little strategy, however, and through the providence of the Almighty, he succeeded in getting on board the steamship passing Hals on its way from Aalborg to Copenhagen. The mob called out in angry tones from the shore, commanding the boatmen to cast him overboard. On boarding the ship he found his tried friend, Elder George P. Dykes, who had come to Aalborg on another visit, but who had been compelled to take refuge on the steamer and depart from the city without seeing the Saints.

While visiting in England, Elder Erastus Snow, under date of July 10, 1851, wrote to President Brigham Young in Salt Lake City, Utah, giving an interesting report of the introduction of the gospel into the Scandinavian countries. Referring to the opposition in Copenhagen, he wrote:

"Our hall and the streets about us were thronged by a great crowd of journeymen, apprentices, sailors, etc., led on by the theological students who turned our meeting into a 'pow wow,' dealing out all manner of threats and abuses until finally we were obliged to cease our public meetings; the police refused interference in our behalf. Some private houses, where we had small gatherings, next became the objects of vengeance. About the same time, also, evil spirits attacked some persons in the Church and manifested their power in many strange ways, and it took some time to subdue them entirely; all of this, however, afforded lessons of wisdom and experience to the young Saints. They also made an angry demonstration upon John E. Forsgren and myself in our room at night, somewhat similar to that upon Elders Orson Hyde and Heber C. Kimball in Preston. My eyes were opened to behold them, and through humble prayer we obtained power to withstand them and to rebuke them from our presence and room. It seemed, indeed, as though the powers of earth and hell were combined to crush the work of the Lord in that land, but through prayer and fasting we received strength, and the clouds began to disperse. "We sent a deputation to the king with a memorial, a Book of Mormon and my pamphlet. I shortly after heard of the Book of Mormon in the possession of the queen dowager (who is reputedly pious and a lover of the Bible). She, as the maids reported, was so wrought up by the presentation of the book that excitement and alarm spread through her palace, and she was unable to leave her room for several days. We were afterwards informed through the 'Kultus minister,' who has the superintendency of all schools and church affairs, that the government was disposed to allow us our regular course and interpose no obstacles. After this the police officers in Aalborg, by order of the 'Kultus minister,' restored to the Saints their privileges and we began also to enjoy peace and quiet at our meetings in Copenhagen. * * Before the adjournment of the Danish Rigsdag (legislature) a law passed in a modified form, sustaining religious freedom, and abrogating the old law which denied the rights of matrimony and all other civil and social privileges to native subjects unless

sprinkled, educated and confirmed in the Lutheran Church. Yet there is nothing in the constitution or laws that guarantees us that protection in our worship and in the exercise of our religious rights which is afforded by the laws of England and America. I now feel that the 'shell is broken' in old Scandinavia, and that the work of the Lord will advance. Probably an earlier mission to that country would have proved a failure."

After Elder Snow's departure for England, Elder Peter O. Hansen visited the Saints in the southern part of Jutland, giving needed counsel and instruction, and rendering the local brethren such aid as he found necessary. After that he visited Aalborg, where he comforted the Saints who had recently been exposed to persecution. During this visit Hans Frederik Petersen was ordained an Elder and appointed president of the Aalborg Branch. Others of the local brethren were ordained Teachers. The Aalborg mob, having discovered that something important was going on among the Saints, gathered one night and made disturbances. A large stone weighing about three pounds was thrown through the window in the house where Brother Hans F. Petersen lived, and struck the cradle in which their baby was sleeping, but, fortunately, no damage was done. After setting things in order in Aalborg and vicinity, Brother Hansen returned to Copenhagen.

CHAPTER 7 (1851)

Elder Erastus Snow returns from England—First conference held in Copenhagen—New branches of the Church organized—First missionaries on the island of Falster—Elder Snow visits Aalborg—The first Norwegian baptized—The publication of "Skandinaviens Stjerne" commenced.

Elder Erastus Snow returned to Copenhagen from his visit to England August 3, 1851, after having been absent from his field of labor about ten weeks. He was hailed with heartfelt welcome and great joy by the Danish Saints. Soon after his return, he and the other American Elders were invited to live with a Brother Rasmus Petersen who resided on Gammeltorv No. 37. Consequently, the brethren moved their residence from the home of Lauritz B. Malling, where they had lived since their first arrival in Copenhagen. Soon afterwards they commenced the translation of Orson Pratt's "Remarkable Visions," which was published in the Danish language under the title "Mærkværdige Syner." It was printed in octave form and subsequently found such a wide circulation in the Scandinavian Mission that 14,000 copies in Danish and 16,000 copies in Swedish had been distributed up to 1881.

Soon after his return from England, Elder Snow called a general conference in Copenhagen, which was held in the Saints' hall on Christianshavn, August 16th, 17th and 18th. At this conference over three hundred Saints in Scandinavia were reported in good standing and over thirty had been excommunicated for cause. A number of local brethren were ordained to the Priesthood. While the conference was in session, Elder John E. Forsgren, who had been sent to the island of Bornholm to assist Priest Andreas Ågren there, returned to Copenhagen and reported that thirteen persons had been baptized. Elder Snow then, with the sanction of the conference, organized a branch of the Church on Bornholm, and also organized the Saints in and near Aalborg into three branches, namely, Aalborg, with Hans F. Petersen as president. Hals, with Nils P. Domgaard as president, and Kjeldgaard, with Niels Petersen as president. The Saints in Copenhagen were organized into two branches, the second to meet on

Christianshavn, where a hall had been secured for holding meetings. At this conference also, it was decided to publish a monthly periodical in the Danish language as the organ of the Church in Scandinavia, and also to publish a larger edition of the hymn-book. Elder John E. Forsgren was appointed to open the gospel door on the island of Falster, and to be accompanied by one of the local brethren.

Soon after this conference Elder George P. Dykes, according to his own desire, left Denmark to continue his missionary labors in Germany.

Agreeable to appointment, Elder John E. Forsgren and Priest Johan

JOHAN FREDERIK FERDINAND DORIUS

Born June 15, 1832, in Copenhagen, Denmark; died July 18, 1901, in Ephraim, Utah.

F. F. Dorius, proceeded as the first Latter-day Saint missionaries to the island of Falster. They arrived in the little city of Nykjöbing, Sept. 4, 1851. A sister by the name of Ludvigsen, the only member of the

Church on the island, met the brethren at the landing place. She had
previously been baptized while on a
visit to Copenhagen, and she now
became a great help to the missionaries during their sojourn on Falster.
Brother Dorius says, in his journal:

"Soon after our arrival on the island, we
commenced holding meetings in various
places and these were generally well attended, curiosity causing a great many to
come out to see and hear us. Very soon
we became the object of general attention
by the inhabitants, and some of them be-
lived our doctrine, while a great many became offended and hostile to us, in consequence of which we soon had a few
friends and many enemies. A Lutheran
priest by the name of Peter Kock was one
of our most energetic opponents; he met
to oppose us in nearly every meeting we
held and used every means in his power to
hinder the progress of the gospel, but not
being very successful by these methods, he
wrote and published a scurrilous article
about the 'Mormons' and 'Mormonism,'
which was published in the local paper,
'Lolland og Falsters Stiftstidende.' The
article was entitled, 'Vogter Eder for de
falske Profeter' (Beware of the false Prophets), and its publication had considerable effect upon the people, who to a great
degree were stirred up against us, and we
came very near being horribly maltreated
by a mob, as the following account will
show: At Nykjöbing, one evening, we
were going out to visit some people who
desired to have a talk with us about the
gospel, but we had hardly arrived at our
destination before several persons entered
the house and sat down, being closely
followed by others; more and more came
in, till the thouse was filled to its utmost
capacity by people who seemed bent on
mischief. Soon, also, the street outside the
house was full of people and the whole
town seemed to be in a general uproar.
Both Brother Forsgren and I made several
attempts to talk to the people, but to no
purpose on account of the great tumult
and shouting both in and outside of the
house. The mobbers then commenced to
break in the doors and windows, and many
of them crowded in upon us, cursing and
swearing at us fearfully. We were also
subjected to ridicule, but we kept ourselves
passive and were silent throughout. Our
situation was indeed disagreeable and it
looked as if we certainly would meet with
harsh treatment. The Lord, however, came

to our deliverance. We were secretly informed that by passing through a small
chamber and the kitchen we could get
away from the house unobserved by our
enemies. This we succeeded in doing, and
as soon as the crowd found we were gone,
they also left, a few at a time, so that by
11 o'clock at night we could leave the town
unmolested. We continued our missionary
labors on Falster for several weeks and
finally returned to Copenhagen to attend
the general conference which had been
appointed for November."

In the latter part of August, Elder
Christian J. Larsen and William O.
Andersen left Copenhagen for the
southern part of Jutland, where they
engaged in successful missionary
labors, and organized a branch of
the Church at Greis, near Veile.
Among the first membership of that
branch was the family of Larsen,
who afterwards figured prominently
in the Church both in Denmark and
Utah.

About this time Elder Erastus
Snow arrived in Aalborg on a visit,
and on the 31st of that month he
held a special conference, or general
meeting, with the Saints at Kjeldgaard, in the parish of Gudumlund,
about twelve English miles southeast
of Aalborg. Among the business attended to on this occasion was the
further organization of the Saints in
Hals and Kjeldgaard into branches
of the Church. The Saints in Aalborg, who constituted the main
branch of the Church in Jutland,
were left in charge of Elder Hans F.
Petersen. Missionaries were called
to visit Dronninglund in Vendsyssel,
Lögstör, Jetzmark and other localities.

In the meantime some of the enemies of the Saints learned of the
presence of Elder Erastus Snow in
that part of the country and that an
important meeting at Kjeldgaard was
in session. A messenger dispatched
by a friend in Aalborg suddenly appeared in the meeting in Kjeldgaard

and informed the Saints that the mob was lying in wait, ready to fall upon them on their way back to Aalborg. The Saints, therefore, scattered and those belonging to Aalborg returned on different routes. Thus, instead of the Saints encountering the assault of their enemies, a company of Baptists, whom the mob mistook for Saints, were shamefully maltreated.

Elder Erastus Snow, while visiting with Hans Peter Jensen in Nörre Sundby, September 3, 1851, had a conversation with a Norwegian sailor, about which Elder Snow journalizes as follows:

"A Norwegian by the name of Svend Larsen, the master of a small merchant

SVEND LARSEN
Born Jan. 26, 1816, at Österrisör, Norway; died April 3, 1886, in Mount Pleasant, Sanpete Co., Utah. He was the first convert to "Mormonism" in Norway, emigrated to Utah in 1853-1854, and filled a mission to Norway in 1865-1867.

vessel, came to visit me. He said he had heard of me and my religion, and had come with a view to learn more about it. I improved the opportunity to explain to him the principles of the gospel and the order of the kingdom of God as it had been revealed from the Lord; he received my testimony with gladness. His vessel being ready to sail for Norway on his return next day, I called and appointed Elder Hans F.

Petersen to go with Mr. Larsen to his home in Norway to open up the gospel door in that country. The two sailed together from Aalborg on the 4th of September, well supplied with the Book of Mormon and tracts."

The little vessel encountered stormy weather. It seemed as if the "prince of the air" was determined to hinder the servant of God from reaching his destination; twice the little craft had to seek shelter against the storm in the harbor of Frederikshavn; but, after a prolonged contest

HANS FREDERIK PETERSEN
Born February 7, 1821, near Aalborg, Denmark; died Jan. 9, 1882, at Ephraim, Utah.

with the elements, Österrisör, in Norway, was finally reached in safety on Thursday, September 11, 1851.

Captain or "Skipper" Larsen, as he was familiarly called afterwards, offered Brother Petersen the hospitality of his home as long as he remained in the town. The following day (Sept. 12th) Elder Petersen commenced to visit the people in Österrisör and distribute tracts. On the 13th Captain Larsen went to the dean (Provsten) and asked if he would permit the "Mormon" Elder, who had just arrived in the land, to hold meetings in the school house on the Sunday. The priest became perfectly astonished at such a bold request and asked with considerable emotion if the "Mormons" really had now come to Norway.

Owing to the hasty departure from Aalborg, Elder Petersen had not secured a passport, or a traveling permit from the authorities of that city and, consequently, he was summoned to appear before the mayor in Österrisör and questioned very closely in regard to his object in visiting Norway. He explained that he had come to preach the gospel of Jesus Christ, but that, if it was contrary to the laws of the land to hold public meetings, he would confine his labors to private conversation with the people. On Captain Larsen giving good security for him, Elder Petersen escaped arrest and imprisonment and was permitted to stay for a few days, but was instructed to secure a passport as soon as possible, or leave the country. After this, Elder Petersen resumed his labors without holding public meetings and made acquaintances and friends among different classes of people. Among those visited, to whom he bore testimony, were the Danish consul, the "Provst" Wittergren, and other distinguished citizens.

Through the neglect of the authorities in Aalborg, Elder Petersen did not receive his passport, in consequence of which he found it necessary to return to Denmark to obtain it. He therefore sailed with Captain Larsen from Österrisör September 20, 1851, and arrived in Aalborg on the 23rd. In the evening of that day Captain Larsen was baptized by Elder Ole Christian Nielsen. Thus he became the first fruit of the true gospel from Norway, with the exception of the few Norwegians who had previously been baptized in La Salle County, Illinois.

On Wednesday, October 1, 1851, the first number of "Skandinaviens

Stjerne" (the Scandinavian Star) was published by Erastus Snow in Copenhagen. It was a single sheet of sixteen pages octavo size, and was issued as a monthly periodical the first year. Elder Peter O. Hansen had been appointed translator as well as clerk of the mission, while Erastus Snow was the responsible editor. The second year it was decided to publish the periodical semimonthly, on the 1st and 15th of every month, and thus it has appeared up to the present time.* The typographical work was done by F. E. Bording, who subsequently printed nearly all the publications of the Scandinavian Mission as long as he lived, and the same firm, Mr. Bording's heirs and successors, are yet printing literature for the Church in Denmark. The wife of Elder Peter O. Hansen recommended Mr. F. E. Bording, after some of the bigger

---

*Up to the close of Volume 76 (the volume printed in the year 1926), 1794 numbers of "Skandinaviens Stjerne" (each number containing 16 pages) has been published, aggregating 28,704 pages of printed matter altogether. Until 1877 when the publication of "Nordstjärnan" was commenced in the Swedish language, the "Skandinaviens Stjerne" was the only organ of the Church of Jesus Christ of Latter-day Saints in the Scandinavian countries. Since 1877 "Nordstjärnan" has been the Church organ in Sweden, or for the Swedish-speaking people, and "Skandinaviens Stjerne" the Church organ for the Saints in Denmark and Norway, or those speaking the Danish-Norwegian language. The subscription price for "Skandinaviens Stjerne" for the first year of its publication was 8 skilling (4 cents a copy, or 24 skilling per quarter, but when the paper became a semi-monthly periodical in 1852, the price was reduced to six skilling (three cents) per copy or one rigsdaler and 3 mark (about 75 cents) per annum. When the money system of Denmark and Norway was changed in 1875, the old denomination of "rigsdaler," "mark" and "skilling" was dropped and the new coins denominated "kroner" and "öre" were substituted for the old coins. The subscription price for "Skandinaviens Stjerne" was then placed at 12 öre per copy, or 3 kroner per annum. As prices have been advanced in Denmark, as well as in nearly all other countries, on nearly every article, the subscription price for the periodical at the present time is 25 öre per copy, or 6 kroner per annum for subscribers in Scandinavia. The subscription price in America is $2 per annum.

The circulation of "Skandinaviens Stjerne," in the beginning, was 1000. This gradually increased to 2,700 in 1861. At present the circulation is less than 1000.

and older firms of the city had refused to do work for the "Mormons." Mr. Bording, who had just established himself as a young printer and was seeking patronage, was thankful for the increase in his business, and his subsequent prosperity as a printer dates from the time he commenced to work for the Church. He died as a prosperous and well-to-do business man in Copenhagen, February 3, 1884.

The first number of "Skandinaviens Stjerne," bearing date of October 1, 1851, contained a brief account of the organization of the Church, also a translation of the 5th General Epistle of the First Presidency, a translation of Orson Pratt's writings on the Articles of Faith and a brief editorial.

On Sunday, October 5th, the first baptism by divine authority took place on the beautiful island of Fyen when William O. Andersen baptized Lars Nielsen. This was the beginning of a great missionary work performed by the Elders of the Church

WILLIAM OVE ANDERSEN

Born Dec. 23, 1826, in Copenhagen, Denmark; died Aug. 24, 1907, in Kamas, Summit Co., Utah.

on that island. Among the early missionaries who labored successfully there were Jens Hansen of Spanish Fork, Utah, and Niels Hansen, who was Bishop of Etna, Canada. A number of branches were soon raised up on Fyen and the neighboring island of Langeland, and from 1856 to 1864 there was a conference on Fyen with headquarters at Odense, the principal city on Fyen. The Odense Branch is still in a healthy and prosperous condition.

CHAPTER 8 (1851)

First Latter-day Saint missionaries in Norway—First baptisms in Norway—Persecution in Österrisör—Opposition on the part of civil authorities in Norway—Elder Hans F. Petersen's voyage along the Norwegian coast.

Elder Hans F. Petersen, accompanied by Elder Johan August Ahmanson, arrived in Österrisör on his second missionary trip to Norway, October 7, 1851. As Captain Larsen's wife refused the brethren the hospitality of her home, Brothers Petersen and Ahmanson ascended a neighboring cliff and prayed earnestly to the Lord to open up the way so that they might find a home and an opportunity to preach the gospel in Norway. In the evening they met a blacksmith by the name of John Olsen, with whom Elder Petersen had become acquainted on his first visit to Norway. This man at once invited the brethren to go with him to his house, were they found a good home. A few days later Elder Petersen had the opportunity to preach and bear testimony to a large crowd of people who unexpectedly gathered in Mr. Olsen's house. They listened with great attention to what they heard. After that the two missionaries commenced to give Bible readings and to spread books and tracts among the people and converse about the gospel to many who came in both from the city and the country to see them.

On October 17, 1851, Elder Petersen traveled to Rod in Söndelev parish, where quite a number of laborers were engaged in an iron working establishment and he sold them a number of pamphlets treating upon the principles of the gospel. Not having brought his passport with him, he could not be permitted to stop over night at the tavern, but he succeeded in obtaining shelter for the night with a poor family living in the vicinity. The head of police at Österrisör had kept his passport undoubtedly for the purpose of preventing him from going out into the country.

The following day Elder Petersen sailed with the master or foreman of the mechanical establishment back to the town, where he soon discovered that John Olsen's wife no longer would extend to him or Brother Ahmanson her hospitality. However, they found another home in the house of Svend Larsen, whose wife now became kindly disposed towards the missionaries. Toward the close of the month, October, 1851, Brother Ahmanson, who had grown tired of missionary life in Norway, returned to Denmark, and Elder Petersen was left to continue his labors there alone. On Sunday, November 2nd, he held the first public meeting at Rod, and the day following he visited the iron works at Ekland, distant about sixteen English miles from Österrisör. Here he was cast out by the foreman and was compelled to leave the place in a rain-storm. In his attempt to cross the cliffs to Söndelev he lost his way, but fortunately happened upon a little hamlet called Skaavog, where he after some difficulty obtained lodgings for the night. In the evening he took advantage of the oppor-

tunity afforded him and bore testimony to the people of the house. He also sold them some pamphlets, but in the morning the master of the Gaard (farm) politely requested him not to speak to the women about "Mormonism" for fear that he might convert them to his creed. At Söndelev, Elder Petersen had a chance to talk to a number of people who gathered one evening. After his return to Österrisör, he held several public meetings.

On Wednesday, November 26, Elder Hans F. Petersen baptized two men, viz., Peter Adamsen and John Olsen, at Österrisör, Norway. These were the first baptisms in Norway by divine authority. On the night of the day after the baptism (Nov. 27th) persecution commenced in real earnest. Though the baptisms were administered as privately as possible, the news thereof spread, and a mob soon gathered under the leadership of a young man by the name of Knud Olsen, a brother of John Olsen, who had been baptized. This man was excited because, as he claimed, Elder Petersen had led his brother astray. The mobbers had strengthened their nerves by partaking freely of intoxicants and they soon attacked the house of Svend Larsen, where Elder Petersen stopped. After knocking for some time for admittance, while uttering vile oaths and threats, they at length broke the door, but before they entered, Brother Petersen had hid himself so successfully in an upper room that they had to leave the house without finding him. Hoping to secure him later, they kept guard around the house until 1 o'clock at night. Similar scenes were continued for several evenings in succession, but the mobbers failed in getting Elder Petersen in their power.

On the 29th of November, 1851,

Brother Petersen wrote a letter to the civil authorities of the town (Österrisör) asking for protection according to the laws of the land. On the same day he was summoned to appear before the mayor to explain why he had performed the ordinance of baptism without being acknowledged by the civil authorities as a clergyman; he was now forbidden in the strongest terms to baptize or hold meetings as long as his case was pending before the court. The mob had determined to transport him out of town that day, but by the interference of the police this was prevented, as the people were forbidden to gather in a greater number than two or three persons at the same place.

On the 1st of December, Elder Petersen was requested by "Byfoged" Finne to send his credentials as a Church officer with all possible haste to the "Amtmand" (county judge) at Arendal. To the officer who brought him this order he promptly delivered his Elder's certificate and two letters of recommendation, all of which were sent to the "Amtmand."

The evening disturbances continued until the 4th of December, when a popular wedding, which was celebrated in the town, absorbed the attention of the people.

"Sunday evening, December 7, 1851," writes Elder Petersen, "we four brethren, Svend Larsen, Peter Adamsen, John Olsen and myself, assembled in an upper room at the house of Brother Larsen. On this occasion I confirmed Peter Adamsen and John Olsen members of the Church by the laying on of hands for the reception of the Holy Ghost. After this the four of us partook of the Sacrament, it being the first time the Lord's Supper was administered by divine authority in Norway. I felt truly thankful for this blessed day and praised the name of the Lord for hearing my prayers."

Thus was the ice broken in "Old Norway" and the first converts made in that land, which, as one of the three Scandinavian countries, has since figured so prominently in the history of the Latter-day Saint missionary operations; but the events which followed immediately after these first baptisms were calculated to put the first Elders and the first converts in that land on their true mettle. Through mobbings, persecutions, imprisonments and hardships the road led to the successful establishment of the Church of Christ in Norway.

On the occasion of the little confirmation meeting, Elder Petersen composed hymn 148 of the Danish hymn book, "Hör os, Immanuel, vi dig anraabe" (Hear us Immanuel, we call upon thee). Previously, during his sojourn at Österrisör, he had written No. 27, "O hörer I Slægter paa Jorden et Ord" (Listen, oh nations of earth), and No. 78, "Zion naar paa dig jeg tænker" (Zion, when of you I think).

On the 8th of December, Elder Petersen was called up before the mayor and, according to a communication which had been received from the "Amtmand," he was ordered to comply strictly with chapter 21, paragraphs 17 and 18, of the criminal code of Norway, where it is specified that none but such as the law recognizes as clergymen are permitted to baptize or perform any church ordinance. Elder Petersen was threatened with imprisonment, if he failed to comply with the law.

About three weeks later, he received a communication from the mayor of Österrisör of which the following is a translation:

"According to order of the Nedenæs and Robygdelagets Amt of the 17th inst., I hereby return the documents which were delivered to me on the 1st inst., namely, "Kaldsbrev" (Elder's certificate) and letters of recommendation dated Sept. 4th and Oct. 1st, 1851, and also No. 2 of the periodical "Skandinaviens Stjerne," and I hereby also inform you that you are not acklowledged as a priest or president of any denomination of dissenters in this nation, and consequently you are not authorized to perform any act in such a capacity; and the amt reserves the right to determine hereafter whether you will be prosecuted for having performed the act of baptism. * * Österrisör, Dec. 27, 1851. Finne. To Mormon Master-Tailor Petersen."

Owing to opposition on the part of the civil authorities of Österrisör, Elder Petersen had previously decided to leave that town and select another field of labor; but before he could carry out his resolution in this regard, he was subjected to another attack by a mob. About 9 o'clock in the evening of Dec. 11, 1851, the house of Captain Svend Larsen, where Elder Petersen still resided, was surrounded by a motley and noisy crowd, which soon burst the door open and filed into the house, demanding with terrible oaths that the "Mormon" priest be given into their hands. They lighted a candle and ransacked the house for him, closely examining every nook and corner in the building except the narrow chimney into which Elder Petersen had crawled and where he kept himself secreted until the danger was past. During the night the door was burst open twice, but the mobbers could not find their man. Later, the mob was dispersed by the police, when Elder Petersen ventured out from his rather uncomfortable hiding place in a plight which necessitated the use of a liberal supply of soap and water. On the following day, the mobbers were summoned to appear before the court; but they were never punished.

On Sunday, Dec. 14, 1851, a man by the name of Svend Peter Larsen, a resident of Frederikstad, came to Österrisör to have an interview with Elder Petersen. Mr. Larsen was a religious man and soon became interested in the doctrines taught by the missionary who had prayed earnestly for several days that the Lord would enable him to get away from Österrisör and find a place where he could do more good. Mr. Larsen was bound for Bergen and Elder Petersen, who looked upon him as a God-sent messenger, decided to go with him at once. Consequently, after taking affectionate leave of the few Saints at Österrisör, he sailed from that place in the sloop "Den gode Hensigt," commanded by his new friend, Svend Peter Larsen. This was on December 16, 1851. The next day they arrived at the little city of Arendal, where the master of the vessel laid by a couple of days, which gave Elder Petersen an opportunity to converse with a number of religiously inclined people in the town; among them was a merchant by the name of Scheveland, to whom he bore a faithful testimony and gave him several pamphlets. The voyage was continued from Arendal December 20th. During the night between the 22nd and 23rd the vessel came near running on a blind rock and the voyagers were only saved from destruction through the efforts of Brother Petersen who was at the helm and who, by calling into requisition all his physical strength, succeeded in turning the little craft around.

The sloop landed its passengers in Mandal, January 4, 1852.

CHAPTER 9 (1851)

Persecutions on Bornholm—Second conference held in Scandinavia—The Scandinavian Mission divided into three conferences—Several new branches of the Church raised up in Denmark—Persecutions on Falster—Mobbings at Bröndbyöster, on Sjælland—Introduction of the gospel in Salling—Elder Erastus Snow's report.

Elders Hans Peter Jensen and Hans Larsen, accompanied by Jens

Jörgensen, a Teacher, landed upon the island of Bornholm, October 10, 1851. Andreas Ågren who labored there had been ordained an Elder while on a visit to Copenhagen. The brethren felt strong enough in faith and power to enter the principal city of the island, Rönne, and for that purpose rented a hall in which to preach to the people. They soon found out, however, that the power of opposition and evil was not asleep. At first, opposition came only in the shape of false statements and illogical argumentation, but these had the effect of raising the ire in the more thoughtless and unruly class of people, which resulted in a great uproar and the mobbing of the missionaries. While Elder Hans. P. Jensen and his companion, Hans Larsen, w e r e

HANS PETER JENSEN

Born March 3, 1815, near Holbæk, Sjælland, Denmark; died in Brigham City, Utah, May 29, 1883.

preaching to a large congregation in their rented hall in Rönne, October 24, 1851, the storm of persecution broke loose in earnest. A man by the name of Beck gave the signal and ignited the evil fire in the mobbers

who had come to the meeting, and the brethren were at once dragged out of the house into the street, surrounded by the mobbers and insulted. By the interference of a Mr. Wulf and a Mr. Hermansen, who took the brethren out of the hands of the mob, they escaped further bodily injuries and reached their lodging place in safety. Soon after these experiences, however, Elder Jensen had the pleasure of baptizing eleven persons on the island of Bornholm; eighteen had previously been baptized there.

Elder Christian J. Larsen and Priest William O. Andersen who had continued their missionary labors in the southern part of Jutland and on the island of Fyen, held a meeting in the house of Lars Jensen in the village of Strib on Fyen, November 9, 1851. At the close of the meeting, Mr. Lars Jensen and one of his daughters and another woman were baptized by Elder Larsen, who also confirmed them. At another meeting held in the evening at the same place, the Saints residing in Fredericia and vicinity and the three members just baptized on Fyen, and one previously baptized on that island, were organized into a branch of the Church called the Fredericia Branch, with Knud Hansen Bruun as president, Lars Jensen was ordained a Priest and Ebbe Jessen a Teacher and appointed to assist Priest Bruun in managing the affairs of the branch. The few Saints also partook of the Sacrament and had a most joyful time together. Several strangers, who attended this meeting, shortly afterwards joined the Church, among whom was the late Lars S. Andersen who was Bishop of Ephraim, Utah.

The second general conference of the Scandinavian Mission convened in Copenhagen, on Saturday, November 15, 1851, presided over by

Apostle Erastus Snow, who gave the Saints interesting news about Elder John Taylor's labors in Hamburg, Germany, and Parley P. Pratt's mission to South America; he also stated that the Elders had recently been called to open up a mission in Australia, the East Indies, Switzerland, Italy and France.

The Saints living in the southern part of Jutland and on the island of Fyen were organized into a conference called the Fredericia Conference, with Elder Christian J. Larsen

CHRISTIAN J. LARSEN

Born March 31, 1831, at Greis, Veile amt, Denmark; died Sept. 15, 1915, in Logan, Utah.

as president. Priest Peter Beckström reported his late mission to Sweden and was appointed to labor in the country districts near Copenhagen. The conference was continued the following day (Nov. 16th) when the general authorities of the Church were presented, and Erastus Snow was sustained as president of the Church in Denmark with Elder John E. Forsgren and Peter O. Hansen as his assistants.

The Saints who lived in the north-

ern part of Jutland were organized into a conference called the Aalborg Conference, with Elder Christian Christiansen as president. The newly-made converts to the Church on the islands of Sjælland, Falster and Bornholm, etc., were organized into a conference called the Copenhagen Conference. A number of the local brethren were ordained to the Priesthood and several called to take special missions to different parts of the country. At this time there were twelve organized branches of the Church in Denmark, viz., Copenhagen, organized September 15, 1850; Aalborg, organized November 27, 1850; Hirschholm, organized March 10, 1851; Christianshavn, organized August 18, 1851; Bornholm, organized August 18, 1851; Hals, organized August 31, 1851; Kjeldgaard (Jutland), organized August 31, 1851; Sönder Oredrev (Sjælland), organized September 14, 1851; Frankerup, (Sjælland), organized September 14, 1851; Greis (Jutland), organized October 5, 1851; Fredericia organized November 9, 1851, and a temporary branch in Nörre Sundby (Jutland). Since the opening of the mission 532 persons had been baptized in the mission, but of that number 60 had been excommunicated. This interesting conference was held in the Saints' hall in Christianshavn because Mr. Nehm had refused to rent his hall in "Lille Kongensgade" to the Saints any longer. Consequently, the Saints of both branches (Copenhagen proper and Christianshavn) had to hold their meetings conjointly in the Christianshavn hall.

After the November conference, Brothers Johan F. F. Dorius and Knud H. Bruun, returned to the island of Falster, arriving there November 28, 1851. Several believed their testimony and on the 3rd of December.

1851, Brother Dorius baptized Hans Tönnesen, the first person, as far as known, baptized on the island of Falster. Elder John E. Forsgren and Johan Swenson (a Swede by birth) joined Brothers Dorius and Bruun at a village called Virkede. Brother Swenson had also been appointed at the late conference held in Copenhagen to labor on the island of Falster. They now divided up in twos, Brother Forsgren taking Brother Brüun with him, leaving Brothers Dorius and Swenson to work together; they visited many villages on Falster, while Elders Forsgren and Bruun extended their labors to the neighboring island of Lolland. The two last named brethren returned from their first visit to that island after remaining one week, during which they had had many good opportunities to preach the gospel in private. The four missionaries spent Sunday, December 21, 1851, together in a meeting on Falster and partook of the Sacrament as a fit conclusion. Brother Knud H. Bruun was ordained an Elder on that occasion by John E. Forsgren.

On Sunday, November 23rd, the hostile element broke out in open violence in Bornholm. Brother Jens Jörgensen, who at that time labored as a missionory on the island, had arranged to hold a meeting in the home of Brother Jens Peter Didriksen in the village of Aaker, when the house was filled with people, but as soon as Brother Jörgensen commenced to speak, he was interrupted by several of the rabble present and subjected to mockery and threats; soon they also laid violent hold on him and dragged him outside of the house by the hair, tearing his clothes to pieces and otherwise ill-treating him. Elder Ole Christian Nielsen, who had been appointed to preside over the Saints on Bornholm, in con-

nection with Brother Jens Jörgensen, arrived on the island November 24, 1851.

On Thursday, November 27, 1851, while the two missionaries (Ole Christian Nielsen and Jens Jörgensen) were peaceably passing along the road leading toward Aaker, they were stopped by ruffians who said that they were sent out to arrest them. These men, who were armed with heavy clubs, asserted that the principal men of the parish wanted to have a talk with the "Mormons," but when they arrived at the appointed place, they were only insulted and threatened with whipping and beating and ordered to leave the neighborhood forthwith; they were even told their lives would not be safe, if they ever again appeared in Aaker parish. Between forty and fifty men were present on this occasion and the parish justice of the peace only promised them temporary protection. The brethren pleaded that they, as peaceable citizens, had the right to travel on the public highways of the country wherever they pleased, but he would not, for one moment, listen to their plea; in an angry tone he ordered them to leave the place, and so the brethren were obliged to follow his men as prisoners. While walking on the road, Elder Nielsen was struck on the cheek by one of the mobbers and wounded so that the blood flowed freely. Having reached the parish line, the brethren were permitted to go free, but the mobbers, who seemed to regret this, pursued them anew, but did not overtake them. Following the admonition of the Savior, "When they persecute you in one city, flee to another," the missionaries continued their labors with unceasing energy in other parts of the island.

While Elders Ole Christian Nielsen and Jens Jörgensen were stopping over night Dec. 2, 1851, at the house of Jens Nielsen (the first Latter-day Saint convert on Bornholm), in the small fishing village of Arnager, the people of the neighboring farming district, having heard of the presence of the "Mormon" Elders, made an attempt to enter the village for the purpose of whipping the "Mormons." But as soon as the villagers became aware of this, they hastily armed themselves with clubs, axes, iron rods, an old shotgun, etc., and drove the mobbers away, "for," said they, "the Mormons teach us correct doctrines, and therefore we will defend them." Most of the men who defended the missionaries on that occasion soon afterwards embraced the gospel and emigrated to Utah. Among them were the late Didrik Jacobsen Funk (Lund) of Plain City, Utah, Mons P. Ipsen, Jens Kofod, Peter Poulsen, George K. Riis, Hans Thorsen and others. Arnager was for several years one of the main resting places for the missionaries who labored on the island of Bornholm.

In December, 1851, a number of Saints were mobbed in the village of Bröndbyöster (East Bröndby) a suburb of Copenhagen, where a family of Saints named Knudsen resided. The man was a tailor in whose home meetings had previously been held on several occasions, and as a rule no disturbances had taken place, except once or twice when some young people had been a little noisy, but one evening in December, 1851, while two brethren (Fred C. Sörensen and a Brother Möller) were preaching repentance to the people, the lights were suddenly extinguished and both the brethren named were roughly handled by a mob which had gathered. In the fracas Brother Möller's coat was torn to pieces. On Sunday, December 14th, four of the brethren

held a meeting and many of the Saints had come out from Copenhagen to attend the services. As soon as the meeting was dismissed, and the visitors began to disperse and start on their return trip, they were greeted with a shower of stones, potatoes and other missiles from a crowd which lay in ambush waiting for them. After proceeding a little farther on their way, someone gave a signal to announce that the Saints were coming, and when these were within the firing-line they received another salvo of stones and potatoes: still farther on men and women who had posted themselves along the hedges, and in trenches, came out to take an active part in the unequal battle between Saints and sinners. Some of the assailants were armed with heavy sticks and clubs, and stones and dirt flew thick and fast around the Saints. Some of the women of the assaulting party carried the missiles in their aprons and skirts with which to supply their male companions while they in a blasphemous manner cried out: "Now call on your God to defend you!" Several of the brethren were knocked down, rolled on the muddy road and beaten with sticks and fists; their coats were torn to pieces in several instances and even one of the sisters was abused and handled very roughly. For more than half a mile the mob pursued the Saints in this way, and when they at last came to a farmhouse by the roadside, they sought shelter within, but as they were not safe there either, they fled across the fields in the darkness, still pursued by their "Christian friends" till they reached another large farmhouse where they once more sought shelter. Here, however, the occupants refused them protection, but a friendly disposed girl kindly showed them a way out through the garden into the fields, and by this means they finally escaped from their pursuers.

One of the sufferers on this occasion says: "For three quarters of an hour we were seemingly in the absolute power of the devil, but while God permitted him to have power over our flesh, our spirits rejoiced, for we knew we suffered for the cause of truth. We cannot describe the sufferings we passed through, but for a short time it certainly looked as if none of us would escape with our lives."

A complaint was at once entered before the district judge (Birkedommeren), but that official, after reading it, made use of abusive language towards the sufferers, and in an angry tone said that he would give them as little protection as possible. He also told them that his sheriff had spoken to him several times about the meetings and the disturbances in the village. It seemed that both he and the sheriff were acquainted with the conspiracy against the Saints before the actual mobbing took place. At all events, no steps were taken by the authorities to bring the perpetrators of these unlawful acts to justice. The Saints who suffered on that occasion were twelve in number and some of them presented the complaint personally to the judge.

In December, 1851, Elder Christian Christiansen moved his family from Aalborg to the little city of Skive (in Salling) where he commenced active missionary operations. Great excitement among all the people followed and large numbers of them gathered to learn something of the new religion. Among the visitors was the parish priest, Mr. Möller, who came to Brother Christiansen's house and threatened him

with the consequences of preaching "Mormonism" in the city of Skive, assuring him at the same time of his hostile intent. Brother Christiansen told the priest that he might use his influence all he wanted to against the work of God, but he should not succeed, for the Lord would stop his opposition. This proved to be a prophetic utterance. The priest left in a rage, but died a few days later.

The following extracts from a letter written by Elder Erastus Snow in Copenhagen, December 15, 1851, will give the readers a general idea of the condition existing in Denmark about a year and a half after the first Elders arrived in Scandinavia:

"We have been endeavoring to extend our operations into all the principal islands and provinces of this little State (Denmark), as also to Norway, and in most places where we have tried we have gained a footing, although the difficulties we have to encounter cannot be realized by those who have only labored in England. * * In many places here, to embrace the gospel is almost equal to the sacrifice of one's life; and to travel and preach it, a man carries his life in his hands. The Danish Constitution guarantees the right, but it is not sustained by collateral laws, nor backed up by the moral force of the country; and when you except Copenhagen and the principal merchant towns, it is scarcely known that such a right exists. It is in the interest of the priests to keep the people ignorant of the fact, and their influence in the country towns and settlements is almost boundless. The masses are not a reading people. We have to preach the constitution to prepare the way for the Bible, and the Bible to prepare the way for the Book of Mormon. * * The more I become acquainted with the Danish people the better I know them; they are the true descendants and living representatives of the ancient Goths and Vandals. They are jealous and excitable, deadly enemies, but warm friends. * * We have recourse to the law, sometimes, when we can find an officer bold enough and honest enough to undertake to do his duty. * * Elder Forsgren and his fellow-laborer ran the gauntlet for some weeks upon the island of Falster and made some narrow escapes, but they weathered the storm, made many friends, and now have a good prospect before them. Upon the island of Bornholm there seems to have been a regular and concerted war waged against the truth. It began in the chief town and spread through the island. It is some months since the seed was first sown on the island and five different brethren have labored more or less among the people, until, after baptizing between thirty and forty, they have been entirely driven from the island. The last two arrived here on the 5th inst. The missionaries, after having been watched and waylaid, were hunted and driven from place to place, and sustained considerable personal injury. Their friends attempted to rally to defend them, but their enemies, armed with various weapons and in large bodies, began the destruction of property, and the work of vengeance upon their friends with such threats that to save the effusion of blood their friends sent them away. * * The way the Danish priests and editors avail themselves of the old lies of Bennett, Caswell, Turner and others, might well put to shame even Bowes himself, and besides these trans-Atlantic wares, there seems to be an abundance of supply of domestic manufacture. Instead of attempting with my limited means and language to check this tornado of trash that has swept through the land, I have contented myself with publishing the plain, simple story and faith of the Saints. * * The young Saints of this country have already been tried with apostasy as well as with persecution. About sixty were reported at our last conference as having been expelled in this country. Some of these have manifested the old, wicked apostate spirit. * *

"We had an excellent conference on the 15th, 16th and 17th ultimo. Most of the Priesthood and a large congregation of Saints assembled; great union and love prevailed. The Holy Spirit was poured out bountifully, numbers were ordained and much needful instruction given to young sprigs of the Priesthood. Several of these have a good common education and knowledge of the Scriptures. A few only read the English."

At the end of 1851, the Scandinavian Mission consisted of 12 organized branches grouped into three conferences, viz., Copenhagen Conference, with six branches (Copenhagen, Christianshavn, Hirschholm, Sönder Oredrev, Frankerup and Bornholm;

Fredericia Conference, with two branches (Greis and Fredericia), and Aalborg Conference, with four branches (Aalborg, Kjeldgaard, Hals, and Nörre Sundby). The total membership in the whole mission was about five hundred, including twelve local Elders and quite a number of Priests, Teachers and Deacons.

CHAPTER 10 (1852)

Elder Hans F. Petersen extends his voyage to Bergen, Norway—Elder Knud H. Bruun mobbed on Falster—First Scandinavian Saints emigrate to Utah—Another general conference —Farewell feast in honor of Elder Erastus Snow—His departure for America.

On Sunday, January 4, 1852, and the following day, the first conference was held in Aalborg, Denmark. Elder Christian Christiansen, who had arrived from Salling, presided. He and Hans Peter Jensen took an active part in the proceedings and preached the gospel with power. The reports given by the local missionaries showed that the prospects for the spread of the gospel were good in the city of Randers, the province of Vendsyssel and other places. The Saints in Vendsyssel were organized into a branch of the Church with Hans Peter Jensen as president. Niels Christian Schou was ordained an Elder and appointed to preside over the Aalborg Branch. Missionaries were called to labor in Randers, Salling, Hjörring, etc., and several ordinations to the Priesthood took place.

A few days later, Pres. Chr. Christiansen wrote that thirty persons had been added to the Church by baptism in and near Aalborg. He found it necessary to remain in Aalborg for the purpose of making needed arrangements in the newly-organized branches, as there was much opposition to the truth, especially on the part of the Baptists. He had just received a letter from his wife in

Skive, telling him how a mob had broken the windows of the house, and compelled her to leave the premises with her child. His father had been threatened with injury if the priest or his colleagues should see a "Mormon" enter his house. Elder Hans F. Petersen, who arrived in Mandal, Norway, Jan. 4, 1852, en route from Österrisör, to Bergen, spent a week in Mandal while the vessel in which he traveled lay at anchor there. He utilized the time by making himself acquainted with the people, and preaching the gospel to them. On one occasion, when he was invited to dinner in the house of a master carpenter by the name of Larsen, the room was suddenly filled with people to whom he, by invitation, commenced to preach the gospel. A "provst" (head priest) Vogt, a member of the "Storthing," who was reputed one of the best speakers in Norway, entered the house while Elder Petersen was speaking, and soon endeavored to create a disturbance by telling the crowd that a part of what had been said was untrue. When Elder Petersen requested him to point out the falsehood, the priest invited him to meet him the next day at his office; but as he had made his accusation publicly, Brother Petersen desired that he should produce his proofs in public. Mr. Vogt refused to do this, under the pretense that he could not remember all that had been said, as the sermon was so long. He still sought to cause disturbance until that part of the congregation which was in sympathy with him pressed forward as if to take Elder Petersen by force. The owner of the house then declared that, as the stranger was his guest, he would not permit any harm to befall him as long as he was under his roof. The priest withdrew, together with his friends, after which Elder Petersen conversed a long time with

those who remained. He made a number of friends, of whom several embraced "Mormonism."

Continuing the journey, Elder Petersen in due time arrived at Bergen, on the west coast of Norway, where he spent the remainder of the winter. He lived with a brewer by the name of Magnus, who, together with his family, treated Elder Petersen with kindness and hospitality, notwithstanding their poverty. The civil authorities in Bergen would not allow Elder Petersen to hold public meetings, unless he hired a large hall for the purpose, and this he could not do, through lack of means, but he spent a couple of months visiting from house to house and bearing testimony of the gospel wherever the people would receive him. He was compelled to live very economically, and on different occasions he suffered for want of the necessaries of life.

In the meantime his friend Larsen returned to Bergen from his fishing expedition in the North and was on his way to Copenhagen, Denmark. Elder Petersen made ready to accompany him. They sailed from Bergen in the latter part of March and arrived in Copenhagen about the 1st of April, 1852. Soon after their arrival in Denmark's capital, Captain Svend Peter Larsen, who, through his association with Elder Hans F. Petersen on the voyage had been converted, was baptized by Elder Andreas Ågren and confirmed by Elder John E. Forsgren. This took place April 2, 1852. Four days later (on April 6, 1852) Captain Larsen's wife, Bethine Randine Larsen, who had accompanied her husband on his voyage, was baptized in Copenhagen. Thus Svend P. Larsen and his wife, on their return to Norway, became the first Latter-day Saints in Fredrikstad.

Knud H. Bruun, Jens Jörgensen, Ole C. Nielsen and Johan Swenson, missionaries laboring on the island of Falster, Denmark, who previously had been subject to much persecution and many hardships, held a meeting in the house of a respectable farmer in the village of Falkerslev, on Falster, January 20, 1852, and while Brother Nielsen was reading from the Gospel of St. John the meeting was interrupted by a mob, among whom was a Lutheran priest. The lights were blown out and the brethren assaulted in a most brutal manner. Elder Bruun, particularly, was beaten with clubs, knocked down, tramped upon and dragged through several rooms out into the yard; his coat was torn from his back and he lost considerable blood. Some of the mobbers proposed that he should be thrown into a well, but as the village school-teacher intervened, the mobbers became divided and began to quarrel among themselves, and Brother Bruun escaped. For some time afterwards he suffered excruciating pains from his wounds, but through the faith and prayers of the Saints he was healed, and continued his missionary labors.

Up to the beginning of 1852, the subject of emigration had scarcely been mentioned by the American missionaries, but by degrees it dawned upon the minds of the Saints through the light of the spirit which had been conferred upon them after baptism, that this was a gathering dispensation, and the Elders had, therefore, no difficulty in introducing that doctrine. The Scandinavian Saints were as eager to cast their lots with the Saints in America as were the converts in England and other parts of the world. As a large company of Saints prepared to emigrate from the British Isles in the month of February, 1852, Apostle Franklin D. Richards, who presided over the British Mission, wrote to President Erastus Snow, that if any of the Saints in the Scandinavian Mission desired to go to Zion, they might have the privilege of joining that company. When Elder Snow made this known a few days previous t the time appointed for the emigrant to leave England, he found nine persons ready to respond at once. Hurriedly they arranged their affairs and commenced their long journey January 31, 1852.

The names of these first nine who proved to be the forerunners of tens of thousands of Saints who have subsequently wended their way from Denmark, Sweden and Norway to the Valleys of the Mountains, were Rasmus Petersen, wife and adopted child; Conrad Emil Edward Schvaneveldt, wife and two children, and two unmarried men, Wilhelm Knudsen and Nils Olson. They traveled by stage from Copenhagen to Korsör, whence they crossed "Storebelt" and "Lillebelt" on ferries; they then traveled through Schleswig by stage to Rendsborg in Holstein, where they arrived in the evening of February 2nd. The following day they continued the journey by rail to Altona where Elder George P. Dykes was on hand to receive them. After treating them to dinner, he took them on board the steamship, "John Bull," which on the morning of the 4th sailed for London, England, where arrived on the 5th, in the evening. After much inquiry in London, the little company of foreigners at length succeeded in finding Elder Jacob Gates, who presided over the London Conference, and to whom they had a letter of introduction from Apostle Erastus Snow. Elder Gates rendered them necessary aid and assisted them to continue the journey by rail to Liverpool on the 7th. Arriving there they were informed that they were too late to sail on the "Ellen Maria as had been their intention, for that ship had just cleared port the same day. Consequently the little company had to wait in Liverpool over a month to find an opportunity to sail on another vessel. Brother Rasmus Petersen was detained one day in London to get the luggage passed through the customhouse. In the meantime Elder Snow arrived in Liverpool with nineteen more Scandinavian emigrants, and with these the first nine embarked in the ship "Italy" on the 11th of March, 1852, and commenced the voyage across the Atlantic.

On account of the approaching departure of Apostle Erastus Snow, a conference of the Scandinavian Mission was held in Copenhagen, commencing on Friday, February 20th, and ending on Sunday, February 22, 1852.

During this conference much important business was transacted for the benefit of the Saints and for the further advancement of the work of God in the Scandinavian countries. Elder John E. Forsgren was appointed to preside over the Scandinavian Mission after the departure of President Snow, and Elders Peter O. Hansen and Hans Peter Jensen were appointed to act as his counselors. The subject of the Perpetual Emigrating Fund recently established in Zion and also in the British Mission, was explained to the Saints, and it was proposed to establish branches of said fund in the various conferences and districts of the Scandinavian countries. This proposition was received with characteristic alacrity by the assembled Saints and a foundation was laid at once by donations to the amount of 450 Danish dollars ($225 American). It was decided to petition the King of Denmark for redress for the persecutions and wrongs that the Saints had been suf-

fering from mobs in various places in Denmark, and to which the officers of the law had paid no attention, although petitions and complaints had been brought before them, substantiated by witnesses. A committee was, therefore, appointed to draft and present such a document to his Majesty in person.

Several brethren were called during this important conference to go on missions into new fields. Elders Anders W. Winberg, Nils Capson and Ola Nilson were appointed to labor in the southern part of Sweden. Elder Hans Peter Jensen was ordained a High Priest and called on a mission to Norway, where a few had already been baptized. Johan F. F. Dorius was ordained an Elder and appointed to labor as a missionary in the Aalborg Conference.

During the conference, Apostle Snow gave much valuable instruction to the Saints in general and to the Priesthood in particular. He urged the people to lay their grievances before the King and the Diet, when in session, that these might be held accountable before God if they neglected their duty in behalf of the Saints. The reports read to this conference showed that more than seven hundred persons had been baptized since the gospel was introduced into the Scandinavian countries. This splendid conference was held in a large hall in "Hotel du Nord," in Copenhagen.

On Tuesday, February 24, 1852, the Saints arranged a farewell social in honor of the much-beloved Apostle, Erastus Snow. A beautiful and spacious hall in "Hotel du Nord" had been rented for this purpose and had been decorated by appropriate mottoes, among which was one "Herrens Löve" (Lion of the Lord) which was very pleasing to Brother Snow. Many were the tokens and expressions of pure, affectionate love bestowed upon him on that occasion; not in jewelry or gifts of moneyed value, but from genuine appreciation of his mission and the eternal blessings he had bestowed by bringing to them the gospel in its purity and authority. A sumptuous banquet, which had been prepared, was partaken of by perhaps three hundred guests and many of the poor Saints said that that day was the happiest of their lives. With all who attended it was a day always kept in pleasant remembrance. That this love for Apostle Snow did not die with his departure was exhibited on a later occasion of a similar kind when Elder John E. Forsgren was about to leave with a large company of Saints for Zion and a feast was arranged by friends. On that occasion, one of the young Saints composed a song, which was sung with much feeling and spirit to a well-known national tune, and in which was sent affectionate greeting to the beloved Apostle in Zion from the Saints in Scandinavia.

Having finished his work in Scandinavia, Apostle Erastus Snow sailed from Copenhagen March 4, 1852, on his return to America, accompanied by nineteen emigrating Saints whose names are as follows: Ole Ulrick Christian Mönster (one of the first fifteen persons baptized in Denmark), wife and child; Christian Hildur Raven, wife and three children; Niels Jensen, wife and one child; Frederik Petersen, Ferdinand F. Hansen, Hans Hansen, Carl Jörgensen, Bertha S. Hansen, Augusta Dorius, Cecelia Jörgensen and Johanne Andersen. The company took steamer from Copenhagen to Kiel, in Holstein; thence traveled by rail to Altona, took steamer from Hamburg to Hull, in England, and thence went by rail to Liverpool, where they

arrived March 8th, and found the previously named nine persons waiting for them. Apostle Erastus Snow, who had some important business to attend to in England before he could

AUGUSTA DORIUS STEVENS

One of the first 28 Latter-day Saints who emigrated from Scandinavia, was born Oct. 29, 1837, in Copenhagen, Denmark; died in Salt Lake City, Utah, July 28, 1926.

return home, placed Ole U. C. Mönster in charge of the little company of Danish Saints, now numbering twenty-eight souls, and saw them safely on board the ship "Italy," on which they sailed from Liverpool, March 11, 1852. After a safe passage, they arrived at New Orleans, May 10th. Proceeding up the Mississippi and Missouri rivers, the Danish emigrants reached Kanesville (now Council Bluffs), Iowa, in good health and spirits. There they were again met by their beloved Apostle Erastus Snow, who had reached the Bluffs by way of New York, and in the beginning of July, 1852, attached to a large company of Saints under the leadership of Eli B. Kelsey, the twenty-eight Danish emigrants commenced the journey across the plains with ox-teams; they arrived in Salt Lake City, Oct. 16, 1852.

CHAPTER 11 (1852)

Petition to the Danish Rigsdag—First branch of the Church organized on Fyen—Elder Jens Hansen's remarkable experiences—The Doctrine and Covenants and numerous pamphlets published in Danish.

A petition was written to the Danish "Rigsdag" March 16, 1852, which presented in detail the persecutions to which the Saints had been subjected in Denmark, and the petitioners asked for redress and protection. Eight hundred and fifty Saints subsequently signed the petition.

On March 16, 1852, also, the first branch of the Church on the island of Fyen was organized under the name of Tröstrup-Korup Branch and made a part of the Fredericia Conference. Elder Jens Hansen gave the following details of the introduc-

JENS HANSEN

Born Oct. 13, 1823, in Otterup parish, Odense amt, Fyen, Denmark; died in Spanish Fork, Utah, June 28, 1897.

4

tion of the gospel on the island of Fyen:

"At the general conference held in Copenhagen November 15 and 16, 1851, I was ordained a Priest and, together with Elder William O. Andersen, appointed to labor as a missionary on the island of Fyen. We went to work immediately in our field of labor and commenced talking to the people, selling tracts and holding meetings; we generally had a fair attendance and quiet audiences. One of the first villages that I visited was Sulkendrup. Just as I entered a certain house I was met by a woman who said: 'These are my brethren.' She had never seen us before, and we had not told her who we were. This woman's name was Gjertrud Hansen and soon afterwards (Dec. 5, 1851) I baptized her as the first fruit of my labors and those of Brother Andersen in that field. We next visited my parents, who received us with much joy and several well-attended meetings were held in their house. In a dream which my father had had a long time previous, he was shown that I should become a savior to his household, but for some time he never was able to comprehend the meaning of the dream. One evening, however, after I had held a well-attended meeting, he walked out into his garden where he bent his knee and prayed earnestly to God for a testimony that he might know if the message which I had delivered was from God. When he re-entered the house he received the sign, which had been given him in answer to his prayer and with tears in his eyes and a trembling voice he asked for baptism which ordinance I administered to him and my mother that same evening. Soon afterwards four of my brothers joined the Church by baptism.

"Meanwhile, the spirit of persecution began to show itself. One evening, as we held our usual meeting in my father's house, a number of intoxicated men, armed with clubs, surrounded the house and stated that a certain person had offered them money if they would give us a thrashing. One of the ruffians attacked me with his cane, but Brother William O. Andersen and I both succeeded in getting out of the door and fled across the fields. My aged parents, who remained in the house, then became the objects of their abuse. They wrote with chalk upon my father's back, and in other ways made him the scape-goat of their tirade and sacrilegious ridicule. Our persecutors next ran out to hunt for us, but we had hidden ourselves in a ditch behind a fence, where we could hear them swear and utter threats to the effect that they would not go home until they had killed us. We prayed to God that he would strike them with blindness, which he literally did, for they did not find us, although they searched for us till past midnight. When they finally gave up the search, we re-entered the house and joined in songs of praise to the Lord, rejoicing exceedingly because we were counted worthy to suffer persecution for Christ's sake.

"Being possessed of a burning desire that all should hear the gospel, Elder Andersen and I concluded to separate. Consequently, he went to the south and I to the north. I visited many of my relatives and friends who received my testimony with joy, and several of them afterwards became faithful members of the Church. One day, while I was on my way to my father's home, I became suddenly impressed with a feeling that I should quicken my pace. I did not know why, but no sooner had I opened the door till the cause of this impression was made plain to me. My brother Jörgen Peter had been attacked by an evil spirit which caused him to shake and tremble. For some time I stood and looked at him, wondering what could be the cause of this unpleasant occurrence. It finally struck me that he must have sinned in some way and thereby given the evil one a chance to attack him, and after I had questioned him somewhat closely, he confessed that when the parson had asked him if he had been baptized, he had answered no. I reproved him a little and, as I then held the Priesthood of an Elder, I laid my hands upon his head and in the name of Jesus commanded the evil one to depart. I was obeyed instantly. By thus witnessing the power of God manifested as in former days, we rejoiced exceedingly.

"From this time on I continued my labors with much success and I became an instrument in the hands of the Lord of bringing many souls to a knowledge of the truth. One day, as I was walking on the road between Nyborg and Svendborg, I heard a voice close by my side calling me by name, saying: 'How do you dare to say by authority from Jesus Christ when you baptize?' This voice had a peculiar effect upon me, but after I had prayed fervently to the Lord I remembered a vision that I had had previously and I was firmly convinced that the ordinance of baptism was performed with perfect consistency."

Soon after Apostle Erastus Snow had left Denmark for England, the first edition of the book of Doctrine and Covenants was issued from the press in the Danish language. In the first edition, consisting of 1,000 copies, the Lectures on Faith were omitted. The translation had partly been done by the same Miss Mathiesen who assisted in translating the Book of Mormon, but before her manuscript was allowed to go to press it was carefully read and revised by President Snow and Elder Peter O. Hansen. Since that time five editions of the book have been published in the Danish language. The last edition, which was carefully revised by Apostle Anthon H. Lund, was printed in the "Deseret News" establishment, Salt Lake City, Utah, in 1900. Early in 1852, also, an enlarged edition of the Danish Hymn Book was published; likewise a pamphlet in Swedish entitled "En röst från landet Zion" (A Voice from the Land of Zion), which contained a brief sketch of the establishment and progress of the Church and its status at that time; besides an outline of the doctrines and faith of the Latter-day Saints. This little work containing fifty pages, octave, has seen several editions. Besides the above mentioned publications, Apostle Snow had, previous to his departure, published "En Sandheds Röst" (A Voice of truth), "Mærkværdige Syner" (Remarkable Visions), "Guddomelig Myndighed" (Divine Authority), "Troes-Artikler" (Articles of Faith), and six numbers of "Skandinaviens Stjerne."

CHAPTER 12 (1852)

A branch of the Church organized in Salling, Denmark—Persecution and mob violence; neither position nor sex spared—Missionary driven out of the district—Missionary work resumed in Sweden—Mikael Johnson arrested and banished—Anders W. Winberg in Skåne, Sweden.

A branch of the Church was organized April 18, 1852, in a district of Jutland, Denmark, called Salling, in the neighborhood of the little city of Skive. This part of the country constituted a part of the Aalborg Conference over which Elder Christian Christiansen acted as president. About the introduction of the gospel in Salling, Elder Christiansen gives the following account:

"In the month of December, 1851, I moved my family to Skive that I might have a better opportunity for opening the gospel door in that part of the country; but no sooner had it become known who I was than the whole town was in commotion and the people turned out in crowds to hear about our doctrines. Among this class of visitors was also the parish priest, Mr. Möller, who came to my house to warn me of the consequences of preaching 'Mormonism' in his parish, and he told me that he would exert all his influence against me. I answered that he was welcome to do so, if he so desired, but I assured him that his attempt would be of no avail, as God could easily stop him in his efforts. He went away very angry and a few days later he died. The Lord only knows the cause of his demise.

"For three months I continued my labors in that neighborhood, almost continually exposed to persecution, but I baptized about forty persons, among whom were my own parents, my brother and his family, and also an unmarried brother and two sisters. After that, mob persecutions became so frequent and severe that I was compelled to move away, in order to save my life. My windows were smashed by stones and blocks of wood thrown by the mob, and even the new converts were frequently subjected to annoyance and persecution, so much so, that most of them moved to Aalborg. My father had for a number of years been a highly respected school-teacher and chorister in Dölby and Hindberg parishes, but after his baptism he became a subject of disrespect and persecution and was forced to sell his effects. He then moved to Aalborg. He finally emigrated to Utah, where he died a faithful Latter-day Saint."

The first person baptized in Salling was Karen Petersen Höstgaard, her son, Frederik Jensen Holst, having been baptized in Copenhagen. Pres. Christian Christiansen ordained

his brother, Niels C. Christiansen, in Skive, a Priest and appointed him president of the branch, and after having baptized a few more, Elder Christiansen returned to Aalborg, as stated, in order to escape mob violence. The mob, however, expended their wrath upon his brother, Niels C., and several times smashed his windows and damaged other property.

At last, he with his family, were compelled to leave their home in the middle of the night, to save their lives, and flee to Aalborg. So fierce had the spirit of persecution become that Brother Christiansen could not appear in the street without being assaulted by the mob, who flung stones and dirt at him. A Brother Frenze also suffered much. His windows were smashed by mobs several times; it even went so far, that the police had to place a guard by his house in the night. At length, three missionaries, Johan F. F. Dorius, Anders Andersen and Niels Milkjær arrived in that district of country and commenced to hold meetings. This enraged the populace still more and mob violence was again resorted to. A meeting had been appointed in the village of Dommerby, and in order to reach that place, the missionaries and some of the Saints had to pass through the city of Skive; but when they had reached a point a short distance beyond the town, a mob led by a Mr. Borup, a hatter, caught up with them, and assaulted them most furiously. Brothers Dorius and Milkjær especially received rough treatment. After first pelting the brethren with stones the mobbers laid violent hands on them, tore Brother Dorius' coat to pieces and at length pushed both missionaries into a peat bog. Fortunately there was not sufficient water in the bog to drown them, and so they soon came out of it alive.

Having appeased their hatred for

the present, the mob at last permitted the brethren to go, but on their return the mobbers met a number of the Saints on their way to the meeting in Dommerby. Among them was a man by the name of Christian Willardsen, from the village of Dölby, who at that time was not a member of the Church, but was baptized soon afterwards. The mob handled him in a most fearful manner. Notwithstanding the bad treatment the brethren thus received, they concluded to proceed to Dommerby and commence their meeting, but during the opening prayer an armed mob surrounded the house and manifested their wicked intentions against the Saints, and the missionaries in particular. The poor man, who owned the house, begged the Saints to leave his premises, which they did, but by so doing they were placed at the mercy of the infuriated mob on the outside. The Saints immediately fled across the fields in every direction while Brothers Dorius and Milkjær reached a farm near the road, where they asked for shelter and protection, but as the proprietor refused them this, they were again captured by the mob and brought back to the city of Skive. On the road the mob made all kinds of hideous noises and continued the same after reaching the town, where the brethren finally succeded in seeing the district judge (Herredsfogden), to whom they stated their case in a straight forward manner, Brother Dorius exhibiting his torn ooat in evidence. While this scene took place in the office of the judge, the street outside was packed by a clamorous rabble. After studying the matter over for a while, the judge concluded contrary to law to send the missionaries home to their respective places of birth. He at once summoned one man to take charge of each of the brethren and conduct them to their homes. Thus

Brother Andersen was taken to Aalborg, Brother Milkjær to Jetzmark and Brother Dorius to Copenhagen, and as they passed through the various towns and villages along the road they were continually exhibited to the populace as prisoners and criminals.

When Elder Christian Christiansen heard of the persecutions in Salling, he, as president of the Aalborg Conference, at once set out from Aalborg to visit Salling with a view to straighten up, as well as he could, the affairs of the Church there, and to give comfort and encouragement to the remaining Saints in the vicinity of Skive; but while endeavoring to perform these duties as quietly as possible, the enemies of the Saints learned of his presence, and so he and his younger brother were mobbed and had to flee to save themselves. Elder Christiansen writes:

"Notwithstanding the threatening aspects before me, I concluded to visit Skive, and officiate in the ordinances of the gospel. In company with a younger brother of mine, I left my father's house in Dölby about midnight on June 15, 1852, and passed through Skive about 1 o'clock a. m., hoping that our enemies were all asleep; but in this we were sadly disappointed, for they had been lying in wait for us for three nights concealed under a bridge that we had to cross. Consequently, when we reached the bridge, three men suddenly sprang upon us, threw me off the bridge and violently dragged my brother with them back to town. On the way thither they treated him in a most barbaric manner, thinking all the time that they were handling me. When I regained consciousness from my fall from the bridge and saw that my enemies had gone, I jumped over a fence and traveled by out-of-the-way paths some four English miles till I reached the house of some friends, who received me kindly and administered to my wants. After having washed and warmed myself (for I was wet through) I sent word to an old sister, Kirsten Smaalerup, asking her to send word of these happenings to my father's house. When she arrived there, she found that my brother had already reached the house and he returned with the sister to the place where I had found shelter. From that place we traveled southward, and, after visiting some Saints living in the neighborhood of Veile, we continued our journey over the island of Fyen until we reached the home of a widowed sister who lived near the town of Nyborg, on the east side of the island. Soon a large crowd of intoxicated men and boys gathered around the house bent on mischief. As the mob entered the front door, we retreated through a back entrance, but the rabble followed us and finally caught hold of my brother, who was again fearfully ill-treated, and as the old sister whose name was Gjertrud rushed in between him and the mobbers to shield him with her person, she, too, was beaten and abused in a brutal manner. This time I escaped from bodily harm. Being impressed with the power of the spirit of God, I commenced talking to the mob, commanding them in the name of the Lord. They left us, and we remained in the house over night. It has been my firm belief that the sufferings to which my brother was subjected during that trip caused the early termination of his mortal career. After the trouble in Nyborg was over, we proceeded on our journey unmolested and reached Copenhagen July 22nd."

In the spring of 1852, another attempt was made to continue missionary work in Sweden. A Brother Mikael Johnson, a native of Sweden, who had received rough treatment at the hands of mobs in Denmark, was sent as a missionary to Sweden. Agreeable to instructions, given him by the presiding brethren in Copenhagen, he went to Gefle, the place of Brother John E. Forsgren's nativity and former labors. He found Peter A. Forsgren and the others, who had been baptized a year and a half previous, holding on to the faith, and the arrival of Elder Johnson in their midst was a great comfort to them. It appears that the seed sown in the beginning had commenced to spring up and that many of the words spoken by Elder Forsgren previous to his banishment were remembered by some of the people. On the arrival of Elder Johnson, these were anxious to

learn more of the principles of the gospel, but just as he had commenced baptizing he was arrested and transported to Stockholm. On his arrival at the capital he demanded a trial, but, after a preliminary examination, he was told by the police that his papers from Gefle were sufficient to send him on. He was, therefore, transported in chains—part of the way between two thieves—a distance of about five hundred miles overland to the city of Malmö, in Skåne. On this toilsome journey his only food was coarse bread and water and his suffering from exposure and insult was very severe. On his arrival in Malmö in a half-starved and weak condition, he was thrust into one of the prisons, which were originally royal castles, but afterwards became state prisons. After remaining there for some time, he was visited by a Lutheran priest who, on conditions, offered to help him out of his difficulties. Inviting him into a more comfortable apartment, the priest, upon discovering that Elder Johnson possessed some learning, proposed to assist him in getting into a high school, to complete his education, provided he would associate himself with the Lutherans, renounce "Mormonism," and cease to preach its doctrines. Brother Johnson answered: "You make me think of the 'gentleman' who was with Jesus on the mountain when he was an hungered."

"What," said the astonished divine, "do you liken yourself to Jesus and me to the devil? You shall go out of the country." Accordingly, the police authorities of Malmö took him over Öresund (the sound between Sweden and Denmark) and delivered him to the police authorities in Copenhagen on the 9th of September, 1852. This action on the part of the Malmö police was the more inconsistent because Elder Johnson was a native-born subject of Sweden, and had neither been tried nor condemned by any judicial court. His crime consisted in having baptized several respectable citizens at their own request. About the same time Elder Forsgren's brother and sister and one of those baptized by Elder Johnson arrived in Copenhagen. Thus ended the second attempt to introduce the gospel into Sweden.

Elder Anders W. Winberg may be classed as one of the first successful missionaries in Sweden. The missionary efforts of Elders Forsgren and Johnson in Gefle and Stockholm having terminated in their banishment from the country, it was reserved for Skåne, the southernmost province of the kingdom, or that part lying adjacent to Denmark, to become the cradle of "Mormonism" in Sweden.

At the general conference of the Scandinavian Mission, held at Copenhagen, Denmark, in February, 1852, just previous to the departure of Erastus Snow on his return to America, a number of Elders were called to labor as missionaries in different parts of Denmark, and three, Anders W. Winberg, Nils Capson and Ola Nilson, were appointed to open up a missionary field in the province of Skåne, Sweden. For some unknown reason, Brother Nilson did not go, but the other two brethren responded to the call.

Elder Winberg left Copenhagen April 21, 1852, crossed Öresund and wended his way to Lund, his native town, where his parents still resided. There he commenced his missionary operations with success, and on the 7th of June, 1852, he had the pleasure of baptizing his sister and brother-in-law (Peter Peterson and wife), who resided in the village of Dalby, about seven miles east of the city of Lund. This is supposed to be the first baptism performed by divine authority

in southern Sweden. Mr. Peterson was a tanner by trade, and he and his wife were baptized in a new tanner's vat, which had not been used for tannery purposes.

CHAPTER 13 (1852)

Arrival of Willard Snow—Johan F. F. Dorius mobbed in Jutland, Denmark—Elders Hans Peter Jensen and Johan A. Ahmanson in Norway—Branches of the Church organized at Österrisör, Frederikstad and Brevig—"Zions Löve"—Opposition in Brevig.

On Monday, April 26, 1852, Elder Willard Snow arrived in Copenhagen from England, having been appointed by the presidency in Liverpool to take charge of the Scandinavian Mission. He was a brother of Apostle Erastus Snow and was cordially received by the Saints. He took full charge of the mission when Elder John E. Forsgren, with a company of emigrants, left for Utah in December, 1852.

WILLARD SNOW

Born May 6, 1811, in St. Johnsbury, Caledonia Co., Vermont; died on the North Sea, Aug. 21, 1853.

Elder Willard Snow, in speaking of his arrival in Copenhagen and his first impressions of the country and its people, writes:

"I left Hull on the 21st of April and landed in Copenhagen on the 26th, making my voyage across the North Sea in five days. I paid £3 or $15 for my passage. Captain Lund, the master of the vessel, appeared quite friendly and spoke English as well as Danish. We encountered headwinds and rough seas on the voyage and I was seasick all the way. I felt rather lonesome, as I was the only passenger on board, and having left the English people, and the Saints with whom I could converse, I was now mingling with people of whose language I did not understand a single word. This, coupled with the realization that I was so far away from my home, made me feel most 'sublime' and solemn, especially when I contemplated the mission upon which I had been called. I fully realized that I should have to obtain a knowledge of the language, manners, customs and laws of the Danish people. On my arrival in Copenhagen I found Elders Peter O. Hansen and John E. Forsgren in good spirits; they welcomed me with such a warm reception that I felt quite at home. Hans Peter Jensen, the other counselor, could not converse with me in English, but he seemed to be a man of good countenance and possessed the spirit of his calling. He had just returned from Hamburg where he had seen Elders George P. Dykes and Daniel Garn. Bro Jensen stayed a day or two after my arrival in Copenhagen and then left for his home near Aalborg, accompanied by Elder John E. Forsgren, to attend a conference. He then expected to go to Norway to open up a mission there, according to an appointment given him by Erastus Snow before he left. I found that persecution raged in some parts of the country, but the Elders continued their labors, and quite recently thirty-five members had been added to the Church by baptism in Copenhagen. Some indications of hostilities had been manifested in Copenhagen since Brother Snow left, and in several of the country branches some of the brethren had been abused and taken up for vagrancy and sent to the police courts in Copenhagen, but they had all been given their liberty. The large hall which the Saints had when Erastus left was refused them, the proprietor seemingly afraid of disturbance."

In the beginning of July, 1852, President Willard Snow received a note from Bro. Johan F. F. Dorius, giving an account of how he had been maltreated in Vendsyssel, Denmark. He was holding a meeting with some of the Saints in a farmer's hiouse, when some lawless fellows came in and commenced pricking him with awls and broke up the meeting. Having driven him out of the house, they ran after him and beat him with clubs and sticks. However, he succeeded in getting into a house, although in a suffering condition, being soiled with his own blood. He was washed and anointed with oil and sent to bed, but the mob broke into the house, tore off the bedding and dragged him out into the field, intending to throw him into the creek, but an unseen power prevented them from carrying out their evil intent, and so they left him almost naked. However, he was healed by the power of God, so that he was able to preach and baptize again the next morning.

On Thursday, June 10, 1852, Elder Hans Peter Jensen, accompanied by Johan A. Ahmanson, landed in Brevig, one of the coast cities of Norway, as Latter-day Saint missionaries from Denmark. They had sailed from Nörre Sundby on the 6th. Almost immediately after their arrival at Brevig, they commenced to hold meetings, circulate tracts and converse privately with the people. Mr. Trane (a newspaper editor), the town priest, and a school teacher, soon became their bitter opponents.

After staying in Brevig six days, Elder Jensen traveled on to Österrisör, where he arrived June 16th and was warmly received by Bro. Svend Larsen and two Saints who had previously been baptized by Brother Hans F. Petersen. Soon after Elder Petersen's departure from Österrisör, in December, 1851, Brother Svend Larsen returned home from a visit to the eastern parts of Norway (Östlandet) and learned that Brother Petersen had left for the west coast on account of persecutions. Svend

Larsen spent the winter at home, laboring as best he could to continue the work which had been commenced by Elder Petersen. Together with the other two converts (John Olsen and Peter Adamsen) he held fast meetings regularly every Sunday, at which they spent their time praying for and with one another; they also read in the Bible and Book of Mormon and bore testimony to the truth of the gospel. Henrik Evensen, the master of a small vessel, was a constant visitor in these little meetings. He soon afterwards joined the Church. Also the wives of the three brethren opened their hearts to believe the truth; and as the meetings were continued, more strangers met with them, and though none of the brethren had yet been ordained to the Holy Priesthood, the spirit of testimony rested upon them as they addressed the people and the hearts of many were softened to believe the words spoken. On one occasion a member of the clergy and a school teacher came to the meeting to oppose them, but they went away confounded.

Brother Larsen also spread the printed word, including "Skandinaviens Stjerne." He also posted himself in regard to the so-called dissenter law and found that, according to the provisions of said law, people who differed with the State Church on religious matters could be organized into a society with as small a number as six members. Consequently, three of the men, viz., Svend Larsen, John Olsen and Henrik Evensen, together with their respective wives, withdrew their names from the Lutheran Church. Their next step was to petition the diocese of Christiansand and the church department of the state (Kirkedepartementet) to be organized into a Christian dissenter society, according to the laws of the land, but though

Mayor Finne of Österrisör assisted Brother Larsen in formulating the petition, and instructed him how to proceed in order to obtain the government permission, their petition was denied.

Three days after the arrival of Elder Hans P. Jensen at Österrisör, June 19th, he ordained Svend Larsen an Elder, and on the 24th he blessed his four children. At a meeting held on Sunday, June 20th, the brethren administered the Sacrament to the few Saints in Österrisör. On the 25th Elder Ahmanson baptized six persons and Elder Jensen ordained two of the brethren (John Olsen and Henrik Evensen) Priests.

After these labors, Elder Jensen made a missionary trip to Arendal, Christiansand and Mandal, bearing testimony of the truth in these places. On his arrival at the last named town, he was fatigued and his feet were blistered so badly that he was unable to proceed any further. As the inhabitants hardened their hearts against him and refused to receive his testimony, he decided to walk back to Österrisör, a distance of about 130 English miles. Following the advise of a friendly lady, he wrapped his feet in rags and commenced his march on foot, and, strange to say, when he arrived at Österrisör on the 8th of July, his feet were free from sores and he felt himself as strong and healthy as ever before.

In the meantime, Elders Hans Peter Jensen and Svend Larsen continued their labors in Norway, and on the 16th of July, they organized a branch of the Church in Österrisör with eighteen members. Elder Jensen ordained John Olsen an Elder and appointed him to preside over the branch, which was the first branch of the Church of Jesus Christ of Latter-day Saints established in Norway. The following day, Elders Hans Peter Jensen and Svend Larsen returned to Brevig from Österrisör. Finding a large number of people in Brevig who were anxious to hear them preach, and not being permitted to hold meetings in halls used by other denominations, they secured a meeting place of their own. From a Mr. Jörgen Christensen they hired a hall in an upper story of a house located in the central part of the town, for which they agreed to pay an annual rent of forty "speciedaler" ($40). The holding of meetings was at once commenced in the hired hall and they were well attended. Among those who came to listen were several priests, some town officials, merchants, etc. At one of the meetings the clergymen, some from the city and some from the country, were bent on having a discussion, and while the brethren spoke, they were exceedingly busy taking notes. Elder Jensen bore a powerful testimony to the truth of the gospel, and, referring to those who were writing, he said that he, by the power of God, would write the words of truth in their hearts in a manner that it could never be effaced. Hearing this, the scribes ceased their note-taking and listened attentively to the rest of the sermon. After the meeting was closed, all went away in peace.

From Brevig, Elders Hans Peter Jensen and Svend Larsen proceeded by water to Frederikstad. While laboring in the ministry in Österrisör, Elder Jensen advised Svend Larsen to purchase a vessel to be used for carrying the missionaries from place to place in Norway, and between that country and Denmark. Brother Larsen, whose zeal for the truth was unbounded, and who considered no sacrifice too great in the interests of God's cause, readily consented to this proposition, and consequently made a visit to Frederikshavn, in Denmark, where he purchased one of the best and swiftest pilot boats in the country

for the sum of 400 "rigsdaler." He fitted up the vessel as a pleasure yacht and named it "Zions Löve" (Zion's Lion). It was a splendid sailer and bore on the masthead a white ensign on which was painted a lion holding a radiating eye in a golden circular halberd, under which the letter Z was painted in blue colors. The whole was a symbol of strength and light and represented Zion spreading its light by divine power over the nations.

The brethren soon put their vessel to good use and for some time Capt. Larsen was kept busy sailing with missionaries from place to place, both in Norway and Denmark. The first trip made with "Zions Löve" in the interest of missionary work was between Brevig and Frederikstad. On that occasion Elders Jensen and Larsen sailed from Brevig July 22nd, leaving Elder Ahmanson in Brevig to continue the meetings and do other missionary work. Arriving at Frederikstad on the 23rd, they found Priest Jeppe J. Folkmann from Bornholm, Denmark, who had been sent to Norway by the president of the Scandinavian Mission to strengthen the mission there, and who had already spent a short time in Frederikstad endeavoring to make an opening for preaching the gospel in that city. He had been kindly received in the homes of Brother Svend Peter Larsen, who, as before stated, had been baptized in Copenhagen, and Emil Larsen, a dyer and brother of Svend Peter Larsen, both of whom lived in Vaterland, a suburb of Frederikstad. These two families also extended a warm welcome to the two Elders (Hans Peter Jensen and Svend Larsen), who at once commenced missionary work. The following day, (July 24th) they held a meeting at the home of Jacob Jensen, a gardener, who lived near Frederikstad, and where the seed fell in good soil, as a number of those people were so wrought upon under the influence of the power of truth that they received the testimony in their hearts with joy and thanksgiving. On Sunday (July 25th), Elders Jensen and Larsen held another spirited meeting in the house of Emil Larsen, and in the afternoon, they attended a meeting of certain revivalists, who were called "Kirke-troende," where the door at first was closed against them, but finally opened, and Elder Jensen was given the privilege of speaking. In the course of his remarks, he endeavored to prove that the State Church of Norway was not the true Church of Christ. A number of those present, among them the mistress of the house, taking umbrage at hearing their old religion thus attacked, Elder Jensen was interrupted in his talk, but as there were several persons present who desired to hear more, a neighbor by the name of Guttorm Baardsen, opened his house for the speaker, who then continued his discourse. At the close of the meeting several persons expressed themselves convinced of the truth of the principles they had heard, and that same night witnessed the baptism and confirmation of five persons, the first converts to "Mormonism" in Frederikstad. Among them was Johan Johansen, who had presided over the local branch of "Kirketroende." He was ordained a Priest and appointed to preside over the little branch of seven members, which was organized on the same occasion and named Frederikstad Branch. In the evening of the 26th, three other persons were baptized in Frederikstad, and in the morning of the 27th, Elder Jensen and Larsen took their departure on board "Zions Löve" for Brevig, where they arrived on the 28th, accompanied by Priest Jeppe J. Folkmann, who was appointed to labor in

Brevig and vicinity under the direction of Elder Ahmanson.

Elder Hans Peter Jensen, after having founded the Church in Norway, and spent his means freely for the welfare of the mission, left for Denmark in the latter part of July, 1852, sailing with Captain Svend Larsen in their own vessel, "Zions Löve." Elder Johan A. Ahmanson was left in charge of the Norwegian Mission. During the voyage to Denmark, Elders Jensen and Larsen encountered the full fury of a terrific storm, but on July 31st they arrived in Aalborg, Denmark, where they attended a conference August 1, 2 and 3, 1852. They then continued the voyage to Copenhagen, taking with them in their vessel President John E. Forsgren, Willard Snow and Christian J. Larsen and a number of other Danish Saints, who, like themselves, went to Copenhagen to attend the general conference of the mission, arriving in Copenhagen August 11th.

After the departure of Elders Jensen and Larsen from Norway, Elder Ahmanson continued his missionary labors in Brevig, and on Monday, August 9, 1852, the first four converts to "Mormonism" in Brevig were baptized. The names of these first converts were Knud Larsen, Bertha Katrina Larsen, Iver Mikkelsen Uglestad, and Susanne Uglestad.

At this time meetings were held in Brevig twice on Sundays and on every Tuesday and Wednesday evening in the hired hall. Small meetings were also held in private houses in and near Brevig and Skien. Elder Ahmanson was a good and influential speaker, and several believers were soon numbered among the regular attendants at the meetings.

No sooner had these first believers yielded obedience to the initiative ordinances of the gospel than the Lutheran clergy and newspaper editors in Brevig united in a crusade against

ie work of God, and did all in their
ower to embitter the minds of the
eople, by circulating all kinds of
alsehoods and slurs against the
Mormons." Their opposition, how-
ver, availed them but little, as a
umber of other converts were soon
aptized. In the meantime a con-
piracy was inaugurated with the in-
ntion of taking Brothers Ahmanson
nd Folkmann out of the town by
orce, but the plot proved unsuccess-
il. On the 24th the two mission-
ries were arraigned before a local
ourt and forbidden to preach and
aptize, but on the 3rd of September,
lder Ahmanson held an audience
ith the "Amtmand," whose name
as Aal, who agreed to receive a
etition from Brother Ahmanson and
nd it to the Church department
Kirkedepartementet). Consequent-
, Elder Ahmanson wrote such a
etition in which he prayed that the
hurch he represented might, as soon
s possible, obtain recognition as a
hristian denomination and thus be
ntitled to protection under the Nor-
egian dissenter law.

On Sunday, September 5th, Elder
hmanson called the newly-baptized
iembers in Brevig together and or-
anized them (eight in number) into
branch of the Church called the
revig Branch. After ordaining
nud Larsen a Priest he appointed
im president of the branch. This
ave Brother Larsen authority to con-
nue preaching and baptizing, in
ise brothers Ahmanson and Folk-
ann should be cast into prison. In
ie evening, the two missionaries
ent to Gjerstad to hold a meeting,
or which they were arrested and im-
risoned on the 7th of September.
owever, after four days in prison,
iey were liberated on the 11th on
ondition that they in the future
ould not perform any act connected
ith the doctrines of the "Mormons"
i that amt (county). The brethren

submitted to these conditions because
they expected a number of other
Elders from Denmark, who, on their
arrival, would become acquainted
with the situation, and if they
(Brothers Ahmanson and Folkmann)
should remain in prison, the new missionaries would, on their arrival, be
at a loss to know what to do. The
imprisonment of Elders Ahmanson
and Folkmann in Brevig was the first
of many imprisonments of Latter-day
Saint missionaries in Norway for
preaching the gospel and administering its ordinances.

CHAPTER 14 (1852)

Fourth general conference held in Scandinavia—The Brevig, Bornholm, Vendsyssel and
Lolland conferences organized—Voyages of
"Zions Löve;" council meeting on board—The
missionaries in Norway arrested and imprisoned; experiences in prison.

On Thursday, August 12, 1852, the
fourth general conference of the
Scandinavian Mission convened in
Copenhagen. The large hall, known
as "Enighedsværn," situated a short
distance outside of the city of Copenhagen, had been rented for the occasion, and here a large number of
missionaries, Saints and friends assembled in the afternoon. Pres. John
E. Forsgren presided, and among
those present were two High Priests
(Willard Snow and Hans Peter Jensen) and two Seventies (John E.
Forsgren and Peter O. Hansen), 23
Elders, 15 Priests, 5 Teachers and 3
Deacons. At this conference splendid reports were made by the missionaries, who reported great success
in different parts of the mission.

The conference was continued the
next day (August 13th), when Hans
Peter Jensen, Christian Christiansen
and Johan F. F. Dorius were appointed to formulate a petition to
the Danish government, asking for
protection against the mal-treatment
and persecution to which some of
the Saints in Denmark had been sub-

jected. The Elders who had labored as missionaries reported baptims and great success on the island of Sjælland, Lolland, Falster, Fyen, Bornholm, and other places, while Elder Hans Peter Jensen gave a most interesting report of the introduction of the work into Norway. On the third day of conference, August 14th, it was decided to change the mission periodical, "Skandinaviens Stjerne," from a monthly to a semi-monthly periodical. The branches in Norway were organized into a conference called the Brevig Conference, and Christian J. Larsen was called to go to Norway to preside over that conference, after he had finished his labors in Fredericia. The Saints in Bornholm were organized into a conference called the Bornholm Conference, with Ole Svendsen as president. The Saints in Vendsyssel were organized as the Vendsyssel Conference with Elder Niels Christian Schou as president, and the Saints on the islands of Lolland, Falster and Möen were organized as a conference called the Lolland Conference, with Johan Swenson as president. The Schlesvig Mission was attached to the Fredericia Conference.

On the fourth and last day of the conference, held August 16th, Elders Anders W. Winberg and Nils Capson were called to labor as missionaries in Sweden. Priest Ole Olsen was called on a mission to Norway.

President Forsgren, in summing up the business of the conference, remarked that there were now seven organized conferences in the mission. The general authorities of the Church and mission and conference authorities were sustained by unanimous vote, and quite a number of young men were ordained to the Priesthood and called to labor as missionaries in different parts of the mission. According to the reports made at this conference, there were now 934 per

sons in the mission belonging to the Church, of whom 95 had been ordained to the Priesthood.

On Thursday, August 19th, Elders John E. Forsgren, Hans Peter Jensen, Christian J. Larsen, Svend Larsen and others (14 persons altogether), boarded the little sailing craft or sloop, "Zions Löve," and set sail for Fredericia, where they arrived the next day. They held a conference on Sunday, August 22nd, at which Elder Niels Mikkelsen was sustained as president of the Fredericia Conference, succeeded Elder Christian J. Larsen who had been called to Norway. A new branch of the Church was organized at Store-Lihme. After the conferene, Elders John E. Forsgren and his companions returned to Copenhagen on "Zions Löve," arriving there August 26, 1852.

On Thursday, September 2nd, the sloop "Zions Löve," with a number of missionaries on board, who had been called to labor in Norway, sailed from Copenhagen for Aalborg, where they arrived on the 3rd. After attending meetings in Aalborg, the voyage was continued to Norway, where they landed on Sunday, September 12th.

The mission to Norway, consisting of Elders Christian J. Larsen (newly-appointed president of the Brevig Conference), Johan F. F. Dorius, Peter Beckström, Svend Larsen and Ole Olsen, Priest Christian Knudsen (later known as Nielsen) and Teacher Niels Hansen, arrived in the Brevig-fjord on the sloop, "Zions Löve." They had sailed from Copenhagen, Denmark, September 2nd. Elder Christian J. Larsen writes:

"When we came near the city of Brevig, perhaps two or three miles from the town, we were very much surprised, at about 10 o'clock a. m., to meet two of our brethren, Elder John A. Ahmanson and Priest Jeppe J. Folkmann, coming out in a small skiff, not aware of our arrival; they were on their way to visit a family of investigators living across the water. These two missionaries had just been liberated from four days' imprisonment in Brevig for preaching the gospel. They were expecting us, but did not know when we would arrive, besides, the town of Brevig was in an uproar, and the mob had threatened to kill the 'Mormon Priest' who might attempt to set foot on shore. It had already been rumored that some more 'Mormon Priests' were coming from Denmark. Upon hearing this intelligence, we all felt to give thanks to God, our Heavenly Father, for it was now clear to our understanding that the Lord knew the plans of our enemies and had frustrated them by keeping us out of their power, and now we were placed in communication with our brethren in a convenient place and at a suitable time. We accompanied our brethren to a fishing village called Bauen, and I, with some others of the brethren, went up among the rocks and implored the Lord for his guidance under our peculiar circumstances. We had a very interesting conversation with one family in that place upon the principles of the gospel, and they showed their good will and appreciation by treating us to a good meal. When we again boarded our own vessel, 'Zions Löve,' we found the other brethren, whom we had left on board, engaged in singing and prayer, which was a source of joy to me. We now held a council meeting on board, at which it was decided that Elder Johan F. F. Dorius should remain and labor in Brevig and vicinity quietly, while the rest of us would proceed to Frederikstad, where we would be assigned to our respective fields of labor. I advised the brethren to work with wisdom, always seeking the guidance of the Spirit of God. Several of the brethren also gave expression to their feelings, and we had a very pleasant time together. The Spirit of God rested upon us in a very great degree, although that important meeting was held in the 'bowels of a lion,' the cabin of the 'Zions Löve.' After the meeting was dismissed Johan A. Ahmanson, Johan F. F. Dorius, Jeppe J. Folkmann, Fred. Anderson and I sailed to a place called Satre, near Brevig, but not in sight of the town, and in the evening we held a good meeting with the Saints who lived in that vicinity, speaking encouraging words to them. We then went to our rented hall and slept there that night."

The next day (Sept. 13th) Elder Christian J. Larsen and fellow-mis-

sionaries confirmed two recently baptized members in Brevig, and blessed three children. Leaving Elder Johan F. F. Dorius in Brevig to continue missionary labors there, the other brethren resumed the voyage on "Zions Löve" to Frederikstad, where they arrived the next day. To their great joy they found that the few Saints in Frederikstad were doing well. A meeting was held with the Saints the same evening, on which occasion Elder Peter Beckström and Priest Christian Knudsen were appointed to labor in Frederikstad and vicinity, while Elder Ole Olsen, Priest Jeppe J. Folkmann and Teacher Niels Hansen were appointed to travel eastward to open up a new field of labor. After making the necessary arrangement in Frederikstad, Elders Christian J. Larsen, Johan A. Ahmanson and Svend Larsen sailed in the "Zions Löve" for Österrisör. There they remained eight days, held ten meetings, baptized seven persons, administered to a number who were sick, organized the branch more fully, and enjoyed themselves among the Saints. When Elder Larsen called at the police station to show his pass, he was warned under threats of imprisonment against preaching his doctrine in Österrisör, but this only gave him an excellent opportunity to bear testimony to the members of the police force. The missionaries next returned to Brevig, where they arrived Oct. 2nd. Later they went to Frederikstad.

While Elder Christian J. Larsen and others were holding a meeting in the house of Emil Larsen at Vaterland, a suburb of Frederikstad, Oct. 13, 1852, a theological candidate (Kjærulff) opposed the brethren, claiming that he had permission from the mayor of the city to appear against the "Mormons" anywhere, and at all times, to oppose the doctrines advocated by them. With this object in view Mr. Kjærulff and his companions repeated a string of old lies and accusations which were circulating against Joseph Smith and the Book of Mormon. A long discussion ensued, during which the brethren got the best of the argument on every point. Soon the mayor himself appeared on the scene, and the brethren asked him if anyone could with impunity oppose and insult them in their meetings without permission, and if they did not have the same right as any other religious society to the protection of the civil authorities, provided they did nothing in opposition to good Christian morals and proper order and decorum. To this the mayor answered in a low tone, "Yes, but opposition to 'Mormon' doctrines is permissable." The next day, Oct. 14, as Elder Chr. J. Larsen and Svend

NIELS HANSEN

Born Aug. 11, 1832, at Tröstrup, Fyen, Denmark; died Dec. 13, 1902, at Etna, Canada.

Larsen, in company with Jeppe J. Folkmann and Niels Hansen, were walking towards Ingelsrud (a large farm near Frederikstad, Norway), to visit some Saints at that place, they met the "Amtmand" or county magistrate, Mr. Birch Reichenwaldt, who accosted the brethren in a most abrupt manner, when he learned that they were "Mormons." He ordered them to go back with him to Frederikstad to be arrested. This the brethren refused to do on the grounds that they had not transgressed any law, and they understood that prisons were built for criminals, and that the tribunals of justice were appointed to punish lawlessness, to protect the rights of citizens and maintain order in the community. And as they had not transgressed any rules or laws in this connection, nor had any intention of doing so in the future, they bade the "Amtmand" goodbye and continued on their journey to Ingelsrud. But they had scarcely got inside the door before the son of the sheriff stepped in, accompanied by ten or twelve persons belonging to the peasantry, who at once, in a gruff manner, questioned the brethren as to who they were, ordering them to show passports. Fortunately for Elder Larsen, he had a note with him signed by the mayor, stating that his passport was at Frederikstad. By this means he was permitted to retain his liberty, after some further questioning, but was ordered to return to Frederikstad at once. Brothers Folkmann and Niels Hansen, whose passports had been left at Moss, where they had intended to go the following day, were at once ordered to prison, all protests on their part being fruitless. The Norwegian Brother, Captain Svend Larsen, who had not his pass with him, but had his vessel lying at Vaterland, was also ordered to prison, but, after considerable parleying, he was permitted to go to the town in the evening to look after his boat, on condition that he would meet ʾn court the following day. Elder Larsen, however, was prevented from keeping his promise, for he had scarcely got up the next morning when the mayor's deputy (Underbyfoged), Mr. Fjeldstad, accompanied by a police officer, appeared at the residence of Brother Emil Larsen at Vaterland, where Brothers Svend and Christian J. Larsen stopped over night, with orders from the mayor that these two brethren should accompany them to the mayor's office. The brethren complied with the request, but the moment they opened the door the mayor, addressing himself to Elder Chr. J. Larsen, said: "You are a prisoner." Hearing no cause given for his arrest, Elder Larsen asked what he had done to deserve imprisonment. The answer was, "You have administered the Sacrament and preached. Go with the officer at once." The police officer, to whom he had reference, already stood by Elder Larsen's side. Elder Larsen asked for the privilege of returning to his lodgings for his clothes and to arrange his affairs before going to prison, but he was told that he could send for them. Realizing that further remonstrance would be in vain, he accompanied the officers to the court house, where he was duly imprisoned in the so-called citizen's jail (Borgerarresten). While Elder Chr. J. Larsen was thus cast into prison, Brother Svend Larsen was retained at the mayor's office for some time, being requested to explain the principles and doctrines believed in by the "Mormons." This request Brother Larsen readily complied with, and thus the mayor had an opportunity of listening to something which he no doubt remembered as long as he lived. The straightforward testimony given by Elder Larsen on this occasion ought to have

saved himself and fellow-laborers from further arrest and imprisonment, but it seemed, on the contrary, to make matters worse. Though Elder Svend Larsen had neither baptized nor administered the Sacrament in Frederikstad, or the vicinity, the mayor said to him, "I'm compelled to arrest you. You will have to follow the officer." Elder Larsen answered, "If it were not that I am being arrested for the sake of the testimony of Jesus Christ, you would find it no easy task to get me into the prison." He then willingly accompanied the officers and was a prisoner after that hour for five months. Elder Chr. J. Larsen writes:

"I rejoiced in being counted worthy to suffer for the gospel's sake, like my co-religionists in far-off America; but I felt grieved in my spirit when I thought of the many noble souls who were anxious to learn of the things pertaining to the Kingdom of God, and that I was now deprived of the opportunity to instruct them. I also felt quite sure that my fellow-missionaries would be compelled to share my fate, and this apprehension I was soon to realize, for a few hours after my own imprisonment, Brother Svend Larsen was brought in as a prisoner by the same officer who had placed me in durance vile. He was ignorant as to the cause of his imprisonment, as he had neither administered Sacrament nor any other ordinance of the gospel. But we clearly saw that the sole object which the authorities had in view was to get us under arrest on whatever pretext might be suggested in order to hinder and stop the progress of truth."

On the same day, Elder Johan F. F. Dorius and Chr. Knudsen were arrested by Lehnsmand Printz. The following account is given by Johan F. F. Dorius:

"On Friday, Oct. 15, 1852, we visited Brother Mons Petersen and about noon Elder Beckström started for Frederikstad, while Brother Knudsen and I went to Aale (a farming district) with the intention of holding a meeting there; but on our arrival we could not obtain a room for that purpose. Toward evening we walked to Kjölbergbro (a farm and inn) where we asked for lodgings, but when the matron of the place learned that we were "Mormons," she said, that the Amtmand had given her strict orders not to entertain that class of people. While we were yet conversing, a uniformed officer stepped in from a side room and, without further introduction, he at once asked me who I was and if I had a passport. To which I replied that my pass was in Frederikstad. He then said to me, "You are under arrest." He then turned to Brother Knudsen and asked him for his passport, but receiving a similar reply to the one I had given, Brother Knudsen was also made a prisoner. We were then brought into another room where we understood we were to remain until the preliminary hearing was over. But what a surprise awaited us when we entered; the room was nearly full of Saints, who had been summoned to appear for examination. We also found Brother Ole Olsen, who had already been imprisoned about two weeks, and Brothers Folkmann and Niels Hansen, whom they had arrested the day before and now brought to Kjölberg for examination. While our feelings were peculiar at meeting under such circumstances, yet an unspeakable joy filled our hearts, for we knew we were guilty of no crime. After the trial or preliminary examination, Brother Olsen was imprisoned at Elverhöj, in charge of Sheriff (Lehnsmand) Mikkelsen, while Brothers Folkmann and Niels Hansen and I were placed in confinement with Lehnsmand Printz, about ten miles from Frederikstad. A guard was kept over us all night."

On Saturday, Oct. 16th, in the forenoon, Elder Johan F. F. Dorius was brought in a vehicle to the court house in Frederikstad, where he arrived about noon, and was delivered to Officer Fjeldstad, who conducted him into the jail. Here Elder Dorius was surprised to meet his beloved brethren, Elders Christian J. and Svend Larsen, who had been arrested the previous day. In the afternoon the number of "Mormon" prisoners was further increased by the arrival of Elder Peter Beckström, who was arrested at Vaterland by an officer who conducted him to prison. Thus the police officers had arrested eight of the brethren for no other cause than this, that they had preached the

gospel of repentance and sought to do good to their fellowmen.

It may seem strange that the "Mormon" Elders should be thus treated by the liberty-loving people of Norway; but it must be remembered that the Lutheran religion had at that time become so fully established in that land, and in the hearts of the people, that any deviation from its "well beaten track" seemed unlawful and unwarranted. A law, however, had been passed some years previously granting certain liberties and privileges to dissenters, that is, those who differed with the State Church on points of doctrine, but who, nevertheless, were considered Christians. Under this provision the Catholics, Methodists, and perhaps other sects, had already obtained a foothold in Norway, and their several congregations had full liberty to worship the Lord according to the provisions of their respective creeds. But when the "Mormon" Elders appeared in the land and commenced to preach about new revelation, the Book of Mormon and kindred topics, the people and authorities were confronted with something so entirely new to them, and so different from all orthodox religion, that they at first did not know what to think of it, or how to meet it. The query soon arose, whether the "Mormons," with their peculiar doctrines, could be classed as Christian dissenters. If they were such, they were entitled to the same protection under the law as other dissenters; but if not, all their acts were unlawful and their baptisms and other ordinance work were punishable with fines and imprisonment. The great majority of the clergy, who in all the countries visited by the "Mormon" Elders have ever shown the most bitter opposition, took the stand in Norway from the beginning that the "Mormons" were not Christians, and consequently the clergy exercised all the influence they possessed with the civil authorities to have the "Mormon" Elders arrested and imprisoned; and we have already seen, in the foregoing, to what extent they succeeded, by having all the active missionares, who had commenced successful operations in the land, placed behind lock and key, pending a more thorough examination of "Mormon" doctrines.

The apartment in which the brethren in Frederikstad were incarcerated was what in some American prisons would be termed the debtors' apartment. It was an upper room, well lighted, clean and tidy; and Mr. Fjeldstad, the jailer, and his family treated the missionaries with considerable kindness and consideration; he granted them all the privileges he was permitted to give them under the prison rules. The brethren spent their time in reading, singing, writing, praying and in interesting conversation. Though their writing-materials were taken from them in the beginning, they were soon restored, through Elder Svend Larsen's earnest request. Thus the time passed away swiftly and pleasantly, the brethren having a clear conscience that their cause was a just one, and worthy of all their sufferings. The Holy Ghost gave them comfort at all times, and when they finally emerged from the prison-house, their faith in the principles of the gospel was stronger than ever before and their zeal for the cause had increased manifold.

When the brethren first entered the prison, they found there a sea-captain (skipper) by the name of Johan Andreas Jensen and a Mr. Jacobsen, the latter also having been imprisoned on account of his religion. These two men lived in the same apartment as the missionaries from the 15th of June, 1852, till the 22nd of October, 1852. They were

adherents of Methodism. Mr. Jacobsen, who was a bitter opponent of the missionaries, was finally removed

JOHAN ANDREAS JENSEN

Born Nov. 16, 1795, near Frederikstad, Norway, lost his father when five years old and went to sea; during the following twenty-four years he advanced from cabin boy to the captaincy of a large ship and navigated nearly all parts of the world; in 1849 he became deeply impressed with religion, gave nearly all his goods to the poor and preached repentance; in his zeal he rebuked the king and was imprisoned in Frederikstad, at the same time that the "Mormon" Elders were imprisoned there for preaching, became a convert and was baptized by Carl Widerborg, Feb. 25, 1854, emigrated to Utah in 1863, and located in Ephraim, Sanpete Co., Utah, where he died Jan. 26, 1882.

to a room by himself on the 22nd of October, while Mr. Jensen continued to share the room with the brethren a little longer. They commenced to preach the gospel to him, but at first he would not receive their testimony.

On Sunday morning, April 24th, Mr. Fjeldstad, the jailer, and his son visited the missionaries in their room, and a lengthy religious conversation took place. Elder Chr. J. Larsen in particular testified to the truth of the gospel under the influence of the Holy Ghost and made a lasting impression on them. After Mr. Fjeldstad left the cell, the brethren continued to converse with Mr. Jensen until they were all brought under a most pleasant and divine influence, and joy indescribable filled their hearts. Mr. Jensen gave way to a sudden outburst of tears and declared that he was convinced that the gospel as explained to him by his fellow-prisoners was true, and his face literally shone with joy. The brethren and their new convert thanked and praised the Lord together, sang songs of joy and had throughout a most glorious experience. This Mr. Jensen was baptized afterwards and remained a faithful member of the Church to the day of his death.

CHAPTER 15 (1852)

The imprisoned missionaries in Norway receive kind treatment, but choose imprisonment rather than to cease preaching—Life in the prisons, at Frederikstad and Elverhöi—Series of examinations and trials—Answers to questions—Christmas in Norwegian prisons.

On Saturday (Nov. 1st) Elder Chr. J. Larsen received a note from the brethren who were imprisoned at Elverhöi, the note being signed by Ole Olsen, Jeppe J. Folkmann, Christian Knudsen and Niels Hansen, and brought by Brother Emil Larsen. The imprisoned brethren at Elverhöi sought Brother Larsen's advice as to whether they should accept an offer from the police to be liberated from their imprisonment on condition that they would return to Denmark and not come back to Norway. To this proposition Elder Larsen was constrained by the Spirit to say, that so far as he himself was concerned, he would not return to Denmark until he was released by the same authority which had sent him to Norway. Even if he was compelled to remain in prison during the rest of his mortal life, he would, if the Lord would sustain him, stand the test rather than shirk the responsibilities of his mission. All his fellow-prisoners in the Frederikstad jail signed a decision

to that effect, as a reply to their imprisoned brethren at Elverhöi.

During this time, the brethren in the Frederikstad jail spent much of their time singing and bearing testimony to the visitors who were permitted to come in and see them. They also fasted and prayed considerably, and enjoyed themselves very much in the society of the few Saints who were admitted to their prison room. Under date of November 10th, Birch Reichenvaldt, the county magistrate, and Mr. Berg, the mayor of Frederikstad, and a priest by the name of Buch, visited the brethren in prison. The magistrate especially treated the brethren in a most impolite manner, as if they were criminals, and when they made any reply, he would roughly tell them to shut up. Nevertheless, they took advantage of every opportunity they had to show these officers that the doctrines advocated by the Elders were in perfect harmony with the Bible and true Christianity.

The brethren asked the jailor for permission to go out once in a while to visit among their friends. This request was granted on condition that they would be accompanied by a police officer. During their imprisonment, the Elders spent considerable time in writing and corresponding with President Willard Snow of the Scandinavian Mission, and others.

On Friday (Nov. 12th) Elder Christian J. Larsen was on trial in Frederikstad. Brothers Ole Olsen, Jeppe J. Folkmann, Chr. Knudsen and Niels Hansen were also on trial before Sorenskriver Bing, the district judge. The three last named brethren had been removed to Elverhöi, to share prison apartments with their fellow-missionary, Ole Olsen. Their place of confinement, unlike the prison in Frederikstad, was uncomfortable and their food was very poor.

On the same day (Nov. 12th) Brother Johan A. Ahmanson was brought as a prisoner from Österrisör and placed in the same apartment as his brethren at Frederikstad. All these arrests and changes were ordered by the magistrate (Birch Reichenvaldt). With Brother Ahmanson's imprisonment, there were five of the brethren confined in Frederikstad, viz., two Danes (Chr. J. Larsen and Johan F. F. Dorius), two Swedes (Peter Beckström and Johan A. Ahmanson) and one Norwegian (Svend Larsen); also their new convert, Mr. Jens Andreas Jensen, who had not yet been baptized. They all occupied the same room. A short time after his conversion, Mr. Jensen received his sentence to imprisonment in the penitentiary in Christiania for one year. His alleged crime consisted in having written something which was construed as an insult to the king. Elder Chr. J. Larsen gives the following details concerning the court proceedings in Frederikstad, November 12, 1852:

"At 2 p. m. I was brought before the 'Amtmand' at his office, and there I found that the other brethren had been brought in from their prison, which was some miles distant from the city of Frederikstad. Besides the "Amtmand" we found ourselves confronted with quite an array of legal dignitaries, all interested in our case, to wit.., Birch Reichenvaldt, the superior chief of the district (Amtmand) ; Mr. Bing, the chief clerk; Mayor Berg, Secretary Cherming, Mr. Ask (the constable) and a Lutheran clergyman. Brother Jeppe J. Folkmann and I were the first of the prisoners to be examined, and the following colloquy took place:

Q. What is the relation of the "Skandinaviens Stjerne" to you and your religion?"

A. It is a publication in which the Saints can present and advocate their religious views as we find them sustained by the doctrines of our faith and the Bible." (I added that I was willing to answer any and all questions that the court might put to me, God being my helper.)

Q. Were you present at a conference held in Copenhagen, August 12th, at which it was decided to have "Skandinaviens Stjerne" issued twice a month?

A. Yes.

Q. Did you answer in writing the several questions which were submitted to you on a former occasion?

A. Yes. (I then produced the papers, which were read, but that did not seem to be entirely satisfactory to the court, and I was therefore interrogated further concerning certain points in our reply, but in such a threatening and crafty way, that it became evident that they were only trying to ensnare me in the meshes of the law, wherefore I again referred them to written statements and the Bible. To this the "Amtmand" tauntingly replied, "Why did you not send the Bible instead of coming yourself into court, inasmuch as you have always referred to the Bible as your answer to legal interrogations?" He wanted me to know that I was here arraigned before a civil court, and that I would be judged according to the laws of the land, and not according to the Bible, and it was their desire that truth and justice might prevail. To this last expression of the judge I replied that this was a source of joy to me, for I was here for no other purpose than to promote righteousness and proclaim the truth, and that we, like the Apostles of old, taught the people to honor God and to respect and obey all good laws and the legal authorities of the land, and that the Bible did not teach anything contrary to this.)

Q. For what purpose have you come to this country?

A. We have come here to teach the people the true gospel of Jesus Christ and to warn them, so as to prepare themselves for the second coming of Christ.

Q. What about the insufficiency of the written word or revelations? (As this point had been explained in our written reply, I only referred to that again, and the accompanying quotations from the Bible.)

Q. Who of you hold the Melchizedek Priesthood and who only the Aaronic Priesthood, and what is the difference between the two, and what is the difference between a president and an Elder, and can the same person hold both of these positions?

I informed them that in their Bible they could find the difference between the Priesthood which John the Baptist held and that which the Apostle Peter held, and as they continued in a sneering way to call me president, I at last said: "You call me so, and that is just what I am in the name of Jesus Christ and to his honor

The "Amtmand" in a very insulting tone then exclaimed: "I am not Felix and you are not Paul," to which I replied, "You, yourself, compelled me to answer you."

Q. Have you had any revelations concerning me (the "Amtmand") while you have been confined?

A. If God should see fit to give me one and command me to inform you about it, then I should surely do so.

Q. Would you return to Denmark if you were liberated from prison?

A. Not till God shall release me through His servants who sent me here.

Q. Will you refrain from preaching and baptizing, as well as from performing any other acts or ordinances pertaining to your faith?

A. If you or any of your priests can convince me that our doctrines and faith are not in accordance with the doctrines of Christ, then I will; for I desire to obtain salvation and to do the will of God and would advise you to do the same.

To this the chief contemptuously replied: "We consider it beneath the dignity of our priests to argue with you, and for this reason we have brought you before the civil court to investigate your doctrines and your belief, and I now forbid you to mislead any more souls by your false doctrines, for I have a great responsibility resting upon me, if I do not stop it; people have come to me by the hundreds to thank me for what I have done towards stopping this heresy, and wherever I come, I am requested to do my best to stop it."

Q. Where do you believe your Zion is located?

A. Zion consists of the pure in heart, and wherever they are, there would be a Zion.

Q. Do you believe it is by the Great Salt Lake in North America?

A. Yes. (And then I referred them to the Scriptures where the Prophets of old had spoken of the gathering of the Gentiles, as well as of the Jews, and I asked them to read for themselves about this.)

Elder Ole Olsen was next asked if he would desist from performing any ceremony or ordinance pertaining to our religious belief here in Norway, and if he would leave the country and return to Denmark. He answered that he would, if he could be released inside of the present month, and if I would give my consent. He then added that he had written to me about that proposition some time ago and that said letter had been forwarded to me through the mayor. I was then asked if I had said letter in my possession, to which I answered in the affirmative and that I

had received it all right. A constable was then sent for it in our prison room, but returned without it. I was asked if I would permit Olsen to leave the country. I was, meanwhile, sent back to our prison in charge of a constable to bring Brother Olsen's letter into court, and after producing it, it was read in court while I was absent.

Priests Folkmann and Knudsen had been asked if they would leave the country and return to Denmark, and they had given a similar answer to that of Elder Ole Olsen. I was again asked if I would give my consent to their departure. I answered that each one of them had his own free will and choice in that respect and could do as he pleased, but, as for myself, I would stay in prison for the cause of truth and the testimony of Jesus as long as God would require it of me, and I hoped that He would give me strength to endure it. I was again asked if I believed that all people should go to Zion in order to be saved. In my reply, I referred them to the prophecies of Joel, 3rd chapter, Isaiah, 2nd and 6th chapters, Jeremiah, 16th chapter, Ezekiel, 20th chapter, and Micah, 4th chapter. They tried in various ways to bring me to say something that would enable them to bring us under the ban of the law as an un-Christian sect, and again I was asked, if I and the brethren would emigrate to that Zion, and if we did not try to persuade the people to emigrate to that place also? My answer was that we were teaching the people the gospel of Christ as it is found in the Bible, and if that sacred Book taught people to flee to Zion in order to escape the destructive judgments of God that will precede the second coming of our Savior, we would go there; and all others who would obtain a like testimony could do the same, if they wished to, and we would have no need to use persuasion. They continued their interrogations, however, in various ways, trying to catch me and even threatened me with imprisonment on "bread and water diet" for contempt, if I did not answer their questions by a straight yes or no; but I continued as previously to refer them to the Bible.

The other brethren were then remanded back to the sheriff's prison at Elverhöi.

Brother Svend Larsen was next brought into court and asked if he had administered baptism to anyone, etc. He was also interrogated concerning the "Skandinaviens Stjerne" and the Book of Mormon, and he answered these questions very properly as a whole. I was then asked if I agreed with him in what he had stated. I answered that I did not believe that the Bible had been corrupted as they had made Brother Larsen say by their tricky interrogations, and I did not believe that Brother Larsen carried such an idea, but that our views in regard to the two books, the Bible and the Book of Mormon, was that the Bible had been translated by uninspired men, while the Book of Mormon had been translated by revelation and the power of God, and yet we believed in and taught the doctrines and principles contained in the Bible, and that all men who would believe and obey these precepts would be saved; and we also believed that all men who did not do so would be punished according to what is written in that sacred book. Brother Larsen was permitted to explain what he meant by his expression "corrupted" in reference to the Bible, and he did that in a very intelligent and consistent manner. The court adjourned at 9 p. m. that day. I felt as though I had been greatly blessed and sustained by the Lord during these court proceedings, and felt in my heart to pray for those men who were thus trying to deprive us of our liberty, and I gave the glory to Him, who is Alpha and Omega, the Beginning and the End. On my return to prison, I found Elder Ahmanson there, as he had been brought there from Österrisör, but he was not permitted to remain in the same room with us until after he also had been tried before the court. Together with my brethren I gave thanks to our Heavenly Father and praised Him in song before retiring for the night."

After that, the imprisoned brethren were repeatedly brought before the court for examination. Otherwise the brethren continued fasting and praying in prison and studied the principles of the gospel. Brother Chr. J. Larsen wrote an encouraging letter to the Saints in Österrisör, where four new converts had recently been baptized; three other converts had been baptized at Brevig.

On Sunday, Nov. 14th, the imprisoned brethren, by permission of the jailer, were visited by some of the local Saints, on which occasion the Sacrament was administered and a regular meeting held, at which there was preaching, praying and singing. Both missionaries and Saints rejoiced

in the blessings of the Lord. On the 19th Elder Chr. J. Larsen was invited to take dinner with the jailer and his family and thus had a fine opportunity to preach the gospel. After dinner, the jailer's son, Mr. Fjeldstad, accompanied the brethren on a visit to the Saints in Vaterland. At this time the brethren received many visits from Saints and strangers. The visits by the brethren to their friends on the outside became more frequent and they were given more liberty to go and come as they liked, the jailer and his family having become very friendly toward them.

On Sunday, Dec. 5th, Peter Beckström was restored to liberty on condition that he would not officiate in any ordinance pertaining to his religion. Brothers Emil Larsen and Johan Johansen (the latter president of the Frederikstad Branch) gave bonds for Brother Beckström. The other imprisoned brethren had labored hard to bring this release about, in order that one of their number might quietly labor among the Saints and friends on the outside. On the same day the sad news reached the imprisoned brethren to the effect that two of the brethren, Henrick Evensen (one of the first converts to "Mormonism" in Österrisör) and Halvor Torgersen had met their death by drowning at sea.

On the 14th of December, the imprisoned brethren finished writing a report of their trials in court. They spent that day, as they had done many days before, in prayer and singing the songs of Zion, and felt themselves exceedingly blessed and happy.

On the 19th, Elders Chr. J. and Svend Larsen, by permission of the jailer, visited the imprisoned brethren at Elverhöi and remained with them five hours. On their return, they visited the Saints in Frederikstad and spoke words of comfort and consolation to them.

On Christmas Day (Dec. 25th) eight of the Saints from the outside were permitted to visit the brethren in prison, where all enjoyed themselves together in songs, prayer and conversations. Later in the day, Elder Chr. J. Larsen, in company with Elders John A. Ahmanson, Svend Larsen and Mr. Johan Andreas Jensen, were permitted to go out and visit friends. On that occasion, they had a conversation with Carl Widerborg, who subsequently joined the Church and became a most important factor in the history of the Scandinavian Mission. Elder Chr. J. Larsen remarks, that "this was indeed a day of liberty to us prisoners."

The close of the year 1852 found Brothers Chr. J. Larsen, John A. Ahmanson, Johan F. F. Dorius and Svend Larsen imprisoned in Frederikstad, and Ole Olsen, Niels Hansen and Christian Knudsen at Elverhöi.

The imprisoned brethren at Frederikstad spent New Years Eve singing and praying. Elders Larsen, Dorius and Ahmanson sang 24 hymns.

CHAPTER 16 (1852)

Scandinavian Saints anxious to gather to Zion—the first large company emigrates to America—Experience on the Ocean—Arrival at New Orleans—Crossing the Plains—Arrival in Great Salt Lake City.

An earnest desire on the part of the Scandinavian Saints to emigrate to Zion soon became quite general, an increased interest in that direction having been manifested by many of them since the first little company had left for the mountains a few months previously. Consequently, the Elders had been busily engaged for some time past in making preparations to send off a large company. About the beginning of December, 1852, the emigrants from the respective conferences in the mission began

to gather in Copenhagen, Denmark and on Monday, Dec. 20, 1852, 29 Saints, including children, went on board the steamship "Obotrit" and sailed from "Toldboden" (the custom-house) at 4 o'clock p. m., under the leadership of Elder John E. Forsgren, one of the Elders who in connection with Apostle Erastus Snow first introduced the gospel into Scandinavia two years before. A great multitude of people had gathered on the wharf to witness the departure of the "Mormons," and many of the rabble gave utterance to the most wicked and blasphemous language, while they cursed and swore because so many of their countrymen were disgracing themselves by following to America "that Swedish Mormon Priest," an appellation they gave Elder Forsgren. No violence, however, was resorted to, and the ship got safely away. After a rather stormy and unpleasant voyage, the "Obotrit" arrived safely at Kiel, in Holstein on the evening of the 22nd. The following day the journey was continued by rail to Hamburg, where a large hall had been hired and supper prepared for the emigrants. In the afternoon on the 24th the Saints went on board the steamship "Lion," which glided slowly with the tide down the River Elbe to Cuxhaven, where the captain cast anchor, owing to the heavy fog that prevailed. The emigrants now celebrated Christmas Eve on board with songs and amusements of different kinds.

In the morning of the 25th, anchor was weighed, and the "Lion" sailed to the mouth of the river, where it was met by heavy headwinds that made it impossible to reach the open sea until midnight. Finally, the passage from the river to the sea was made in the moon light. Early in the morning of the 26th, the ship passed Heligoland, soon after which a heavy gale blew up from the southwest which increased in violence until the next day when it assumed the character of a regular hurricane, the like of which old sailors declared they had never before experienced on the North Sea. The ship's bridge and part of the gunwale was destroyed and some goods standing on the deck were broken to pieces and washed overboard; otherwise, neither the ship nor the emigrants were injured. On the 28th, in the evening after the storm had spent its fury, the "Lion" steamed into the harbor of Hull, England. About 150 vessels were lost on the North Sea in the storm and the people of Hull were greatly surprised when the "Lion" arrived there safely on the 28th, as it was firmly believed that she had gone under like the many other ships that were lost.

From Hull the emigrating Saints continued their journey on the 29th by rail to Liverpool, where lodgings and meals previously ordered were prepared for them, and on the 31st of December, 1852, they went on board the packet ship "Forest Monarch," which was hauled out of the dock and anchored in the River Mersey. There it lay about two weeks because of storms and contrary winds. In the meantime, three of the company died, two babies were born, and three fellow-passengers were united with the Church by baptism. One man, who had been bitten by a dog, was left in Liverpool, to be forwarded with the next company of emigrating Saints. One night the ship became entangled with another vessel and sustained some damage; and a few days later, during a heavy storm, it got adrift, pulling up both anchors, and was just about to run aground when two tugboats came to the rescue and saved it. On the 16th of January, 1853, the "Forest Monarch" put out to sea. The emigrants

now numbered 297 souls who were placed under the direction of Elder John E. Forsgren, in connection with whom Elders Christian Christiansen and J. Herman Christensen acted as counselors. Elder Willard Snow and Peter O. Hansen, who had accompanied the emigrating Saints to Liverpool, now returned to Copenhagen.

During the voyage across the Atlantic Ocean the "Forest Monarch" was favored with very pleasant weather, but for several days there was a perfect calm. In many respects the emigrants, who were nearly all unaccustomed to seafaring life, found the voyage trying and tedious. The provisions were poor and their fresh water supply gave out before the journey was ended. Four deaths also occurred on board, and three children were born during the voyage. On the 8th of March, 1853, the ship arrived safely at the mouth of the Mississippi River, where five of the company died, and on the arrival at New Orleans, March 16th, two others departed this life; one family, which had apostatized, remained in that city.

From New Orleans the journey was continued by steamboat up the Mississippi River to St. Louis, Missouri, where the emigrants landed March 31st. In that city, tents and other commodities needed for the overland journey were purchased. After tarrying about a month, during which time six of the emigrants died and two couples were married, the company left St. Louis and proceeded by steamboat about two hundred miles further up the Mississippi River to Keokuk, Iowa, where the emigrants pitched their tents for the first time and lay in camp for several weeks before starting for the Plains.

In the meantime, the emigrants received their teams of oxen and wagons. Some of the Scandinavian emigrants, who disliked the American way of driving oxen in yokes, made harness in regular Danish fashion; but no sooner were they placed on the animals than they, frightened half to death, struck out in a wild run, refusing to be guided by the lines in the hands of their new masters from the far North. As they crossed ditches and gulches in their frenzy, parts of the wagons were strewn by the wayside; but the oxen (many of which had never been hitched up before) were at last stopped by men who understood how to manipulate that most important article of all teamsters' outfits—the whip—and the Danish emigrants, profiting by the experience they had gained, soon concluded that, although harness might do well for oxen in Denmark, the yoke and whip were preferable in America, and they readily accepted the method of their adopted country.

With 34 wagons and about 130 oxen, the company rolled out from the camping-ground near Keokuk on the 21st of May, and after three weeks' rather difficult travel over the prairies of Iowa, the town of Council Bluffs, on the Missouri River, was reached. Here the company rested for several days, but on the 27th of June, the emigrants resumed their journey by crossing the Missouri River, after which they were soon out on the Plains. In the overland journey a number of the emigrants died, and more children were born, while a few lost the faith in the midst of the hardships and trials of the long march. Finally, on the 30th of September, 1853, the company arrived safely in Great Salt Lake City.

On the 4th of October the emigrants were nearly all rebaptized by Apostle Erastus Snow, and they were counseled by President Brigham Young to settle in different parts of the Territory with people of other nationalities, so as to become useful in developing the resources of the new country. Most of them located in Sanpete Valley, whither other companies from Scandinavia subsequently followed them yearly, and that valley has ever since been known as a stronghold of the Scandinavians in Utah. Still, President Young's advice has not been unheeded, as the people from the three countries of the North, Denmark, Sweden and Norway, are represented to a greater or less extent in nearly every town and settlement of the Saints in the Rocky Mountains.

CHAPTER 17 (1853)

The missionaries in Norway on trial—All the imprisoned Elders in Norway liberated—Progress of the work of the Lord.

When the brethren at the headquarters of the Scandinavian Mission in Copenhagen were praising the Lord for the glorious introduction of the fulness of the gospel in Denmark, and also for the fair prospects in southern Sweden, they felt very much concerned about the Norwegian Mission. The wholesale imprisonment of the Elders in that land was something unlooked for, and now they could only hope and pray that the spirit of freedom and liberty which for years past had characterized the Norwegians, would assert itself and frown down religious bigotry and intolerance, with which a selfish and hateful clergy was endeavoring to enthrall the people.

On Tuesday, Jan. 4, 1853, the brethren imprisoned at Frederikstad and Elverhöi, Norway, were again brought before the court for trial. About fifty witnesses were examined, all of whom were questioned very closely in the hope on the part of the authorities to prove something for which the prisoners could be punished; but all testified in positive terms that the missionaries were moral and honest in the highest degree.

On Friday, Jan. 14th, the imprisoned brethren were again on trial, this time at Kjölbergbro, the place where Elders Johan F. F. Dorius and Christian Knudsen were first arrested. Again on January 19th, the brethren were brought into court for examination.

Once more, on Feb. 17th, the brethren were subjected to an examination at the court-house in Frederikstad, but all that could be proved against them was that they had administered the ordinances of the gospel according to the teachings of the Bible. Nevertheless a preliminary judgment was read to them, which imposed upon each of them a fine of eight ounces of silver or eight "speciedaler" (about $8) in Norwegian money. They were also to pay the costs of court, and defray the expenses connected with their arrest and imprisonment. A declaration from the church department of the government, endeavoring to show that they were not Christians and therefore denying them protection under the dissenter law, was read to them. This declaration was founded on numerous false accusations and interpretations of the principles advocated by the Latter-day Saints. The brethren soon afterwards wrote a communication, in which they answered some of the most absurd of these accusations and filed the same as a part of the court proceedings on the 21st of February, when the last trial was held. To this document, however, the judge paid no attention; nor did he notice the testimonies and explanations given by the prisoners and their witnesses in open court, but he followed strictly the interpretations and declarations given by the clergy. Consequently, the brethren were sentenced, as already stated.

The findings of the lower court were read, on March 4, 1853, to the imprisoned brethren. They at once appealed the case to the higher court.

On Thursday, March 31, 1853, Elder Chr. J. Larsen was released from prison in Frederikstad on bail, on conditions that he would not attend to any official ordinance pertaining to his Church pending the findings of the Supreme Court. Elder Larsen accepted these conditions, agreeable to advice which he had received from the brethren in Copenhagen. He at once visited the Saints in Frederikstad and vicinity, giving them such advice and encouragement as the circumstances seemed to demand. And on the 6th of April, 1853, a conference was held on the "Gaard" Ingolsrud, about three miles from Frederikstad. This was the first conference of Latter-day Saints held in Norway. Besides Chr. J. Larsen, who had just been liberated from prison, there were six other Elders and also three Priests, one Teacher and quite a number of lay members present. The authorities of the Church were, on this occasion, sustained by vote of Saints for the first time in Norway, and considerable business was attended to in the interests of the good work in that land. The Saints enjoyed the meetings exceedingly.

On Saturday, April 23rd, the decision of a higher court was read to the brethren, who were still imprisoned in Norway. It sustained the findings of the lower court, but Birch Reichenwaldt, the "Amtmand," himself had appealed the case to the Supreme Court. The decision was accompanied by a communication from Mr. Reichenwaldt, dated Moss, May 3, 1853, stating that the "Mormons," who were still in prison, could be liberated, if they would obligate themselves not to perform any ordinance or act pertaining to their religion.

After having thoroughly considered Birch Reichenwaldt's communication, the brethren at Frederikstad (having also consulted their fellow-prisoners at Elverhöi in the matter) all agreed to accept liberty on the terms offered. Accordingly, on the 5th of May, 1853, in the forenoon, the brethren at Frederikstad left their prison house, where they had spent nearly seven months, and walked to the residence of Brother Johan Johansen, the president of the Frederikstad Branch, where they received a most hearty greeting. In the evening of that day, quite a number of brethren assembled in council to deliberate upon their future movements. Most of those who had been liberated spoke on this occasion and there was great rejoicing.

Among the strangers who visited the brethren in prison was Carl Widerborg. His first visit was in November, 1852, and from that time he began a thorough investigation of the principles of the gospel, both by reading the books and pamphlets, which had been published by the Church, and by conversing with the Saints in Frederikstad. When he first met the brethren, he was a merchant in that town, but had formerly been a school teacher and had devoted his youth to study. Consequently, he was a well educated man and also possessed considerable natural ability, while he at the same time was meek and humble. Being above prejudice, he took great interest in the brethren during their imprisonment and rendered them efficient service in having their case properly brought before the courts, he being well posted in law and politics. In January, 1853, he made a trip to Christiania solely for the purpose of speaking in behalf of the brethren before the church department. He was finally baptized on March 4, 1853, and the following day, when he visited the brethren in the Frederikstad prison, he was ordained by them to the office of a Priest. From that time on he labored successfully in connection with the brethren who had been liberated (mainly Brother Beckström) to spread the gospel; and when the Elders were released from prison, they found that the membership in Frederikstad and vicinity had doubled since the time they were deprived of their liberty. "Thus it is plain," writes Elder Dorius, "that whenever the Almighty wants a certain work accomplished, no effort on the part of men can hinder it. 'Amtmand' Birch Reichenwaldt and his colleagues, no doubt, thought that by casting us in prison, they would put an end to the progress of 'Mormonism' in Norway, but all who entertained such a hope were indeed doomed to disappointment."

Brother Widerborg subsequently became a very important factor in the Scandinavian Mission, presiding over the same two long terms.

As soon as Elder Beckström had regained his liberty, in December, 1852, he resumed his missionary labors and continued the same with good success until April 28, 1853, when he was again arrested by Mayor (Byfoged) Berg, because he would not cease preaching the gospel. However, he was soon liberated again.

After Elder Svend Larsen's release from prison in March, 1853, he made a missionary trip to Christiania, after which he did much missionary labor in Österrisör and vicinity.

Elder Johan F. F. Dorius, accompanied by Johan Johansen, made a trip into the country near Frederikstad early in May, 1853, to hold a meeting at a farm called "Myrvold," where some people had joined the Church recently. Among these was a young girl by the name of Anna Christine Mouritsen and her brother, Niels Arent. The girl was afterwards forced to leave her parental home for the sake of her religion. In due course of time she emigrated to Utah, where she became

ANNE CHRISTINE MOURITZEN
Born Dec. 19, 1834, at Brekke, Norway, baptized in 1855, emigrated to Utah in 1855, married Bishop Abraham O. Smoot, Feb. 17, 1856, became the mother of seven children, including Apostle Reed Smoot, figured prominently in the Primary Associations in Utah County, and died in Provo, Utah, Jan. 20, 1894.

the wife of Bishop Abraham O. Smoot of Provo, to whom she bore a number of children, one of these being Apostle Reed Smoot.

CHAPTER 18 (1853)

Persecutions on Lolland (Denmark)—Disturbances on Bornholm—Mobbings on Sjælland —New branches organized at the general conference at Copenhagen—A hired hall on Gothersgade, Copenhagen, demolished by a mob— "Mormonism" discussed in the Danish "Rigsdag."

Persecution continued to rage against the Saints in different parts of Denmark. Thus while Elder Jacob J. M. Bohn was addressing a meeting of Saints in Thoreby on the island of Lolland on Sunday, Jan. 9, 1853, a Mr. Gjersing entered the house with a number of ruffians to break up

the meeting. He restrained himself while the Sacrament was being administered, but as soon as that was over, he commenced by abusive language to stir up excitement among the people, and finished with the suggestion that the people might do as they pleased. Some of the more ignorant people immediately began their disturbances by imbibing the whisky which they had brought with them. Then, when they were joined by another company of ruffians led by a school teacher, pandemonium reigned supreme, where, shortly before, songs of praise and prayer to God had ascended from a few Latter-day Saints. Windows, doors and furniture were summarily demolished: one of the sisters was hit by a stone in the face and hurt quite seriously, and the others fled for safety. After having finished the work of destruction at the meeting place, the mob went to a farmer's house, near by, where they were treated to brandy and encouraged to go ahead with their vandalism. They then proceeded from place to place where Saints were living, destroying property, breaking doors and windows, and even the stove in one house, scattering the fire on the floor regardless of the danger of a conflagration and the total destruction of the premises. Complaint was afterwards entered against the principals in these dark deeds of violence towards peaceable citizens, including the parson, but only two of the whole gang were considered guilty and they received only a light punishment.

Also on the island of Bornholm the persecutions continued in the early part of 1853. Thus at a meeting held at Klemmensker Parish on Sunday, Jan. 30th, a mob numbering about fifty men, broke up a meeting, and ill-treated Elders Chr. G. Larsen and Christopher O. Folkmann and one sister in a fearful manner. On several other occasions the Saints, and particularly the missionaries, were subjected to harsh treatment, but amidst the persecutions some of the honest in heart were added to the Church by baptism on Bornholm.

President Willard Snow and Elder Peter O. Hansen, who had accompanied the emigrants to England the previous December, returned to Copenhagen in the latter part of January, 1853, and resumed their missionary labors.

About this time a branch of the Church was organized at Ishöi, a village about 11 miles southwest of Copenhagen, with Hans Hansen as president.

Two Elders from Zion, both natives of Norway, namely, Erik G. M. Hogan and Canute Peterson, who had joined the Church in America, arrived in Copenhagen, Feb. 12, 1853. They were both appointed to labor as missionaries in Norway. Another brother, Hans Peter Olsen, generally called Bro. Piercy, arrived with Elders Willard Snow and Peter O. Hansen when they returned from England.

At a meeting held in Copenhagen, Feb. 13, 1853, Bro. Hans Peter Olsen preached in the Färroe tongue. Elders Canute Peterson and Erik G. M. Hogan in Norwegian, Peter O. Hansen and Hans Peter Jensen in Danish and others in Swedish, and Brother Willard Snow, according to his own statement, a little of all mixed with English. The spirit of the Lord was with the brethren and five or six new members were added to the Church the following week.

At another meeting held in one of the suburbs of Copenhagen, about a dozen rude fellows of the basest sort entered the house where services were held. Brother Canute Peterson, who was speaking, was interrupted by the mob asking a number of silly questions. Willard Snow tried in vain to

quiet the mobbers, and Bro. Poulsen, the owner of the house, requested them not to disturb the peace of his family in his own house, but they declared that three of the persons present should not get out of the house until they had received a flogging. At once they began to beat and kick a Bro. Jensen, an old gentleman, and filled the house with their uproar, confusion and rage. Brothers Olsen and Hogan succeeded in slipping out one way and Brother Peterson another, and finally Elder Snow, after watching the movements of the mob, and leaving his cloak in the hands of some of the sisters, succeeded in making his escape through the darkness unhurt. One or two of the local brethren were knocked down, and others abused.

On Sunday, March 12th, a branch of the Church was organized on West Sjælland, with Carl C. A. Christensen as president, and about thirty members. Another branch of the Church was organized on March 14th, at Laasby, near Aarhus, with thirteen members. Still another branch was organized March 24th in the village of Thoreby, on the island of Lolland.

On Wednesday, April 6, 1853, a general conference of the Scandinavian Mission was opened in Copenhagen, Denmark, it being the 23rd anniversary of the organization of the Church. The first meeting commenced at 10 o'clock a. m., and after the opening exercises, President Willard Snow gave the Elders who presided over the different conferences an opportunity to report. Elder Niels Chr. Schou, president of the Vendsyssel Conference, Johannes Larsen, president of the Aalborg Conference, and Anders Andersen, president of the Fredericia Conference, reported their labors and the progress made in their respective conferences, as well as the condition of the Saints. Notnet them almost everywhere, the gospel had spread throughout the land and missionaries had gone as far north as Skagen, the northernmost point of Jutland, and everywhere the message declared by the Elders caused a great stir among the population. In the vicinity of Aarhus, where the people hitherto had shown a most bitter opposition to the gospel, a number of persons had recently been baptized and organized into a branch of the Church. All the speakers encouraged the Saints to be humble, patient and faithful. "We have suffered long enough for our own sakes," said Elder Schou, "and we ought to rejoice now that we can suffer for the sake of Christ."

In the afternoon session, Johan Swenson, president of the Lolland conference, and Peter O. Hansen, president of the Copenhagen Conference, gave their reports. On Lolland and Falster the preaching of the gospel had engendered opposition on the part of the people, and those who had received it had been subject to a great deal of persecution. It had become a common saying that all who joined the "Mormons" should have their windows broken. Since the previous conference, about thirty persons had been baptized in the Lolland Conference. In the Copenhagen Conference there had been less persecution, and many had been baptized recently, mostly in Copenhagen and in the country districts on West Sjælland.

The conference was continued the following day (April 8th), at which other Elders gave reports. Elders Hans Peter Jensen and Willard Snow (the latter speaking through an interpreter) spoke encouragingly to the Saints, and explained that the persecutions which raged against the Elders in all three Scandinavian countries was based on opposition to the truth and the testimony borne by the

withstanding the persecution which Elders that Joseph Smith was a Prophet of God.

The conference was concluded on Sunday, April 10th. Elder Erik Gustaf Erikson gave a report of the mission in Sweden, where the brethren and the local Saints had also been subject to persecution, but mostly by the civil authorities, who used every opportunity to arrest and imprison them. Yet, the work of the Lord made progress in Sweden. About seventy souls had been added to the Church since the last general conference, but as yet no branch of the Church had been organized in Sweden.

Elder Johan P. Lorentzen, who had been called on a mission to Iceland, spoke encouragingly about the prospects of preaching the gospel in that far-off land where Bro. Gudmund

GUDMUND GUDMUNDSON

Born March 23, 1825, in Iceland, died Sept. 21, 1883, in Lehi, Utah Co., Utah.

Gudmundson had remained faithful since 1851 and had encouraged the believers.

In the afternoon session of the conference, the general authorities of the Church were sustained and Willard Snow was sustained as president of the Scandinavian Mission, with Elders Peter O. Hansen and Hans Peter Jensen as his counselors. Niels Chr.

WILLARD SNOW

Third president of the Scandinavian Mission, with Peter 'O. Hansen as his first and Hans Peter Jensen as his second counselor.

Schou was sustained as president of the Vendsyssel Conference, Johannes Larsen as president of the Aalborg Conference, Anders Anderson as president of the Fredericia Conference, Peter O. Hansen as president of the Copenhagen Conference, Christian G. Larsen as president of the Bornholm Conference, Johan Swenson as president of the Lolland Conference, and High Priest Erik G. M. Hogan as president of the Norwegian Mission, called the Brevig Conference, with Elders Canute Peterson and Chr. J. Larsen as his assistants, Elder Anders W. Winberg as president of the Swedish Mission, Johan Peter Lorentzen as president of the mission in Iceland and Hans Peter Olsen from Zion as a missionary in Denmark.

According to the statistical report read during this conference the Saints in Scandinavia, at this time, numbered 1,331, of which number 1,133 were in the six Danish conferences, 88 in Norway and 110 in Sweden.

On Sunday, April 24, 1853, the Saints in Copenhagen held their first meeting in a new hall which they had rented on Gothersgade. At this meeting, an interesting letter was read from Elder John E. Forsgren, who had led the first large company of Scandinavian emigrants across the Atlantic. Several converts recently baptized were confirmed. Then a large mob entered the hall just as the brethren were administering the Sacrament. Some of these mobbers

ERIK GOUDASON MIDBOEN HOGAN

Was born June 23, 1802, in Tim Præstgjld, Hallingdal, Telemarken, Norway; died June 21, 1876, in Bountiful, Davis Co., Utah.

carried rocks in their pockets. They began their vandalism by splitting open one side of the door and flinging in a bottle of vitroil or some similar acid. The bottle broke and injured a sister so severely in the face that her blood flowed profusely. Women and children screamed, and the whole meeting became a complete uproar.

Willard Snow writes: "I arose and spoke to the people, asking them to sit still and fear nothing. We held them to their seats as silent as possible while we proceeded with the services as if nothing had occurred. We succeeded in preserving some degree of order until we got through with the Sacrament and had dismissed the meeting, after which the mob tore down the whole of the door and burst into the hall. They piled the benches in heaps hither and thither, stripped the hall of the cleats which were nailed upon the sides for the hanging of the hats and coats, and continued their spoliations until they were measurably satisfied. At last, after repeated solicitations, a police officer made his appearance, and the mobbers began to leave."

On Saturday, July 16th, the Danish Diet (Rigsdag) had under consideration the question of "Mormonism," or what rights and privileges the Latter-day Saints were entitled to under the newly-adopted constitution of Denmark. Mr. Hjort, one of the members of the Diet, called attention to the solid organization and vigorous activity exhibited by the "Mormons" for the promulgation of their creed. In a congregation of 1000 members, he said, there were 38 Elders, 59 Priests, 40 Teachers and 17 Deacons. He believed that many of the people had become converts to "Mormonism" from honest motives and belief, but he also thought that many were joining them in hopes of temporal gain. He had no intention to call upon the secular powers to oppose a religious sect, but he did desire a strong impression from the government to the effect that "Mormonism" was something fearfully corrupt and false. The common people, he said, would generally put much stress on what the government had to say in such matters. To this query, the Kultus min-

ister replied that the government did not consider itself justified in interfering with the preaching of "Mormonism," but had only to guard against anything being practiced which was repulsive to public morals and good order in general. This duty devolved upon the minister of justice, he said. He wished that the established church would take hold of opposition to that sect with more energy than had been shown in the past. Mr. Haas, a minister, thought it right that the "Mormons" should enjoy perfect liberty, even to the taking of more wives, as this was allowed the Mohammedans, and, he queried: Could not a Mohammedan claim to live in Denmark with a number of wives? Mr. Lindberg spoke in favor of perfect religious liberty and Mr. P. Hansen thought that the "Mormons" should have the right to worship God as it suited themselves best, but that they should not be allowed to travel all over the country to persuade people to join them. This proposition was met with a lively opposition from different parts of the assembly. Mr. Lindberg finally summed up his peroration by declaring that when "Mormonism" claimed to be founded on a revelation given only a few years ago, it could not be one with the eighteen-hundred year old Christianity.

CHAPTER 19 (1853)

Persecutions in Sweden—First branches of the Church in Sweden—The Skåne Conference organized—A special conference held in Copenhagen—Sickness and death of President Willard Snow—John Van Cott appointed president of the mission.

On Sunday, April 17, 1853, Bro. Nils Capson arrived in Copenhagen from Sweden, he and Bro. Åke Svenson having been exiled for baptizing in that land. Brother Capson's brother had also been arrested for giving lodgings to Brother Swenson in his house, and for not telling the police that he had been baptized by his brother. He was fined five Swedish dollars, and notice given that the "Mormons" were prohibited from holding meetings in their own houses under a penalty of fifty "riksdaler." The next day, Brother Peter Björk, another intelligent young Elder, arrived in Copenhagen from Sweden. Before he and other brethren were banished, they had made a solemn appeal to the "landshöfding" of the district of Skåne for protection. This officer seemed to be a gentleman of fine feeling, and he confidentially told the brethren that it was his personal wish that the "Mormons" should enjoy the right to worship the Lord and administer the ordinances of the Church as they desired, but, he added, that the law was against it, and that the Lutheran clergymen were constantly complaining, and thus it was impossible for him to grant them protection from their enemies.

Under date of April 20, 1853, President Willard Snow, in a letter addressed to his brother, Erastus Snow, reported that seventy persons had been baptized in the Swedish Mission since the previous August conference, that another Elder had been driven out of Sweden and that three or four more were under arrest for preaching the truth. All these, though native-born subjects of Sweden, were banished from their native land, through the influence of priestcraft. These brethren were advised to follow the example of Brother John E. Forsgren, by emigrating to a free land. During the past winter, 150 persons had been baptized in Copenhagen, and in the whole mission about 600 had been added to the Church by baptism since the previous August conference. All the copies of the Doctrine and Covenants and hymn books had been sold and new books and pamphlets were con-

tinually being printed in the interest of the mission.

At the general conference of the Church in Scandinavia, held a Copenhagen, Denmark, April 10 1853, Elder Anders W. Winberg was appointed to preside over th Swedish Mission, and on the 21st o April following he took passage from Copenhagen to Ystad, Sweden whence he proceeded on foot to Skönabäck, a large estate situated about thirty miles east of Malmö Being closely watched, he found i impracticable to attempt to hold an public meeting, as a proclamation had been issued by the local civi authorities forbidding any privat persons to hold religious meetings i their houses, under a penalty of fift "riksdaler." However, he stayed tw nights, during which eight person were baptized. On the night of Apri 24, 1853, he called a council meetin and organized the first branch of th Church of Jesus Christ of Latter-da Saints in Sweden. It was called th Skönabäck Branch and numbered 3 members at the time of its organiza tion. Several of the newly baptize converts were also ordained to dif ferent positions in the Priesthoo and a Brother Petter Pettersson wa appointed president of the branch All this was, of necessity, done in th silent hours of the night, in order t avoid arrest. Not until the nightin gale in her sweetest melody had ar nounced the dawning of another day did the brethren break up their ir teresting meeting. It was then foun necessary for them to scatter at onc as the people in the neighborhoo were watching very closely for "Mor mon" Elders, but when they com menced to gather with evil inten early in the morning, the missio aries were gone.

From Skönabäck, Elder Winber proceeded to the city of Malm where he, in the evening of April 2

1853, held another council meeting, and organized the second branch of the Church in Sweden, with Hans

The house near Skönabäck, Skåne, Sweden, in which the first branch of the Church was organized, April 24, 1854.

Lundblad, who was ordained an Elder, as president. On the same occasion seven Saints residing at a small seacoast village called Lomma, about seven miles north of Malmö, were organized into a third branch. Priest Åke Jönsson was ordained an Elder and appointed to preside. From Malmö, Elder Winberg proceeded to the city of Lund where he, assisted by his fellow-missionaries, o r g a n i z e d a branch of the Church over which Carl Capson was appointed president, after first being ordained an Elder. This was the fourth branch of the Church organized in Sweden.

Commencing on Saturday evening, June 25, 1853, a conference was held in the barn of Carl Capson in the city of Lund, Sweden, this being the first gathering of that kind which ever took place in Sweden. The meeting was continued all night, or until 7:30 o'clock the next morning, Sunday, Jan. 26th. Elders Peter O.

Hansen and Ola N. Liljenquist from Copenhagen participated in this important meeting, which was attended by about one hundred people. On this occasion the four branches, viz., Skönabäck, Malmö, Lomma and Lund, recently established in Skåne, Sweden, were organized into a conference with Elder Hans Lundblad as president. This was the commencement of the famous Skåne

Carl Capson's premises at Lund, Skåne, Sweden, where the Skåne Conference was organized June 25, 1854.

Conference, which is still in existence, and has had a most interesting history covering a period of more than seventy-four years. In due course of time the gospel in its fulness radiated from Skåne into the more northern provinces of Sweden through the administration of some of the most e a r n e s t mssionaries which the Church of Jesus Christ of Latter-day Saints ever had. Other branches and conferences were organized later, and at the close of the century, the Swedish Mission, particularly the Stockholm Conference, was one of the most fruitful fields of labor in which the average "Mormon" Elder ever had the privilege of promulgating the principles of truth and salvation.

On Friday, Aug. 12th, a special conference was commenced in Copenhagen which was continued for several days. Willard Snow was sustained as president of the Scandinavian Mission, with Peter O. Hansen as his first and Hans Peter Jensen as his second counselor. Erik G. M. Hogan was sustained as president of the Brevig Conference, Norway, with Canute Peterson and Carl Widerborg as his counselors.

While Pres. Willard Snow was addressing a meeting on Monday, Aug. 15th, he was suddenly attacked by some evil power which caused him to fall to the floor in front of several of the brethren, who at once kneeled by his side and prayed for his recovery. The next morning, August 16th, Brother Snow requested that Elders Peter O. Hansen and Hans Peter Jensen should take him to England by the first steamer leaving Copenhagen. Soon afterwards Brother Snow was again violently attacked by an evil power to such a degree that it took four or five strong men to hold him. After several similar attacks during the afternoon and evening, he was taken to the hospital. The Elders held several fast and prayer-meetings and asked for divine assistance in behalf of Elder Snow. Their prayers were answered in part, but the president did not get well; consequently, the brethren succeeded in getting Brother Snow on board the steamer "Transit," accompanied by Elders Peter O. Hansen and Hans Peter Jensen. While on board the steamer, Elder Snow was again prostrated and became unconscious. Everything possible was done for him, but it seemed to afford no permanent benefit. He exhibited considerable derangement of mind. On Saturday, the 20th, he received food with apparent relish, but on Sunday morning, August 21st, he relapsed, became almost unconscious and remained in that condition during the day. A general collapse ensued and about 5 o'clock p. m. he fell asleep, to all appearance with entire ease and composure. About two hours afterwards he breathed with difficulty and a little before 8 o'clock in the evening he passed away without a struggle. In compliance with the captain's orders, Elder Snow's body was consigned to a watery grave the same evening. Thus Willard Snow, who was much beloved by the Scandinavian Saints, became the second Elder in the Church who found a watery grave, the first being Elder Knowlton F. Hanks, who died at sea, on his way to the Society Islands, Nov. 3, 1843. The death of Pres. Snow was a heavy blow to the young, inexperienced Elders and Saints generally in the Scandinavian countries.

As soon as the news of Elder Willard Snow's death reached the presiding brethren in Liverpool, England, Elder John Van Cott was called to succeed him as president of the Scandinavian Mission. He arrived in Copenhagen, Sept. 4, 1853. President Van Cott, although at first

JOHN VAN COTT

Fourth president of the Scandinavian Mission, was born Sept. 7, 1814, in Canaan, Columbia Co., New York, and died Feb. 18, 1883, in Salt Lake City as one of the first seven presidents of Seventies.

ınable to speak the Danish language, soon proved himself a stalwart, efficient and wise president, who gained the hearts of the Scandinavian people, and by the assistance of the local Elders, of which there were many faithful and true ones in the different conferences of the mission, he soon brought the mission up to a better condition than for some time previous, and the work in all three countries made wonderful and rapid progress. New branches were organized in different parts of Denmark, Sweden and Norway.

Another general conference of the Scandinavian Mission was held in Copenhagen, Oct. 6, 1853, at which Pres. John Van Cott delivered a sermon full of good counsel and instruction. At this conference also Elder Chr. J. Larsen was released as president of the Copenhagen Conference and he, together with Carl C. A. Christensen and Chr. G. Larsen, were appointed to labor in Norway under the direction of Erik G. M. Hogan. Peter Björk, Petter Pettersson, Anders Peter Öman, Niels Johnsson, Jeppe Jeppeson and Ola Nilsson were appointed to labor in Sweden under the direction of Anders W. Winberg. Olof Lövendahl, Johannes Björk, Niels Johan Öman and Johan Rosengren were also ordained to the Priesthood and appointed to labor in Sweden. Elder Ola N. Liljenquist was appointed to preside over the Copenhagen Conference, succeeding Chr. J. Larsen, and L. H. Schouby and Johan F. F. Dorius were appointed to labor in the Copenhagen Conference under the direction of Ola N. Liljenquist. Elder Hans Peter Olsen was appointed to preside over the Bornholm Conference and others of the local brethren were ordained to the Priesthood.

After this conference, the Elders in Denmark renewed their diligence in spreading the gospel upon the different islands and on the peninsula of Jutland. Well-attended meetings were held in Copenhagen, Aalborg and many other places. A branch of the Church was organized on the island of Möen on Sunday, Oct. 16th, and called the Speilsby Branch. In Copenhagen, especially, the meetings were well attended and many were baptized. Preparations were also made to organize another large company to emigrate to America and many of the Saints made haste to become members of said company.

CHAPTER 20 (1853)

Arrival of first American Elders in Norway —Elder Carl C. A. Christensen in Norway— Latter-day Saints classed as non-Christians in Norway—Organization of the Christiania branch—Carl C. N. Dorius in Drammen.

Elders Canute Peterson and Eric G. M. Hogan from Utah, and Carl C. N. Dorius from Denmark, arrived in Österrisör, Norway, May 10, 1853. This was only a few days after the last of the brethren had been released from prison. Elders Peterson and Hogan had arrived in Denmark about three months previously, but left Copenhagen for Norway, April 13, 1853. They were the first missionaries from Utah to visit Norway. Their arrival gave a fresh impetus to the missionary work in that land, and the brethren, who had been imprisoned so long, felt greatly encouraged over this important addition to their strength. From now on the Norwegian Mission became a decided success; the Elders renewed their diligence; new fields of labor were opened, many meetings were held and quite a number of converts baptized, notwithstanding the interference of the police and the frequent disturbances by mobs. At Frederikstad, in particular, the brethren were opposed and insulted by the citizens, the civil authorities refusing to render them any protection. In Österrisör the persecutions assumed such dimensions, that the mayor at last took the matter in hand and issued a proclamation in favor of the Saints.

Elder Carl C. N. Dorius had left Copenhagen on his mission to Norway early in the year, but on account of weather conditions he stayed in Aalborg until May, when he, in company with Elders Peterson and Hogan, went by ship to Norway. Soon after his arrival in Österrisör he went to Brevig, where he met his brother, Johan F. F. Dorius; later he labored at Frederikstad and Drammen, where he subsequently was arrested several times. Still later he succeeded Elder Carl Widerborg as president of the Brevig Branch.

Elders Chr. J. Larsen, Johan F. F. Dorius and Svend Larsen and family sailed from Österrisör, Norway, August 2, 1853, on board the "Zions Löve" (Bro. Svend Larsen, captain), and after a quick and pleasant voyage they arrived at Hals, Denmark, on the 3rd. The next day, some of the brethren arrived in Aalborg, where they met President Willard Snow who was there on a visit, and on Thursday, Aug 5th, Pres. Snow and Elders Chr. J. Larsen, Johannes Larsen, Niels Chr. Schou, Johan F. F. Dorius and Svend Larsen and family sailed from Aalborg on board the "Zions Löve." After a successful voyage they arrived in Copenhagen late in the evening of August 6th. On Sunday, Aug. 7th, interesting meetings were held in Copenhagen, which were addressed by Pres. Snow and the brethren who had arrived from Aalborg the previous day.

Elder Carl C. A. Christensen, who had labored for some time as a missionary in Frederikstad, Norway, traveled, together with Elder Johan F. F. Dorius. to Christiania, arriving there Oct. 30, 1853. They found Elder Canute Peterson living at a cheap boarding house on Slotsgade, together with Mathias Olsen, his missionary companion. Both of them

CARL CHRISTIAN NIKOLAI DORIUS

Born April 5, 1830, in Copenhagen, Denmark; baptized Jan. 2, 1852; labored as a missionary in Denmark and Norway about four and a half years, and emigrated to Utah in 1857. He filled a mission to Scandinavia in 1860-1862, acted as Bishop of Ephraim South Ward from 1877 to 1894, and died in Ephraim, March 4, 1894.

were somewhat despondent, as the city of Christiania seemed to present a very discouraging outlook, so far as success in preaching the gospel was concerned, and their financial resources were very limited. They only found two local members of the Church in Christiania, one of whom was Carl J. E. Fjeld, who had joined the Church in Copenhagen, Denmark. Elder Christensen gave his passport to the police in Christiania and soon found a more suitable boarding place at the house of a Mr. Iversen, who resided on Brænderi-Bakken. He seemed to be guided by the Lord to that place, where he soon made converts among the other boarders. One of these was the late Peter O. Thomassen, who become so well known in Scandinavia and Utah for his literary ability.

The brethren next sought to find a hall for holding meetings. They finally secured a private house for that purpose, but Elder Christensen was summoned by the chief of police to meet him at his office. This he did, Nov. 4, 1853, and had a preliminary examination, at the close of which he was told by Chief Carl Morgenstjerne that he was forbidden to hold meetings. A decision had just been rendered by the Supreme Court of Norway, to the effect that the "Mormons," or Latter-day Saints, were not considered Christian dissenters, and therefore were not entitled to enjoy any protection under the law. Consequently they would be vigorously prosecuted if they attempted any religious exercises. This decision also sustained the judgment passed upon the Elders by the lower courts to the effect that each of the missionaries, who had been arrested and had spent months in prison the previous winter, should pay a fine of ten speciedaler and cost of court, amounting to $25.00 in each case. Being thus instructed by the court, Elder Christensen made short trips out into the farming districts, accompanied by Bro. Mathias Olsen, while Elder Canute Peterson labored quietly among the few friends found among the laboring companions of the two brethren already baptized. In this way also the current expenses of the Elders were reduced to a minimum, the few friends they had in the city being very poor. When the two Elders spent some of their time in Christiania, their meals usually consisted of a piece of bread and a drink of water from a public fountain in the market place. They selected a certain place in a grove in the outskirts of the city, where they engaged in prayer, there being no opportunity to pray at their place of lodging.

Priest Mathias Olsen left Norway, Nov. 18th, to join the Saints in Denmark who were emigrating to Zion; but before he boarded the steamer, he baptized Andreas Weihe and wife, the parents of Willard Weihe, the late noted violinist of Salt Lake City. After that, Elder C. C. A. Christensen held small meetings in private houses, where some investigators, trusty friends, would meet with the Saints and where the preaching was done by the Elders in a sitting position. In this way they answered questions and read from the Bible such passages as would elucidate the principles of the gospel. This method was necessary in order to avoid the letter of the law, for if the Elders had delivered a regular discourse in a standing position they would have been considered guilty of preaching, but speaking while occupying a sitting position could only be classed as conversation.

Elder Canute Peterson left Christiania Dec. 1, 1853, by steamer for Frederikstad, where he took charge of a small number of Saints who, emigrating to Zion, were to join other emigrants in Copenhagen, Denmark.

After Elder Peterson's departure for Denmark, Elder Carl C. A. Christensen was left alone to look after the welfare of the Church in Christiania and endeavor to make more converts. But as his means of subsistence were nearly gone, he tried (but in vain) to obtain work at his trade as a painter, while at the same time he used every opportunity that presented itself to preach the gospel.

On Thursday, Dec. 8, 1853, he met with the few Saints and friends in the humble home of Brother Carl J. E. Fjeld and explained the first principles of the gospel to those assembled. Late in the night, when the people in the neighborhood were supposed to be enjoying their natural slumbers, he led two converts into the river and baptized them. When this was done, they all assembled again at Brother Fjeld's house, where Elder Christensen confirmed the two sisters first baptized and afterwards blessed their children.. He also ordained Carl J. E. Fjeld a Priest and organized the little flock into a branch of the Church, to be known as the Christiania Branch. The spirit of prophecy on that occasion rested upon the young Elder, Carl C. A. Christensen, who stated that what had been done during that evening would yet prove one of the most important missionary acts performed, so far, in Norway. The newly-organized branch numbered nine members in all, besides children. Carl J. E. Fjeld was set apart to preside.

CARL JOHAN ELLEFSEN FJELD

First president of the Christiania Branch, Norway, was born Jan. 26, 1825, in Drammen, Norway, emigrated to Utah in 1860, and located in Lehi, Utah Co., Utah, where he died a faithful Latter-day Saint, Jan. 8, 1883.

The names of the nine constituting the original membership of the Christiania branch were the follow-

ing: Carl Johan Ellefsen Fjeld, Johannes Olsen, Andreas Weihe and wife (Bolette Sophie), Carl R. Granholm, Lars Andersen, Christoffer Andersen, Helene Granholm (wife of Carl R. Granholm), and Maren Oline Fjeld (wife of Carl J. E. Fjeld). They had been baptized into the Church in the order her given. The four persons first named were baptized by Mathias Olsen, th next four by Carl C. A. Christensen

Meanwhile, Elder Carl C. N. Dorius had reached the city of Drammen, about thirty miles west o Christiania, and together with hi native companion, Hans Larsen, h commenced holding meetings in private houses; Brother Dorius, however, soon found it necessary to see employment at his trade as a carpenter, in order to subsist. Such employment he found with a M Erik Johnsen, who lived a short distance outside the city. Mr. Johnse and his wife were soon convinced o the truth and made Elder Dorius a home in their house, which was large enough for holding meetings. Th house afterward served as a splendi base of missionary operations, n only for the city of Drammen b also for the surrounding country di tricts. Elder Dorius generally worke at his trade in the daytime and spe the long winter evenings in visiti among and conversing with the pe ple. He also held cottage meetin in different places and occasional found friends, some of whom afte wards joined the Church. Two fa ilies are especially entitled to me tion, viz., the above-mentioned Er Johnsen and his wife, and Amu Dahle and his wife. They all ca to Utah, where they subsequent died as faithful members of t Church.

At the end of the year, 1853, E G. M. Hogan, the presiding Elder Norway, was living at Frederikst where he had spent most of his time since he arrived in Norway. Elder Carl C. A. Christensen also went to Frederikstad, after having organized the branch in Christiania, and all the Elders who had been imprisoned during the preceding winter had either gone to Denmark or had emigrated to Utah. Thus the missionary force in Norway was very small at the close of 1853. Elder Canute Peterson, who had gone to Denmark with the Norwegian emigrants, was still in that country at the close of the year.

CHAPTER 21 (1853)

The principle of gathering cherished by the Scandinavian Saints—Two large companies of emigrants leave for America—A prosperous mission.

Quite a number of the recently-baptized converts in Denmark possessed considerable means, and as the spirit of emigrating to America was universal in all the branches of the Church throughout the mission, the well-to-do Saints made almost immediate preparations to sell their property and wend their way Zionward. The incessant persecutions which prevailed against the members of the Church in nearly all parts of the country also increased the desire to emigrate, and, rather than tarry, a number preferred to sell their homes at half price, if by so doing they could only obtain sufficient means to defray the expenses of the journey. Under these circumstances the spirit of brotherly love also manifested itself in its best form, and under its divine influence the rich Saints remembered their poorer fellow-religionists and extended to them that material help and succor which has always characterized the Saints of the Most High. Thus hundreds of the poor, whose chances to migrate to Zion with their own means were almost beyond reasonable expectations, were assisted by

their wealthier brethren. Through the columns of "Skandinaviens Stjerne," the Church organ in Scandinavia, plain and minute instructions were given to the emigrants who nearly all were unacquainted with the incidents of travel. In fact, there were many among them, who, during all their previous experiences in life, had never had occasion to go farther from their homes than to the nearest market town. It was, therefore, no easy task for the Elders, who presided over the different branches and conferences in the mission, to plan and arrange everything for the emigrants, and the burden rested heavily especially upon the presiding brethren in Copenhagen, where the headquarters of the mission was located.

In the latter part of December, 1853, however, Pres. John Van Cott succeeded in making the necessary contracts for transportation, etc., and in the afternoon of Dec. 22, 1853, the first emigrant company of the season and the third emigrating company of the Saints from Scandinavia (301 souls) set sail from Copenhagen on board the steamship "Slesvig," under the presidency of Chr. J. Larsen, who had been released from his appointment to Norway with permission to emigrate to Zion. A large concourse of people had assembled at the wharf in Copenhagen to witness the departure of the "Mormons," and a great deal of bitterness and hard feelings were manifested. When Elder Peter O. Hansen, after the vessel had left the harbor, was walking back to the mission office, he was followed by a mob who knocked him down and beat him considerably about the head. He lost a quantity of blood, but received no dangerous injuries. Pres. John Van Cott accompanied the emigrants as far as England, and during his absence from Scandinavia Elder Peter O. Hansen took temporary charge of the mission. By way of Kiel, Gluckstadt, and Hull, the emigrants reached Liverpool, England, in safety on Dec. 28th, and on the first day of January, 1854, they went on board the ship "Jesse Munn," which had been chartered by the presidency in Liverpool for the transportation of the Scandinavian Saints, and also a few German Saints, which swelled the total number of souls to 333. The company sailed from Liverpool Jan. 3, 1854, and after a prosperous voyage, arrived at the mouth of the Mississippi River, Jan. 16th. During the voyage twelve of the emigrants died, namely, two adults and ten children. Three couples were married. On Monday, Feb. 20th, the "Jesse Munn" arrived at New Orleans, where Chr. J. and Svend Larsen made a contract for the further transportation of the company to St. Louis, Missouri, and on Saturday, Jan. 25th, the river journey to that city was commenced. Owing to unusual low water in the Mississippi the passage was slow and tedious, which, in connection with the change of climate and difference in the mode of living, caused cholera of a very malignant type to break out among the emigrants, resulting in an unusual number of deaths.

After arriving in St. Louis, March 11th, houses were rented for the temporary occupation of the emigrants who tarried there about a month until the next company of Scandinavian emigrants, under the direction of Hans Peter Olsen (Piercy) arrived. During the stay in St. Louis sickness continued among the Saints and many more died of the cholera.

On Monday, Dec. 26, 1853, another company of Scandinavian Saints, consisting of more than 200 souls, sailed from Copenhagen, Denmark, by the steamship "Eideren," bound for Utah, under the leadership of Hans Peter Olsen, who had labored about ten months on the Island of Bornholm. Like the preceding company, these emigrants traveled by way of Kiel, Gluckstadt and Hull to Liverpool, where they arrived January 9, 1854. Here they were compelled to wait nearly two weeks, during which time the greater portion of the children were attacked with fever, resulting in the death of twenty-two of the little ones; two adults also died. On the 22nd of January the emigrants went on board the ship "Benjamin Adams," together with a few German Saints. On the 24th, the doctor, who examined the condition of the emigrants, declared that fifteen of them were unfit to proceed on the voyage, and they were consequently landed in Liverpool, with the understanding that they would be sent on to New Orleans when sufficiently recovered to travel.

The "Benjamin Adams" sailed from Liverpool Jan. 28th, with 384 Saints on board, and arrived in New Orleans on the 22nd of March, after a very pleasant and prosperous voyage. Eight deaths occurred during the voyage, namely, two very old persons and six children; two children were born on board and nine couples were married.

On the 25th of March the company continued the journey from New Orleans by the steamboat, "L. M. Kennet," and arrived in St. Louis, Mo., on the 3rd of April. During the passage up the river considerable sickness prevailed and fourteen of the emigrants died. From St. Louis, where many members of the Church resided at that time, the emigrants continued the journey up the river April 5th, to Kansas City, where they arrived April 10th. A few days later they were joined there by the company which had crossed the Atlantic in the "Jesse Munn." Westport, now part of Kansas City, Jackson County, Missouri, had been selected as the outfitting place for the Saints who crossed the Plains that year, and the Scandinavian emigrants made their encampment near Westport, situated a short distance south of the Missouri River.

After the arrival of the "Jesse Munn" company from St. Louis, the two companies were amalgamated and organized for the journey across the Plains, May 9th. Hans Peter Olsen was chosen leader of the amalgamated company and Christian J. Larsen as chaplain, while Bent Nielsen was chosen wagon master, Jens Hansen camp captain and Peter P. Thomsen captain of the guard. The company, which consisted of sixty-nine wagons, was divided into six smaller companes with ten or twelve wagons and a captain in each company. To each wagon were attached four oxen and two cows. There were also in the company a number of reserve oxen. From ten to twelve persons were assigned to each wagon. Elders Carl Capson, Anders Andersen, Peter Beckström, Jens Jörgensen, Anders W. Winberg and Valentine Valentinsen were appointed captains of the six divisions. Oxen, wagons, tents and other traveling equipment, which the emigrants bought in St. Louis and Kansas City or vicinity, cost more than had been expected, on account of which a number of the emigrants ran short of means and were unable to furnish a full outfit.

The more well-to-do, however, among whom we might mention Bro. Bent Nielsen from Sjælland and Peter P. Thomsen from Falster, contributed freely of their means, so that none were left in the States through lack of money. Toward the close of May, another camping place was chosen about eight miles west of Kansas City, from which place the emigrants commenced their long journey over the Plains on Thursday, June 15, 1854. This company of emigrants traveled over a new but shorter road than previous companies had done. After traveling about twenty miles from Kansas City, a halt was called because nearly all the teams were too heavily loaded, owing to the fact that the emigrants had taken too much baggage along, contrary to instructions or counsel given. At the suggestion of Bro. Olsen some of the brethren went to Leavenworth City, about thirty miles from the camping place, to consult Apostle Orson Pratt, who, in his capacity of emigration agent, had located temporarily in said city. Elder Pratt advanced the company sufficient money to buy fifty oxen, after which the journey was continued. A few days' journey west of Fort Kearney the company, on the 5th of August, met Apostle Erastus Snow and other Elders from the Valley who had been called on missions to the States. Elder Snow held a meeting with the Scandinavian Saints and addressed them in their own language, which caused great rejoicing in the camp.

Of all the emigrant companies, who this year crossed the Plains, the Scandinavians suffered the most with sickness (cholera), and during their temporary sojourn at the camping place near Westport, as well as on the steamboats, fatalities were more numerous. Scores fell as victims of the dreadful disease and many of the Saints were compelled to bury their relatives and friends without coffins on the desolate plains. So great was the mortality among them that of the 680 souls who had left Copenhagen the previous winter only about 500 reached their destination. The others succumbed to the sickness and hardships of the journey. The survivors reached Salt Lake City, Oct. 5, 1854.

The condition of the Scandinavian Mission at the close of 1853 was reported by President John Van Cott as follows:

"In Denmark there is more religious liberty than in any other part of the mission. I can say that the prospect is flattering in every part where the servants of the Lord have found an opening, notwithstanding they have to come in contact with that ignorant prejudice which always characterizes those who are opposed to the revelations of God. It is not an opposition by argument, * * but a contemptible sneer, a shriek at the highest key of the voice, sometimes the smashing in of doors of our meeting places; occasionally also a few will be bold enough to stand upon the benches during meetings, and smoke cigars with their hats on. This appears to be the greatest opposition. The Sunday previous to the first ship load of emigrating Saints leaving Copenhagen this season, I witnessed a scene of that kind, but I suppose the devil was angry, because we that day confirmed eleven persons into the Church of Jesus Christ. * * Our hall was crowded to excess and hundreds went away and tarried in the streets, as they could not obtain admittance. This turn out, I concluded, was the result of the hallooing of men and boys, as the Saints were retiring from their meeting place. The shouting is better than a number of bells to attract the attention of passers by, for the streets in front of our meetings are blocked with people who stop to enquire into the matter, and of course learn where the Latter-day Saints hold meetings. The people are thus induced to come, out of curiosity. The result with many is, that they are led to embrace the truth. Numbers are baptized weekly, and I see nothing to prevent the rapid spread of the work of the Lord until the honest-in-heart in Denmark are numbered with the covenant children.

"In Norway, the question in relation to tolerating religious liberty has for a length of time been under consideration by the authorities of that country, and reports of a flattering nature have been circulated from time to time. But alas! the scene has changed. The case growing out of the brethren being imprisoned for a length of time has been decided against them, which subjects them to a heavy fine, or imprisonment. The authorities are now more rigid and severe than ever; the brethren are forbidden even to mention "Mormonism," much more to teach it. Should anyone to whom they teach or read the Bible, betray them, it would subject them to an immediate fine or imprisonment. No mercy whatever is shown to anyone professing the faith of the Latter-day Saints. One of the Elders appointed at the October Conference to labor in Norway had arrived there previous to my learning the change that had taken place; the other two were on their way. After receiving the above information, I thought it not advisable for them to go, as one of them, Christian J. Larsen, would on his arrival be immediately thrust into prison, as he was one of the number who had been imprisoned formerly, and had been released while the subject of religious liberty was under consideration. I accordingly intercepted them by letter, giving one of them (Chr. J. Larsen) liberty to emigrate and the other (Chr. G. Larsen) an appointment to the presidency of the Bornholm Conference, in the place of Elder Hans P. Olsen, whom I had called upon to go home in charge of the Saints. Could the servants of the Lord have liberty to preach the gospel in Norway, thousands would embrace the same. I instructed Elders Erik G. M. Hogan and Canute Peterson not to give up the mission, but to continue to petition for liberty until they succeeded; or else not give the authorities any rest; also to use every necessary precaution in conversation, etc., so that the law would not be brought to bear upon them.

"The work in Sweden has prospered, notwithstanding the opposition of the authorities of the land. After some of the missionaries were sent back to Copenhagen, "Mormonism" still prospered. The authorities forbade the Elders traveling about, confining some of them in town, under the scrutinizing eye of the police, who, if they caught any of them instructing the people, would impose a fine of 25 Swedish dollars for each offence, or 26 days' imprisonment on bread and water without intermission. Some of the brethren were punished to that extent; 28 days was considered by law equivalent to death. In some instances, the brethren have been beaten with clubs. Some of the missionaries who were sent to Sweden from the October Conference, were compelled to leave; they have since emigrated. * *

"As regards the emigration, we do not have to urge that in the least, for there is no lack of the spirit; only give the Saints the means. And I am happy to inform you that many have been blessed with that, so that they have been enabled to emigrate; we have the names of 678 who have emigrated this season."

CHAPTER 22 (1854)

Imprisonment of Elders in Norway for baptizing—Preaching the gospel under difficulties—First baptisms in Drammen, Norway—Progress in Christiania—Elder Canute Peterson in Stavanger—Branches of the Church organized in Drammen and Stavanger.

In 1854 missionary work was continued successfully in Norway. Elder Carl C. A. Christensen left the kind-hearted Saints in Frederikstad Jan. 20, 1854, for Drammen, where he found Elder Carl C. N. Dorius with the Johnsen family. The Johnsens received Elder Christensen with the greatest kindness, though they had not yet been baptized. Previous to this, Elder Dorius had come in contact with the police officers in Drammen and had been arrested for preaching, but, as some of his friends gave security for his appearance in court, he was allowed to enjoy his liberty, until he received his sentence. This came while Elder Christensen visited him in Drammen. The two Elders left Drammen Jan. 20th, but separated on the way to Christiania, about seven miles out of town, as Elder Dorius had then to enter the premises of the county sheriff, whose guest he became, to be fed on bread and water for five days, instead of paying a fine of 10 speciedaler ($10.00). It was rather a touching moment for the two Elders, to separate under such circumstances, but there seemed to be no other way. Elder Christensen continued his journey to Christiania, while Elder Dorius went to prison.

On his arrival in Christiania, Elder Christensen held meetings, visited investigating friends and distributed tracts. He also baptized a number of people, most of whom later emigrated to Utah and died as faithful members of the Church.

Elder Christensen again left Christiania Feb. 1st, setting his face toward Drammen. After a long day's travel on foot, during which he disposed of tracts in many places along the road, he received a hearty welcome in the home of Mr. Johnsen, where he also again met his fellow-laborer, Elder Carl C. N. Dorius, who had regained his freedom after expiating his "crime" of preaching the gospel. After holding two well-attended meetings in the home of the Johnsen family, Elder Christensen went out to find a suitable place for the performance of the ordinance of baptism, but no open water could be found anywhere; all was ice and snow. On the 5th of February, Elders Christensen and Dorius left their friends in Drammen to visit the Saints in Christiania. There they found their little flock of Saints happy and thankful for the gospel truths they had received. In the evening the two Elders met with the Saints in the home of Bro. Carl J. E. Fjeld. Just as they were about to commence their meeting they were startled by the appearance of three policemen in the doorway, sent by their chief to be present at the "Mormon" meeting. Elder Christensen respectfully informed them that this was not a public meeting, but invited them to take a seat, which they did. An inspired thought flashed upon the minds of both missionaries at the same time as to how they might extricate themselves from their embarrassing situation. There was no opportunity for the two Elders to communicate with each other, but Elder Dorius instinctively, assuming the role of a stranger, began to argue with Brother Christensen on the principles of Christianity from a Lutheran point of view. This gave Elder Christensen an excellent opportunity to explain some of the doctrines of the Latter-day Saints as compared with Bible teachings. In this manner even the police officers received a strong testimony, without giving them any cause to interfere. After thus entertaining the people for about two hours, Elder Christensen proposed that all should separate and go to their respective homes. The police bade Elder Christensen a very polite goodnight, shaking hands with him before leaving. Although it was quite late, the missionaries afterwards sang a few hymns with the Saints and then went to the opposite side of the city to stay over night.

Elder Canute Peterson, accompanied by Elder Carl Widerborg, returned to Christiania from his visit to Denmark, Feb. 6th, and found Elders Carl C. A. Christensen and Carl C. N. Dorius actively engaged in missionary labors.

Three days later, Elders Christensen and Dorius left Christiania for Drammen. On their journey they passed through a district of country called Röken, distributing tracts. Soon after their arrival in Drammen, Elder Carl Widerborg arrived in that city to work up an interest among the people in favor of absolute liberty for all men, including the Latter-day Saints, and he pleaded with the people in a very forcible way to this end. While holding crowded meetings in various parts of the city and its environments, advocating religious liberty on general principles, he also preached the gospel to the people in a most interesting manner, assisted by the other Elders. A number of signatures was obtained to a petition which was forwarded to the Storthing, then in session in Christiania. In some of the meetings the local parsons endeavored to counteract the efforts of the missionaries, but they invariably met with signal defeat, as Elder Widerborg was well posted on the theological points of the Lutheran Church, and was familiar with all the defects of its system. By these bold movements on the part of the Elders, great interest was awakened in Drammen and the streets were sometimes crowded o u t s i d e the houses in which meetings were being held, the rooms being inadequate to accommodate the people.

Elder Widerborg soon returned to Christiania, while Elders Christensen and Dorius quietly continued their labors in Drammen and vicinity among their friends, being aware that the police officers were watching their movements. The threatened cloud finally appeared in the form of a policeman, who on March 2nd, 1854, appeared on the scene with a summons for Elders Dorius and Christensen to appear before the magistrate the following day.

When the two Elders responded and appeared in court, they found that some of their friends had been summoned as witnesses. The preliminary trial was very brief, but when the magistrate, Mr. Chr. Schive, asked the missionaries if they would refrain from promulgating their doctrines, they both answered no. The magistrate then, in a somewhat sympathetic tone, said, "I am then under the necessity of arresting you."

This was consequently done. Calling in the jailer, the magistrate ordered him to give the missionaries the best cell in the prison, which proved to be a new, clean room. And he furthermore allowed their friends to bring them bedding and other things for their personal comfort, as well as books and writing material. This made the prisoners quite comfortable. The following day, March 4th, Elders Christensen and Dorius were again on trial and once more they were offered their freedom, if they would agree to be passive while their case was pending before the courts. To this they again gave a negative reply. One reason why the Elders so stubbornly refused to submit to the legal authority was that President Willard Snow had once written a letter to the Elders when they were imprisoned in Frederikstad the previous winter, expressing himself to the effect that he would rather remain in prison during his whole life, or until they picked him out piece-meal through the keyhole, than promise to cease preaching the gospel. Influenced by this assertion on the part of President Snow, Elders Christensen and Dorius deemed it obligatory upon them to refuse liberation under the conditions offered them; they were therefore returned to jail.

While in prison, the two Elders studied the Scriptures continually and also an ecclesiastical history, by which they became familiar with many important events connected with the decay of the Christian Church under Popery and with the disputes and schisms which later took place among the sects at various times, as well as with the horrible persecutions that it called forth. The jailer showed his good will towards the imprisoned Elders in various ways; thus one day, when the Elders were preparing an appeal of their case from the police court, he put an educated lawyer, confined for a small offense, into the room in which the missionaries were confined and this man willingly assisted them in making an able plea in writing, which, when it was presented in court along with some of the published tracts, caused great astonishment. The judge remarked: "I did not know that these men were also lawyers." A few days later the judge himself called upon the Elders in prison, and when he first saw them he exclaimed, "Why, they are only

very young men," and added, "but what did you come here for?" The Elders answered that they had not come from choice, but because—. Here the judge interrupted them by saying, "I wish you were located on Mount Zion, every one of you." To this wish the Elders most readily acquiesced. On the 18th of March the sentence of the lower court was read to the Elders. It was to the effect that Elder Christensen should pay 10 speciedaler and Elder Dorius 20 speciedaler as a fine and cost of court. The double fine imposed on Elder Dorius was due to the fact that he had once previously been punished for a similar offense.

On Sunday, March 19th, the imprisoned brethren were visited by Mrs. Dahle, and by a note, smuggled to them, they were advised by Elders Erik G. M. Hogan and Carl Widerborg, who at that time constituted the presidency of the missionary work in Norway, that they might accept the offer of liberation on the terms laid down by the magistrate in the first place. The following day, the imprisoned missionaries therefore wrote a petition to the proper court, asking for their freedom, and agreeing to comply with the terms proposed to them. On the 21st their petition was granted, on condition that the Elders would give security for their appearance in court, whenever wanted. Such security was easily obtained from their noble friends, Amund Dahle and Erik Johnsen. Consequently the Elders left their prison home March 22, 1854, and the same evening a feast in their honor was given by their devoted friends in Drammen.

In the evening of March 30, 1854, Amund Dahle and wife and Erik Johnsen and wife, the faithful friends to the missionaries in Drammen, were baptized by Hans Larsen, who first accompanied Elder Dorius to Drammen. He had walked all the way from Frederikstad to Drammen, a distance of about 100 miles, for the purpose of doing that which Elders Christensen and Dorius had agreed not to do, and thus a nucleus was formed in Drammen, around which many honest souls subsequently gathered and joined the Church.

On Friday, April 21, 1854, Elder Christensen was notified by the police in Drammen that he might come and occupy his former room in the prison to spend five days living on bread and water diet, inasmuch as he did not intend to pay the fine and cost of court. Consequently, he went to prison that same evening, after having enjoyed a good supper; he remained in jail the required time, and came out on the 26th a free man. Elder Dorius did not expiate his sentence at that time as his place of lodging was outside the city and under the jurisdiction of another judge.

Elder Carl Widerborg was notified by the police in Drammen, April 28th, to meet in court and submit to imprisonment on bread and water for six days for having preached and baptized.

In May, 1854, Elder Carl C. A. Christensen was called to labor as a missionary in Frederikshald, about twenty miles south of Frederikstad. Here, during the following months, he labored in the daytime at his trade as a house painter, thereby earning the necessary means to pay for his board and lodging, while in the evening and on Sundays he expounded the Scriptures wherever he found an opportunity to do so.

After laboring four months in Frederikshald, he was again appointed to labor in Christiania, where he arrived Sept 13th. During the summer of 1854, Elder

Carl C. N. Dorius labored much of the time in Christiania and Drammen. President Erik G. M. Hogan and Elder Carl Widerborg had made a missionary trip to the district of Telemarken, the birthplace of President Hogan, without any apparent results, but in Christiania quite an addition had been made to the Church by the labors of Elders Widerborg and Dorius. One of the local Saints, Jonas Otterström, who lived at the base of a high hill called Egebjerg, overlooking the city, bore testimony to his customers and others, and thus Gustav Anderson, a good and highly respected man who lived on the top of said hill, became a convert to "Mormonism."

It is interesting to note the various localities in or on the outskirts of Christiania, where the gospel took root in the beginning. The Elders, having found their first converts among the laborers in the factories along the falls of the river, next commenced propaganda in the extreme opposite edge of the city where Gustav Anderson and his wife joined the Church and became ardent supporters in the work of God. They owned a small but neat dwelling, and, having only two children, they were glad to have the Elders make their home with them free of charge, and to let their house be used as a meeting place for the Saints and strangers at all times. Besides this, they would bear testimony to the truth to any and all with whom they came into contact, and thus they became the means of leading others into the fold of Christ. Being a good stone-mason, Bro. Andersen was employed by the city engineer, and by degrees he gained such influence with his superiors through his skill that he was made the trusted foreman of large gangs of workingmen, among whom he engaged several of the brethren.

At length he was engaged as foreman in building a large bridge near the city of Trondhjem, and thus he became the indirect means of introducing the gospel into the more northern parts of Norway, for he bore testimony to all who would listen to him and thereby established faith in the hearts of a few honest souls.

From Trondhjem Brother Andersen, who only held the Aaronic Priesthood, wrote to the president in Christiania, requesting that an Elder be sent as a missionary to Trondhjem. In response to this request Elder Carl C. N. Dorius was sent to Trondhjem, and thus it fell to his lot to introduce the gospel in that city and vicinity. Brother Andersen supported the Norwegian mission with his means and influence as long as he remained in Norway.

Elder Canute Peterson, who had been called to labor as a missionary on the west coast of Norway, arrived in Stavanger Sept. 1, 1854. Here he found a Brother Johansen, a hatter, who had embraced the gospel in Denmark. Brother Peterson held his first meeting Sept. 10, 1854. The few who attended seemed to be interested and well pleased, and when he held his next meeting on the 17th, quite a congregation was present. After that he held several other meetings in Stavanger and vicinity. He baptized his first converts Oct. 13th, viz., Lars Johnsen and his wife, as the first fruits of his labors in Stavanger. After baptizing three other persons in Stavanger, he was ordered by the magistrate to quit holding meetings, or leave the city.

On Nov. 6th, Elder Peterson received a letter from President John Van Cott appointing him to succeed Erik G. M. Hogan as president of the mission in Norway. This made it necessary for Elder Peterson to leave his little flock in Stavanger, and he, therefore, proceeded to organize his converts into a branch of the Church, Nov. 8, 1854, with six members; he ordained Jörgen M. Siau an Elder and appointed him to preside over the new branch.

During the year 1854, Elder Canute Peterson wrote a small pamphlet or tract consisting of Bible references. It was the first pamphlet of that kind published in the Scandinavian Mission, and was used by the missionaries to great advantage for several years afterwards.

Elder Carl C. N. Dorius, being arrested and sentenced a third time, lived exclusively on bread and water for nine days in prison, in lieu of paying a fine of 40 Norwegian speciedaler. His prison life commenced Dec. 10, 1854, but when he was released Dec. 19th, he was well and hearty and immediately renewed his missionary labors.

The Saints residing in the city and neighborhood of Drammen were organized into a branch of the Church Sept. 29, 1854, called the Drammen Branch. Bro. Amund Dahle was ordained a Priest and appointed president of the same by Carl C. N. Dorius and Carl C. A. Christensen. Many good people have since joined the Church in Drammen and vicinity, and this branch is still one of the best branches in Norway, although made up of new members, as all the original members emigrated to Zion long ago and died faithful to the Church.

Elder Johan F. F. Dorius, accompanied by Mathias Olsen, arrived in Norway from Copenhagen, Denmark, Oct. 6, 1854. Brother Olsen was a Norwegian who had embraced the gospel in Denmark and had been traveling in that country as a missionary, but he had been arrested by the police on a charge of vagrancy and banished. Together with Elder Dorius he was appointed to labor in Christiania. Since his departure from Norway in August of the previous year, Elder Dorius had labored energetically, and with success, in Denmark, especially in the northern part of Sjælland. After his arrival in Norway, Mathias Olsen worked awhile at his trade, but he was soon called to labor as a missionary in the Drammen Branch and the country round about.

Elder Erik G. M. Hogan left Norway, Nov. 10, 1854, to return to his home in Zion, accompanied by some 30 or 40 Norwegian Saints emigrating to America. These emigrants first went to Copenhagen, Denmark, whence they sailed Nov. 23rd, for Liverpool, England, where they later joined the other emigrant companies of the season which left Copenhagen, Denmark, respectively Nov. 24th and 27th. Elder Carl C. A. Christensen was left in charge of the mission in Norway until Elder Canute Peterson should arrive from Stavanger.

CHAPTER 23 (1854)

More new branches organized—Anti-Mormon literature—Apostle Franklin D. Richards visits Scandinavia—Elder Peter O. Hansen leads a large company of Scandinavian emigrants to Utah—A stormy voyage across the North Sea—An important council meeting in Copenhagen—The Stockholm Conference organized.

In the beginning of 1854, persecutions and disturbances by mobs became so frequent in Copenhagen, Denmark, that public meetings had to be discontinued for about three months. The police authorities, by their reluctance to interfere with this lawlessness, plainly showed their sympathy for the mobbers. Later in the year, however, the disturbances ceased, and the Elders in the capital, and also in some of the provinces, met with success. Pres. John Van

Cott returned from his visit to England, February 10, 1854, and resumed his official duties.

During the year a number of new branches were raised up. Among them were the Ledöv Branch on Sjælland, organized Jan. 22, 1854, the Roholte Branch on Sjælland, organized March 1, 1854, the Quistgaard Branch on Sjælland, organized March 19, 1854, the Benstrup Branch on Sjælland, organized March 19, 1854, the Arnager Branch on Bornholm, organized June 5, 1854, the Vig Branch on Sjælland, organized Aug. 6, 1854, the Brasserup Branch on Falster, organized Aug. 13, 1854, the Aarhus Branch and the Læborg Branch in Jutland, organized Sept. 10, 1854, and the Gjötterup Branch in Hanherred, Jutland, organized Oct. 15, 1854.

In Sweden, the Elders extended their fields of labor northward and met with considerable success. Three new branches of the Church were raised up during 1854, namely, the Neflinge Branch and the Riseberga Branch in Skåne, and the Hjo Branch in Skaraborgs län. They were organized at a conference held at Malmö, Sweden, April 16, 1854.

In June, 1854, the Danish government, alarmed because of the rapid progress of "Mormonism," appointed a committee of five members to investigate the new religion. The investigation, however, led to no important results.

About this time, an anti-"Mormon" pamphlet, by Dr. H. C. Röhrdam, caused considerable opposition to the work of the Lord in Denmark, the author resorting to all kinds of misrepresentations and falsehoods. An answer to some of his attacks was published in the mission periodical, "Skandinaviens Stjerne." Mr. Röhrdam's pamphlet was the forerunner of scores of other books and pamphets which later were published against the work of God in the Scandinavian countries.

In September, 1854, Apostle Franklin D. Richards, who presided over the European Mission, made a hurried visit to the Scandinavian Mission. He arrived in Copenhagen, Sept. 27, 1854, and left Oct. 5, 1854. During his short visit in Denmark, he preached in one important conference held in Copenhagen and also addressed a number of other well-

APOSTLE FRANKLIN D. RICHARDS
Born April 2, 1821, at Richmond, Berkshire
Co., Mass.; died Dec. 9, 1899, at Ogden, Utah.

attended meetings in Copenhagen, his discourses being translated into Danish by Elder Carl Widerborg, who arrived from Norway Sept. 25, 1854, to succeed Elder Peter O. Hansen as translator and writer for "Skandinaviens Stjerne." The Saints in Denmark were overjoyed at being visited by an Apostle, and even strangers turned out in large numbers to hear him.

At this time, the Saints began to hold quarterly conferences in the different conferences of the mission, on which occasions the traveling as well as the local ministry usually reported their labors.

On Friday, Nov. 24, 1854 about 300 Scandinavian Saints sailed from

7

Copenhagen, Denmark, on board the steamer "Cimbria" bound for Utah, under the direction of Elder Peter O. Hansen. All the emigrants were in good health and excellent spirits, but had an exceedingly rough passage over the North Sea. At 10 o'clock on the morning of the 25th, the "Cimbria" arrived at Frederikshavn, on the east coast of Jutland, where 149 more emigrants from the Aalborg and Vendsyssel conferences came on board. With these additional passengers the voyage was continued on the morning of the 26th. The prospects were fair until about 2 o'clock in the morning of the 27th, when the wind turned south-west, and began to blow so heavily that the captain, an experienced s a i l o r, deemed it necessary to turn back and seek the nearest harbor in Norway. C o n s e q u e n t l y, the course was changed, and about 4 o'clock in the afternoon the "Cimbria" put into the port of Mandal, which is an excellent natural harbor, surrounded by very high and steep granite cliffs. This romantic place and its surroundings were as much of a curiosity to the Danish emigrants as a shipload of "Mormons" were to the people of Mandal. In this harbor the emigrants tarried for several days, while the winds outside spent their fury on the troubled sea. Some of the Saints went ashore to lodge; they found the inhabitants of Mandal very hospitable, and, by request, some of the brethren preached several times to the people on shore. The result of this was that some of the inhabitants became interested in the gospel.

On the morning of Dec. 7th, when the weather seemed to be more favorable, the "Cimbria" again put to sea, and steamed off towards England once more; but the captain and all on board soon learned that the change in the weather was only a lull preceding a more violent outburst of a long winter storm. Towards midnight of the 7th, the wind became a terrific gale, which increased in violence till it shattered the ship's bulwarks and broke a number of boxes. About 2 o'clock in the morning of Dec. 8th, the captain decided to turn back to Mandal, but as the wind, waves and strong current rendered it very dangerous to turn the vessel in the direction of Norway, it was deemed necessary to go clear back to Frederikshavn, where the ship arrived on the 9th about 4 p. m. By this time the emigrants were suffering severely, but with the exception of two or three individuals, who decided to remain behind, the Saints bore their hardships with great fortitude and patience. While laying weatherbound in Frederikshavn, most of the emigrants went on shore to refresh and rest themselves after their rough experience at sea, and while waiting for the weather and wind to change in their favor, a number of meetings were held which made a good impression upon the people of that seaport town, who hitherto had been unwilling to listen to the preaching of "Mormonism."

On the 20th of December the weather moderated, and the captain made a third attempt to reach England. By this time the emigrants were rested and in good spirits, but in the night between the 21st and 22nd, a worse storm than any of the preceding ones arose, threatening the ship and all on board with utter destruction. For many hours the noble "Cimbria" fought her way against the raging elements, but was at length compelled to change her course, and for the third time the company was turned back. But while the captain and crew began to feel discouraged, most of the Saints continued cheer-

ful and thanked the Lord for their preservation. About 2 o'clock in the afternoon of the 22nd, the wind suddenly changed to the north and the captain immediately steered for Hull once more, amid the rejoicings of the Saints, and on the 24th, about noon, the ship anchored safely in the Humber. On the following day (Dec. 25th) the emigrants continued their journey by rail from Hull to Liverpool, where they joined two smaller companies which had left Copenhagen about the same time as the "Cimbria," and had waited for the arrival of the latter for several weeks.

The Presidency in Liverpool chartered the ship "Helios" to take the Scandinavian emigration to New Orleans, but the company being detained so long on account of the storms, the "Helios" had been filled with other passengers, and the "James Nesmith," Captain Mills, was secured for the transportation of the Scandinavians. Consequently, 440 (or 441) emigrating Saints, all from Scandinavia except one, sailed from Liverpool, England, Jan 7, 1855, bound for New Orleans. The ship arrived at the mouth of the Mississippi River Feb. 18, 1855, after a successful voyage, during which, however, thirteen deaths occurred. At New Orleans, where the company landed on the 23rd, most of the emigrants went on board the large steamboat "Oceana" and sailed from New Orleans on the 24th. On the journey up the Mississippi River, seven of the Saints died; on the 7th of March the company arrived at St. Louis, Missouri. From that city about 150 of the Scandinavian Saints continued their journey on the 10th of March for Weston, Missouri, with the intention of remaining somewhere in that section of the country until they could obtain means to go through to the Valley; and 175 others, under the leadership of Peter O. Hansen, left St. Louis March 12th by the steamboat "Clara" for Atchison, Kansas, but owing to low water in the river, they were compelled to land in Leavenworth, where they tarried until the company led by Elder Hogan arrived. During the stay in Leavenworth, about twenty of the emigrants died, and after selecting a new camping place, cholera broke out in the company and caused nine more deaths. In the latter part of May the emigrants removed to Mormon Grove, situated about five miles west of Atchison, Kansas, which place had been selected as the outfitting point for the emigrants who crossed the plains in 1855. They arrived at Mormon Grove, May 22nd, 1855. Most of the Scandinavian emigrants, who continued the journey to the Valley that season, left Mormon Grove, June 13, 1855, in Captain Jacob. F. Secrist's company and arrived in Salt Lake City Sept 7, 1855.

Commencing with December 28, 1854, and continuing for three days, a general council, consisting of representative brethren from various missionary fields in the Scandinavian countries, convened in Copenhagen, President John Van Cott presiding. He had extended an invitation to the missionaries to meet in a grand council, in order that he might learn the conditions, prospects and wants in the various parts of the Scandinavian Mission, and impart such instructions and counsel to the brethren as might be found necessary. In response to this invitation nearly all the conference presidents and many other missionaries had gathered in Copenhagen.

In the first meeting, held in the forenoon of the 28th, Elder Ola Nilson Liljenquist, president of the

Copenhagen Conference, reported that about five hundred persons had been baptized in his field of labor during the preceding 15 months. The

OLA N. LILJENQUIST

President of the Copenhagen Conference, and a group of Elders laboring with him. On the picture Elder Liljenquist is the man on the right, sitting down.

conference consisted of fifteen branches, of which 14 were on the island of Sjælland. Each of these branches was presided over by a good, faithful man. Thirteen Elders were traveling and laboring as missionaries among the Saints in the organized branches, besides the local Priesthood in each branch. There was need of six more faithful Elders to labor in the conference. Elder Liljenquist was highly pleased with the Copenhagen Branch, presided over by Elder Ole Christopher Olsen, whom he regarded as a most faithful shepherd over the flock entrusted to his care. He praised the Saints for their liberality in sustaining the work of God with their temporal means, and many of the Saints that were poor had thus been assisted to emigrate to Zion.

Elder Jens Jensen, president of

the Aalborg Conference, reported that said conference contained eight branches and that a number of young brethren were laboring in that field. The gospel had made satisfactory progress lately and quite a number had been baptized, some in Randers and vicinity. There had been some persecutions in certain places and some of the brethren, who were sent to the City of Viborg, had been arrested and sent away. He needed more Elders to assist in the work in his field of labor.

In the afternoon session, Johan Swenson, president of the Lolland Conference, brought greetings from the Saints in his field of labor, which comprised the islands of Lolland, Falster and Möen. The conference contained seven organized branches. He also needed more Elders to assist in promulgating the work in those islands. The missionaries had been subject to considerable hardship and persecution; yet the conditions were not as bad as they were when he commenced to labor in that field. On the island of Möen, where the people were stirred up against the gospel by their priests, the opposition was the greatest and most severe, and he himself had often experienced the hatred and animosity of the wicked, but had been delivered from many dangers by the kind providence of God. He desired three efficient Elders to assist him in his field of labor. At present, he said, there were 103 members in good standing, and the missionaries did not suffer for want of the necessities of life, because the Saints living in the districts where missionary work was done, were glad to take care of them. He hoped to see more branches of the Church established on Falster, where many people were interested in the gospel principles.

Elder Lauritz Larsen, president of the Vendsyssel Conference, reported that the work of God in that field was prosperous, the Saints being alive in faith and good works. The conference consisted of eight branches with a total of 257 members; ten brethren were laboring in pairs, preaching and distributing tracts among the people. He missed a number of the Saints who had recently emigrated to Zion, but expected soon to see many new converts added to the Church.

Elder Nils Nilsson, president of the Skåne Conference, Sweden, reported eight small branches in his field of labor (Skåne), besides two other branches farther up in Sweden. Fifteen Elders were laboring as missionaries in Sweden. Sometimes the brethren would be arrested and beaten and treated as the worst of criminals, according to the so-called Christian laws of the land. Nevertheless, he felt happy in the work, inasmuch as the spirit and power of God were manifested in their behalf, especially in the city of Malmö, where those who had come to make disturbances had been overpowered by the truth on several occasions. The Swedish Mission stood in need of missionaries who were not afraid to meet the consequences of preaching the gospel in the face of rigorous laws and their unmerciful administration, and who would put their trust in God while performing their duty as his servants, regardless of the treatment they might receive from the opposing forces.

The general conference being continued on Friday, Dec. 29th, Elder Jens Jörgensen, president of the Fredericia Conference, who spoke in the forenoon meeting, reported that his field of labor was in a prosperous condition. His conference included the island of Fyen and some smaller islands, besides a very large portion of Jutland; he would like to get four good, energetic Elders to assist him, if possible. The Saints who constituted the membership in his conference were liberal in paying tithing and subscribing towards the Perpetual Emigrating Fund, and as a rule the Saints, as well as many strangers, appreciated the printed word through which they derived much spiritual benefit.

Elder Chr. G. Larsen, president of he Bornholm Conference, expressed himself in a happy way and reported that his conference was prosperous. The missionaries and most of the Saints were faithful and true to their covenants. There was less opposition to the truth than before, and the spirit of the Lord seemed to be gaining an influence for good over its former opponents.

Elder Erik G. Erikson, who had been laboring in different parts of Sweden, reported that he had met with considerable opposition and persecution from the people, as well as from the clergy and the civil authorities. He said that Sweden was a hard country for missionary labors, because the laws would not permit men to worship God according to the doctrines laid down in the Bible; nevertheless, the gospel had found its way into some of the middle provinces of Sweden, and some had already been baptized in the Skaraborg län, and one person also in Stockholm, the capital of Sweden. He considered the prospects for the promulgation of the gospel fairly good, and energetic, faithful Elders would find a fruitful field in that part of Sweden.

In the afternoon session, Pres. John Van Cott explained that owing to the great distance and the irregularities of the steamship traffic between Denmark and Norway, Elder Canute Peterson, president of the Brevig Conference, Norway, could not be present, but a written report prepared by Elder Carl C. A. Christensen was read to the council, from which it was learned that conditions in Norway with regard to the gospel were fairly good and promising, notwithstanding the stringency of the laws. The branch in Christiania had now fifty members and a smaller branch in Drammen had recently been organized. In Stavanger, where Elder Canute Peterson had labored for some time, a small branch numbering six members had been organized, and Elder Carl C. N. Dorius had recently been called to labor there. Elders Carl C. A. Christensen and Johan F. F. Dorius were laboring in Christiania and vicinity, while Mathias Olsen, a Norwegian who had embraced the gospel in Denmark, was laboring in Drammen. The brethren were occasionally "treated" to bread and water in prison for preaching repentance and baptizing people for the remission of their sins. Yet, they gladly accepted such treatment over and over again, although the penalty was increased each time they were arrested and convicted. The Norwegian Saints were very kind to the missionaries and as a rule faithful in the performance of their duties; and if there had been more religious liberty in the land the people in general would have listened gladly to the testimonies of the Elders. As in nearly all other countries, the teachers of religion in Norway were the principal opponents of the truth; finding themselves unable to conquer the Elders by arguments, or Bible proofs, they would call upon the civil authorities and officers of the law to aid them, by arresting and imprisoning the missionaries.

The general council was continued on Saturday, Dec. 30th, at which Elder John Van Cott, in the forenoon session, gave timely instructions to the presiding Elders, in regard to proper and accurate bookkeeping.

In the afternoon session, on motion of Pres. John Van Cott, Sweden was divided into two conferences, the new conference to include the Kalmar Branch and the middle provinces of Sweden, including the capital of the country, to be known as the Stockholm Conference, with headquarters in Stockholm. President Van Cott explained that the northern boundaries of the new conference could be extended as far north as the Lord should be pleased to open the way. Elder Åke Jönsson was appointed to go to Stockholm to take care of the new conference.

During these three days' council meetings, Pres. John Van Cott and other brethren gave good and wise counsel, and a number of the presiding Elders and other missionaries delivered brief addresses. A spirit of union and love was manifested in all of the sessions.

According to the statistical report dated Dec. 31, 1854, the Scandinavian Mission now consisted of nine conferences, namely, six (Copenhagen, Aalborg, Vendsyssel, Fredericia, Lolland and Bornholm) in Denmark, one (Brevig) in Norway, and two (Skåne and Stockholm) in Sweden. In the 69 branches of the mission there were 2 Seventies, 106 Elders, 95 Priests, 93 Teachers, 53 Deacons, and 2,099 lay members, or a total membership of 2,447. During the past nine months 902 persons had been added to the Church by baptism; 237 had been excommunicated, 337 emigrated and 12 died.

CHAPTER 24 (1855)

Hard winter in Scandinavia—Canute Peterson presides in Norway—Report of general conditions in Norway, Sweden and Denmark—Visit of Elders Daniel Spencer and Joseph A. Young to Scandinavia.

The winter of 1854-1855 was hard in Scandinavia. Many people were, consequently, out of employment. This led to considerable suffering and want among the laboring classes. Nearly all the Saints being poor, they shared the fate of the general public. About this time, also, labor became scarce, and the price of the necessaries of life went up, because all traffic on the sea ceased for several months on account of ice. Thus Öresund froze entirely over, so that the people could travel on foot, and even by teams, between Sweden and the island of Sjælland. Not until the middle of April, 1855, could the traffic on the seas be continued from Copenhagen, and it was still later before the steamers could run regularly to Stockholm and Christiania.

On Jan. 11, 1855, Elder Canute Peterson arrived in Christiania from the west coasts of Norway. He had left Stavanger Nov. 10, 1854, starting eastward over the mountains toward Christiania. At this time of the year snow had dressed the mountains in their winter garb, but there was no other way for Elder Peterson to reach the headquarters of the Norwegian Mission at Christiania from the west coast overland than to cross these mountains. Hence on Jan. 2, 1855, he traveled a distance of some 45 miles over the mountains on snow shoes in company with a Mr. Knud Nielsen, whom he had hired to serve him as guide and pilot him over the trackless waste on a cold blustering day. The drifting snow made the journey very dangerous and toilsome indeed, and it had a detrimental effect on Bro. Peterson's health ever after

On his arrival in Christiania, Elder Peterson assumed the presidency of the Brevig Conference.

The work of the Lord in Norway at that time was more prosperous than ever before. In Christiania the Saints held well-attended public meetings, although it was contrary to law. The police officers were friendly and said: "Let the Mormons alone, they are peaceable and well disposed; they do not make us any trouble." This friendly feeling, however, was mostly confined to Christiania, for at other places in Norway arrests and imprisonments were still the order of the day. Thus Elder Johan Johansen was arrested at Frederikstad in January, 1855, and fined 40 speciedaler, which he atoned for in prison on bread and water. A Bro. Fleisher paid ten speciedaler in the same way. Priest B. Petersen was arrested and imprisoned from Jan. 20 to March 15, 1855, five days of which he was compelled to subsist on bread and water. In March Elder Carl C. A. Christensen was arrested at Drammen and imprisoned for five days on bread and water. About the same time Elder Johan F. F. Dorius was arrested and imprisoned two and a half days, after which he was brought before the court and fined 25 speciedaler, which he atoned for on bread and water imprisonment. All these fines were imposed upon the brethren named for preaching the gospel and for baptizing.

According to a letter written by Pres. John Van Cott under date of July 15, 1855, the persecutions in Sweden were severe at that time. The brethren were continually hunted by the police, and the citizens who gladly and willingly would have treated the brethren with hospitality and kindness, dared not do so in many instances, owing to the stringent laws which existed, and the determination on the part of some of the officials to enforce them. The Lutheran clergy had the laws of Sweden practically at their command, and in order to bring trouble upon the brethren, some of the statutes which had laid dormant for ages were brought to bear upon the case of the missionaries. Thus many of the brethren were arrested and transported from one place to another, while some were fined and imprisoned. In the Skåne Conference Bro. Andreas Isgren was arrested and cast into prison; afterwards he was brought into court and sentenced to pay a heavy fine, all for no other crime than that of holding a meeting in his own house and preaching the gospel. Three other brethren, namely, Lars Larson, P. Jönson and O. Mattsson, were arrested and brought to an inn, and while in custody of the law they were abused a whole night. Some of their tormentors tried to force the missionaries to drink whisky and were also in favor of giving them a brutal thrashing, but others, more humane, prevented such actions. Two of the brethren were finally dismissed, but Bro. Larson was brought to Malmö, where he was confined in prison for several days and then set at liberty. A few days later Elder Nils Nilsson, president of the Skåne Conference, was caught by a gang of ruffians. He was threatened with personal violence, and while he was being led by two men to the same inn where other brethren had previously been abused, he, who possessed the right grit and was withal a little springy, slipped out of their hands, and as he was rather too swift on foot for them, he escaped. But in order to give vent to their spite the gang captured another brother who dwelt in that part of the country and beat him unmercifully. A Bro. C. A. Stenström was arrested near Halmstad in June, 1855, and after being imprisoned for a short time, he was transported to his home. A number of the peasantry in Sweden were also brought into court because they had allowed "Mormon" meetings to be held in their houses, and others were arrested because they had attended such meetings. The court treated them as if they were great criminals, and imposed upon them fines varying from 30 to 120 "riksdaler." On the 26th of June, Andreas Isgren was again arrested and sentenced to imprisonment on bread and water for 25 days. Elder A. Nyborg was similarly arrested and imprisoned on a bread and water diet. In the city of Malmö, where the missionaries held large meetings every Sunday for some time, the Saints were gradually increasing in number, but finally the police, through the instigation of the priests, broke up these meetings and forbade the Saints to gather in larger numbers than ten persons. The police officers also warned the local brethren against opening their houses for holding meetings, for if they did they would become subject to a fine of 300 riksdaler. This arbitrary order resulted in many small meetings being held instead of large gatherings, in order to keep within the limits of the law. In Malmö it happened frequently that some of the brethren were knocked down in the streets, while others were stoned and had their clothing torn to pieces by mobs who understood that the "Mormons" had no rights. Yet in the face of all these occurrences, many honest and upright people, who desired to serve the Lord, became converts to the restored gospel.

In the Stockholm Conference there was less persecution. During the winter and spring of 1855 Pres. John Van Cott appointed four brethren to go to the capital of Sweden and labor there. This led a number of people to investigate the work of the Lord, some of whom were baptized and a branch of the Church was organized. A number of the new converts, who were very zealous for their religion, sacrificed much to sustain it. On one occasion two of the brethren were invited by a Baptist minister to converse upon the subject of religion. When they arrived at the appointed place, they found two other Baptist ministers awaiting them, and six hours were then spent in an animated discussion of religion. The ministers, who were unable to refute the Bible truths presented by the Elders, were finally led to the conclusion that the doctrines of "Mormonism" could not be contradicted by Bible arguments.

In Denmark the missionaries and Saints enjoyed more liberty; yet in many places there was considerable persecution. Meetings were frequently broken up and many of the local brethren, who had been sent out on missions, became quite conversant with arrests and imprisonments on bread and water. In Copenhagen Conference alone upwards of twenty arrests were made in 1855. Some of the brethren were imprisoned for weeks, while others were transported to their native towns or permanent dwelling places. The arrests were generally made on the charge of vagrancy, as the civil authorities could find no other law which could reach their case.

Speaking of the faithfulness of the Elders, Elder John Van Cott writes: "Notwithstanding the power of darkness are great, and the adve sary is continually busy, through his emissaries (the hireling priests), to stop the work of the Lord, it still prospers. New places are being opened with good prospects, additions to the Church are continually being made and many are investigating the work. The brethren of the Priesthood, as a general thing, are very faithful and true in their posts. I have full confidence in them, and can bear testimony that they labor to build up the kingdom of God. They take hold unitedly, when called upon, and the co-operation of the Saints, with the good feeling which exists, and the love of God in their hearts, feeling an interest for the prosperity of his work, causes them to do all that their ability will allow. Our publications are read with interest by the Saints, as well as by many strangers, and they are doing good. We have done everything possible to circulate the printed word. And it is not a little that has been spread around during the last six months. Much labor has been performed, and testimony borne. What the fruit may be, the Lord only knows. Not so many have been added to the Church as I had expected, but, were I to judge, I would say that the mission is in a healthy and prosperous condition with good prospects ahead. In Copenhagen we have full meetings every Sunday, and have good order, too. Many strangers attend with an apparent interest."

Elder Daniel Spencer, counselor to President Samuel W. Richards of the British Mission; Joseph A. Young, eldest son of Pres. Brigham Young, and Hector C. Haight, appointed to succeed John Van Cott in the presidency of the Scandinavian Mission, arrived in Copenhagen Sept. 9, 1855, and there received a hearty reception from Pres. John Van Cott, Elder Carl Widerborg and the local Saints generally. After spending a few days in Copenhagen, the two visitors, accompanied by Pres. John Van Cott and Elder Ola N. Liljenquist, president of the Copenhagen Conference, visited some of the country branches on the island of Sjælland. On the trip several meetings were held and the American Elders had a splendid opportunity to study the habits and customs of the Danish peasantry while partaking of their unstinted hospitality. The visiting brethren were enthusiastic about the high state of the agriculture of the Danish farmers. On the trip they visited the historic city of Roskilde, where the sarcophagi of a long line of Danish kings are housed in the old cathedral.

On Sept. 19th and 20th an interesting conference was held in Copenhagen, at which the visiting brethren addressed large congregations of Saints and strangers through interpreters.

On the 24th of September, Elders Spencer and Young, accompanied by Pres. John Van Cott, left Copenhagen on a visit to Sweden. Landing at Göteborg, where there were no Saints at that time, the brethren took the canal route through the heart of Sweden to Stockholm, where they arrived on the 28th. There they found a branch of the Church numbering eighteen members, and the visiting brethren attended several meetings, held in private houses, as the laws of Sweden at that time forbade the assembling of more than ten persons at one place. The few Saints rejoiced exceedingly to have the American Elders visit them, and a few specially invited friends, who could be trusted, also enjoyed the powerful testimonies borne in these small meetings. After visiting the Saints, and taking in the sights of the Swedish capital, the Elders returned to

Copenhagen by steamer, landing on the way at Ystad. Although there were a few Saints in that little city, the visiting brethren had no time to look them up and so, after landing, they retired to the hills, a short distance from the city, and knelt before the Lord in prayer for his blessing upon the people of Sweden, pleading to the Lord to open the way so that his servants in the near future might be permitted to preach the gospel unmolested. The brethren arrived at Copenhagen Oct. 6th and, after attending a council meeting in that city, and also arranging matters of importance in the interest of the Scandinavian Mission, Elders Daniel Spencer and Joseph A. Young sailed from Copenhagen Oct. 11, 1855, returning to England. They were exceedingly well pleased with their visit to Scandinavia.

CHAPTER 25 (1855)

Another large company of emigrating Saints leaves Copenhagen—A general mission conference held in Denmark—Fyen Conference organized—Summary of Pres. John Van Cott's mission to Scandinavia.

On Thursday, Nov. 29, 1855, a company of Scandinavian Saints numbering 447 souls sailed from Copenhagen, on board the steamship "Löven," bound for Utah, under the direction of Elder Canute Peterson, who returned from his mission to Norway. After a pleasant voyage, Kiel, in Holstein, was reached, and thence the emigrants continued their journey by rail to Gluckstadt, thence by steamer to Grimsby, England, and thence by rail to Liverpool, where the Scandinavian emigrants were joined by 42 British and 30 Italian Saints, and went on board the ship "John J. Boyd."

Elder Charles R. Savage, one of the emigrating missionaries, gives the following report of the voyage:

"We left Liverpool on Wednesday, Dec. 12th, 1855, at 7 a. m. and had a fine run down the channel, sighted Cape Clear on the Friday morning following, and had mild weather with a fair wind for three days after. During this time we had leisure to devise plans for the maintenance of order and cleanliness during the voyage. Notwithstanding that our company consisted of Danes, Norwegians, Swedes, Icelanders, Italians, English, Irish and Scotch, the rules adopted proved efficient in maintaining a strict *entente cordiale* among us all. The Saints were by the sound of the trumpet called to prayer morning and evening. Meetings were also frequently held in the Danish, English and Italian languages during the voyage. On the whole we enjoyed ourselves first-rate, notwithstanding the gales and hurricanes we experienced, from the breaking up of the fine weather in longitude 15 degrees to our anchoring off Sandy Hook.

"About midway on our passage we fell in with the clipper ship "Louis Napoleon," from Baltimore to Liverpool, laden with flour, with all her masts and spars carried away and leeward bulwarks stove in; upon nearing the ship we found her in a sinking condition. The captain and crew desired to be taken off, which was done. This acquisition was of great advantage to us, as the bad weather, sickness and exhaustion from overwork had made quite a gap in our complement of sailors. We had much sickness on board from the breaking out of the measles, which caused many deaths among the Danish, chiefly among the children. In the English and Italian companies we lost three children. The weather got worse after crossing the Banks, so much so, that we were driven into the Gulf Stream three times, and many of our sailors were frost-bitten. Our captain got superstitious on account of the long passage and ordered that there should be no singing on board; the mate said that all ships that had preachers on board were always sure of a bad passage; however, the Lord heard our prayers, and ·in his own due time we arrived at our destination. On the evening of the 15th of February we were safely anchored, having been 66 days out from Liverpool.

"Our supply of water was almost exhausted. We had on our arrival only about one day's water on board. The provisions were very good and proved abundant to the last. On our taking the pilot on board he informed us that there had been many disasters during the months of January and February; many ships had been wrecked.

We had made the passage without the loss of a single spar."

On the 16th of February, 1856, the emigrants landed in New York, and after tarrying a few days at Castle Garden, the journey was continued on the 21st or 22nd by rail via Dunkirk and Cleveland to Chicago, where the company, according to previous arrangements, was divided into three parts, of which one, consisting of about 150 souls, went to Burlington, Iowa, another to Alton, Illinois, and a third to St. Louis, Mo. Most of those who went to Burlington and Alton remained in those places, or near them, a year or more, working to earn means wherewith to continue the journey to Utah. The part of the company which went to St. Louis arrived in that city on the 10th of March and soon afterwards proceeded to Florence, Nebraska, where they joined the general emigration that crossed the Plains in 1856.

Elder Chr. Christiansen, who was sent as a missionary from Utah to preside over the Scandinavian Saints in the Western States, relates the following about the emigrants who stopped in Burlington:

"On the 29th of February, 1856, about 150 Scandinavian emigrants arrived in Burlington, Iowa, to be placed under my jurisdiction, as they, through lack of means, were unable to continue the journey to Utah that year. I assisted them in the transportation of their luggage across the Mississippi River on the ice, and brought them to a house belonging to an apostate 'Mormon' by the name of Thomas Arthur, of whom I had hired a room for the accommodation of the emigrants—the only one I could secure in the whole town. On that day the editors of the Burlington papers announced to the public the startling fact that the town had been 'taken' by the 'Mormons.' Without friends or money I stood in the midst of my poor brethren, not knowing what to do; but I set to work in earnest and succeeded in finding employment for some of the brethren as wood choppers in the country,

where I also rented a number of empty cabins for the Saints, who subsisted on corn meal, bacon and other articles of food which they received as advance payment for their labors. For the young men and women I also secured places as servants, and in Burlington alone I found places for 50 of them. I also hired wagons and took some of the emigrants to Montrose and Keokuk in search of employment. Thus, in less than a week after the arrival of the emigrants at Burlington, all who were able to work had found something to do. But there was a number of other persons who needed financial aid, and as I had no money I approached one of the emigrants who had a twenty dollar gold piece, but he was an unbeliever and refused to lend his money to me, or anyone else, even for the relief of the sick. A few days later he died, and his widow promptly advanced me the means; thus I secured the necessary medicines and other things needed by the sufferers. My next step was to organize the Saints into branches of the Church, over which I appointed presidents. After a little while everything went well, and in a remarkably short time the emigrants earned means enough to continue their journey to the Valley."

On Thursday, Dec. 27, 1855, and the three following days, a general conference of the Scandinavian Mission was held in Copenhagen, Pres. John Van Cott presiding. Among those present were Elder Hector C. Haight from Zion, who was to succeed John Van Cott in the presidency of the Mission. Elders from different parts of the mission and a good-sized congregation of local Saints were present. Owing to the cessation of steamship traffic during the dead of winter, some of the presiding Elders from Norway and Sweden could not be present.

At the first meeting Elder Ola N. Liljenquist, president of the Copenhagen Conference, reported that the police officers had arrested a few of the brethren under the pretense that they had no passports, and on this pretext, Bro. Gudmund Gudmundson had been imprisoned for some time, while Bro. Jens Madsen had been sent to Jutland and Bro. Nils P. Lindelöf to Sweden. But this opposition on the part of the police officers had not impeded the work at all, but rather helped the Elders in gaining influence among the people. Elder Chr. D. Fjeldsted, who had labored as traveling Elder on Sjælland, and other Elders had rendered Pres. Liljenquist great assistance. New fields of labor had been opened, but the inhabitants of Copenhagen were, as a rule, less inclined to accept the gospel than the country people, and also rendered greater opposition. Elder Chr. A. Madsen had been compelled to leave Præstö on account of mob violence.

Elder Johan Svenson, president of the Lolland Conference, reported that the Lord has blessed the Lolland Conference greatly and the Elders had labored with great diligence and considerable success. Nearly every town on the island of Lolland had been visited by the Elders, and quite a number had joined the Church. The Saints, who lived in a scattered condition, were, as a rule, very hospitable and kind to the brethren. Two of the Elders had been arrested on a trumped-up charge in the western part of Lolland, but during their imprisonment they had a splendid opportunity of preaching the gospel to the guards, of which one, together with his wife, soon afterwards was baptized. The officers had also sought to arrest Bro. Johan Svenson, but the Lord had, on different occasions, protected him from lawless mobs, against which the officers in the past had neglected to render protection. However, the mob violence during the past two years had been less frequent than formerly. Yet only quite recently Elder Jens Jensen was handled so roughly by the mob that his life was despaired of.

The labor in the conference demanded more missionaries.

In the afternoon meeting, Elder Chr. G. Larsen, president of the Bornholm Conference, reported that the Saints on the island of Bornholm were doing well. Nearly every city and village on the island had been visited by the Elders.

Elder Jens Jörgensen, president of the Fredericia conference, said that the Elders in his field of labor, had been successful in circulating the printed word among the people, and had obtained a good foothold in most of the cities along the east coast of Jutland. Recently a new branch had been organized on the island of Fyen. A hall for holding meetings had been hired in Odense.

Bro. Jens Jensen, traveling Elder on Lolland, gave a detailed account of how he had recently been handled by a lawless mob. The mobbers seemed to have no respect for either God or the authorities.

The conference was continued on Friday, Dec. 28th, when two meetings were held, at which a number of the Elders gave reports showing splendid progress in the respective missionary districts.

The next day, (Dec. 29th) Elder Johannes and Lauritz Larsen, who had just arrived, reported. Elder Johannes Larsen, president of the Aalborg Conference, brought greetings from the Saints in his field of labor, where he had met with success during the past three years. Some of the brethren who labored as missionaries in his conference had been arrested, but as the police had found no cause against them, they had been liberated. Elder Lauritz Larsen, president of the Vendsyssel Conference, who spoke in the afternoon meeting, testified that many in the northern part of Jutland had been rought from darkness into the light nd now basked in the full sunlight f the restored gospel.

By request, Elder Johan A. Ahman- on made an attempt to speak to ae assembly in English, a task which e filled to the great satisfaction of ll, considering the little opportunity e had had to study the English lan- uage. President Van Cott gave this ractical demonstration to show the candianavian Saints how easy they ould acquire the English language –that language in which the Lord ad revealed his will in these last ays. He recommended to the Saints ae study of English and all present oted heartily in favor of that propo- ition.

Pres. John Van Cott spoke a num- er of times in the conference meet- ngs, and so did Brother Hector C. Iaight, whose speeches in English ere translated.

This interesting conference closed ith well-attended meetings on Sun- ay, Dec. 30th, at which President ohn Van Cott referred to the dili- ence of Elder Johan A. Ahmanson, hom he nominated as traveling El- er in the whole mission. * * El- er Ola N. Liljenquist was then ustained as president of the Copen- agen Conference, Lauritz Larsen f the Vendsyssel, Jens Jörgensen of ae Fredericia, Chr. G. Larsen of the Bornholm, Carl C. A. Christensen f the Brevig, Åke Jönsson of the tockholm, and Nils Nilsson of the kåne Conference. It was then de- ided by vote that the islands of yen and Langeland should be sep- rated from the Fredericia Confer- nce and organized into a separate onference to be called the Fyen Con- erence, with Elder Peter Nielsen as resident. Elder Johan Svenson as released from presiding over the olland Conference with permission

to emigrate to Zion and Elder Jens Jensen appointed his s u c c e s s o r. Johannes Larsen was released as president of the Aalborg Conference, with permission to emigrate, and Elder Christian D. Fjeldsted ap- pointed his successor.

In the afternoon of that day, Pres. John Van Cott delivered his farewell address. In all the meetings there was a rich outpouring of the spirit of the Lord and the hearts of the Saints were made to rejoice.

Speaking of this conference, Pres- ident John Van Cott wrote the fol- lowing:

"The reports of the presidents and travel- ing Elders were, altogether, of a favorable nature. The spirit of peace and union pre- vailed among the Saints; there was a universal willingness on their part to give heed to the teachings of those who were appointed to preside over them. They in- creased in faith and understanding, and improved upon every means within their reach to gain information in the things pertaining to their salvation and were, as a general thing, willing to do all in their power to help extending the work of the Lord, and roll forth his kingdom on the earth.

"The Priesthood were united, and felt in a great degree the responsibility that rested upon them; consequently, they labored with much zeal and perseverance. The willing and obedient spirit which they manifested clearly showed that the spirit of Zion was with them. Through the blessings of the Lord, and the faithful labors of the Priest- hood, the Scandinavian Mission has pros- pered. I feel to express the gratitude of my heart to them and to all the Saints, for their confidence and united co-operation to extend the kingdom of God in these north- ern countries.

"The Saints gladly received Elder Haight as their president, and agreed to sustain and uphold him as such. He expressed much satisfaction in finding the mission, with its financial affairs, in a prosperous condition; and felt to enter upon his labors with joy and satisfaction. He was making considerable progress in the language."

President John Van Cott left Co- penhagen, January 29, 1856, to re- turn to his home in Utah. He had gained the love and confidence of the Scandinavian Saints who reluctantly said goodbye to him. After his arrival in England, he wrote quite a lengthy report of his missionary experience in Scandinavia, of which the following is extracted:

"In consequence of the sudden death of our beloved brother, Elder Willard Snow, who presided over the Scandinavian Mission, it became necessary that someone should be appointed to preside in his stead. Pres. Samuel W. Richards and his counselor, Elder Daniel Spencer, lost no time in taking the matter into consideration, the result of which led to my appointment as president for the time being, or until otherwise directed by the Twelve, or the First Presidency in Zion. I immediately repaired to the field of my labors and landed in Copenhagen, Sept. 4, 1853. Unexpectedly, and for reasons as yet unknown to me, I was continued in that field of labor until the 1st of January, 1856, making about two years and three months' residence there, instead of a short time, as was first contemplated.

"The time, although apparently long, has appeared a very short time to me, owing, I presume, to a multiplicity of business and care. Notwithstanding my lot was cast in a foreign land, among a people whose language I was at first unacquainted with, I have labored with a great deal of satisfaction. I have witnessed the gradual progress of the work of the Lord. The Holy Spirit has accompanied the word and borne witness of the truth. It has strengthened and sustained the servants of the Lord on trying occasions, and enabled them to combat opposing powers, and come off triumphant."
* *

"Many of the Elders engaged in the ministry have had to endure much. The enemy of all righteousness has been on the alert, and has resorted to almost every possible means to hinder the spread of the work of the Lord.

"In Denmark there has been a universal and almost simultaneous effort made to prevent our Elders from preaching and from traveling to circulate the printed word. The practice was to arrest them as vagrants, or for any other supposed offense, such as a defect in their pass, etc. * *
Last fall the authorities arrested Elder Jens Madsen, and sent him to Jutland. He was afterwards appointed to labor in the Vendsyssel Conference. Elder Lindelöf was arrested, ill-treated and then sent to

Sweden. At our General Conference which was held soon after, he was appointed to labor in Göteborg. I had previously contemplated sending him there, and afterwards learned that he had desired for a long time, to go there and labor consequently, that which the authorities designed as evil has resulted in good Elder Gudmundson was arrested and imprisoned for several weeks, and no one was allowed to speak to him except the officer that had him in charge; finally he was sentenced to serve as a soldier for four years and commenced to serve his time in the latter part of December (1855) at the garrison in Copenhagen.

"In the Lolland Conference there has been considerable persecution. Some of the people are so very bad that they do not appear to have respect for either God or the authorities of the land; consequently the servants of the Lord have often been abused. A traveling Elder, Jens Jensen was attacked by a mob and beaten until they supposed he was dead. While lying in a helpless condition, yet conscious of what was transpiring, the mob were consulting upon the best way to dispose of him, but his friends came to his rescue. The parties who had treated him thus were arrested, and a doctor called to Brother Jensen, who, after examining his wound pronounced him mortally wounded, and certified to the magistrate to that effect The doctor prescribed for him, but he declined taking anything. He resorted to the ordinances of the gospel, from which he derived immediate relief, and finally was restored to health and soundness, but not left without scars.

"The magistrates, upon investigating the matter, became quite indignant at those who had perpetrated such a crime, and assured them that they should suffer the full penalty of the law, which, no doubt from last accounts will be the case.

"Several other Elders there met with very narrow escapes from those who sought their injury. Doors and windows were broken open, and the brethren hunted as though they were wild beasts. A traveling Elder by the name of Sören Peter Gul had his life threatened repeatedly. The mob sought by night to waylay him as he traveled from one branch to another; one night, supposing that they had him for certain, they nearly killed a man not in the Church. I mention this circumstance as one of many wherein the servants of the Lord have been shielded from the power of their enemies, and in which the evil designed fell upon the heads of those who, perhaps, deserved it. Since the things have transpired there, the Elders have gone forth with renewed vigor and strength, relying more fully upon the arm of the Almighty who has thus delivered them. They stand forth boldly, and bear testimony of the truth, and the Spirit accompanies the word to the conviction of many of the honest-hearted.

"In the month of August last (1855), Elder Nils Nilsson, the president of the Skåne Conference, Sweden, was arrested when out in the conference a day's journey from Malmö. He was chained hand and foot, placed on a two-wheeled cart, beside a thief, and brought to Malmö. At every stopping place on the way, it was made known that he was a 'Mormon' Elder; consequently he was made an object of ridicule and abuse. The police had his hair cut short, and cast him into prison at Malmö, from which he obtained his release in a few days.

"The authorities being more rigid during the summer, the Saints there were not allowed to hold public meetings, as they had previously done; but notwithstanding all this, they could not stop the spirit of inquiry. The Spirit of the Lord was at work upon the honest, who were seeking for the truth, and the Elders were doing all that was possible, in their limited sphere, to enlighten the minds of the people. Finally, the Lord softened the hearts of the authorities, so that the Saints commenced holding public meetings again without molestation. Many strangers attended, and the work of the Lord extended with renewed vigor. During the last half year, 78 were baptized in the conference, and the prospect for the future spread of the work was extremely good.

"The work at Stockholm exhibited a favorable aspect, many were investigating the subject of 'Mormonism' and more were favorably disposed. Two Elders had been appointed to Göteborg, and from last accounts the prospect was good for establishing the work there.

"In behalf of the Saints of Norway and Sweden, I addressed a petition to their King, Oscar I. The object of this petition was the attainment of *religious liberty*, praying that His Majesty would grant to his subjects, belonging to the Church of Jesus Christ of Latter-day Saints, the right to administer the ordinances of the gospel according to the New Testament. Could the Saints but have that right, the work in those lands would break forth on the right and left, for there are thousands of honest in heart there.

"In Norway the work has prospered and gradually increased under the wise counsels of Elder Canute Peterson, who has labored faithfully in that land almost three years. He was released to return to his family in Zion, and to take charge of the Saints that emigrated in November last. He had the faith, confidence and blessing of the Saints. Elder Carl C. A. Christensen was appointed to succeed him in the presidency of the work in Norway." * *

"While I have been in Scandinavia, two conferences and 31 branches of the Church have been organized. * * Elder Carl Widerborg has labored faithfully in the office at Copenhagen since September, 1854. He has given perfect satisfaction, and the Lord has blessed him in the discharge of his duties. * *

"Elder Johan A. Ahmanson has labored in the mission generally, under my direction. He has been faithful and obedient, has magnified his calling, and been the means of doing much good."

CHAPTER 26 (1856)

Hector C. Haight presides—Another emigration—Scandinavian Saints cross the Plains with handcarts—President Haight's first report.

With the beginning of the year 1856, Elder Hector C. Haight took charge of the Scandinavian Mission, succeeding Elder John Van Cott.

HECTOR C. HAIGHT

Born Jan. 17, 1810, in Windham, Green Co., New York, baptized in 1845, went to Utah in 1847, and died in Farmington, Davis Co., Utah, June 26, 1879.

The new year opened with a very promising outlook for the spread of the gospel in Norway. New fields were being worked by faithful missionaries, both Norwegian and Danish, but after the departure of Elder Canute Peterson in October, 1855, Norway was left without Utah Elders for several years. Christiania was still the most flourishing branch in that country, and the prospects were also very good in Drammen and environments, where Niels Chr. Poulsen, a Danish Elder, labored with much success.

New Year's Day was observed as a fast day by the Saints in Christiania and good meetings were held, attended by many strangers, who exhibited much interest in the testimonies and sermons of the brethren.

On Wednesday, April 23, 1856, under the leadership of Elder Johan A. Ahmanson, 161 emigrating Saints bound for Utah, sailed from Copenhagen per steamship "Rhoda." The route taken by this company of emigrants was by steamer to Kiel, by railroad to Hamburg, by steamer to Grimsby in England and by railroad to Liverpool. The company arrived safe and well at Liverpool, April 29th.

On Sunday, May 4, 163 Scandinavian emigrants sailed from Liverpool per ship "Thornton," together with about 600 Saints from Great Britain. The whole company was placed in charge of Elder James G. Willie with Millen G. Atwood, Johan A. Ahmanson and Moses Cluff as his assistants. During the voyage Captain Collins showed himself a considerate and pleasant gentleman, as he allowed the emigrants all the liberty and privileges which could be expected, and praised them for their cleanliness and good order, and also for their willingness to conform to

all his requests. He also gave th Elders unlimited liberty to preac and hold meetings on board, and, to gether with the ship's doctor an other officers, he listened repeatedl to the preaching by the Elders an occasionally joined them in singin the songs of Zion. Considerabl sickness prevailed among the em grants, of whom quite a number wei old and feeble. Seven deaths (amon which two Scandinavian children three births and two marriages too place on board.

On Saturday, June 14th, the beaut ful ship "Thornton" arrived at Ne York, and a little steam tug brougl the emigrants to Castle Garde where they were heartily received b Apostle John Taylor and Elder N thaniel H. Felt. On the 17th of Jur the emigrants left New York an traveling by rail arrived at Dunkir Ohio, on the 19th. Here they wei on board the steamship "Jersey City and sailed to Toledo, where the arrived on the 21st. The followin day they were in Chicago, Ill. Toledo, the emigrants were treated a most unfriendly manner by tl railroad men and in consequeno were subjected to much unpleasan ness. On the 23rd the company le Chicago in two divisions, of whic the one started a few hours befoi the other. At Pond Creek it wა ascertained that the bridge at Roc Island had tumbled down while railway train was passing over i Apostle Erastus Snow and oth brethren from Utah happened to l on board when the accident ha pened, but they escaped unhurt. Tl emigrants left Pond Creek on tl 26th and arrived the same day Iowa City, Iowa, which at that tin contained about 3,000 inhabitan and was the western terminus of tl railroad. The place had been chose

by the Church emigration agents that
year as an outfitting place for the
Latter-day Saint emigrants who crossed the Plains. In order that as many
of the poor Saints as possible should
get the opportunity of emigrating at
a small expense, the First Presidency
of the Church had suggested in their
13th general epistle, which was dated
in Salt Lake City, Oct. 29, 1855, that
the emigrants who in 1856 were assisted to emigrate to Zion by the
Perpetual Emigrating Fund should
cross the Plains with handcarts. Consequently this cheaper but difficult
method of traveling was tried for
the first time. The first handcart
company, under the direction of Elder Edmund Ellsworth, left Iowa
City, June 9, 1856. About 100 Scandinavian emigrants constituted the
fifth division of the fourth company
of the handcart emigration which,
under the direction of James G. Willie, left Iowa City, July 16th. John
A. Ahmanson was appointed leader
of the Scandinavian division.

After almost untold suffering and
hardships this company of handcart
emigrants arrived in Salt Lake City
Nov. 9, 1856. About sixty of the
emigrants died on the journey across
the plains, among whom were a number of Scandinavian Saints.

On Monday, June 23, Pres. Hector
C. Haight and Elder Carl Widerborg
left Copenhagen for England to attend a grand council meeting, which
was held in Birmingham, July 21st,
22nd and 23rd, 1856. This council
meeting was attended by nearly all
the presiding Elders of the European
missions, and President Haight was
able to give a very favorable report
of the Scandinavian Mission. Under
date of July 10, 1856, while in England, he reported as follows:

"The Scandinavian Mission was in a prosperous condition when I, on the 1st of
January, 1856, succeeded Elder John Van

Cott, whose faithful labor is duly felt and
appreciated by the Saints, and my efforts
have been to keep that good order which
I found established, and, furthermore, to
promote the cause wherein I am engaged.
I can truly say that the Lord has blessed
my feeble efforts in all things; and I
am also happy to say, that the Priesthood,
with few exceptions, have faithfully carried out the instructions given, and the
Saints generally have been obedient and
done with willingness what has been required at their hands, and facilitated my
labor in so doing. The traveling Priesthood, especially, have sometimes much to
combat, in consequence of the opposition,
which, in many places, occasionally breaks
out in persecution, imprisonment, mobbing,
etc., on account of the illiberal laws, or
rather an intolerant clergy, urging the
civil authorities and people to rather in-
human conduct towards the Saints, especially in Sweden.

"Scandinavia, consisting of three different kingdoms, though peopled by kindred
nations, which are living under different
institutions of government, presents three
different phases which the servants of the
Lord have to study, and in each of those
lands they have to go forth with all that
cautiousness and wisdom which experience,
faithfulness and the guidance of the Holy
Spirit will impart.

"Denmark, having a liberal constitution,
has hitherto maintained its pre-eminence in
the Scandinavian Mission. It affords missionaries to the other parts, especially the
Copenhagen Branch, which numbers 800
members, and is headquarters, wherein
the Elders can take refuge in times of
trouble and persecution. There the Saints
enjoy more freedom than throughout the
country, where, in many places, the authorities try to stop the Elders from spreading
the truth by applying a law which pro-
hibits anybody from traveling without a
passport, or to stay in any place without
being an official character, or driving some
business or trade. The applying of this
law sometimes causes the Elders to be imprisoned or sent back to their respective
homes. They seek to avoid such emer-
gencies by procuring a passport when they
can get it, which is not always the case, or
else by hiring themselves out as servants,
as in this manner they gain protection.

"An effort of another kind, to prevent
or stop the progress of the kingdom of God
in Denmark, has been made in the Lolland
and Falster diocese, by a chamberlain,
Esquire Wickfeldt, who presented a petition to the king, invoking that measures

8

may be taken to stop that awful delusion, 'Mormonism.' Said petition was signed by several hundreds of the peasantry, and when it was handed to his Majesty the King, by a deputation, he answered in a courteous manner 'that he would take the matter into consideration, as it had been a long time upon his mind.' This undertaking has brought forth an interesting article in the leading paper of the democratic party, the editor of which took a stand against the issue of the unconstitutional petition, showing Wickfeldt and the signers thereof their ignorance of certain paragraphs in the constitution, and ridiculing them for taking a step against their own interest and religious liberty, misguided by the influence of the said Wickfeldt; advising them to keep the constitution sacred and inviolate and leave it to the learned and well-paid clergy to carry on the war against the 'Mormons' with spiritual weapons. 'For,' said he, 'if the brethren priesthood cannot defend the State Church, and the principles thereof, without the help of the police authorities, then let it fall to the ground.' * *

"Concerning the mission in Norway, I can also say, with great satisfaction, that the Elders who labor there are doing exceedingly well. Elder Carl C. A. Christensen, who was appointed to succeed Elder Canute Peterson, as president, has managed very wisely. The gospel is pressing forward and beginning to gain entrance into several new places, through the faithfulness and perseverance of the brethren, who willingly and gladly suffer imprisonment, now and then, rather than give up their preaching and baptizing. The authorities are somewhat tolerant, especially in Christiania; and, even in executing the laws, they treat the Elders with some degree of respect and humanity. Fifty-six members have been added to the Church in Norway during the past half year.

"In Sweden the State Church and the clergy have so great an influence, supported by the old intolerant laws, and the strict and rigid executors of the same, that the people are living under fear and bondage, and have no religious liberty, which makes it very difficult to spread the gospel. The Elders in that land have indeed a hard mission; nevertheless it seems as if the Lord, having mercy on scattered Israel in that country, has operated upon the minds of the people, so that a desire for religious liberty is awakened with full force, and different parties and sects have arisen, especially in Stockholm, and the members thereof petition the government for free religious worship. Among the parties

which have made the greatest progress a the Baptists; they, as it were, break t way for other dissenters, and I believe th the Legislature in the next Riksdag w have to discuss the subject of religio liberty. Under these movements our E ders have also labored in Stockholm, Skån and other places, with more or less succes and the branch in the capital is increasin The police, being aware of the progre of the work, brought the Elders before t court, and finding that the president the Stockholm Conference, Elder Christi A. Madsen, was a Dane, and had no oth employment than preaching the gospe they banished him and sent him to Cope hagen in May. I immediately appointe several Elders, who are mechanics, a natives of Sweden, to go to Stockholm ar other places, and secure their stay, in th first place, by taking labor, or hiring o to men, who drive some kind of busines and thus protected labor in the gospel the circumstances will allow. Working this manner, and by spreading the writte word, I hope that, by and by, many plac will be opened for the gospel in that lan as the people in general are very desiro to hear and read. Notwithstanding t unfavorable circumstances, there were ba tized in Sweden, in the past half year, persons.

"As a fair specimen of the present pos tion in Sweden, I will mention, that I, company with Elder Carl Widerborg, ma a trip over the Baltic to Malmö, in Skån to attend a conference meeting, on th 28th of March, not neglecting to procu our passports. The police in Malmö, bein informed by some of our enemies, that the was a meeting of the Saints, came in ar broke up the meeting, and the Saints we obliged to disperse. The police took o names and then left, but soon returned search of us, which we avoided. In t afternoon, Brother Carl Widerborg got o passport signed for the return the next da and went in the evening at 8 o'cloc with the president of the Skåne Conferenc Elder Nils Nilsson, to a place out of th town to finish up the business of the co ference. Feeling safe, as we had got ou passport signed, I stayed in the conferenc house, but a few minutes after the bret ren had left the police came and carrie me as a prisoner to the police office; ar as Bro. Widerborg had the passport wit him, I had to remain in custody until h came to my relief, which was about tw hours. We were permitted to leave th town the next day without further molesta tion. * *

"I have issued a second edition of the 'Voice of Warning' in Danish, also of the book of 'Doctrine and Covenants,' and added to the same the Lectures on Faith, and the alphabetical index, so that now the Danish edition contains the same as the English. In these and other labors in the office I have been faithfully assisted by Elder Carl Widerborg. As the labor was considerably increased, I found it necessary, in April, to call to our assistance in the office a young brother from Norway, Peter Olof Thomassen, who, if he continues as he has begun, bids fair to be a useful laborer. I can also say that Elder Ola N. Liljenquist and the presidents of the several conferences have been faithful, and one with me in our efforts to roll forth the kingdom of God. I consider it a great blessing and privilege to preside over so good a people, and my greatest desire is, by the aid of the Spirit of the Lord, to bless them and do them good.

"The Scandinavian Saints are very anxious to emigrate and be gathered with the Saints in Zion, where they can be more fully instructed in the way of life and salvation. They rejoice in the newly adopted mode of emigration with handcarts, seeing that so many more can yearly be delivered from the land of oppression, and they are not at all afraid of the trip over the Plains.

"The most favorable season for our emigrants to leave Copenhagen seems to be in the spring, instead of the autumn, as far as I can judge, all things taken into consideration, the long and more dangerous journey over the sea in the winter, the expense of their support in the western countries, provided they should not obtain labor, and the bad influence on their health in a foreign clime, if they should have to stay some months before they could continue their journey."

CHAPTER 27 (1856)

Visit of Apostle Ezra T. Benson and Elder John M. Kay—The law of tithing introduced—statistical report.

Apostle Ezra T. Benson and Elder John M. Kay arrived in Copenhagen Sept. 10, 1856, on a short visit from England and received a hearty reception from Pres. Hector C. Haight and the brethren in Copenhagen. This was the second time the Scandinavian Mission was visited by an Apostle since Erastus Snow left in February, 1852. Hence the presence of Brother Benson, and also of Bro. Kay, who was a fine singer, caused the Saints to rejoice greatly.

APOSTLE EZRA TAFT BENSON

Born Feb. 22, 1811, in Mendon, Worcester County, Mass.; died Sept. 3, 1869, in Ogden, Utah.

On the following Sunday (Sept. 14th) a very well-attended meeting was held in a large hall in Copenhagen, where Apostle Ezra T. Benson spoke in English, with Elder Carl Widerborg as translator. On this occasion, the Copenhagen Branch was divided into four separate branches to be known respectively as the Copenhagen East Branch, the Copenhagen West Branch, the Nörrebro Branch and the Christianshavn Branch.

On the 17th, Apostle Ezra T. Benson, Pres. Hector C. Haight and Elders John M. Kay and Carl Widerborg sailed from Copenhagen for Göteborg, Sweden, whence they traveled on the canal route to Stockholm, where they arrived on the 23rd. Here they were received with open arms by the Swedish Elders and Saints. The visiting brethren were delighted with the beauties of Sweden and its capital. After attending meetings in Stockholm, the brethren returned by way of Ystad, Sweden, arriving at

Copenhagen, Sept. 29th. On Saturday, Oct. 4th, these same brethren left Copenhagen on a visit to the conferences in Jutland, Denmark. They attended interesting conferences in Veile and Aalborg, and returned to Copenhagen on the 12th. After that, Apostle Benson and the other Elders attended meetings with several of the branches on the island of Sjælland, and finally left Copenhagen for England, Oct. 14, 1856.

The following is extracted from the report written by Apostle Benson and Elder Kay after their return to England:

"We attended meeting in Copenhagen in a large and commodious hall and preached to about 1000 people. * * * At Göteborg, Sweden, we went to the house of Elder Frantz Theo. Grönberg, the president of the branch. He had all the Saints in the branch, numbering seven souls, and about five strangers, who were friendly, invited to his house in the afternoon. While we were engaged in prayer together, we heard the noise of persons coming into the room, but paid no attention to it, until we had done praying, when we found three large policemen in our company. The first, after talking to Brother Grönberg, took a seat at the table, wrote down all our names and demanded our passports. One brother living a few miles away, who had no passport, they took to the police station, and ordered the rest of us to disperse. After they had gone, we stayed a short time, comforting the Saints, while we were bidding them farewell and laying hands on a sick child by the desire of its mother, who was not in the Church. The newspapers noticed the circumstance of our meeting and said the young man who was taken up was so full of "Mormonism" that he preached it before the police court. Before leav-

ing Göteborg, we laid hands on Brother Grönberg and blessed him. He had been before the police many times for preaching the gospel, but he feels more determined than ever. On the 19th of Sept., we set sail up the Götha River, across the country for Stockholm. The scenery on the trip between Göteborg and Stockholm was extremely grand and beautiful. There are 75 locks and 7 lakes to pass through. * * * * Stockholm is a beautiful place. It is built on seven islands and is rendered still more interesting by its splendid buildings, rich groves of timber, and fine bay intersected with islands. * * * * We attended meeting on the 24th and addressed the Saints who met together, numbering 30. Brother Widerborg acted as interpreter."

After his return to England, Apostle Ezra T. Benson, in a letter written to President John Taylor under date of Nov. 26, 1856, writes:

"Since my arrival in this country I have visited the Scandinavian Mission, in company with Elder John M. Kay. * * * * President Haight enjoys richly the spirit of his mission and has the full faith and confidence of the Saints. We spent about six weeks, and traveled through most of the conferences in that mission, visited Sweden and Denmark, and had many happy seasons with the Saints.

"The Saints composing the Scandinavian Mission are not of the wealthiest portion of the community but they are rich in faith and ready and willing to do all they can to further the interests of the Kingdom. The Elders are under much restraint in preaching the gospel and are often cast into prison, but they are determined under all circumstances to call upon their countrymen to repent of their sins and be reconciled to God through obedience to his will."

During the last three months of the

year 1856, the law of tithing was introduced among the Saints in Scandinavia. A number of articles treating on the subject and nature of that principle were published in "Skandinaviens Stjerne," and the traveling Priesthood gave the necessary counsel and advise in the conferences held in the different parts of the mission, and also in the general meetings of the Saints as well as in private conversation. Most of the Saints accepted the law willingly and the Scandinavian Saints, generally speaking, have, since that time both in the old countries and after their arrival in the mountains, been numbered among those members of the Church who have been most conscientious and punctual in their adherance to the law of tithing.

The statistical report of the Scandinavian Missions for the year 1856 showed that during that year 575 persons had been baptized, viz., 367 in Denmark, 153 in Sweden and 65 in Norway. The mission consisted of 10 conferences of which 7, namely, Copenhagen, with 19 branches, Aalborg with 10 branches, Vendsyssel with 12 branches, Fredericia with 8 branches, Lolland with 8 branches, Bornholm with 4 branches, and Fyen with 4 branches, were in Denmark; one, namely, Brevig with 8 branches, in Norway, and two, Skåne, with 13 branches, and Stockholm with 7 branches, in Sweden. The Priesthood in the mission was represented by 1 Seventy, 310 Elders, 118 Priests, 118 Teachers and 73 Deacons. The organized branches in the mission now numbered 94, of which 66 were in Denmark, 8 in Norway and 20 in Sweden.

CHAPTER 28. (1857)

Change of officers in the Scandinavian Mission—A general reformation takes place—English schools established in the mission—Many new branches organized.

"Skandinaviens Stjerne" of Jan. 1,

1857, announced several changes, releases and appointments which were intended to go into effect at the beginning of the new year. The following Elders were released, with permission to emigrate to America: Carl C. A. Christensen, Ola N. Liljenquist, Lauritz Larsen, Chr. G. Larsen, Jens Jörgensen and Jens Svendsen. These Elders had all labored long and faithfully in the ministry. The following appointments were made: Elder Niels Wilhelmsen to take the pastoral charge of the Copenhagen, the Lolland and the Bornholm conferences, Elder Hans P. Lund to succeed Elder Carl C. A. Christensen as president of the Brevig conference in Norway, Elder Lars Eriksen to succeed Elder Ola N. Liljenquist as president of the Copenhagen Conference, Elder Peter A. Fjeldsted to succeed Lauritz Larsen as president of the Vendsyssel Conference, Elder Christoffer O. Folkmann to succeed Elder

CHRISTOFFER OLSEN FOLKMANN

Born Feb. 8, 1827, on Bornholm, Denmark; baptized Nov. 29, 1851; labored as a missionary in Denmark about six years, and emigrated to Utah in 1858. He filled two missions from Utah to Scandinavia (1865-1868 and 1886-1888), and died at Farr West, Weber Co., Utah, Nov. 14, 1915.

Jens Jörgensen as president of the Fredericia Conference, Elder Mads Jörgensen to succeed Elder Jens Jensen as president of the Lolland Conference, and Elder Hans Jensen to succeed Elder Chr. G. Larsen as president of the Bornholm Conference.

About this time, the so-called Reformation, which had been commenced in Utah the year before, was introduced in the Scandinavian Mission. It was a time for confession and repentance, as well as a renewal of covenants on the part of the Elders and Saints generally, by rebaptism. The missionaries were no exception to the rule. They confessed to one another and renewed their covenants. Yet no very serious offenses were brought to light, which was indeed very gratifying to the presiding officers, as all seemed to be open and honest in their confessions.

Under date of Jan. 26, 1857, Pres. Hector C. Haight, in reporting to Pres. Orson Pratt in England, stated that 575 persons had been baptized in Scandinavia during the past six months. He writes:

"The Elders have much opposition to encounter from the priests and authorities in different places, though not as much as formerly. The work is progressing and spreading abroad, and the Lord indeed blesses the efforts of the Elders and the Saints who are generally faithful in bearing testimony and spreading the written word. Those holding the Priesthood are obedient to counsel and persevere in their labors. * We are very thankful to you and President Benson for his visit to us, in company with Elder Kay. It was indeed a cheering time to us all—one long to be remembered, and beneficial to the Saints and the work in general. From the accompanying emigration lists we learn that 788 souls are preparing to leave Scandinavia in the spring. The spirit of gathering prevails among the Saints, and those who have a little more means than they need themselves are very willing to assist their friends and acquaintances who have not means of their own. The law of tithing was introduced the last quarter, and the spirit thereof penetrates the hearts of the Saints: the rejoice in it; it will help to roll on th work, and release the conferences fror debt."

At this time so-called Englisl Schools were commenced in differ ent parts of the Scandinavian Mis sion. Elder Christian A. Madsen writing from Aalborg, Denmark, un der date of Feb. 17, 1857, stated tha an English school had been estab lished at Aalborg under the directio of Sister Madsen and that those wh were studying under her were expect ed, after finishing their course, t go out and establish schools in othe branches of the conference.

During the year 1857, a numbe of new branches of the Church wer organized in Denmark. Thus at a conference held at Veile, Jan. 4 1857, the Læborg Branch of th Fredericia Conference was divide and the Saints residing in the vicinit of Hesselho were organized as th Hesselho Branch, with Rasmus Niel sen (formerly president of the Stor Lihme Branch), as president. An other part of the Læborg Branch, in cluding the town of Ribe and ad jacent districts, was organized as th Ribe Branch, with Elder S. Madser Vad as president. The Saints living in the vicinity of Kolding were or ganized as the Kolding Branch, with Elder H. Sörensen Schou as pres ident. A part of the Laasby Branch was organized as the Skanderborg Branch, with Elder Niels Sörenser (formerly president of the Laasby Branch) as president. Another par of the Laasby Branch, including the city of Silkeborg and vicinity, was organized into a separate branch called the Silkeborg Branch, with Peter Andersen Just as president. A a conference held at Bredstrup, nea Bogense, on the island of Fyen, Jan 12, 1857, the Bredstrup Branch was divided and a part of it organized into a new branch to be known as e Fillerup Branch, with J. Johansen s president. A part of the Fröbjerg ranch was separated from said ranch and organized as the Sarup ranch, with Elder Jörgen Nielsen s president. On Sunday, Jan. 25, e Speilsby Branch on the island f Möen (Lolland Conference) was ivided, and a part of the same or-anized into a new branch named the aarbölle Branch, with Sander Pe-ersen as president.

At a conference held in Veile, larch 2nd, a part of the Aarhus ranch was organized into a separate ranch called the Ravnholt Branch, ith Elder Niels Christiansen as pres-lent. Another new branch was or-anized by dividing the Silkeborg ranch, to be known as the Zörkild ranch, with Lars Svendsen as pres-lent. A part of the Greis Branch as organized into a new branch alled the Hvissel Branch, with Hans lathias Nissen as president. One of e speakers at this conference was onrad Edward Emil Schvaneveldt, ho emigrated to Utah in 1852 and fterwards went to California as an postate and subsequently returned Denmark where he, after locating n Veile, was re-admitted into the hurch by baptism. After his return the Church he did some missionary ork in Denmark.

At a conference held at Harritslev, ear Hjörring, Denmark, March 15, 857, a new branch, called the Aaby branch, was organized by dividing he Jetsmark Branch; Elder Niels hristensen (Underlein) was ap-ointed president of the new branch, eing a part of the Vendsyssel Con-erence.

At a conference held in Aalborg, March 22nd, the Saints living at Hasseris and Freilev parishes, were rganized into a branch of the hurch called the Freilev Branch, with Ole Sonne as president. The Saints residing in the villages of Östersundby and Nörre Uttrup were organized into a branch to be known as the Nörre Uttrup Branch, with Peter C. Christensen as president. The south part of the Salling Branch was separated from said Branch and organized as the Hjerm Branch, with Elder Jens Chr. Christensen as president. The Veddum Branch was divided and the western part thereof organized into a branch to be known as the Astrup Branch, with Peter Mortensen as president.

At another conference held March 22nd, the Saints residing at Kappin-drup, in the northern part of the island of Langeland, were organ-ized as the Tranekjær Branch of the Fyen Conference, with Elder Ole Nikolai Klemmensen as president. These Saints had previously belonged to the Longelse Branch. The Saints residing in the city of Odense and vicinity were organized as a branch to be called the Odense Branch, with Elder Jens Frederiksen as president. This branch has had a continued existence ever since. A new branch called the Middelfart Branch was also organized on the island of Fyen, with Elder Lars Nielsen as president.

At a conference held in Veile, (Fredericia Conference), a new branch of the Church was organized in Mols called the Tved Branch with Lars Svendsen (formerly president of the Zörkild Branch) as president. The Saints living in Herslev parish were organized into a branch to be known as the Herslev Branch, with Elder Ole Svendsen as president. The Saints living in Stenderup and Stöv-rup were organized as a branch call-ed the Stenderup Branch, with Elder L. Larsen as president.

At a conference held at Odense, Denmark (Fyen Conference), July 12, 1857, the Saints living at Jers-öre on Fyen were organized into a branch of the Church to be known as the Jersöre Branch, with Jens Andersen (formerly president of the Bred-strup Branch) as president. The Saints living in Hindsholm, Nyborg and Sulkendrup on Fyen, were organized into a branch called the Nyborg Branch and Elder Peter Madsen (released from presiding over the Odense Branch) was appointed to preside over said branch.

At a conference held at Willestrup, near Hjörring (Vendsyssel Conference) Sept. 20, 1857, a part of the Frederikshavn Branch was organized into the Gjerum Branch, with Elder Christen Jensen (formerly president of the Frederikshavn Branch) as president. A new branch was formed and organized from parts of the Taars and Sindal branches to be known as the Ugilt Branch, with Niels C. Christensen as president. A part of the Taars Branch was organized into the Jerslev Branch, with Mads C. Petersen as president.

At a conference held at Napstjert, near Frederikshavn, Denmark, June 21, 1857, the Hörmested Branch was divided, the north part retaining the old name, with Elder Jens Christensen as president, and the south part organized as the Skjæve Branch, with Elder Christian Jensen (Grönholt), formerly president of the Hörmested Branch, as president.

At another conference held in Aalborg, June 28, 1857, the Saints residing in Öster Sundby and vicinity were separated from the Aalborg Branch and organized into the Öster Sundby Branch. The Saints residing in Smedie and vicinity were separated from the Kjeldgaard Branch and organized as the Smedie Branch, with Niels Petersen as president. The Saints residing in the village of Horsens and vicinity in Vendsyssel were separated from the Hals Branch and organized as the Horsens Branch with Elder Jens Nissen as president. The Morsö Branch was divided and the Saints residing in Thyland organized

as a separate branch with Jens Chr. Hansen as president. The Hjerm Branch was divided and a part of it organized as the Fousing Branch with Elder Knud Mortensen as president. The Havbro Branch was divided and a part of it organized as the Kjölby Branch with Mads Chr. Gregorsen as president. The Rold Branch was divided and a part of it organized as the Hobro Branch, with Elder Sören Chr. Christensen as president. The Randers Branch was divided into three branches, one of the new branches being called the Nielstrup Branch with Niels C. Christensen as president, and the other new branch called Vinge Branch with Elder Frederik Ludvigsen as president. Elder Mads Jörgensen was appointed president of the Randers Branch.

CHAPTER 29. (1857)

Another company of emigrants—Aarhus. Conference organized—Hector C. Haight reports conditions in the mission—New branches raised up in Sweden.

On Friday, April 18, 1857, a company of emigrating Saints, numbering 536 souls, bound for Utah, sailed from Copenhagen on the steamer "L. N. Hvidt," in charge of Elder Hector C. Haight, who accompanied the emigrants to England. Among the emigrants was the late Simon Peter Eggertsen of Provo, Utah. After a successful voyage the ship arrived at Grimsby, England, April 21st in the afternoon, thence the journey was continued the following day by rail to Liverpool, where the emigrants, together with four returning Utah Elders from Great Britain, went on board the ship "Westmoreland" and sailed from Liverpool, April 25th. In the evening of the 24th, while the ship still lay at anchor in the River Mersey, five young couples were married, namely: Carl C. A. Christensen and Eliza Haarby, Johan F. F. Dorius and Karen Fransen, Carl C. N.

orius and Ellen G. Rolfsen, Lauritz Larsen and Anne M Thomsen and Jacob Bastian and Gertrud Peter-

SIMON PETER EGGERTSEN

Born on Fyen, Denmark, Feb. 7, 1826, was the son of Peter Eggertsen, from Schleswig-Holstein, and Caroline Larsen, from Odense, Denmark, the youngest of six children. He joined the Church, June 18, 1853; was ordained a Priest, June 6, 1854, by Peter O. Hansen, performed a three years' mission; emigrated to Utah in 1857, crossing the Plains in a handcart company which arrived in Salt Lake City, Sept. 13, 1857. In 1858 (Feb. 7th) he married Johanne Andreason, the daughter of Thomas Andreason and Sarah Louisa Nygren, from Hais, Jutland, Denmark, born Jan. 2, 1825. He located in Provo after "the move," where his wife had gone while he was doing military service in Echo canyon. Bro. Eggertsen sent his children to the best schools; kept two of his sons on missions, one of them (Lars Echert) in Denmark, where he also filled a short mission himself in 1887. He died Sept. 27, 1900, in Provo, Utah.

sen. Matthias Cowley was appointed by the presidency in Liverpool to take charge of the company, with Henry Lunt and Ola N. Liljenquist as his counselors. The Saints were divided into four districts under the presidency of Elders George W. Thurston, Lorenzo D. Rudd, Chr. G. Larsen and Carl C. N. Dorius. The following discipline or order was observed during the voyage: The emigrants went to bed between 9 and 10 o'clock in the evening and arose about 5 o'clock in the morning. Prayers were held morning and evening, and, as far as possible, also at noon. The Sundays were occupied with fasting, prayers and preaching. Schools were also organized in each district for the purpose of giving the Scandinavian Saints instructions in English. A musical company was organized and the Saints frequently enjoyed themselves in the dance and other innocent diversions. Splendid health as a rule existed among the emigrants and only two small children and an old man (82 years of age) died during the voyage. A child was born May 3, 1857, which was named Decan Westmoreland, after the captain and the ship. After a successful voyage, which lasted 36 days, the company arrived in Philadelphia, Pa., May 31, 1857. Here they were received by Elder Angus M. Cannon, who, during the absence of Pres. John Taylor, acted as emigration agent; he made the necessary arrangements for the journey of the company through the States. On the 2nd of June, the emigrants continued by rail from Philadelphia, and, traveling via Baltimore and Wheeling, they arrived safely in Iowa City, Iowa, July 9, 1857. This place was the outfitting point for the Saints who crossed the Plains in 1857 the same as in 1856. During the railroad journey, a Brother Hammer from Bornholm and three children died. About the 15th of June, a part of the company commenced the journey toward the Valley from Iowa City with an ox-train, under the captaincy of Elder Matthias Cowley, while another fraction of the company, about the same time, commenced the journey aross the Plains with handcarts under the leadership of Elder James P. Park. Several of the emigrants who had not sufficient means to continue the journey to the Valley that year, remained in the

States for the purpose of earning money with which to continue the journey later. The ox-train, which consisted of 198 souls, 31 wagons, 122 oxen and 28 cows, arrived at Florence, Neb., July 2, 1857, in pretty good health; but when the handcart company reached that place the following day a number of the handcart emigrants were sick, owing to the change of food and climate, and also because of over-exertion. Consequently, a council was called for the purpose of considering their condition, and, after some discussion, it was decided by unanimous vote that the company should continue the journey at once and that all who were not strong enough to stand the journey should remain behind, so as not to become a burden to the company. The ox-train rolled out of Florence, July 6th, and the handcart company, which consisted of 330 souls, with 68 handcarts, 3 wagons and 10 mules, continued the journey from Florence, July 7th, under the leadership of Elder Chr. Christiansen, who returned home from a mission to the Western States. Both companies arrived safe and well in Salt Lake City, Sept. 13, 1857.

The second division of the season's emigration from Scandinavia, consisting of 286 souls, sailed from Copenhagen, May 20, 1857, en route for Utah. The company arrived at Liverpool, England, on the 24th, being accompanied that far by Pres. Hector C. Haight. Together with a large number of emigrating Saints from the British Mission, the Scandinavian emigrants sailed from Liverpool, on the ship "Tuscarora," early on the morning of May 30, 1857, under the leadership of Richard Harper. After a pleasant voyage of about five weeks, the "Tuscarora" arrived in Philadelphia, July 3, 1857. From that city the journey was continued by railroad westward to Burlington,

Iowa, from which place the emigrants scattered in their endeavors to find employment and earn means wherewith to continue their journey to Utah as soon as possible.

At the April conference held at St. Louis, Mo., that year, it was decided that the Scandinavian Saints who were stopping temporarily in the States, should be advised to move from St. Louis, Mo., and Alton, Illinois, to Omaha and Florence, Neb., which places at that time were being built up with great energy, and the brethren stood a good chance to find remunerative employment there until they could travel further west. This move was carried out almost immediately, and in a remarkable short time all the Scandinavians had left Missouri and Iowa for Nebraska. About the same time a number of temporary settlements were founded by the Saints west of Florence on the route to Utah, according to instructions from President Brigham Young.

After the departure of the two companies of emigrants, the Elders who were left in the different Scandinavian conferences continued their missionary labors with renewed zeal, and soon new converts took the places of the many who had emigrated to Zion. In Denmark, two Elders, namely Lauritz Larsen and Hans Peter Iversen, were arrested for vagrancy and sentenced to pay a fine. They appealed their cases to the higher court at Viborg, which court rendered a decision May 2, 1857, and sentenced each of the two Elders to pay a fine of 10 rigsdaler.

At a conference held at Veile, July 6, 1857, a new conference called the Aarhus Conference was partly organized by taking the branches of Laasby, Aarhus, Hesselho, Skanderborg, Silkeborg, Ravnholt, Zörkild and Tved from the Fredericia Conference and organizing them into the new conference. The f o l l o w i n g branches remained in the Fredericia Conference: Greis, Fredericia, Store-Lihme, Veile, Horsens, Læborg, Ribe, Kolding, Hveissel, Herslev, Stender-up and Stohl.

The first conference council meeting held in the Aarhus Conference after its organization convened in the house of Sören Christiansen in the village of Grundför, Aug. 2, 1857, at which the organization of the Aarhus Conference, which had been effected at a conference held in Veile, July 5th, was accepted with joy and satisfaction by the assembled Saints. Arrangements were made to hold monthly Priesthood meetings in the several districts into which the conference had been divided according to locality. The Aarhus Conference at the time of its organization comprised the f o l l o w i n g ten branches. to-wit: Aarhus, Ravnholt, Skanderborg, Tved, Silkeborg, Laas-by, Zörkild, Randers, Nielstrup and Vinge. The last three branches were taken from the Aalborg Conference, all the others from the Fredericia Conference. Aarhus Conference has had a continued existence ever since its first organization and is still one of the largest and best conferences in the Scandinavian countries.

Under date of July 16, 1857, Pres. Hector C. Haight reported the Scandinavian Mission to Pres. Orson Pratt as follows:

"I can truly say with a thankful heart that the God of Israel has blessed and prospered my feeble efforts to spread and establish the gospel in the various regions in Scandinavia, which differ so much from each other with regard to their laws and customs. In Denmark we are at present enjoying much freedom, compared with the past, both in preaching and spreading the written word. When I first came here, which was a year and a half ago, it was a frequent occurence for the Elders to be whipped, mobbed and driven from their fields of labor. I soon found that much of this was occasioned by the course pursued by the Elders themselves in harsh preaching, reproving and reproaching both priest and people for their religion. I forthwith counseled them through our "Star" ("Skandinaviens Stjerne") and in public meetings, that they should go forth in the spirit of meekness and kindness, proclaiming the simple truth of the gospel, showing the people the principles and materials wherewith they could build a better habitation, before commencing to pull down the one in which they were living. In this they have been obedient, and are now able to go into many towns and villages, where before they were afraid to enter. Through the cautiousness with which our Elders have labored of late, much of the prejudice against us has abated, and our enemies have expressed through the papers that 'Mormonism' was on the wane, and that they had no more to fear, as it would die out, when at the same time we were baptizing over two to one to what we were before. I will also mention that an act, passed in the Diet (Rigsdag) last winter, gave liberty to parents to baptize their children or not, whereas, before, their baptism was compulsory. We feel that this also will greatly tend to facilitate the work of the gospel in Denmark. Everything is moving on satisfactorily in Denmark under the present circumstances, and in the last half-year 700 souls have been baptized.

"As to Sweden the circumstances are different. The Elders are often arrested, dragged before both civil and clerical authorities, sentenced with fines and imprisonment on bread and water, and ill-treated, as a consequence of illiberal laws. A proposition for religious liberty, to a certain degree, has lately been presented before the Diet, assembled in Stockholm, but it is doubtful whether it will pass this term, as the members in the legislative assembly are not satisfied with the many restrictions contained therein. The act was rejected by three classes, namely, the nobility, the priests and the peasantry, and only accepted by one class, namely, the citizens (Borgarne). The people in general are longing for freedom of conscience and worship, as there are many dissenters from the State Church, but the priestly caste and nobility are afraid that too much liberty will be given to the people, who they say are liable to be deceived by proselyting emissaries. In spite of all the combined opposition in that country, the gospel is spreading and finding its way

to the hearts of many of the honest, and
the prospects are cheering in the two conferences, Skåne and Stockholm, which lately
have been visited by Brother Carl Widerborg, whom I sent to counsel and assist
the native Elders in carrying out my instructions for the further spreading of the
work. He found the brethren doing well,
considering the unfavorable circumstances
they labor under, and the Lord had blessed
their efforts; 216 members were added to
the Church in the past half-year, and we
entertain the best hopes for the future.

"With regard to Norway, it is a rocky
land, and the Saints are, figuratively speaking, to be hewn out of the rocks, and it
costs the Elders much labor, and almost
every soul has to be bought with fines and
imprisonments. The only difference between Sweden and Norway is that the
authorities are more humane, never suffering the Elders to be ill-treated, though
strict in executing the laws. Eighty-two
members have been added to the Church in
that part of the mission, making 998 in all.

"Lately two new conferences and twenty-
nine branches have been organized in the
mission. These additions, with our past
emigration of 829 souls, show that the work
is onward in these northern countries.
The Elders and the Saints in general are
faithful in bearing testimony and spreading
the written word, and are also obedient in
responding to every call and giving heed to
the counsels of the Prophets of the Lord.
They are also willing to learn the English
language, and schools for that purpose are
established where circumstances will permit. One can travel through the mission,
and in most places find some who can
read, understand and speak a little English.

"Our writings are read with great interest by both Saints and sinners, and
'Skandinaviens Stjerne' is taken by many
outside the Church, who are influential
men.

"If the experience of this year's emigration proves favorable, and our people arrive early enough in the States to cross the
Plains before the cold weather overtakes
them in the mountains, it would be a
great favor to us, and very desirable, if we
could leave here in the spring instead of
the fall."

At a conference council meeting
held at Falkenberg (Göteborg Conference), Sweden, Dec. 18, 1857, the
Halmstad Branch was divided, and
a part of it organized into a branch
of the Church called the Falken-

berg Branch, with Elder A. Johanson as president.

At a conference held in Stockholm, Sweden, July 5, 1857, two new
branches were organized, namely
one in Vestergötland, called the Ul-
rikshamn Branch with Elder Swen
J. Petterson as president, and the
other in Vestervik called the Vestervik Branch with Elder Anders Göranson as president.

CHAPTER 30 (1857)

Arrival of Elders Joseph W. Young, John
Y. Greene and Iver N. Iversen—A general
council meeting—Imprisonments in Norway—
Statistics.

On Sunday, Aug. 16, 1857, Elders
Joseph W. Young, John Y. Greene
and Iver N. Iversen arrived in Copenhagen from Utah as missionaries
to Scandinavia. These brethren had
left Salt Lake City, together with
other missionaries, April 23, 1857,
and traveled over the Plains in 48
days, without horses, mules, oxen or
cows, as they hauled their own provisions, bedding, tents, cooking utensils, etc., on handcarts. On their arrival in Scandinavia, these Elders
were filled with the inspiration and
spirit of the Lord and took hold of
their missionary labors with great
zeal. Their arrival was hailed with
much joy on the part of the Scandinavian Saints.

On Friday, Sept. 4th, a general
council of the Scandinavian Mission
convened in Copenhagen, Denmark.
Besides Pres. Hector C. Haight and
his counselor, Carl Widerborg, there
were present the three newly arrived
Elders from Zion, viz., Joseph W.
Young, John Y. Greene and Iver N.
Iversen, and about 200 members of
the local Priesthood, among whom
were the following presiding Elders:
Carl A. Madsen, pastor of the Jutland district; Lars Eriksen, president of the Copenhagen Conference,

Peter A. Fjeldsted, president of the Vendsyssel Conference, Christian D. Fjeldsted, president of the Aalborg Conference, Lars Chr. Geertsen, president of the Aarhus Conference, Lars Jacobsen, president of the Skive conference, Christoffer O. Folkmann, president of the Fredericia Conference, Sören Peter Guhl, president of the Fyen Conference, Lars Jörgensen, president of the Lolland Conference, Hans Jensen, president of the Bornholm Conference, Hans Peter Lund, president of the Brevig (Norway) Conference, Nils B. Ädler, president of the Skåne Conference, and Lars Nilsson, president of the Stockholm Conference. The presiding Elders reported their respective fields of labor and gladdened the hearts of all present by showing how the Lord had blessed his servants in their endeavors to spread the sacred truths of the gospel, which so many in the three Scandinavian countries had received with joyful hearts. Next the blessings of heaven and the preaching of the living word, the spreading of books and tracts, treating upon the principles of the gospel, had specially promoted the work of the Lord; the printed word was read with much interest and had opened the eyes of many. While many of the Elders in different parts of the country had been treated as if there were no law or justice in the land, yet by the miraculous interposition of the Almighty, the Elders had been delivered from the hands of their persecutors and their lives saved. The prospects for the further progress of the work were good, and the Elders all hoped that the seed which had been sown the past year would take root and by careful nursing grow to become a powerful factor in the work of the Lord, and at some future day bear manyfold. Numer-

ous testimonies were given to the effect that the Priesthood and the Saints generally had been faithful in the discharge of their duties. The Saints had been diligent in keeping the commandments of God, had obeyed counsel, paid their tithes and donations liberally, and appreciated the gospel which they had received. Pres. Haight and the other brethren gave timely instructions, and presented the newly arrived Elders from Zion.

The council meeting was continued the following day (Sept. 5th), at which a new conference .was organized in Sweden, called the Göteborg Conference, with Elder Mathias B. Nilsson as president. A number of brethren were called and appointed to labor in the ministry in different parts of the mission, and

MATHIAS B. NILSSON

Born March 8, 1829, at Vemmenshög, Malmöhus län, Sweden; died May 8, 1926, in Salt Lake City, Utah.

every one thus called expressed their willingness to do the best they could

to advance the cause of the Lord.
Pres. Haight informed the council
that Elder Jos. W. Young would
probably be his successor, when his
own time should expire.

At a conference held in Aalborg
Sept. 27, 1857, attended by Pres
Hector C. Haight and Joseph W.
Young, the latter addressed the congregation in English, his sermon being translated by Elder Peter O.
Thomassen. Anthon H. Lund, then
about 14 years of age, who afterwards became prominent in the
Church, is mentioned in the report of
this conference as a successful
teacher of the English language.

The year 1857 witnessed increased
vigilance on the part of the civil authorities in enforcing the law against
Latter-day Saint propaganda. At this
time quite a number of Danish Elders were laboring in Norway, together with several of the native sons
of that country. Baptisms and imprisonments followed in quick succession, but the good work still progressed. In the spring of 1857, Elder Hans O. Magleby, one of the
Danish missionaries who labored in
Norway, came in contact with the
police authorities at Drammen, for
preaching the gospel. He was opposed by a school-teacher, who reported him to the legal officers, by
whom he was arrested and somewhat
abused and insulted. Two men
finally brought him to the sheriff,
who lived several miles away. He
was hauled about from place to
place in a little two-wheeled carriage, but finally set free. Elder
Magleby was again imprisoned in
Drammen, Nov. 28, 1857, for preaching and baptizing.

Elder Carl J. E. Fjeld and other
brethren were summoned to appear
in the police court in Christiania,
July 1, 1857, to answer to charges

made against them for having per-
formed the ordinance of baptism.
Elders Fjeld, Peter Halversen and
Peter Christensen were cast into pris-

HANS OLSEN MAGLEBY

Born April 14, 1835, at Dragör, on the island
of Amager, Denmark; was baptized Oct. 24,
1865; labored as a successful and energetic missionary in Denmark and Norway about three
years; was imprisoned several times in Norway for the gospel's sake, emigrated to Utah
in 1859, and crossed the Plains in Captain
George Rowley's hand cart company. He filled
a most successful mission to Scandinavia in
1881-1883, and died Aug. 16, 1903, at Monroe,
Sevier Co., Utah, leaving a large family. Elder
Magleby was a man with marked ability and
a most faithful servant of God.

on in Christiania, to settle their several accounts with the police authorities for these so-called unlawful
religious exercises. On Saturday,
June 13th, Elder Lars Larsen, who
was laboring as a missionary in
Hedemarken, was arrested and taken
by the sheriff to a prison in the
parish of Vang, where he was kept
for eleven weeks awaiting trial. He
was finally released July 28, 1857.
Elder Lars Petersen was imprisoned
in Trondjem, Oct. 20, 1857, to expiate a fine of 90 speciedaler by

seven days on a bread and water diet. Elder Anders Larsen was fined 10 speciedaler for having performed the ordinance of baptism. He also expiated this fine by serving five days in prison on a diet of bread and water.

On Tuesday, Sept. 15, 1857, the Saints living in a country district west of Christiania were separated from the Christiania Branch and organized into a branch of the Church to be known as the West Aker Branch, with Elder Anders Rasmussen as president. On Sunday, Oct. 11, 1857, the Saints living inland in the vicinity of Lake Mjösen in Hedemarken (including Löiten and other places) were organized into a branch of the Church to be known as the Hedemarken Branch, with Elder Anders Olsen as president. A branch of the Church was also organized in Trondhjem, Nov. 15, 1857, with 25 members, including 2 Elders and 2 Teachers.

In December, 1857, John Y. Greene, who had labored a short time as a missionary in Jutland, Denmark, left Scandinavia to return to his home in Zion.

At the close of the year 1857, there were 3,353 members of the Church in the Scandinavian Mission, viz., 2,317 in Denmark, 726 in Sweden and 310 in Norway. The mission was divided into 13 conferences, of which 9, viz., Copenhagen, with 19 branches, Aalborg with 18 branches, Vendsyssel with 17 branches, Fredericia with 11 branches, Lolland with 9 branches, Bornholm with 4 branches, Fyen with 1 branches, Aarhus with 10 branches, and Skive with 7 branches, were in Denmark. There were three conferences in Sweden, viz., Skåne with 14 branches, Stockholm with 7 branches and Göteborg with 7

branches, and one conference in Norway, namely, the Brevig Conference with 11 branches. From this it will be seen that at the close of the year 1857 there were 101 branches of the Church in Denmark, 25 in Sweden and 11 in Norway. During the year, 623 had been baptized in the mission, viz., 417 in Denmark, 151 in Sweden and 55 in Norway. The Priesthood in the whole mission was represented by 2 Seventies, 201 Elders, 159 Priests, 140 Teachers and 73 Deacons.

CHAPTER 31 (1858)

Utah Elders called home on account of the Johnston Army troubles—Hector C. Haight and Joseph W. Young report conditions in the mission—A small company of emigrants leaves Scandinavia for Zion—Persecution and imprisonment of Elders.

On account of the so-called Johnston Army troubles all Utah Elders were called home early in 1858, and, consequently, Pres. Hector C. Haight and the three other American Elders who labored in Scandinavia were released with instructions to return to America.

Elder Carl Widerborg, counselor in the mission presidency, was appointed to succeed Elder Haight as president, with Elders Niels Wilhelmsen and Peter O. Thomassen as his counselors.

Elder Joseph W. Young, referring to this change, wrote:

"When I arrived in this country in August, of last year, I expected that I would remain with you for a period of some two or three years, but since that time important events have taken place, and the future appointments of the Elders have been changed in order to conform to the circumstances surrounding them."

Then follows a brief account of the troubles that had arisen between Utah and the United States, which caused all the Elders in the different missionary fields throughout the

world to be called home. Undoubtedly Elder Joseph W. Young would
have made a splendid president of
the Scandinavian Mission; he took

CARL WIDERBORG

Born May 11. 1814, in Göteborg, Sweden,
was baptized by Svend Larsen, March 4, 1853,
in Norway; he labored a short time as a missionary in Norway and after that for several
years as translator and writer at the mission
office in Copenhagen, Denmark. When the
American Elders were called home in 1858,
on account of the Utah war, Elder Widerborg
was called to preside over the Scandinavian
Mission; this presidency was continued till 1860,
when he emigrated to Utah, and located in
Ogden, Weber County. In 1864-1868 he filled
a mission to Scandinavia, again presiding over
the mission. Soon after his return he took
suddenly sick and died March 12, 1869. Elder
Widerborg was perhaps the ablest public speaker
which the Scandinavian Mission has produced
up to the present time.

kindly to the Saints and the Scandinavian people in general, and, in
return, the local Elders and Saints
had been very favorably impressed
by his personality and kind ways.

Elder Hector C. Haight, who had
presided over the Scandinavian Mission about two years and one month,
and Elder Joseph W. Young, who
during the few months he had been
in Scandinavia, had labored in the
mission office most of the time,
left Copenhagen Feb. 4, 1858, to return to their homes in the Rocky
Mountains. During the presidency
of Elder Haight, 2,610 souls had

been baptized in Scandinavia and 990
members had emigrated to Zion. The
Scandinavian Saints donated liberally towards assisting these brethren
financially to return.

In a communication by Hector C.
Haight, dated Copenhagen, Jan. 18,
1858, to President Samuel W. Richards in Liverpool the following oc-
curs:

"You will see by the statistical report
that this mission numbers 3,353 souls. The
greater part of these are very poor as to
the things of this world, yet they are rich
in faith. Wages are low, and the many
calls which are made on the Saints for
money to carry on the work, and the great
number of Elders who are traveling and
preaching, make the burden pretty heavy;
but the willingness which they manifest
in meeting these calls, according to the
best of their ability, cannot, I think, be
surpassed. They are humble, willing to
be taught, and are ready to do all in their
power to build up the kingdom of God: in
short, they are a good people and I am
proud of them. The brethren from Zion,
who have been laboring here the last few
months. have done the Saints much good.
Elder Iverson has spent a considerable
part of his time among his relatives on
the island of Als in Schlesvig. He has
baptized three persons on the island, which
has created great excitement. He came
over to see me and visit among the Saints
in Copenhagen during the Christmas holidays, after having visited among the conferences since he left Als. His knowledge
of the language enables him to do much
good. The Saints and many who are not
in the Church have desired for a long time
to see some of the Danish brethren return
from Zion, for they know that one of their
own countrymen, who has lived for a few
years in the Valley, can give them a better
idea of things there than anybody else;
hence, Brother Iverson's testimony will do
much good.

"Elder John Y. Greene, who was with
us a short time, labored in the province of
Jutland. Notwithstanding he could not
speak the language of the people, the
Saints were glad to see him, and, through
the aid of an interpreter, he bore many
faithful testimonies.

"Elder Joseph W. Young remained with
me until Brother Greene left here to return home. He then went to Jutland, where

he labored until within a few days, when he returned to this place. He has visited all the principal conferences in the province, and has had a good time in testifying of the truth and counseling the Saints.

* *

"In closing my labors in this country, I can look back with a good deal of satisfaction upon the prosperity which has attended the work in this mission during the time in which I have had the honor to preside over it. The Lord has truly blessed me in my labors; and I am thankful that I can leave the mission with such good prospects for the future.

"I cannot close this report and do justice to my feelings, without speaking of Elder Carl Widerborg, who has been my counselor and junior editor of 'Skandinaviens Stjerne.' His labors have been of great service to me and the work of the Lord in these lands; and I, as well as all the Saints in this mission, appreciate them very highly. His knowledge of the Danish, Swedish and English languages renders him very efficient in translating the publications of the Church and the counsels of the First Presidency in Zion. His labors have been very arduous, but he has gone through them with zeal and determination, which are truly commendable."

Elder Joseph W. Young, in giving a summary of his labors in Scandinavia and his impressions of the Scandinavian people, writes:

"The people are very industrious and certainly the most strictly honest people that I have ever met with. The country people are very plain and simple, and their dress as primitive as their manners. * * "The Scandinavian Mission has justly been considered the most prosperous of all our foreign missions. There has probably been more persecution attending the propagation of the gospel here than elsewhere—indeed, the history of the mission establishes that beyond doubt; but with it all, never has there been such success attending the labors of the Elders."

About 75 Saints, who had gathered in Korsör, Sjælland, Denmark, left that place en route for Utah, Feb. 21, 1858. They had intended to take a steamer to Kiel, in Holstein, but when they found that navigation between Korsör and Kiel had ceased for the

time being on account of ice, they crossed Storebelt to the island of Fyen, and thence traveled from Nyborg, via Odense, to Assens, whence they crossed Lillebelt to Haderslev in Schleswig. From Haderslev they went overland by way of Apenrade to Flensborg where they were robbed by an unscrupulous hotel-keeper who charged them 65 rigsdaler for serving each of the emigrants with a cup of coffee, a few "tvebakker" and a quart of family beer. From Flensborg they continued the journey by rail to Hamburg, where they found the river Elbe frozen over, with no prospect of opening up for some time to come. The emigration agent, who met them in Flensborg, succeeded, however, in making the necessary arrangements for their embarkation at Bremerhafen in Hanover. Consequently, they left Hamburg March 3, 1858, and traveled by wagons to Bremerhafen, arriving there the following day. Here they secured passage on a steamer and sailed for England. Elder Iver N. Iversen was made captain of the company. On account of the "Utah War," he returned to his mountain home, after having labored only a short time in the mission, and most of this time he had spent among his relatives on the island of Als, where he baptized three persons. Elders Christian A. Madsen and Christoffer O. Folkmann were appointed assistants, or counselors, to Elder Iversen. President Carl Widerborg accompanied the emigrants to Hamburg. Among the Saints in this company were the following brethren who had labored as missionaries in different parts of the Scandinavian Mission: Christian A. Madsen, who had presided over the Stockholm Conference and, since September, 1856, acted as pastor over the missionary labors in Jutland; Christian D. Fjeldsted, who had labored as a traveling Elder on

9

the island of Sjælland two years and as president of the Aalborg Conference two years; Christoffer O. Folkmann, who had labored as a missionary on Bornholm four years, on Lolland six months and as president of the Fredericia Conference one year; Hans Peter Lund, who had labored as traveling Elder on Sjælland nearly two years, and as president of the Norwegian Mission since December, 1856; Niels C. Poulsen, who had labored as a missionary in Denmark from December, 1853, to September, 1855, and afterwards in Norway; Nils B. Ädler, who had first labored as traveling Elder and later as president of the Skåne Conference; Lars Göranson, who had labored in the Skåne Conference since 1854; Anders Petter Ömann, who had labored in the Skåne Conference since October, 1853; A. Andersen, who had labored on Sjælland, Denmark, since March, 1855; Hans Peter Olsen, who had labored in Jutland (Fredericia Conference) since November, 1854; Peter P. Meilhede, who had labored in the Vendsyssel and Fyen conferences since July, 1855; A. Nielsen, who had labored in Jutland since September, 1857; Ole C. Sonne, who had labored in the Aalborg Conference since December, 1856; Mads Christian Gregersen, who had labored in the Kjölby Branch, Denmark, since March, 1857; Knud Svendsen (Weibye) who had labored in the Vendsyssel Conference since December, 1856, and R. Olsen, Niels Petersen and Lars Svendsen. These brethren had all labored faithfully in the missionary fields in their respective localities and now emigrated to Zion with the blessings of the Lord and the Saints upon their heads.

Owing to storms, contrary winds and ice, the little company of emigrants were tossed about upon the North Sea for four and one-half

days, and suffered a great deal from seasickness. Once they were compelled to return to Bremerhafen to take in more coal. During their

KNUD SVENDSEN

Born in Veiby, Hjörring Amt, Denmark, April 11, 1827, was the son of Svend Larsen and Ane Pederson, his father's second wife. In 1849 he enlisted in the Danish army and until February, 1851, participated in the war against Germany. In November, 1855, he heard the gospel preached by Elder Lars C. Geertsen, and on April 28, 1856, he was baptized by that Elder and was confirmed by Lauritz Larsen May 4, 1856. During the year 1857 he performed local missionary work in his native land. In February, 1858, he emigrated to Utah, traveling by way of Hamburg and Bremerhafen, in Germany, and Hull and Liverpool, in England. He crossed the Atlantic in the ship, "John Bright," which arrived in New York April 24, 1858. He arrived in Salt Lake City, April 9, 1858, crossing the Plains in Horace S. Eldredge's company. He married Johanna Hansen June 24, 1860. On June 7, 1877, was ordained a High Priest and set apart as second counselor to Bishop John Brown, of Pleasant Grove. On April 20, 1890, he was made Bishop of the Pleasant Grove 3rd ward (now Manila). Bishop Svendsen died at Pleasant Grove, March 14, 1902.

temporary stay in Bremerhafen, Sister Anna Louisa Madsen, wife of Elder Christian A. Madsen, who had suffered on account of poor health for a long time, died March 10, 1858. The next day (March 11th) an attempt was made to get the steamer through the ice out into the open sea, but it did not prove successful until the 12th. Having finally reached open water, the voyage to Hull in England was continued and the emigrants arrived in that city on the 14th. The following day (March 15th) they went by rail to Liverpool, where quarters were secured for them in an emigrant hotel, and here the company remained until the 18th, when they went on board the ship "John Bright" and sailed from Liverpool on the 22nd. After a successful voyage, the ship reached New York harbor, April 23, 1858. Besides the Scandinavian emigrants, who now numbered eighty souls, and nine English saints, about 600 Irish emigrants crossed the ocean in the same vessel. During the voyage a young girl from Jutland and a little child died. The emigrants landed in New York April 24th.

From New York the company continued the journey on April 26th, and, traveling by rail via Dunkirk, Buffalo, Cleveland and Chicago, they arrived in Iowa City, Iowa, May 1st. Here the company was disorganized and the young, unmarried brethren, fourteen in number, commenced their journey westward May 9th, with four wagons, drawn by mules, under the direction of Hector C. Haight. In Florence they were amalgamated with a number of returning missionaries and others, after which the company consisted of 40 brethren with 14 wagons and 47 mules and horses, under the leadership of Horace S. Eldredge. After 39 days' journeying from Florence, they arrived in Salt Lake City, July 9, 1858.

The other emigrants remained a short time in Iowa City and vicinity. A number of them, however, commenced their journey towards the mountains under the leadership of Elder Iver N. Iversen, and reached the Valley Sept. 20, 1858. The re-

mainder of the company (two families excepted), under the guidance of Capt. Russell K. Homer, Christoffer O. Folkmann and others, commenced their journey westward and crossed the Plains with a number of English emigrants; they reached the Valley Oct. 7, 1858.

Under date of April 13, 1858, Pres. Carl Widerborg wrote from Copenhagen to Pres. Asa Calkin in England that several of the Elders in Sweden and Norway had lately suffered persecution by mobs and imprisonment, and that several of the Saints of both sexes had been fined for taking part in religious exercises. Elder Niels Wilhelmsen was traveling in the conferences and did much good in preaching, exhorting, counseling and assisting the Elders and Saints. Elder Peter O. Thomassen, who assisted Pres. Widerborg in the mission office, was a most efficient and faithful worker.

CHAPTER 32 (1858)

Important council meeting in Copenhagen—President Carl Widerborg reports general conditions in the mission.

On Tuesday, Wednesday and Thursday, May 11, 12 and 13, 1858, a series of council meetings were held in Copenhagen, at which interesting and encouraging reports were given by the presiding Elders of the different conferences and others.

Elder Lars Eriksen reported the Copenhagen Conference, which consisted of 19 branches, and Elder Peter Nielsen, president of the Fredericia Conference, reported that his conference consisted of 9 branches.

Elder Mads Jörgensen, president of the Lolland Conference, reported that his conference consisted of nine branches, and that there were three traveling Elders, namely, one on Lolland, one on Falster and one on Möen. The people on the last named island were, as a rule, hard-hearted and prone to persecution, but on the islands of Lolland and Falster the tendency to mobocracy had in the main ceased.

Elder Peter A. Fjeldsted, president of the Vendsyssel Conference, reported that his conference contained 364 members, organized into 18 branches, and that there were four traveling Elders. The Elders were faithful in their labors and had great influence among the people, who permitted the missionaries to hold meetings in private dwellings.

Elder Johan F. Klingbeck, president of the Aalborg Conference, reported 19 branches, 4 traveling Elders and much success in their labors. The landlord of whom the Saints had rented their meeting hall in Aalborg was worthy of mention on account of the good order which he preserved, and the police authorities had also been kind to the Elders. Among the opponents to the work of the Lord were a number of Baptists living outside of Aalborg, but they were divided among themselves.

Elder Hans Jensen, president of the Skive Conference, reported five branches with 52 members.

Elder Lars Chr. Geertsen, president of the Aarhus Conference, reported that his conference was organized ten monthh ago, and now consisted of 10 branches with 171 members.

Elder Mads Andersen, president of the Bornholm Conference, reported that the Saints on that island, although they were poor, were liberal in their donations, and the conference was without debt.

Elder Sören P. Guhl, president of the Fyen Conference, reported that his conference had a total membership of 112, organized into 11 branches. The Elders had gained access to the city of Odense, where,

notwithstanding mobs, a branch had been organized with 30 members.

Elder Saamund Gudmundsen, president of the Norwegian Mission (called Brevig Conference), reported that there were 11 organized branches in Norway with a total membership of 376. In some places the people were persecuting the Elders, and in other places the civil authorities cast them into prison, or fined them heavily. In Christiania the authorities were more humane, and open meetings were held continually. He praised his co-laborers because of their faithfulness in the service of the Lord.

Elder Johan Fagerberg, president of the Skåne Conference, reported that his conference consisted of 14 branches with a total membership of 481. Sixty had been added to the Church by baptism since New Year. As an example of how the public opinion was manifested towards the Elders, he cited an instance where a certain Swedish bishop had composed a prayer which was being read in the churches in behalf of those who had left the state church to join the "Mormons." The names of these were mentioned under the hypocritical pretense that all in the parish should pray for them, but the real object was to advertise to the public the names of those who had been baptized, in order that they might be generally shunned and hated by their fellow-men. And in some instances in the country, the leading men had entered into a kind of conspiracy, binding themselves to sell nothing to those who had joined the "Mormons," or give them employment. By thus depriving them of a chance to earn a livelihood, they hoped to force them back into the state church and make hypocrites of them.

President Widerborg remarked

that the police authorities in Sweden, with a few honorable exceptions, had always exhibited more bitterness towards the Elders than the authorities in Denmark and Norway. They had treated the missionaries as if they were the lowest kind of criminals, beaten them, placed them in irons, clipped their hair, dressed them in prison garb and cast them into dirty cells. Yet the good work of the Lord made progress, and the Elders were not discouraged.

Elder Mathias B. Nilsson, president of the Göteborg Conference, reported four branches with 78 members. In Ulricehamn and vicinity the Elders had found a good people and 12 persons had recently been baptized there. The resident Elder, who had charge, was a faithful man and had suffered much for the gospel's sake, as the persecutions were carried on by both the clergy and the police. In Göteborg, Elder Nilsson, together with several of the brethren and sisters, had been called before the court and fined 100 riksdaler, or 14 days imprisonment. But he had appealed the case to the king. The brethren could hold no public meetings in Göteborg, as the police officers would invariably interfere. In some other parts of the conference, the people were eager to hear the testimonies of the Elders, and good and well attended public meetings were held.

Elder Lars Nilsson, president of the Stockholm Conference, remarked that his conference consisted of nine branches. On account of the great area of country included in the conference, he suggested that the six branches of the Church in Östergötland, Vestergötland and Småland, namely, the Kalmar and Vexiö läns, be separated from the rest of the conference and organized into a new conference. In the city of Stockholm the police authorities were strict and watchful as to the movements of the Elders; thus they had closed the Saints' meeting hall, forbidden the holding of meetings, summoned the brethren before the police authorities and threatened them with banishment. In Norrland and Dalarne, and also in Vermland, the people were peaceable. As a rule, a tolerant religious sentiment p r e v a i l e d in Sweden. At a certain place, not very far from Stockholm, there was a young woman who was subject to violent fits. She would often fall over and remain in a prostrate condition, cold as a corpse for some time, and while in this condition every limb of her body would be useless, except the organs of speech. Her mouth would be in perpetual motion and she preached with a voice so strong and loud that she, who otherwise spoke in an undertone, could be heard by the large concourse of people assembled. At times the attendance at her meetings was so great that scores remained outside the house, listening. The peasantry believed that this woman was a prophetess, and when she was possessed of this preaching spirit, she usually cried out in a loud voice, telling the people to repent of their sins, go to church often, and beware of "Läsarne," and those leaving the state church. Thus the devil tried in every possible way, with the assistance of editors, priests, police, and possessed people, to hinder the progress of the true gospel.

In the evening session held May 12th it was decided by unanimous vote that the Linköping, Kalmar and Vexiö läns, as well as Västergötland (between Lakes Vänern and Vättern), should be separated from the Stockholm Conference and organized into a separate conference under the name of Norrköping Conference, and that Elder Ole Nilsson (Stohl) be appointed as president of the same.

The general council meeting closed on May 13th, when the authorities of

OLE NILSSON STOHL

Born Nov. 9, 1835, in Malmöhus Län, Sweden. In 1853 his brother Nils Nilsson explained the gospel to him, and on Jan. 6, 1854, he was baptized at Malmö. Soon afterwards he went to Copenhagen, and in September, 1855, having been ordained a Priest by Ola N. Liljenquist, went on a missio to Sjælland. In May, 1856, he was called to Stockholm, but on account of persecution he and Elder Burgston, went to Westmanland. In the fall of 1856 he took charge of the Norrköping Branch. In May, 1858, when the Norrköping Conference was organized, he was appointed president. He was released in 1862, the confernce having grown to several hundred members. Emigrating to Zion, he left Copenhagen, April 14, 1862, and arrived in Salt Lake City Sept. 22, 1862. His first labor in Zion was for President Brigham Young on a molasses mill. In October, 1866, he moved to Brigham City. From 1874 to 1879 was a member of the United Order under President Lorenzo Snow. In 1879-1881, he filled a mission to Scandinavia, during which he presided over the Göteborg Conference. In August, 1885, he was ordained a High Priest and appointed second counselor in the Bishopric of the Brigham City 4th Ward. For many years, commencing with 1897, he presided over the Scandinavian meetings in Brigham City, where he died, Nov. 13, 1926. He left a large posterity.

the Church and the Mission were unanimously sustained.

From a communication written June 25, 1858, by Carl Widerborg

to President Asa Calkin in England, we extract the following:

"The General Council met on the 11th of May, 1858, in Copenhagen, Denmark, and, besides the conference presidents, a number of the traveling Elders were also present.

"I can say that we rejoiced in coming together, and felt a considerable portion of that spirit which the Lord in his mercy is pouring out upon his covenant people in these last days. My heart felt to praise him when I heard the cheering reports from the conferences, the hopeful prospects for the future, the willingness manifested to receive and obey counsels, and the prevailing unison in all things.

"With regard to Denmark, the Elders can travel and preach in many places and regions without being disturbed or molested in any way, and our writings are read and patronized by many strangers. The spirit of persecution is very much abated, and we are not opposed with such bitterness and hatred as we had experienced before, as our opponents and countrymen in general begin to learn and observe that the Saints are not such a bad people as they have been represented. False stories and misrepresentations are still circulating to some extent about us and Utah, and the Elders are sometimes mobbed, driven and beaten, but not so frequently as in past years, yet a more peaceable spirit is prevailing, and more indifference also, especially in places where the gospel has been preached for some length of time. I therefore directed the Elders to break new fields as much as possible, that the gospel seed might be spread over the length and breadth of the country. For this purpose the conferences are divided into suitable districts, and a traveling Elder appointed in each to counsel and assist the local Priesthood in the branches, and to preach and spread the written word in every direction where the Lord may open the way.

"In Sweden there is a harder work for the Elders to perform. The opposition is very great; imprisonments are frequent; conference meetings have to be held in the night time, and as privately and secretly as possible. I attended such a conference meeting in Malmö, Skåne Conference, on the 16th instant. We assembled at 12 o'clock midnight, enjoyed much comfort of the spirit, transacted our business, and dispersed quietly at 5 o'clock in the morning. From Stockholm I have lately received the intelligence that the police, finding out the place of our meetings, came to the house, dispersed the little congregation, closed the door, took possession of the key, summoned the president of the conference before the court, forbade him to hold meetings and threatened him with banishment. I shall soon appoint another president, and the work of the Lord will roll on, in spite of all the police in Sweden "As Stockholm Conference was too large in circumference, I found it wisdom to divide it into two, and organize another conference by name of Norrköping, consisting of the middle provinces. In the Göteborg Conference there has also been some persecution, and the presiding Elder is under trial.

"The usual manner of proceeding against the Saints is as follows: When it becomes known that a person has embraced our faith, he or she is called before the clergy (first the parson's then the bishop's court) and examined, admonished and threatened. If they do not then return to the bosom of the state church, the eyes of the police are upon them, watching for an opportunity to imprison them, or get them sentenced and fined. The hypocritical priests have begun the seemingly Christian-like conduct not alone to visit the erring sheep, but also to pray for them in the churches, as they do for the sick, publishing their names from the pulpit, that their good fellow-men also can pray for them. A cunning plan of the evil one and his servants. But they will not gain much thereby; the faithful will abide in the truth.

"As a striking sample of the religious intolerance in Sweden, I will mention that lately six women, who have left the Lutheran church and embraced Catholicism, have been banished from their native country. If it had happened with 'Mormons,' certainly all would have been right; but because it was done with children of the 'mother harlot,' a hué and cry is raised in all Christendom protesting against such cruelty of Christians towards Christians, and subscriptions are gathered for those expelled.

"From Norway we have had a cheering report. The progress is sure, but rather slow, as the Elders are so frequently imprisoned; but as soon as they are liberated they go to work with all their strength and are spreading the testimony as fast as they can. I had the pleasure of forming an acquaintance with two brothers from the northern part of Norway, two skippers, masters of crafts running between Norway,

Sweden and Denmark, who had been lately baptized and were full of faith, spirit and love for the cause. They had come for the express purpose of attending the general council, and desired, if it was the will of the Lord, through me, to be appointed a mission in their native country. The spirit bore testimony that they were men of the right stripe, and they were called, ordained and set apart for the northern part of Norway. It is a rocky land, and it is rather hard work to hew the Saints out of the rocks.

"The substance of the reports of the Elders from the various parts showed that they have enjoyed much of the spirit of their respective callings, and the spirit bore testimony of their faithfulness and integrity, which Elder Niels Wilhelmsen and myself have witnessed under our travelings in the conference.

"During the months of January, February, March and April, there were baptized in this mission five hundred souls.

"The Saints in general are faithful, obedient to counsel, willing and ready to pay their tithing, with few exceptions, and to meet every necessary call for the promotion of the work. But the past and present season have been rather unfavorable for many of the Saints, who are out of employment and are scarcely able to procure the most necessary articles for their support, and, to some extent, this is still the case. Some of the conferences I found almost too weak and poor to defray the necessary expenses and pay some debts accumulated in times past, not through mismanagement, but rather on account of the great willingness to borrow money and donate to emigrating Elders, Saints and traveling Elders. The financial matters were taken under earnest consideration, and the spirit assisted us in our deliberations and counselings, so that I believe we shall soon be able to lift, or by and by to lighten, the burden of the weaker conferences, through a good management and some assistance from the wealthier part of the mission. I was glad to learn that, from the beginning, when the principle of tithing was introduced, tithing books have been kept, in which are recorded the names of every individual and the amounts paid.

"Our council lasted three days, and we felt from the beginning to the end the strength and power of the spirit of Zion, of Joseph, of Brigham, Heber, Daniel and the European presidency. We were much instructed, edified, comforted and strengthened. It was a joyful time—an affecting sight to see the radiant faces and the uplifted hands, when the authorities of the Church in Zion and Europe were presented. You could feel the votes come from their hearts; and when the Elders expressed fervent wishes for the prosperity of the authorities for the cause of Zion, for the kingdom of God and for their own deliverance, together with that of all the faithful, and their gathering with the people of God, the tears arose in my eyes, and I responded with a hearty "amen."

CHAPTER 33 (1858)

Choirs organized in Scandinavia—More new branches organized in Denmark, Sweden and Norway—Pres. Carl Widerborg visits Sweden—Pres. Asa Calkin visits Scandinavia—More imprisonment of Elders in Norway—Pres. Widerborg visits England—Statistical information.

On Sept. 11, 1858, a male chorus was organized in the Copenhagen Branch to sing in the meetings of the Saints, with Herr Frantz Michaelsen as teacher. Singing has always been a most important feature of Latter-day Saint worship both at home and abroad. In Copenhagen as in most other places, where branches of the Church were organized, the Saints engaged in congregational singing, but after awhile regularly instructed choirs were organized and harmony singing introduced.

At a conference held at Dahl, near Frederikshavn, Denmark, March 21, 1858, a branch of the Church was organized on the island of Læsö, called the Byrum Branch, with Elder Chr. Jensen (Grönholt) as president, and six members who had all been converted and baptized by Elder Jensen.

At a conference held in Aalborg, August 1, 1858, a part of the Jetzmark Branch was organized into a new branch called the Öland Branch, with Elder Jens Christensen as president.

At a conference held at Odense on Fyen, Sept. 12, 1858, the Saints residing in the city of Bogense and vicinity on the island of Fyen were organized into a branch, called the Bogense Branch, with Elder Jens Jörgensen as president.

President Carl Widerborg, who arrived in Stockholm on a visit from Copenhagen, August 30, 1858, wrote the following to Asa Calkin in England, after his return to Denmark:

"Lately I returned from a trip to Sweden. * * On my journey to Stockholm, I first visited Göteborg, where I had an interview with the conference president, Mathias B. Nilsson, and learned from him that the Elders and Saints had to move very cautiously, and in order not to excite the police too much, they had to gather in smaller assemblies, with friendly neighbors and acquaintances, whom they could trust. The traveling Elders also meet with this difficulty that they cannot move from place to place without passports; and the authorities who are acquainted with them and their business often refuse to give them passports, except they have a certain place of destination, where they will stop and labor for their support; for if they are found without passports, or without employment, they are taken up as loafers and idlers, treated accordingly and transported to their respective homes.

"Having strengthened and encouraged the Elders and Saints, I set out from Göteborg by steamer for Stockholm, via the Göta Canal, passing the falls of Trollhättan, the lakes of Väneran, Vettern and Mälaren, and after traveling three days and nights I arrived in Stockholm, where I was kindly received by the president of the Stockholm Conference, Lars Nilsson, and some Elders. I held the usual council meeting with the brethren and was introduced to and visited some of the Saints, and as we could not meet in public, a private meeting was arranged in the house of a friend, who was kind enough to offer us one of his apartments for the purpose. Accordingly, about thirty Saints gathered in the evening of the 1st instant. We prayed, preached and had a good time. Elder Lars Nilsson, threatened with banishment, was released, and Elder Gustaf A. Ohlson was appointed in his stead as president of the conference. * *

"While in Stockholm, I learned that the Baptists are gaining ground, and as there are among them many wealthy people, they command greater influence than other dissenters, and are probably making friends with the "unrighteous Mammon," as the police are not so hard upon them as they are upon us.* In fact, several parties of dissenters are raising their heads in Sweden, and the clergy of the state church are almost puzzled to know what to do, as the regulations of the illiberal laws and police authorities (strong as they aie brought to bear upon the several cases and parties) seem to be inefficient. By-and-by they will have to give up the struggle and let the dissenters alone, and then, I hope, we also will have a share of freedom. * *

"Having instructed the Elders to act in wisdom for the promotion of the cause, I left Stockholm on the 3rd inst., with a steamer for Norrköping. Arriving there in the evening, I had the satisfaction to attend a little branch meeting, and felt a good spirit among the Saints. The president of this conference, Ole Nilsson (Stohl) had just returned from a trip through the middle countries (läns) of Sweden. and he made me acquainted with the condition of the scattered Saints, who have been rather behind in their practical duties, as they, on account of unfavorable circumstances, had not been visited or instructed sufficiently."

During the year 1858, several new branches of the Church were organized in Sweden. Thus a few members of the Church, who belonged to the Stockholm Branch, but who lived too far away to attend meetings in the capital, were organized into the Ljungstorp Branch Jan. 13, 1858, with Elder Erik Johan Pehrson as president. At a conference held at Norrköping, June 22, 1858, the Saints residing in the town of Risinge, who had formerly belonged to the Norrköping Branch, were organized as the Risinge Branch, with Adam Swenson as president; and the Saints in Linköping and vicinity were organized into a branch to be known as the Motala Branch, with H. J. Dahlström as temporary president.

Elder Asa Calkin, president of the European Mission, and wife, arrived in Copenhagen Sept. 27, 1858, on a

visit to Scandinavia. Accompanied by President Carl Widerborg, who acted as interpreter, Brother Calkin visited and preached in a number of meetings in Denmark, Norway and Sweden. They returned to Copenhagen on the 24th of October and Elder Calkin left that city on the 29th, returning to England via Belgium and France.

The "Skandinaviens Stjerne" of Dec. 1, 1858, announced that the question of religious liberty had again been under consideration in the Swedish Riksdag and that three classes, the royalty, the priests and the peasantry, had rejected it. while only one class, namely, the citizens (Borgarne), had voted in favor of it.

A special conference was held in Christiania, Norway, Feb. 2, 1858, at which Elder Saamund Gudmundsen was sustained as successor to Elder Hans P. Lund, as president of the Brevig Conference.

At a meeting held at Bergen, Norway, August 13, 1858, the few Saints who had embraced the gospel in that city, were organized into a branch of the Church with Elder Ole Jacobsen as its president.

At a council meeting held in Drammen, Wednesday, Sept. 1, 1858, the Drammen Branch was divided and a part of the same organized into a new branch called the Hurum Branch with Elder Johan Johansen as president.

Elder Hans O. Magleby, who had already been incarcerated twice, was again imprisoned in Drammen, Jan. 19, 1858, for preaching the gospel and administering its ordinances. After serving nine days in prison, he was released Jan. 28th. While in prison, he had opportunity to bear testimony to some of his fellow-prisoners, upon whom he made a very favorable impression. In July and

---

*The pioneer leaders of the Baptist movement in Sweden were such men as the Rev. A. W. Wiberg, Colonel Broady, Dr. A. Drake, Dr. Erik Nyström, and others. They were men of great learning and intelligence, as well as zeal, and their success was due to this fact rather than to wealth.—J. M. S.

September following, he served other terms of imprisonment.

President Saamund Gudmundsen was arrested and imprisoned in Christiania April 21st, for five days, in lieu of paying a fine of 15 speciedaler, for having preached the gospel and administering in its ordinances. Elder Peter Christiansen, Hans Thoresen and Ole Christiansen were incarcerated in the city prison in Christiania April 24th, to expiate a fine for having preached and baptized. Elders Carl J. E. Fjeld, Johannes Olsen and Johan Johannesen were imprisoned in Christiania April 25th, according to a sentence which the court had previously passed upon them.

Elder Frederik G. S. Lyngberg was r e l e a s e d from imprisonment in Trondhjem August 30, 1853, after having paid his fine of 65 speciedaler by imprisonment for 11 days.

Elders Niels Petersen and Knud Halversen were incarcerated in prison at East Aker, near Christiania, Sept. 25, 1858. A Mr. Stormund was fined 10 speciedaler for having rented his hall to the "Mormons" in which to hold meetings, and a Mr. Berg was fined 2 speciedaler for complicity in renting said hall.

Elder Oluf C. Larsen was imprisoned for five days in Drammen, Dec. 16th, to settle for a fine of 10 speciedaler.

The sentence to imprisonment in most of these cases included a diet on bread and water.

In December, 1858, Pres. Carl Widerborg went to England to represent the Scandinavian Mission at a special council meeting held in Birmingham Jan. 1, 1859. On that occasion he reported as follows:

"In Denmark the people are greatly blessed with freedom and liberty, political and religious, in comparison to former times. In the last half-year we have not been molested in any way, except that the authorities sometimes try to hinder the Elders from preaching in certain localities. When an Elder moves from one place to another, he must have his book of testimonials signed by the parson of the parish in which he has last lived; and when he moves to another parish, he must also report himself to the parson there and get his book properly signed; for he has no right to stay in any region of country till these formalities have been complied with. In Sweden there is much more to contend with and the Elders have much to endure there. During the last half-year, however, we have not had such severe persecution as before. I may mention that the Bishop of Skåne, in whose diocese is our largest conference in Sweden, has issued a proclamation to the priests, forbidding them to persecute our Elders through the police; but they are to go to the 'poor deluded people' who have embraced 'Mormonism,' talk to them, pray for them in the churches, and try to convert them again to the 'holy evangelical religion.'

"In Norway the civil authorities have regard for humanity and generally respect a man in his position; but they say, 'We can't let you preach as you please.' At the time the mission was opened in Norway, I had the honor to labor there for two years. I was imprisoned thrice, but I agreed exceedingly well with the judges, for, when I was brought before them, they would say, 'Have you been preaching?' 'Yes, sir.' 'Have you been baptizing?' 'Yes, sir.' 'Well, you know these things are contrary to the laws of the land.' 'Yes, sir; but they are in accordance with the laws of God.' 'Yes, but I must judge you after the laws of the land.' 'Yes, sir, you do your duty, and I will do mine.' We were very polite to each other. I respected them in their position, and to some extent they respected me in mine. They gave me the nicest rooms they had in their prisons, and clean sheets, and came to see that I did not want for bread and water; and I had that very comfortably. I remember the first four days I was in prison I was so intent in reading pamphlets belonging to the Church that I scarcely knew whether it was four days or four minutes. That was in the beginning of my career in the Church. When I was as a child, and the Spirit of the Lord was opening my mind and showing me things pertaining to this work, my joy was so great that I heeded not the prison, * * and though my fare was bread and water, I can say that I got quite fat in prison, spiritually, I mean. The Elders who are still preaching and baptizing in Norway get bread and water for it. But, if the authorities imprison one Elder, we send out another. This the people do not understand, they do not know that we can confer the Priesthood upon men and send them out as the work demands.

"The Scandinavian people are a humble, obedient, law-abiding people. The great hindrance to their obeying the gospel is sectarianism. There are many sects and parties there and consequently the people are very religious. In fact, they have gone from one extreme to the other; for even among the mountaineers, where once scarcely ever a social party terminated without cruelty, bloodshed and murder, they are now so 'holy' and so full of 'Christianity' that they scarcely dare look up. Yet there are many honest people among them and my soul is often grieved because they do not receive the truth. In my conversations with them, they have nothing to say against the principles we teach; but they hear so many bad things concerning us, that they think we must be a wicked people. However, we are gradually gathering out of these nations the honest in heart. * *

"My mission is about 2,100 English miles in length, and of various breadths, being intersected by water and mountains. This makes travel very expensive, for the people are not everywhere sufficiently hospitable to give our Elders lodging at night, or food. Sometimes the Elders have to give the writings of the Church in exchange for lodging and the necessities of life.

"The law of tithing takes more and more hold of the people, and the faithful among them rejoice in it. I may also say that this law has been a means of cleansing the Church in that mission; the rejection of the law of tithing by some of the Saints caused the spirit to be withdrawn from these and through this negligence and indifference, they finally lost their standing in the Church. * * The majority of the Saints, however, rejoice in the principle. * * We begin to feel that we stand on a firm basis. Obstacles are moving out of the way and our Elders will soon be experienced men. I do not feel at all discouraged; but, taking all things into consideration, our hopes are stronger and our prospects brighter for the future advancement of the work of the Lord in those countries than ever before."

A statistical report of the Scandinavian Mission dated Nov. 30, 1858, showed that the mission now contained 3,709 baptized members, namely, 2,492 in Denmark, 756 in Sweden, and 461 in Norway. Included in this number were 492 Elders, 184 Priests, 167 Teachers, and 88 Deacons. During the past 11 months, 1,038 had been baptized, 70 had emigrated to Zion and a number had been excommunicated; 55 had died. The mission consisted of 14 conferences, segregated into 125 organized branches of the Church. Of these, 9 conferences (including 102 branches) were in Denmark; one conference consisting of 13 branches in Norway, and 4 conferences containing 10 branches in Sweden. The names of the conferences were the following: Copenhagen, Aalborg, Vendsyssel, Fredericia, Lolland, Bornholm, Fyen. Aarhus and Skive, in Denmark, Brevig in Norway, and Skåne, Stockholm, Göteborg and Norrköping in Sweden.

CHAPTER 34 (1859)

Emigration reopened—Crossing the Plains with handcarts—Scandinavian Saints advised to save means towards their emigration to Zion—Important council meetings in Copenhagen.

In January, 1859, Pres. Carl Widerborg returned to Copenhagen from his visit to England.

To the great joy and satisfaction of the Scandinavian Saints, a communication was received from President Brigham Young towards the close of the year 1858, announcing that the emigration to Utah, which, on account of the "Utah War," had been temporarily interrupted, could now be resumed, and that the Saints would have the privilege of crossing the Plains either with handcarts or ox-teams. Pres. Carl Widerborg and his co-laborers went to work at once to make the proper preparations for the migration of a large company of Saints the following spring. And as the more well-to-do Saints exhibited an usual liberal and kind spirit towards their poorer co-religionists, a great number of names were placed on the emigration list for 1859.

"Skandinaviens Stjerne" of Jan. 1, 1859, announced that the cost for each adult who intended to cross the Plains with handcarts in 1859, would be about 150 rigsdaler ($75), and that those who expected to cross with oxen and wagons would need about 200 rigsdaler ($100), if eight persons were reckoned to each wagon. Those who expected to emigrate under those terms were advised to send their names, with ages, date and place of birth, occupation, etc., to their respective conference presidents, and at the same time, advance 40 rigs· daler ($20) for each handcart emigrant and 80 rigsdaler ($40) for each wagon emigrant. This money was to be sent to America in advance to purchase the necessary outfit for the journey across the Plains, such as handcarts, wagons, oxen, provisions, etc.

On Friday, April 1, 1859, a company of Scandinavian Saints, consisting of 355 souls, namely 224 Danes, 113 Swedes and 18 Norwegians, sailed from Copenhagen, Denmark, on the steamer "L. N. Hvidt," in charge of Elders Carl Widerborg and Niels Wilhelmsen. After a rather stormy voyage over the North Sea the company reached Grimsby, England, on the 6th. From Grimsby the emigrants continued the journey by rail the same day to Liverpool, where they, on the 7th, went on board the ship "William Tapscott," Captain Bell, and were joined by British and Swiss emigrants. Elder Robert F. Neslen was appointed president of the company, with Henry H. Harris

and George Rowley as counselors. Under them Elders Sören P. Guhl, Johan F. Klingbeck, Peter A. Fjeldsted, Anders Petersen, Lars Petersen and Morten Petersen presided over the Scandinavians. Brothers Christian Jeppesen and Niels Jacobsen acted as interpreters and Hans O. Magleby and Anton Petersen as cooks. On Monday, April 11, 1859, the ship lifted anchor and was tugged out of the Mersey into the open sea with its precious cargo of 726 souls. Songs of joy resounded from all parts of the ship as it was pulled out to sea, but these were subsequently succeeded by a chorus of those who, during the first days of the voyage, yielded to the usual attack of seasickness, in which most of the passengers participated to a greater or less extent.

After going through the process of government inspection, clearing, etc., Pres. Neslen, in connection with his counselors, proceeded to organize the company into ten wards, namely, five English and five Scandinavian, appointing a president over each to see to the faithful observance of cleanliness, good order, etc. The Scandinavian Saints occupied one side of the vessel and the British and Swiss the other. The company was blessed with a most pleasant and agreeable voyage, which lasted only 31 days. The health of the passengers was exceptionally good, which was demonstrated by the fact that only one death occurred on board, and that was an old Swedish sister by the name of Inger Olson Hagg, 61 years old, who had been afflicted upwards of four years previous to her embarkation. This single loss by death was counterbalanced by two births. In the matrimonial department the company did exceedingly well, as no less than nineteen marriages were solemnized on board; of these five couples were

glish, one Swiss and thirteen Scan-
navian. Every day during the voy-
e the people were called together
prayers morning and evening at
o'clock. On Sundays, three meet-
gs were usually held on deck, and
lowship meetings in each ward two
ghts a week. The monotony of the
yage was also relieved with sing-
g, instrumental music, dancing,
mes, etc., in which, as a matter of
urse, the young people took a
ominent part, while the more
late enjoyed themselves in witness-
g and hearing the happifying rec-
itions. Elder Neslen writes that
felt it quite a task, when he was
pointed to take charge of a com-
ny composed of people from so
ny countries, speaking nine differ-
: languages, and having different
nners, customs, and peculiari-
s, and thrown together under such
se circumstances; but through the
thfulness and diligence of the
ints, which was universally mani-
ted, he soon found the load far
ier than he had anticipated, and
on the arrival of the company in
w York, it was pronounced by
tors and government officers to
the best disciplined and most
eeable company that ever arrived
that port.

Arriving safely in New York har-
r, the emigrants were landed in
tle Garden on Saturday, May 14th.
the same day, in the evening,
st of them continued the journey
steamboat up the Hudson River
Albany; whence they traveled by
l via Niagara, Windsor in Canada,
troit in Michigan, and Quincy, Ill.,
St. Joseph, Missouri, where they
ived on the 21st. In the afternoon
that day they boarded the steam-
t "St. Mary," which brought them
the Missouri River to Florence,
braska, where they arrived on the

25th in the morning. The whole route
through the States was one which no
former company of emigrating Saints
had ever taken. Brother George Q.
Cannon and those who assisted him
in the emigration business that year,
were quite successful in making arrangements for their transportation
by rail direct to St. Joseph, instead
of, as first contemplated, shipping
them to Iowa City.

On their arrival at Florence the
Saints were organized into temporary
districts and branches, with presiding officers over each, whose duty
it was to look after the comfort and
welfare of the people while en-
camped at or near that place. Prayer
meetings were held regularly twice
a week in most of the temporary
branches. About fifty of the Saints
who crossed the Atlantic in the
"William Tapscott" stopped temporarily in New York and other
parts of the United States.

On the 1st of June the Scandinavian handcart emigrants were organized into three companies with
Hans O. Magleby, Jens Jensen and
Mathias B. Nilsson as captains, and,
together with the English Saints,
they commenced their journey from
Florence on the 9th of June. The
whole company consisted of 235
souls with 60 handcarts, under the
leadership of Capt. George Rowley.
For each handcart there were from
4 to 6 persons, with 20 pounds of
baggage and some provisions for
each. Eight wagons hauled by oxen
followed the handcarts with the rest
of the provisions and were expected
also to give the tired and sick an
opportunity to ride in case of necessity. After a successful journey,
the company reached Salt Lake City
on Sunday, Sept. 4th.

As soon as it became known in
the Valley that the handcart com-

pany was approaching, thousands of the inhabitants of the City went out to meet them, and, led by two bands of music, the brave wanderers marched through the streets of the City, which were filled with people, to Union Square, where they were greeted by the multitude, and Apostle Ezra T. Benson gave a short speech of welcome. A bounteous supply of all kinds of food was brought the emigrants, agreeable to arrangements made by the Bishops of the different Wards of the city. The reception was very touching and full-hearted, and many tears of joy were seen trickling down the cheeks of the new arrivals and their friends who received them. The emigrants were soon settled and treated in a most hospitable and kind way by their relatives, friends and acquaintances.

An ox train, consisting of about 56 wagons, was organized at Florence with nearly 380 Scandinavian Saints, segregated into five divisions, for each of which a captain was appointed, while Elder Robert F. Neslen was appointed captain of the whole. The five captains of Ten were George D. Keaton, C. Kidgell, Sören P. Guhl, Lars Nilsson, and Christian Jeppesen. The company left Florence June 26, 1859, and arrived after a successful journey, in Salt Lake City, Sept. 15th. Six deaths and three births took place on the journey and 24 of the animals died en route by sickness and poisoning. Among the brethren who died was Elder Peter A. Fjeldsted who, prior to emigrating, had presided over the Vendsyssel Conference.

In 1859, the Saints in the Scandinavian Mission were advised by the Elders to do all within their power to save means for their emigration to Zion. This counsel was followed

with great willingness, so much so that Pres. Carl Widerborg in his report, dated June 30, 1859, could state, that he had already placed in the bank the sum of 3,029 rigsdaler which the Saints in Scandinavia had saved for emigration purposes. Since that time the poor Saints in Denmark, Sweden and Norway were repeatedly urged to practice economy and by a wise expenditure of their earnings, hundreds of Saints were enabled by their own effort to emigrate to Zion.

On Friday, June 24, 1859, and the two following days, a series of council meetings were held in Copenhagen, attended by many of the presiding Elders of the Scandinavian Mission. The meetings were held in the Saints' hall at Nörrebro, and the Elders reported the different conferences and missionary districts in Denmark, Sweden and Norway. The reports were satisfactory, showing progress, although a variety of spirits, both carnate, and incarnate had been encountered in all parts of the mission. The Saints had experienced many trials and had suffered much opposition, but most of them were faithful and rejoiced in their afflictions.

Referring to this council, Pres Carl Widerborg writes: "The report of the presiding Elders filled our hearts with satisfaction and thanksgiving, because the Lord our God had prospered his work with the aid of the humble and meek of the earth, by which his name has been glorified and his purposes promoted, resulting in great blessings to those who, in the spirit of meekness and peace, had investigated the principles of truth and had accepted the same, through their obedience to the laws of the kingdom. It was indeed a great feast for us to thus a sociate with our brethren and participate with them in the spirit which encourages and strengthens men in their good resolution.

Under date of April 22, 1859, Pres. Carl Widerborg wrote the following:

"Since I received the joyful information from you that the way was open for the gathering of Israel, and you gave me instructions about the proceedings of our emigration, my attention has been materially directed to that business, and to get as many of the Saints ready to go out from these countries this season as possible. My counselors and the ministering Priesthood in general have effectively assisted me in carrying out the necessary measures. Even the Saints themselves, being anxious to improve the opportunity of going home to Zion, have, many of them, as their means and circumstances would allow, lent a helping hand to others, which made the company larger than I at first expected. I had, therefore, the great satisfaction of bringing over to you 355 souls, * * who are now on the great Atlantic with the English and Swiss Saints. * *

"Through reports from the various parts of the mission, I am happy to say that the prospects are good and that the Lord has blessed the faithful Elders in their endeavors to spread the gospel truths."

CHAPTER 35 (1859)

Conditions in Norway and Sweden—The Elders in Norway continue to suffer imprisonment for preaching and baptizing—New branches of the Church organized in Sweden—Progress of the work in Denmark—Arrival of Elders John Van Cott and Ola N. Liljenquist—Important Priesthood meeting—Statistical report.

President Carl Widerborg reported to Pres. Asa Calkin in England (under date of June 30, 1859), as follows:

"Brothers Niels Wilhelmsen and Peter F. Thomassen have faithfully aided me in the duties of the presidency. Most parts of the mission have been visited and the Priesthood and Saints encouraged, instructed and edified; and the Lord has prospered us, for which we feel exceedingly grateful. * *

"With regard to Denmark, I have before mentioned that we have comparatively great liberty in the exercise of our religion, and we have not this year met with any opposition or persecution worth mentioning.

"In Norway some of the Elders have been sentenced and imprisoned, but in Christiania they have had much peace. It seems that the government there intends to lay before the legislature (Storthing), which will be in session next winter, a proposition or bill regarding 'Mormons.' What may result therefrom, I do not know at present, but I believe the legislators are inclined to give us more liberty, or at least the same liberty as others (dissenters) enjoy. I am judging from the fact that the government has charged the clergy to send in statistical reports and information of the increase or decrease of 'Mormonism.' The parson in Christiania applied to the presiding Elder, Brother Gudmundsen, for his help in giving correct statements as required by the government. Brother Gudmundsen offered to give him the necessary information regarding not only our Church in Christiania, but over the whole country, which was accepted with thankfulness. Accordingly, Brother Gudmundsen made out a statistical report, such as is used among us, both for last year and for this, and the parson declared himself very much obliged to Gudmundsen for the same, and said that we had good order amongst us, and that he in his report could not but speak in favor of the morals of the 'Mormons' as far as he knew. The police authorities in Christiania also speak highly of the orderly behavior of the members of our Church.

"Concerning Sweden, I may say that I have visited the conferences there and found the Priesthood and Saints doing well, considering what they have to grapple with, as the priests, through the police, have done their utmost of late to hinder and break up our public meetings; wherefore the Saints have had to gather in a more private capacity and with as little stir as possible. It was, therefore, a great treat to them to come together in the capacity of conference meetings, which we held in Malmö on the 25th of May, in Norrköping on the 5th, in Stockholm on the 12th, and in Göteborg on the 19th of June. * * We were not disturbed in any place, our meetings being held in private houses by ourselves, and the Lord favored us with peace and joy, and poured out his Holy Spirit upon us, making us to rejoice and prophesy good things about the kingdom.

"In the conference meeting in Stockholm, I felt prompted by the Spirit to organize a conference in the northern part of Sweden, by the name of Sundsvall."

A brother, Anders Andersen, was imprisoned in Drammen, Norway, Feb. 23, for administering the gospel ordinances in that city, and thus became a companion of Elder Hans O. Magleby for about five days.

Elder Ole E. Örstad was incarcerated June 26, 1859, for fourteen days on Hasselöen to expiate a fine.

Elder Hans O. Magleby was imprisoned in Drammen, Feb. 15, 1859. This was his fifth experience of the kind. While in prison he wrote on the 18th: "Today it is two years since I was sitting here the first time." Elder Magleby was liberated March 9, 1859, after having expiated a fine of 150 speciedaler. This time Elder Magleby left his prison, never more to return to it as he was now free and ready to emigrate to Zion.

Elder Frederik G. S. Lyngberg was released from confinement in Trondhjem, Norway, Feb. 10, 1859, after serving 14 days in prison. Elder Lars Petersen was liberated in Österrisör, after having been imprisoned April 23rd, for 20 days to settle for a fine of 150 speciedaler. Elder Niels Petersen was imprisoned in Land parish, Hedemarken, to serve six days, in lieu of paying a fine of 15 speciedaler.

All these imprisonments carried with them a diet on bread and water, and were imposed upon the Elders for preaching and baptizing.

At a conference council meeting held in Göteborg, Sweden, June 19, 1859, it was reported that no public meetings had been held in Göteborg or Halmstad for several months, because of police interference. In other places the Elders had been arrested on charges of vagrancy and deported. In these persecution against the Elders, the Luthera clergy had as usual taken an activ part.

A new branch was organized in th Göteborg Conference, called th Vänersborg Branch, Feb. 23, 185 with Swen J. Pettersson as presiden

At a conference held at Valb Sweden, August 31st, the Saints li ing in the province of Blekinge we organized into a branch of th Church called the Karlshamn Branc and the Saints residing in or ne Kullenberg were organized as th Kullenberg Branch.

The different localities in th Skåne Conference were organized i to districts and the necessary presi ing officers appointed. Similar visions of conferences into distric were done about the same tin throughout the entire Scandinavi Mission.

Arrests and imprisonments of El ers in Sweden for preaching we not as numerous as before; yet May, 1859, Elder Nils Bengtson w imprisoned on bread and water f advocating true Christianity.

Denmark continued to be a fru ful field of the Elders, and sever new branches of the Church we organized. Thus, at a conferen held in Aalborg, Feb. 13, 1859, new branch of the Church w organized on the south side of t Mariager Fjord, called the Stru holm Branch, and at a conferen held at Aalborg, Sept. 25th, n branches were organized at Br derslev, Skjæve, and Hellevad, all Vendsyssel.

Occasional arrests and impris ments of Elders also took place Denmark in 1859. Thus Elders L Larsen and Hans Peter Iversen w imprisoned in Veile, March 1, 18 to expiate a fine to which they l been sentenced for having preached the gospel. They spent five days in prison.

In April, 1859, Elder Jabez Woodard, of the Swiss and German Mission, arrived in Copenhagen on a visit. After spending a few days very pleasantly with the brethren and local Saints in Copenhagen, he returned to his field of labor.

On Tuesday, Oct. 18, 1859, (the regular Danish "Flyttedag" (moving day), the mission office in Copenhagen was moved into the well-known suite of rooms in Lorentzensgade (later named St. Paulsgade) No. 14, 1st Sal, which was used continuously for a mission office for 43 years, or until the year 1902, when the Church built a house of its own in Korsgade No. 11.

Elders John Van Cott and Ola N. Liljenquist arrived in Copenhagen, as missionaries from Zion, Nov. 23, 1859. Elder Van Cott had been called by the Presidency of the Church to take charge of the Scandinavian Mission, a second time. Brother Liljenquist was the first man among those who had embraced the gospel in Scandinavia to return to his native land as a missionary from Zion. These two brethren, who were so well and favorably known to the Saints from their former labors as missionaries in Scandinavia, received a most hearty and affectionate welcome by both Saints and strangers, and their inspired sermons, which they delivered afterwards in visiting the different conferences and branches in the mission, did much to give a fresh impetus to the work of the Lord in the northern countries.

Another council meeting of the Priesthood of the Scandinavian Mission was held in Copenhagen Dec. 22nd, 23rd and 24th. Encouraging reports were given in these meetings

by the respective presiding Elders. Elder Jens C. A. Weibye reported splendid progress in Vendsyssel, where he presided over the conference. Elder Hans Jensen, president

OLA NILSON LILJENQUIST

Born Sept. 23, 1825, in Inaberga, Malmöhus Län, Sweden, was baptized by William Andersen; ordained to the Priesthood and called into the local ministry, in which he labored about four and one-half years, part of the time a president of the Copenhagen Conference. He emigrated to Utah in 1857, and located in Goshen, Utah County. In filling a mission to Scandinavia, in 1859-1862, he was the first of the converts in Scandinavia who returned from Zion to preach in his native land; he labored as traveling Elder in the mission and led a large company of emigrating Saints to Utah in 1862; removed to Hyrum, Cache County, where he acted as Bishop for many years. He filled a second mission to Scandinavia in 1876-1878, presiding over the Scandinavian Mission. Later he was appointed a general missionary and Patriarch in all the Stakes of Zion. He died April 24, 1906, at Rexburg, Idaho.

of Aalborg Conference, reported that schools in which the Saints were taught the English language were doing a great deal of good. Elder Gustaf A. Ohlson, president of the Stockholm Conference, reported that two of his fellow-laborers were compelled to spend Christmas in prison, as they had been sentenced to imprisonment for one month for having preached the gospel. He believed that a great work would be done in Sweden when the people were given religious liberty.

Elder Lars Chr. Geertsen, president of the Aarhus Conference, stated that the brethren had introduced the gospel into many parts of the country, where it had not formerly been preached. Elder Peter Nielsen, president of the Fredericia Conference, reported that the Elders had obtained a foothold in the city of Horsens.

Elder Ole Nilsson (Stohl), president of the Norrköping Conference, reported well-attined meetings during the winter months. In Göteborg, Sweden, a Lutheran clergyman (Vieselgren) had stirred up the people to mob violence by his misrepresentation and false accusations of the Saints and their religion. In the Skåne Conference, the Saints had enjoyed comparative peace of late, which was partly due to the fact that a certain Lutheran bishop, who had recently located in the city of Lund, had instructed the clergy under him not to persecute the "Mormons," but endeavor by persuasion and prayer to show them the error of their way.

As Brother Saamund Gudmundsen, president of the Brevig Conference, could not attend the council, owing to the irregularity of the steamship traffic in the dead of winter, Pres. Widerborg reported that the Elders in Norway had succeeded in obtaining openings for preaching in different parts of the country where missionary labors had not been done before. But the opposition was great and a number of the Elders had been imprisoned on bread and water for preaching and administering gospel ordinances. At one place where an Elder held a meeting, an officer (Lensmand) appeared with 40 men to arrest him. They put him in chains and carried him away as if he was

a hardened criminal, because he ha preached repentance, faith and ba tism for the remission of sins. Mar sincere people in Norway were pr vented from joining the Chur through fear of the priests and t police authorities. Pres. Widerbo also reported the Sundsvall Confe ence and stated that the people northern Sweden were peaceable ar the civil authorities humane. T few Saints who lived in these nort ern regions in a scattered conditic were generally good and faithfu

Elder Chr. P. Rönnow, preside of the Fyen Conference, stated th the Saints had suffered some pe secution in different places, partic larly in the city of Assens, whe both clergy and civil authorities o posed the brethren with great enmit

On the last day of the conferen quite a number of changes in t presiding officers were made.

According to the official statistic report of Dec. 31, 1859, the Scand navian Mission at the close of t year 1859 contained 3,934 baptiz members of the Church, namel 2,512 in Denmark, 562 in Norw and 860 in Sweden. Of these 5 were Elders, 191 Priests, 165 Teac ers and 82 Deacons. The Missic was divided into 15 conferences ar 145 branches. During the past ye 929 had been baptized, namely, 5 in Denmark, 153 in Norway and 2 in Sweden. During the year 460 ha been excommunicated, 263 had em grated and 40 died. The Saints ha been very diligent in doing their du temporally, so much so that Pre Widerborg during the year had bee enabled to send 11,000 rigsdal ($5,550) in tithing and about 9 rigsdaler ($450) in book money the office in Liverpool. Pres. Wide borg and Elder Niels Wilhelms had traveled much in the missic nd visited the different conferences, while Elder Peter O. Thomassen had abored almost continuously at the ffice in Copenhagen. Good and aithful Elders presided over the respective conferences.

In Denmark the persecutions had lmost ceased, while the Elders in orway were frequently subjected to rrest and imprisonment on bread nd water. Christiania, however, was 1 exception to that rule, for there 1e civil authorities had learned to 1ow the Saints as men and women ho were exemplary and moral in l their deportment, and consequent- ' they were not disturbed.

Owing to the bitterness of the olice officers in Sweden, the Saints that country were compelled to old their meetings in secret, but rests were not as frequent as pre- ously, and, in the province of kåne, the persecution had nearly ased altogether, the same as in enmark. Pres. Widerborg had sited all the Swedish conferences ring the summer, and conference eetings had been held by him in almö, Norrköping, Stockholm and öteborg. During the conference in ockholm on June 13, 1859, he had ganized the Sundsvall Conference, northern Sweden, and appointed lder Carl E. Lindholm as president the same. The new conference, 1ich at the time of its organization ly numbered 26 members, included orrland clear up to the boundary Finland (then Russia). With the ganization of the Sundsvall Con- rence, all of the three Scandinavian untries were divided into branches d conferences.

While a number of new branches re organized in the Scandinavian ission in 1859, a number of the aller branches were discontinued d their membership added to the larger branches in their respective localities.

CHAPTER 36 (1860)

John Van Cott again presides over the Scandinavian Mission—Swedish hymn book published—Elder Mads P. Sörensen imprisoned—Emigration of Saints.

With the beginning of 1860, Elder John Van Cott succeeded Elder Carl Widerborg as president of the Scandinavian Mission. This gave the latter a chance to visit relatives and rest up a little before emigrating to Zion. For seven years he had labored faithfully and unceasingly in the ministry, and during the past two years presided over the mission. He was highly beloved by the Saints, and his fellow-laborers in particular, and all felt that his departure was a great loss to the mission. In his last report to Liverpool, he spoke very feelingly about Elders Niels Wilhelmsen and Peter O. Thomassen, who had acted as his counselors and who, together with the conference presidents, had been his chief aids, as they had labored with great diligence and ·faithfulness in their respective positions. Elder John Van Cott chose no counselors, but appointed Ola N. Liljenquist as traveling Elder in the whole mission and Elders Peter O. Thomassen and Carl Larsen as his assistants in the mission office. Brother Larsen had labored at the mission office since July 1, 1859.

In the early part of 1860, a hymn book for the use of the Saints in Sweden was published in the Swedish language. It was compiled by Elder Jonas Engberg under the direction of the mission president. The first edition, consisting of 2000 copies, contained 126 hymns. Three other editions of the book were afterwards published, namely, the second edition of 4000 copies in 1863 by Jesse N.

Smith; the third edition (3000 copies) in 1873, by Canute Peterson, and the fourth edition (3000 copies) in 1881 by Niels Wilhelmsen. The three later editions each contained 252 hymns, twice the number published in the first edition. At least three other, editions have appeared subsequently.

In May, 1860, Elder Mads P. Sörensen, who had been fined for selling religious tracts, etc., in Denmark, served a term of imprisonment in Veile, Denmark. He was arraigned before the court in that town Dec. 8, 1859. His case was appealed to the higher court in Viborg, and in March, 1860, this court sentenced him to pay five rigsdaler in fine and five rigsdaler to each of the lawyers, but the case was appealed to the supreme court of Denmark. In the final judgment, Brother Sörensen was sentenced to pay a fine, or serve a term in prison in lieu of the fine. He had not transgressed any law of the land, except one which was not intended to cover such a case, but which, through prejudice and hatred on the part of the civil authorities toward the "Mormons," was applied to his case by a most unique and strained legal interpretation.

On Wednesday, May 2, 1860, 301 emigrating Saints, viz., 182 Danish, 80 Swedish and 39 Norwegian, sailed from Copenhagen, Denmark, on board the new Prussian steamship "Pauline," under the leadership of Carl Widerborg, who now emigrated to Zion. The voyage over the Cattegat and North Sea being stormy, a number of the emigrants suffered with seasickness, but the company arrived safe and well in Grimsby, England, May 5th. From Grimsby, the emigrants continued the journey to Liverpool, where they arrived Sunday afternoon, May 6th,

and secured lodgings in a hotel on Paradise Street. On Monday, May 7th, they boarded the "William Tapscott" a freight ship, which the previous year had brought a large company of emigrating Saints across the Atlantic. Besides the Scandinavian Saints, 85 Swiss and a large company of Welsh and English Saints went on board the same ship bound for America. Among the English were Elders Asa Calkin, who had presided over the European Mission, and Thomas Williams, both accompanied by their families. When all were on board, the emigrating Saints numbered 730 souls. Asa Calkin was appointed president of the company, with Elders William Budge and Carl Widerborg as counselors. The company was divided into nine districts, each with a district president. The district presidents of the Scandinavian contingent were Lars Eriksen, assisted by Hans Jensen; Mads Poulsen from Copenhagen, assisted by Carl J. E. Fjeld from Norway; Elder Christensen (Dannebrogsmand), assisted by Paul Stark from Sweden, Jöns Jönsson from Malmö, assisted by Sören Möller, and Ingvardt Hansen from Aarhus, assisted by Hans M. Nisson from Lohland. Swen Lövendahl was appointed captain of the guard and Nils Larson from Skåne, Sweden, cook.

The "William Tapscott" sailed from Liverpool, May 11, 1860. It was a fine ship and a splendid sailer but, owing to contrary winds, the voyage consumed 35 days. Union and good order prevailed during the whole voyage. Prayer was held every morning and evening, and on Sundays religious services were held on the deck. Owing to cold and a change of diet, considerable sickness prevailed among the emi grants, and ten deaths occurred, most of them among the Scandinavian Saints. Four children were born on board and nine couples married, among whom were Hans Christian Heiselt and Larsine Larsen from the Vendsyssel Conference, Denmark. On the 3rd of June, the smallpox showed itself among the emigrants, seven cases of this disease were reported, none of which, however, proved fatal. On Friday evening, June 15th, the ship arrived at the quarantine dock in New York harbor. The next day two doctors came on board and vaccinated, with but very few exceptions, all of the steerage passengers, a part of the cabin passengers, and the ship's crew. This was done to prevent a further outbreak of the disease, though all the sick had nearly recovered by this time. On the 20th, after being detained in quarantine five or six days, the passengers were landed at Castle Garden, New York. The smallpox cases had previously been taken ashore and placed in a hospital. On the 21st the emigrants left New York per steamboat "Isaac Newton" and sailed up the Hudson River to Albany, where they arrived on the 22nd. From Albany the journey was continued via Rochester to Niagara Falls, where the train stopped about seven hours in order to give the emigrants the pleasure of seeing the great waterfall and the grand suspension bridge. The journey was continued through Canada along the north shore of Lake Erie to Windsor, where the river was crossed to Detroit in Michigan. Thence to Chicago, which city was reached June 25th.

From Chicago, the emigrants traveled by railroad to Quincy, Ill., whence they crossed the Mississippi River to Hannibal in Missouri, and thence traveled by railroad to St. Joseph, Mo. Here 13 persons were placed in a hospital, but upon close examination they were found to be well enough to join the company the following day on the trip up the Missouri River, to Florence, Neb., where the company arrived in the night between June 30th and July 1st.

Elder George Q. Cannon, who this year acted as Church emigration agent, made splendid arrangements for the journey across the Plains. It was deemed wisdom to send the emigrants as far as possible by steam and avoid the toilsome and harrassing part of the team journey from Iowa City to Florence, a distance of nearly 300 miles, which in former years had required from 15 to 20 days' travel. It had been learned by experience that the distance between Iowa City and Florence, at the season of the year when the emigrants had to travel it, was, in point of toil and hardship, by far the worst part of the journey, owing to its being a low, wet country, which in the opening of the year was subject to heavy and continued rains. These storms, owing to the nature of the soil (being clay most of the distance), rendered the roads almost impassable. Arriving at Florence, the emigrants found shelter in a number of empty houses while they made the necessary preparations for crossing the Plains.

A handcart company consisting of 126 souls, traveling with 22 handcarts and 6 wagons, left Florence on their westward journey July 6th, under the leadership of Capt. Oscar O. Stoddard. The company was divided into three parts under Elders D. Fischer, Anders Christensen and Carl J. E. Fjeld, respectively. After a journey of 81 days, the company arrived in Salt Lake City, Sept. 24, 1859, having suffered the ordinary hardships and difficulties incident to all handcart travel. Considerable sickness prevailed among the emigrants during the journey, and a number of animals died, which made the latter part of the journey particularly difficult.

The last ox-train of the season, with which a number of the Scandinavian emigrants crossed the plains, left Florence soon after the handcart company and arrived in Salt Lake City, Oct. 5th. This company consisted of about 400 souls, traveling with 55 wagons, 215 oxen and 77 cows, all under the leadership of Elder William Budge, but the Scandinavian and Swiss contingent traveled under the immediate direction of Elder Carl Widerborg, part of the way separate from the rest of the company. Four deaths and four births took place on the journey.

A company of English and Scandinavian Saints, who had been temporarily located at different places in the United States, principally in Iowa and Nebraska, left Florence for the West July 3rd. This company, which consisted of 123 souls, was led by Elder John Taylor, assisted in the Scandinavian division by Elder Jens Peter Christensen, who had spent about five years in the States and presided for one year over a Danish branch of the Church at Alton, Ill. After a successful journey across the plains, this company arrived in Salt Lake City, Sept. 17, 1860.

CHAPTER 37 (1860)

Arrival of ten missionaries from Zion—Visit of Apostles Amasa M. Lyman and Charles C. Rich—Catechism for children published—Traveling without purse and scrip—A growing mission.

The year 1860, which marked the first decade of the Scandinavia Mission, witnessed the work of th Lord somewhat thoroughly esta lished in all three Scandinavian cou tries.

At a conference held in Stoc holm, Sweden, in June, 1860, th Saints residing in a certain part c Westmanland were organized into branch of the Church called th West Löfstad Branch, with Eld Elias Eliasson as president. A other branch, called the Fahlu Branch, was organized with Eld Lars S. Spongberg as president.

Among the faithful Elders wh had labored in Norway as mi sionaries was Elder Anders Pete sen, who died at Sarpsberg Jan. 1 1860, in the home of his parent Elder Petersen was a most energeti missionary, and a man of nobl character in every respect and muc beloved by the Saints and all wh knew him. Until he was taken sick he labored as a missionary in th Drammen and Hurum districts.

On Monday, Sept. 3, 1860, the fo lowing named Elders arrived in Co penhagen as missionaries to Scandi navia: Christian A. Madsen, Carl C N. Dorius, Sören Christofferser Peter Beckström, Knud H. Bruun and Hans Peter Lund. These Elder had left Salt Lake City, April 27 1860, and crossed the Plains togethe with other missionaries called to dif ferent parts of the world. They ar rived in Florence, Neb., July 1, 186 and in New York July 18th, saile thence, Aug. 3rd, for Liverpool, Eng land, where they arrived Aug. 26th After receiving instructions from Apostle Amasa M. Lyman, they lef Liverpool Aug. 27th, sailed from Hull by steamer "Urania" Aug. 30th occupying a nice stateroom by them selves and had good board. The were favored with beautiful weather nd after a voyage of 47 hours across ne North Sea, they landed in Hamnurg on Sunday, Sept. 2nd. Thence rey traveled by train to Kiel, by

KNUD HANSEN BRUUN

Born Jan. 1, 1921, in North Schleswig, was naptized Aug 17, 1850, by Geo. P. Dykes, labored as a local missionary in Denmark about hree years, suffered much persecution, emigrated to Utah in 1853-54, and filled two missions from Utah to Scandinavia (1860-1863 and 1875-1877).

teamer to Korsör, and by rail to Copenhagen.

Elders Anders Christensen and and Hans Chr. Hansen, who had left Utah together with the other missionaries April 27, 1860, but had been delayed on the journey through lack of means, arrived in Copenhagen as missionaries to Scandinavia Sept. 24, 1860. These brethren, together with those who arrived Sept. 3rd, and two who arrived in Christiania, Norway, Sept. 4th, were all natives of the Scandinavian countries who labored as missionaries before they emigrated to Utah. Their return to their native countries as witnesses of Zion and her cause sent a thrill of joy to

the hearts of the Saints throughout the mission.

Apostles Amasa M. Lyman and Charles C. Rich, who presided over the European Mission, arrived in Copenhagen on a visit to Scandinavia, Oct. 10, 1860, after having attended meetings on Nörrebro and Enighedsværn (Copenhagen). The Apostles, accompanied by Pres. John Van Cott, visited Christiania in Norway, where Elders Carl C. N. and Johan F. F. Dorius labored as missionaries and where the visiting brethren attended conference Oct. 19th and 21st. From Christiania the brethren went to Göteborg, Sweden, where they held a meeting and then proceeded to Stockholm. Here they attended a conference Oct. 28th, and returned to Copenhagen Nov. 2nd, where they, on Sunday, Nov. 4th, addressed a large congregation on Enighedsværn, and on the evening of the same day left Copenhagen on their return to England. The visit of these two Apostles in the Scandinavian Mission cheered and comforted the Saints very much.

In the beginning of December, 1860, a Danish translation of John Jaques' splendid little work "Catechism for Children" was published, in Scandinavia. The book was translated by Elder Peter O. Thomassen, and the first edition consisted of 3000 copies. Another edition of 3000 copies was published by Pres. Canute Peterson late in 1872. For a number of years this book was used very extensively in the Scandinavian Mission, especially in the Sunday schools, which were organized in the interest of the children of the Latter-day Saints.

Until the close of the year 1860, a part of the tithing contributed to the Church in the European Mission was used for the sustenance of the missionaries, traveling expenses, and the maintenance of the branches and conferences, etc. But, according to a communication from President Brigham Young, dated Salt Lake City, Sept. 13, 1860, and addressed to President Amasa M. Lyman and Charles C. Rich, the Elders were advised not to use the tithing for these purposes. The letter says: "The tithing must be credited to those who pay it, to the utmost farthing; and then Elders must not be lovers of money, but must, at all times, hold every farthing of tithing strictly subject to advice from here, and on no account use it without such advice. The Elders are invariably instructed to travel and preach without purse and scrip as did the Elders anciently, and should, therefore, in all cases sustain themselvees as far as possible, and in no manner and way oppress the brethren nor the cause." This communication was published in "Skandinaviens Stjerne" of Dec. 1, 1860, and the new order of things was introduced at once in the Scandinavian Mission. From that time on the brethren laboring as missionaries had to sustain themselves by manual labor, or by free-will offerings from the Saints. The expenses connected with the maintenance of the respective branches and conferences had to be borne in a similar way, which often was no easy matter, as the great majority of the Saints were poor. It also put the faith of the missionaries to a severe test, and several who had not faith enough to travel without purse or scrip were, according to their own request, released from their missionary labors. But the more influential and diligent Elders continued their activities with the same energy as formerly, and the Lord opened the way so that they very

seldom suffered for the necessities of life. After the enforcement of this order of things, it became impossible for any one to labor without being directed and strengthened by the influence of the Holy Spirit, for the brethren had to proceed with their labors in such a way that their faithfulness could win the approbation of God and his Saints, as well as strangers. After that, a considerable portion of the tithing paid was used for the emigration of the poor, while at the same time large sums were sent to the headquarters of the Church and there spent for the building of the Temple and for other purposes connected with the kingdom of God.

The year 1860 was a prosperous one for the Scandinavian Mission, 1,107 persons were baptized throughout the mission, which was a greater number than had joined the Church in any previous year since the mission was commenced. At the close of 1860 twelve Elders from Zion were engaged in missionary labors in Scandinavia, besides a large number of able and faithful local Elders who had been chosen for the ministry from among the converts. The mission at that time had a total membership of 4,416 and was divided into 15 conferences and 136 branches. Following is a list of the conferences and their presiding officers and missionaries from Zion laboring in the Scandinavian Mission at the close of 1860:

DENMARK

Aalborg Conference (Rasmus Nielsen, president) with 379 members, divided into 9 branches.

Aarhus Conference (Lars Chr. Geertsen, president) with a membership of 229 and divided into 9 branches.

Bornholm Conference (Mads Andersen, president) with a membership of 99, divided into 4 branches.

Copenhagen Conference (Niels Wilhelm-n, president) with 1,023 members, divided into 15 branches.

Fredericia Conference (Peter Nielsen, president) with 204 members, divided into branches.

Fyen Conference (Christian P. Rönnow, president) with 149 members, divided into branches.

Lolland Conference (Jens Hansen, president) with a membership of 162, divided into 6 branches.

Skive Conference (Aaron G. Ömann, resident) with a membership of 55, divided into 5 branches.

Vendsyssel Conference (Jens C. A. Veibye, president) with 419 members, divided into 20 branches.

NORWAY

Christiania Conference (Carl C. N. Dorius, president) with a membership of 695, divided into 14 branches.

SWEDEN

Göteborg Conference (Rasmus Berntzon, president) with 138 members, divided into 5 branches.

Norrköping Conference (Ole Nilsson Stohl, president) with 905 members, divided into 10 branches.

Skåne Conference (Johan Fagerberg, president) with a membership of 533, divided into 13 branches.

Stockholm Conference (Carl Johan Sund-bäck, president) with a membership of 102, divided into 6 branches.

Sundsvall Conference (Carl Erik Lindholm, president) with 37 members, divided into 2 branches.

The Elders from Zion laboring in the mission at the close of 1860 were the following:

1. John Van Cott, president of the mission.

2. Ola N. Liljenquist, traveling Elder in the whole mission.

3. Christian A. Madsen, pastor of Aalborg and Vendsyssel conferences.

4. Carl C. N. Dorius, president of the Brevig Conference, Norway.

5. Sören Christoffersen, pastor of Aarhus and Skive conferences.

6. Peter Beckström, traveling Elder in Sweden.

7. Knud H. Bruun, traveling Elder in the Fredericia and Fyen conferences.

8. Hans Peter Lund, traveling Elder in the mission.

9. Johan F. F. Dorius, missionary in Norway.

10. H. Olin Hansen, missionary in Norway.

11. Hans Chr. Hansen, traveling Elder in Jutland, Denmark.

12. Anders Christensen, traveling Elder in Jutland, Denmark.

CHAPTER 38 (1861)

Vendsyssel, Denmark, as a fruitful missionary field—Arrival of Elders Jesse N. Smith, Wm. W. Cluff and Johan P. R. Johansen—The spirit of gathering prevails—A large company of emigrating Saints leaves Scandinavia.

Elder Anders Christensen, in a communication dated Aalborg, Jan. 4, 1861, wrote the following:

"This place (Vendsyssel) is a curious place; it extends to the North Sea on the west, and on the east to Cattegat, and it is separated from the rest of Jutland by a bay on the south, called Limfjorden. In the times when the Roman Catholics made their conquests in Germany and these northern lands, they were never able to conquer this little place, which contains now only about 60,000 inhabitants, and at that time much less. The people were brave and fearless for the threatening tyrants, and took up their arms, and finally succeeded in redeeming this little Vendsyssel from their intruders; Catholicism was consequently never introduced here, and the ancient saying was, that the north side of said bay (Limfjorden) was the north side of righteousness.

"To look at the situation of this people, and see their liberality, kindness and freedom of spirit, I think it is very plain to see the good effects of their never having been under the mother church and like influences. Greater numbers have been baptized here, according to its population, than in any other place I know of, and there are still greater numbers who believe the gospel; and in general the Elders are treated very kindly by a great many people here. A good many of those who embrace the gospel have been in possession of means, and been very liberal in assisting the Elders to send off the poorer class to the Valley. All the Elders who come here admire the freedom of spirit, and in general feel desirous of proclaiming the gospel."

On Friday, Jan. 11, 1861, three Elders from Zion arrived in Copenhagen, Denmark, as missionaries to Scandinavia, viz., Jesse N. Smith of Parowan, Utah, and Elders Wm. W. Cluff and Johannes P. R. Johansen (Johnson) of Provo, Utah. They came direct from London and had been 11 days on the way from that city, traveling by way of Holland and Germany. They had a very rough passage across the North Sea.

JOHANNES PETER RASMUS JOHANSEN

Born April 10, 1824, at Lindved, Veile Amt, Denmark; acted for many years as Bishop of the Provo Second Ward, and died July 9, 1910, at Provo, Utah.

Under date of March 3, 1861, President John Van Cott reports as follows:

"There is no lack of spirit to gather out of this land (I mean among the Saints). We are not under the necessity of preaching the gathering, for as soon as any of the Saints can obtain sufficient means to take them to America, they want to go. * * As regards the prospect for the spread of the gospel in this land, it never was better than at the present time. The spirit of inquiry is quite prevalent. Our meetings as a general thing, are well attended by strangers. As far as I have received reports from the conferences for the last quarter, they represent the people, together with the authorities, as a general thing, humane; and the prospect is good. During the last quarter many have been baptized, notwithstanding the cold weather.
* *

"The missionaries from Zion are all well and doing well, as far as I know. Brother Peter Beckström has traveled very extensively in Sweden during the winter. * * Brothers Ola N. Liljenquist and Jesse N. Smith are now in Aalborg. Brother Knud H. Bruun is in Fredericia, Hans C. Hansen in Lolland, and Sören Christoffersen in Aarhus. Brother Johansen, who was one of the last that came, is now president of the Fredericia Conference. The Brothers Dorius were well, and give a flattering account of the work in Norway. * * Brothers Jesse N. Smith and Wm. W. Cluff are making great progress in the language."

On Thursday, May 9, 1861, a company of 565 Scandinavian Saints (373 Danish, 128 Swedish and 64 Norwegian) sailed from Copenhagen by steamer "Waldemar." Pres John Van Cott, who accompanied them to England, joined the emigrants at Kiel. Elders Hans Olin Hansen, Niels Wilhelmsen, Jens Nielsen, Gustaf A. Ohlson, Saamund Gudmundsen, Carl W. J. Hecker, Anders Frantzen and others returned home or emigrated with this company, after having labored faithfully as missionaries in the Scandinavian Mission. After a successful voyage the company arrived at Kiel in the morning of May 10th, and were at once forwarded by special train to Altona, where they arrived about noon. In Altona the company was divided in two parts, of which one (about 200 Saints) immediately boarded the steamer "Brittania" and departed for Hull, England, about 3 p. m. the same day. They arrived at Hull May 12th. The second division (169 souls), having been quartered in a large hall over night, left Hamburg May 11, 1861, at about 3 p. m. by steamer "Eugenia," which, after a pleasant voyage, arrived at Grimsby, England, on the morning of May 13th. The captain of this vessel treated the emigrants with all due respect and kindness, while the opposite was the case on the steamer "Brittania." The two companies joined together again at Grimsby, where they were comfortably cared for until the morning of May 14th, when they proceeded by special train to Liverpool, arriving in that city about 2 p. m. Two hours later they were placed on board the ship "The Monarch of the Sea," the largest vessel that had carried Latter-day Saint emigrants across the Atlantic up to that date. This company of Saints was also until then the largest to cross the Ocean on one ship. On May 16th, the company was organized by Presidents Amasa M. Lyman, Chas. C. Rich and Geo. Q. Cannon, who appointed Elder Jabez Woodard from Switzerland, president, with Hans Olin Hansen and Niels Wilhelmsen as his counselors. At 11 a. m. the great vessel lifted anchor, and, amid great cheers of parting friends, the ship left the wharf and began its long voyage. Later the large company was divided into districts, the Scandinavian in seven and the English and Germans into three or four, each under a president. The names of these presidents were: Edward Read, John J. P. Wallace, Horace Pegg, Peter Nielsen, Saamund Gudmundsen, Gustaf A. Ohlson, Aaron G. Öman, Lars C. Geertsen, Johan Fagerberg and Rasmus Nielsen; the latter also acted as marshal for the Scandinavians. Elias L. T. Harrison was appointed chief

secretary, while Lars C. Geertsen was chosen to act as clerk for the Scandinavians. The emigrants were kindly treated by both officers and crew on shipboard and the provisions were good and sufficient. Some inconvenience was experienced in getting the food cooked on the ranges, on account of the great number of pots and kettles to be served in the kitchen, and on this account each family could only cook five times each week. The sick were treated to wine and beer; the adults received boiled sago and the children had milk. On the voyage from Copenhagen to New York nine persons, most of whom were children, died; 14 couples were married and four births took place on board. Of the marriages 11 couples were Scandinavians. Among them were Anders Frantzen of the Aarhus Conference and Maren Mortensen of the Copenhagen Conference. Saamund Gudmundsen and Ellen Maria Mörk of the Brevig Conference, and Carl W. J. Hecker and Karen Marie Madsen of the Vendsyssel Conference. The weather was favorable most of the time during the voyage; the ship, however, had to battle against the wind a couple of days. Large icebergs were passed among which was one judged to tower 200 feet high above water. On June 19th the "Monarch of the Sea" arrived in New York, where the company was met by Elders Jones and Williams and lodged at Castle Garden. Apostle Erastus Snow, who also happened to be in New York at the time, spoke to the Scandinavians in the Danish language.

From New York the company traveled by rail and steamboat (part of the way in two divisions) to Florence, Neb., the first division arriving at Florence July 1st, and the second July 2nd. The route taken was

about the same as the year before
(via Dunkirk, Cleveland, Chicago,
Quincy, St. Joseph, etc.).

Preparations for the journey across
the Plains were at once made and
all who had not the means to fit
themselves out for the long journey
were assisted by teams from Utah,
which this year for the first time
were sent in large companies by the
Church to the Missouri River to assist the poor Saints in gathering to
Zion. Most of the Scandinavians
grants assisted in this manner crossed
the Plains in Capt. John R. Murdock's company, which left Florence
in the beginning of July and arrived in Salt Lake City, Sept. 12th.
The rest of the emigrants—those who
possessed sufficient means to help
themselves—left Florence a few days
later under the leadership of Captain
Samuel A. Woolley with about 60 ox-
teams. After traveling for some distance, the company was divided into
two sections, and Elder Porter was
appointed captain of the second division. On Sunday, Sept. 22nd, this
company arrived safely in Salt Lake
City.

Between 4000 and 5000 emigrants
crossed the Plains in 1861, destined
for Utah. The Church sent out 200
wagons, with four yoke of oxen for
each, and taking along 150,000
pounds of flour and other provisions.
By this arrangement 1900 Saints,
who were not able to provide their
own outfits for the long journey, but
who wished to leave Florence, were
assisted by the Church.

Pres. John Van Cott returned to
Copenhagen, May 22, 1861, from his
trip to England. While in Liverpool,
it was decided to attach the Hamburg Branch to the Scandinavian
Mission; it had previously belonged
to the German Mission. Soon afterwards Pres. Van Cott appointed Peter

Wilhelm Poulsen to visit the Sain
in Hamburg and set things in ord
there as far as possible. After i
forming the few Saints there of th
transfer of the Hamburg Branc
from the German to the Scand
navian Mission, Elder Poulsen o
dained one of the local brethren a
Elder. A month or so later, Eld
Georg Petersen of Copenhagen wa
appointed president of the Hambur
Branch. On his way to Hamburg
Bro. Petersen baptized one perso
in Kiel.

About this time, Pres. John Va
Cott printed a small tract in th
German language and sent Bro
Petersen 1000 copies of the same t
circulate among the people in Han
burg and vicinity as soon as circum
stances would permit.

CHAPTER 39 (1861)

A second visit to Scandinavia by Apostle
Amasa M. Lyman and Charles C. Rich—Elde
Lyman's graphic description of Denmark—Loca
Elders praised—Nearly 2,000 souls added t
the Church by baptism in one year—A branc
of the Church organized on the island o
Gotland, Sweden.

Apostles Amasa M. Lyman an
Charles C. Rich, presidents of th
European Mission, arrived in Co
penhagen on another visit to Scandi
navia, Aug. 21, 1861, accompanied
by Pres. John Van Cott, who had
gone as far as Hamburg to mee
them. After spending several days
sight-seeing and attending meetings
in Copenhagen, the two Apostles, and
Pres. Van Cott, visited Jutland, Denmark. Elder Lyman writes:

"Of our journey from Copenhagen to
Aalborg I need only remark that no thrill-
ing incidents were connected with its con-
summation. Brother Van Cott was with us.
We passed the night very pleasantly in
unbroken sleep, and at a quarter past 7
o'clock we arrived at Aalborg, where we
were met and welcomed by Elders Christian A. Madsen and L. P. Larsen, who
conducted us to the residence of Brother

Larsen, where we met Elders Jesse N. Smith and Hans C. Hansen. During the day several of the Saints called to see us and gave us a hearty welcome and a good Danish shake of the hand, which, by-the-by, is no sickly, indifferent affair; for, with a warm heart and stalwart frame, the

APOSTLE AMASA M. LYMAN

Born March 30, 1813, at Lyman, Grafton County, New Hampshire; died Feb. 4, 1877, at Fillmore, Utah.

soul's affections, of necessity, sought expression in the strong grasp of earnest, honest friendship, as it was denied the privilege of more intelligible utterance to us.

"On the day following our arrival in Aalborg, we were furnished with a carriage and team for traveling in the country. At 4 o'clock we crossed the Limfjord in a small boat, while our carriage and team passed over in a larger one. Joining our carriage, we rolled away on a very good road to Hjörring. The country through which we passed was generally flat, with slight undulations, somewhat resembling, in this respect, the prairies of the great West. Like them, it is destitute of timber, save here and there some isolated small groups of the native forest growth; in contrast with the green foliage of which were sometimes to be seen the white walls of the residences of the better class of farmers. This contrast affords a pleasing variety to break the monotony that in its absence would meet the eye of the traveler. The highest parts of many of the low ridges, joined by the undulating character of the country, were crowned with numerous tumular mounds resembling those so common in parts of the continent of America,

and their excavation discloses similar historic evidences of their origin and uses.

* *

"The character of the soil over which we passed was poor (as compared with the soil of the valleys of Utah), sand predominating in its composition. The cultivation bestowed upon it by the hardy husbandman brings only partially remunerative crops to compensate his toil and meet his most pressing requirements. After a ride of some 29 English miles, we arrived in Hjörring, where we were welcomed by the president of the Vendsyssel Conference, Elder Jens C. A. Weibye, with whom we had our lodgings.

"On Sunday, August 25th, we traveled about 11 miles to the residence of Mr. Johan Petersen, who had kindly extended the use of his large barn to the Saints (at Tidemensholm) for the holding of their conference. At 10 o'clock some five hundred of the Saints were assembled. The entire number of Saints in the conference was six hundred. The meeting was addressed by Elder Rich, myself, Brother Van Cott and several of the members of the local and traveling ministry. A good spirit pervaded the assembly, which makes the prospects bright for future increase to

APOSTLE CHARLES C. RICH

Born Aug. 21, 1809, in Campbell County, Kentucky, died Oct. 24, 1880, at Paris, Bear Lake County, Idaho.

the Church in this district of country. Conference over, we returned to Hjörring.

"Early on the morning of Monday, the 26th, we took a brief stroll to inhale the morning air, and from an elevated point near the town we had a pleasant view of the surounding country, which seemed one

extended plain, slightly diversified, with
gentle undulations, stretching itself around
us until it met the bright blue of the distant horizon. The blue sea in the northwest was in sight from our pleasant perch
on the heights of Hjörring. We returned
from our stroll refreshed, and in a condition to do ample justice to the breakfast
provided by our kind host. This done, we
were moving on our return to Aalborg,
during which we spent two nights with
some farmers in the country, which incident
was not without its interest to us, as it
afforded us a chance of seeing something
of rural life in the northern portion of the
kingdom of the Danes.

"The habitations of these sons of toil
are very rude, and not generally encum-
bered with any large amount of furniture,
or even floors; yet in these hovels (the
low ceilings of which keep one in constant
remembrance that it is not good to hold the
head too high) with all their indications
of squalor and poverty, the spirit of genial
friendship shed its cheering light; and,
although there were no bedsteads, a liberal
supply of fresh clean straw, placed on the
earthy floor of the best apartment, afforded the traveler an opportunity to think
of the rude and humble entertainment
extended to the Sinner's Friend, and in
sleep to forget the rude couch on which
he finds repose. Thatch is the general
covering of the tenements of the tillers
of the soil; some of the comparatively
wealthy have tile. Among the hardy and
poor class, the gospel at present finds its
votaries—a hardy and sound material or
element for the development and increase
of that world-wide nationality, in the broad
shadow of which the saved of the world
shall repose in the full enjoyment of that
liberty which the gospel promises to the
honest disciple of the truth.

"We returned to Aalborg, where we remained until Sunday, the 1st of September,
when we attended a meeting of the Saints
in Aalborg Conference, which numbers in
full 462, and had a very pleasant time, the
place of meeting being some four miles
away from Aalborg, in the country (Nörre
Uttrup). We remained with our friends
in Aalborg until 5 o'clock on the 3rd, when
I and Brothers Rich, Van Cott, Jesse N.
Smith and Hans C. Hansen bade our kind
friends on the banks of the Limfjord farewell and took passage on board the steamer
"Dania" for Copenhagen, where we arrived
safely and in good health on the morning
of the 4th. We remained here until the
evening of the 7th, when I, with Brothers

Rich and Van Cott, passed over the Sound
(Öresund) to Sweden, landing at Malmö,
where we had a most interesting conference with the Saints, who number 610 in
the conference. On the 9th we returned
to Copenhagen. * *

"At Copenhagen, on the 14th and 15th,
we held a most agreeable and pleasant
conference, on which occasion there were
convened, of the 1,136 Saints contained in
the conference, about 900. The conference
being over, we extended our stay in Copenhagen to the 21st of September. Then myself and Brothers Rich, Van Cott and Jesse
N. Smith started by rail en route for the
island of Fyen, via Korsör, at which place
we took passage on the mail steamer to
Nyborg on Fyen, from which place we
proceeded by carriage to Odense, a distance
of about 18 miles, over a most beautiful
and highly-cultivated country, abounding
in the elements of wealth and rural beauty
in every direction around us. The highly
cultivated farm, with its embellishments
of shrubbery and timber, reminded us of
the best cultivated and richest portions of
the rural districts of England and Scot
land.* *

"On our arrival in Odense we were met
and welcomed, and our wants kindly cared
for, by the president of the conference
Elder Christian P. Rönnow. We also met
at this point the district president, Knud
H. Bruun. The Saints were happy to meet
us, and all seemed to vie with each other
in making us sensible of this by minister
ing in various ways to our comfort and
refreshment during our stay with them.

"On the 21st we held a conference with
the Saints of Fyen, who numbered 170
We protracted our stay in Odense until the
26th, when, with the addition to our party
of Elders Bruun and Rönnow, we left our
friends in Odense and rolled away in an
open carriage over a good road to Brastrup
This was the most pleasing and really in
teresting travel we have had since we
crossed the Atlantic. The entire country
over which we were passing presented to
us, as we passed along, a sea-girt picture
of rural loveliness and beauty. When we
arrived at Brother Andersen's we were
kindly welcomed by himself and family
with whom we tarried until the next morn
ing. While here, one woman was baptized
and on the following morning, by the
kindness of our host, we were conveyed
to the town of Middelfart, where we left
the island and crossed to the continent
While in Middelfart we were provided with
dinner by a sister and a family who did

not then belong to the Church, but have since joined.

"The work is moving on well throughout the island of Fyen. There is a good harvest, and good-spirited laborers are in the field, devoted to the good work.

"After landing on the continent, another brief ride brought us to the small town of Veile, situated at the head of the bay of he same name. On our arrival we were made welcome and comfortable by Brother Johan P. R. Johansen, president of the Fredericia Conference. On Sunday, 29th, we had a pleasant and interesting conference in Veile. The work is on the increase here."

From Veile, the visiting brethren went to Aarhus, where a conference was held on the 5th and 6th of October. They then returned to Copenhagen, whence they started on the 9th for Norway. A conference was commenced in Christiania on Friday, Oct. 11th, and continued on Sunday the 13th. After having spent eight days in Norway, during which the visiting brethren received most expressive proofs of the hospitality and brotherly love on the part of the Norwegian Saints, the visitors returned to Copenhagen, whence Apostles Lyman and Rich on the 25th started on their return trip to England. They arrived in Liverpool, Oct. 29th. During their sojourn in Scandinavia, the Apostles visited altogether eight of the fifteen conferences in the mission and were exceedingly well pleased with their visit among the Saints."

Under date of June 27, 1861, Pres. John Van Cott wrote a long letter to Pres. Geo. Q. Cannon, of which the following is an extract:

"Those who have been engaged in the ministry (in Scandinavia) have, as a general thing, honored their callings, exerting every power and faculty which they possessed in order to enlighten the children of men and lead them in the way of life and salvation. No labor has been considered too arduous, nor has opposition or privation deterred them from pursuing that course which has been marked out. The scoffs and frowns of the wicked have been regarded as emanating from a source or beneath their notice; consequently there has been less time expended on useless objects than otherwise would have been. The Priesthood in general have begun to learn to devote their time to the best advantage, so that when they come into con-

versation with individuals not inclined to receive the truth, they bear a faithful testimony and leave them in the hands of God, devoting their time upon those who are susceptible of the truth."

Elder Chr. A. Madsen, who labored as a missionary on the northern conferences of Jutland, wrote a communication from Aalborg, dated July 24, 1861, to the effect that nearly all the converts made in that part of Denmark were of the poorer class, mostly peasants from the country districts, but they were faithful, and would gladly travel from ten to fifteen miles on Sunday, in rain or shine, to attend meetings. Elder Madsen writes:

"Many times, when I consider the people's poverty and their weary toil during the six week days, I have thought they were worthy of better things, and I have been astonished to see them so glad and happy and full of good works. We have no railroads or other extraordinary means of conveyance, so we go on foot. * * The Saints pay their tithing and respond with ungrudging willingness to every requirement. We have some opposition and persecution from priests and rich men, but generally the country and village population are very liberal-minded. We have the privilege of preaching wherever we come and the people willingly hear us. * * We hold our conferences and district meetings in private houses, barns and out-buildings around in the country. * * Everywhere among the Saints the next years' emigration is almost their every thought; this circumscribes their prayers, their anxieties and their exertions."

Under date of Dec. 28, 1861, Pres. John Van Cott reported to Pres. Geo. Q. Cannon in England, that the Elders in most of the conferences were baptizing weekly, if not almost daily. The labors of the brethren engaged in the ministry in Scandinavia were crowned with unparalleled success, notwithstanding the circumstances under which they had to labor. They manifested a

zeal and perseverance truly characteristic of the servants of God and, with very few exceptions, were faithful and true to their callings as messengers of life and salvation. The field of their labors had been an extensive one, when the vastness of the country over which they had to travel was considered, as well as the circumstances which had attended them, and the opposition with which they had to cope.   * *
Pres. Van Cott writes:

"During the past year the gospel of salvation has been proclaimed in many a sequestered place hitherto unopened, and its benign influences felt by many of the benighted sons and daughters of Adam. The testimony of the servants of the Lord has been faithfully borne in many places in the northern regions almost to the borders of Russia.   * *

"In Sweden, during the last year, we have enjoyed more liberty than at any previous period, owing, I suppose, in a great measure to the passport law being repealed. Our Elders there have felt as though a great bond had been broken, and as though they were scarcely under any restrictions in relation to the law of the land touching religious liberty. The people there, as a general thing, are more liberal-minded than heretofore, and the spirit of liberty is at work upon them, so that they are petitioning for more liberty. * *

"In Norway religious liberty remains the same as heretofore, though the repealing of the law in relation to passports saves our Elders much trouble; yet they have many difficulties to encounter, especially in the rural districts. Religious superstition and prejudice remain about the same, and it requires the patience of Job, coupled with perseverance and the spirit of truth, to remove it. Then they only succeed with but very few, when compared with the mass. * *

"In Denmark, where we enjoy the greatest religious liberty, the work has been more successful, and the opposing power has been manifested in the shape of mobs in many places of late, so that our brethren have been under the necessity of taking 'leg-bail' for security, or seek to seclude themselves from the eyes of demons in human shape, in order to escape their vengeful hands, yet sometimes not without a garment rent, an arm wrenched, or a bloody face.

"Our meetings, as a general thing, are well attended by strangers, many of whom listen with apparent interest, and many are investigating the doctrines as taught by the Latter-day Saints. * * The Spirit of the Lord is at work upon the hearts of the honest, and preparing the way for the reception of the truth."

During the year 1861, 1,954 persons were added to the Church in the Scandinavian Mission by baptism. About 2,000 meetings were held in the houses of strangers and a great many books and tracts distributed. "Skandinaviens Stjerne" had nearly 500 subscribers outside the Church. Almost everywhere the Elders were successful in their missionary labors and many new fields were opened. An Elder was even sent to Finland, which belongs to Russia. He traveled as a business man and preached the gospel wherever he found an opportunity to do so. In Sweden and Norway, where the law requiring passports had been recalled, liberty seemed to gain more and more ground, and the King himself seemed, after a tour abroad, to have become more liberal-minded than before. In Denmark some opposition had been encountered in places. Thus, for some time, it was almost impossible to hold meetings in Aalborg in the hall used by the Saints, on account of disturbances by mobs. Nowhere in the whole mission did the gospel spread better than in the Vendsyssel Conference, where nearly every parish and village contributed its share of converts to the Latter-day gospel. In the summer of 1861, Elder Peter W. Poulsen, president of the Copenhagen Conference, sent Elder Osterlin and Priest Lars Petersen to Samsö (an island in the Cattegat) to inroduce the gospel there. During he following winter (1861-1862) a quantity of tracts were sold on Samsö; many meetings were held and three persons baptized on the island.

A general longing to emigrate to Zion was manifested among the members of the different branches and conferences, and many preparations for a large emigration were made during the winter of 1861-62.

During the year 1861, several new branches of the Church were organized in the Scandinavian Mission. Thus, in the beginning of the year 1861, two Elders, who were appointed missionaries to the island of Gotland, succeeded in opening up a missionary field there by baptizing four persons and afterwards more. During the summer a branch of the Church was organized on that island. Gotland is the largest of all the islands belonging to Sweden, and is situated about 50 miles from the east coast of Sweden in the deepest part of the Baltic Sea. The area is about 1000 square miles and had a population in 1861 of about 50,000 people.

At a conference held in Aarhus, Denmark, June 16, 1861, the Aarhus branch was cut in two, the north part being organized into the Grundför branch. On the same occasion, the Saints in the town of Grenaa and vicinity was organized into a branch called the Grenaa Branch.

At a conference held in Norrköping, Sweden, July 14, 1861, the Saints in Linköping and vicinity were organized into a branch of the Church called the Linköping Branch with Carl Gustaf Ahlquist as president.

At a conference council held in Norrköping, Sweden, Dec. 30, 1861, the Saints at Quillinge and vicinity, who had formerly constituted a dis-

11

trict of the Norrköping Branch, were organized into a branch called the Quillinge Branch with Samuel Krohn as president.

CHAPTER 40 (1862)

Elders Chr. A. Madsen and Hans C. Högsted arrested—The large emigration of Saints from Scandinavia to America cross the Atlantic in four ships—Many die on the voyage—Difficulties in crossing the Plains.

The new year (1862) dawned upon the Elders and Saints in the Scandinavian Mission under the most favorable circumstances so far as the prospects for missionary work were concerned. The Elders felt jubilant over the success of the previous year, which had been a banner year in the history of the mission, and they naturally looked forward to the accomplishing of great things also in the new year.

About this time a Lutheran priest (a Mr. Lund) published in a popular Norwegian newspaper a series of slanderous articles against the Saints under the caption "A visit to the capital of the Mormons," which caused considerable excitement and led to the arrest of several of the brethren.

Elders Chr. A. Madsen and Hans C. Högsted, while holding a meeting Jan. 30, 1862, in the home of Peter Carlsen, a blacksmith, at Udbyneder, about 10 miles east of Mariager, Denmark, were arrested by a constable and taken as prisoners to Mariager, where they were immediately released. The brethren entered suit against the officers for unlawful arrest, but obtained no redress.

The number of Saints emigrating from Scandinavia in 1862 was greater than in any previous or subsequent year. No less than 1,556 souls, in four different companies, sailed from Hamburg on four chartered vessels destined for Utah. The presidency of the Scandinavian Mission had made a contract with a Mr. Robert M. Sloman of Hamburg to carry the Latter-day Saint emigrants from the port of Hamburg to New York that year, and he seemed to have filled his contract with perfect satisfaction to the representatives of the Church and the emigrating Saints generally. For several months, the preparation for this large emigration had been going on in the different conferences throughout Denmark, Sweden and Norway. The emigrating Saints from the Jutland conferences in Denmark went direct to Hamburg, while most of those from the other conferences first gathered in Copenhagen and thence made their way to Hamburg in different companies. Thus the steamer "Albion" sailed from Aalborg, April 6, 1862, with over 400 Saints from the Aalborg and Vendsyssel conferences. Sailing southward, the ship took up the emigrating Saints from the Aarhus and Skive conferences at Aarhus in the morning of the 7th, and at Fredericia later the same day they picked up the emigrating Saints from the Fredericia and Fyen conferences at Fredericia; the ship reached Kiel in Holstein on the eve of the 7th. Here they were joined by a small contingent from Copenhagen, and the journey was then continued the same day (April 8th) to Altona and Hamburg; in the evening the emigrants went on board the ships "Humboldt" and "Franklin," which were anchored in the Elbe.

The steamer "Albion" sailed from Copenhagen April 14, 1862, with about 500 emigrating Saints on board, and, after a successful voyage, arrived at Kiel at 8 o'clock a. m. of April 15th. After spending about two hours in transferring the baggage of the emigrants to the railway cars, the company left Kiel on an extra train for Altona, where they arrived at 1:30 p. m. Pres. John Van Cott, assisted by other brethren, proceeded immediately to read the list of the emigrants and bring them on board the ships "Electric" and "Athenia" which, like the "Humbolt" and "Franklin," were anchored in the Elbe off Hamburg.

The last of the Latter-day Saint Scandinavian emigrants of that season sailed from Copenhagen, April 17, 1862, on board the steamer "Aurora," which arrived at Kiel in the morning of the 18th and later the same day continued the journey by rail to Altona, where the emigrants spent a few hours attending to their baggage, and were then taken by a tender to the ship "Athenia," which lay at anchor down the Elbe near Gluckstadt.

On Wednesday, April 9th, the ship "Humbolt," Capt. H. B. Boysen, sailed from Hamburg with 323 emigrating Saints, in care of Elder Hans C. Hansen, who now, after laboring as a missionary in Scandinavia, was returning to his home in Zion. After a successful voyage this company of emigrants arrived in New York May 20th, thence the journey westward was continued by railroad and steamboat to Florence, Neb., which was the outfitting place for the journey across the Plains this year, and where the emigrants of that company arrived in the beginning of June. Fourteen persons died on sea and land up to the date of the company's arrival at Florence

On Tuesday, April 15th, the ship "Franklin" (Capt. Robt. Murray) sailed fom Hamburg with 413 emigrating Saints, nearly all from the Aalborg and Vendsyssel Conferences. They were in charge of Chr. A.

Madsen, an Elder returning home. He chose Jens C. A. Weibye and Lauritz Larsen as his counselors. On board the ship the company was

CHRISTIAN AUGUST MADSEN

Born July 23, 1822, near Copenhagen, Denmark, acted for many years as Bishop of Gunnison, Sanpete Co., Utah, where he died Aug. 16, 1907.

organized into eight districts with the following brethren as presidents: Jens C. Thorpe, Jens Christensen Kornum, Niels Mortensen (Lynge), Lars P. Fjeldsted, C. P. Börregaard, Jens C. S. Frost, Thomas Larsen and Jens Andersen. Jens F. Mortensen was appointed baggage master, Anthon H. Lund, interpreter, and Chr. Andersen captain of the guard.

Elder Jens C. A. Weibye gives the following account of the voyage across the Atlantic:

"We went on board the "Franklin" in the evening of Tuesday (April 8th) and I was appointed to-locate the emigrants in their bunks below deck. These bunks, 160 in number, were so wide that three persons easily could have room in one of them side by side. After getting our baggage in order, we received our rations of provisions. These consisted of beef, pork, peas, beans, potatoes, pearl barley, rice, prunes, syrup, vinegar, pepper, cof-

fee, tea, sugar, butter, rye bread, sea biscuits, water, flour, salted herring, salt, and oil (for the lamps). We lighted 11 lanterns every night, 6 of which belonged to the ship and 5 to the emigrants. We hired an extra cook in Hamburg for 90 rigsdaler, and besides him two of our brethren served as assistant cooks. We thus had our dinners nicely cooked in about the following routine, viz., Sunday we had sweet soup, Monday pea soup; Tuesday and Wednesday, rice; Thursday, pea soup; Friday, barley mush, and Saturday herring and potatoes.

"Some of the emigrants carried the measles with them from home and the disease soon spread to all parts of the ship, so that no less than 40 persons, mostly children, were attacked at once. Many of the emigrants were also suffering with diarrhea, which caused very much weakness of body. We lost the appetite for sea biscuits, but learned to soak them in water or tea from 8 to 12 hours, which softened them so that they could become more palatable. The sick were served twice a day with porridge made from barley, rice or sago, and almost every day pancakes could be had by the hundreds for the sick who could not eat the "hard tack" (sea biscuits). Wheat bread was also baked for some of the old people. We held a council meeting every night, and the sanitary conditions of the ship's

JENS CHRISTIAN ANDERSEN WEIBYE

Born Sept. 26, 1824, at Veiby, Hjörring Amt, Denmark, acted as tithing clerk for many years in Manti, Sanpete Co., Utah, where he died Feb. 25, 1891

apartments were attended with great care. Three times a week the decks were washed and twice a week the ship was thoroughly fumigated by burning tar. A spirit of peace prevailed and very few difficulties occurred. The captain and crew were good-natured and obliging, and so were the cooks, who even served the sick when they were not on duty.

"We held at times meetings of worship on the upper or lower decks, and every morning at 5 o'clock the signal for rising was given by the clarionet, or accordeon. At 7 a. m. and 9 p. m. a similar signal was sounded calling the Saints to assemble in their several districts for prayer. Most every day we amused ourselves a short time by dancing on the deck to music played by some of our brethren or members of the crew. We could thus have had an enjoyable time, had it not been for the sorrow occasioned by the many sick and dying among us, on account of the measles. Up to this date (May 27th) 3 adults and 43 children have died, nearly all from measles. During the last few days the chicken pox has also broken out among us and four cases have already developed. We have had head winds most of the time, otherwise we could have been in New York before now, for the 'Franklin' is a first-class ship. We have been very little troubled with sea sickness."

On Thursday, May 29th, in the forenoon, the "Franklin" arrived at New York. The emigrants were placed on a transport steamer to be landed at Castle Garden, but on arriving at the wharf, they were not permitted to go ashore, because of some cases of measles yet existing among them. After 18 of the sick had been taken into the hospital, the rest were returned to the "Franklin" and there remained on board two more nights and a day. Finally, on May 31st, they were landed at Castle Garden, where they were met by Elders Chas. C. Rich, John Van Cott and other brethren.

A part of the emigrants did not have means to carry them further on their way to Zion than New York, but through the generosity of some of the Saints who were more

fortunate, a sufficient sum was raised to take all these poor Saints along, and with rejoicing the journey was then resumed, leaving New York May 31st, at 9 p. m., by extra railway train to Albany, where they arrived the next morning (June 1st). From there the journey was continued by train via Syracuse, Rochester, Niagara, Windsor, Detroit and Chicago to Quincy, Ill., and thence by steamboat across the Mississippi River to Hannibal, Mo., and again by train to St. Joseph, Mo., where they arrived June 6th. The following day they boarded the steamboat "Westwind" and left St. Joseph at 10 p. m., after having spent the "Day of Pentecost" in a way that was anything but pleasant (as there was very poor and crowded accommodation for so many people on this comparatively small vessel). The company arrived at Florence, Neb., on Monday, June 9th, at 10 o'clock p. m. Hans C. Hansen's company, which crossed the ocean in the "Humboldt," arrived there a week before. Among the 43 persons who died in the "Franklin" company during the voyage on the sea was Bro. Jens Andersen from Veddum (Aalborg Conference), Denmark, who with his own means had assisted 60 or 70 poor Saints to emigrate. He died on the North Sea on the 25th of April, soon after the ship had left Cuxhaven. On the way from New York to Florence, two children died, of whom one was the 15 months old daughter of Jens C. A. Weibye. Eleven persons (4 adults and 7 children) died while staying at Florence and a young girl died on the Plains, making in all 62 of the "Franklin" company · who died between Hamburg and Salt Lake City.

On Tuesday, June 10th, the emigrants pitched their tents a short distance north of Florence, and the necessary purchases of oxen, wagons, cows, etc. were attended to. Those who crossed the Plains by the Church teams were organized into messes to receive their provisions from the commissary of the company. A few of the emigrants had become apostates on the way and remained in the States. Among these were a blacksmith, J. P. Jacobsen, and Lauritz Larsen from Höjen, Christopher Thomsen from Gaardsholt, Vendsyssel, Denmark, and others with their families. The rest of the emigrants remained in camp for several weeks before beginning the journey across the Plains. A few days before the company left camp, Florence and vicinity was visited by a terrible tornado, accompanied by rain, thunder and lightning, by which two of the brethren were killed and Elder Jos. W. Young received severe wounds from a wagon-box which blew down upon him; after the accident, he was carried to a place of safety in an unconscious condition, but recovered after awhile. The tents and wagon covers of the company were badly torn and shattered on that occasion.

On Friday, April 18th, the ship "Electric" (Capt. H. J. Johansen) sailed from Hamburg with 336 emigrating Saints bound for Utah, in charge of Elder Sören Christoffersen. The emigrants were from the Lolland and other conferences in Denmark, and from Norrköping Conference in Sweden. The original plan was that the Norrköping Conference contingent should have sailed on the "Athenia," but this arrangement was changed so that some of them sailed on the "Electric" instead.

The "Electric" sailed down the Elbe to Gluckstadt Roads, arriving there about noon. Here anchor was cast near the ship "Athenia," which had another company of emigrating Saints on board. At this time there were 335 emigrants on board the "Electric" and 486 on the "Athenia." The "Electric' lifted anchor April 22nd and sailed to a point off the coast of Hanover, where anchor was again dropped and the ship waited for the wind to change. Favored at last with a good wind the "Electric" made the final start for America, April 25th, sailing out into the North Sea. Before sailing, Pres. John Van Cott came on board and assisted in organizing the emigrating Saints, who were divided into nine dstricts, in each of which there were from 25 to 40 persons.

During the voyage a number of the emigrants died. Following is a partial list of the dead: A woman from Lolland, Denmark, who was sick before she left her home, died May 2, leaving her husband and a child; a 15-year old girl died of throat disease May 3rd; a little girl from Lolland died May 5th; Sophia Maria Sörensen, the 2-year old daughter of Knud Sörensen, from Jutland, died May 8th; Hilma Anderson, a daughter of Sister Susanna Anderson, of Sweden, died May 14th; Jörgen Lydersen from Jutland, Denmark, 48 years old, died May 17th, leaving a wife and one child; on the same day, Augusta Caroline Johanson, the one-year old daughter of August Johanson of Sweden, died; also a little girl named Sophia Katrine Johansen from Denmark died; Lars Petter Pehrsson died May 19th; he was from Vesterplano, Sweden. Pauline Mortensen, a daughter of Carl Fred Mortensen, died in the evening of May 25th; she was the third of the Mortensen family to die on board the "Electric."

At least one marriage took place

on board, that of Frederik Bernhardt Thyberg and Sister Mathea Josephine Nordfors; they were married May 10th.

On the 31st of May, one of the sisters gave birth to a child who received the name of Electric Sophia Sörensen.

A number of meetings were held on board during the voyage and union and harmony existed among the emigrants during the entire journey.

The ship arrived safely in New York and the emigrants landed at Castle Garden on Friday, June 6, 1862. Here the company met the Saints who had crossed the Atlantic in the ship "Athenia" and who landed on the 7th. Both companies left New York June 9th and arrived at Florence, Neb., June 19.

On Monday, April 21, 1862, the ship "Athenia" (Capt. D. Schilling) sailed from Hamburg with 484 emigrating Saints on board in charge of Elder Ola N. Liljenquist, and before noon the ship was on the broad face of the North Sea. Elder Ola N. Liljenquist, in giving a report of the voyage, writes:

"We steered to the North of Scotland, had fine weather, doubling a cape of Scotland on the 29th in the afternoon, passing the light tower in the evening. Before midnight we were sailing on the Atlantic Ocean. We had favorable winds for several days with considerable motion of the sea, and therefore many suffered with sea sickness. Two weeks after leaving Gluckstadt we had covered about half of the distance to New York, but from that time the wheel of fortune rather turned against us. While we hitherto had been favored with good winds, these now turned, and then at other times we had a perfect calm. The captain steered towards the southwest until we reached the Gulf Stream, about 300 miles south of Newfoundland Banks. After that we had such a calm for a whole week that not even a feather stirred and the temperature of the water and air varied between 70 and 80 degrees Fahrenheit. This sudden change from the cool north, together with the bad water, which becomes stagnant from the heat, caused the sickness, which already had a hold among us, to increase rapidly. The measles, which had been brought on board and already had claimed several victims, took away 33 of the little ones, and several of the adults also suffered with bowel complaints and diarrhea. The first winds that blew the captain utilized to take us farther north into a cooler climate. Now we are all well, thanks to Him, who holds our destiny in his hands. Five adults have died, namely, Ole Nielsen, 37 years old; Christine Poulsen, 29 years old; Hans Nielsen from Amager, 52 years old; Ane Nielsen, 70 years old, and Kaisa Jensen, 65 years of age. The captain ordered the cook to make oat meal porridge for the sick in the morning, rice at noon, and sago porridge in the afternoon."

On the 7th of June, the "Athenia" arrived in New York, where Elder Sören Christoffersen's company was met, it having arrived the day before. Both companies left New York June 9th by train for Florence, where they arrived safely on the 19th.

The emigrants who sailed across the Atlantic in the four ships mentioned came together in Florence, from which place those who had not the means wherewith to equip themselves for the journey across the Plains were assisted by the teams sent there from the Valley by the Church, while those who had means wherewith to help themselves were organized into two independent companies. One of these was placed in charge of Elder Chr. A. Madsen and was composed of 264 persons, 40 wagons, 14 horses, 174 oxen, 99 cows, 37 heifers, 7 calves, 6 dogs and 10 chickens, and brought along 22 tents, 32 cooking stoves, 5 revolvers and 37 rifles. Hans C. Hansen was captain of the guard and Jens C. A. Weibye secretary for the company, which was divided into six divisons with the followng brethren as captains: Sören Larsen, Jens C. A. Weibye, Niels Mortensen (Lynge), Thomas Lund, Lauritz Larsen and Chr. H. Grön. The first mentioned had charge of five horse teams and the others eight ox teams each.

The other company, which also counted about 40 wagons, with its quota of persons, animals, etc., was in charge of Elder Ola N. Liljenquist, and Elder John Van Cott was placed as general leader of both companies, which broke camp at Florence, July 14, 1862. The first few days some difficulty was experienced, as the oxen, who were not used to Scandinavian orders and management, would often follow their own inclination to leave the road and run away with the wagons, but after some practice on the part of their inexperienced teamsters, the difficulty somewhat disappeared. The journey from Florence was via Elkhorn River, Loup Fork, Wood River, Willow Lake, Rattlesnake Creek, Fort Laramie, Upper Platte Bridge, Devil's Gate, South Pass, Green River, etc., to Salt Lake City, where the company safely arrived Sept. 23, 1862.

Elder Jens C. A. Weibye, from whose journal most of the information in regard to the journey across the Plains was obtained, gives the following details:

"Capt. Chr. A. Madsen advised us to take along several needful articles, which we did, and we were well organized when we began the journey from Florence. To begin with, we traveled only a few miles each day, which was a good thing for us, who were unaccustomed to drive oxen. We generally had good camp grounds and only occasionally we had to camp where we could not obtain water. As a rule there was an abundance of grass for the oxen, and at times also sufficient fuel to be found, but a great part of the way the sisters had to content themselves with cooking over fires made from sunflower stems and 'buffalo chips.' Nearly all able-bodied men and women had to walk most of the way; some of the women rode in the wagons only across the larger rivers, while they would wade across the smaller streams like the men. Sometimes the women and children were carried across the streams by the men when it was feared the oxen could not pull the wagons with their heavy loads. We did exactly what our leaders told us to do, and consequently everything went well with us, for we could not read in books how and what to do, either on the voyage across the ocean (which took 51 days) or on the journey across the Plains (which lasted 71 days). On the journey across the Plains, the weather was generally fair and a good spirit prevailed among us. The health of the company was also good as a rule, and only one death occurred on the Plains. We always kept up a guard and lost but a few head of cattle."

Concerning the arrival in Salt Lake City of this company, the "Deseret News" of Sept. 24, 1862, published a short sketch:

"Of the Scandinavian Saints who crossed the Plains with the Church teams 384 souls went with Capt. John R. Murdock's company, which left Florence July 24th and arrived in Salt Lake City, Sept. 27th. The whole company consisted of about 700 souls and 65 teams. On the journey 14 persons died, 2 couples were married and 2 children born.

"Another division of the Scandinavian emigrants crossed the Plains in Capt. Joseph Horne's company (the 3rd company of the Church teams) containing 570 souls and 52 ox-teams, which left Florence July 29th and arived in Salt Lake City Oct. 1st. A third division crossed the Plains in the 4th company of the Church teams under Capt. Ansel P. Harmon, arriving in Salt Lake City on the 5th of October. This latter company was from the start infested with measles from which about 15 children died on the Plains. Two children were killed by the overturning of a wagon.

The Church sent in all six companies (262 wagons, 293 men, 2,880 oxen, 143,315 pounds of flour, etc.) to the Missouri River in 1862, to assist poor Saints immigrating to the Valley.

CHAPTER 41 (1862)

Elder Jesse N. Smith succeeds John Van Cott as president of the Scandinavian Mission—Visit of President George Q. Cannon and other American Elders—The zenith of prosperity reached in the Scandinavian Mission.

After having attended to the business of sending the large emigration away from Hamburg, Pres. John Van Cott returned to Copenhagen and prepared for his own journey home. In accordance with instructions from President Brigham Young, he turned over the presidency of the mission to Elder Jesse N. Smith, who had labored as a mis-

JESSE NATHANIEL SMITH

Born in Stockholm, St. Lawrence County, New York, Dec. 2, 1834, and baptized in Nauvoo, Ill., by Patriarch John Smith, Aug. 13, 1843, arrived in Great Salt Lake Valley Sept. 25, 1847. He was called on a mission to colonize Southern Utah, Oct. 1, 1851, and was for many years a prominent citizen of Parowan, Iron County; filled a mission to Scandinavia in 1860-1864, presiding most of the time over the mission; filling a second mission to Scandinavia in 1868-70 he again acted as mission president; presided over the Eastern Arizona Stake from 1878 to 1887; filled a special mission to locate colonies in northern Mexico in 1885; presided over the Snowflake Stake, Arizona, from 1887 to 1906, and died as president of said Stake June 5, 1906, leaving a large posterity.

sionary in Scandinavia about 16 months, and on the 9th of May,

Brother Van Cott bid farewell to the brethren and Saints in Copenhagen and started on his homeward journey. He had, on this his second mission to Scandinavia, presided over the mission about two years and four months and was held in high esteem by the Scandinavian Saints, with whose traits of character he had become well acquainted; he had learned how to gain the love and good will of the people. On the 13th of May he arrived in Liverpool, England, from which place he, together with Apostles Amasa M. Lyman, Chas. C. Rich and other Elders, sailed by the steamer "Kangaroo" to New York. Here they met with a part of the Scandinavian emigration. From Florence, John Van Cott journeyed along with the companies led by Elders Madsen and Liljenquist to Green River, where they were overtaken by Elders Lyman, Rich, Wm. H. Hooper, Jos. W. Young and others who traveled with horse teams. Along with these brethren, Elder Van Cott traveled the rest of the way to Salt Lake City, where he arrived Sept. 16, 1862.

On Thursday, Sept. 14th, 1862, Elder Geo. Q. Cannon, President of the European Mission, and wife, and also Elders John Smith, Samuel H. B. Smith and Joseph F. Smith, arrived in Hamburg from England. The two last-named brethren accompanied Pres. Cannon on a visit to Scandinavia, while John Smith came to labor in the mission. Following is Pres. Cannon's own report of his visit to Scandinavia:

"From Hamburg we did not proceed directly to Copenhagen—the headquarters of the mission—but, being advised by Pres. Jesse N. Smith that he had appointed a conference to be held at Aalborg on Sunday, Sept. 7th, and that we would barely have time to reach there for the meetings, we took rail to Kiel, and from there, steamer to Korsör, where we found a steamer going to Aarhus, Jutland, on which peninsula Aalborg is situated. We went by coach from Aarhus to Aalborg, a distance of about 70 English miles, reaching the latter place at 4 o'clock in the morning

GEORGE QUAYLE CANNON

Born Jan. 11, 1827, in Liverpool, Lancashire, England; died April 10, 1901, in California.

of the day appointed for the conference. Our meetings with the Saints and friends during this day were very interesting. The people were very glad to see us. Our inability to talk freely with them in their own language was the only drawback to our pleasure, but as Elders Smith, Cluff and Anders Christensen were with us, who could speak Danish perfectly, we did not feel this to be so much of a want. Elder Christensen interpreted in our meetings, and was much blessed in so doing. Returning to Aarhus we held conference there on the 10th of September. It was a time of rejoicing with the Saints; and that they appreciated our visit was evinced by their glad countenances and their kindness to us. Here we took steamer again for Korsör, from which place we crossed the island of Sjælland by rail to Copenhagen. While at Copenhagen we met with the Priesthood and Saints (who with the strangers numbered about 1,000) in conference in a large hall which they had rented expressly for the occasion. This

was on the 14th of September. On the 15th and 16th we met with the Elders in conference. All the officers, from all parts of the mission, who were exclusively devoted to the ministry—with the exception of one or two who were too far distant to receive notice of the conference in time to be there—with a number of the local Priesthood, met with us on that occasion. So profitable did we feel this Elders' conference to be to all, myself included, that these two days' meetings alone, we thought more than repaid us for our journey. There were many points upon which the Elders needed instruction, and the Spirit of the Lord was poured out, inspiring our hearts to impart and receive his counsels respecting them. We met with the Saints another day in that city (the 21st) and in the evening took our departure for Hamburg, en route for Holland and Switzerland.

"While we remained in Denmark we were treated with the greatest possible kindness by all with whom we came in contact. The Saints all seemed to vie with one another to make the Elders who visited them feel comfortable. Every one of the Elders who spoke in public to the people enjoyed a good degree of freedom. Indeed, we do not recollect ever having had greater liberty in speaking, and more of the spirit of instruction, than we had on some occasions while in this land. The people appeared to listen with eager attention to all that was said; their desire to hear and the faith they exercised helped the Elders in laying before them the principles of truth. The Elders are very successful in their labors throughout the Scandinavian Mission, the people freely receiving the gospel when it is preached unto them. In many places in Sweden and Norway, however, the Elders cannot preach, nor officiate in any of the ordinances of the gospel without incurring risk and they are not infrequently incarcerated in prison. Still the work spreads, and as liberal ideas and views are gradually gaining ground, and there are prospects of a greater toleration being granted by government, it is to be hoped that the time is not far distant when the Elders will be able openly to preach the principles of the gospel to those nations without fear of molestation. If that day shall come, thousands will come forward and readily embrace the principles of truth. In Denmark there is considerable freedom. This has been the case since the gospel was first carried there by Elder Erastus Snow. The people generally have but little respect for, or confidence in, their old religious guides, and they do not have those priestly traditions and influences to contend with to so great an extent as the people do in some lands where priestcraft flourishes. They do not, however, on this account enjoy an immunity from evil influences. Satan is by no means bound in that country. The people prove this occasionally by mobbing the Saints. When banded together as a mob they are outrageously violent, not hesitating to inflict the greatest abuses upon those who may fall into their hands. Generally speaking, at such times, they are inclined to be very sullen and desperate, and to talk but little and entirely deaf to reason and argument. The Elders there have many difficulties to contend with in preaching the gospel. It is a very cold country in the winter season, and to travel from place to place—frequently in the snow—to meet with the Saints, with no other means of conveyance than those which nature has furnished, requires a resolute and patient mind, a strong constitution and an active, hardy body. The food eaten generally by the humbler classes is also very coarse. We think it would startle many of our Elders and Saints in this country (England) if the food that is almost universally eaten throughout Denmark were put before them with the expectation that they would make a meal of it. The gospel will not only bestow spiritual benefit upon many of those who embrace it in those lands, but it will benefit them temporally. However, this is true of more lands than Scandinavia. But we were struck, in traveling through that country, with what we saw and what we had described to us respecting the style of living common in the country. The people have much to learn before they will know how to appreciate and put to a right use all the blessings which God has surrounded them with. In this respect the gathering will be advantageous to the Saints. Transplanting them to Zion will benefit them in every way, if they will do right. With all the rest their physical beauty will be increased. They already are strong and robust; but handsome forms and faces will, among the Saints who shall be gathered to Zion, become common. The heavenly influence of the Spirit of the Lord, with more favorable circumstances and a more generous diet, will effect this. As it is in other lands, so it is there; the Lord is gathering out the best and the most pure material for his own use. His Spirit is moving upon the honest and pure in heart, and they are embracing the truth. With them will he build himself a people and name in the earth. From every nation where the gospel is being preached the Lord is assembling people whom he will yet make the mightiest power that has ever had an existence on the earth. Scandinavia will doubtless furnish her quota to make up this mighty kingdom."

If it can be said consistently that the Scandinavian Mission at any time has had a real flourishing period, it certainly was in the years 1861 and 1862. In 1861, 1,954 persons were added to the Church by baptism and in 1862 the total number of baptisms was 1,977. At no other period in the whole history of the mission has such an abundant harvest of souls been realized. At the close of the year 1862, the mission consisted of 15 conferences, subdivided into 155 branches, and notwithstanding the large emigration in the spring there was a total membership of 5,800 in the mission at the close of the year. Of these 595 were Elders, 216 Priests, 215 Teachers and 97 Deacons. Fourteen Elders from Zion labored in the mission at the close of the year, namely, Jesse N. Smith (president of the mission), Wm. W. Cluff and Hans Peter Lund (traveling Elders in the mission), Anders Christensen (pastor of the Aalborg and Vendsyssel Conferences), Carl C. N. Dorius and Johan F. F. Dorius (missionaries in Norway), Knud H. Brunn (pastor of the Fredericia and Fyen Conferences, Peter Beckström (missionary in the Swedish Conferences), Johan P. R. Johansen (president of the Fredericia Conference), Anders W. Winberg (traveling Elder in Jutland), Johan Swenson and Christoffer Holberg (traveling Elders in

Sweden), Hans C. Hansen (missionary in the Aalborg and Vendsyssel Conferences), and John Smith (assistant in the mission office in Copenhagen). Of local Elders, P. Wilhelm Poulsen presided over the Copenhagen Conference with a membership of 1,202, Niels C. Edlefsen over the Aalborg Conference with a membership of 350, Hans Chr. Högsted over the Vendsyssel Conference with 685 members, Johan P. R. Johansen over the Fredericia Conference with 278 members, Jens Hansen over the Lolland Conference with 182 members, Peter C. Nielsen over the Bornholm Conference with 87 members, Peter C. Carstensen over the Fyen Conference with 185 members, Peter C. Geertsen over the Aarhus Conference with 296 members, Christoffer S. Winge over the Skive Conference with 82 members, Carl C. N. Dorius over the Christiania Conference with 908 members, Nils Rosengren over the Skåne Conference with 757 members, Nils C. Flygare over the Stockholm Conference with 220 members, Anders P. Söderborg over the Göteborg Conference with 214 members, Lars Nilson over the Norrköping Conference with 299 members, A. Svedlund over the Sundsvall Conference with 47 members and Gustaf Pegau over the Hamburg Branch with 8 members.

Besides the presiding brethren mentioned, a great number of others labor in the mission as traveling missionaries, presidents of branches, etc., laboring diligently for the spread of the gospel, doing honor to God and themselves.

In Göteborg, Sweden, where for some time not much had been accomplished, Pres. Anders P. Söderborg succeeded in securing a new hall in the summer of 1862, and commenced again to preach in spite

of the opposition from the police authorities. About the same time Elder Borgeson was fined in the sum of 300 riksdaler, or 28 days' imprisonment on bread and water, for having preached the gospel, and another brother was fined in the sum of 25 riksdaler, or 14 days' imprisonment, for the same "offense." The imprisonment was chosen in both cases, as cash was scarce.

In Norway four brethren were likewise imprisoned in the month of July to atone for fines which were imposed upon them the previous winter for preaching and baptizing. Pres. Carl C. N. Dorius, during the summer and fall, made a round-trip in the conference and went as far north as Hassel Islands. At a conference held in Christiania Oct. 18th, it was decided that the Norwegian Mission no longer should be called the Brevig Conference, as the headquarters were in Christiania, but that from that time on it should be called the Christiania Conference.

CHAPTER 42 (1863)

False reports of apostates cause some excitement in the Mission—Visit of Brigham Young, jun.—Arrival of American Elders—President Geo. Q. Cannon again visits Scandinavia.

In 1863, 1,587 new members were added to the Church in Scandinavia by baptism, namely, 789 in Denmark, 621 in Sweden and 177 in Norway. The emigration of Saints to Zion that year numbered 1,458 souls, including children.

Some of the Scandinavian emigrants who, the preceding year, had ended their journey at Omaha and vicinity as apostates, wrote letters to their friends in Scandinavia concerning the previous year's emigration. containing false reports which turned many people against the missionaries. who, on that account, were badly treated on several occasions. The priests and other sympathizers caused some of these letters to be published in the newspapers and tracts, with their own interpretations and comments added, and scattered them gratis among the people.

Elder Wm. W. Cluff, who was laboring in Jutland, Denmark, acquired the Danish language to a wonderful degree of perfection. Of all the American Elders who were sent to Scandinavia as missionaries, he and Elder Jesse N. Smith, became so proficient in the use of the Danish tongue that only a few could detect they were foreigners. Consequently, they became very influential as missionaries and did much good. Elder Cluff writing from Aalborg, under date of Feb. 16, 1863, stated that the Aalborg Conference was in a flourishing condition. The hired hall rented by the Saints for meeting purposes in the city of Aalborg had been enlarged and greatly improved. At a conference held there on Feb. 15th, more than 600 people were in attendance, of whom 100 were strangers, who listened with great attention and interest to the principles advanced by the Elders. The missionaries in the Aalborg Conference had, of late, paid particular attention to breaking new grounds and were preaching the gospel with excellent results in localities where it had not been preached before.

Elder Brigham Young, jun., president of the European Mission, and Elder Chauncey W. West of Ogden, Utah, arrived in Copenhagen, July 18, 1863, on a visit to Scandinavia. They attended a few meetings in Copenhagen and also, in company with President Jesse N. Smith, made a short visit to Malmö, Sweden. The two visitors left Copenhagen July 23rd, returning to England.

Four young American Elders, namely, Samuel L. Sprague and John Gray of Salt Lake City, George M. Brown of Provo and John E. Evans of Salt Lake City, arrived in Copenhagen, August 8th, 1863, having been appointed to labor as missionaries in the Scandinavian Mission. Elder Sprague was appointed to labor in the Copenhagen, Elder Evans in the Skåne, Elder Brown in the Christiania and Elder Gray in the Fredericia Conference. Elders Sprague and Brown studied the Scandinavian languages with success and became efficient missionaries. The other two Elders were soon afterwards released because of transgression.

Apostle Geo. Q. Cannon, president of the European Mission, arrived in Copenhagen, August 19, 1863. After attending meetings in Copenhagen, visits were made to Göteborg, Stockholm and Christiania. In Copenhagen, an important council meeting was held on the 18th and 19th of September and a splendid conference on Sunday, September 20th. On that occasion, about one thousand people attended the public meeting at which President Cannon and other Elders preached. Anders W. Winberg acted as translator for the brethren who spoke in English.

According to the reports given by the presiding Elders at a council meeting, success had attended the efforts of the Elders in nearly all parts of the mission. In Norway, the brethren continued, however, subject to imprisonment for preaching the gospel and administering its ordinances. In Christiania, where hired halls were secured, the meetings were filled to overflowing. There had been considerable persecution in the Göteborg Conference, Sweden. In Schleswig there was no religious liberty, in consequence of which the Elders there ad not met with much success. There were a few scattered Saints in Hamburg. In Aalborg Conference, many of the well-to-do Saints had during the previous year assisted a great number of poor Saints to emigrate to Zion. This had reduced the membership of the conference very much. In Stockholm Conference, Sweden, the Saints were doing well, and while there was no religious liberty in Sweden, opportunities for holding meetings and having religious conversations with the people were good. There were only a few Saints left in the Skive and Bornholm conferences, Denmark, owing to the large emigration which had taken place this year. The same was the case in the Göteborg Conference, Sweden.

After his return to England, Pres. Geo. Q. Cannon gave an interesting account of his visit to Scandinavia and wound up by saying:

"We are quite unable, in a brief sketch like the present, to do justice to the feelings we entertain towards the Elders and Saints in Scandinavia, for the kindness universally shown on all hands to Brother Smith and myself while visiting them, and the pleasure we have experienced in their society in public meetings and in social intercourse. The visit has been one of unalloyed pleasure to us, and has made such an impression upon us, we trust, as will never be erased. The presence and the teachings of the Elders from Zion are very highly valued by the Saints throughout those lands; they honor their counsels and receive with eagerness the instructions they have to impart to them, and bear testimony by their actions that they have had the love of God implanted in their hearts, whereby they are enabled to value the truth, and the Priesthood which he has again restored to the earth. They are exerting themselves with all diligence to procure the means necessary to emancipate themselves from Babylon, and the prospect, so far as we could learn from the reports of the Elders, is that the emigration for the coming season, from the most of the conferences in that mission, will be but little, if any, below that of the past spring. The calls for Elders are very numerous—more than

can be supplied at present, and there is every reason to think that thousands will yet receive the gospel in those lands and be gathered therefrom to Zion. In Sweden and Norway there are large fields stretching out before the Elders to the far North, which, for the want of time, they have not yet been able to penetrate. They have only been able to skirt along the edges and labor in a few places which have been most convenient and accessible. But what they have accomplished warrants the belief that many of the inhabitants of the places yet unvisited will yield a ready acquiescence to the principles of truth when they shall have the privilege of hearing them. They are a kind-hearted, simple-minded, noble race, and when they comprehend the truth are very firm in clinging to it. Freedom of conscience is enjoyed to a far greater extent than formerly in Sweden and Norway, yet there is still room for considerable more liberty in this direction.

"The meetings in which we had the privilege of participating with the Saints, in the various places which we visited, were of a very interesting character. The Spirit of the Lord was there and was felt in a goodly extent by all who assembled with pure motives. The spirit of instruction rested upon all who spoke. Particularly was this the case during the days when we met in general conference; and we have cause to anticipate that much good will result from the counsels and instructions imparted to the Priesthood on that occasion."

In the latter part of 1863, quite a number of the young local brethren, who had labored as missionaries, left Denmark in order to avoid drafting into military service, as a war had broken out between Prussia and Austria on one side and Denmark on the other. Some of these young men emigrated to America.

About this time, the Skive Conference was dissolved and the remnant of its membership divided into two districts, so that a part of it lying north of the Limfjord would in the future belong to the Aalborg Conference, and that part lying south of the Limfjord to the Aarhus Conference.

CHAPTER 43 (1863)

Three ship-loads of Saints emigrate to Zion
—Incidents of the voyage across the Atlantic
—Life on the Plains.

About four hundred Saints, emigrating to Utah, sailed from Copenhagen, Denmark, April 20, 1863. This was the first division of a large emigrant company of Scandinavian Saints which left Copenhagen that spring. The emigrants, after a pleasant voyage on the Baltic, landed at Kiel, Holstein, whence they traveled by railroad to Altona and there boarded the steamer "Tiger," bound for Hull, and the steamer "Lord Cardigan," bound for Grimsby, England, and sailed the same evening. President N. Smith and the mission clerk (Carl Larsen) left Copenhagen by rail in the evening of the 20th for Korsör and thence traveled by steamer to Kiel, where they joined the emigrants and then accompanied them to Altona. Brothers Smith and Larsen went on board the "Tiger" at Altona in order to accompany the larger company of the two to England. Stormy weather caused delay of 36 hours at Cuxhaven, at the mouth of the Elbe, but at last the ship put to sea. The magnificent vessel fought bravely against the strong contrary wind and the angry sea, and, though the voyage was long and unpleasant, the emigrants arrived safely in Hull in the morning of April 26th. At the landing the emigrants were met by Elder John M. Kay, who was awaiting them with a small steamer, which after an hour's sailing landed the passengers from the "Tiger" at Grimsby, where a large and convenient house had been hired for the use of the emigrants during their brief stay in Grimsby. The emigrants who had sailed from Altona on the steamer "Lord Cardigan" arrived in Grimsby April 27th. On both steamers the officers and crews treated the emigrants with all due courtesy. From Grimsby the journey was continued by rail to Liverpool, where the company arrived April 28th, and there joined the second division of Scandinavian Saints which left Copenhagen April 23rd.

A second company of emigrating Saints (about 200 souls), bound for the gathering places of the Saints in the Rocky Mountains, sailed from Copenhagen, April 23, 1863, per steamship "Aurora." This was the second division of a large company of emigrating Saints who left Scandinavia that spring for Utah. The steamer "Aurora" arrived in Kiel in the morning of April 24th, and the same day the Saints went by special railway train to Hamburg where lodgings were secured for them in a large emigrant building, while their baggage was being transferred to the large and beautiful steamer "Grimsby," on which they went on board in the evening. This steamer sailed from Hamburg on the 25th and after a successful voyage of two days on the North Sea arrived at Grimsby England, Monday morning, April 27th. Here the emigrants spent the night in a freight house. The following day (April 28th) the company went by train to Liverpool where the Scandinavian emigrant and 113 English Saints boarded the ship "John J. Boyd," the total number of souls now being 766. The company was organized by President George Q. Cannon, who appointed Wm. W. Cluff leader, with Elder Knud H. Bruun and William S. Baxter as his counselors. Later the company was divided into seven districts The ship sailed from Liverpool on the evening of April 30th, but anchored out in the river until the next morning (May 1st), when the "John J. Boyd" lifted anchor and started on its voyage across the Atlantic. The voyage proved a pleasant one and lasted only 29 days. On board, the emigrants received good food in abundance. Every seventh day a ration for each person was issued consisting of one and one-half pounds of rice, two pounds of peas, one pound of pork, two pounds of beef, three pounds of potatoes, three pounds of oatmeal, one-fourth pound of tea, two ounces of pepper, two ounces of mustard, one-half pint of vinegar and a quantity of English sea biscuits. Besides this the sick obtained wine, milk, sago, sugar and soup from the captain's kitchen. Elder Peter O. Thomassen writes that Brother Wm. W. Cluff won for himself the admiration of the Saints and gave perfect satisfaction in performing his difficult duties as leader of the company. The sanitary condition on board was very good; only four or five persons died on the sea. The monotony of the voyage was one day (May 21st) broken by seeing eight mighty icebergs swaying in majestic grandeur upon the shining billows, glittering in forms of purest crystal. They were accompanied by a wintry degree of cold, and to make the illusion of the polar seas more effective five whales were seen playing about the ship, sending the water like springing fountains high in the air.

The "John J. Boyd" arrived safely with its precious cargo of souls in New York harbor, and on Sunday, June 1st, the emigrants were landed at Castle Garden. In the evening of the same day the journey was continued to Albany, New York, and on to Florence, Nebraska.

Peter O. Thomassen writes:

"The journey by railroad was more pleasant than we had expected to find it, as the train stopped often and at some length at some of the principal cities we passed through, giving us opportunities to straighten our legs and move about, see some of the country and satisfy our ever increasing appetite for sightseeing. An old conductor, who claimed to have been acquainted with Joseph, the Prophet, was clever enough to stop the train when we arrived at Palmyra, N. Y., where the Prophet first entered upon his remarkable career. He showed us the house in which the Prophet resided, the woods in which he received heavenly visions and the hill Cumorah, where he obtained the Book of Mormon plates. This information went like wildfire from car to car and

PETER O. THOMASSEN

Born Aug. 29, 1836, at Drammen, Norway; baptized June 9, 1854; acted as translator for "Skandinaviens Stjerne" from 1858 to 1863; emigrated to Utah in 1863; filled a mission to Scandinavia in 1870-1872, and died Oct. 28, 1891, in Salt Lake City.

all who possibly could do so got out to have a view of these dear historic places, and to pluck a flower or blade of grass from the locality as a memento to carry away with them. A few moments later, after the whistle of the engine had signalled for 'all aboard,' the train again glided onward towards the object of our journey."

The emigrants arrived in Florence June 11th, all well. Here some of them remained about six weeks. Soon after their arrival in Florence they were joined by the emigrants who had sailed from Copenhagen April 30, 1863.

About two hundred emigrating Saints from the Christiania, Lolland and Bornholm conferences sailed from Copenhagen per steamer "Aurora," April 30, 1863, bound for Utah, under the leadership of Elders Carl C. N. Dorius, Johan F. F. Dorius and Hans Peter Lund.

Some of the Norwegians emigrating in this company (28 souls) had sailed from Christiania April 13, 1863, per steamer "Excellensen Toll." A strong and contrary wind on the Skagerak and Cattegat made the voyage very uncomfortable, but the emigrants were safely landed in Copenhagen April 15th.

Another company of emigrating Saints (about one hundred souls) left Christiania, Norway, April 28th, under the direction of Elder Johan F. F. Dorius and arrived in Copenhagen, April 29th, where the Norwegians joined the emigrants from other parts of the mission. About a dozen Saints emigrating to Zion went direct from Stavanger to Hull where they joined those who had sailed from Copenhagen.

When the emigrating Saints left Copenhagen April 30th the weather was fine, and a great number of people congregated on the wharf to see the Saints leave, but there were no disturbances, as a number of police had been detailed on special duty to keep order. The emigrants made themselves as comfortable as they could on the deck and in the second cabin of the "Aurora," which on the morning of Friday, May 1st, arrived at Kiel, where the emigrants walked to the railway station and left at 11 o'clock a.m. by railroad for Altona, where they arrived at 3 o'clock in the afternoon. From Altona to Ham-

burg the emigrants walked in abou half an hour to the ship "Roland," o which they went on board, togethe with about four hundred emigratin Saints from Jutland and Fyen (or th Saints from the Vendsyssel, Aalborg Skive, Aarhus, Fredericia and Fye conferences) who, on June 30, 186? had boarded a steamer at Aalborg Aarhus and Fredericia, and like thos who commenced the voyage from Cc penhagen, landed in Kiel, whenc they traveled by rail to Altona. Afte the emigrants, numbering nearly si hundred souls, had gone on boar together with about forty steers an several hundred sheep(which mad the atmosphere on board anything bt comfortable for the emigrants), th ship "Roland" sailed from Hambur May 1st about midnight. The weathe was very fine, but the emigrants, i their crowded quarters, nevertheles were uncomfortable. Early on Su day morning, May 3rd, the "Roland cast anchor off Grimsby, and a littl later sailed to the wharf, where mos of the emigrants landed, with som of their baggage; the balance of th baggage, together with forty of th brethren, remained on board, as th ship went to Hull, where they arrive at 6 o'clock in the evening and r mained on board all night. The ne: morning (May 4th) a small steame ran up to the side of the "Roland and took the rest of the baggage, b longing to the emigrants, back Grimsby, while the forty brethr went to the same place by rail. E der Carl C. N. Dorius, however, r mained in Hull where he, about 1 o'clock the same day, received son emigrants (seven adults and six chi dren) who arrived direct from Sta anger, Norway, per steamer "Skanc navien." In the afternoon, after s tling with the captain of the steam for their passage, Brother Dorius l these emigrants by steamer and tra to Grimsby, where they were united with the other emigrants.

At Grimsby the emigrating Saints were made quite comfortable in a large building erected for the use of emigrants. On the 6th all the emigrants, except the Norwegians, made themselves ready for the journey to Liverpool. They left, nearly seven hundred strong, by rail for that city at 5 o'clock in the afternoon. A young Danish sister who was sick was carried in a chair into the cars.

The exact number of emigrants who arrived in Liverpool May 6, 1863, was 681. At this port 644 Scandinavian and 13 English Saints were taken on board the ship "B. S. Kimball" (Capt. H. Dearborn), while thirty-seven Scandinavians were placed on board the ship "Consignment." Elder Anders Christensen was placed in charge of this little band.

President George Q. Cannon organized the company on the "B. S. Kimball," with Elder Hans Peter Lund as president, Elder Peter Beckström and Christoffer S. Winge were chosen as his counselors. Elder P. Wilhelm Poulsen was appointed secretary for the company, which was divided into seven districts with a president and a captain of guard over each. Other helps were also appointed. Both ships sailed from Liverpool on the 9th of May. Four deaths occurred on board the "B. S. Kimball" during the voyage; two children were born and the following couples were married: Christoffer S. Winge and Anna Marie Salvesen, John Ness and Christine Andersen, Jorgen Dinesen and Christine Christensen, Sören Petersen and Ane Nielsen, Sören Mikkelsen and Christine Weibel, J. H. Hendricksen and Maren Rasmussen, Rasmus Nielsen and Maren Sörensen, Lars Gustaf Bergström and Johanna Engström,

Peter Christian Steffensen and Mariane Berthelsen, S. J. Christensen and Ane M. Nielsen, Niels Larsen and Wilhelmine Hövinghoff.

The "B. S. Kimball" cast anchor in the harbor of New York in the evening of Saturday, June 13th, and on the 15th the passengers were permitted to go ashore. In the evening of the same day the emigrants continued by train to Albany. There a fine boy was born. The company then proceeded to Florence, Neb., from which place the journey across the plains was commenced in connection with the other company from Scandinavia.

The ship "Consignment", having on board 37 Scandinavian Saints, arrived (after a successful voyage) in New York on the 20th of June, having spent one month and 12 days on the ocean. These emigrants were at once forwarded to Florence by train.

Elder Anders Christensen, who returned to his home in Zion with this emigration, had labored diligently and with good success in Aalborg and Vendsyssel Conferences under the direction of Elder Christian A. Madsen. Later, he succeeded Elder Madsen as traveling missionary in the two conferences named. While most of the missionaries laboring in Scandinavia had been rather slow and indifferent about reporting their labors and experiences in the missionary field, Elder Christensen had shown himself as an exemplary servant of God in this respect. He wrote a number of letters for publication to "Skandinavians Stjerne", "Millennial Star" and other periodicals in relation to the progress and happenings in his field of labor.

While the majority of the emigrants left Grimsby for Liverpool, May 6, 1863, the Norwegians remained in Grimsby in charge of Elder Carl C. N. Dorius until May 20th,

12

when they also traveled by rail to Liverpool, and on the same day went on board the ship "Antartic," on which also 60 passengers from Switzerland and many English emigrants went on board, making a company of 450 passengers. The "Antartic," which was a fine ship and well equipped for the voyage, sailed from Liverpool May 23rd. Before leaving Liverpool, President Geo. Q. Cannon and other Elders came on board and organized the company, appointing Elder John Needham president, with Philip De La Mare and Samuel H. B. Smith as his counselors. Carl C. N. Dorius was appointed steward, and together with his brother Johan F. F. Dorius given charge of the Norwegian Saints. Several deaths occurred on board, and several couples were married. The ship arrived in New York July 10, 1863, and the same day the journey was continued via Albany, Niagara, Detroit, Chicago and Quincy to St. Joseph, Mo., and thence by steamer to Florence, Neb. A child (Jensen) died on the steamer and was buried in Holt County, Missouri. Sister Anneken Larsen's child died as the emigrants landed; it was buried at Florence. The greater part of the Scandinavian emigrants journeyed across the Plains in three of the ox-team companies sent out by the Church that season to the Missouri River after immigrants. The first of these left Florence June 29, 1863, led by Capt. John R. Murdock, and arrived in Salt Lake City, Aug. 29th. The second company, led by Capt. John F. Sanders, left Florence July 6th and arrived in Salt Lake City Sept. 5th. The third company, led by Capt. Wm. B. Preston, left Florence July 10th and arrived in Salt Lake City Sept. 9th. The Church sent altogether 10 ox-trains from the Valley that year to bring the poor

Saints home to Zion and haul freig[h]t from the Missouri River.

The Norwegian emigrants crosse[d] the Plains in Captain Peter Nebeker['s] company, consisting of 50 wagon[s.] This company arrived in Salt Lak[e] City, Aug. 24, 1863. On the journe[y] across the Plains, 2 adults and [some] children died and were buried by th[e] wayside.

The Scandinavian Saints wh[o] crossed the Plains with their ow[n] teams, left Florence in Capt. John [F.] Young's company July 7th and a[r]rived in Salt Lake City, Sept. 1[?] 1863. This company experienced [a] terrible stampede, all their oxe[n] speeding over the prairies in fu[ll] fright. Some of the emigrants wer[e] killed and several severely injured.

Elder Anders Christensen, in a le[t]ter written at Salt Lake City to Pre[s.] Jesse N. Smith under date of Sep[t.] 18, 1863, gives the following accoun[t] of Capt. Preston's company:

"Of the company which numbered 3[00] souls, besides the teamsters, only thre[e] children died and these were sickly b[e]fore starting out on the Plains. Sever[al] were run over by the stampeding tea[m] because they were not careful enough [to] get out of the way, and their death seem[ed] evident; but through faith and pray[er] all were saved except a Swedish girl, wh[o] suffered a broken leg a few days befo[re] reaching Salt Lake City. The hot an[d] dry weather caused the waters of the Platt[e] and Sweetwater rivers to dry up in man[y] places. The cattle were kept in good co[n]dition all the way, but a sudden disea[se] killed about 25 of them, when we came [to] the Sweetwater. With these few exce[p]tions, the journey across the Plains wa[s] a success. Besides our 55 wagons, heav[i]ly laden with passengers, baggage an[d] freight, there were 12 independent team[s] traveling with our company. Union an[d] brotherly love prevailed, especially [among] among the Scandinavian Saints. Th[e] teamsters were kind and generous, willi[ng] to assist the emigrants all they could."

Elder Peter O. Thomassen, wh[o] after having remained in Florence si[x] weeks, started with other Scandina[-]

ian and English emigrants across
he Plains in Capt. Nebeker's company July 25, 1963, gives the followng report of the journey across the
Plains:

"The company I traveled with counted
no less than 70 wagons, nearly all of
which were drawn by eight oxen each.
It is remarkable to see how easy the
teamsters guide these heavily loaded
wagons and long strings of oxen without
reins or harness, using only a long whip
and the three words 'Haw,' 'Gee' and
Whoa' (which the oxen, through serious
lessons, have learned to understand).

"The journey across the Plains was successful, but somewhat monotonous, and
most of the travelers were glad to see the
wagons drawn up to form the corral and
rest their weary feet; but the young people, as a rule, were bent on having their
lively sports before retiring at the call of
the horn. Then all sang, music and dancing ceased, and the utmost quiet prevailed
throughout the camp, while one of the
Elders offered up a prayer and thanksgiving to the Almighty for his Fatherly guidance.

"On the 16th of August, we found a
buffalo skull, * * * having the information written thereupon that a company of
more than 50 wagons had experienced a
frightful stampede resulting in three persons being killed and several injured. The
names of these, all Scandinavians, I have
been unable to learn.

"The same day on which we found the
skull, an extended prairie fire, which had
started from one of our camp fires, spread
with great rapidity, fanned by a high
wind. It was a great sight to see this
mighty mass of flames travel over hill and
dale to the extent of many miles, while
herd of antelope, frightened by the blaz-
ing fires, sought refuge among our cattle,
where they scarcely were discovered before every one who possessed a gun or
pistol was ready to shoot down these pretty animals. Most of them, however, escaped unharmed—thanks to their swift
legs.

"On August 21st a German sister was
struck by lightning and fell to the ground
dead. A small bundle of keys, which she
carried on a string around her neck, could
not be found, and this, no doubt, had attracted the lightning which killed her.
With the exception of a small hole in the
head and a little mark under one foot,
no marks of injury to the body were

found, wherefore it was supposed that the
electric current had passed directly
through her body. The same stroke of
lightning felled seven of the oxen to the
ground, although without serious damage
to them. The company lost 50 oxen on the
journey.

"With weary feet but glad hearts we
arrived at the pleasant homes of the Saints
in Zion, September 24th, 1863, after the
long tramp over the wide deserts of America. It was a pleasant and delightful
sight to see the beautiful city spread out
before us when we passed out of Parley's
Canyon, a rough pass about 12 miles in
length. The city far exceeded my expectations, both as to extent and beauty; the
streets are wide and bordered with shade
trees, which already have reached a considerable size; the houses, which are of
course all new, are built in a nice, and in
many cases elegant, style."

The total number of Saints who
emigrated from Scandinavia in 1863
were 1,458, besides eight returning missionaries, namely, Wm. W.
Cluff, Hans Peter Lund, Johan F. F.
Dorius and Hans C. Hansen. These
Elders had all labored faithfully
as missionaries in Scandinavia. Elder Peter O. Thomassen, who for several years had labored in the mission
office in Copenhagen as writer for
"Skandinaviens Stjerne", also emigrated with his family that year, and
so also did Elders P. Wilhelm Poulsen, Nils Rosengren and Christoffer
S. Winge, who had acted as presidents of conferences.

CHAPTER 44 (1864)

The war in Denmark makes a break in
missionary labors—A number of young
Danish Elders, liable to military service, emigrate to America—Elder Samuel L. Sprague
takes temporary charge of the mission after
Jesse N. Smith—Another large emigration—
Arrival of Carl Widerborg to preside over
the mission.

In the beginning of 1864 the war,
which had been threatening for some
time, between Denmark on one side
and Prussia and Austria on the other,
broke out, and on the 1st of February, 1864, the allies crossed the Eider
as a commencement of hostilities

against the Danes. This war, which ended with defeat to the Danes, was caused by the Schlesvig-Holstein controversy. Among the Danish brethren subject to military duty were a number of young missionaries, who were forced to leave their missionary fields to take up arms in defense of their country, but a few of these young men were able to emigrate to Utah before they were drafted. Altogether, the events associated with the war tended to retard the progress of the missionary work in Denmark for a short time.

Meanwhile, the brethren laboring in Sweden were pushing their missionary labors with considerable success and many interesting incidents occurred in the experience of the Elders in that country. At Södra Rörum in Skåne, for instance, a priest, or minister, announced that the "Mormons" might be permitted to preach in his church; but after a large audience had assembled and the Elders were about to address them, the minister pounded on a table with a hammer with such violence that he deafened the remarks of the Elder who was speaking. He then opened a Greek Testament, asking the Elders to read from it, but as the Elders could neither read Greek nor the audience understand it, the meeting was dismissed and the people dispersed. Many of the people who had come together seriously objected to being fooled in this manner by the minister, whose object was apparently to receive a greater collection than usual, knowing that many people would of curiosity come out to hear the "Mormons" preach in the Lutheran church.

During the year a number of the smaller branches in the mission were disorganized or consolidated to make larger branches.

In March, 1864, Elder Thomas Taylor, who had been appointed by the European Mission presidency to succeed Elder Jesse N. Smith as president of the Scandinavian Mission, arrived in Copenhagen, but as instructions were received direct from Pres. Brigham Young early in April to the effect that the young Elder Samuel L. Sprague should occupy that position temporarily, Elder Taylor left Copenhagen for England April 13th; he had been a great help in arranging for the season's emigration, and had in several ways rendered Pres. Jesse N. Smith able assistance.

Elder Samuel L. Sprague, on receiving his appointment by Pres.

SAMUEL LINDSAY SPRAGUE

Born March 23, 1843, in Lowell, Norfolk Co., Mass.; died May 11, 1900, in Salt Lake City, Utah.

Brigham Young to succeed Jesse N. Smith as president of the Scandinavian Mission, writes: "I was completely surprised, and told Bro. Smith that I would rather continue laboring as a common missionary, as I was but a boy and unacquainted with the language of the people. The mission comprises Denmark, Norway and Sweden, and some parts of Germany, and the vast amount of business connected with the office, such as publishing 'Skandinaviens Stjerne,' keeping books, answering correspondence in foreign languages, traveling, preaching, counseling, and other matters too numerous to mention, caused me to shudder and wonder in my soul how a poor, unlearned boy could attend to all the duties devolving upon me in such a position."

On April 10th, at 5 p.m., the Swedish steamer "L. J. Bager" sailed from Copenhagen, carrying 350 emigrants from Sweden and Norway and some from the Fredericia Conference, Denmark, in charge of Johan P. R. Johansen. This company of Saints went by steamer to Lubeck, thence by rail to Hamburg, thence by steamer to Hull, in England, and thence by rail to Liverpool, where the emigrants joined another company of emigrating Saints which sailed from Copenhagen three days later.

On April 13, 1864, the English steamer "Sultana" sailed from Copenhagen, Denmark, with 353 emigrants from the different conferences in Denmark, excepting a few from Fredericia, who, on account of the war, had to go direct to Hamburg. This company was in charge of Pres. Jesse N. Smith, who returned home from a successful mission to Scandinavia. Elder John Smith, who on account of poor health had labored in the mission office in Copenhagen, and Christoffer Holberg, who had labored in Sweden, also left with this company, returning to their homes in Zion. The following Elders, who had presided over conferences, were among the emigrants: Niels C. Edlefsen, Peter C. Geertsen, Peter C. Carstensen, Nils C. Flygare, Anders Swedlund, Jens Hansen, Lars Nilsson, Anders Pontus Söderborg and Jens

C. Olsen. A number of the traveling Elders, who had diligently labored in the ministry, also emigrated with this company, which, like the preceding one, went by way of Lubeck, Hamburg and Grimsby to Liverpool, where they were joined by the company that sailed from Copenhagen, April 10th.

On Tuesday, April 26th, the ship "Monarch of the Sea" cleared for sailing, and on Thursday, April 28th, sailed from Liverpool, England, with 973 souls on board. Patriarch John Smith was chosen president of the

PATRIARCH JOHN SMITH

Born Sept. 22, 1832, at Kirtland, Ohio; died Nov. 6, 1911, in Salt Lake City, Utah.

company with Elders John D. Chase, Johan P. R. Johansen and Parley P. Pratt, Jun., as his counselors. Elders were also appointed to take charge of the different divisions of the company. During the voyage there was considerable sickness and some deaths, mostly of children. In the morning of June 3rd the "Monarch of the Sea" arrived at New

York where the landing of the emigrants at Castle Garden at once took place. In the evening they boarded a steamer for Albany, N. Y., and from there they traveled by train to St. Joseph, Missouri; thence by steamer up the Missouri River to Wyoming, Neb., from which place most of the Scandinavian Saints were taken to the Valley by Church teams, of which 170 were sent out by the Church that season. Thus about four hundred Scandinavian emigrating Saints crossed the Plains in Capt. Wm. B. Preston's company of about 50 Church teams, that left Wyoming, Neb., in the beginning of June, and arrived in Salt Lake City, Sept. 15, 1864.

The marching of the retreating Danish forces through Jutland in May, 1864, and the victorious Prussians who followed them, caused all kinds of trouble to the missionaries who were laboring in that part of Denmark; thus in Aalborg, the German troops took possession of the Saints' meeting hall, and thus prevented meetings being held there for some time. The Danish soldiers, fleeing before the superior forces of the Prussians, hastened to Frederikshavn, where they embarked for Copenhagen or other points on the Danish Islands. The German troops followed in close pursuit and overran the entire peninsula of Jutland, some of them going as far as the extreme northern point (Skagen).

On Sunday, July 31, 1864, Elder Carl Widerborg arrived in Copenhagen, having been appointed by the Presidency of the Church to take a mission to Scandinavia and there resume his former position as president of the Scandinavian Mission. It was only four years and two months since he had left Copenhagen to emigrate to Ziun. Elder Widerborg at once took charge of the mission, succeed-

ing Elder Samuel L. Sprague, wh had presided temporarily. Presiden Widerborg chose Samuel L. Spragu to act as his first and Anders W. Win berg as his second counselor; thes two brethren were to travel an preach throughout the mission. El der Sprague reports that he on Aug 1, 1864, delivered everything pe taining to the mission office to Pres dent Widerborg, giving a full accoun of the financial affairs, etc.

At this time, news reached the mi sion office in Copenhagen that th missionaries on Fyen had a har time because of the Danish troop being stationed there. Some of th brethren had been taken prisone and tried as spies, followed by short imprisonment.

President Carl Widerborg, repor ing the Scandinavian Mission, unde date of Dec. 23, 1864, writes:

"Our increase in Denmark this yea has not been so large as in former yeat on account of the unhappy war, whic tore many of our best Elders from the fields of labor, and in some measure su pended the labors of the few Elders th remained in the field. Since the Germa troops evacuated Jutland we have resume our labors with success, and I enterta the best hopes for the future in tho parts of the mission. * * *

"According to my own observations, a the favorable reports of the presiding a traveling Priesthood, the work is in prosperous condition, everything consi ered. It is true, we have more or less encounter—persecutions from opposi priests and mobs; but the Lord has, neve theless, protected his faithful servants a blessed their labors. Our meetings are the most places attended by attenti strangers, and we are always adding our numbers by baptism. Our 'Stars', boo and pamphlets have a wide circulatic spreading the truth and bearing testimo where our Elders cannot go.

"With regard to our Valley Elders boring in this mission, they are in go health and spirits, exerting themselves honor their Priesthood and calling. Eld Samuel L. Sprague has traveled consid ably in Norway, preaching and beari faithful testimony. He and Elder Geo.

Brown are doing a good work there. Elder Anders W. Winberg, who still continues his labors in the conferences of Jutland, has been a great blessing to the Elders and Saints in that part of the country. Elder Johan Swenson in Sweden is in a perpetual motion, as it were, hard to beat in walking and traveling, always on hand, and indefatigable in his labors. Elder John Sharp, jun., traveling in Sweden in company with Elder Swenson, is determined to learn the Swedish language as fast as possible. We were together at a good conference meeting in Malmö, Skåne, on the 30th ult. Elder Geo. W. Gee begins to feel quite at home in Stockholm, making himself useful, trying his best to acquire the Swedish tongue, though it is a jaw-breaking business. Elders Mons Petersen and John Gindrup, my assistants in the office, have labored to my satisfaction, and are native Elders, as a general thing, are faithful and obedient, trying to do their best, and have sometimes a great deal of difficulty and hardship to encounter.

"The spirit of gathering is great among the Saints, and those that can are preparing to emigrate next season. Would to God we had means enough to emigrate the poor, honest and faithful souls who are struggling here in poverty, hardly able to support themselves, work being scarce and wages low."

CHAPTER 44 (1865)

A severe winter in Scandinavia hinders the progress of the Elders—Pres. Daniel H. Wells visits Copenhagen—Many Saints emigrate to Zion.

In the latter part of January, 1865, an unusual hard winter set in with snow storms and cold in the Scandinavian countries, freezing the Baltic and the Belts, breaking off all steamboat communication, as well as stopping the railroad trains for several days. This made the sending of mails and traveling not only inconvenient, but very irregular, on account of the great depth of the snow and the ice. This state of affairs continued through February and March. But notwithstanding the cold weather the Elders labored faithfully; sometimes they had to wade through heavy snow and endure severe cold, especially in Sweden and Norway, where the cold

made baptisms in the open impossible for some weeks.

Elder Joseph H. Felt, a Utah Elder, arrived in Copenhagen, March 20, 1865, as a missionary to Scandinavia. He had already labored about one and a half years as a missionary in England.

A company of emigrating Saints, numbering 557 souls, left Copenhagen by the steamer "Aurora," May 4, 1865, accompanied by Anders W. Winberg (who was returning to his home in Utah) and Johan Swenson. President Carl Widerborg went with the emigrants to Hamburg. The company arrived at Kiel the next morning (May 5th). In the afternoon the journey was continued by train to Altona, whence the emigrants went up the Elbe on a small steamboat to a place off Hamburg, where the company was at once placed on board the double-decked ship "B. S. Kimball," an American vessel (Capt. Dearborn). On their arrival in Altona, the company was met by President Daniel H. Wells and Elder George Reynolds from England, who were both present when the company boarded the vessel. On Sunday, the 7th, a meeting was held on deck, on which occasion President Wells dedicated the ship with its captain, crew and passengers to the Lord and gave instructions and admonition to the Saints. Elder Anders W. Winberg was appointed leader of the company with Johan Swenson and Hans C. Högsted as his counselors. The ship was divided into eight districts, each with a president. Among the emigrants were the following Elders who had acted as presidents of conferences in Scandinavia: Hans C. Högsted from the Copenhagen, Sören Jensen from the Aalborg, Gustaf Pegau from the Fredericia, P. O. Holmgren from the Stockholm, John C. Sandberg from the Göteborg, and

Swen Nilsson from the Skåne Conferences. Among a number of other Elders who had labored as missionaries in Scandinavia and who as emigrants crossed the ocean in the "B. L. Kimball," was the late Martin Lundwall.

On Monday, May 8th, about noon, the ship lifted anchor and was drawn by a tender down to Gluckstadt, where President Carl Widerborg and Elders Samuel L. Sprague and Geo. M. Brown (who had accompanied the emigrants from Copenhagen), took leave of the emigrants and returned to Copenhagen, accompanied by President Daniel S. Wells and Elder Geo. Reynolds.

On Wednesday, May 10th, the ship with its precious cargo, sailed from Gluckstadt, and as the captain thought the colder climate would be better for the passengers, he chose the route north of Scotland. With the exception of one single day's storm the weather was very fair and favorable during the entire voyage. The captain was kind to the emigrants and the sick received good treatment. Three meals of warm food each day were served to all. Three adults died on the sea and about twenty-five children died of measles and scarlet fever. Besides the Scandinavian Saints, a number of other emigrants crossed the Atlantic on that ship. "While peace and good will reigned among the Saints," writes Elder Christoffer J. Kempe, "the others, who were Lutherans, Baptists and Methodists, lived more like cats and dogs together; some had disputes and engaged in fights, others played cards and swore, while some preached, and altogether there was a real pandemonium."

On June 14th the ship arrived in New York harbor, and the following day the emigrants landed at Castle

Garden. In the afternoon most of them continued the journey by train and then traveled via Albany, Niag-

MARTIN LUNDWALL (LUNDVALL)

Born in Ystad, Sweden, May 25, 1842 (the eldest of eight children), accepted the gospel when presented by Elder A. W. Winberg, and was baptized by Elder A. Peterson, Nov. 15, 1857, at Ystad, Sweden. He was ordained to the Priesthood and labored as a missionary until 1865 in the Ystad and Skönabeck branches, presiding over these branches, distributing tracts, preaching and baptizing. Emigrating to America in 1865, he crossed the ocean on the ship "B. S. Kimball," tarried in Omaha, Neb., for several years; thence went to Montana, where he became a staunch defender of the truth; received his endowments Oct. 14, 1908, in Salt Lake City, and died a faithful member of the Church, July 2, 1912, in Bozeman, Montana. To his devoted wife, Hannah Larson, ten children were born, three of whom now (1927) survive him, namely, Mrs. Ellen Maxwell, Olof and Nels B. Lundwall, all residing in Salt Lake City. Olof holds a position in the U. S. Government service and Nels B is secretary of the First Council of the Seventies.

ara, Detroit and Chicago to Quincy, Ill., where they arrived on the 20th. Here they were ferried across the Mississippi River and then spent two days and nights in the woods on the Missouri side without tents or other shelter, while the rain poured down in torrents. They had in a hurry fixed some small huts of brush, which, however, afforded them but very little shelter. The unpleasant delay was caused by the bridges on the railway being washed away, so he trains could not proceed. Finally he traveling was resumed on the 22nd, the cars conveying the company being very commonplace and dirty. The emigrants reached St. Joseph the following day. On the 25th they started by steamboat up he Missouri River and arrived at Wyoming, Neb., June 26th, bringing with them the corpses of three persons who had died on the steamer. Four others had died between New York and St. Joseph.

Several of the emigrants had only paid their fare to New York and therefore had to remain in that city for the time being. Elder Thos. Taylor, who was emigration agent for the Church, however, subsequently succeeded at a considerable sacrifice to complete arrangements so that all could proceed to Wyoming. But as the Church did not send any teams to the Missouri River that season to assist the poor Saints to reach Utah, and the price of oxen was much higher than in past years, some of the emigrants had to remain on the frontiers until the following year. Elder Taylor arranged matters as well as he could by purchasing oxen and loading each wagon with 1000 pounds of freight and 2000 pounds for the Saints, three yoke of oxen being provided for each wagon. In this way about 150 persons were taken across the Plains who otherwise would have been left on the frontiers. The price of a wagon at the outfitting place that year was 200 in greenbacks ($100 in gold), and a yoke of average oxen cost $150. It took about five weeks before everything was in order for starting the journey across the Plains. During his time the emigrants at Wyoming suffered much on account of the excessive heat and a few of them died. A Danish brother, Lars Petersen, about 30 years of age, who had as-

sisted about twenty poor Saints to emigrate, was accidentally drowned in the Weeping Water, a stream near Wyoming, where he, together with others, went to bathe. He was buried June 29th, with much expression of sorrow by the sympathizing Saints.

On the 31st of July most of the Scandinavian emigrants left Wyoming in a company consisting of forty-five ox-teams. The company was organized Aug. 1st by appointing Miner G. Atwood, captain; Charles B. Taylor, assistant captain; Anders W. Winberg chaplain and interpreter, Johan Swenson commissary and assistant to Winberg, and John Gindrup secretary. The following were appointed captains of ten: Hans C. Högsted, Hans Hansen, Christoffer Jensen Kempe and John Everett. At first the traveling was slow, as the roads were bad on account of the great amount of rain that had fallen. On Sept. 19th the company passed Fort Laramie, and three days later, when stopping at noon for lunch and rest, and while some of the brethren were driving the oxen to the watering places, fourteen or sixteen well-armed Indians suddenly sprang forth from their ambush in the woods and tried to take the cattle, but when the brethren opened fire upon them and the frightened oxen ran back to the camp, the theft was prevented. Seven of the brethren, however, were wounded by bullets and arrows, and a woman by the name of Grundtvig (an emigrant from Copenhagen, Denmark), who was lingering some distance behind the train, was taken captive and carried off by the Indians. Her fate has never become known. The wounded brethren all recovered from their wounds. Some days previous to this affray, the Indians, who this year were very hostile and had killed a number of travelers, stampeded the oxen of the company while grazing at night, but after two days' search the animals were all found, except three head.

Elder Thomas Taylor, having meanwhile completed all arrangements in Wyoming for the outfitting of the emigrants, passed by all the companies on his way to the Valley, where he secured forty-four mule teams, loaded with provisions, and with these went back to assist the emigrants. Capt. Atwood's company, which arrived in Salt Lake City all well, did not receive any assistance from that source, except some provisions.

Elder Hans C. Högsted, who emigrated to Zion in this company and who kept a journal of the doings on the way, states that it took the company 190 days to travel from Copenhagen, Denmark, to Salt Lake City, Utah, namely, 42 days from Copenhagen to New York, 12 days from New York to Wyoming, 36 days preparing for the journey across the Plains, and 100 days' travel from Wyoming to Salt Lake City. "On board the ship," writes Elder Högsted, "I earned the title of Doctor, as I distributed medicine to the sick and very frequently administered to them by virtue of the Priesthood. President Carl Widerborg had also appointed me second counselor to our president, Anders W. Winberg, who was a good man and much beloved by the Saints."

Elder Peter A. Nielsen, another of the emigrants, gives the following account of the journey:

"We left Gluckstadt, Germany, May 10, 1855, on the sailing ship 'B. S. Kimball'. Our company consisted of 557 souls. Three adults and 25 children died and were buried in the ocean. One day a fire started on the vessel, which created a panic among the passengers, but the fire was soon put out.

"Meeting a ship going east from America, we were informed of the victory of the Union Army. We were all ordered on deck and gave many cheers for the Red, White and Blue.

"Capt. Dearborn gave us many privileges in the way of amusements, dancing and theater-playing. But, best of all, he gave

PETER ANTON NIELSEN

A successful missionary in Scandinavia, was born May 12, 1845, in Odense, Denmark; baptized Feb. 22, 1862, by J. J. Jörgensen; ordained to the Priesthood and labored successfully as a local missionary in different branches of the Copenhagen Conference. While thus engaged he was imprisoned in Frederiksvärn twelve days for preaching the gospel. He emigrated to Utah in 1865; participated in the fight with the Indians in which a Sister Grundtvig was kidnaped by the Indians; married Olivia Jensen, Nov. 16, 1865, who bore him eleven children. In 1879-1881 he filled a mission to Scandinavia, laboring principally on the island of Bornholm. He suffered two days' imprisonment in Rönne for selling tracts. Returning to Utah, he led a company of emigrating Saints. In 1897 he performed a mission to California. At home he has always been active in Sunday school work. For thirty-two years he presided over the Scandinavian meetings at Draper, Utah. After filling another short mission to Denmark in 1907-1908, laboring in the Aarhus Conference, he was ordained a High Priest, July 6, 1909, by Joseph Keddington. In civil life Brother Nielsen has acted as a school trustee, postmaster, etc., and is now honored as one of the veteran Elders of the Church.

us leave to put our own cook, the best we could find, in the kitchen to prepare food for the sick. In the latter part of the journey the drinking water got so bad that we had to mix it with vinegar in order to swallow it, and many were sick on this account.

"What I called the worst trouble on the

ocean was the fact that we had no air pipes; all the air had to come through the stairways. The stench coming from below was very bad indeed, and the place was so infested with vermin that we could not rest. * * * At Wyoming we stopped five weeks before continuing our journey across the Plains. At this place wagons cost $200 in greenbacks and oxen $50 per yoke. Of these, at least 80 per cent had never borne a yoke upon their necks, which was the cause of our slow travel.

"On July 31st we started to cross the Plains with 45 wagons (ox teams), under Capt. Miner G. Atwood, with Charles B. Taylor as his assistant, Johan Svenson, commissary, and John Gindrup, secretary. On September 19th, the company arrived at Fort Laramie. Here we were called together in a meeting and warned by the U. S. officers at the Fort that the Indians were on the war path, and that we had better not go further; a free passage was offered us to any part of the United States where we wished to go. This announcement was made in three different languages. After all of us had been made aware of conditions and of the offer made by the U. S. officers, a vote was called by Elder Anders W. Winberg, but we all voted to refuse the kind offer of the U. S. officials, preparing to take a chance of reaching Zion in safety. On September 22nd. when about three days journey from Fort Laramie (at a place called Cottonwood Hollow, where we had camped for noon), while the men were driving the teams to a watering place about three-quarters of a mile from camp, the Indians came upon us from their hiding place and seven of our company were badly wounded. Thus Johan Swenson came into camp with two arrows in his left arm and Peter "Doctor" with one arrow in his cheek and one clear through his neck. A Swedish brother came in with an arrow in the small of his back and was not able to walk again on the journey. All we could do to relieve the sufferers was to let them sit down on a wagon hub with their backs against the spokes while we, using as surgical instruments common blacksmith's pincers or nippers, extracted the arrows from all except Peter "Doctor". The arrow in his neck could not be moved until we found a pair of pincers with extra long handles. Then laying the man on the ground with his head resting upon an ox yoke, two men sat upon him while Albert W. Davis, with one strong jerk, managed to pull the arrow out. Bro. Holmgreen, later of Corinne, was shot by a bullet and taken up for dead, but he recov-

ered. A man named Anderson was shot by a bullet which took off a little bit of his cheek and a piece of his nose. These two men lay. as dead while we cared for the others. John Holmgren, later of Bear River City, was then a new-born baby lying in a wagon with his mother. Bro. Frederick Gruntvig came into camp with an arrow fastened in his right hip. His wife had been carried off by the Indians.

At Sweetwater, a relief train, consisting of 44 mule-teams, met us, laden with provisions to relieve us of our sick and invalids. Some of the company then went forward to shovel the snow before we could put up our tents. We reached Green River one day at noon and decided to cross at once, and it took until after dark, and even then one wagon with a husband, wife and children, was left on a sandbank in the middle of the river all night, the kingbolt of their wagon having come out or was broken. At daylight the captain asked me to go and bring the family in, which I did. I found them all well, but they had passed a very restless night in their lonely position. We had to swim our teams over the river and many a teamster had to hold on to the oxen, or to the wagon, to keep from drowning.

"On the 8th of November we arrived on the Eighth Ward Square, Salt Lake City, where the City and County Building now stands. Pres. Brigham Young and Elder Wm. W. Riter came and shook hands with us. Besides our company of emigrants with 45 wagons, a company of 10 more wagons, carrying freight, joined us on the journey on account of the Indians being on the war path. This company was in charge of Albert W. Davis (later Bishop of Center Ward, Salt Lake City), with Lewis Romney as his assistant."

CHAPTER 45 (1865)

More Elders arrive from Zion to labor as missionaries in Scandinavia—The Norrland Conference organized in Sweden—Agitation for religious liberty in Norway.

The following Elders from Zion called to labor as missionaries in Scandinavia, arrived in Copenhagen Aug. 2, 1865: Niels Wilhelmsen of St. Charles, Idaho; Chr. Christiansen, Fred C. Sörensen and John Fagerberg of Ephraim; Sören Iversen and Gustaf A. Ohlson of Salt Lake City; Peter Hansen and Hans Hansen of Hyrum; Niels Nielsen of Brigham City;

Morten Lund of Fountain Green;
Hans Jensen (Hals) and Anders
Nielsen of Manti; Anders Larsen and
Lars Peter Edholm of Weber Val-
ley; Svend Larsen of Mt. Pleasant,
and Christoffer O. Folkmann of
Plain City, Utah.

Elder Carl C. A. Christensen of
Mt. Pleasant and Elder Jens Hansen
of Spanish Fork, Utah, arrived in
Copenhagen Aug. 20th, and Elder
Fred C. Anderson of Salt Lake City
arrived in Copenhagen Aug. 23rd, as
missionaries to Scandinavia.

Under date of Sept. 27, 1865,
President Carl Widerbòrg wrote the
following in reporting conditions in
the Scandinavian Mission to President Brigham Young, Jun.:

"I have visited and attended conference
meetings at Göteborg on the 26th and 27th
ult., at Veile on the 9th and 10th inst.,
at Aarhus on the 16th and 17th, and àt Aalborg on the 23rd and 24th. In all these
places I met with large congregations of
Elders and Saints, and a considerable
number of strangers, who all paid
good attention to the teachings of the
Priesthood. The Spirit of God assisted us
to bear a faithful testimony, and to give
such counsel as the people needed in the
various places. It was very interesting
to witness the warm-heartedness of the
Saints in pressing the hands of the Elders
from Zion, their faces beaming with joy
and satisfaction. It did my heart good
to look at the people, and to witness their
willingness in voting for the authorities
at home and abroad. Several of the Saints,
and among them aged men and women,
had walked from 60 to 70 English miles
to come to the meetings, and though the
majority of them are poor, they are nevertheless willing to sustain the Work by
their donations.

"The Scandinavian Elders from the Valley are exciting considerable interest a-
mong their friends and acquaintances, and
are pretty busy in traveling, holding meetings and conversing with those who are
seeking information about the things and
matters in famous Utah. Some strangers
only wish to satisfy their curiosity, I admit, but still many of the honest will be
led to investigate the truth of the gospel
and obey it."

President Widerborg also wrote
the following:

"On the 28th and 29th of October, 1865
I attended conference convened in Stockholm, where Elders Samuel L. Sprague
Joseph H. Felt, John Sharp, jun., Geo
W. Gee, Gustav A. Ohlson, Magnus
Cedertsröm, president of the conference, together with the traveling Priesthood, the
Saints of the Stockholm Branch, and several strangers were present. The Elders
represented the Saints in their various
fields of labor as in good standing, with
few exceptions, and the openings to
preach the gospel increasing. Our pam
phlets and work were having a wide circulation, and assisted considerably in pre
paring the way for the Elders. In the city
of Stockholm itself, the gospel was not
preached with the same success as in the
country districts, where the people are
more desirous to hear and obey, especially when they begin to see the incorrect
ness of the principles of the state church
and the corrupting influence of the priestcraft that has held them in bondage and
fear by means of illiberal laws, threatening everybody with fine and imprisonment
who dissented from the state church, or
opened their houses for religious meetings
It takes time to break down the barriers
that obstruct the progress of the gospel
requiring men of integrity, courage and
perseverance to overcome the manifold
opposition that meets the dissemination of
the truth. The work of God is, nevertheless, advancing steadily and surely, though
in some places it takes more time and re
quires greater efforts than in others, according to existing circumstances. We are
trying to distribute the printed word as
much as possible, and the Lord has favor
ed our efforts in that direction. Besides
the opposition of the clergy of the state
church, we have another class of people
to grapple with, the so-called Bible-read-
ers.

"It is almost impossible to reason with
them, as they spiritualize the meaning of
the clearest passages of the Holy Writ
Still, among all those classes there are
honest and upright individuals, yea, thou
sands of them, who will embrace the gos
pel and engage themselves in the great
and glorious cause of establishing the
Church and the Kingdom of our God. * *
"While at Stockholm in council with
the Elders, I found it necessary to organize
the northern part of Sweden into a con
ference, by the name of Norrland Confer
ence, and appointed Lars Peter Edholm to
preside over the same. He is a worthy

man, wielding a good influence among his former friends and acquaintances, who treated him coldly when he embraced the truth and emigrated to Utah; but now, since his return as a missionary, they are beginning to listen to his testimony, and inclined to examine for themselves. Upon the whole, I can say with regard to Sweden, that the Church is gaining ground, for which I am thankful to the Lord, who has opened the way thus far for us, causing the king and the government to grant us, in fact, more freedom than their laws and institutions in their present form admit. I clearly see that the Lord is gradually loosening the bonds and breaking the fetters of bigotry and intolerance, that for a long time have bound these northern nations, among whom such a great portion of the scattered house of Ephraim seems to be diffused.

"From Norway, Elder Geo. M. Brown writes me that the work is prospering and that lately a member of the Church, Elder Isacksen, has had an interview and conversation with the president of the Storthing (the Diet) now in session in Christiania. Said gentleman had expressed himself favorably in our behalf, counseling us to send in a new petition for religious liberty, as we have not the right to administer any ordinances of the Church, and also advising that our members, before being baptized, should report themselves as dissenters from the state church, thereby depriving the clergy of any right or power over them. Following his advice, the Norwegian Saints have sent in a petition for religious liberty to the Diet, accompanied with a copy of each of our standard works. The Christiania morning paper stated afterwards, that said petition had been referred to the committee on church affairs. What result it will have I do not know, but I am inclined to think that they will grant us a little more liberty than we have hitherto enjoyed. Our Elders will then not be subject to imprisonment and fine, as these things have often been their lot in the past, when the clergy made any complaint against them. I acknowledge, however, that the majority of the priests as well as the government officers and police authorities, have been very liberal in their treatment towards us, giving us liberty to hold meetings, and even protecting us.

"As a general thing the spirit of liberty and of freedom of conscience is penetrating the masses, so I suppose the clergy will have at last to give way, and loose the grasp upon the people, who in their hearts despise the hirelings whom they by custom and tradition show a degree of respect.

"In Denmark we are enjoying all the liberty we can expect, the clergy, of course, doing their best to prejudice their parishioners against us, using all the ciculating stories, lies and apostate letters they may pick up; but in spite of all this trash, the gospel of the kingdom is spreading to every nook and corner, revealing the scattered sheep of the fold of Israel. The Danes are not naturally a religious people, and do not read the Bible much; therefore, when in combat with the Elders, in the absence of Scriptural proofs, they sometimes use striking arguments—namely fists, rocks and sticks, and occasionally disturb our meetings by rough and boisterous behavior; but, after all, the people are honest and upright as a general thing, and embrace the truth when they have had sufficient time to be enlightened.

"Our missionaries, the Scandinavian brethren from the Valley, are respected among the people, wielding a good influence.

"I have now visited all the principal parts of this widespread mission. I have also tried to make 'Skandinaviens Stjerne' as interesting and instructive as possible, both for the Saints and the readers in general; and I am happy to say, that of the 2030 copies we issue semi-monthly, 215 are taken by outsiders."

CHAPTER 47 (1866)

Elders from Zion succeed local Elders in the presidency of conferences—Carl Widerborg arrested on a trumped-up charge, tried and acquitted—A large emigration of Scandinavian Saints sail in three ships from Hamburg for America.

With the beginning of the year 1866 there was a greater number of Utah Elders in the Scandinavian Mission than ever before, and it had been decided to appoint these Elders from Zion to preside over the various conferences. Previous to this time most of these positions had been filled by local Elders, in order to give the few Utah Elders in the mission a better opportunity to travel and preach. But now Elder Niels Nielsen was appointed to preside over the Copenhagen Conference, Peter Hansen over the Islands (Öernes), Fred C. Sörensen over the Fredericia, Anders Nielsen over the Aarhus, Hans Jensen (Hals) over the Aalborg, Morten Lund over the Vendsyssel, John Fagerberg over the Skåne, Gustaf A. Ohlson over the Norrköping and Fred C. Anderson over the Göteborg Conference. Lars Peter Edholm was made president of the Stockholm and Norrland conferences and Carl C. A. Christensen of the Christiania Conference. Most of these appointments went into effect with the beginning of the new year (1866) or soon afterwards.

Under date of March 17, 1866, President Carl Widerborg wrote the following:

"The numbers of our emigrants are increasing daily, and will probably amount to upwards of eight hundred souls. We have good news from the conferences; the meetings are well attended, and the brethren are laboring faithfully, causing the enemies of the work of God to raise a little disturbance here and there, but this only tends to stir up and advance the cause. Here, in Copenhagen, we have had an attack from the emissaries of the adversary, thinking they would strike a heavy blow against our Church. Some malicious person, an old apostate probably, managed under cover of the police authorities, to get me arrested on the 8th inst., on the false and abominable charge—'That I, last summer, had tried to seduce a young girl, and did my best to induce her to embrace 'Mormonism.' (Said girl had called twice at my office to inquire for letters from her mother, who emigrated last spring.)

"Under the examination I told the judges, that the accusation was a hellish plan, laid by some secret enemy to destroy my reputation and influence in my position, and to throw a shade over us as a religious community, but that that enemy would fail in his undertaking, as neither he nor any man could prove that I had perpetrated any immoral act whatever in the course of the eight years I had resided in Copenhagen.' The Spirit of the Lord assisted me in defending myself, as well as the truth of 'Mormonism', in all its principles and bearings.

"Among other things they inquired into our organization here, how many we numbered, and how many we had emigrated since the introduction of the doctrines of the Latter-day Saints in these countries, &c. I gave them true statements, and said that we did not work in the dark, all our transactions were well known to the public.

My clerks, Brothers Mons Petersen and August W. Carlson, were examined, and as their testimonies corroborated mine, also in that very important point of my never being alone in the office, as always one of them, at least, was present at a time, and no proofs could be found against me, I was released on the 13th inst.

"In further conversation with the gentlemen of the court, I asked them why they thought me guilty of such a damnable act? Their relpy was 'Because the talk is about you Mormons, that you are seeking after the women and have that peculiar institution, polygamy, amongst you.' Having asked for the liberty of giving my explanation, which was granted, I represented the matter to them in the light of the gospel, referring them to Holy Writ, and showing them what the law of God was in that respect among his chosen people, the Patriarchs and Prophets. I told them that we abhorred the peculiar institution of Christianity, licensed prostitution, that we considered the crime of illegal sexual intercourse as a capital crime, which could only be atoned for by the shedding of blood. I asked them if it would not be better for society if a man had the privilege of honorably sustaining in matrimonial relaticn more women than one, and their offspring, instead of, as the case now is in Denmark, and other civilized countries, to prostitute thousands upon thousands of females, causing depravity, corruption, sickness and crimes of various kinds? I remarked that I would rather see my daughter the fourth or fifth wife of an honorable man, or else dead and buried, than see her as a licensed whore among the Christians. I told them that I had never seen a better community than the 'Mormons' in Utah, and was glad to have the privilege of returning home to that people, when the labors required at my hands in these countries were finished. They heard me with patience all through, only remarking that they preferred their own institutions.

"Since my release I have been moved to tears by the many marks of affection, sympathy and respect that have been showed me not alone by the Saints, but also by outsiders, who have been acquainted with me for years, and who have said that they thought it was calumny. Last evening we had a crowded meeting of straners and Saints in our hall here. I gave them a short description of my trial, and preached to them the principles of the gospel of the Son of God, as revealed through his servant Joseph Smith the Prophet; of the persecution his people had suffered, and will suffer until the kingdom of God should conquer. The tears were listening in the eyes of many, and I hope the truth spoken that evening has, through the conviction of the Spirit of God, penetrated many a heart with good results. I thank God, my Heavenly Father, for the protecting care that he has over me for good: that he has delivered me from the hands of my enemies and permitted me to bear a faithful testimony of his work and of his people before policemen, judges, and many others. The servants of God have had to go and preach to the spirits in prison; why not preach in the prisons of men here on earth?"

As the transportation of the emigrants in 1865 from Hamburg direct to New York had proved a success, it was decided by the presidency of the European Mission in Liverpool that the larger emigration from Scandinavia in 1866 also should embark at Hamburg and sail direct to New York, and with this object in view President Brigham Young, jun.. and Elder John W. Young personally went to Hamburg in the month of May to assist President Carl Widerborg to make the necessary arrangements to that end.

A company of emigrating Saints (the first of the year's emigration) left Copenhagen by steamer "Aurora" May 17, 1866, and arrived early on the following day (May 18th) in Kiel, from which city the company went by train to Altona. From there the women and children continued in a small steamer to Hamburg, while the men walked to the same place. On their arrival in Hamburg, the emigrants were lodged for the night in a large emigrant building, and the following day went on board the double-decked ship "Kenilworth" (Capt. Brown). On Tuesday, May 22nd, more emigrants (who had left Copenhagen the preceding day) together with Elders Carl Widerborg, Niels Wilhelmsen, Geo. M. Brown and Chr. Christiansen, arrived in Hamburg, and on the 23rd the ship sailed a few miles down the river Elbe, where it anchored. On the 24th President Carl Widerborg, accompanied by Elders Niels Wilhelmsen and Christian Christiansen, came on board and organized the company, appointing Samuel L. Sprague president with Elder Morten Lund as his assistant. Fred R. E. Berthelsen was appointed secretary and Elder Ole H. Berg captain of the guard. The emigrants were divided into forty-two messes, each containing from twelve to seventeen persons, and a president appointed over each mess.

The ship "Kenilworth" lifted anchor in the River Elbe at Hamburg May 25, 1866, and commenced its long voyage across the North Sea and Atlantic Ocean, with its precious cargo of 684 souls on board; of these 583 were from Denmark, 23 from Norway, 73 from Sweden and five from Germany. The route around the north of Scotland was chosen and one day the ship, driven by contrary winds out of its course, got so close to the west coast of Norway that its rocky cliffs were plainly seen. The Shetland and Orkney Islands were soon passed and the winds were favorable for about three weeks. After that there was continuous headwinds and fog for five weeks, which made the voyage both long and dreary. Capt. Brown and the ship's crew treated the passengers in a kind and generous manner, allowing them all the privileges that could reasonably be expected. The provisions were satisfactory and the sick received good attention. Eleven or twelve persons died during the voyage. Among these was a man who wilfully jumped overboard on July 15th, just as land was in sight. A boat was launched in an endeavor to save him, but without success. The following night the ship anchored off Staten Island, and on the 17th of July the emigrants

OLE HENDRIKSEN BERG

Born Sept. 12, 1840, in Smaalenenes Amt, Norway, learned the trade of a cabinet maker in Christiania, became a convert to the gospel and was baptized in 1861. Being ordained to the Priesthood, he labored as a local missionary in Odalen, Kongsvinger and Solör and later presided over the Risör Branch. He also labored as a traveling Elder in Drammen and Röken, Norway. Being called to Denmark, he presided over the Öernes Conference, and emigrated to Utah in 1866, crossing the Atlantic in the ship "Kenilworth;" located in Provo, where he served as a member of the Board of Education, city councilor, county coroner, etc. He filled a mission to Norway in 1889-1891, presiding most of the time over the Christiania Conference. At home he acted as a High Councilor in the Utah Stake and as president of the Scandinavian meetings. He died in Provo, Feb. 23, 1919. Elder Berg was an able man, a good speaker and a faithful Latter-day Saint.

were landed at Castle Garden, the weather being exceedingly hot.

Elder Thos. Taylor, who again acted as emigration agent for the Church in 1866, had experienced much trouble in making the necessary arrangements for transporting the emigrants from New York to Wyoming, Neb. The railroad companies, whose lines went out from New York, had apparently planned to speculate at the expense of the "Mormons", and hence asked an unusual high price for conveying the emigrants westward. At length, after making a trip to Boston, Elder Taylor succeeded in closing a satisfactory contract for their conveyance, by an entirely new route, which was several hundred miles longer, but much cheaper than the more direct route used to be.

On the evening of the same day that the passengers of the "Kenilworth" were landed at Castle Garden, the emigrants proceeded on their journey on a large freight steamer to New Haven, Conn., where they arrived on the morning of July 18th. After staying there a few hours, the journey northward by train was begun, passing through the States of Connecticut, Massachusetts and Vermont to Montreal in Canada. Here the emigrants had to accept passage in some very uncomfortable and dirty freight and cattle cars, in which they traveled through Canada, the route of travel being along the north bank of the St. Lawrence River and the shores of Lake Ontario and Lake Erie, to the St. Clair River. On the evening of July 20th, a part of the train jumped the track near Port Hope on the banks of Lake Ontario, but through the interposition of a kind Providence no one was hurt. The emigrants were ferried over the St. Clair River to Port Huron in the State of Michigan, where better cars were obtained, and they wended their way via Chicago to Quincy, Ill. A steamer took them across the Mississippi River to the Missouri side, where they found temporary shelter from the burning sun in a nearby grove. While stopping there, a young oy who ventured too far out while bathing was drowned in the river. After a very disagreeable ride through the State of Missouri, where the inhabitants at nearly every station did all they could to insult the emigrants, the company arrived at St. Joseph July 27th. From this place they sailed two days on a steamboat up the Missouri River. On this most unendurable passage up the river they suffered all kinds of insults and abuses from a wicked crew. Finally, the company reached Wyoming, Neb., Sunday morning, July 29th, and in the afternoon camped on the heights in and near the town. The 450 teams sent by the Church in 1866 to the Missouri River to assist the poor had already waited some time for the arrival of the emigrants in Wyoming, wherefore the necessary preparations were hurriedly attended to in order to begin the journey across the Plains as soon as possible.

Another company of emigrating Saints, bound for Utah, sailed from Copenhagen at 1 o'clock p.m. on May 28, 1866, on the steamship "Aurora". The weather was fine and continued thus during the following night. On the morning of the 29th the emigrants arrived at Kiel (Holstein), where a stop of about three hours was made in order to bring their luggage to the railway station. The journey was then continued to Altona, where the emigrants arrived at 1 p. m. The Norwegians and others went on board the ship "Humboldt" three hours later, while others boarded the ship "Cavour". Of the large company of Saints which had sailed from Copenhagen, May 28th, 201 souls, who boarded the Norwegian ship "Cavour", sailed from Hamburg June 1, 1866. The "Cavour" was commanded by Capt. Floyn, and Elder Niels Nielsen, a Utah Elder, was appointed president of the company with Jens

Gregorsen and Carl Fred. Rundquist as his assistants. This ship had, on account of head winds, calm and fog, a long voyage, notwithstanding the vessel took the shortest route, viz., through the English Channel. The emigrants were organized into four districts in charge of Elders Jens Gregorsen, Carl F. Rundquist, a Bro. Jacobsen and Ole Nielsen. Two old sisters, who had been sick for several years, and two children died during the voyage. The "Cavour" arrived in New York July 31st, and the emigrants were at once conveyed over the same route as the one taken previously by the "Kenilworth" company; they arrived at Wyoming, Aug. 11, 1866. Already, on board the "Cavour", cholera had broken out among the emigrants. It made its first appearance in Brother L. Larsen's family, of whom most of the members died later. But on the travel by railway that terrible malady raged fiercely among the emigrants, claiming its victims one by one. The rough treatment the emigrants received was in part responsible for the heavy death rate. Just before the train arrived at St. Joseph, Mo., one of the passenger cars took fire, and it was with great exertion that the sick were removed from it to escape from being burned to death. At St. Joseph a number of sick and dying had to be left in the hands of wicked people. Their friends obtained no further knowledge as to their fate, and never learned whether they were buried alive, or killed by force, for the people there were seemingly so hateful, that they actually thirsted for the blood of the Saints. On the voyage by steamer up the Missouri River nine of the emigrants died, four of them being buried one night and five of them the next.

The ship "Humboldt" (Capt. Boyson) sailed from Hamburg, June 2, 1866, with another company of Saints bound for Utah. This was the third division of the emigration of Scandinavian Saints that year and numbered 328 souls, who were organized with George M. Brown, Sven S. Jonasson and Christian Hansen as leaders. The company was organized into four districts, which were subdivided into nine lesser divisions with a president appointed for each of them. Besides the Saints, sixty or seventy other passengers were on board. The "Humboldt" was tugged down the River Elbe to the North Sea by a steam-tug boat. Taking the route north of Scotland, the ship passed the Shetland Islands on the 6th of June with Cape Telsit on the right and the small island Fair on the left. In the b e g i n n i n g of the voyage much seasickness prevailed among the passengers. Passing the New Foundland Banks the fog was intense, and with the exception of the first ten days, the ship encountered headwinds most of the time. The captain, who was very kind to the Saints, admitted that he had never witnessed so good and orderly a company of emigrants crossing the Atlantic before, and he was very kind and sympathetic to the sick, sending them extra food from his kitchen. Five persons, two adults and three children, died during the voyage. On July 18th the "Humboldt" arrived safely in New York, and the emigrants were at once started westward by steamer and railway to Wyoming, Neb., arriving there on Aug. 1st.

A part of the Scandinavian emigrants crossing the ocean that year in the ships "Kenilworth" and "Humboldt" crossed the Plains in Capt. Jos. S. Rawling's ox train, which left Wyoming Aug. 2nd and arrived in Salt Lake City Oct. 1st. Another part of them left Wyoming with Capt. Peter Nebeker's ox train, Aug. 4th and arrived in Salt Lake City Sept. 29th. A third division left Wyoming with Capt. Andrew H. Scott's company, Aug. 8th, and arrived in Salt Lake City Oct. 8th.

When the "Cavour" company arrived at Wyoming there was no time to rest, as the last train of the Church teams had already waited a long time for the arrival of these emigrants, and it was now so late in the season that the start across the Plains could be postponed no longer, with any hope of getting across the mountains that year. Consequently, this cholera-infested company had to get ready in the greatest haste for the long and wearisome journey, and on Aug. 13th the emigrants left Wyoming with sixty ox-teams, in charge of Capt. Abner Lowry.

If the details of the journey across the Plains of this company were written, it would probably present one of the most pitiable and heart-rending chapters in the history of the Church, but it is perhaps better to close the episode and not revive the memory of something so touching and sorrowful. At some future day, undoubtedly, more details will be published about the experience of that ill-fated company, and in the great hereafter those who laid down their lives on the way will have an opportunity to give an accurate and truthful account of their sufferings. The survivors of Captain Lowry's company arrived in Salt Lake City Oct. 22, 1866.

Only a few of the Scandinavian Saints crossed the Plains this year with their own teams, nearly all going with the Church trains. The death list among all companies was quite heavy, the cause being, chiefly, cholera. Thus ten persons died in Capt. Rawlings' company, about thirty in Capt. Nebeker's company and about the same number in Capt. Scott's company. It was the last year that emigrants traveled all the way from the Missouri River to Great Salt Lake City with ox-teams, as the Union Pacific Railroad was being built from Omaha westward, and the following year (1867) was opened for several hundred miles west of the Missouri River.

Elder Brigham Young, jun., and John W. Young of Salt Lake City, both sons of President Brigham Young, arrived in Copenhagen June 17, 1866, on a visit to Scandinavia. President Carl Widerborg met these brethren in Hamburg and accompanied them via Lubeck and Korsör to Copenhagen. In the afternoon of the day of their arrival the visitors attended a meeting of the Saints in Copenhagen, where they spoke well and intelligently to the large audience.

After spending a few days in Copenhagen, Elders Brigham and John W. Young, accompanied by Carl Widerborg, visited Christiania, Norway, where they held two good meetings with the Saints, and also participated in a number of excursions through the interesting mountain country which surrounds the capital of Norway. From Norway the visiting brethren went to Göteborg, Sweden, where they held an interesting meeting with the Saints and their friends, and thence proceeded by canal route via the Trollhättan Falls, Lakes Venern and Vettern, and the canal system to Stockholm. Here the brethren took in the sights and met with the Saints in several meetings. From

GROUP OF MISSIONARIES LABORING IN NORWAY IN 1866

Top row, left to right: Anders Poulsen, Jonas Johannesen, John Larsen, *. Middle row: *, Peder Nielsen, *, Anthon L. Skanchy, *, Borre Jensen. Lower row: Christoffer O. Folkmann, Svend Larsen, Carl C. A. Christensen, Niels Wilhelmsen, *, Theodor M. Samuelsen.

*Names not obtainable.

Stockholm the visitors made a trip to St. Petersburg, Russia, thence to Moscow, the old capital of Russia, thence they traveled by railroad to Berlin, the capital of Prussia, and thence to Hamburg, where President Carl Widerborg took leave of the two Elders Young, August 1st, they to return to England and President Widerborg to Copenhagen.

President Carl Widerborg, in reporting to President Orson Pratt in England, Oct. 5, 1866, stated that the Elders from Zion were doing a splendid work in the Scandinavian Mission. On the following day (Oct. 6th) a general council of the Scandinavian Mission convened in Copenhagen, at which it was stated that the meetings in that city were well attended by strangers as well as by Saints. The Elders in Norway had labored with great success and the civil authorities there were not so vindictive in persecuting the brethren as they had been in years gone by. A branch of the Church had been organized at Namsos, Norway, Sept. 30, 1866, with sixteen members.

In Sweden, the Elders had extended their missionary labors to Haparanda, the northernmost city in Sweden, where one person had already been baptized. In Schleswig-Holstein, where the Prussians held control, the Elders found it very hard to prosecute missionary labors. One of the brethren who had recently visited the few Saints there had been driven out by the civil authorities. Brother J. T. Pytcher, who could speak the German language, was appointed to labor as a missionary in Schleswig-Holstein.

CHAPTER 48 (1867)

Apostle Franklin D. Richards visits Denmark—Elder Sven Larsen imprisoned in Norway—Return of American Elders and arrival of others—The first company of Scandinavian Saints cross the Atlantic by steamer.

Apostle Franklin D. Richards,

president of the European Mission arrived in Copenhagen, Jan. 12 1867, on a visit from England. Together with President Widerborg who met him in Hamburg, he made a tour through Sweden, visiting all the conferences in that country, and also held special meetings in Malmö Jönköping, Norrköping, Stockholm and Copenhagen. As the weather would not permit them to visit the Danish conferences, or Norway, Elder Richards left Copenhagen, Feb 12th, for England, President Widerborg accompanying him to Hamburg

Under date of Feb. 6, 1867, Franklin D. Richards wrote the following from Stockholm, Sweden:

"I have, in company with Elders Carl Widerborg and Niels Wilhelmsen, visited and held meetings in each of the conferences in the kingdom of Sweden. As deep snow covered most parts of Denmark and Norway, being in places so deep as to cover the telegraph wires, it was concluded that the greatest good would be accomplished by our taking this course, as Bro. Widerborg had intended to visit the Swedish Saints, if I did not accompany him, and the road in this direction was open for travel; besides, Bro. Widerborg thinks the work in this nation has not had the opportunities for extension and advancement which it has had in Denmark and in Norway. True, there were a goodly number of Elders appointed to the Scandinavian Mission, but it happened that nearly all of them were Danish, and therefore not adapted to the peculiar mode by which the gospel has to be introduced and promulgated in this kingdom.

"In Denmark the Elders stand forth with holy boldness, claiming and maintaining their rights, under their constitution, to preach and worship according to the dictates of their own consciences. Not so here, in Sweden. A dissenter has no right in law, or by the constitution, to worship any hour when the State Church, which is Lutheran, shall be holding services. A provision of the law grants to resident dissenters, members of other churches, the privilege of holding meetings on Sunday, provided that such meetings are not intended to make proselytes to such dissenting faiths; all religious dissenters being tolerated except the Saints. Thus you see that instead of having contitutional or legal guarantees or inducements for furthering our work, we are entirely on sufferance in our labor of love to this portion of the human family, and our Elders are liable at any time to be taken up and imprisoned at the instigation of the priests.

"Our only safe and certain mode hitherto, has been for some Elder, a mechanic, to obtain employment in the place where it was designed to introduce the gospel, and thus, while employed at his work, disseminate the revealed truth among the hands until, without let or hindrance from the enemy, a branch was organized, and the fire once kindled soon won its widening way. In this manner, mostly, have the 38 branches, which compose the four conferences in Sweden, been built up, and which, besides those who have emigrated, now number about 1600 members.

"It is not by any means that our Swedish brethren lack the pluck to use bolder means, but that this appears the only prudent method. Recently two of our Elders, thinking it too slow a process for so important a work, concluded to call on the minister of the parish, offer him the truth, and, if possible, get liberty to hold meetings among his flock. The result was that after staying over night with him, his reverence told them that they must leave his parish, and not come into it again to teach such heretical doctrines; if they did, he would send them to prison. Not content with this captious mode of closing up their way, they quietly visited in another parish, and succeeded in awakening an interest to hear more, and in view of a meeting a gentleman offered his house for preaching, whereupon the minister was respectfully invited to attend. Demanding to know why they had presumed to do such a thing in his parish, without his knowledge, he received for a reply, that they did not come to contend with him, but to inform him there was to be a meeting, and to invite him to attend, if he pleased. Thus getting the truth before a part of his people, it took root in their hearts and became impossible of extinction.

"In most places where the gospel can be revealed to the people, it finds believers readily; but the law establishing the Lutheran church in these northern countries has given the priests almost unlimited authority to compel the adoption of that faith, making their mode the only legitimate form of marriage, etc. Indeed, in their constraint of religious opinion, as well as many of their rites and ceremonies, they are but one step removed from their ancient Catholic mother; for example, a brother went to a Lutheran priest to be married, but was refused the ceremony because he was a heretic, and applied to the president of the mission, who advised him to get a writing from the priest stating the fact, which he did, when Bro. Widerborg married him, and gave him a certificate of the same, since which his neighbors consider him an honorably married man. Thus, while the priests are willing to exercise their power to an extent that bastardizes or renders illegitimate 42 per cent of the population, as shown by the statistics of this city, there is an insatiable thirst on the part of the people, that is growing with the ruler and sovereign also, for an extension of human rights, and freedom of thought, of speech, of the press, and of conscientious worship of Almighty God. * * *

"I had the happy privilege last Sunday evening to meet with about one hundred Saints and fifty strangers, in a pleasant little hall in this city (Stockholm), and to address them with great freedom and pleasure, although through an interpreter. It seemed singularly strange to me, that I was nearly eight thousand miles from my home, preaching the gospel to the Goths, the Swedes of northern Europe—that in Sweden alone nearly 2,000 persons had obeyed the gospel, and accepted all the doctrines of the Church, not excepting tithing, consecrations, and polygamy in the faith, with the same right good will that you and I have and call Utah their home with as heartfelt sincerity as do either of us. How could I help speaking to them by the Spirit, while its effects caused smiles and tears to alternate in their countenances. The strangers gave the best attention, and we could see and feel that the truth was gaining place in their hearts.

"On Monday it came to our ears that the Royal Theatre, which had been closed for a time, was to be opened that evening, and the King, ministers and members of parliament were expected to be present. Though not much of a theatre-going man, I did not need much urging to accept a ticket for the parquette. Punctually at 7 o'clock, the King, attended by the queen, queen dowager, princes and princesses of the family, appeared in the royal box. The audience arose and faced their majesties. The orchestra of 50 performers struck up the national anthem, at the close of which the King bowed acknowledgment of the honor, and all were seated.

"Thus I found myself in the midst of nobility and gentry, the beauty, elite, and authority of Sweden, composed of bishops, barons, counts, ministers, officers of the army, princes and royal personages of the crown, with their beautiful ladies by their sides. It was an impressive scene, and gave rise to many interesting reflections, which I cannot now write you.

"When I thought how much I should like to impart to His Majesty the testimonies of the gospel restored, and the work of God as it is now progressing on the earth, and inform him how he could assure the stability of his throne, the perpetuity of his dynasty, with the peaceful prosperity of his realm, the spirit whispered it were well I could not, for if I were to, it would probably prevent the liberty now enjoyed by the Elders in preaching the gospel throughout the State, and perhaps cause expulsion of both Elders and Saints from its borders. I breathed a silent, earnest prayer that he who is the King of kings, would vouchsafe peace and increase of liberty to the dominion of Carl XV of Sweden, until those of his subjects who are the seed of Israel shall obtain a renewal of the promises made to the fathers upon their own heads. The theatre was about the same size as the one in Salt Lake City. * * * There are Saints 200 miles north of here, but the difficult traveling prevents our visiting them."

Under date of April 23, 1867, Elder Carl C. A. Christensen writes:

"Norway constitutes but one conference, called Christiania Conference, and we, three Elders from the Valley, have been laboring here. Christoffer O. Folkmann labors as a traveling Elder in the north, and Svend Larsen in the south. Last winter Elder Christoffer O. Folkmann was tried by the courts at Trondhjem for preaching 'Mormonism' and was fined; he appealed to higher courts, but to no avail, and will shortly atone for the crime of preaching by the usual mode of paying for that offense.

"At present Elder Svend Larsen is in prison for preaching in Frederikshald and will, according to law, be fined and treated to bread and water.

"As Elder Larsen is released to return to his home in Zion this season, and Elder Folkmann is called to preside over the Göteborg Conference, in Sweden, I shall be left alone with the native Elders to enjoy all the blessings that our 'Christian' brethren will bestow upon us. according to law."

Inasmuch as the Church did not send teams for emigrants in 1867,

only such of the Saints as could help themselves with means had opportunity to emigrate that year. For this reason the whole year's emigration from Scandinavia was only 290 souls, who left Copenhagen June 13, 1867, by the steamer "Waldemar", accompanied by the following returning Elders from Zion: Niels Wilhelmsen, Christian Christiansen, Lars Peter Edholm, Anders Nielsen, Hans Hansen, Sören Iversen, Jens Hansen, Frederik C. Sörensen, Gustaf A. Ohlson and Svend Larsen who had labored as missionaries in Scandinavia since their arrival in August, 1865. After a successful voyage across the North Sea, the "Waldemar" arrived in Hull, England, June 16th. Thence the journey was continued by railway to Liverpool, from which city the Scandinavian emigrants, together with 190 English Saints, sailed June 21st on board the beautiful steamer "Manhattan", a vessel of 2000 tons, equipped to carry one thousand passengers. Elder Archibald N. Hill was appointed to preside over the company with Elders Niels Wilhelmson, James Ure and Francis Platt as his assistants. The Saints were located from midships to stern by themselves and were divided into seven divisions, over which Elders Christian Christiansen, Anders Nielsen, Lars Peter Edholm, Stephen Hales, Gustaf A. Ohlson, Jens Hansen and Henry Cooper were placed to preside. Robert R. Anderson from the mission office in Liverpool was appointed secretary. About seven hundred other emigrants were on board. This was the first Scandinavian emigrant company which crossed the Atlantic in a steamship. After a voyage of twelve and one-half days, the "Manhattan" arrived in New York July 4th. The next day (July 5th) the emigrants landed at Castle Garden and continued the journey by steamer up the Hudson River to Albany. From there they were conveyed by railway via Niagara, where they stayed over night and thus were afforded a splendid opportunity to view the great Niagara Falls. They then proceeded westward, via Detroit and Chicago, to St. Joseph, Mo., and from that city up the Missouri River by steamer to Omaha. Three Scandinavian children died on the way. From Omaha the emigrants traveled on the Union Pacific Railroad 291 miles westward to North Platte, from which place, after a stay of four weeks, the journey across the Plains was begun with an ox-train, in charge of Capt. Leonard G. Rice, and arrived in Salt Lake City Oct. 5th, after a successful journey.

In 1867, eleven Elders from Zion arrived in Copenhagen, to labor as missionaries in Scandinavia. They were Saamund Gudmundsen of Fairview and Lauritz Larsen of Spring City, Utah, who arrived July 27, Chr. D. Fjeldsted of Sugar House Ward, Ole C. Olsen and Morten Mortensen of Gunnison, Jens Johansen, George K. Riis, Samuel Petersen, Jens Jensen and Arne Christensen Grue, all of Salt Lake City, who arrived July 31st, and Carl C. Asmussen, also of Salt Lake City, who arrived later.

Elder Saamund Gudmundsen was appointed to labor as a traveling Elder and later as president of the Christiania Conference, Norway. Elder Larsen was appointed to preside over the Aarhus Conference, later over the Aarhus and Fredericia conferences and still later to labor as a traveling Elder in the whole Scandinavian Mission. Elder Fjelsted was appointed to preside over the Aalborg Conference, later to labor as a traveling Elder in the whole mission and still later to preside over the Christiania Conference. Elder Olsen was appointed to labor as a traveling Elder and later as president of the Stockholm Conference. Morten Mortensen was appointed to labor as a traveling Elder in, and later as president of the Öernes Conference. Elder Jens Johansen was appointed to labor in the Vendsyssel Conference and later as president of said conference, and when the Aalborg conference absorbed the Vendsyssel Conference, he was chosen president of the amalgamated conference. Elder Geo. K. Riis was appointed to labor as a traveling Elder in, and later as president of, the Norrköping Conference, Sweden. Elder Petersen was appointed to labor as a traveling Elder in the Skåne Conference and later as president of the Göteborg Conference, Sweden. Elder Jens Jensen was appointed to labor as traveling Elder in the Fredericia and Aarhus conferences and later as president of the Aalborg Conference. Elder Arne Christensen Grue, after working for some time at his trade as watchmaker in Denmark and Norway, was appointed to labor in Norway as a traveling Elder and still later to preside over the Jönköping Conference, Sweden. Elder Carl Chr. Asmussen, who arrived from New Zealand, where he had labored as a missionary for six months, was appointed to labor in the Copenhagen Conference.

CHAPTER 49 (1868)

Conferences in Scandinavia amalgamated.— Last sailing vessel brings Scandinavian emigrants across Atlantic: the death toll on voyage very heavy on board the "Emerald Isle"—Last Scandinavian emigrants cross the Plains with teams.

At a general conference of Elders held April 13, 1868, in Copenhagen, Hans Jensen (Hals) was released from his position as traveling Elder and appointed to lead the year's emigration to America. Elders Peter Hansen, John Fagerberg, Christoffer O. Folkmann and Carl C. A. Christensen were also released with permission to return home. Christian D. Fjelsted was appointed to labor as a traveling Elder in Scandinavia. The Aalborg and Vendsyssel conferences were amalgamated under the presidency of Jens Johansen to be known as the Aalborg Conference. The Fredericia Conference was also discontinued and its few remaining branches amalgamated with the Aarhus Conference under the presidency of Lauritz Larsen and James Jensen as traveling Elders. Morten Mortensen was appointed to preside over Öernes and Saamund Gudmundsen over the Christiania conferences, and Samuel Peterson, Geo. R. Riis, Ole C. Olsen and Peter T. Nyström were appointed to take charge of the Swedish conferences. Elder Halvorsen was appointed to preside in Copenhagen.

In 1868 a strong effort was made in Zion to gather means to assist the poor Saints who wished to emigrate, and large sums of money were sent to the British Islands to assist members of the Church to this end, especially faithful Saints of many years' standing. Besides this, the Church sent for the last time teams out to the terminus of the Union Pacific Railroad to bring them thence across the deserts and mountains. Although scarcely any of the means collected was applied to assist the poor from Scandinavia, a goodly number (820) souls emigrated from the Scandinavian countries in 1868, viz: 544 Danes, 209 Swedes and 63 Norwegians; also 4 German emigrants.

Of the above-named number 104 Swedish Saints sailed from Göteborg May 29, 1868, by the steamer "Hero" in charge of Elder Christoffer O.

Folkmann, arriving in Hull, England, May 31st. Here they were joined by a small company of Danish Saints in charge of Elder Carl Widerborg and along with these continued the journey to Liverpool by railroad. On the evening of the next day (June 1st) Elder Carl C. A. Christensen arrived in Liverpool with some emigrating Saints from Norway, about 50 in number. They had sailed from Christiania by steamer for England, where they joined the main body of emigrating Saints from Scandinavia. On June 3rd all were on board the ship "John Bright" (Capt. John Towart). Elder James McGaw was appointed president of the company, of which 17 were Scandinavian and more than five hundred British Saints. Christoffer O. Folkmann and Fred C. Anderson were chosen for assistant president. The Scandinavian Saints, who were located on the lower deck, were placed under Elder Carl C. A. Christensen's special charge.

The "John Bright" sailed from Liverpool June 4th. It was intended that the emigrants this year should have crossed the Atlantic by steamers, but on account of the high price demanded for steamship passage, the voyage had to be made by sailing vessels as in previous years, so that those of only limited means could be accommodated. During the voyage there was very little sickness and only an aged sister from England, who was sick when she went on board, died. A Swedish couple were married during the voyage. The captain was very kind and obliging towards the Saints. The company arrived safely in New York July 13th, and on the following day was conveyed by railroad westward. The emigrants traveled via Chicago and Omaha, and on the Union Pacific Railroad to Laramie City. The far from New York to Omaha was $14 and to the terminus on the Plains $35, but those who would stop to labor on the Union Pacific Railroad were conveyed all the way for $14. The company arrived at Laramie, 573 miles from Omaha, July 23rd. At that time, Laramie City was the western terminus of the Union Pacific Railroad, and also, temporarily, the outfitting place for the journey across the mountains with teams. Here the emigrants met the Church teams and most of the Scandinavian Saints went with Captain Horton D. Haight's company, which left Laramie July 27th, and arrived in Salt Lake City, August 24, 1868.

Elder Folkmann acted as' leader of the Scandinavians in this company and also as chaplain for the whole company. Two Swedish emigrants died on the journey across the mountains.

Elder Carl C. A. Christensen, together with some Norwegian Saints, crossed the Plains with Captain John R. Murdock's company, which left Laramie a little before Captain Haight's company and arrived in Salt Lake City August 19th. The fare by the Church teams from the railroad terminus to Salt Lake City was $29, which the emigrants were required to pay later.

About 630 emigrants left Copenhagen by the steamer "Hansia," June 13, 1868. On the departure the brethren had considerable trouble with the police authorities in Copenhagen. After a successful voyage across the North Sea, the company arrived in Hull, England, on Tuesday, June 16th, and in the evening of the same day they went by train to Liverpool. Here they found accommodations in seven different hotels, where they, with the exception of one place, received anything but decent treatment; and when they on the 19th went on board the ship "Emerald Isle," they were insulted in most every imaginable way. On the 20th the ship sailed from Liverpool, carrying a company of emigrants consisting of 877 souls, of

HANS JENSEN (HALS)

Born June 24, 1829, at Hals, Aalborg Amt, local missionary about eight months and emigrated to Utah in 1853-1854. After his mission Denmark, was baptized in 1853, labored as a to Scandinavia in 1865-1868, he acted for many years as Bishop of the Manti South Ward, where he died as a Patriarch, June 10, 1911.

whom 627 were Scandinavians, all in charge of Elders Hans Jensen (Hals) as president with James Smith and John Fagerberg as assistants. Elder Peter Hansen was appointed commissary for the Scandinavians, and Elder Mons Pedersen, who had labored faithfully for four years in the mission office in Copenhagen, was chosen as secretary. Eighteen other Scandinavian emigrants sailed this year by other ships, some of them from Hamburg and some from Norway.

On June 26th the "Emerald Isle" sailed into the harbor of Queenstown to take fresh water on board, as a certain machine on the vessel used to distill seawater for culinary purposes was out of commission and could not speedily be repaired. While the ship waited at Queenstown Elders Hans Jensen (Hals) and James Smith had an excellent opportunity to accompany the captain on a railway trip to Cork. On the 29th the ship left Queenstown, but the voyage after that was anything but pleasant. The emigrants received very rough and harsh treatment, both from officers and crew, and only by the strong protest of Elder Hans Jensen (Hals) in their behalf did they succeed in getting a part of their rights according to the contract made. On one occasion, when one of the ship's mates attacked a sister by the name of Sander, Brother Jensen took hold of the mate and pulled him away, while sharply reproving him for his conduct. Soon a lot of sailors came up ready for a fight, but the incident ended when the offender got a severe reprimand from the captain, whom Brother Jensen reminded of the promises made. No other company of emigrating Saints from Scandinavia are known to have met with such bad treatment as this on board any ship in crossing the Atlantic Ocean. Fortunately it was the last company of Scandinavian Saints which crossed the Atlantic in a sailing vessel. From that time on only steamers were employed in the transportation of the Saints. It was not alone the rough treatment which the emigrants received from the ship's crew that made the voyage so unpleasant, but the water taken on board at Queenstown soon became stagnant and unfit for use, causing much sickness among the passengers, and no less than 37 deaths occurred on the voyage. Many of these, however, were caused by measles among

the children, but the stagnant water which all the passengers had to use was undoubtedly the real cause of the heavy death rate.

On August 11th the ship arrived at the entrance of New York harbor and 30 of the sick were taken ashore on Staten Island. The following day (August 12th) eight other sick people were landed, and finally, after being held in quarantine three days, the rest of the emigrants were landed at Castle Garden, August 14th. On the same day a steamer conveyed the emigrants a few miles up the Hudson River, where they found shelter in a warehouse for a couple of days, while their baggage was being weighed. While staying there a boy belonging to the company died. On the 17th the journey was resumed by railway from New York and the emigrants traveled via Niagara, Detroit and Chicago to Council Bluffs, where they arrived on the 21st. The following day (August 22nd) they were taken across the Missouri River by a steamboat and thence they traveled by the Union Pacific Railroad to Benton, seven hundred miles west of Omaha, arriving there in the morning of August 25th. Here the Church teams met the emigrants and took them to their camp on the Platte River, about six miles from Benton, where they remained till August 31st, when the Scandinavian Saints took up the journey across the mountains by ox train led by Captain John G. Holman, while the English emigrants about the same time left by mule teams. Elder Hiram B. Clawson acted this year as emigration agent for the Church. The English Saints traveling with mule teams could ride while the Scandinavians traveling with slow ox-teams, walked most of the way to Salt Lake City. Sickness continuing to rage among the Scandinavian emigrants, about thirty died between New York and Salt Lake City, where the surviving part of this, the 28th, company of emigrating Saints from Scandinavia arrived on the 25th of September, 1868.

With this company ended the emigration of Latter-day Saints from Europe by sailing vessels and ox teams. The long, tedious and trying journey to Zion, under which so many brave sons and daughters from northern Europe succumbed, was now a thing of the past, but hundreds of noble men, women and children, who left their native lands for the sole purpose of obeying the counsels of God by gathering with his Saints in his own appointed place, had during the past years lost their lives in their attempt to carry out his will. Surely these martyrs will receive their rewards in the great hereafter.

Only two Elders arrived from Zion to labor as missionaries in Scandinavia in 1868, viz: Hans Petersen of Hyrum, who arrived in Copenhagen, August 15th, and Jesse N. Smith of Parowan, Utah, who arrived September 19th. Elder Hans Petersen was appointed to labor in the Copenhagen Conference. Elder Jesse N. Smith had been called by the First Presidency to succeed Elder Carl Widerborg in the presidency of the Scandinavian Mission. Elder Smith had left Salt Lake City August 17, 1868, in company with Apostle Albert Carrington. They traveled by mail coach about 300 miles to the terminus of the Union Pacific Railroad, whence they continued their journey by rail to New York, and thence by steamer to Liverpool, where Elder Smith spent a few days before proceeding on his way to Denmark.

CHAPTER 50 (1869)

Hard times in Sweden—Nine Missionaries from Zion arrive in Scandinavia—The completion of the Union Pacific Railroad makes emigration from Europe to Utah easier, but more expensive.

The crops in certain parts of Sweden having failed in 1868, there were famine and great distress in the land the following year, especially among the peasantry in several country districts. A local Elder, S. J. Larson, who labored as a missionary in Småland, wrote to Pres. Jesse N. Smith from Dädesjö, Kronoborgs län, under date of April 15, 1869, that the poverty of the people made missionary work very hard indeed.

The people in many places had only water to use with their "moss bread." The night previous to writing his letter Elder Larson was denied lodging on account of the scarcity of food. But when he finally told the people that he would do without food, if he could only be sheltered, he was permitted to stay for the night. The next morning he tried at another place to buy a little food, but the housewife said, "We have only five small loaves which we have made from hazel buds mixed with a little rye meal." Elder Larson asked her to sell him one of these, but she said she could not afford to sell any of her scanty supply. Elder Larsen then went to another place and succeeded in obtaining two kinds of bread, one made from barley chaff and a little rye meal, and the other from heather and a little rye meal. The people told Elder Larsen that they had made bread from a kind of moss called "lav," but that they dared not eat it because it made them sick. Mush or porridge made from hazel buds was better, as it did not have any sickening effect. The people even made bread by grinding up bones; nothing but absolute starvation could induce them to eat such food. Many animals died of starvation.

In 1869, nine missionaries from Zion arrived in Copenhagen to labor as missionaries in the Scandinavian Mission, viz., Carl Larsen of Salt Lake City, who arrived May 18th, John Holmberg, John Ehrngren and Erik Peterson of Salt Lake City, and Erik Johan Pehrson of Tooele, Utah, who arrived June 29th; Lars P. Borg of Salt Lake City, who arrived July 2nd; John H. Hougaard of Man-\ti, and Jacob H. Jensen of Salt Lake City, who arrived July 10th, and Hans P. Olsen of Fountain Green, Utah, who arrived Dec. 19th.

Elder Carl Larsen was appointed to preside over the Copenhagen Conference and John Holmberg over the Skåne Conference. John Ehrngren was appointed to labor as traveling Elder in the Stockholm Conference and later to preside over the Jönköping Conference. Erik Petersen was appointed to preside over the Stockholm, Erik Johan Pehrson over the Norrköping and John H. Hougaard over the Aarhus Conference. Elder Jacob H. Jensen was appointed to labor as a traveling Elder in and later as president of the Aalborg Conference. Elder Lars Peter Borg was appointed to labor as a traveling Elder in Norway and later in the Skåne Conference, Sweden, and Elder Hans Peter Olsen was appointed to labor in the Aarhus Conference.

The Union Pacific Railroad having been completed all the way to Utah, crossing the American Desert with teams was a thing of the past, and when the presidency of the European Mission decided not to send the emigration any longer by sailing ships, a new chapter in the history of the emigration of the Saints began. It

no longer meant a journey of six or more months' duration to get from Europe to the gathering place of the Saints in the mountains of the far west; but on the other hand it re-

JACOB HANS JENSEN

Born Dec. 6, 1845, at Haverup, Sorö amt, Denmark, is the son of Hans Jensen and Sidsel Marie Petersen. He was baptized about 1855 by Ole Hansen and emigrated with his parents to Utah in 1857, crossing the plains in Christian Christiansen's hand-cart company. The family located in the Tenth Ward, Salt Lake City. Jacob H. made a trip to the Missouri River after emigrants as a Church teamster in Joseph S. Rawiins' train. While filling his mission in Scandinavia, 1869-1872, he presided over the Aalborg Conference, Denmark. In the fall of 1872 he married Juliane Marie Andersen who after bearing him nine children, died Oct. 14, 1912. Elder Jensen has changed places of residence several times and now (1927) lives in Holiday, Salt Lake County, Utah. As to date of arrival he is now the oldest living missionary who has labored in the Scandinavian Mission as an Elder from Zion.

quired more means than before, as the emigrants had to pay for the entire journey themselves. This, of course, hindered many poor Saints from emigrating. Nevertheless, preparations were made during the fore-part of the year 1869 for a large company of emigrating Saints, and thus a company, numbering 567 souls, besides five returning missionaries, viz., Ole C. Olsen, Saamund Gudmundsen, Jens Johansen,

o. K. Riis and Hans Petersen,
iled from Copenhagen July 10,
69, bound for Utah. A severe storm
seat necessitated the ship seeking
fety near land, anchoring near
agen. On the 12th the voyage was
ntinued and the steamer arrived at
ill, England in the afternoon of the
th. At 10:30 p. m., the same
y, the company proceeded by rail-
iy to Liverpool, where it arrived at
a. m. on the 15th. Here the Saints
re at once transferred to the steam-
"Minnesota," which sailed from
verpool the same day about 11:45
m. Elder Ole C. Olsen was ap-
inted president of this company
th Saamund Gudmundsen and Jens
hansen as his counselors. Chris-
n H. Halvorsen was appointed cap-
in of the guard with Johan B.
esse as his assistant. The com-
ny was divided into four divisions
th Elders Geo. K. Riis, Hans Peter-
n, L. Johansen and Peter T. Ny-
öm in charge, the latter also acting
interpreter. The fore-half of the
amer was set aside for the com-
ny, while the after-half was as-
ned to about 600 other emigrants,
aking a total of about 1200 pas-
igers on board besides a crew of
5 men. The unmarried men were
aced in the foremost part of the
ip, next to them the families, and
in midships the unmarried sisters.
iring the voyage prayers were reg-
arly attended to by the Saints in
ch division at 7 a. m. and 8 p. m.
ur couples were united in mar-
ige during the voyage, and only a
ry little sickness prevailed among
e passengers, and no deaths. After
successful voyage of 13 days the
linnesota" arrived safely in New
ork on the 28th of July. The fol-
wing day the emigrants proceeded
stward by train, and on Aug. 8th
rived at "Tailors Switch" near
gden, Utah. Two children died on
e train. This was the first com-

pany of Scandinavian Saints who
traveled all the way from New York
to Utah by railroad. The whole
journey from Copenhagen to Utah
took 27 days. From Ogden the emigrants were conveyed by teams north
and south to their destinations, as
the railroad from Ogden to Salt Lake
City was not yet completed.

CHAPTER 51 (1870)

Apostle Albert Carrington visits Scandinavia—Ten missionaries from Zion arrive—
William W. Cluff succeeds Jesse N. Smith as
president of the Scandinavian Mission—Sunday schools first established in the mission.

Albert Carrington, president of the
European Mission, accompanied by
Elder Lewis W. Shurtliff, arrived in
Copenhagen, April 25, 1870, on a
visit to Scandinavia. In company
with Pres. Jesse N. Smith, these
brethren visited Malmö, Norrköping,
Stockholm, Göteborg and Christiania,
at which places good and successful
meetings were held. After returning
to Copenhagen, an unusually well-
attended meeting was held May 15th
in that city, where the leading brethren in the Danish conferences and
Skåne, Sweden, were present by invitation. Timely instructions and
proper encouragement were given by
the visiting brethren and others.
Elders Carrington and Shurtliff left
Copenhagen May 16th, to return to
England.

In 1870, ten missionaries from
Zion, who had been called to labor in
the Scandinavian Mission, arrived in
Copenhagen on the following dates:
Peter Madsen of Provo, Mons Ander-
son of Lehi, Sören Chr. Thure of
Ephraim and Mikkel C. Christensen
of Mt. Pleasant, Utah, June 5th;
Peter O. Thomassen of Salt Lake
City, June 12th; Wm. W. Cluff of
Provo, Utah, June 21st; Niels C.
Edlefsen of Ovid, Idaho, July 2nd;
Peter Andreas Bruun of Coalville,
and Peter F. Madsen of Brigham
City, Utah, July 5th, and Erik Mag-

nus Caste of Salt Lake City, Utah,
Dec. 4, 1870.

Elder Peter Madsen was appointed to preside over the Aarhus Conference. Elder Mons Anderson was
appointed to preside over the Christiania Conference and later to labor
as a traveling Elder in the same conference; Sören Chr. Thure and Mikkel C. Christensen were appointed to
labor in the Aalborg Conference. Elder Peter O. Thomassen was appointed to labor as a writer and translator

SÖREN CHRISTENSEN THURE

Born Dec. 17, 1796, at Harritslev, Hjörring amt, Denmark, was baptized by Jens C.
Thomsen Jan. 28, 1856, became an enthusiastic
Latter-day Saint, and even before joining the
Church, he, being a giant in physical strength,
frequently protected the Elders against mob
violence. He emigrated to Utah in 1862 and
became a resident of Ephraim, Sanpete County,
where he died as a faithful Latter-day Saint,
Dec. 29, 1877.

in the mission office in Copenhagen,
a position which he had filled before
he emigrated to Utah, in 1863. Elder
Wm. W. Cluff, who came to fill his
second mission to Scandinavia, had
been appointed to succeed Elder Jesse
N. Smith as president of the mission.
Elder Niels Chr. Edlefsen was appointed to labor as a traveling

Elder in the whole mission and late
as president of the Odense Con
ference, Denmark. Elder Peter A
Bruun was appointed to labor as
traveling Elder in and later as pres
dent of the Christiania Conferenc
Elder Peter F. Madsen was appointe
to preside over the Copenhagen Con
ference, and Erik Magnus Caste t
labor in the Stockholm Conferenc

About the 1st of July the Island
(Öernes) conference was dissolve
and that part of the same containin
Fyen and Langeland was joined t
the Aarhus Conference, while the res
(Lolland, Falster and Möen) wa
made a part of the Copenhagen Con
ference. About the same time th
Göteborg and Norrköping Confer
ences in Sweden were joined tc
gether in one and called the Jönköj
ing Conference. A couple of yeai
later, however, the name was chang
ed to that of Göteborg Conferenc
After these changes there were onl
seven conferences in the Scandinavia
Mission, viz., the Stockholm, Göt
borg, and Skåne conferences i
Sweden; the Copenhagen, Aarhu
and Aalborg conferences in Denmar
and the Christiania conference i
Norway.

Pres. Jesse N. Smith, after a su
cessful mission in Scandinavia, lei
Copenhagen, July 15, 1870, returnin
to his home in Utah as leader of
company of 348 emigrating Saint
The following returning missior
aries left with the same company o
board the steamer "Milo:" Chr. I
Fjeldsted, Jens Jensen, Morten Moi
tensen, Samuel Petersen, Carl La
sen, Eric J. Pehrson, John H. Hou
gaard and Lars Peter Borg. Elde
Lauritz Larsen had left a few day
before to transact some business i
England. The emigrants arrived a
Hull, England, in the evening c
July 18th. The same night they pr
ceeded by railway to Liverpool, a
riving there on the 19th, in the mon

ng. A seven-year old girl (Ida Kirstine Outzen) died on the train and was buried in Liverpool. On Wednesday morning, July 20th, the company embarked, together with even English Saints and two returning missionaries, on the steamer, "Minnesota," which sailed from Liverpool the same day in the afternoon. Besides the Scandinavian Saints, there were on board 350 Irish and German emigrants who, however, were entirely separated from the Saints during the voyage. After a successful voyage, the "Minnesota" arrived safely in New York on the 1st day of August, 1870, and the emigrants proceeded westward by railway train the following day; they arrived in Salt Lake City, Aug. 10th. Pres. Brigham Young, Daniel H. Wells, George A. Smith and other Church leaders met the company between Salt Lake City and Ogden, and on their arrival in Salt Lake City the emigrants were received by Bishop Edward Hunter and others.

A small company of Saints (19 souls) left Copenhagen, Sept. 3. 1870, migrating to Utah. These Saints reached Liverpool, England, in safety on the evening of Sept. 8th, and sailed from Liverpool Sept. 14th on board the steamer "Nevada" in charge of Elder Bonde N. Walter.

In the fall of this year the first Sunday school in the Scandinavian Mission was founded in Copenhagen. It was organized on the same plan as such schools at that time were organized in Zion, with a superintendent and two assistants or counselors. The school was divided into classes with six or eight pupils, and a teacher for each class. Later, similar schools were organized in all the large branches of the mission. These schools from the beginning proved a great help to the mission and they still continue their activities.

CHAPTER 52 (1871)

Nine Elders arrive from Zion—Canute Peterson succeeds Wm. W. Cluff as president of the mission—A conference house built and dedicated in Christiania, Norway—Several companies of emigrating Saints sail for America.

The Elders from Zion and the Scandinavian Saints generally commenced another decade full of hope and aspiration in regard to the future. The "Skandinaviens Stjerne" of that date, in summing up the labors of the previous year, mentions that 853 new members had been added to the Church by baptism in 1870.

The same "Stjerne" announced that the districts of Fyen, Schlesvig and Holstein were organized into a conference called the Odense Conference, the organization to take effect with the beginning of the year 1871. Elder Niels C. Edlefsen, who previously had labored as a traveling Elder in the whole mission, was appointed to preside over the new conference. In passing, it may be stated that this conference only existed about 18 months, after which it was dissolved and its branches added to the Aarhus Conference.

In the beginning of the year 1871 the winter was very hard in Scandinavia and the traffic, both by railroad and steamship, was for a time obstructed on account of snow and ice. Even the ice boats were at times unable to get across the straits between Sjælland, Fyen and Jutland. In consequence of the great lack of employment for the laboring class, much distress was experienced; also among the poorer Saints there was much suffering.

Nine Elders from Zion, called to labor in the Scandinavian Mission, arrived in Copenhagen in 1871. Of these Canute Peterson of Ephraim, Jens C. A. Weibye of Manti, Chr. Willardsen of Ephraim, Chr. Madsen of Gunnison, Paul Dehlin of Mt.

Pleasant, Poul Poulsen of Fountain Green and Anthon H. Lund of Ephraim, Utah, arrived May 6th. Niels P. Jensen of Mt. Pleasant, Utah, arrived May 28th and Anders P. Söderborg of Salt Lake City, Utah, arrived Dec. 4th.

Elder Canute Peterson, who came to fill his second mission to Scandinavia, had been appointed to preside over the Scandinavian Mission, succeeding Elder Wm. W. Cluff. Elder Jens C. A. Weibye was appointed to labor as a traveling Elder in Norway; later he presided over the Christiania Conference. Elder Chr. Willardsen was appointed to do missionary labors in Jutland. Elder Chr. Madsen was appointed to preside over the Aarhus Conference,

Elder Poul Poulsen was appointe to labor in the Aalborg Conferen and Anthon H. Lund as busine manager at the mission office Copenhagen. Elder Niels P. Jense was appointed to labor in Swede

PRESIDENT ANTHON H. LUND
As he looked while filling his first m sion to Scandinavia as an Elder from Zion 1871-1872.

and Elder Anders P. Söderborg the Jönköping Conference, Swede later he labored in the Stockhol Conference.

Elder Horace S. Eldredge, pres dent pro tem of the European Mi sion, accompanied by his wife ar Elder Lorin Farr, arrived in Cope hagen, April 7, 1871, from a rour trip through Italy and Switzerlan They attended a conference in Cope hagen, April 9th and 10th, and the 16th, Pres. Eldredge attended meeting in Malmö, Sweden, whi Elder Farr made a trip to Norway visit his wife's relatives in Frederi stad, where they also attended a mee ing, together with Pres. Peter Bruun. On the 22nd, Pres. Farr r turned to Copenhagen and then left for Hamburg. Pres. Eldred had left Copenhagen two days pr viously to return to England.

CANUTE PETERSON

Born May 13, 1824, in Hardanger, Norway, emigrated to America in 1837, was baptized in La Salle County, Illinois, Aug. 12, 1842, labored as a missionary in the States, migrated to Great Salt Lake Valley in 1849, and settled in Lehi, Utah, being one of the founders of that settlement. He filled two missions to Scandinavia (1853-1855 and 1870-1873) acting as mission president on the latter mission. After serving as Bishop of Ephraim, Utah, in 1867-1877, and president of the Sanpete Stake in 1877-1902, he died in Ephraim, Oct. 14, 1902.

Denmark, and Elder Paul Dehlin over the Skåne Conference, Sweden,

An important meeting of the Christiania Conference was held in Christiania, July 23, 1871, on which occasion the upper floor of the newly erected conference building in Christiania was dedicated with great solemnity. About 400 Saints and strangers attended the meeting.

CHRISTIANIA CONFERENCE HOUSE

Erected by the local Saints in the Christiania Conference in 1871.

Among them were 75 of the Saints from the Frederikstad Branch, who had hired a steamer to convey them to Christiania. A few had also come from Drammen. The new hall was beautifully decorated with flowers and evergreens, which, together with the trained choir and new organ, lent an impressive festal air to the occasion. After the opening hymn was sung, the dedicatory prayer was offered by Pres. Peter A. Bruun. The conference president read the names of those who had contributed to the furnishings of the hall. The donations for this purpose amounted to about 125 speciedaler.

The speakers in the dedicatory meeting were Pres. Peter A. Bruun, Jens C. A. Weibye, Mons Andersen, Chr. Andersen, Halvor H. Berg, Martin Christoffersen, Erik Chr. Grön-

14

beck (now Erik Chr. Henrichsen,) Emil Hartvigsen, Emil Nökleby and Anton Olsen. Bro. Engebregt Olsen, the builder, was presented with a beautiful Bible as a token of appreciation of his successful efforts. A real feast it was to all present.

This was the first edifice of its kind ever built by the Latter-day Saints in the Scandinavian Mission. The following details of its erection will be of interest:

On the 1st day of November, 1870, Elder Peter A. Brunn, who at the time presided over the Christiania Conference, decided together with the brethren in Christiania to have a house erected in which to hold meetings. With the assistance of Elder Engebregt Olsen, a builder, a plan was made for a three-story building, the upper floor to be used for meetings of the Saints, while the first and second floors should be fitted up as apartments for renting in order to assist in the payment of erection and to defray current expenses.

The building-site was bought from Mr. N. O. Young, a merchant, on Nov. 7, 1870, for the sum of 850 speciedaler. The erection of the building was begun on the 9th of November and, with the exception of the two coldest winter months, the work proceeded energetically until it was finished in July, 1871. Elder Olsen, who was an experienced builder, had the contract and did all in his power to make the house strong and tasteful as well as a success financially.

Most of the means expended in its erection was borrowed in various places, a considerable amount being obtained from "Hypothek-Banken" in Christiania. The building was 60x33 feet and (besides a basement) had its first, second and third floors. The assembly hall was 43 by 30 feet and had six windows on each side; it was furnished with a nice pulpit and a raised platform, 8x16½ feet, for the Priesthood, and a gallery for the choir. The Christiania Branch choir at this time had forty members. One room on the second floor was set apart for a conference office and another one for the use of the president of the conference.

The various conference presidents who for years afterwards presided in Norway had charge of the building, which from various reasons at different times was in danger of passing out of the hands of the Saints, until Pres. John Taylor came to the rescue with help from the Church, so that the house became Church property. The premises, including the original cost of the site, was valued at 30,000 kroner, in 1900, and was insured in 1880 for 26,000 kroner.

The first company of this season's emigration of Scandinavian Saints sailed from Copenhagen in the evening of June 23, 1871, bound for the land of Zion, on board the steamship "Humber" in charge of Pres. Wm. W. Cluff. Besides Pres. Cluff there were on board the following returning missionaries: Peter Madsen, Mikkel C. Christensen, Johan Holmberg and John Ehrngren. The whole company consisted of 387 souls. After a successful voyage the "Humber" arrived safely in Hull, England, June 26th, from which place the emigrants were conveyed by rail to Liverpool the following night. After arriving safely in Liverpool in the morning (June 27th) the emigrants, 397 souls, including a Scotch family, embarked on the steamer "Minnesota," which sailed the following day (June 28th) with its precious cargo for New York, where it arrived 14 days later (July 12th). An aged sister from Scandinavia died July 5th and was buried in the Atlantic Ocean. Besides the Saints, about four other emigrants from England and Ireland were passenge on the ship.

The day after the arrival of t emigrants in New York (July 13t a desperate fight between conserv tive Irish and Orangemen took pla in the city of New York, in whi many persons were killed and woun ed, but the emigrants were not mole ed in any way. From New York t journey westward was resumed the 13th and the company arrived Ogden, Utah, July 21st. Here t company was dissolved, some of t emigrants going north, many Salt Lake City, and others farth south to other cities and towns. T journey from Copenhagen to Ut was made in four weeks.

Another company of Scandinavi Saints emigrating to Utah (the seco company of the season) sailed Se 1, 1871, from Copenhagen per stea ship "Humber." The weather w ideal and the emigrants (170 in nu ber) were made quite comfortab on board. Elder Anthon H. Lu accompanied the emigrants to Live pool, to render necessary help those who were unaccustomed travel. The voyage across the Nor Sea was pleasant and the weath favorable during the whole pas age, and scarcely any sea sickne occurred. On Sunday, Sept. 3rd, meeting was held on board, attende by all the Saints and some no members of the Church. A splendi spirit was dominant and quietne and peace prevailed. The ship a rived safely at Hull, England, Mo day afternoon, Sept. 4th. The ne day (Tuesday, Sept. 5th,) the em grants continued their journey t Liverpool. The Elders from Zio who returned to their America homes with this company wer Chr. Willardsen, Sören Chr. Thur and Eric M. Caste, who had labore in Jutland (Denmark) and Nor land (Sweden), for some time, visi

g among their relatives and acquain-
nces of former days. The emi-
rants sailed from Liverpool Sept.
, 1871, under the presidency of
ohn I. Hart, on the steamship
Nevada." After a successful voy-
ge, the ship arrived in New York,
ept. 18th, and the emigrants im-
ediately continued their journey
estward by rail to Ogden, Utah,
here they arrived Sept.   27th.
hose of the emigrants who were
oing south continued their jour-
ey by the Utah Central Railway to
alt Lake City the same evening.

Still another company of emigrat-
g Saints from Scandinavia, number-
g 71 souls (the third company of
e season), sailed from Copenhagen
er steamer "Najaden" Oct. 13, 1871,
a charge of Elders Peter A. Bruun,
iels C. Edlefsen and Niels P. Jen-
en (the latter having visited rela-
ves in Skåne, since May 28, 1871).
his little company of Saints had a
uccessful voyage to England, and in
iverpool the Scandinavian emigrants
oined about 230 British Saints and
ailed from that port per steamer
Nevada" Oct. 18th, in charge of
lder Geo. H. Peterson. Elder Peter
. Bruun was placed in charge of the
candinavian Saints. After a rather
ough and unpleasant voyage across
he Atlantic, the company arrived
afely in New York, Nov. 1st. Thence
he journey westward was resumed
n the 3rd by railway, via Pittsburg
nd Chicago. On the plains, at Pole
odge station, the train got stuck in
he snow for 12 hours. Finally, by
he assistance of four locomotives
vith snow plows, the track was
leared and the train proceeded on its
vay, arriving in Ogden and Salt
ake City, Nov. 11, 1871.

When the Elders laboring in the
candinavian Mission looked back
pon the results of their activities
uring the year 1871 they had reason
o rejoice exceedingly, as their mis-

sionary efforts had not been in vain.
In the three Scandinavian countries,
Sweden led in the number of baptisms, Denmark and Norway followed closely. In Norway a number of
missionaries had been imprisoned
for preaching and baptizing. Thus
Elder Martin Christoffersen had been
incarcerated three days in Frederikstad. In Sweden and Denmark there
was less opposition than ever before.

CHAPTER 53 (1872)

Seven missionaries from Zion arrive in Scandinavia—Further emigration to Utah—Elders
imprisoned in Sweden.

Seven missionaries from Zion, call-
ed to labor in the   Scandinavian
Mission, arrived in Copenhagen, May
28, 1872, namely, Chr. F. Schade of
Huntsville, Peter C. Christensen of
Manti, Jens Mikkelsen of Spanish
Fork, Mathias B. Nilsson of Tooele,
Sören   Christiansen   of   Fountain
Green, Peter C. Carstensen of Ogden,
and Nils P. Lindelöf of Plain City,
Utah. Elder Chr. F. Schade was appointed to preside over the Aarhus
and Peter C. Christensen over the
Aalborg Conference.   Elder Jens
Mikkelsen was appointed to do missionary labor in Jutland, while visiting among his relatives.   Elder
Mathias B. Nilsson was appointed to
preside over the Stockholm Conference, and Elder Sören Christiansen
to do missionary labors in Denmark.
Peter C. Carstensen was appointed to
labor in, and later to preside over,
the Copenhagen Conference, and Elder Niels P. Lindelöf was appointed
to preside over the Göteborg Conference.

A large company of emigrating
Saints (397 souls) sailed from
Copenhagen, on the fine steamship
"Otto," June 21, 1872, in charge of
Elder Eric Peterson. Elders An-
thon H. Lund, Poul Poulsen, Sören
Christiansen and Jacob H. Jensen re-
turning home from their missions.

went along with this company, which, after a successful voyage across the North Sea, arrived in England and proceeded by railway to Liverpool, arriving there June 25th. The Scandinavians, together with 28 British and 22 Dutch Saints, immediately embarked on the ocean steamer "Nevada" and sailed from Liverpool June 26th, under the direction of Elder Eric Peterson. On the 10th of July they arrived safely in New York, and the following day continued their journey westward by railway. They arrived in Ogden, and in Salt Lake City July 17, 1872, at 11 p. m. Arrangements were made for their entertainment in Salt Lake City by their Scandinavian friends. Four children had died on the journey from New York to Salt Lake City.

To show how the emigrating Saints at times were treated by their enemies in the United States the following is taken from a letter written by Elder Anthon H. Lund:

"In Chicago we stayed a few hours; the people there were very hostile. Brother Peterson went with a few of the younger brethren to watch the baggage, which had to be transferred to other cars, leaving me in charge of the emigrants. I told a man who wanted to get into our car that he had no business there, upon which he threatened me, saying I should not get out of Chicago alive. They were the worst lot of scoundrels I have ever come in contact with, and a mob of thieves and pickpockets swarmed around us. One of the brethren was robbed of $28 and others lost valuable things. Dealers in provisions and fruits made their trade as profitable to themselves as possible, not giving the full amount of change to the purchaser. One of our people was refused the money due him in exchange because the dealer claimed he had given him the money. As our brother insisted that he had not received his change, and I had no reason to believe he was telling an untruth, I clapped my hands and told the emigrants to do no more trading until the brother had received his money. To this all acceded, and you may imagine the dealer's surprise when all trading immediately stopped. The man then found it to his best interest

to pay the claim and I heard no complaint after that incident.

"There were not enough cars to convey us out of Chicago, and we were on the point of having to stay there until the next morning, but we preferred to use a couple of freight cars, in order to get away from this band of robbers, although it was not easy to satisfy those who had to occupy these cars. But all agreed that it was best to get away from Chicago as soon as possible. We made a stop five miles outside the city where Elder Peterson joined us the next day.

"In Omaha we encountered a lot of apostates, who sought to raise a disturbance. The baker, to whom I had sent my order by telegram for bread, had not made a sufficient quantity, so we had only half a loaf to the man, and it being Sunday there was not much to be had of other bakers, but on our arrival in Cheyenne we obtained a sufficient supply of nice fresh bread."

On Friday, Aug. 30, 1872, at o'clock p. m., a company of 260 emigrating Saints sailed from Copenhagen, per steamer "Cato," accompanied by the following returning missionaries: Peter O. Thomassen, Christian Madsen, Arne C. Gru and Mons Andersen. On the 2nd of Sept. this company arrived at Hull, England, where the emigrants were served supper at Mr. Lazarus' hotel, and the following day they took train to Liverpool, arriving there on the 3rd at 11 a. m. The sisters were at once conveyed by omnibus to the steamer "Minnesota," while the brethren assisted in the handling of the baggage. At 9 p. m. all went on board, and the following day (Wednesday, Sept. 4th) the ship sailed from Liverpool, Elder Geo. W Wilkins having charge of the company. No deaths occurred at sea, but the company was increased by the arrival of two babies. On the 16th the steamer anchored near Castle Garden, New York, and the next day (Sept. 17th) the emigrants went ashore. On the 18th they boarded the train and traveled via Pittsburg, Chicago, Omaha, etc., to Salt Lake

City, Utah. One child died on the train and was buried in Chicago. Halfway between Ogden and Salt Lake City the company was met by President Brigham Young, Elder Daniel H. Wells and other leading men, who immediately went through the cars, bidding their brethren and sisters from afar a hearty welcome to Zion. On their arrival in Salt Lake City, Sept 26, 1872, the emigrants were taken to the Music Hall, where a sumptuous dinner was awaiting them. In course of the two following days the company was dissolved, friends and relatives taking the new-comers to temporary homes.

About $10,000 were sent from private sources in Zion to bring poor relatives and friends to Zion in 1872.

At the close of this year, 1872, the Elders laboring in the Scandinavian Mission again had occasion to feel satisfied with their efforts. Not only the Elders from Zion, but the many local brethren who had been ordained to the ministry and sent out to preach the gospel, had labored with great success. Thus the work had made splendid progress in Sweden, especially in the Stockholm Conference, where 165 members had been added to the Church during the year. But several of the missionaries were hard pressed by their enemies and some were imprisoned. One Elder in the Stockholm Conference was fined 175 riksdaler for testifying that Joseph Smith was a true prophet of God. As he had not the money wherewith to cancel his fine, he had to endure imprisonment for 14 days. It was a hard sentence, but he asked the Lord to bless the bread and water that constituted his diet, and his prayer was answered so that he felt stronger when he left the prison than when he entered it. This was a wonder to the jailer and others who after his release accompanied him part of the way to his home. The authorities felt afterwards ashamed over the incident and blamed the priests, while the priests blamed the authorities.

In Denmark several successful moves had been made to renew missionary labor in old, abandoned fields, of which several had for a long time shown very small results. The missionaries succeeded in several of these places to infuse new life into missionary work, while it was found necessary to excommunicate a number of cold and indifferent members.

CHAPTER 54 (1873)

Apostle Erastus Snow visits Scandinavia—Arrival of new Elders from Zion—Elder Chr. G. Larsen succeeds Canute Peterson as president of the mission—Reopening of missionary labors on Iceland.

Apostle Erastus Snow and his son, Erastus W. Snow, of St. George, Utah, arrived in Copenhagen, May 15, 1873, on a visit to Scandinavia. Elder Snow, in his communication to the press, wrote the following about his visit to Scandinavia:

"On the afternoon of the day I left you (Elder Geo. A. Smith and party) at Berlin, we met Elder Charles H. Wilcken and his brother at the Lubeck station, and accompanied them until the next afternoon, when we took steamer for Copenhagen, where we landed in the morning of May 15th, and were welcomed at the mission office by Elder Peter F. Madsen, from Brigham City, President Canute Peterson having gone to Sweden. We rested and refreshed ourselves until the following day, when we took steamer across the Sound (Öresund) to Malmö, Sweden, where we took train at 2 p. m. and arrived by express at this place (Stockholm) next morning at 8 o'clock. Here we found Pres. Peterson and Elder Mathias B. Nilsson of Tooele City, president of the Stockholm Conference, and a couple of other Swedish missionaries from America, and also a large assembly of Saints gathered for conference. * * Elder Peterson had just closed praying for our arrival when we put in our appearance. We had three meetings on Saturday, two on Sunday and two on Monday, and an excellent spirit prevailed. There were representatives from branches high up in Sweden, and a few persons from Finland. The Elders and Saints seemed devoted and earnest and full of joy and the Holy Ghost. Some eight or ten persons were baptized during our stay in Stockholm. It has been over 21 years since I was in Scandinavia and when here confined my labors chiefly to the Danish language; consequently, I found myself quite awkward among those who spoke Swedish; yet most of them could understand what was spoken in Danish on religious subjects. I have spóken to the Saints and Elders in Danish at several of the meetings, and although the Swedish is quite different, yet they have been in the habit of hearing Elders preach in Danish so much that most of them said they could understand me. I do not clearly understand the Swedish native speakers, but sufficient to keep track of the subject. * * We arrived in Stockholm amid the festivities attending the coronation of Oscar II, and the town was full of guests from abroad. It is about 480 English miles from Copenhagen, and the railway runs through a cold and barren-looking region; small pine timber with rocks, rock-bound lakes and ponds, with a few villages along the line, and a few patches of grass and grain just coming up. The ground was covered with new-fallen snow when we landed in Stockholm. On Wednesday morning (June 21st) we left Stockholm by express train for Norway; slept at Karlstad and arrived in Christiania about noon the following day. The Christiania Branch numbers about 350 members, and the conference is second in size in the mission. The Saints have the finest hall and an excellent choir. The conference office is in the same building, which was built expressly for the benefit of the conference and is owned by the Church. The conference meetings were well attended on Saturday, Sunday and Monday and all seemed happy. * * I find this mission in a thrifty condition. I am daily refreshing myself in the language and doing what good I can while trying to recruit my health."

After attending the conference in Christiania, Apostle Erastus Snow and his son, together with Pres. Canute Peterson, returned to Copenhagen, and Erastus W. Snow started for England May 28th.

On Friday, May 30th, 1873, the fol-

lowing Elders from Zion arrived in Copenhagen to labor in the Scandinavian Mission: Chr. G. Larsen, Lars S. Andersen, Andrew S. Nielsen and

CHRISTIAN GRIES LARSEN

Born Dec. 17, 1828, at Greis, Veile Amt Denmark; baptized March 15, 1851; labored as a missionary in Denmark four and a half years and emigrated to Utah in 1857. He acted as Bishop of Spring City, Utah, from 1860 to 1868, presided over the Scandinavian Mission in 1873-1875, presided over the Emery Stake of Zion from 1882 to 1899, and died June 1, 1911, in Castle Dale, Emery Co., Utah. Bro. Larsen was an excellent speaker and a man of distinct leadership.

Nils Anderson of Ephraim, Elder John Frantzen of Spring City, Andrew Jenson of Pleasant Grove, Elders Magnus Bjarnason and Loptur Johnson of Spanish Fork, and Elder Even Torgesen of Tooele, Utah.

In the afternoon of the same day a general council meeting was held at the mission office in Copenhagen on which occasion Elder Chr. G. Larsen was appointed by Apostle Erastus Snow to succeed Elder Canute Peterson as president of the Scandinavian Mission. Elder Lars S. Andersen was appointed to succeed Elder Jens C. A. Weibye as president of the Christiania Conference. Nils nderson to succeed Paul Dehlin as esident of the Skåne Conference, d Elder John Frantzen to succeed

LARS S. ANDERSEN

Born April 16, 1829, at Avlby, Veilby parish, lense amt, Fyen, Denmark, followed the cation of sailor and fisherman, and participed in the war of 1848-1850 between Denmark d Germany. Becoming a convert to the spel he was baptized Feb. 6, 1852; married nna Sophie Larsen, May 10, 1852; was orined to the Priesthood and presided over a anch of the Church; emigrated to Utah in 55-1856 and located at Ephraim, Sanpete unty; filled two missions to Scandinavia 873-1875 and 1887-1889); acted as counselor Bishop Canute Peterson at Ephraim from 68 to 1877 and as Bishop of the Ephraim orth Ward from 1877 to the time of his death, ich occurred Sept. 8, 1901. Bishop Andersen so served in the Ephraim City council eight ars, and was throughout his entire life an ergetic and successful leader.

eter F. Madsen as assistant in the ission office in Copenhagen. Eldrs Loptur Johnson and Magnus jarnason were appointed to Iceland s missionaries; Elder Andrew Jenon was appointed to labor as a aveling Elder in the Aalborg Conrence to assist Elder Peter C. Chrisnsen, and Elder Andrew S. Nielsen as sent to the Aarhus Conference assist Elder Chr. F. Schade; Eldr Even Torgesen was appointed to bor in Norway, under the direction f Pres. Weibye. Elder Peter C. arstensen was appointed to succeed

Elder Peter F. Madsen as president of the Copenhagen Conference. Elder Peter F. Madsen and Paul Dehlin were released to return home with the first emigration, and Jens C. A. Weibye was appointed to take charge of the second emigration, together with Elder Anders P. Söderborg.

Besides Elder Chr. G. Larsen's company of Elders from Zion (9 in number) the following additional Elders arrived in Copenhagen as missionaries to Scandinavia in 1873: Peter O. Hansen, who arrived in Copenhagen, on his second mission to Scandinavia, June 10th, Peter C. Geertsen of Huntsville, Jens Hansen of Brigham City, Christoffer S. Winge of Hyrum, and John C. Anderson of Grantsville, who arrived Nov. 15th, and Knud Petersen of Logan, and Samuel Johnson and John F.

ANDREW JENSON

Born Dec. 11, 1850, at Torslev, Hjörring amt, Denmark, was baptized Feb. 2, 1859; emigrated to Utah in 1866, crossing the Atlantic in the ship "Kenilworth"; located in Pleasant Grove in 1867 and in Salt Lake City in 1882; has filled nine missions for the Church (1873-1875, 1879-1881, 1888, 1893, 1895-1897, 1902-1903, 1904-1905, 1909-1912, and 1921). He has circumnavigated the globe twice, is the publisher and author of several books and periodicals and has been sustained as Assistant Church Historian since 1898.

Oblad of Salt Lake City, who arrived Nov. 29th.

Elder Peter O. Hansen was appointed to labor in the Copenhagen Conference and later to preside over the Aalborg Conference, Peter C. Geertsen was appointed to labor in and later to preside over the Aarhus Conference, Jens Hansen to labor in the Copenhagen Conference, Elder Christopher S. Winge to labor as traveling Elder in Norway and later to preside over the Aalborg Conference, Elder John C. Anderson to labor as a traveling Elder in and later to preside over the Stockholm Conference, Elder Knud Petersen to labor as traveling Elder in and later to preside over the Copenhagen Conference, Samuel Johnson to labor as a traveling Elder in and afterwards to preside over the Göteborg Conference, and Johan F. Oblad to labor as traveling Elder in and afterwards to preside over the Stockholm Conference.

On Sunday, June 1, 1873, Apostle Erastus Snow attended conference in Malmö, Sweden, after which he, in company with Elders Chr. G. Larsen and Lars S. Anderson, made a visit to Jutland, Denmark, where they held meetings in Aalborg, Hjörring, Randers, Aarhus, Odense and Slagelse. After this Bro. Snow spent several days in Copenhagen, until June 27th, when he left Denmark, returning to England with an emigrant company. His visit to Scandinavia meant good cheer to the Saints, who all knew him by name as the founder of the mission, but only a few of them had ever seen him personally. He gave splendid counsel and instructions to the laboring Priesthood and the Saints in general in all places where he visited.

A company of Scandinavian Saints emigrating to Zion (870 souls) sailed from Copenhagen on the steamers "Pacific" and "Milo" June 27,

1873, Apostle Erastus Snow, Pres Canute Peterson and Elders Pete F. Madsen and Paul Dehlin re turned to their homes in Zion with this company of emigrants. The "Pacific," which left Copenhagen a 12:30 p. m. and on which Apostl Snow had charge of the Saints, ar rived at Hull, England, on the 30th at 8:30 p. m. A child was born on this voyage. The same day the com pany went by train to Liverpool where they immediately embarked on the steamship "Wisconsin." The "Milo," on which Elder Canute Peter son had charge of the Saints, lef Copenhagen three hours later than the "Pacific" and arrived at Hull on the 1st day of July, 24 hours late than the other ship. At 9 p. m. this company arrived in Liverpool and also embarked on the ocean steamer "Wisconsin" which sailed from Liver pool July 2nd with 976 souls on board, in charge of Elder David O Calder, assisted by Elders Canute Peterson, Peter F. Madsen, S. S Jones and Paul Dehlin. Of the emi grants 104 were English. After a successful voyage the "Wisconsin" arrived safely in New York, July 15th. The number of the passengers had increased, one child being born on board, and decreased by the loss of two, as a Brother Knud Mortensen was missed at Liverpool and a child was killed by accident. From New York the journey westward was re sumed by railway, and the company arrived in Salt Lake City on July 24th.

Another company of emigrating Saints from Scandinavia (the second company of the season) sailed from Copenhagen August 29, 1873, on the steamer "Pacific" in charge of Elder Jens C. A. Weibye, assisted by Elder Anders P. Söderborg (both returning missionaries). The com pany, numbering 219 souls, arrived safely in Hull, England, on Sept.

st, about noon. The night followng, the journey was continued by
ailway to Liverpool, where the
migrants arrived on the 2nd, about
a. m., and at once embarked on
the ocean liner "Wyoming," on which
lso a company of British Saints
ook passage. Elder John B. Fair-
anks was placed in charge of the
whole company, with Elders Jens C.
A. Weibye, Anders P. Söderborg and
Samuel Snow as his assistants. On
the 3rd of Sept., about 5 p. m., the
ship sailed from Liverpool, but a
couple of hours later some of the
machinery broke down and had to be
repaired, which took two days. Having again resumed the voyage, all
went well until the 15th, when the
ship ran aground on a sand bank
near Sable Island, 700 miles from
New York. The captain immediately
sent the third mate with five others
of the crew ashore for help; he also
fired several shots and sent up 14
skyrockets as signals of distress.
Then he proceeded to cast overboard
ironware, telegraph wire and other
heavy articles (with which the ship
was in part laden) to the value of
about $40,000, which act, together
with the coming tide, lifted the ship
off the bank, and it proceeded again
on its way by midnight, after having
stuck in the sand about six hours.
The boat sent out to obtain help did
not return, but it was supposed, as
the weather was fair and the sea calm,
that it had either safely reached
shore, or that the crew had been
taken aboard another vessel. On the
16th the ship passed Sable Island,
at a distance of about two miles with
the island on the left. After the
danger was past, the Elders came
together and offered thanksgivings
and prayers to the great Deliverer
from the threatened danger. Most
of the emigrants did not realize the
danger to which they had been exposed until it was all over. On the

19th the ship arrived at the place
of quarantine, near New York, and
the following day the emigrants were
landed at Castle Garden. At 5 p.
m. the same day the journey was resumed by rail, via Philadelphia,
Pittsburg, Chicago and Omaha to
Ogden, Utah, where the company
arrived Sunday, Sept. 28th. Those
who were going south went to Salt
Lake City on Monday (Sept. 29th).
A little child had died on the train
and been buried at Altoona, Penn.

CHAPTER 55 (1874)

President Joseph F. Smith and other American Elders visit Scandinavia—A branch of the
Church organized in Iceland—"Mormonism"
again discussed in the Danish Rigsdag—Large
emigration of Saints—Seven missionaries arrive
from Zion.

During the year 1874, the Elders
continued their missionary labors in
Scandinavia with unabated zeal and
good success. In Norway they were
permitted, in most places, to preach
without much hindrance, though a
Bro. Petersen, at Drammen, was
fined in the sum of 10 speciedaler
for having baptized one believer; in
Odalen another Elder had to suffer
for having administered the Sacrament. At a meeting held in Laurvik,
March 3rd, two hundred persons were
present, and among them three Lutheran priests. It was the first "Mormon" meeting held in Laurvik for
years. After the brethren had borne
a powerful testimony about the restoration of the gospel, one of these
clergymen exclaimed, "false prophet;" and immediately one of the
visitors cried out, "Prove it, Mr.
priest." Complying with this request,
he endeavored to do so, but was entirely unsuccessful in producing sufficient proofs. At last the priest
turned to the proprietor of the house,
who was a widow and not a member
of the Church, forbidding her to let
the "Mormons" hold meetings in her
house. Her answer was, "When I

was sick and poor, you never visited me; now I do not need you." One of the Elders then announced that their next meeting would be held in the same place the following Thursday evening at 7:30. Elder Christoffer S. Winge was soon afterwards summoned to appear in the town court, charged with the "crime" of preaching the gospel. But upon his showing them his American citizen papers, they decided to let him alone. Apostle Joseph F. Smith, president of the European Mission, arrived in Copenhagen May 27, 1874, on a visit

JOSEPH FIELDING SMITH
Born Nov. 13, 1838, in Far West, Caldwell County, Missouri, visited Scandinavia several times and died as the sixth president of the Church, Nov. 19, 1918, in Salt Lake City, Utah.

to Scandinavia, accompanied by Elders Geo. F. Gibbs and Junius F. Wells. They attended a conference held in Copenhagen May 23rd and 24th, where they enjoyed their association with Saints and strangers and gave the active Priesthood valuable instructions. The remarks of the English-speaking brethren were translated into Danish. The visitors left Copenhagen May 29th to return to England.

Under date of March 1, 1874, Elder Loptur Johnson wrote from Vestmanöen, Iceland, to Pres. Chr. G. Larsen, stating that he and his missionary companion, Elder Magnus Bjarnason, had experienced hard times during the past winter and had suffered much with cold. They had been summoned into court three times for preaching "Mormonism," although there was religious liberty in Iceland. They were, of course, acquitted. So far they had baptized no one since their arrival on the island.

A Brother Einar Eiriksson, a new convert to "Mormonism," on Iceland, wrote from Vestmanöen, under date of August 24, 1874, to the effect that he had been converted to the gospel through the labors of Elders Loptur Johnson and Magnus Bjarnason, who had baptized seven persons on Vestmanöen, and before their return to their homes in Utah had organized these few converts into a branch of the Church with Einar Eiriksson as president. Bro. Eiriksson stated that on Aug. 28th, he had the pleasure of baptizing three more persons on the island, making a total of 10 persons who had been baptized on Vestmanöen. He wrote that most of the new members were poor as to this world's goods and that Bro. Eiriksson and the other Saints were very anxious that other Elders from Zion should be sent to continue missionary labors in Iceland.

Elder Peter C. Geertsen, president of the Aarhus Conference, Denmark, called a special meeting of the Saints in Aarhus, Sept. 11, 1874, in order to consult with them in regard to securing a more permanent and suitable place for a conference home and meeting hall, the need of which had been apparent for a long time. The proposition met with universal approval by the Saints and a small sum of money was subscribed in that initial meeting, and considerably more afterwards, until the amount of 418 rigsdaler (about $225) was raised. Of this amount, 400 rigsdaler were paid to Knud Emmertsen, a member of the Church and owner of the place, at Nörregade 8, Aarhus, for a meeting hall and dwelling, at the rate of 80 rigsdaler per annum.

In the fall of 1874 the civil authorities in several cities of Denmark decided that they would forbid the "Mormon" missionaries to hold meetings. The case was submitted to the Rigsdag which took the matter under advisement Nov. 10th. A lively and warm debate on the question arose, lasting until 6 p. m., with the result that the "Venstre" (or Left) party, who wanted the "Mormons" to have the same privileges as other religious sects, came off victorious. In the course of the debate one man went so far as to declare that the "Mormon Elders" had done ten times more to enlighten the people on religion than all the Lutheran priests together had done; another said he thought it out of place for the honorable members of the Rigsdag to trouble themselves with questions of a religious nature, which belonged to the priests to settle, and that these ought to be able to prove to the people what was right or wrong in such matters.

A company of Scandinavian emigrants bound for Zion, numbering 703 souls, sailed from Copenhagen, June 18, 1874, together with five returning Elders, namely, Peter C. Carstensen, Chr. F. Schade, Peter C. Christensen, Mathias B. Nilsson and Jens Hansen. The first company of 517 souls left by the steamer "Milo" and arrived safely in Hull, England, Monday, June 22nd, in the forenoon, and the same day were taken by rail to Liverpool. Another company of 186 souls, in charge of Elder Chr.

F. Schade, left on the steamer "Humber" and had a hard voyage across the North Sea on account of rough weather, for which reason the captain ordered a lot of cattle to be thrown overboard; but the ship arrived nevertheless safely at Hull on the 22nd in the evening, and on the following day the emigrants arrived by train in Liverpool, where all the Scandinavian Saints, together with a number of other emigrants, went on board the steamer "Idaho," which sailed from Liverpool on Wednesday afternoon June 24th. There were 810 Saints on board and about 300 other emigrants, who occupied the forepart of the ship. Elder Peter C. Carstensen was appointed leader of the company with Elders John Clark and George F. Gibbs as his assistants. With the exception of one stormy day, the weather was favorable all the way. On that day the waves rolled like mountains, and a mighty wave rushed over the deck, and (the hatchway happening to be open) a great volume of water went down below, so that mess boxes, baskets and the like were seen floating about, while the passengers were forced into the bunks till the water was pumped out. A remarkable calm was observed among the Saints on that occasion, while the opposite was the case with the other passengers, who were badly frightened. Capt. Forsyth, relating the occurrence on the following morning at the breakfast table, said that he went down to the people in the forepart to allay their fears, as they were crying aloud, "Lost, we are lost!" But after he had assured them that there was no danger, because there were too many "Mormons" aboard for the ship to be harmed, order and quiet was restored. A Catholic priest, who was present, took exception to this statement, but the captain said that he had now for 18 years conveyed the

"Mormons" safely across the Atlantic, and he had never heard of the loss of any ship carrying "Mormons."

On the 6th of July the company arrived safely in New York and on the following day proceeded by rail from Jersey City westward, arriving in Ogden and Salt Lake City, all safe, on the 15th of July. Two children had died of measles on the journey.

Another company of Scandinavian Saints (214 souls) emigrating to Utah, sailed from Copenhagen per steamship "Cato," Aug. 27, 1874, accompanied by four returning missionaries, namely: Nils P. Lindelöf (leader of the company), John F. Oblad, Christoffer S. Winge and Andrew S. Nielsen. The company arrived at Hull on the 31st, about 11 a. m., and proceeded by rail the same day to Liverpool, where they, together with 320 British and a few German, Swiss and Dutch Saints, embarked on the steamer "Wyoming" which sailed from Liverpool Sept. 2nd and arrived in New York on the 14th. Elder John C. Graham was in charge of the whole company, assisted by Elders Nils P. Lindelöf, Robert W. Heybourne and nine other returning Elders from Zion. Christian Glade of Aalborg, with his wife and one child, were left in Liverpool on account of sickness. On the 15th the company proceeded by train westward and arrived in Salt Lake City, Wednesday, Sept. 23rd.

Seven missionaries from Zion, appointed to labor in the Scandinavian Mission, arrived in 1874, viz., Peter Hansen of Huntsville, Utah, who arrived in Copenhagen June 20th, and Andrew R. Andersen of Lehi, Carl J. Gustafson of Salt Lake City, Sören Christoffersen of Manti, Sören L. Petersen of Huntsville, Nils C. Flygare of Ogden, and John M. Larsen

of Salt Lake City, Utah, who arrive Nov. 22, 1874.

Elder Peter Hansen was appointe to labor in the Copenhagen Conference, Elder Andrew R. Anderse was appointed to labor as travelin Elder in North Jutland, Denmark and later to preside over the Aarhu Conference. Elder Carl J. Gustafso was appointed to labor as a travelin, Elder in, and later as president o the Skåne Conference, Sweden. Elde Sören Christoffersen, who came on a second mission to Scandinavia, wa appointed to labor as a traveling Eld er in the Copenhagen Conference Elder Sören L. Petersen was appoint ed to labor as traveling Elder in, an later as president of the Christiani Conference, Norway. Elder Nil Chr. Flygare was appointed to pre side over the Stockholm Conference Sweden; and later he succeeded Chr G. Larsen as president of the Scandi navian Mission. Elder John M. Lar sen was appointed to labor in the Copenhagen Conference.

The "Skandinaviens Stjerne" of Jan. 1, 1875, published a New Year editorial, in which the editor referred with satisfaction to the labors done in the Scandinavian Mission during the past year. It stated, among other things, that during the year, 915 souls belonging to the Church had emigrated to Zion, namely: 515 from Denmark, 302 from Sweden and 98 from Norway, besides 9 Utah missionaries returning to their homes, and a small company of 11 persons who emigrated from Iceland, going direct to Liverpool on their way to Zion.

CHAPTER 56 (1875)

Pres. Joseph F. Smith and Elder John Henry Smith and others visit Scandinavia— Nils C. Flygare succeeds Chr. G. Larsen as president of the Scandinavian Mission—Pamphlets published in the Icelandic language— Missionary labors commenced in Finland— Fifteen Elders arrive from Zion.

On Sunday, May 22, 1875, Apostle

Joseph F. Smith, president of the European Mission, arrived in Copenhagen, from England, on a short visit to Scandinavia, accompanied by Francis M. Lyman (a son of the late Amasa M. Lyman), John Henry Smith (a son of the late Geo. A. Smith), Milton H. Hardy and Elijah N. Freeman. They attended conference, which on the same day in the evening was commenced in the Saints' hall in Frederik den Syvendes Gade," and was continued on Sunday, in Mr. M. Hansen-Gissemanns' large social hall at Frederiksberg.

Pres. Smith writes: "On Sunday we assembled in a very fine new hall, capable of seating 600 people, which was well filled in the morning, and· over-flowing in the afternoon and evening. I never saw better attention. The conference was remarkable for the excellent spirit abounding, the large number attending, and the good attention paid throughout the day. It was a time of rejoicing. The native Elders spoke with great freedom and power. On Monday evening the choir gave a concert. On Wednesday evening (May 26th) we held a Priesthood meeting, which was attended by forty or fifty of the local Priesthood and fifteen Elders from Zion. After the reports of the various branches were given, which were very encouraging, Pres. Chr. G. Larsen and myself addressed the brethren at some length, John Frantzen interpreting for me. Again we had an excellent time. The Elders were feeling well and happy in their labors. We had the pleasure of seeing the kings and queens of Denmark and Sweden, the Swedish rulers being on a visit in Copenhagen."

On Friday, May 28th, Apostle Jos. F. Smith and companions left Copenhagen by steamship for Stettin, Germany.

Under date of Nov. 30, 1875, Eld-ers Theodor Didrikson and Samuel Bjarnason, who labored as missionaries in Iceland, reported that the printers had refused to print tracts for the Elders, in consequence of which the manuscript had to be sent to Copenhagen to be printed there in the Icelandic language. So far, the Elders had met with but little success in their labors on the mainland of Iceland.

At a conference held in Stockholm Oct. 3, 1875, two Elders were called to labor in Finland, where the gospel had not previously been preached. As a special feature worth mentioning in connection with this conference, was the fact that the Stockholm Conference at that time had an emigration fund representing 5,-700 kroner, which had already done much good in assisting poor Saints to emigrate to Zion.

On Friday, June 25, 1875, about 3 o'clock a. m., the first company of the season's emigration of Scandinavian Saints (658 souls) sailed from Copenhagen, on two steamers, namely, the "Pacific" and the "Cato." The "Pacific" took on board 383 Saints from the Christiania, Copenhagen and Skåne conferences, who were placed in charge of Elder Chr. G. Larsen, assisted by Elders John Frantzen, Lars S. Andersen and Nils Anderson. The "Cato" took on board 275 Saints from the Aarhus, Aalborg, Stockholm and Göteborg conferences, with Elders Peter C. Geertsen and Andrew Jenson in charge. Both ships arrived in Hull on Monday, June 28th. The same day the emigrants were conveyed to Liverpool by rail. Here, together with 98 English Saints and one returning missionary, they went on board the ocean steamer "Idaho," commanded by Capt. Beddoe, and sailed from Liverpool on Wednesday, June 30th.

Pres. Jos. F. Smith appointed Elder Chr. G. Larsen, leader of the company, to be assisted by all the other returning missionaries, namely, John Frantzen, Lars S. Andersen, Nils Anderson, Peter C. Geertsen, Andrew Jenson and M. J. Williams. The company was divided into six districts and a president appointed for each of these; Andrew Jenson was appointed captain of the guard. After a successful voyage, the company arrived safely in New York, July 14th. The overland journey by railway was begun on the 15th, and on the 22nd the company arrived, all well, in Ogden and Salt Lake City. A Swedish sister, 73 years of age, died on the Atlantic Ocean and was buried at sea, and a child, 15 months old, died before arriving in Ogden, July 22nd. A young Norwegian sister who was left in New York on account of sickness came on to Utah later.

The second and last company of the year's emigration of Scandinavian Saints, consisting of 168 souls (of whom the majority were Danes), sailed from Copenhagen, Sept. 10, 1875, per steamer "Hero," accompanied by two returning missionaries, namely: Peter O. Hansen and Evan Torgesen. Pres. Nils C. Flygare accompanied them to England, where the emigrants arrived at the port of Hull on the 13th, and, taking train from there, arrived in Liverpool in the morning of the 14th. The same day the emigrants embarked on the steamship "Wyoming," together with 118 English Saints and six returning missionaries. The "Wyoming" sailed from Liverpool on the 15th of September. Elder Richard V. Morris was appointed leader of the company, assisted by the other returning missionaries. Pres. Jos. F. Smith, who had been succeeded as president of the European Mission by Elder Albert Carrington, also returned home with this company, which ar-

rived in New York Sept. 27th, and in Ogden and Salt Lake City, on Oct. 5th.

Elder Samuel Johnson and three emigrating Saints left Copenhagen Oct. 8, 1875, for Zion, sailing on the steamship "Cato."

In 1875, fifteen Elders from Zion were called to labor as missionaries in the Scandinavian Mission. They arrived in Copenhagen in the following order: Chr. Jensen of Ephraim, Hans Peter Iversen of Washington, Theodore Didrikson of Spanish Fork and Samuel Bjarnason of Spanish Fork, Utah, arrived May 24th; Mads Christensen of Farmington and Mons Pedersen of Provo arrived June 5th; Knud H. Bruun of Nephi, John A. Anderson of Ephraim, Rasmus N. Jeppesen of Mantua and Hans Thunnesen of Gunnison, Utah, arrived Nov. 17th; and John C. Sandberg of Salt Lake City, John N. Larson of Moroni, Erik M. Larsen of Salt Lake City, Sven Nilsson of Tooele, and Erik F. Branting of Salt Lake City, Utah, arrived Nov. 27th.

Elder Chr. Jensen was appointed to labor as traveling Elder in Aarhus and later as president of the Aarhus Conference. Hans Peter Iversen was appointed to labor as traveling Elder in the Aalborg Conference, where he baptized 110 persons. Elder Theodore Didrikson was appointed to preside over the Icelandic Mission, with Samuel Bjarnason as his assistant. Elder Mads Christensen was appointed to preside over the Aalborg Conference. Elder Mons Pedersen was appointed to labor as translator and writer for "Skandinaviens Stjerne" in the mission office in Copenhagen. Elder Knud H. Bruun (who came an a second mission) was appointed to labor as a traveling Elder in the Aarhus Conference and later as president of the Aalborg Conference. Elder John A. Anderson was appointed to labor in the

Göteborg Conference, and Rasmus N. Jeppesen in the Copenhagen Conference, all as traveling Elders. Elder John C. Sandberg was appointed to preside over the Göteborg Conference, and later to commence the publication of "Norstjernan" in Göteborg, under the direction of Pres. Ola N. Liljenquist. Elder John N. Larson was appointed to labor in the Skåne Conference, and Erik M. president of, the Skåne Conference and later in Norway. Elder Swen Nilsson was appointed to labor as a traveling Elder in, and later as president of, the Skåne Conference and Erik F. Branting was appointed to labor as a traveling Elder in, and later as president of, the Stockholm Conference.

CHAPTER 57 (1876)

Local Elders make excellent showing in racting in Aarhus—Miraculous case of healing—Attempt to build a conference house in Aarhus—A branch of the Church organized in Vinland—Sixteen Elders from Zion arrive in Scandinavia—Elder Ola N. Liljenquist succeeds Nils C. Flygare as president of the Mission.

During the winter of 1875-1876, some 18 or 20 local brethren in the city of Aarhus were appointed to ravel as missionaries a couple of ours after regular labor hours, two and two, making a door-to-door canvass, offering tracts and endeavoring to get gospel conversations with the people. A young brother was also appointed as a regular missionary in the city. Missionaries were sent to Langeland and Samsö, where the gospel had not been preached for several years. Occasionally the brethren were invited by the clergy to public discussions. An occurrence of this kind happened in the Aarhus Conference where Pres. Andrew R. Andersen and Elder Knud H. Bruun, at the request of the priest, attended such a meeting for debate Feb. 27, 1876, in the Tranberg School. The

discussion between the priest and teacher on the one side and our Elders on the other ended in a victory of truth over error.

Under date of Sept. 13, 1876, Elder Hans Peter Iversen, who labored as a missionary in the Aalborg Conference, related how an old sister in Nörre Tranders, who had walked by the assistance of crutches for three years, was miraculously healed by the administration of Elders Knud H. Bruun and Hans Peter Iversen. Immediately after the administration, she threw away her crutches and never used them afterwards.

The attempt of the Saints in Aarhus to build a house for meeting purposes proving unsuccessful, the unfinished building became the property of Bro. Knud Emmertsen. But in 1875-1876, after Elder Andrew R. Andersen had succeeded Peter C. Geertsen as president of the Aarhus Conference, the building project was taken up again, and the brethren in Aarhus organized themselves into a co-operative company with Thomas Sörensen as president. Opportunity was given the Saints to take shares in the building, and Pres. Andersen headed the list for 100 kroner, while Thomas Sörensen signed for 500 kroner. About 2000 kroner were subscribed in this way; besides, the 800 kroner which had been paid to the building previously attempted, could now be applied on the proposed new enterprise. A site was then purchased in the newly platted part of the city near the railroad station. In the course of the following winter and spring of 1876, the work was commenced with Knud Emmertsen as builder, and the building was completed the same year. It was a three story structure, and the upper floor, arranged as a meeting hall, had a seating capacity for 300 persons, while the two lower stories were intended for tenants. ex-

\cept some rooms which were reserved for the use of the Elders and for a conference office. There were also some rooms in a smaller building belonging to the property. Altogether the premises known as Borupsgade 14 cost about 18,000 kroner, including 2000 kroner paid to Lawyer Winge in Aarhus for the site. Thomas Sörensen lent the company 5200

AARHUS CONFERENCE HOUSE

Erected by the local Saints in Aarhus, Denmark, in 1876.

kroner, and the balance was secured from a credit association on very reasonable terms.

The missionary labors in Norway were carried on successfully in the early part of 1876. The meetings in Christiania were generally well attended and a number of young brethren were doing efficient missionary work on Sundays by distributing tracts among the people. One of the missionaries was incarcerated for having performed the ordinance of baptism. Among others Andreas Peterson was imprisoned in Drammen Feb. 20, 1876, for baptizing and administering the Sacrament the year before.

The Elders laboring in Sweden were meeting with considerable success in 1876. A new branch of the Church was organized in Vermland.

At that time, there were twenty-two missionaries (mostly natives), besides the local Priesthood, engaged in preaching the gospel in the Stockholm Conference alone. Elder John Anderson, in speaking of conditions in Sweden at that time, remarked that drunkenness, immorality and vice of every description were increasing among the lower classes of the people, and although times had been good for some years in Sweden, hundreds of families were suffering from cold and hunger. The middle classes had apparently become very religious and many of them were joining the Methodists, Baptists and other sects, separating themselves from the State Church or Lutheran Church. The upper classes were drifting into infidelity very fast, and society generally presented a sad picture.

In July, 1876, Elder Erik F. Branting explained that the Stockholm Conference emigration fund had already assisted 28 Saints in emigrating to Utah, in sums ranging from 20 kronor to 1,000 kronor. He also spoke of the success which had attended the Elders laboring in Finland.

Elder Albert Carrington, president of the European Mission, accompanied by his wife, Elders Ernest I. Young and Arta D. Young (sons of President Brigham Young), James Sharp and Brigham W. Carrington, arrived in Copenhagen April 20, 1876, on a visit to Scandinavia. They attended conferences in Copenhagen, Göteborg, Christiania and Stockholm. From the latter place, the visitors returned to Copenhagen, whence they on May 19, 1876, continued their journey to Germany and Switzerland.

The first company of the season's Latter-day Saint emigration from Scandinavia, consisting of 405 souls left Copenhagen by steamship "Otto," June 22, 1876, having on board also the following returning missionaries: Nils C. Flygare, leader of the company, Knud Petersen (of Logan), John C. Anderson, Carl J. Gustafson, Andrew R. Andersen,

NILS C. FLYGARE

Born Feb. 3, 1841, at Ruuthsbo, Bjerresjö parish, near Ystad, Malmöhus län, Sweden; baptized Sept. 5, 1858; ordained an Elder in 1859, and spent three years as a missionary 'in the Skåne conference, laboring in the province of Blekinge, and in the Nefling and Wiggarum branches. From 1861 to 1864 he presided over the Stockholm conference; emigrated to Utah in 1864, and located in Ogden; filled a mission to Scandinavia in 1874-1876, presiding over the Stockholm conference, and the last year over the Scandinavian Mission; filled another mission to Scandinavia in 1877-1879, and a third mission from 1885-1888, each time presiding over the mission. At home he acted as Bishop of the Ogden Fifth Ward from 1877 to 1883, and as second counselor in the Weber Stake presidency from 1883 to his death, which occurred in Ogden, Feb. 19, 1908. He also served the city of Ogden as building inspector, city councilor, fire and police commissioner, and filled numerous other positions. Pres. Flygare possessed an impressive personality and was a natural leader of men.

Sören Christoffersen and Rasmus N. Jeppesen; also Johan A. Bruun, who had labored as translator in the mission office in Copenhagen. After a voyage of about 63 hours, the "Otto" arrived at Hull, England, in the morning of June 25th, and the

15

following day (June 26th) the company went by train across England to Liverpool, where, together with some German, Swiss and English Saints, they went on board the steamer "Idaho" and sailed on the 28th for New York. Nils C. Flygare was appointed president of the whole company of Saints with Geo. L. Farrell, John U. Stucki and Wm. H. Maughan assisting. Elders John C. Anderson and Andrew R. Anderson were appointed chaplains for the Scandinavian Saints. The company arrived in New York in the morning of July 10th, just in time to see the smoking ruins of the old well-known "Castle Garden," which had been destroyed by fire the previous night. Had it not been for the head winds, which materially hindered the progress of the steamer "Idaho," it would probably have arrived and disposed of the baggage of the emigrants at Castle Garden in time to be destroyed in this fire, as happened to the property of some other emigrants, who were detained there at the time of the fire. Upon their arrival in New York, the emigrants immediately boarded the train in Jersey City for the West, arriving in Ogden, July 18th. A Danish child, who had been sick about six months, died in Pittsburg and was buried in that city.

A company of 150 emigrating Saints left Copenhagen by the steamer "Cameo," Sept. 8, 1876, together with the following returning Elders: Sören L. Petersen (leader), Mads Christensen, John M. Larsen of Salt Lake City, Nils J. Grönlund and John N. Larson of Moroni. After a voyage of 61 hours the "Cameo" arrived in Hull, Sunday, Sept. 10th, at 8 p. m. The following day, the emigrants were conveyed by train to Liverpool, where they, together with other emigrating Saints and returning missionaries, embarked on the steamer "Wyoming" and sailed on the 13th. After a successful voyage of ten days, they landed safely in New York. Elder Wm. L. Binder was leader of the whole company which left Jersey City by railroad train for Salt Lake City, where they arrived Oct. 3rd. One death occurred on the train.

During the year 1876, the number of missionaries laboring in the Scandinavian Mission was increased with the arrival of sixteen new Elders from Utah, called to labor in that mission. They arrived in Copenhagen in the following order: Ola N. Liljenquist of Hyrum, who came to fill a second mission in Scandinavia, Johan F. F. Dorius of Ephraim (also on a second mission), Jens Keller of Mantua, Nils J. Grönlund of Salt Lake City, Axel Tullgren of Spring City, Sören Jensen of Salt Lake City, Ola Hanson of Logan, and Sören P. Neve of Salt Lake City, Utah, arrived June 3rd; Rasmus Christensen of Bear River City, Utah, arrived June 9th, Niels Mortensen (Petersen) of Richfield arrived June 10th; Ola Olson of Millville, Alfred Hanson of Logan, and Ingvald C. Thoresen of Hyrum, arrived Oct. 17th, and Jens C. Nielsen of Moroni, John E. Christiansen of Ephraim, and Bendt Jensen of Bear River City arrived Dec. 2nd.

Elder Ola N. Liljenquist came to preside over the Scandinavian Mission after Elder Nils C. Flygare. Elder Johan F. F. Dorius was appointed to labor as traveling Elder in the whole mission, and later as president of the Christiania Conference. Elder Jens Keller was appointed to labor in the Copenhagen Conference. Nils J. Grönlund in the Skåne Conference, and Axel Tullgren in the Stockholm Conference. Elder Sören Jensen was appointed to pre-

side over the Aarhus Conference, and later to labor on the island of Bornholm. Ola Hanson was appointed to

INGWALD CONRAD THORESEN

Was born May 2, 1852, in Christiania, Norway, the son of Hans Thoresen and Karen Andersen, who joined the Church in 1855. Ingwald understood and believed the gospel in early boyhood and was baptized Aug. 14, 1860. He received a good education in the Christiania schools, including the study of English and German. Emigrating to Utah with his father's family in 1863, he crossed the Plains with Peter Nebeker's Church ox train which arrived in Salt Lake City Sept. 25, 1863. Ingwald and his sister Marie worked for Apostle Wilford Woodruff, and the family moved to Hyrum, Cache County, in November, 1863, which was their home for many years. Ingwald was employed at farming, railroading and mining, and attended schools. In 1870-1872 he was a student of the Cache County Academy at Logan. Later he became principal of the Hyrum Academy. In 1873 (April 14th) he married Margrethe Christine Nielsen who bore him 14 children. Brother Thoresen followed school teaching for twelve years in Utah and Idaho and also studied law and surveying. On his mission to Scandinavia in 1876-1878 he labored successfully as a missionary in Denmark and Sweden. He has held the offices of surveyor, attorney, school trustee, mayor of Hyrum City, attorney and surveyor and commissioner of Cache County. He was also a member of three constitutional conventions (including the successful one of 1895) and of the Legislature of the State of Utah of 1897. He served as U. S. Surveyor-General for the State of Utah in 1913-1921. Being ordained a High Priest Aug. 26, 1901, he served as a counselor in the Hyrum Stake presidency for several years. In 1904 he moved to Logan and in 1911 to Salt Lake City. Since his earliest youth Elder Thoresen has been active as a Church worker.

labor as a missionary in the Göteborg Conference, Elder Sören P. Neve to preside over the Copenhagen Conference, and Rasmus Christensen to labor in the Aarhus Conference. Elder Niels Mortensen (Petersen) was appointed to preside over the Christiania Conference, Norway, and later over the Aalborg Conference, Denmark. Elder Ola Olsson was appointed to labor as traveling Elder in and later as president of the Skåne Conference. Elder Alfred Hanson was appointed to labor as traveling Elder in and later as president of the Stockholm Conference. Elder Ingvald C. Thoresen was appointed to labor at the mission office in Copenhagen and also to preside over the Copenhagen Branch; still later he was called to preside over the Göteborg Conference, Sweden. Elder Jens C. Nielsen was appointed to labor as a traveling Elder in and afterwards as president of the Aarhus Conference. Elder John E. Christiansen was appointed to labor in the Aalborg Conference and Elder Bendt Jensen in the Copenhagen Conference.

At a conference held in Stockholm, Sweden, Oct. 3, 1875, two local brethren, Carl August and John E. Sundström, were called on missions to Finland, where the gospel up to that time had not been preached. They at once proceeded to their field of labor, and notwithstanding the great opposition they encountered on account of the strong arm of the law against unpopular sectarianisms, they succeeded in holding several meetings. Before long, however, a Lutheran priest was on their track, forbidding them to preach and hold meetings. In order to keep within the limitations of the law, the brethren had to remain seated while preaching and thus bear testimony to the truth of the gospel to their in-

vited friends. This mode of procedure went very well after they got used to it, and their hearers generally listened with great interest to the explanations of the principles of the gospel by the Elders. In the course of the summer four persons were baptized in the vicinity of St. Nikolaistad. The first baptism was performed on May 7, 1876. Some time afterwards a small branch was organized in Finland and Elder Axel Tullgren from Zion was sent there in October (1876) to further the mission work. The following extracts from a letter, written by Elder Tullgren at Nikolaistad, Finland, to Pres. Ola N. Liljenquist in Copenhagen, under date of Dec. 19, 1876, describes the existing condition at that time:

"In company with Bro. Sundström I have been sixteen miles north, and have held meetings with Baptists and other so-called "believers," and also in the towns we have passed through. I believe that many will in time embrace the gospel, when they are labored with considerably; for the people are in a very low and ignorant condition as to religion. They seem to think the "old leaven" is the best, for there are not many sects here; the only one of consequence is the Baptist church, and it has but very little growth. We made ourselves well known among the people where we went, and I believe we have fair prospects for the future. Shortly after I wrote you my last letter, one of the sisters called some friends together and we had a little meeting. But her cousin, who, on account of this sister's connection with our Church, had become her bitter enemy, went at once to the priest, informing him about our meeting. This man, together with a doctor, then came and endeavored to disturb us, and two days later the governor sent two policemen to bring us before him. He received us in a very rough and impolite manner and forbade us to preach, telling the police to watch us. He went so far as to threaten to have us arrested and sent to Siberia, if we did not cease our preaching, but I do not think his authority extends that far. We then went farther north and have just returned home. It is uncertain how long we shall enjoy liberty, as a policeman may at any moment come and arrest us; for the priest here has published all kinds of lies against us, so that many feel ashamed of his procedure in proclaiming such outrageous falsehoods. But, by the assistance of the Lord, we will be patient and suffer whatsoever we will have to meet. There is no religious liberty here, and the law is so rigid, that we dare not sell tracts for fear of being arrested. The priest was here and took away the books this sister had bought of us last year. I have for this reason sold very few tracts, but given away some in order to spread the truth among the people. I am in hopes that more liberty will soon be given, for the "Riksdag" will convene on Jan. 28th, and the deputy from this city is a liberal and unbiased man. Right now the town marshal and two policemen have been here and taken some of our tracts, in order to further investigate our doctrines, after which they will return them. Hence, I do not know what the result will be, but we hope for the best. All they can do is to banish us from the land and send us away."

CHAPTER 58 (1877)

The publication of "Nordstjernan," a mission organ in the Swedish language, was commenced in Scandinavia—Arrival of 18 Elders from Zion—Four companies of emigrating Saints leave for Utah.

The first number of "Nordstjernan" was published in Göteborg. Sweden, Jan. 3, 1877. As the gospel continued to spread in the north of Sweden, where the people were unable to read or understand the Danish language, it became very necessary that a Church organ should be published in the Swedish language. Pres. Ola N. Liljenquist, being himself of Swedish birth, could easily see the need of his countrymen in this regard, and in 1876 he made the preliminary arrangements for the publication, with Ola N. Liljenquist as publisher and Elder John C. Sandberg as assistant editor. The following annoucement in relation thereto is found in "Skandinaviens Stjerne," Vol. 26, page 109:

"Coincidentally with this number of the "Skandinaviens Stjerne" the first number

of "Nordstjernan," an organ in the Swedish language, which, like the Danish organ, will represent the interests of our Church in spreading the truths of the gospel among the inhabitants speaking that language, has been issued. Many may suppose that the people of Scandinavia all speak the same language and easily understand each other in speech and print, but without entering upon any further discussion of that question, we will say that a great portion of the Swedish people, to whom we have had opportunity to preach the gospel, does not understand one who speaks in Danish, and only in part understands the Danish tracts. The young could soon learn, but not so with the older people; and, in fact, but few take enough interest in the heavenly truths to trouble themselves much with studying them in a foreign tongue. As the gospel is beginning to spread among the Swedish people farther north in the provinces along the Baltic Sea, we have felt it expedient to publish this organ in their own language, in order that the Saints and other truth-seekers may have the privilege of reading in the language they understand, what Prophets and Apostles proclaim in our time; that they may understand the signs of the times and the honest of heart may obtain a knowledge of the ways of the Lord and be led to embrace the gospel. * * The Swedish brethren are expected to use their best endeavors in behalf of the "Nordstjernan," so that the printed word, which often speaks where we must be silent—and which may counsel and guide some who would not receive our advice—may be spread, and the glad tidings of salvation be proclaimed to all people."

The first seventeen numbers of "Nordstjernan" (which is issued semi-monthly, of the same size and form as the "Skandinaviens Stjerne," but printed with the English type) were printed at "Förpostens" Aktiebolags printing office in Göteborg, Sweden, Elder John C. Sandberg having the oversight of the work. But as he returned to his home in Utah the following year, the place of its publication was changed to the mission office in Copenhagen, the printing thereof being let to the long-patronized firm of F. E. Bording. In 1877-1878, one thousand copies were printed; in 1879-1880 only 800, and in 1881 the issue was 850 copies. "Nordstjernan" has well performed its mission to date (1927). Since its establishment, the gospel work has spread continuously in north and middle Sweden, and the Stockholm Conference was for many years the most prosperous in the Scandinavian Mission. It is especially in the northern parts that the people do not understand Danish; for as long as Skåne and the southern provinces were the most fruitful fields for "Mormonism," the Danish literature to some extent answered the purpose, which fact may be cited as one reason why a Swedish organ was not started at an earlier date. As assistant workers in the "Nordstjernan" office, laboring under successive mission presidents, may be named the following: John C. Sandberg, in 1877; August W. Carlson, in 1877-1878; Gustaf Pettersson, a native Elder who died at the mission office in Copenhagen, April 13, 1881, 1878-1881; Hugo D. E. Peterson (a native Elder who emigrated in June, 1883), 1881-1883; Olof Hellquist (a native Elder who emigrated in 1885), 1883-1885; Edward Hanson, a Utah Elder, June, 1885, to October, 1886; Otto Rydman, a native Elder, 1886-1888; Adolph Anderson, a Utah Elder, 1888-1890; John A. Forslund, a local Elder, 1890; John A. Hellström, a Utah Elder, 1890-1892; August Carlson, a Utah Elder, 1892; Gustaf A. Anderson, a Utah Elder, 1892-1893; Charles J. Wahlquist, a Utah Elder, 1893-1894; Nils Forsberg, a Utah Elder, 1894-1895; Swen Swenson, a local Elder, 1895-1896; Anton P. Peterson, a Utah Elder, 1896-1897; Gustaf A. Brandt, a Utah Elder, 1897-1899; Carl A. A. Augustson, a Utah Elder, 1899; Henry F. Fernström, a Utah Elder, 1899, to January 25, 1900; Albert H. Berg-

man, a Utah Elder, Jan. 25, 1900, to July 23, 1900; Carl A. Carlson, a Utah Elder, July 23, 1900; Carl A. Krantz Oct., 1905; Swen Swenson (second term), May, 1905; Victor E. Krantz, 1908; Emma S. Tendt, 1909; Dan A. Swenson, 1911; Swen Swenson (third term), 1913; Oscar W. Söderberg, Dec., 1915; August W. Lundström, Sept., -1917; Swen Swenson (fourth term), July, 1919; Oscar W. Söderberg (second term), 1920; Elon Keding, April, 1921; Oscar V. Johanson, Sept., 1921; Gideon N. Hulterström, July, 1922; Carl Simon Fors, Nov., 1922; Hugo D. E. Peterson (second term), Aug., 1923, and Andrew Johnson, Sept., 1925.

The first company of the season's emigration from Scandinavia sailed from Copenhagen, June 21, 1877, in two steamships, namely, the "Argo" and the "Pacific." There were 471 souls of emigrants and eight returning missionaries, namely, Erik F. Branting, John A. Anderson, Sven Nilsson, Christen Jensen, Hans Peter Iversen, Eric M. Larsen, Hans Thunnesen and Jens Keller. For several days prior to the departure the emigrating Saints had gathered in Copenhagen from the different conferences, and the Elders who had the emigration affairs in hand were very busy at the mission office, making their arrangements. The emigrating Saints seemed very satisfied and happy in saying good-bye to the lands of their nativity, to gather with the people of God in the Valleys of the Mountains. The embarkation of the Saints took place without accident or the least disturbance. The greater part of the emigrants went on board the "Argo," while a small company, mostly emigrants from the Christiania and Göteborg conferences, took passage on the "Pacific." About 6:30 p. m. the "Argo" steamed out of the harbor and was soon afterwards followed by

the "Pacific." After a successful
voyage across the North Sea, both
ships arrived safely in Hull, England, on Sunday, June 24th, the
"Argo" at 9 o'clock a. m. and the
"Pacific" at 8 o'clock p. m. The
emigrants landed the following day
(June 25th) and proceeded at once
by railroad to Liverpool, where they
boarded the steamship "Wisconsin,"
together with a number of British,
German, Swiss and Dutch Saints.
Bishop John Rowberry was appointed
captain of the whole company, while
Elder Erik F. Branting was continued
as captain of the Scandinavian emigrants. The "Wyoming" sailed from
Liverpool, June 27th, and arrived in
New York, July 7th. From New
York the journey was continued by
rail westward the same day and the
emigrants arrived safe and well in
Ogden and Salt Lake City, July 14th.
Three Scandinavian couples were
married en route and an hour after
the arrival in Salt Lake City, the
wife of Martin Christensen, from the
Aalborg Conference, gave birth to a
daughter.

The second company of this season's Latter-day Saint emigration
from Scandinavia sailed from Copenhagen, Sept. 13, 1877, per steamship
"Argo," according to appointment,
consisting of 211 Saints, under the
leadership of Elders John C. Sandberg and Knud H. Bruun, returning
missionaries. The embarkation took
place in good order and without any
disturbance, and at 5 o'clock p. m.
the "Argo" sailed from the wharf,
while the Saints on board sang farewell hymns and cheered as the ship
left the harbor. The leave-taking of
the emigrating Saints with their
friends and relatives who were left
behind was indeed most impressive,
and tears of both joy and sadness
flowed freely. After a successful
voyage over the North Sea, the "Ar-

go" arrived safely in Hull, England,
on Monday, Sept. 17th. The journey
was continued the same day to Liverpool, where the Scandinavian emigrants, together with about 260 British Saints and ten returning missionaries, went on board the steamship
"Wisconsin," which sailed from
Liverpool Sept. 19th and arrived in
New York Sept. 30th. Elder Hamilton G. Park was appointed leader of
the whole company, and Elders John
C. Sandberg and Knud H. Brunn
acted as his counselors. From New
York the journey was continued the
same day (Sept. 30th) by rail, and
the emigrants arrived safe and well
in Ogden and Salt Lake City, Saturday evening, Oct. 6th. The Scandinavian emigrants were, on their arrival, given a reception by their fellow-countrymen, who had prepared a
supper for them in the large hall in
which the Scandinavian meetings
were held in Salt Lake City. The
company which had arrived in Salt
Lake City the previous July was
given a similar reception.

In 1877, eighteen Elders from
Zion, who had been called to labor
as missionaries in Scandinavia, arrived in Copenhagen, Denmark, in
the following order:

Jöns Anderson of Ephraim, John
Petersen of Spring City, Carl Olson
of Mayfield, and Bengt Nilson of
Cedar City, Utah, arrived June 2nd,
1877; Jacob Rolfsen of Mt. Pleasant
and Andrew F. Petersen of Lehi,
Utah, arrived June 26th; August W.
Carlson of Salt Lake City, arrived
Sept. 27th; Andrew Hendriksen of
Levan, Olof A. T. Forsell and John
F. Olson of Salt Lake City, Rasmus
Nielsen of Logan, Otto E. W. T.
Christensen, of Fairview, Waldemar
Petersen of Salt Lake City, Jonas E.
Lindberg of Tooele, John Larson of
Gunnison, Johan A. Ekman of Salt
Lake City, John A. Quist of Big

Cottonwood and Jens Christensen of Spring City, Utah, arrived Nov. 27th.

Elder Jöns Anderson was appointed to labor as a traveling Elder in the Göteborg Conference, Sweden, later in the Aalborg Conference, Denmark, and still later to preside over the Skåne Conference, Sweden. Elder John Petersen was appointed to labor in the Christiania Conference and Carl Olson and Bengt Nilson in the Skåne Conference. Jacob Rolfsen was appointed to labor as traveling Elder in and afterwards as president of the Christiania Conference. Andrew F. Petersen was appointed to labor in Norway. Elder August W. Carlson was called to translate the Book of Mormon into the Swedish language, and he presided for a short time over the Scandinavian Mission, succeeding Elder Ola N. Liljenquist. Elder Anders Hendriksen was appointed to labor in Norway and Denmark. Elder Olof A. T. Forsell was appointed to labor as a traveling Elder in the Stockholm Conference. He spent part of his time in Finland, from which country he was banished by the Russian government. Elder John F. Olson was appointed to labor in the Göteborg Conference. Rasmus Nielsen was appointed to labor as a traveling Elder in Aalborg and later in the Aarhus Conference; still later he presided over the latter conference. Elder Otto E. W. T. Christensen was appointed to labor in the Aarhus Conference and later as president of the Copenhagen Conference. Elder Waldemar Petersen was appointed to labor in the Copenhagen and Jonas E. Lindberg in the Göteborg Conference. Elder John Larson was appointed to labor as a traveling Elder in and later as president of the Stockholm Conference. Elder Johan A. Ekman was appointed to labor in the Stockholm Conference, and Elder John A. Quist to labor as a traveling

Elder in and later to act as president of the Göteborg Conference. Elder Jens Christensen was appointed to labor as a traveling Elder in the Aarhus Conference and later as president of the Aalborg Conference.

On Sunday, Aug. 26, 1877, a new branch of the Church was organized from parts of the Lund and Christianstad branches in the Skåne Conference, Sweden, called the Ystad Branch.

CHAPTER 59 (1878)

Elder Nils C. Flygare succeeds a second time to the presidency of the Scandinavian mission—The Book of Mormon published in the Swedish language—President Wm. Budge visits Scandinavia—Twenty-one Elders from Zion arrive in the mission—Progress of the work in Sweden.

The Elders from Zion, as well as the many local missionaries who had been called into the field in Scandinavia, commenced the new year with the determination that they would renew their efforts and, if possible, labor with greater energy than ever. The death of President Brigham Young, a few months before, did not impress them with the idea that there would be any relaxation in their activities, but that the Twelve Apostles, who once more stood at the head of the Church, were fully authorized to direct the affairs of the same, both at home and abroad, as in the days of President Brigham Young.

On Jan. 7, 1878, Elder Nils C. Flygare of Ogden, Utah, arrived in Copenhagen, Denmark, having been called by the Apostles to preside over the Scandinavian Mission. Considering the time of the year, Elder Flygare had had a successful journey, both on land and on sea, from Utah to Denmark.

Under date of March 11, 1878, Elder Nils C. Flygare reports that 240 persons had been baptized in the Mission since New Year's. On the island of Bornholm, Elder Sören Jensen held 44 meetings in six weeks, causing quite a stir on that island,

SÖREN JENSEN

Born June 14, 1838, in Hvirring, Skanderborg amt, Denmark, was baptized by Jens Hansen Oct. 12, 1857; ordained a Teacher Nov. 1, 1857, and labored as a local missionary more or less for about two years. He emigrated to Utah in 1860 and located in Salt Lake City. In 1876-1878 he filled a mission to Denmark, laboring first in the Copenhagen conference and subsequently presided over the Aarhus conference; he finished his missionary labors on the island of Bornholm. After his return home he labored at his trade as a carpenter in Salt Lake City until 1884, when he was called to go to Arizona, where he stayed two years, built a tithing office and Relief Society hall, after which he was called to the San Juan Stake, and located at Mancos, Colorado, where he spent 22 years working with zeal and success to make that settlement prosperous. In his later life he returned to Salt Lake City, where he died April 27, 1912.

where the Elders had met with poor success for many years, but during his short activity 23 persons were added to the Church by baptism.

On Friday, May 17, at 9:30 a. m. a company of emigrating Saints, 66 in number, bound for Utah, sailed from Copenhagen by the steamship "Cato" in charge of Elder Sören P. Neve and Sören Jensen, returning Elders. The ship arrived safely in Hull, England, in the evening of

May 20th, and the following morning (May 21st) the company of emigrants landed and was conveyed by rail to Liverpool, where it joined about 300 other emigrating Saints and returning missionaries. The united company sailed from Liverpool per steamer "Nevada," May 25th, for New York. Elder Thomas Judd was appointed president of the company with Sören P. Neve and L. Howells as his assistants. On the voyage a boy was born who was given the rather uncommon name, Nevada Atlantic Larsen. After a successful voyage, the company arrived safely in New York June 5th. The next day (June 6th) the journey was continued westward by railroad from Jersey City, and the company arrived safely in Salt Lake City, June 13th.

A company of emigrating Saints, 55 in number, sailed from Copenhagen June 21st, per steamer "Humber," in charge of Elder Bendt Jensen, a returning missionary. The ship arrived at Hull, England, in the evening of Monday, June 24th, and the following day, June 25th, the emigrants continued their journey by railroad to Liverpool, where they joined the larger company of emigrants from Scandinavia, crossing the Atlantic Ocean in the steamer "Nevada."

A company of emigrating Saints, 446 souls, sailed from Copenhagen, Denmark, June 24th, 1878, per steamer "Cameo," accompanied by seven returning missionaries, viz., Niels Mortensen (Petersen), leader of the company, Johan F. F. Dorius, Ola Olson, Rasmus Christensen, Ole Hanson and Andrew Hendriksen. Elder Valdemar Rhode, who had labored as a translator in the mission office in Copenhagen, was also among the emigrants. After a successful and uneventful voyage of fifty-one and one-half hours across the North Sea, the ship arrived in Hull, England, about 11:30 p. m. on the 26th, and the following day (June 27th) the emigrants continued their journey by rail to Liverpool, where they were joined by the smaller company of emigrants which had sailed from Copenhagen June 21st. Their number was further augmented by seventy English Saints and four returning missionaries, and all boarded the steamship "Nevada" which sailed from Liverpool June 29th. Elder Niels Mortensen (Petersen), who had charge of the larger company from Copenhagen, was appointed leader of the two Scandinavian companies, which united numbered 501 souls. When the whole company was organized for further travel at Liverpool, John Cook was appointed to take charge, with Niels Mortensen (Petersen) and Ole Olsson as his assistants. On the voyage Elder Joseph E. Hyde, who had been sick during his sojourn as a missionary in England, died, and his remains were packed in ice and sent to his home in Utah. A child of Scandinavian parentage, six months old, also died. The emigrants arrived in New York City July 10th and the journey was at once continued to Salt Lake City, where they arrived July 18th.

A company of 218 emigrating Saints and eight returning missionaries sailed from Copenhagen on the steamer "Bravo," Sept. 7, 1878, under the leadership of Elder August W. Carlson. The other returning missionaries were the following: Alfred Hanson, Axel Tullgren, Ingwald C. Thoresen, John E. Christiansen, Andrew F. Petersen, Truls A. Hallgren and Bengt Nilson. On Tuesday, Sept. 10th, the company arrived in Hull, England, and the following day continued the journey to Liverpool by rail. Here the Scandinavian Saints, together with 321 British and

57 Swiss and German Saints, embarked on the steamer "Wyoming" and sailed from Liverpool Sept. 14th. Henry W. Naisbitt who, during the absence of Pres. Joseph F. Smith, had presided over the European Mission, was appointed leader of this company, with Daniel D. McArthur and Alfred Hanson as his assistants. Elder Carlson remained in Liverpool until the departure of the next emigrant company. On Sept. 25th the "Wyoming" arrived safely at New York. During the voyage the emigrants encountered three days of stormy weather, which caused much seasickness among the passengers. An old Danish brother died the day before reaching America and was buried at sea. After a somewhat tiresome journey by rail from Jersey City, the company arrived in Salt Lake City, Oct. 3, 1878.

In August, 1878, the last sheets of the Swedish "Book of Mormon" were printed in Copenhagen, Denmark. Following is a brief history connected with the publication of the volume: After the arrival of Pres. Nils C. Flygare in Copenhagen, early in January, 1878, Elder August W. Carlson had a better opportunity to pursue his labors in the translation of the Book of Mormon into the Swedish language. In the month of March, the first of the serial parts of the book was issued, and the following fall the whole book, of which 3,000 copies were printed at a cost of 4,128 kroner, was completed, so that Elder Carlson could begin his homeward journey in the month of September. About 600 subscribers received the book in serial parts from the press. The following is Elder August W. Carlson's report:

"In the year 1877, Elder Ola N. Liljenquist, who at that time presided over the Scandinavian Mission, saw that on account of the steady progress of the Latter-day work in Sweden it had become necessary to have the Book of Mormon published in the Swedish language. Consequently, he called Elder John C, Sandberg, who then labored in Sweden, to assist him in the translation of the book. But as Elder Sandberg soon afterwards was released from his mission to return home, nothing further was done in that regard until the following winter, when it fell to my lot to take the work in hand. On the 16th of Aug. 1877, I received a call from Pres. Brigham Young to take a special mission to Scandinavia to translate and publish the Book of Mormon in the Swedish lan-

AUGUST WILHELM CARLSON

Born in Karlskrona, Sweden, Aug. 28, 1844, became a member of the Church in 1863; labored in the Göteborg Conference as a missionary in 1864 and 1865, in the office at Copenhagen in 1865-1866 and in the "Millennial Star" office at Liverpool, England, in 1867-1871. He emigrated to Utah, in 1871, locating in Salt Lake City, where he became identified with the Z. C. M. I. and occupied the position of secretary of that institution for many years. In 1877, he was called on a special mission to Scandinavia to translate the Book of Mormon into the Swedish language. He also had temporary charge of the Scandinavian Mission and returned to Utah in 1878. At home he was associated with the presidency of the Scandinavian meetings in Salt Lake City. Brother Carlson occupied many positions of trust, both ecclesiastical and civil; thus he acted as a counselor in the bishopric of the 19th Ward, Salt Lake City, for many years, and also as a director of the Deseret National Bank, Deseret Savings Bank, State Bank of Utah, Zion's Benefit Building Society, Trustee for the School for th Deaf and Blind, member of the City Council, etc. On April 22, 1872, he married Miss Mary P. Spencer, and died in Salt Lake City, July 8, 1911.

guage. My instructions were to the effect that I should publish it in conformity with the new English edition, which was then being prepared by Orson Pratt in Liverpool. I left New York Aug. 28, 1877, the day before the demise of Pres. Brigham Young, and on my arrival in Liverpool I found that Apostle Orson Pratt had received orders to return home, together with Pres. Joseph F. Smith, on account of the death of the President, and the publishing of the new English edition of the Book of Mormon in English would, therefore, have to be postponed indefinitely. Inasmuch as I had depended on this edition to translate from, and it was uncertain when it would again be taken in hand, Brother Pratt kindly loaned me one of his books, which already was marked off in chapters and verses, and in order to be more sure of getting it exactly like the one he intended to use himself, the two were closely compared, in which work I had the assistance of Bro. Pratt himself as long as his time permitted, and later I was assisted by Bro. Franklin D. Richards. The references prepared by Bro. Pratt being too copious and numerous for me to copy in the short time allotted to me, they were left in Liverpool, to await further action from the Council of the Twelve.

"When I arrived in Copenhagen, a month after leaving New York, Pres. Liljenquist needed my assistance in the publication of the "Nordstjernan," which was some numbers behind time after the departure of Bro. Sandberg; and as there were many other things connected with the mission, which needed immediate attention, I was not able to do much in relation to the translation of the Book of Mormon until January, 1878, when Elder Nils C. Flygare arrived to preside over the mission. I then took up the work with all my might. The people had expected the book published the preceding year and many, who were preparing to emigrate, wished to get it before leaving, or to have it sent to them by the first emigration of the year. To accommodate such, it was decided to issue a part of the edition in pamphlet form, containing 64 pages each, and to begin the printing as soon as the translation was so far advanced that we could keep the printer supplied with manuscript. The first number of the series was issued from the press in March, 1878, and the 11th and last number in August of the same year. A large number of copies were bound and sold immediately; the total edition was 3,000 copies. It would have been impossible to publish it in so short a time, had not Pres. Flygare lent excellent aid in the accomplishment of the work. In connection with me, he compared the translation with the English edition and assisted me in reading the first proof sheets. The book contains 676 pages, besides the index. It was printed on good paper with large, new type, the text divided into chapters and verses like the latest English editions, but without the references, which, according to instructions from the First Presidency, would appear in a later edition."

On Sept. 22, 1878, Elder William Budge, president of the European Mission, arrived in Copenhagen, on a visit to Scandinavia, and on Wednesday, Sept. 25th, a special meeting was held at the mission office, where Pres. Budge gave good and timely instructions to the Elders and Priesthood. On Sept. 29th, he left Copenhagen for London via Hamburg.

The "Millennial Star" under date of Sept. 23, 1878, under the caption, "Spread of the Gospel," contains the following:

"Speaking in a general sense, the work in the Scandinavian Mission makes good advancement. In Norway the prospects are improving, and with the additional help that will soon be there from Zion, it is thought that much good will be done In some portions of Sweden the work seems to have been infused with new life. Quite a number have been added in and about Stockholm; in Göteborg and the adjoining country large numbers have been baptized, and the missionaries have been building up new branches, one of them numbering 35 members. In the Göteborg Conference some of the Elders were recently summoned before a legal court and fined. The brethren appealed the case, and subsequently it was dismissed without the fines being collected or imposition of costs. The offense charged against the Elders was the holding of public meetings. As this occurred in a small village, everybody was cognizant of the affair, the brethren having the entire sympathy of the people. It caused many to investigate the gospel; a goodly number were baptized and a lively branch was organized. This is another instance of a petty annoyance created by the enemies of the truth serving as an effective advertisement and being productive of the most gratifying results,

the antipodes of those intended to be brought about. In the southern portion of Sweden comparatively little has been accomplished of late, but with new help, shortly expected, the work will there probably receive a renewed impetus. For the first time in the history of the Scandinavian Mission, so we are informed by Elder August W. Carlson, the number of baptisms in Sweden for about a year, has exceeded those during the same period in Denmark. In the latter country, however, the gospel seed continues to take root, grow and bear good fruit. Perhaps in no other country have the people been so fully and faithfully warned. People can be found in nearly every section who have friends or relatives in the Church either there or in Zion. Baptisms in the Danish conferences continue more or less frequent and the servants of God feel encouraged."

In 1878, besides Nils C. Flygare, who came Jan. 7th to preside, 21 Elders from Zion arrived in Copenhagen, as missionaries to Scandinavia. They arrived in the following order: Truls A. Hallgren, of Ogden, and Lars P. Nilsson of Provo, Utah, arrived June 1st. Ole Ellingsen of Lehi, Utah, arrived Sept. 11th. Niels P. Rasmussen of Levan, Goudy Hogan of Orderville, George Frandsen of Mt. Pleasant, Lars Svendsen of Moroni, John Anton Halverson of Salt Lake City, and Christian Jensen of Mt. Pleasant, Utah, arrived Sept. 24th. Niels N. Andersen and Lars M. Olson of Ephraim, arrived Sept. 25th. Jens Hansen (on a second mission) of Spanish Fork, Anders Peter Rose and Gustav Anderson of Hyrum, Chr. H. Monson of Richmond, Peter Andersen of Echo, Carl Magnus Bergström of Salt Lake City, Jonas Halvorsen of Richmond, Anders Hanson of West Jordan, Ola Nilson of Millville, and Charles L. Anderson of Grantsville, Utah, arrived Nov. 20, 1878.

Elder Truls A. Hallgren was appointed to labor in the Stockholm Conference; he spent most of his time in Finland, Russia, and returned home on account of poor health. Elder Lars P. Nilsson was appointed to labor in the Skåne Conference, and Ole Ellingsen in Norway. Elder Niels P. Rasmussen was appointed to labor in the Copenhagen Conference and later to preside over the Aalborg Conference; he returned home as leader of the 52nd company of emigrating Saints from Scandinavia. Goudy Hogan was appointed to labor in Norway, and George Frandsen in the Aarhus Conference. Lars Svendsen was appointed to labor in and afterwards as president over the Aarhus Conference. John A. Halverson was appointed to labor as traveling Elder in Norway and afterwards to preside over the Skåne Conference, Sweden. Christian Jensen was appointed to labor in the Copenhagen and Elder Niels M. Andersen in the Aalborg Conference, both as traveling Elders. Lars M. Olson was appointed to labor as traveling Elder and afterwards as

CHRISTIAN H. MONSON

A missionary to Scandinavia in 1878-1880, was born June 16, 1837, near Frederikstad, Norway, was baptized April 4, 1853, by Svend Larsen, labored in the ministry a couple of years and emigrated to Utah in 1857 and crossed the plains in a handcart company. He died in Richmond, Cache Co., Utah, Sept. 23, 1896.

president of the Stockholm Conference. Jens Hansen (on this his second mission) was appointed to labor as traveling Elder in the Copenhagen Conference. Anders P. Rose was appointed to labor as traveling Elder in the Aalborg and later in the Aarhus Conference. Elder Gustav Anderson was appointed to labor in Norway and Chr. H. Monson in the Göteborg Conference. Peter Andersen was appointed to labor in Norway and Carl M. Bergström in the Stockholm Conference. Jonas Halvorsen was appointed to labor as a traveling Elder in and later as president of the Christiania Conference, Norway. Elder Anders Hanson and Ola Nilson were appointed to labor in the Skåne Conference, Sweden. Elder Charles L. Anderson was appointed to labor as traveling Elder in and later as president of the Göteborg Conference.

At the close of the year 1878, the Elders from Zion, as well as the local Priesthood, who had labored in the missionary field in the Scandinavian countries during the year, had reason to be pleased with the fruits of their labors. No less than 1,255 persons had been added to the Church during the year, and 785 Latter-day Saints, including children, had emigrated to Zion. In some parts of Sweden the work was progressing exceedingly well through the renewed vigor of the Elders. In the Göteborg Conference some of the Elders had been brought before the civil authorities and fined for having held public meetings, but the brethren appealed to a higher tribunal, where the judgments of the lower court were annulled and the costs and fines were not demanded. This persecution on the part of the authorities, which led many to investigate the doctrines advocated by the Elders, resulted in a goodly number of converts being dded to the Church, and a prosper-us branch was founded. Yet, gen-rally speaking, the Elders in Sweden met, during the course of the year, hardly as much opposition from the ivil authorities as previously. But n Norway several of the brethren vere imprisoned and put on the usual bread and water diet for having preached the gospel of Jesus Christ. Pres. Nils C. Flygare had great ympathy for the poor Saints, who or many years had longed for their eliverance from the hardships of he world. In his letters to the residency in Liverpool, and to thers, he often referred to the great overty and distress prevalent among hem, and at the same time showed heir good qualities and faithfulness n the true light. Thus he writes:

"The Saints in Scandinavia are truly a ood people; they generally live their eligion, according to the best knowledge they have, and are united in brotherly love; they show great confidence in the breth-en who are called to watch over them, nd these in turn do all in their power) bless and comfort the Saints. The reat question among the Saints is 'How all we get to Zion?' Many have been n the Church for fifteen or twenty-five ears and have grown old, but they are ot tired of assisting in the good cause. hey have indeed shown the world, God nd angels that they love the truth, and is to be hoped that the Scandinavians in ion will not forget their poor relatives d friends left in their native lands. The aints here entertain hopes of their de-verance in the way of help from Zion."

CHAPTER 60 (1879)

Opposition to the work of the Lord in weden—Twenty-nine Elders from Zion ar-ve—Elder Niels Wilhelmsen succeeds Nils C. lygare as president of the mission—First gular Relief Society and first Y. M. M. I. . organized in Scandinavia—A small book of ible references (Bibelske Henvisninger) was blished in Copenhagen.

Under date of Jan. 10, 1879, Pres. ils C. Flygare reported that the eetings in Copenhagen were very ell attended, and such was also the case in some of the other conferences in the mission. Besides Sunday mis-sions, the brethren in some places, had organized evening missions, at which they had the opportunity to become better acquainted with the people; they found this to be a most effectual way to reach citizens who could not easily be approached in the daytime.

Under date of Feb. 19, 1879, Elder Lars M. Olson wrote from Upsala, Sweden, as follows:

"In this branch within the last three and one-half months, our brethren have had fourteen notifications to appear before the Kyrkoråd (Church Council) for speaking in public. For non-appearance the first time, the fine was only 1 krona (27 cents) ; hence we think it best not to attend, thus avoiding the warning, and the fine is so small that it is never collected. For dis-regarding the second notification, the fine is 5 kronor and the person summoned is brought in by the police; hence we attend by compulsion and receive the warning, but never promise to stop our labors as messengers of the truth."

In February, 1879, Elder Jens C. Nielsen, who at that time presided over the Aarhus Conference, Den-mark, visited Hamburg, but found none there who belonged to the Church. Bro. Nielsen had formerly labored as a missionary in Hamburg, but now found it difficult to speak the language. So he held no public meetings, but was kept quite busy answering numerous questions con-cerning Utah and the Latter-day Saints as a people. Those who had known him, when he was imprisoned and banished from the city for the gospel's sake, 25 years before, were not a little surprised to see him again, and they listened with the greatest interest to his testimony. He dis-tributed some literature, and recom-mended that Bro. Fuhrmann in Ber-lin should make a missionary visit to Hamburg.

During his visit to Germany, Bro. Nielsen also visited the village of

Stohl in Schlesvig-Holstein, where he ordained Brother H. J. Misfeldt, who had been a member of the Church for 20 years, to the office of an Elder.

Pres. Nils C. Flygare, writing from Copenhagen, May 1st, 1879, reported that most of the missionary work in Jutland, Denmark, during the past winter, was done in places where the gospel had never before been preached, and in other localities where it had not been declared for many years. There was an enquiring spirit among the people, and the Elders were not able to respond to all the calls made upon them to preach. Several good openings had been made in the southern part of Jutland, bordering on Schlesvig-Holstein, and quite a few books and pamphlets published in the German language had been sold or gratuitously spread in Hamburg. Quite a number of good native Elders were employed in the ministry, who, in a systematic way, visited every town and village, spreading pamphlets and engaging places for meetings.

In 1879, twenty-nine Elders from Zion, who had been called to labor as missionaries in Scandinavia, arrived in Copenhagen, in the following order: Andrew Hammer of Mill Creek, Utah, arrived May 20, Carl C. Asmussen of Salt Lake City, arrived on May 23rd, on a second mission. Andrew Jenson of Pleasant Grove, Utah, arrived on a second mission, June 11th. Niels Wilhelmsen of St. Charles, Idaho, on a second mission, and Ole C. Sonne of Mendon, Utah, arrived Aug. 19th. John Eyvindson and Jacob B. Johnson of Spanish Fork, Utah, arrived Sept. 12th. Carl J. Oberg of Salt Lake City, Christen Jensen of Moroni, Chr. A. Christensen of Fountain Green, Lawrence C. Mariager of Kanab, Erik O. Bylund of Santaquin, Niels Thomsen of Ephraim, Niels C. Lar-

sen of Manti, Chr. L. Hansen of Gunnison, Chr. Olson of Fairview, Nils B. Ädler of Spring City, and Mons Nilsson of Ephraim, Utah, and Ludwig Suhrke of Soda Springs, Idaho, arrived Sept. 30th. Herman F. F. Thorup and John T. Thorup of Salt Lake City. Ola N. Stohl of Brigham City, Jacob Hansen of Bear Salt Lake City. Ole N. Stohl of Washington, Utah, arrived Nov. 11th. Hans Funk of Lewiston, Isaac Sörensen of Mendon, and Peter Nilsson of Smithfield, Utah, arrived Nov. 29th. Anton L. Skanchy and Fred Lundberg of Logan, Utah, arrived Dec. 20th.

Elder Andrew Hammer was appointed to labor in Norway and Carl C. Asmussen to preside over the Copenhagen Conference. Andrew Jenson was appointed to preside over the Copenhagen Branch and afterwards to labor as translator and assistant at the Mission Office. Niels Wilhelmsen had been called by the First Presidency to succeed Elder Nils C. Flygare as president of the

NIELS WILHELMSEN

President of the Scandinavian Mission from 1879 to 1881, born April 21, 1824; died Aug 1, 1881.

Scandinavian Mission. Ole C. Sonne was appointed to labor in the Aalborg Conference. Elders John Eyvindson and Jacob B. Johnson were assigned to Iceland. Elder Carl J. Öberg was appointed to labor as a traveling Elder in the Stockholm and later in the Göteborg Conference. Elder Chr. Jensen was appointed to preside over the Aarhus branch and later over the Aarhus Conference. Elder Chr. A. Christensen was appointed to labor in the Aarhus and Elder Lawrence C. Mariager in the Aalborg Conference. Erik O. Bylund was appointed to labor in the Stockholm Conference, Niels Thomsen in the Copenhagen Conference, Niels Chr. Larsen and Christen L. Hansen in the Aalborg Conference and Chr. Olson in the Stockholm Conference. Nils B. Ädler was appointed to labor as a traveling Elder in and later as president of the Skåne Conference. Elder Mons Nilsson was appointed to labor

as a traveling Elder in the Skåne Conference, Elder Ludwig Suhrke in the German part of the Scandinavian

HERMAN F. F. THORUP

Born in Copenhagen, Denmark, April 19, 1849, was baptized Aug. 25, 1861, labored as a local missionary on the island of Sjælland and emigrated with his parents to America in 1868. After residing in Chicago, Ill., one year, the family came on to Utah, in 1869, with the first company of emigrating Saints that reached Ogden on the Union Pacific Railway. Brother Thorup resided in Provo until 1874, when he removed to the First Ward, Salt Lake City, his present home. He was ordained a Seventy in 1879, filled a mission to Scandinavia in 1879-1881, laboring in the Copenhagen conference, Denmark. He filled a second mission to Scandinavia in 1899-1901, laboring in the Aarhus conference, part of the time as its president. In Utah he has acted as a home missionary.

Mission, Elder Herman F. F. Thorup in the Copenhagen Conference and John T. Thorup in the Aarhus Conference. Ole N. Stohl was appointed to labor as a traveling Elder in and later as president of the Göteborg Conference. Elder Jacob Hansen was appointed to labor in the Copenhagen and Peder Nielsen in the Aarhus Conference. Elder Hans Funk was appointed to labor in the Copenhagen Conference and later to preside over said conference. Elder Isaac Sörensen was appointed to labor in the Copenhagen Conference and Peter Nilsson in the Göteborg

MONS NILSSON

Born Dec. 19, 1834, in Skåne, Sweden, baptized April 6, 1860, emigrated to Utah in 1862, filled a mission to Sweden in 1879-1881, and died April 2, 1923, in Ephraim, Sanpete Co., Utah.

Conference. Anton L. Skanchy was appointed to labor in Norway and Fred. Lundberg in the Göteborg and

JOHN T. THORUP

Son of Herman A. and Mary C. Thorup, was born May 25, 1856, in Copenhagen, Denmark; emigrated to America in 1868; stayed in Chicago, Ill., till 1869, when he came to Utah with his father's family; located temporarily in Provo but moved to the First Ward, Salt Lake City, in 1873; filled a mission to Denmark in 1879-1881, laboring in the Aarhus and Aalborg conferences, and baptized 49 persons. Jan. 23, 1887, he was ordained a High Priest and set apart as second counselor in the Bishopric of the First Ward, Salt Lake City, and later acted as first counselor. In 1910 he was called to be a member of the High Council of the Liberty Stake. Elder Thorup died in Salt Lake City Dec. 18, 1918, leaving a large and respected family.

later in the Stockholm Conference, Sweden.

Elder John Eyvindson and Jacob B. Johnson left Copenhagen for Iceland Nov 8, 1879. After a voyage of 15 days, they arrived at Reykjavik Nov. 26, and at once commenced missionary labors.

A company of emigrating Saints (331 souls) sailed from Copenhagen per steamship "Cato," bound for Zion, June 23, 1879, accompanied by the following Elders returning to their homes in America: John Anderson Quist, Jöns Anderson, Jacob Rolfsen, Otto E. Wm. T. Christensen,

Jens C. Nielsen, Jens Christensen, Carl Olson, Johan A. Ekman, Olof A. T. Forsell, Jonas E. Lindberg and John Petersen. Pres. Nils C. Flygare accompanied the emigrants as far as England. After a successful voyage across the North Sea, they reached Hull, England, on the 26th, and were then conveyed by rail to Liverpool, where they, together with 145 British, 83 German and Swiss Saints, and two more returning missionaries, embarked on the steamer "Wyoming," which sailed from Liverpool June 28th, and arrived in New York, July 8th. The journey westward was continued by rail and the company reached Salt Lake City, July 16th. Elder Wm. N. Williams was the leader of the company, with Henry Flamm and John A. Quist, as his assistants. The voyage across the Atlantic was stormy and many of the passengers were seasick. One infant died in New York, and an aged brother met with an accident to his leg while traveling by rail. Otherwise all went well with the company.

A company of emigrating Saints numbering 103 souls, sailed from Copenhagen per steamship "Albion" Aug. 30, 1879, under the leadership of Pres. Nils C. Flygare, who now left the mission after presiding over the same about two years. Elders John F. Olson, Lars P. Nilson, Rasmus Nielsen, Jens Hansen and Gusta Anderson, all Elders from Zion, who had labored in the Scandinavian Mission, left Copenhagen with the same company, returning to their homes in Zion. Elder Niels Wilhelmsen succeeded Elder Flygare in the presidency of the Scandinavian Mission. The emigrants from Stockholm Sweden, 24 in number, under the direction of John Larson, did not arrive in Copenhagen until the following day, owing to the storm weather on the Baltic, but sailed from Copenhagen Sept. 1st, at 1 o'clock

p. m., per steamship "Aurora" which took them to Kiel, in Holstein, whence the emigrants continued the journey via Hamburg to Hull, England, where they joined the other Scandinavian Saints. The larger company, which left Copenhagen Aug. 30th, had a very stormy and unpleasant voyage across the North Sea and did not arrive in Hull until Wednesday evening, Sept. 3rd. The steamship "Argo" with the Stockholm Saints on board arrived in Hull Thursday morning, Sept. 4th, soon after the emigrants had landed from the steamship "Albion." The two divisions were united at the railway station in Hull and traveled on the 4th by rail to Liverpool, where they boarded the steamship "Wyoming" and sailed from Liverpool Sept. 6th, together with 188 British emigrants, five Dutch Saints and nine returning Elders. Elder Nils C. Flygare was appointed leader for the whole company with Elders Thomas Child and Rasmus Nielsen as his counselors. During the voyage across the Atlantic the emigrants experienced a severe storm Sept. 8th, during which the sea washed the deck repeatedly. On the 16th of Sept. in the evening the emigrants arrived safely in New York, and the following day the journey was continued by rail westward. The company arrived safe and well in Ogden and Salt Lake City, Sept. 24, 1879.

On Nov. 20, 1879, the first regular Relief Society in the Scandinavian Mission was organized in Copenhagen, with the following officers: Mrs. Johanna Christina Nordström, president; Christine Holm and Annette Sofia Andersen, counselors; Anna Elizabeth Nielsen and Christine Nielsen, secretaries, and Inger Marie Jensen, treasurer. This society has had a continued existence ever since. Soon afterwards similiar organizations were effected in some
16

of the large branches of the Scandinavian Mission.

On Saturday, Nov. 29, 1879, the first Young Men's Mutual Improvement Association in Scandinavia was organized in Copenhagen, with the following officers: Andrew Jenson, president; Gustaf Pettersson, first, and Fred Andersen, second counselors; Chr. A. F. Orlob, secretary, and Sören C. Jensen, treasurer. This organization, the same as the Relief Society, has been re-organized many

CHRISTIAN A. F. ORLOB

Who came to Utah in 1880, was born in Odense, Denmark, June 30, 1860. As a youth he was employed as deputy in the estate office of Count Moltke Hvitfeldt, at Glorup on Fyen, and Chamberlain Scavenius, at Gjörsley Stevns. Having become a convert to the gospel, he was called by President Nils C. Flygare in 1879 to the mission office in Copenhagen to labor as a translator, and after emigrating to Utah he located in Logan, where he was employed by Charles W. Nibley in the office of the United Order Building & Manufacturing Co., later becoming its secretary. Early in 1885 he moved to Salt Lake City to engage in the publication of "Utah Posten" with Andrew Jenson, but in June following he entered the employ of Z. C. M. I. as private secretary to Col. Thos. G. Webber. In 1911 he was elected assistant secretary of Z. C. M. I., and in 1919 as secretary, which latter position he still (1927) occupies, as well as being a director of the institution times since its first organization, has done a great deal of good and is still in existence.

The "Skandinaviens Stjerne" of this date announced that a new edition of "Bibelske Henvisninger" (Bible references) had been issued from the press in Copenhagen, and was highly recommended to the Saints as a work useful for all Bible students.

In the earlier days of the mission in Scandinavia, Elder Canute Peterson had compiled a little tract of Bible references which later was considerably enlarged and re-printed several times; but as it afterwards was found too small and in some respects inadequate to fill the demands of a more advanced state of the mission, Pres. Nils C. Flygare thought it best to publish a new and enlarged edition, in which the most important passages of scriptural proofs of the doctrines taught by the Elders should be printed in their fulness along with the references. The work he had thus begun was carried to completion by Elder Andrew Jenson, and the first edition of the book of 66 pages was issued from the press in November, 1879. This edition, consisting of 2000 copies, was sold in the short period of three months, therefore a second edition of 2000 copies was printed in March, 1880, and a third revised edition of 5000 copies in 1881. A like edition of 2000 copies was printed in the Swedish language in the latter part of 1879, and another of 3000 copies in 1881. The book was sold for the small sum of 25 öre (about 6½ cents) per copy. The great call for the book proved that it fully answered its purpose.

In December, 1879, Elder Ludwig Suhrke wrote to Pres. Wilhelmsen from the German part of the Scandinavian Mission, stating that there were good prospects for successful missionary work being done in the North German and Holstein mis sionary districts, where Elder Suhrke was laboring. Elder Suhrke also stated in a jocular way that a certain school-teacher at Glessien, near Neukloster, actuated by "Christian" feelings towards him, had induced the priest in the town mentioned to pray for Mr. Suhrke in his church, "plead ing with the Lord that he would open the eyes of the 'Mormon,' so that he might see the error of his way and return to the only saving condition in the bosom of the dominant church (Lutheran)."

CHAPTER 61 (1880)

"Ungdommens Raadgiver," a monthly peri odical, was commenced in the Scandinavian Mission—The fiftieth anniversary of the organization of the Church was celebrated in Copenhagen—President Wm. Budge makes a tour of the mission.

Under date of Jan. 2, 1880, Elder Lars M. Olson wrote from Upsala, Sweden, stating that two local breth ren had been imprisoned for preach ing the gospel. One of them, al though a cripple walking on crutches had to suffer 10 days in jail. The other one had a family who suf fered for the want of daily bread during his imprisonment, but the officers paid no attention to that The brethren were happy because they were counted worthy to suffer for the name of Christ.

After the organization of the Y M. M. I. A. in Copenhagen, the idea of publishing a periodical in the in terests of the young men and women of the mission was given considera tion, and as the plan was generally approved, the first number of a monthly periodical "Ungdommens Raadgiver" was issued from the press Jan. 6, 1880. Of the first two num bers only 800 copies were printed, but as the paper won greater favor and patronage than had been expected the number of copies were increased to 1000 with No. 3. Elder Andrew Jenson was appointed editor under the direction of the mission president. The price of the periodical was 72 öre per year, or 6 öre per copy. To subscribers in America the subscription price was placed at 35 cents yearly.

Under date of Jan. 26, 1880, Pres. Niels Wilhelmsen wrote that the Elders in the Scandinavian Mission were laboring most diligently in preaching the gospel in all three Scandinavian countries. Even in Sweden, where the laws forbade baptism for the remission of sins and also to administer the Sacrament, except by authorized clergymen, the Elders held large meetings. In Stockholm, where the Saints had hired a hall, they were very seldom disturbed in their worship. Lately, however, one of the Elders was sentenced to 10´ days' imprisonment, but it seemed that every time the civil authorities undertook to hinder the progress of the work, they only helped to arouse the feelings of the people and further the good cause.

About this time, Elder Hans Funk from Utah and a local Elder visited Samsö, an island in the Cattegat, where they held two meetings. The authorities arrested and imprisoned the brethren for three days. While in prison, Elder Funk received a letter requesting him to call on a family when he came out of jail. He and his companion did so, and baptized and confirmed the family before leaving the island.

Under date of March 20, 1880, Pres. Wilhelmsen reported that Elder Andrew Jenson, who had charge of the Copenhagen Branch, had been released from that position and appointed to translate and assist in editing "Skandinaviens Stjerne." The president also reported that an Elder who was sent to Finland had

been arrested, and so also had Elder Ludwig Suhrke in Germany.

In keeping with the instructions from the headquarters of the Church that the Saints should honor the 50th anniversary of the organization of the Church with some suitable service, commemoration meetings were held in all the larger branches of the Scandinavian Mission. In Copenhagen the Saints met in their commodious branch hall April 6th, and had a season of rejoicing together. Pres. Niels Wilhelmsen gave the following account of the meeting held in Copenhagen on that day:

"The sisters of the Relief Society had very tastefully decorated the meeting hall, and at 8:30 p. m. it was filled to its full capacity with Saints and strangers. After singing and prayer, Elder Andrew Jenson read a poem written by himself for the occasion. He then spoke to the assembly on the history of the Church, showing in a plain and clear manner how the Lord had watched over his Church and people from the beginning, and that during the period of fifty years the Church had grown from six members to about 200,000; he also showed how the Lord in a most miraculous way had sustained his Saints through persecutions, poverty and distress. Pres. Hans Funk, Pres. Carl C. Asmussen and I then spoke to the congregation, and we all bore powerful testimonies to the truth of the Gospel under the inspiration of the Holy Ghost. Every heart rejoiced in contemplating the great kindness of the Lord to his children. This meeting will long be remembered by those of the Saints and strangers who were present."

On April 2nd, 1880, Elders Lars Svendsen and Niels Thomsen, who had labored as missionaries in Scandinavia, left Copenhagen for Utah, accompanied by an emigrating brother. In England they joined a company of emigrating Saints, which sailed from Liverpool April 10th.

Under date of June 5, 1880, Pres. Wilhelmsen reported that 600 persons had been added to the Church by baptism during the past six months. The brethren from Zion, as well as the native Elders, were very zealous and diligent in their labors, and had held hundreds of meetings in private houses with strangers, besides those held regularly in hired halls. The priests, especially in Norway and Sweden, had caused the Elders some annoyance, and several of the brethren had been imprisoned and fined for preaching the gospel, but, generally speaking, the civil authorities, in the three Scandinavian countries had of late years been quite liberal-minded towards the Elders, considering the fact that there was no religious liberty recognized for Latter-day Saints in Norway and Sweden.

A company of 248 emigrating Saints from the Scandinavian Mission sailed from Copenhagen July 5, 1880, at 6 o'clock p. m., as passengers on board the steamship "Leo." They were from the Aalborg, Aarhus and Christiania conferences, and Elder Niels P. Rasmussen acted as their leader to England. A few minutes later the steamer "Cato" sailed from Copenhagen, having on board 346 emigrating Saints from the Stockholm, Goteborg, Skåne and Copenhagen conferences, in charge of Elder John A. Halverson. The other returning missionaries who went with this company, were: Carl L. Anderson, Chr. H. Monson, Carl M. Bergström, Chr. Jensen, Chr. L. Hansen, Niels M. Anderson, George Frandsen, Niels C. Larsen, Chr. A. Christensen, Goudy Hogan, Ole Ellingsen, Ola Nilson and Andrew Hammer. Elder Peter Andersen from Norway sailed, on account of certain circumstances, a couple of days later and crossed the Atlantic on the steamer "Arizona." On the 9th, in the forenoon, the "Cato" arrived at Hull, England, and the "Leo" arrived in the afternoon of the same day. The emigrants con-

tinued by rail to Liverpool and there embarked on the steamer "Wisconsin," together with 113 British Saints and five more returning missionaries. The company was organized with Niels P. Rasmussen as president and John A. Halverson and Hugh Findlay as assistants. Goudy Hogan was appointed chaplain for the Scandinavians and Charles H. French recorder for the company. The "Wisconsin" sailed from Liverpool July 10th, and arrived in New York in the evening of the 20th. Next morning (July 21st) the emigrants went ashore at Castle Garden, and on the 22nd the journey by rail westward was begun. The company arrived in Ogden, Utah, July 24th. A child four-months old died on the cars and was buried at Pittsburg, Penn. But the company was increased by one on July 19th, when Hans Petersen's wife on board the "Wisconsin" gave birth to a daughter. Carl A. Sundström and Emma Erickson were married on board July 16th.

Another company of emigrating Saints (128 souls) and six returning Elders sailed from Copenhagen Aug. 28, 1880, per steamship "Otto" on their way to Zion. The returning Elders were: Jonas Halvorsen (leader of the company), Carl C. Asmussen, Anders P. Rose, Anders Hanson, Ole C. Sonne and Peder Nielsen. Five emigrants had sailed two days previously and a Bro. F. Svenson, with his wife and children from Göteborg Conference, went via Kiel and Hamburg to England and joined the company in Liverpool. These, together with the returning missionaries, increased the number of the company to 147 souls, who all reached Liverpool safely August 31, 1880, and were accommodated in two hotels. On the 3rd of September they, together with 138 British and 38 German Saints, and some more returning missionaries, embarked on the steamer "Nevada." John Rider was appointed president of the company with Geo. H. Taylor and Peter Reid as his assistants. The ship was divided into sections, each having accommodations for 24 persons. For each of these divisions a presiding Elder was appointed with two assistants to look after the well-being of the Saints. The ship sailed from Liverpool Sept. 4, 1880, and arrived in New York on the 15th, after a rather rough voyage. A Swiss brother died on the 11th and was buried in the sea. On Saturday, Sept. 25th, the company arrived in New York safely.

A small company of 22 emigrants bound for Utah sailed from Copenhagen Oct. 15, 1880, per steamer "Cato" for Hull, England. Thence they traveled by rail to Liverpool, which city they reached in time to go on board the steamer "Wisconsin," which sailed from that port Oct. 23rd with a large company of British, German, Swiss, Italian and Dutch Saints. Elder John Nicholson was appointed leader. The company arrived in New York Nov. 2nd, and in Salt Lake City, Nov. 11, 1880.

Elder William Budge, president of the European Mission, arrived in Copenhagen July 17, 1880, on a visit to Scandinavia, accompanied by Elders Lyman R. Martineau and Moroni Snow.

Concerning this visit Elder Moroni Snow wrote the following:

"On our arrival in Copenhagen we were met by Pres. Wilhelmsen and several of the Elders from Utah. Pres. Wilhelmsen and the Elders were looking well and felt well, and were very much pleased to welcome Pres. Budge to Scandinavia.

"Sunday morning we visited the Sunday school and had the privilege of looking upon the bright, intelligent faces of the children of the Saints of God in Denmark. The room had been tastefully decorated for the occasion and over the stand were these

words: 'We welcome to Scandinavia Pres. Wm. Budge.' At the opposite end was suspended on the wall, the American flag. Pres. Budge spoke to the children a short

WILLIAM BUDGE

Born May 1, 1828, in Lanark, Lanarkshire, Scotland; died March 18, 1919, in Logan, Utah, as a Patriarch and president of the Logan Temple.

time, and his remarks were translated into Danish by Elder Andrew Jenson. * *

"At 2 p. m. the hall, which holds about 300 people, was crowded by Saints and strangers, when Pres. Budge addressed them, expressing his pleasure in meeting them, and the manner in which he had been received, and spoke also on the spirit and power of the gospel. His remarks were rendered in the vernacular tongue by Elder Jenson. In the evening Elder Martineau and myself spoke a short time, and were followed by other Elders. A most excellent spirit prevailed during the day, and we all truly enjoyed ourselves. The Saints in this country seem to be so humble and contrite, that it is almost impossible to feel otherwise than well. The spirit of the Lord is indeed with the Saints in Scandinavia. * *

"On Friday morning we bade farewell to Elders Asmussen, Jenson and others of the brethren in Copenhagen, and went on board the S. S. 'Christiania' bound for Christiania. At 9 o'clock we moved out into the Baltic, accompanied by Pres. Wilhelmsen. During the day we passed a castle, situated on the north end of Zealand (Sjælland), the place where Hamlet saw his father's ghost, as represented by Shakespeare. In the evening we arrived on the coast of Sweden and entered an inlet reaching up to Göteborg. The coast is made up of barren rocks breaking into innumerable recesses or inlets and dotted with myriads of rocky islands void of vegetation with an occasional exception as we go inland, when a lone fisherman's cottage crowns the top or is nestled in some crevice amid the rocks where the scanty vegetation furnishes a foothold. Here and there on the shore appears a little green spot as if shut out from the cold blasts and fierce waves by the rugged surroundings, and a picturesque fishing hamlet lies nestled in its quiet recess. Lumber, wood and fish are the principal exports of the country. We stopped for a short time at Göteborg and then continued on our journey.

"On the following morning, on going on deck, the coast of Norway appeared on either side, for we were entering the Christiania Fjord. The country is very rough as in Sweden, but the hills are covered with fir trees. The fjord is studded with innumerable small, rocky islands. About 50 miles from the sea we brought up at Christiania, and were met by Elders Jonas Halvorsen, the president of the Christiania Conference, and Elders Chr. Hogensen and Lars K. Larsen. Christiania is not crowded together as most European cities of its size, but more nearly resembles our American cities in that it is relieved here and there by little gardens and orchards surrounding the dwellings, the latter, many of them, being artistic in design and very beautiful. One of our party had formed a strong attachment for restaurants and as we passed along the street, he did not fail to notice such signs, but at last he was staggered by the following sign, 'Restauration og Brændevinsudskjænkning,' which graced the side of a house near the market place. On inquiry, we found the last word meant 'Drinks sold here at retail.' Being rather weak from the effects of a sea voyage, I thought it best not to try to pronounce the word.

"On Sunday we held meetings in Christiania. The first commenced at 10 o'clock, when the Saints met in our meeting room, at 27 Osterhaugsgaden. The room is the best, I suppose, that is in our possession in Europe. It is about 30 x 40 feet with arched ceiling about 20 feet high in the middle, is nicely furnished and fitted up, capable of seating about 350 people, and on this occasion was very tastefully decorated. The large building in which this room is situated belongs to the Church. The office is on the same floor as the meeting room. Elder Martineau was the first speaker and expressed his pleasure at meeting with the Saints, and also spoke of the obligations we are under to God for his mercy towards us. Pres. Wilhelmsen interpreted his remarks. Pres. Budge spoke a short time, expressing his satisfaction at the cordial manner with which we had been received. At 5 p. m. we again met, when I spoke a short time on the principles of the gospel and the command to gather given to the Latter-day Saints. Pres. Wilhelmsen again came to our assistance as interpreter. Pres. Budge then said he was pleased with the spirit manifested on this occasion. Said we had not come into the world to teach them because we thought we had more learning than they, but we come forth as the servants of God of old, being called of God as was Aaron.

"In the evening there was a little concert, when the choir rendered some anthems and other pieces in a most excellent manner. Great credit is due to their young conductor, as well as to the talent exhibited by the members. The Sunday school choir, composed of children from six to twelve years of age, rendered some pieces in a manner that would have been creditable to those of riper years, executing their different parts with great success. Pres. Budge thanked them in behalf of the company, for the agreeable entertainment tendered us. The Spirit of the Lord was truly manifested in the midst of the Saints and we enjoyed ourselves exceedingly. * *

"On Wednesday morning we took train for Sweden. * * At 3 p. m. we stopped at Charlottenberg, over the line in Sweden and took dinner in Swedish style, which consists in every one seizing a plate from a stack and helping himself to whatever he likes, and eating standing, or retiring to a side table. Traveling is very cheap in these countries, and a capital dinner can be had at quite a reasonable price. We lay over a few hours at Laxå during the night, and arrived in Stockholm the next morning at 10 o'clock, having been met by Elders Olson and Löfgren about twelve miles from the city."

The visiting brethren had an enjoyable time among the Saints in Stockholm and held four meetings with them; two during the week and two on the Sunday. On the Sunday evening Pres. Budge spoke most encouraging to the Saints, Bro. Lars M. Olson translating his remarks into Swedish. The hall, which could accommodate about 250 persons, was beautifully decorated and was well filled with both Saints and strangers.

In the morning of Tuesday, the brethren left Stockholm en route for Göteborg. At Sköfde, the Swedish Crown Prince boarded the train and traveled to Herrljunga. Göteborg was reached in the evening and Elder Ole N. Stohl, who presided over the conference, received the visiting brethren with much kindness. The following day, the brethren went to Trollhättan, where they enjoyed the beautiful scenery, sailing up Götaelven by steamer. At the foot of the locks they met Elder C. H. Lundberg and in the evening held a good meeting with a little branch of the Saints at this place. Many strangers were also present. The following day, the visiting brethren returned to Göteborg and had a splendid meeting with the Saints there in the evening. On Friday, Aug. 6th, they boarded the steamship "Aarhus" and sailed for Copenhagen, where they arrived Saturday morning.

The following day (Sunday, August 8th,) another meeting was held in Copenhagen, in a large hall rented in Römersgade No. 22, where a great gathering of Saints and strangers assembled. Two meetings were held attended by about 300 people. A third meeting was held in the evening in the Saints' own meeting hall, at Store Regnegade. The following day in the forenoon a Priesthood meeting was held at the mission office at Lorentzensgade No. 14, which was attended by twenty Elders from Zion. On Tuesday, Aug. 10th, the visiting brethren, together with Pres. Niels Wilhelmsen and Elder

Andrew Jenson, crossed the sound to Malmö, Sweden, where a meeting was held in the evening. This was the 17th and last meeting which Pres. Budge attended in Scandinavia, and on Thursday, Aug. 12th, he and his companions left Copenhagen per steamship "Titania" for Stettin, whence they returned, through Germany and Holland, to Liverpool.

CHAPTER 62 (1880)

Elder Ludwig Suhrke is arrested and imprisoned several times in Holstein for preaching and baptizing—Thirty-four Elders from Zion arrive.

Under date of Nov. 16, 1880, Elder Ludwig Suhrke wrote to President Niels Wilhelmsen in Copenhagen, as follows:

"In accordance with my appointment I went in October, 1879, to my native land,

LUDWIG SUHRKE

Was born in Mecklenburg-Schwerin, Germany, May 11, 1837, went to Norway and was baptized in Frederikstad in 1864. Emigrating to Utah in 1866, he worked upon the Salt Lake Tabernacle and other buildings as a carpenter; located in Soda Springs, Idaho, in 1870, where he resided until his death, which occurred Sept. 23, 1905. Brother Suhrke left a wife, one son and two daughters. During his mission in 1879-1881, he labored in Denmark and Germany. He died as he had lived, a true and faithful Latter-day Saint.

Germany, and commenced my missionary labor by preaching the gospel in my birthplace, Rambo, in Schwerin-Mecklenburg, where I held several meetings and baptized one person. On this account a portion of the people became angered against me and complained to the police authorities, which resulted in my imprisonment for 48 hours. In the month of March, 1880, I went to Aarhus, Denmark, where I remained about a month and attended the spring conference held there April 24th and 25th. Here I was appointed to begin a mission in Schlesvig-Holstein, where at that time only two families of Saints resided. In the forepart of May, 1880, I arrived in Kiel, where I at once rented a room and asked the police authorities for the privilege of holding meetings. As this request was denied, I commenced to visit from house to house, trying to get into conversation with the people in private, and also embraced every opportunity to bear my testimony to such as I could meet on the roads, at the markets, by the wharfs and other places. I found some who believed my testimony, and in the month of June, 1880, I had the joy of baptizing four persons at Kiel. Meanwhile, I became acquainted with a respected and somewhat well-to-do citizen, whose name was Frederik Max Dahlen, who invited me to come and live with him. I, of course, accepted this offer gladly and shortly thereafter I baptized him and his whole family. This brother has ever since been a great help to me in the further spread of the gospel in Kiel and vicinity. For not only has he been exceedingly kind and generous towards me and Bro. Göthe, who in the month of August was sent here from Sweden to assist me, but he has himself showed the greatest zeal in discussing the gospel principles with all who came into his house. I continued my activity in Kiel a couple of months and baptized altogether about twenty persons. When this became known to the civil authorities, I was (notwithstanding their claim to have religious liberty) summoned before the police court, where a number of questions were asked me as to who I was, what I had come for etc. I told them plainly that I was a missionary from the Church of Jesus Christ of Latter-day Saints in Utah, America, and had come to preach the gospel of Jesus Christ. Staatsrath Lorensen, meanwhile, saw fit to write to the president of the province (Schleswig-Holstein) that I was an impostor and a burden to the inhabitants in Kiel, and he lied and misrepresented me in other ways, which resulted in the said president issuing a decree that I should be banished from the country. Accordingly, I was again summoned to appear before the police court, where I was ordered to leave the country within two days. Knowing that I had not done anything for which I could lawfully be banished, I did not comply with the order, wherefore I, a couple of days later, was arrested and, after having been imprisoned for two days I was, under guard, transported across the line to Hamburg, where they turned me loose. This happened in the latter part of July, 1880. After remaining in Hamburg a couple of days, I went back to Kiel, where I continued my activity quietly four or five days, during which time I baptized seven or eight persons. The authorities were soon informed about my return, and after having hunted for me in vain with 35 policemen, they at last got me and I was, of course, immediately placed under arrest. I was imprisoned 17 days, after which I was transported to Hamburg the second time with the threat, that if I ever came back again, they would send me to America. Inasmuch as I did not consider it wise to go back at once under these conditions, I commenced to labor for the spread of the gospel in Hamburg by going from house to house. I spent a week in that city and became acquainted with several good and upright people and baptized four persons in Altona.

"Meanwhile, I was invited to attend the conference to be held in Copenhagen and immediately started on my journey to that city. As I desired very much to visit the Saints in Kiel, I decided to go that way and I succeeded, by disguising myself as well as I could, in leaving the railroad station without being detected. I spent a few days in a very pleasant way in the company of the Saints. Presumably all would have been well, had it not been for some persons who, while pretending to be my friends betrayed me into the hands of the police. Consequently I was again arrested and had to stay 38 days in prison This time I spent, considering the circumstances, in a pleasant way in singing, reading and praying. The Lord comforted me in my lonely hours and gave me that peace and consolation which always comforts those who suffer persecution for the testimony of Jesus. While thus imprisoned I had opportunity to converse with several persons, prominent in society, to whom I explained how unfair and unlawfully I was treated, but as one feared opposition from the other, no one dared to defend my case. I had also opportunity to preach the gospel to the jailor and others. On the 11th of November (1880) I was liberated without any acknowledgment to the effect that I was innocent, or, on the other hand, to prove that I had violated any law of the land, which I demanded of them to give me. I then started again on my journey to Copenhagen, where I arrived Nov. 13th. I can say in truth that I have felt blessed and happy in everything I have had to go through for a righteous cause, and feel certain that it all will serve to forward the work of the Lord in Germany. There are now about 45 members of the Church in Kiel and vicinity, and the prospects for the future are promising. I intend to go back to Hamburg in a few days and there continue my missionary labors."

At the conference held in Aarhus, Oct. 30 and 31, 1880, while Elder Suhrke was still in prison, a branch of the Church called the Schleswig-Holstein Branch was organized, with Elder Ola Göthe as president. At the same time Elder Suhrke was appointed to labor as a missionary in Hamburg, when he again should obtain his liberty.

Under date of Dec. 24, 1880, Pres. Niels Wilhelmsen reported the Scandinavian Mission as follows:

"There are at present 56 Elders from Zion in this mission, who have been and are still working diligently for the spread of the gospel among the people, and, so far as I know, they are all true and faithful men. Besides them a great many of our good native Elders have been sent out as missionaries into the various branches and conferences. The Lord has blessed his servants. and their labors have borne much fruit. During the year we have, as the statistical report will show, added to the Church by baptism, 1,160 persons, and the future looks promising. Thus we have great reason to feel thankful to our Heavenly Father, and to him we ascribe the honor for what good we have been permitted to accomplish in these lands. During the summer season we emigrated over eight hundred souls; a number of these have been assisted, considerably, by their friends and relatives in Utah, and we feel thankful to see so many delivered from Babylon to gather with the Saints to Zion.

"The governments have been liberal towards us, so that the Elders, as a general thing, have been permitted to preach the gospel and administer in its ordinances unmolested, except in Germany, the province of Schleswig-Holstein, and also in Finland. Elder Ludwig Suhrke has been arrested three times in Kiel, and imprisoned altogether 57 days, for preaching the gospel, but he is now free and is continuing his efforts in Hamburg, where he will labor this winter. Our Elders in Finland have been followed up by the Russian authorities, which have confiscated quite a few of our books and pamphlets; but the people themselves seem to be kindly disposed towards the Elders, and some have also been added to the Church in that country. I have just received a letter from the Elders in Iceland; they hope to do a good work there through this winter, notwithstanding the authorities are against them. They are enjoying good health and feel well.

"Our Relief Societies and Young Men's Associations in the various conferences are in a thriving condition and doing a great deal of good in distributing the printed word from house to house, and inviting the people to our meetings; many of the young men are now on missions and are doing much good. Our Sunday schools in the various cities are also in good operation and are conducted after our pattern at home.

"A great deal of the printed word has been published during the last year; besides publishing 'Skandinaviens Stjerne,' semi-monthly, 'Nordstjernan,' semi-monthly and 'Ungdommens Raadgiver,' monthly, we have, since my arrival here in August, 1879, printed 7,000 copies of 'Mærkværdige Syner' (Remarkable Visions), in Danish and 4,000 ditto in Swedish; 5,000 copies of 'En Sandheds Röst' (Voice of Truth), in Danish and 7,000 copies in Swedish, 4,000 copies of 'Bibelske Henvisninger' (Bible References), in Danish and 4,000 copies in Swedish; 2,000 copies of 'Ægteskab og Sæder i Utah' (Marriage and Morals in Utah), in Danish; 2,000 copies of 'Anskuelser om Ægteskab' (The Marriage Institution), in Danish and the same number in Swedish; 5,000 copies of 'Den eneste Vei til Salighed' (The Only Way to be Saved), in Danish and the same number in Swedish; 3,000 copies of 'Israels Indsamling og Zions Forlösning' (The Gathering of Israel and the Redemption of Zion), in Danish; 2,000 copies of "Er Mormonismen en Vranglære,' in Danish; 16 sheets or forms of the new edition of the Book of Mormon and six sheets of the Swedish Hymn Book, and 2,000 copies of a work called the 'Voice of Warning,' in the Icelandic language. "From the above you will see that we have not been idle in the publishing department. We are as busy now as we ever were, and have the best prospects for continuing so during the remainder of the winter."

In 1880, thirty-four Elders from Zion, called to labor in the Scandinavian Mission, arrived in Copenhagen, in the following order: Peter A. Nielsen of Draper, Utah, arrived Jan. 7th. Lars K. Larsen of Hyrum, Carl Peter Warnick of Pleasant Grove, Ole C. Tellefsen of Hyrum, Hans J. Christiansen and Carl H. Lundberg of Logan, Hans Madsen of Ogden, John Christensen of Brigham City, Nils O. Anderson of Ephraim, Anders G. Johnson of Grantsville, Simon Christensen of Richfield, and Jens Iver Jensen of Elsinore, Utah, arrived May 4th. Peter A. Löfgren of Huntsville, Utah, Chr. Hogensen of Montpelier, Idaho, and John Dahle of Logan, Utah, arrived May 21st. Charles Samuelson of Santaquin, Rasmus Berntzon of Logan, and Nils Henrikson of Richfield, Utah, Martin Jacobson of St. Charles, Idaho, Lars Nielsen of Fountain Green, and Pauli E. B. Hammer of Salt Lake City, Utah, arrived Sept. 14, 1880. Peter O. Hansen (on a third mission) of Manti, Sven Erikson of Grantsville and Jacob P. Olsen of Salt Lake City, Utah, arrived Oct. 6th. Nils R. Lindahl of Union, Lars N. Larson of Moroni, Jens Jenson of Monroe, James H. Hansen and James P. Larsen of Ephraim, Hans E. Nielsen of Hyrum, Andrew Amundsen of South Jordan, James J. Hansen of Hyrum, and John Hansen of South Jordan, Utah, arrived Nov. 6th. Jens C. Olsen of Salina, Utah, arrived Nov. 13th, and James S. Jensen of Redmond, Utah, Dec. 24, 1880.

Elder Peter A. Nielsen was appointed to labor in the Copenhagen,

Elder Lars K. Larsen in the Christiania, Elder Carl P. Warnick in the Skåne, and Ole C. Tellefsen in the Christiania Conference. Hans J. Christiansen was appointed to labor

CARL PETER WARNICK

Was born April 5, 1850, in Forsby parish, Skaraborgs län, Sweden, the son of Anders Peter Warnick and Anna Lina Anderson. He was baptized in the spring of 1866 and emigrated to America with his parents and others of the family, arriving in Salt Lake City, Oct. 22, 1866, after spending twenty weeks on the journey. Several of the family died en route. The survivors located in Pleasant Grove where Carl bcame a permanent resident. He worked on the Union Pacific Railroad in Echo and Weber canyons in 1868, married Christine Marie Larsen March 14, 1874, and became the father of seven sons and three daughters, nine of whom are still (1927) living. He joined the United Order in 1875; filled a mission to Scandinavia in 1880-1882, laboring 27 months in the Skåne conference, presiding successively over the Helsingborg and Christianstad branches. In Utah he has served two terms in the Pleasant Grove City Council, presided over the Scandinavian meetings in Pleasant Grove for 15 years, labored as a ward teacher 17 years, and acted as 2nd counselor to Bishop Joseph E. Thorne of Pleasant Grove in 1891-1895. He moved to Manila in 1895 and acted as Bishop of the Manila Ward nine years. Bishop Warnick still lives at Manila, surrounded by his posterity, and continues active both in Church and civic affairs.

in the Copenhagen Conference and later to preside over said conference. Elder Carl H. Lundberg was appointed to labor in the Göteborg, Hans Madsen in the Aarhus, John Christensen in the Aalborg, Niels O. Anderson in the Skåne and Anders G. John-on in the Göteborg Conference. Elder Simon Christensen was appointed to preside over the Aalborg Conference, Elder Jens I. Jensen to labor in the Aalborg Conference and later to preside over the Aarhus Conference. Elder Peter A. Löfgren, was

SIMON CHRISTENSEN

Was born Aug. 13, 1846, in Bindslev parish, Hjörring amt, Denmark, the son of Christen Simonsen and Anne Jensen. His father served in the war between Germany and Denmark in 1848-1850 and died in October, 1850, as a result of hardship and exposure incident to the war, leaving a widow and three children. Becoming a convert to the restored gospel, Simon was baptized June 28, 1867, ordained to the priesthood and labored four years as a missionary. He presided successively over the Thisted, Hjörring and Aalborg branches and emigrated to Utah in 1871. In 1872 (July 22) he married Berthe Marie Jensen which union was blessed with nine children (five boys and four girls). In 1874 he moved with his family to Richfield, Sevier County, where he was associated with the United Order. In 1880-1882 he filled a mission to Scandinavia and presided over the Aalborg conference, Denmark. During the two years 207 persons were baptized. Returning home he had charge of a large company of emigrants which arrived in Salt Lake City July 10, 1882. In Richfield he was for twenty years a counselor in the Ward Bishopric and for nearly thirty years a member of the High Council in the Sevier Stake and South Sanpete Stake. He assisted in promoting and organizing the Otter Creek Reservoir Company, served as a member of the city council of Richfield for five consecutive terms and as justice of the Peace for over twenty years. In 1907-1908 he filled a second mission to Scandinavia, laboring in the Aalborg conference. His wife died in 1914 and two years later he married Mette Marie Christensen of Manti. Since 1916 he has acted as an ordinance worker in the Manti Temple.

appointed to labor in the Stockholm Conference, Elder Chr. Hogensen to preside over the Christiania Conference, John Dahle to labor in the Christiania Conference and Chas. Samuelson in the Göteborg Conference. Elder Rasmus Berntzon was appointed to labor in the Göteborg Conference and later to preside over the Stockholm Conference. Elder Nils Henrikson was appointed to labor in the Skåne Conference, and Martin Jacobson as a traveling Elder in, and later as president of the Skåne Conference. Elder Lars Nielsen was appointed to labor in the Aarhus Conference. Pauli E. B.

LARS NIELSEN

Born May 3, 1849, at Sönder Vinge, near Randers, Denmark, the son of Jens Nielsen and Mette Christiansen, who were baptized May 4, 1857. Lars was baptized May 18, 1857, and emigrated with his parents to Utah in 1859 and located in Spanish Fork, Utah County. In 1863 the family moved to Fountain Green, Sanpete County. His father died April 8, 1872, and his mother May 26, 1909. In 1871 (Nov. 27th) he married Marie M. Christiansen who bore him fourteen children, of whom four are dead. Brother Nielsen filled a mission to Scandinavia in 1880-1882, presiding over the Veile Branch, Aarhus conference, Denmark. Marie M. Christiansen, wife of Lars Nielsen, was born Sept. 29, 1856, near Aarhus, Denmark, the daughter of Sören Christiansen and Caroline Loft, and emigrated to Utah in 1860. Her parents were baptized at Aarhus in June, 1857, and her grandparents also joined the Church. They all came to Utah and subsequently died at Fountain Green.

Hammer was appointed to labor in the Copenhagen Conference, and later in the German part of the Scandinavian Mission. Elder Peter O. Hansen was appointed to labor in the mission office and also as a traveling Elder in the Copenhagen Conference. Elder Sven Erikson was appointed to labor in the Göteborg and Jacob P. Olsen in the Aalborg Conference. Elder Nils R. Lindahl was appointed to labor in the Stockholm Conference and later as president of said conference. Elder Lars N. Larson was appointed to labor in the Skåne, Jens Jenson in the Göteborg, James H. Hansen in the Copen-

NILS RASMUSSEN LINDAHL

Born May 18, 1837, at Stora Svedala socken, Malmöhus län, Sweden, the son of Nils Rasmussen and Bengta Hansdotter. When a young man he was converted to the gospel and was baptized Sept. 16, 1857, by Johan Holmstedt and ordained an Elder March 18, 1858. For four years he labored as a local Elder before he emigrated to Utah. He crossed the ocean on the sailing vessel "Athenia" in O. N. Liljenquist's company; crossed the plains with Capt. Joseph Horne, arriving in Salt Lake City Oct. 14, 1862. The next year he married Kersti, Per Larsson's daughter; they had four children. For several years he labored as a colonizer in different settlements. In 1880-1882 he filled a mission to Sweden, where he presided over the Stockholm Conference and in 1894-97 he filled a second mission to his native country and again presided over the Stockholm Conference. Jan. 14, 1914, he married Gustava Olson of Sandy and died at Midvale, Salt Lake County, Oct. 13, 1922.

hagen, James P. Larsen and Hans E. Nielsen in the Aalborg and Andrew Amundsen in the Christiania Conference. Elder Jas. J. Hansen, John Hansen, and Jas S. Jensen were appointed to labor in the Aarhus Conference. Jens Chr. Olsen was appointed to labor in Norway and later in the Copenhagen Conference.

CHAPTER 63 (1881)

Death of Elder Gustaf Pettersson—He is succeeded by Elder Hugo D. E. Peterson—Elder Pauli E. B. Hammer in Hamburg—Saints emigrating to Zion—Elder Ola Göthe's experience in Holstein.

The first Young Ladies' Mutual Improvement Association in the Scandinavian Mission was organized in Christiania, Norway, Jan. 10, 1881, with Karen Olsen as president. Later similar organizations were organized in some of the larger branches in the mission.

Elder Gustaf Pettersson, translator and assistant at the mission office in Copenhagen, died April 13, 1881, of inflammation of the lungs, after an illness of about three months. Bro. Pettersson was born in Skedevi, Östergötland, Sweden, Feb. 18, 1850, and baptized Feb. 6, 1876. Soon afterwards he was ordained a Deacon, and later an Elder. After laboring faithfully about two years as a missionary in the Stockholm Conference, he was called to labor in the mission office in Copenhagen, in 1878 and in compliance with that call he came to Denmark in September, 1878. From that time until he was taken sick he labored faithfully about two and a half years as translator for "Nordstjernan" and attended to other duties in the mission office. By his faithfulness and humility, he won the confidence and love of all who became acquainted with him. The funeral took place April 18th, when his remains were interred in "Vestre Kirkegaard," Copenhagen,

Elder Hugo D. E. Peterson succeeded Gustaf Pettersson as assistant editor of "Nordstjernan."

GUSTAF PETTERSSON

Born Feb. 18, 1850; died April 13, 1881.

When Pres. Niels Wilhelmsen visited Stockholm, Sweden, during the summer of 1880, he requested Conference President Lars M. Olson to find a man who was qualified to succeed Elder Gustaf Pettersson as writer for "Nordstjernan," a Swedish periodical published by the Church in Scandinavia, as Elder Pettersson was expected to emigrate the next year to Zion. President Olson suggested Brother Hugo D. E. Peterson, then a type-setter, 19 years of age, employed in the printing establishment of Albert Bonnier & Sons in Stockholm. Brother Peterson was consequently chosen to take the position named in the near future, but the call came sooner than expected, as word was received in December, 1880, that Elder Gustaf Pettersson was seriously ill in Copenhagen, and that his successor was needed at the mission office at once.

Brother Peterson therefore arranged to leave his employers, with whom he had only a few months previously served his apprenticeship, meanwhile having attended the "Jönsson Private School," where he studied orthography and grammar. He left Stockholm Jan. 5, 1881, and arrived in Copenhagen Jan. 7th, where he immediately commenced his labors, gathering up the threads of the work left off by Elder Pettersson when he took sick. "That was a little hard in the commencement," writes Elder Peterson, and would no doubt have been discouraging, had I not received the kind and hearty assistance rendered me by Elder Andrew Jenson, to whom I became and have ever since been very much attached, and whose help and advice were enjoyed and appreciated by me until Elder

HUGO DANIEL EDWARD PETERSON

Born in the city of Visby, Isle of Gotland. Sweden, Aug. 14, 1860, the son of Isak Peterson and Anna Sophia Gardstedt. He was baptized May 11, 1873; ordained a Priest April 27, 1880, and an Elder Aug. 31, 1881.

Jenson's return to Zion later in 1881."

The last sheet of a new and improved edition of the Book of Mormon was printed at F. E. Bording's printing office May 31, 1881, in Copenhagen. The following is from the pen of Elder Andrew Jenson:

"On the 10th of June. 1880. I com-

President Niels Wilhelmsen and Elder Andrew Jenson engaged in translating the Book of Mormon.

menced, together with Pres. Niels Wilhelmsen, to revise the Book of Mormon. The first edition of this book was translated into Danish by Apostle Erastus Snow and Elder Peter O. Hansen, and published in Copenhagen in 1851; a second edition was printed in 1858. As both of these editions had been sold out, it became necessary to issue a third edition, but before a new edition could be printed it was considered wise to divide the book into chapters and verses like the latest English edition, and also supply it with footnotes. And, furthermore, it was considered best to submit the book to a thorough revision in other respects, as the Danish language, both as regards to orthography and style, had undergone material changes since 1851. This work of revision proved a greater task (as the work proceeded) than was anticipated when the work was begun. Every sentence and every verse was carefully compared with the latest English edition. This was done in the following manner. After previously marking off the book into chapters and verses, I would

read one or more verses at a time to President Wilhelmsen, who followed me carefully with the English edition, after which he usually read the same in English to me, while I followed carefully in the Danish translation. In this manner we guarded against possible errors and after I had written such changes as we had agreed upon and had made the necessary corrections in the orthography, etc., we read further. * * A few days after the issuance from the press of the last sheet we received from the bookbinder the first bound copies of the book, which was considered one of the finest books from a mechanical standpoint which had ever been published by our Elders in the Scandinavian Mission.

"Besides revising and publishing this new edition of the Book of Mormon, we also revised and published new editions of a number of books, pamphlets and tracts, which had formerly been issued from the press in the mission. As in the case with the Book of Mormon, a number of errors had crept into these books and pamphlets, through having been reprinted so often, that it was necessary to make many corrections."

Elder Pauli E. B. Hammer of Salt Lake City, who had been laboring in the Copenhagen Conference, was, in the spring of 1881, appointed to go to Schleswig-Holstein, to assist Elder Ludwig Suhrke and Ola Göthe, as he could speak the German language. He at once went to Hamburg, from which city he wrote the following to Pres. Niels Wilhelmsen, dated June 3rd, 1881:

"After Elder Suhrke was banished from Hamburg, everything was quiet for about a month. On May 15th I went to Altona to attend a third meeting with the Saints and a few invited friends. This time, however, we were betrayed by some false friends, and we had not even time to open our meeting before three detectives came in and immediately recorded our names, and, taking us, one at a time, into an adjoining room, they put many questions to us to answer. They also took possession of some of our books and tracts, which lay on the table, and declared me to be their prisoner. I went along with them to the station, and after they had searched me and taken my things, among which were etters in Danish and English (which they proceeded to translate), I was put in prison, where I was kept nine days. I was then brought before the court and found not guilty. Meanwhile, they had opened

PAUL E. B. HAMMER

Was born July 28, 1839, at Faaborg, Fyen, Denmark, emigrated to Utah in 1861 and besides his first mission (1880-1881) he filled another mission to Europe in 1884. Is now (1927) a resident of Salt Lake City.

my trunk, which was left in Hamburg, taken my missionary certificate, letters and other documents of various kinds, which they also had translated and recorded. These were later returned to me in court. They then read to me a decree of banishment, which I was compelled to sign, and I was transported across the Prussian boundary and turned loose in Hamburg, May 24th. They then boastingly published in the papers "how they got rid of 'Mormonism.'" I commenced, notwithstanding, to labor carefully in Hamburg, and all went well for four days; but on the 28th, a detective visited the two places where I held meetings and made inquiries about me; among other things he said that I was not wanted in Hamburg. The next day another detective was sent to the place where they had previously robbed my trunk, leaving a summons for me to appear before the 'Staatsenator,' who

wanted to see me; but as yet I have not gone there. I am at present enjoying liberty, but how long this will last I know not. If I am banished again from here, I intend to go to Lubeck and pursue my labors there till I receive other instructions from my superiors in the Priesthood. In the prison I preached the gospel to the other prisoners and had much conversation with the chief jailer (a Mr. Runge), on whom I made a good impression. I gained his confidence to such a degree that he decided to send one of his children with me to Zion, when I should return home."

Elder Hammer subsequently baptized Mr. Runge, together with his wife and four grown daughters.

A company of 609 emigrating Saints (the 35th company from Scandinavia), together with 12 returning missionaries, sailed from Copenhagen, June 20, 1881, by the steamers "Cato" and "Hero." The "Cato" had on board the Saints from the Göteborg and Skåne conferences (147 souls), in charge of Elders Mons Nilsson, Peter Nilsson and Fred Lundberg. The "Hero' carried 462 Saints from Stockholm, Copenhagen, Aarhus, Aalborg and Christiania conferences, and the following returning missionaries: Peter A. Nielsen (leader of the company), Lawrence C. Mariager, Herman F. F. Thorup, Jacob Hansen, Isaac Sörensen, John T. Thorup, Christian Olson, Erik O. Bylund, and Andrew Amundsen. On Thursday, June 23rd, both steamers arrived safely at Hull, England, and later the same day the company was conveyed to Liverpool by the railway, and the same evening the emigrants embarked on the steamer "Wyoming," which sailed on Saturday, June 25th. Besides the Scandinavians, there were 146 British Saints, seven more returning missionaries and one visitor on board from the British Isles. Elder Samuel Roskelley was appointed leader of the company, while Elders Peter A. Nielsen, Lawrence C. Mariager and Herman F. F. Thorup were retained

as a presidency over the Scandinavian division. After a successful
voyage, the "Wyoming" arrived safely at New York, July 7th, and the
next day the emigrants resumed their
journey westward and arrived in
Ogden, July 15th. Here the company parted, as about half of the
emigrants went to Salt Lake City,
while the rest either remained in
Ogden, or went north. One child
died on the cars while journeying
through the States.

Elder Ola Göthe, who arrived in
Copenhagen, July 20, 1881, reported
as follows:

"I arrived in Kiel in August last year
(1880) to assist Elder Ludwig Suhrke in
the preaching of the gospel in Schleswig-
Holstein. On my arrival there, about 30
persons had already been baptized, and up
to date about 70 persons altogether have
been added to the Church by baptism.
During my sojourn in that part of the
country I labored principally in Kiel and
vicinity, and have succeeded in establishing
a complete organization of the members.
We held regular meetings every Sunday
and besides these a meeting in the middle
of the week. These were, as a rule, attended by 20 or 30 persons, among whom
occasionally were some strangers. Our
meetings had to be conducted with great
caution; for the civil as well as the
ecclesiastical authorities were continually
watching our movements, and were desirous of hindering our progress. For a
long time we succeeded in escaping from
their evil designs upon us, but on Sunday,
July 10th, when we as usual were assembled for worship, a detective came in
and took down the names of all who were
present (some 15 or 20 names), after which
he ordered me to go along with him. I
was at once imprisoned and on the following day (July 11th) I was tried in the
police court. The principal charge was
that I had read the Bible publicly and
explained its passages. I asked if the
reading of the Bible was a crime, to which
he replied that he had no intention of
entering upon any religious discussion with
me. I was taken back to prison again,
where I was detained nine days, after
which I, on July 19th, again was brought
before the court, where a decree of banishment was read to me, requesting my

immediate departure from the country because, as they said, I was preaching a
doctrine *they had no use for.* I took the
liberty to tell them that whether they had
use for it or not, it was the true gospel
of Jesus Christ, and the only one which
could be defended by the Bible. After I
had been detained in prison several hours,
they placed me on the evening of the same
day on board the steamer 'Aurora,' with
which I then sailed to Copenhagen, where
I arrived safely the following day and was
kindly received by the brethren at the
mission office."

CHAPTER 64 (1881)

Death of Pres. Niels Wilhelmsen—Elder
Andrew Jenson in temporary charge of the
mission—Elder Chr. D. Fjeldsted succeeds to
the presidency of the mission—Elder Jenson's
departure—Arrival of 38 Elders from Zion.

Pres. Niels Wilhelmsen died in
Copenhagen, Denmark, Aug. 1, 1881,
after an operation in one of the
hospitals in that city. His death
came unexpectedly, as the operation
had been considered a success. Elder
Wilhelmsen, who was the first Elder
from Zion to die while filling a mission in Scandinavia, was born at
Feuling, Skanderborg Amt, Denmark,
April 21, 1824. He was baptized in
Copenhagen by Elder Fred. Phister,
Aug. 30, 1854, and shortly after ordained to the Priesthood and sent
out on a mission to preach the gospel.
He continued in the ministry, advancing step by step and filling places of
great responsibility, until he emigrated with his family to Utah in
1861. After his arrival in the Territory, he settled on the Weber, according to the counsel of Pres. Young,
and endured the privations incident
to pioneer life in connection with the
rest of the settlers in that region. In
the fall of 1864, he went to Bear
Lake and located in St. Charles,
where his family has resided ever
since. The following spring he was
called to go on a mission to his native
land. Leaving his family under
trying circumstances, he started on

his mission, arriving in Copenhagen in company with 15 other Utah Elders on Aug. 2, 1865. As traveling Elder in the whole Scandinavian Mission and counselor to Pres. Carl Widerborg, he spent about two years in the ministry at that time. He returned home in 1867 as leader of the 26th company of emigrating saints from Scandinavia. On July 21, 1879, Elder Wilhelmsen left his home in Bear Lake Valley the second time, on a mission to Scandinavia, arriving in England on August 15, 1879, and in Copenhagen, August 19th, having been appointed to succeed Elder Nils C. Flygare in taking charge of the Scandinavian Mission, in which important position he was laboring at the time of his death. He was greatly beloved by his family and friends, and particularly was he respected by those closely associated with him in the ministry.

The funeral of Pres. Wilhelmsen took place in Copenhagen, Aug. 7th, 1881. The following is from the pen of Elder Andrew Jenson:

"About 12 o'clock noon the Saints began to assemble at the churchyard for the purpose of showing their last token of respect to the remains of our beloved brother and president, Niels Wilhelmsen; also a great many strangers, who were friends of the deceased, assembled with us. The coffin, containing the earthly remains of him whom we all had so dearly loved, stood on a stand in the upper end of the hall, and was beautifully decorated with some thirty or forty wreaths of flowers, some of which were very handsome and costly. The stand itself was draped in black, and was also decorated with a great variety of wreaths and flowers. Among the wreaths on the coffin we noticed on the upper end a large one made of palms, and upon the attached silk-band was the inscription: "From mourning friends in Stockholm." Inside of this was another handsome wreath decorated with a great variety of white flowers, which had the inscriptions: 'Goodbye from his assistants in the office,' and 'Those who knew you best loved you most.' On the sides of the coffin were hung, among many other wreaths, those

17

with the following inscriptions: 'Goodbye to Brother Wilhelmsen from the Relief Society in Aarhus.' 'Goodbye from the sisters' and 'Goodbye from the young brethren,' and on the lower end the following: 'Last farewell from the choir.'

"At 1 o'clock p. m. the services commenced in the chapel under the direction of Elder Andrew Jenson. The sixteen Elders from Zion who were present had their place behind the coffin to the right, and the choir was stationed on the left. The choir sang an appropriate piece which had been composed for the occasion. Elder Hans Funk then offered prayer. Remarks, brief but timely, pointed and sympathetic, were then made by Elders Simon Christensen, Lars M. Olson, Christen Jensen, Hans Funk and Andrew Jenson. A hymn was then sung by the choir, after which the procession moved out. The coffin was borne by six conference presidents, viz, Hans Funk, Lars M. Olson, Simon Christensen, Ole N. Stohl, Christen Jensen and Nils B. Ädler. Immediately after the bier walked Elder Andrew Jenson and Brother Hugo D. E. Peterson. After them the other brethren from Zion, Peter O. Hansen, Hans J. Christiansen, Martin Jakobsen, Carl P. Warnick, Lars N. Larsen, James C. Olsen, Rasmus Christoffersen, Jens Hansen and Rasmus Olsen. Next came the members of the choir, and finally the multitude of the Saints and strangers, numbering nearly four hundred persons, who all marched four abreast to the grave. The distance from the chapel to the grave was about three hundred yards. Having reached the grave, and the coffin being lowered, the choir sang another selected hymn, after which Elder Hans J. Christiansen dedicated the grave. After this the people walked in single file past the grave, and viewed the coffin after it was lowered. The grave itself was nicely decorated with leaves and flowers. Everything passed off quietly and peacefully, and with the best of order. Nobody tried to disturb us in our proceedings, and we were granted all the privileges both in the chapel and in the churchyard which we asked for, the various officials being very liberal and kind in their feelings and treatment towards us. Everybody present seemed to partake alike in the solemn feelings which penetrated the hearts of the Saints. Surely it was a day that will never be forgotten by those who participated in its mournful proceedings. A meeting was held in the evening, in which several of the brethren spoke words of cheer, comfort and counsel to the assembled Saints and strangers. "A council of the brethren from Zion was held in this office this morning. All the brethren present spoke their feelings unrestrainedly, and the greatest union and best of feelings prevailed. It was decided by unanimous vote of those present to 'sustain Elder Andrew Jenson in our faith and prayers, to take charge of the affairs of the Mission until Pres. Wilhelmsen's successor arrives, or until the Priesthood shall appoint it otherwise.'"

Elder Lars M. Olson, under date of Aug. 18th, 1881, wrote the following:

"Since my arrival in these lands in September, 1878, I have visited 35 Swedish cities and traveled about 7,000 English miles and preached and borne my testimony in 598 meetings. Since August, 1879, my labors have been more confined to the city of Stockholm, owing to the responsibilities that have rested upon me as president of the Stockholm Conference. During the three years that I have spent in the mission, seventeen of our missionaries have been summoned before ecclesiastical councils and six before the civil authorities. It is unnecessary to state the cause. While the clergy have thus shown us unnecessary attention, we have been liberally paid in the joy which we have experienced because of the many honest and upright people who have willingly listened to our testimony, and notwithstanding the persecution to which our co-religionists have been subjected, many have embraced the truth and have been thankful to the Lord for the opportunity. Thus 493 persons have been added to the Church by baptism, of which number 95 have been baptized during the past three months, and when those who have recently been booked for emigration have taken their departure, over 340 persons have emigrated to Zion during my presidency. 'Nordstjernan' and 'Ungdommens Raadgiver' are read with interest, and of the 438 copies of the former and 171 of the latter subscribed for, quite a percentage is read by non-members. Our financial condition is good, only a little money is outstanding and the conference has no debt. We have Relief Societies in the various branches, where regular meetings are held bi-monthly, and in praise of the sisters I will say that much has been done to assist the poor, for which may the Lord bless them. * * Of missionaries laboring in this conference at present there

are four Elders from Zion, namely: Elders Löfgren, Lindahl, Lindvall and myself, and ten local missionaries. They all labor with energy and good will for the welfare of their fellowmen."

On August 29, 1881, a company of 270 emigrating Saints from Scandinavia sailed from Copenhagen, on the steamer "Pacific," under the direction of Elders Lars M. Olson, Hans Funk and Christen Jensen. Five other returning missionaries accompanied them, viz: Ole N. Stohl, Nils B. Ädler, Anthon L. Skanchy, John Dahle and Jörgen Jörgensen, and also Sister Fredrika Nilsson from Tooele, Utah, who had been visiting relatives in Sweden. The whole company numbered 279 souls. After a successful voyage, the steamer arrived at Hull, England, Sept. 1, 1881, and the emigrants proceeded by rail to Liverpool, from which place they, together with 311 British and 37 Swiss and German Saints and 13 returning missionaries, sailed on the steamer "Wyoming," Sept. 3, 1881, and arrived in New York on the 13th. The next day (Sept. 14, 1881), the emigrants continued the journey westward by railroad train and arrived all well in Salt Lake City, Utah, Sept. 21, 1881. An English sister, 67 years of age, died on the train, near Evanston, Wyoming, on the 20th. A child was born of English parentage on the ocean. Elder James Finlayson was leader of the company from Liverpool to Salt Lake City.

Elder Andrew Jenson left Copenhagen, Sept. 7, 1881, on his return to his home in Utah. Following is a personal account of his mission:

"Soon after my arrival in Copenhagen, June 11, 1879, I was called to labor as president of the Copenhagen Branch, which position I held for eight months, but although I had been instructed by Pres. John Taylor and Pres. Wm. Budge to devote a part of my time on this mission to the study of the Danish language, my

ntire time was soon occupied with labors
t the mission office and in taking care
f the branch so that I only succeeded
n obtaining a few lessons from a
rivate teacher until May, 1880, when I
vas released from the presidency of the
ranch, after which I spent about three
nonths studying the Danish language, etc.
About the 1st of May, 1880, I commenced
he work of translating for 'Skandinaviens
Stjerne' and soon afterwards, in connec-
ion with Pres. Niels Wilhelmsen, I com-
nenced to revise the Book of Mormon.
While thus engaged, the most intimate
riendship arose between the president and
nyself, and I soon learned to love him with
a devotion similar to that of a son for
an affectionate father, and he seemed fully
to reciprocate my feelings. He was truly
a good and noble man.

"As the details of our joint labor on the
Book of Mormon is described elsewhere in
the history of the mission, I will here
merely remark that when Pres. Wilhelmsen, July 21, 1881, went to the hospital,
he left the affairs of the mission in my
care and remarked at the time that he felt
perfectly safe concerning the business of
the mission as I had gained his unlimited
confidence. I immediately took hold of
my extra labor and from that time until
my departure for home, I was very busily
engaged with the various affairs which
formerly had demanded all the time and
attention which two men could give to it.
But I did not worry because I was busy;
my only anxiety was in behalf of the condition of my beloved brother, and I visited
him regularly once or twice a day in the
hospital. Conference President Hans Funk
and my fellow-laborer at the mission office,
Hugo D. E. Peterson, rendered me all the
assistance they could under the trying
circumstances. I shall not describe the
sad scene that was witnessed at "No. 14"
when the news of the death of President
Wilhelmsen was communicated to us in
the morning of Aug. 1st. When older and
experienced men's feelings are wrought
upon to such an extent that there is an
outburst of weeping, the conclusion is at
once that something very serious has happened and that the tenderest heart-strings
have been touched. As soon as we recovered from the first shock of grief, I
telegraphed what had happened to Pres.
Albert Carrington in England, and also to
the various presidents of conferences in
Scandinavia, and later in the day by letter.
I sent them a detailed account of Pres.
Wilhelmsen's sickness and death, and in-

vited a number of them to come to Copenhagen to attend the funeral. Next we
ordered a casket for the remains of our
deceased brother and purchased a lot in
the cemetery (Assistents Kirkegaard). For
this lot I paid 72 kroner and obtained the
deed, which could be renewed in 20 years.

"In the meantime the invited brethren
arrived in the city, and after the funeral
had taken place, Sunday, Aug 7th, I called
all the brethren together for a general
council the following day (Aug 8th) at
the mission office, at which such business
was attended to as the conditions demanded. I also wrote a short epistle to
the Saints, which I published in the 'Skandinaviens Stjerne' and 'Nordstjernan,' and
after the brethren had returned to their
respective fields of labor, I commenced to
pay careful attention to the financial condition of the mission. Thus I worked out
a complete statement of the assets and
liabilities of the mission, which showed
that everything was in first-class condition,
and the only inconvenience we experienced
was the fact that the money in charge of
the mission, and which mainly belonged to
private individuals, had been deposited in
a savings bank (Bikuben), and until a
power of attorney could be secured from
the family of Pres. Wilhelmsen in Idaho,
that money had to go into probate (Skif-
teretten), but by the assistance of a Lawyer
Larsen, who formerly had rendered us professional assistance, and by obtaining a
temporary power of attorney from Pres.
Carrington, at Liverpool, I succeeded in
getting sufficient means at my command
to send off a company of emigrants, numbering 270 souls, which sailed from Copenhagen, Aug 20th, accompanied by eight
returning missionaries, among whom was
Hans Funk, who had presided over the
Copenhagen Conference. I own that I felt
somewhat downhearted when I had taken
leave of this company bound for America,
and I myself had to remain behind. I
had already been away from home longer
than any other missionary from Zion then
laboring in Scandinavia. Among the communications which I, during the short time
that I had charge of the mission, received
from Pres. Carrington in Liverpool was also
the following: 'I am well pleased with the
manner in which you conduct the affairs
of the mission, and as for instructions, I
have only this to say for you for the present:
Continue to do the best you can under the
circumstances until a successor to Pres.
Wilhelmsen arrives from Zion. I am glad
to hear that the people at the hospital

were so kind to Pres. Wilhelmsen during his sickness, and I approve of what you have done in relation to buying a lot in the cemetery in which to bury his earthly remains. I am also pleased to learn that the brethren have rendered you such efficient aid, and I suggest that you secure what help you need during the emigration period by calling to your assistance such of the brethren that you may need. In all these affairs I trust that you may be guided by the unerring counsel of the Holy Ghost.'

"On Thursday, Sept. 1st, eleven Elders from Zion arrived in Copenhagen, among whom was Chr. D. Fjeldsted, who had been called by the presidency of the Church to preside over the Scandinavian Mission. I immediately went to work on the financial accounts of the mission and handed over the mission to him on the 3rd. On the following Sunday I delivered my farewell address to the Saints in Copenhagen, on which occasion the most tender feelings were exhibited toward me, and it appeared that I had gained the confidence and respect of all the Saints, to which the numerous little presents which I received plainly testified. On Wednesday, Sept. 7th, I hurriedly drank a cup of chocolate which our new housekeeper at the mission office had prepared for my farewell, and, together with Pres. Fjeldsted and others, I rode to the railway station. Here I found a number of Saints gathered to say goodbye, and after shaking hands with most of them and exchanging a few kind words with each, I left Copenhagen by rail at 7 o'clock a. m. To take leave of the brethren and the Saints at the office and also at the station overwhelmed me in spite of my best efforts, and tears flowed freely. We arrived in Korsör at 9:30 a. m. Here I boarded the steamer 'Adler,' and sailed 15 minutes later for Kiel, leaving Elders Chr. D. Fjeldsted and Hans J. Christiansen on the wharf. To part with these, my last two friends, who had accompanied me thus far on my journey, caused me despondency for a moment, for now, after having labored in the mission for two years and four months during which time many of my fellow-laborers in the mission field had arrived and departed, I, at last, had to take my departure for home alone. After having walked up and down the deck of the good ship 'Adler' a short time and casting a look toward the Danish shore before wending my way to the far west the third time I went down into my cabin and

obtained a refreshing sleep, of which I was very much in need, for I had scarcely slept at all during the two last nights I had spent in Copenhagen. At 4:30 p. m. the ship arrived at Kiel, Holstein, and I soon afterwards continued my journey by rail to Hamburg, where I arrived at 9 o'clock p. m. Here I had to pass through the custom-house, but although I could not speak German I succeeded by hints and signs to make the officer in charge understand that I wished my trunk, which was well roped, to pass through German without being opened, to which he assented

At 11 o'clock p. m. I left the Harburg station in Hamburg and, after crossing the splendid bridge spanning the River Elbe the railroad journey was continued through the kingdom of Hanover. The conductor was kind enough to place a first-class compartment at my service, although I only held a second-class ticket. I slept well during most of the night, passing Bremen Munster, Dusseldorf and other large cities in Germany, and arrived in the morning of the 8th in the old historical Prussian town of Köln, after having crossed the River Rhine on a giant bridge built on five great pillars. The only thing of importance that I saw in this renowned Prussian city was the great cathedral, which stands close to the railway station. After stopping about half an hour in Köln, the railroad journey was continued through a most beautiful and highly cultivated country, and at 2 o'clock p. m. we reached Aachen, one of Germany's oldest and most remarkable cities. Soon afterwards we reached the Belgian frontier at Herbesthal. Thence we traveled further through the Belgian cities of Verviers, Luttish and Leuven, and arrived at Brussels, the capital of Belgium, at 2:15 p. m. This beautiful city, with regular streets, is most romantically situated in the midst of a fine country, and has 300,000 inhabitants. Here I ate my only meal in Belgium, ordering dinner at the railroad hotel, for which I am sure I paid enough. At 3:15 p. m. I left Brussels and arrived at Ostend at 6 p, m. after having passed through the remarkable city of Ghent, which is bui't on 25 islands, connected with 85 bridges. The town is situated on the river Schelde and has about 150,000 inhabitants. We also passed through the renowned city of Brugge, the chief city in the Belgium province of Westflandern. At Ostend, which is a fortified city by the North Sea with 25,000 inhabitants, and which has regular steamship connection with

ngland, I went on board the steamship
'arlement Belge' and sailed from the har-
or at 8:30 p. m. After a pleasant and
uick voyage we arrived at Dover, England,
3 miles from Ostend at 1:30 in the night.
over is a fortified city containing 40,000
ihabitants. It has a romantic situation
nd is a city with many historical mem-
ries.

"The next day (Friday, Sept. 9th), 1
assed through the custom-house without
aving to open my baggage, and after a
rief stop in Dover I traveled by express
rain 70 miles to London, where we arrived
t 4 o'clock in the morning. As the train
topped at Cannon Street Station, I hired
cab and traveled several miles through
he streets of London to Euston Station.
Much as I desired to spend a few days in
his the largest city in the world, in order
o behold its many sights, time did not
ermit me to do so, as I was hastening to
Liverpool in order to secure passage on the
teamship 'Arizona' which sailed on Satur-
lay. Hence I left London at 5:30 a. m. and
ifter a pleasant ride through the middle
rovinces of England I arrived in Liverpool
it 10:30 a. m. I went immediately to the
nission headquarters at 42 Islington, where
. was kindly received by President Albert
Carrington and his associates. I gave him
a brief account of my mission in Scandi-
iavia and spent the night at the office.
"The next day, Saturday, Sept. 10th, I
sailed from Liverpool for America and arrived in New York, Monday, Sept. 19th.
The good ship "Arizona" made the distance
of 2,779 miles from Queenstown, Ireland,
to Sandy Hook in 7 days, 8 hours and 34
minutes which is the quickest trip, except
one, of any vessel which has crossed the
Atlantic up to the present time. I was the
only representative of the Latter-day Saints
on board, but was treated with courtesy
by the other passengers, of whom the
greater number belonged to the better
classes in America and England.

"Soon after my arrival in New York I
visited the Church agent, Elder James H.
Hart, who received me kindly, and after
having eaten supper with him at the
Grand Central Hotel, he accompanied me
to Jersey City, from which place I continued my journey by railroad westward
at 8:30 in the evening. After an uneventful journey I reached Ogden, safe and
well, in the evening of Sept. 24th. The
following day, in the morning, I continued
the journey to Salt Lake City, and in the
afternoon of the same day, to my home in
Pleasant Grove. I made the entire trip
from Copenhagen to Salt Lake City in
about 16 traveling days, which was the
quickest tour ever made by any of our
missionaries between these two places up
to the present time."

A company of 32 emigrating Saints
sailed from Copenhagen, Denmark,
Oct. 14th, 1881, on the steamer
"Milo," led by Elders Hans Madsen
and Jens C. Olsen. After a successful voyage over the North Sea and
by railroad travel to Liverpool, England, this little company was united
with a large company of British
Saints led by Elder Lyman R. Martineau, and sailed from Liverpool,
Oct. 22nd, on the steamer "Wisconsin," which arrived in New York
November 2nd. Thence the emigrants continued the journey westward by railway, and after a successful trip arrived in Ogden and
Salt Lake City, Nov. 11, 1881.

Elder Ola Göthe returned to
Copenhagen (Oct. 22, 1881) from
another missionary trip to Schleswig-
Holstein. He had left Copenhagen
Sept. 4, 1881, to pursue his missionary labors in that province. He
soon met a "gendarm" who at once
demanded to see his papers, and
when he could not find any fault
with them, he demanded to see his
money. Elder Göthe writes: "I was
now reminded of how the missionaries in former days were sent out
without purse or scrip, while now
they are not permitted to go out without money. Even should the Savior
himself come without money, the
civil authorities would arrest and
imprison him. Being possessed of
a little money I was allowed to go
on my way, and arrived in due time
in Kiel. In the town of Sattrup I
found friends, whom I had met before, very good people. I desired
very much to hold a meeting in that
town and appointed one for the following evening. Being told that the
pastor was a pious man, I visited

him, but found him to be an uncivil and uncouth person of a low grade. My spirit bade me be silent, and I left him, thinking that the time would come when he would be glad to hear the testimony which he now rejected. The meeting was held in spite of that man's threats to the contrary. I came to Kiel on the 16th and was there one week before the police found it out; I was then again imprisoned for a period of 23½ days. On Oct. 18th, I was once more banished from Prussia and sent to Copenhagen on a steamer. A furious storm detained the steamer so that I did not reach Copenhagen until the 22nd at noon, and being weak from the prison diet, I had suffered much from sea sickness."

In the latter part of 1881 the Schleswig-Holstein Branch was joined to the North German Conference of the Swiss and German Mission.

In November, 1881, when Bro. Ola C. Tellefsen ventured to preach in Langesund, Norway, he was called into court and sentenced to pay a fine of 32 kroner, besides expenses of court, which was 60 kroner, or 92 kroner altogether.

Elder Hans O. Magleby, about this time, was sick at Trondhjem and called for assistance. In Frederikshald the police summoned the presiding Elder to court because he had held religious services and Sunday school and baptized a 15-year-old boy. He was called into the police court five different times for examination. The officers demanded that he should bring the branch records into court, which he refused to do, in consequence of which he was cast into a dark cellar and confined there one and one-half hours. In Christiania the police officers acted very humanely, and the meetings were very well attended. Young men who were sent out as missionaries

were the means of doing much good in spreading the work.

In 1881, 38 Elders from Zion arrived in Copenhagen, Denmark, a missionaries to the Scandinavian Mission. They arrived in the following order: Hans Jörgensen of Pleasant Grove, Jens Jacobson of Fountain Green, Jens M. Christensen of Moroni, Jens Hansen of Mill Creek, Utah, Jörgen Jörgensen of Ovid, Idaho, Rasmus Christoffersen of Lynne, Lars Peter Christensen of Richfield, Utah, Joseph R. Linval of Paris, Idaho, Jens P. Jensen of Hyrum, Oluf C. Larsen of Ephraim Rasmus Olsen of Draperville, and Tellef J. Israelsen of Hyrum, Utah arrived May 16th. Chr. D. Fjeldsted of Logan (on his second mission) Peter Sundwall of Fairview, Solomon Peterson of Santaquin, Sören Chr. Petersen of Elsinore, Niels Heilesen of Glenwood, Anders Larson of Washington, Niels H. Börresen of Spring City, Chr. Christensen of Big Cottonwood, Hans O. Magleby and James Yorgason (Jörgenson) of Moroni, and Andrew Eliason of Logan, Utah, arrived on Sept. 1st. Jens. Chr. Frost, Andrew C. Nielsen and Andrew L. Andersen of Ephraim, Morten Rasmussen and Thos. Chr. Christensen of Mt. Pleasant, Andreas Hansen of Redmond, Hans C. Hansen of Gunnison, Bendt Larsen of Monroe, Frederik Peterson of Grantsville, and John N. Olson of West Jordan, Utah, arrived Nov. 5th. Hans A. Hansen of Logan and Hans Olin Hansen of Hyrum (on his second mission) arrived Nov. 15th. Chr. Hansen, Lars Mortensen and Henrik C. Jensen of Brigham City, Utah, arrived Dec. 7th.

Hans Jörgensen was appointed to labor on the island of Fyen and later as translator in the mission office. Jens Jacobsen was appointed to labor in the Aarhus Conference.

ens M. Christensen was appointed to labor in the Aarhus Conference and later as president of said conference. Jens Hansen, who had already labored one year as a mis-

JENS HANSEN,
Born March 15, 1837, at Gjerslöv, Holbæk amt, Sjælland, Denmark, was baptized by J. P. Thyggesen April 5, 1857, and labored as a missionary on Sjælland about four years before he emigrated to Utah in 1862. He became a resident of Mill Creek, Salt Lake County; called on a mission in 1880, and after laboring in the United States for about a year he was transferred to the Scandinavian Mission, where he arrived in May, 1881. There he labored in the Copenhagen Conference until June, 1882, principally on the Island of Sjælland. After returning from his mission, he acted as counselor to the Bishop of Mill Creek Ward about seventeen years. Bro. Hansen died at Wilford, Salt Lake County, Sept. 9, 1917.

sionary in the United States, was appointed to labor in the Copenhagen Conference. Jörgen Jörgensen was appointed to labor in the Copenhagen Conference, but returned home shortly on account of ill health. Rasmus Christoffersen was appointed to labor in the Copenhagen Conference, Lars P. Christensen in the Aalborg Conference, part of the time as president. Joseph R. Linvall was appointed to labor in the Stockholm,

Jens Peter Jensen in the Aalborg, Oluf Chr. Larsen and Tellef Johan Israelsen in the Christiania and Rasmus Olsen in the Copenhagen Conference. Chr. D. Fjeldsted came to preside over the Scandinavian Mission. Peter Sundwall was appointed to labor in the mission office in Copenhagen. Solomon Petersen was called to labor in the Göteborg, Sören Chr. Petersen and Niels Heilesen in the Aalborg and Anders Larson in the Skåne Conference. Niels H. Börresen was appointed to labor in Norway, and Chr. Christensen in the Copenhagen Conference, Denmark. Hans O. Magleby was appointed to labor in Norway

CHRISTIAN DANIEL FJELDSTED
Born Feb. 20, 1829, in Sundbyvester, near Copenhagen, on the island of Amager, Denmark, was baptized by Andreas Christian Samuel Hansen Jan. 20, 1852; ordained an Elder, July 25, 1853, labored as a missionary in Denmark about four years, part of the time as president of the Aalborg conference, and emigrated to Utah in 1858; located in the Sugar House Ward, and later in Logan, Cache County; was ordained a Seventy Feb. 5, 1859; filled a mission to Scandinavia in 1867-1870, presiding over the Aalborg Conference, Denmark, and still later in Norway; filled another mission to Scandinavia in 1881-1884, presiding over the Scandinavian Mission; was set apart as one of the First Seven Presidents of Seventies, April 28, 1884; filled a third mission to Scandinavia in 1888-1890. Later he filled several short missions to Scandinavia and died in Salt Lake City, Dec. 23, 1905.

and later to preside over the Copenhagen Conference. James Yorgason was appointed to labor in and afterwards to preside over the Skåne Conference. Andrew Eliason was appointed to labor in the Göteborg Conference, Jens Chr. Frost in the Copenhagen and later in the Aalborg Conference, Anders Chr. Nielsen in the Aarhus and later in the Copenhagen Conference, Andrew L. Andersen and Morten Rasmussen in the Aarhus Conference, Thos. Chr. Christensen and Andreas Hansen in the

Aalborg Conference, Hans. Ch Hansen in the Copenhagen Confe ence, Bendt Larsen in Norway, Fre erik Peterson in the Göteborg Co ference and John N. Olson in tl Skåne Conference. Hans A. Hans« was appointed to labor in and lat to preside over the Christiania Co ference. Hans O. Hansen (on h second mission) was appointed labor as a traveling Elder in Norwa Chr. Hansen and Lars Mortensen the Copenhagen and Henrik C. Je sen in the Copenhagen and later the Christiania Conference.

CHAPTER 65 (1882)

Elders Jens C. Frost and Sören Sörens« imprisoned. in Thisted, Denmark—Three co panies of emigrating Saints leave for Utah Persecutions in Horsens, Denmark—Arrival 51 Elders from Zion.

At a special meeting held in C« penhagen, Jan. 26, 1882, a Y. L. M I. A. was organized in the Coper hagen branch with Inger Marie La« sen as president, Sophie Hansen Eg«

LARS MORTENSEN,

Missionary to Scandinavia, was born Dec. 29, 1831, in North Sjælland, Denmark, was baptized by Rasmus Jensen June 6, 1858, and emigrated to Utah in 1871, walking across the Plains. He married Mary Olsen Sept. 23, 1861, and by her became the father of nine children, namely, Icaac Lars, Anne Mary, Josephine Dorthea, Ellen Johanne, Lise, Caroline, Anders Olof, Lars, jun., and Emma Leonora. Later he married Susannah Mary Jensen, who bore him five children, namely, Rosine, Lawrence Lars, Morten Alfred, Susannah Rosetta and Carl Christian. Lars Mortensen was ordained a Seventy Oct. 12, 1862, and a High Priest July 5, 1890. He filled a mission to Scandinavia in 1881-1883, laboring in the Copenhagen Conference, Denmark. Bro. Mortensen was the pioneer blacksmith of Brigham City, worked in a nail factory in 1860, was the only wheelwright in Boxelder County for several years, and was a member of a military band. He died in Brigham City March 25, 1912.

INGER MARIE LARSEN,

First president of the Y. L. M. I. A. of th« Copenhagen Branch, Denmark, was born Feb 5, 1855, at Nakskov, Maribo amt, Denmark She emigrated to Utah in 1882 and was mar ried to the late Hans J. Christiansen Aug. 30 1883. She is the mother of four children.

sen, first, and Ida Jonasson, second counselor; Marie Hansen, secretary.

A company of emigrating Scandinavian Saints (the 58th company from Scandinavia), sailed from

SOPHY HANSEN EGESEN VALENTINE,

Wife of Bishop August Valentine, was born in 1862 at Nykjöbing, on the Island of Falster, Denmark, her father being a merchant of that town. Her mother died when she was about eight years old and she was sent to America, where she resided with an aunt living in Racine, Wis., and also spent some time with her grandparents in Spencer, Clay Co., Iowa, they being among the pioneers of that part of the state. In Racine she attended the Danish-Norwegian school and at 14 years of age was confirmed a member of the Lutheran Church. She also attended American schools and showed considerable ability in English literature. When she was 18 years of age her father desired her to return to Denmark, which she did, and again prosecuted her literary studies, although much against her father's wishes. Having become acquainted with some Latter-day Saints, she was baptized in 1881 and emigrated to Utah in 1885, and the same year was married to August Valentine and later became the mother of six children. She has published many short stories in both the English and Church and in literary pursuits.

Copenhagen. June 16, 1882, on the steamers "Albano" and "Bravo." "Albano" had on board 573 emigrating Saints, besides 15 returning missionaries, viz., Simon Christensen, Jens Iver Jensen, Christian Hogensen, Jens Hansen, Lars Nielsen, James J. Hansen, Jacob P. Olsen, Lars K. Larsen, James S. Jensen, Ole C. Tellefsen. Chr. Christensen, Peter A.

Löfgren, James P. Larsen, Hans E. Nielsen and Rasmus Olsen. The smaller steamer "Bravo" had on board 125 emigrating Saints and seven returning missionaries, viz., Nils O. Anderson, Martin Jacobsen, Swen Erikson, Carl P. Warnick, Nils Henrikson, James H. Hansen and Anders Larsen. After successful voyages across the North Sea both steamers arrived safely in Hull, England, June 19th, the "Albano" in the morning and the "Bravo" in the afternoon. The emigrants proceeded by train to Liverpool, where all embarked on the steamer "Nevada," which sailed on the 21st with a total of 933 Latter-day Saints on board. Of these 201 were Britishers, 694 Scandinavians, 2 Hollanders, 33 returning missionaries and 3 visitors. The whole company was led by Elder Robert R. Irvine and arrived safely in New York July 2nd. From there the emigrants started by railway the following day, July 3rd, on their westward journey, had a pleasant and speedy journey to Utah, arriving in Ogden July 9, 1882. The next day (July 10th) those who were going south arrived in Salt Lake City. Two children died on the journey.

Another company of Scandinavian Saints (292 souls) sailed from Copenhagen Aug. 28, 1882, by the steamer "Argo," under the direction of Elder Hans J. Christiansen and five other returning missionaries, viz., Carl H. Lundberg, Anders G. Johnson, Rasmus Berntzon, Charles Samuelson and Christian Hansen. After a stormy and unpleasant voyage the "Argo" arrived at Hull, England, and in the afternoon the emigrants were conveyed by railway to Liverpool. There they embarked at once on the steamer "Wyoming" and sailed on Sept. 2nd, together with emigrating Saints from other parts of Europe. The company thus augmented consisted of 298 British, 287 Scandinavian and

54 Swiss and German Saints, besides 16 returning missionaries and seven returning Utah visitors—altogether 662 souls. When the Scandinavians left Copenhagen their number was 292, but a Swedish sister and her children were left in Liverpool, on account of sickness. After a successful voyage the "Wyoming" arrived in New York Sept. 12th, and the next day (Sept. 13th) the company proceeded westward by railroad to Utah, under the leadership of Elder Wm. Cooper and arrived in Ogden and Salt Lake City, Nov. 10, 1882.

A company of Scandinavian Saints (the 60th company from Scandinavia), 108 or 109 souls, left Copenhagen Oct. 13, 1882, on the steamer "Cato" under the leadership of Elder Peter O. Hansen, assisted by Elders Lars N. Larson, Jens Jenson and Andrew O. Anderson, returning missionaries. After a successful voyage across the North Sea, the "Cato" arrived safely at Hull, England, on the 16th, and the Saints were conveyed to Liverpool by train the same day. Together with 279 British Saints and 24 returning missionaries from Great Britain, they embarked on the steamer "Abyssinia," which sailed Oct. 21st. Elder Geo. Stringham was appointed leader of this company. The voyage across the Atlantic Ocean lasted 13 days, on account of unfavorable weather, but the company reached New York safely Nov. 3rd. From there the journey was continued westward by train to Ogden and Salt Lake City, where the emigrants arrived Nov. 10, 1882. One death occurred, that of a two-year-old child, near Laramie. Not for many years had there been so large an emigration from Europe as during 1882.

In the latter part of 1882, the Elders who labored in Horsens, Denmark, were compelled to stop their evening meetings, because a mob had assumed a threatening attitude towards them, and the police denied them protection. The brethren were advised to take legal action against a Mr. Eltsholtz, and through the newspapers prove that he had lied about the "Mormons." But as the papers, as a rule, refused to publish anything in favor of the Latter-day Saints, nothing of that kind was done. The missionaries in Horsens had almost invariably to pay for their food and lodgings, and even then they could scarcely obtain what they needed, except at the regularly licensed public houses.

About this time, also, Elders Christian Poulsen and A. Jensen were arrested in Thisted, Aalborg Conference, Denmark, for preaching the gospel, and, pending trial, they were imprisoned for several days, being held in such close confinement that their friends were not permitted to visit them.

Under date of Jan. 2, 1883, Elder Jens C. Frost, speaking of the two Elders imprisoned at Thisted, writes that he and Elder Sören Sörensen applied for the privilege of attending their trial, but were refused. However, when the examination was over, and the bitterness had somewhat modified, as the brethren refused to pay the fine, preferring to spend three days in prison, Brothers Frost and Sörensen were summoned to appear at the police office, where they were interrogated as follows:

Question: Are you Mormons?

Answer: Yes, we believe in the doctrines of the Latter-day Saints.

Q.—Where are you from?

A.—America.

Q.—What are you doing here?

A.—We visit our friends.

Q.—What are you preaching?

A.—The doctrines of Jesus Christ.

Q.—Where do you hold your meetings?

A.—Anywhere.

Q.—But we suppose you do not hold any here?

A.—Yes, if we get an opportunity to do so.

Remark.—Then you shall be honored with our supervision.

A.—Thank you, we shall be pleased for you to honor us with your presence.

These and other unnecessary questions were put to the Elders, who desired to know what particular paragraph of the law they had violated. This question embittered the chief officer, who in a most uncivil tone commanded them to "shut up," and ordered them out of the police quarters at once, while Elders Chr. Poulsen and A. Jensen were cast into prison. The following day, Brothers Frost and Sörensen asked for permission to visit the imprisoned brethren, but were denied the privilege. They then left the town. The imprisoned brethren rejoiced for having had the privilege to suffer for Christ's sake. The police officers, who kept their books and pamphlets, said that they intended to burn them.

The year 1882 witnessed the arrival of 51 Elders from Zion, who had been called to labor as missionaries in Scandinavia. They arrived in Copenhgen on the following dates: Lars Svendsen of Moroni (on his second mission), Niels Rasmussen of Parowan, Chr. Poulsen of Richfield, and Sören Madsen of Milton, Utah, arrived May 3rd. John Anderson of Fillmore, Johan B. Hesse of Monroe, Gisle E. Bjarnason and Peter Valgaardson of Spanish Fork, Utah, arrived June 3rd. Emil Andersen of American Fork, arrived Aug. 21st. Niels C. Skougaard of Koosharem, Halvor Olsen of Richfield, Utah, Jeppa Monson and Anders Jonsson of St. Charles, Idaho, Hans Jörgen Bruun and Hans Poulsen of Mt. Pleasant. Chas. E. Anderson and

Hans Andersen of Logan, Jeppa Nilsson of Pleasant Grove, Jakob J. H. Jensen of Mt. Pleasant, Chr. John Christiansen of Fountain Green, Chas. A. Tietjen of Santaquin, Lars H. Outzen of Richfield, Peter Christensen of Elsinore, Nils Johnson of Santaquin, John Capson of East Mill Creek, and Nils W. Anderson of Ephraim, Utah, arrived Sept. 12th. Mons A. Rosenlund of Mt. Pleasant, Lars P. Johnson of Hooper City, Andrew O. Anderson of Glenwood, and Peter Anderson of Peterson, Utah, arrived Oct. 3rd. Carl August Ek of Logan, Andrew J. Hansen of Big Cottonwood, Andreas Peterson of Logan, Lars Peter Ovesen of

SÖREN SÖRENSEN

Was born Sept. 10, 1845, in Mygdal, Hjörring Amt, Denmark, the son of Sören Christian Sörensen and Marie Hansen. Becoming a convert to the gospel, he was baptized in March, 1864; was ordained to the Priesthood and labored as a local missionary in the Aalborg Conference about three years. Emigrating to Utah in 1867, he crossed the plains with ox team. Soon after his arrival in Utah he married Anne M. Nielsen in Salt Lake City and after residing in Pleasant Grove two years and in Levan six years, he became a pioneer settler of Elsinore, Sevier County, in 1876. In 1882-1884 he filled a mission to Scandinavia, laboring in the Aalborg Conferece. Elder Sörensen, who is the father of nine children, six of whom are still (1927) living, acted for several years as a High Councilor in the Sevier Stake, and is a farmer and merchant by occupation.

Ephraim, Charles Jensen of Redmond, Gustaf Anderson of Grantsville, Jens Olsen of Ephraim, Bengt M. Ravsten, and Chr. Larsen of Logan, James P. Olson of Ephraim, Andrew Amundsen of South Jordan (on his second mission), Thomas S. Lund and Sören Pedersen of Ephraim, Andrew Anderson of Union, Sören Sörensen of Elsinore, Niels P. Petersen of Richfield, John Olson of Moroni, Jens Peter Jensen of Ephraim, Olaus Johnson Nordstrand and Chr. H. Steffensen of South Cottonwood, and Andrew H. Anderson of Huntsville, Utah, arrived Nov. 6th, 1882.

Lars Svendsen, Sören Madsen, Hans J. Bruun, Hans Poulsen, Hans Andersen, Jacob J. H. Jensen, Chr. Johan Christiansen, Andrew J. Hansen, Charles Jensen, Chr. Larsen and

JEPPA NILSSON

Missionary in Sweden, was born Oct. 28, 1834, at Ullatofta, Sallerup parish, Malmöhus län, Sweden. In 1865 (June 21st) he married Anna Svensdotter, who bore him five children (four girls and one boy). Jeppa Nilsson and wife were baptized April 5, 1871. Emigrating from Sweden, they arrived in Salt Lake City July 24, 1873. He filled two missions to Sweden, one in 1882-1884 and another in 1904-1905, laboring in the Skåne Conference on both missions. Bro. Nilsson died in Pleasant Grove, Utah, Sept. 23, 1914. He had been a faithful Church worker since he was first baptized, was a successful farmer and highly respected in the community where he resided. His son, Sven, performed a mission to Sweden in 1899-1901.

Sören Pedersen were appointed to labor in the Aarhus Conference. John B. Hesse was appointed to labor in, and later to preside over the Aarhus Conference. Niels Rasmussen, Emil

JEPPA MONSON

Born Dec. 17, 1842, at Bertilstorp, Melby parish, Christianstad län, Sweden. He was baptized in September, 1870; emigrated to Utah in 1871; married Nellie Mattsson Oct. 31, 1871, the ceremony being performed by Apostle Joseph F. Smith in Salt Lake City. Bro. Monson has filled two missions to Sweden, one in 1882-1884, laboring in the Göteborg and Skåne Conferences, and another 1898-1900, again laboring in the Skåne Conference. Bro. Monson lived in St. Charles, Bear Lake County, Idaho, for about 44 years and at present (1927) is residing in Smithfield, Utah.

Andersen, Jens Olsen and Jens P. Jensen were appointed to labor in the Copenhagen Conference. Christian Poulsen, Lars H. Outzen, Lars P. Ovesen, Thomas Sörensen Lund, Sören Sörensen and Niels P. Petersen were appointed to labor in the Aalborg Conference. John Anderson, Charles E. Anderson, Peter Christensen, Nils Johnson, and Nils W. Anderson were appointed to labor in the Stockholm Conference, and Carl August Ek was appointed to labor in and later to preside over the Stockholm Conference. Gisle E.

jarnason was appointed to preside
ver the Icelandic Mission with Peter
algaardson as his assistant. Niels
hr. Skougaard, Halvor Olsen, Peter
nderson, Andrew Amundsen, Olaus
hnson and Christian H. Steffensen
ere appointed to labor in the Chris-
ania Conference. Jeppa Monson
ad Anders Jönsson were appointed
· labor in the Göteborg Conference
ad afterwards in the Skåne Conrence. Jeppa Nilsson, Chas. A.
ietjen, John Capson, Mons A.
osenlund, Andrew O. Anderson,
ames P. Olsen, Andrew Anderson
ad John Olson were appointed to
abor in the Skåne Conference. Lars
. Johnson, Gustaf Anderson, Bengt
l. Ravsten and Andrew H. Ander-
n were appointed to labor in the
öteborg Conference.

Andreas Peterson was appointed to
abor in the Stockholm Conference.
uring his mission he walked 3,408
iles, held 190 meetings with straners and baptized 42 souls.

CHAPTER 66 (1883)

Large companies of emigrants leave for
on—Apostle John Henry Smith visits Scan-
navia—Elder Andrew Amundsen in Bergen,
orway—Arrival of 44 Elders from Zion—
der Anthon H. Lund succeeds Chr. D.
eldsted as president of the mission.

A company of Scandinavian Saints
103 souls), the 61st company from
candinavia, with five returning Eld-
s, namely, Nils R. Lindahl (ap-
ointed president or leader of the
ompany), Oluf C. Larsen, Jens P.
nsen, Hans C. Hansen, and Joseph
. Linvall, left Copenhagen, April
1883, on the steamer "Cato" bound
r Utah. The "Cato" arrived in
ull, England, on the 9th. Proceed-
g by train to Liverpool they there
ined a company of British Saints
d by Elder David McKay and sailed
om Liverpool April 11th, on the
eamer "Nevada," which arrived in
ew York on the 22nd. The follow-
g day (April 23rd) the journey

was continued by train to Ogden and
Salt Lake City, where the company
arrived April 30, 1883. The whole
company, numbering 352 souls, was
made up of 235 British and 103
Scandinavian Saints, 13 returning
Elders and one visitor.

A small company of emigrating
Saints (12 persons) sailed from
Copenhagen May 11, 1883, on the
steamer "Bravo," bound for Utah,
together with four returning Elders
from Zion, namely, Lars Mortensen,
Rasmus Christoffersen, Jens Jacobsen and Niels H. Börreson. On their
arrival in Liverpool, England, they
were united with a large company
of British, German and Swiss Saints
(about 400 souls), which sailed from
Liverpool per steamship "Nevada"
May 16, 1883. After a pleasant
voyage, the company landed in New
York, May 27th, and reached Salt
Lake City, Utah, by rail, June 2nd.
While journeying through the State
of Wyoming, an axle broke on a
loaded car, causing five cars to leave
the track, but none of the emigrants
were hurt in the accident.

A large company of the season's
emigrating Saints from Scandinavia,
503 in number, together with 18 re-
turning missionaries, sailed from
Copenhagen June 15th, 1883, on the
steamers "Pacific" and "Milo." The
returning missionaries were: Hans
O. Magleby (leader of the company),
Andrew C. Nielsen, Lars Peter Chris-
tensen, Sören Chr. Petersen, Niels
Heilesen, Andreas Hansen, Thos.
Chr. Christensen, Jens M. Christen-
sen, Morten Rasmussen, Lars Svend-
sen, Tellef Johan Israelsen, Bendt
Larsen, Andrew Eliason, Solomon
Petersen, Lars P. Johnson, James
Yorgason and Hans Olin Hansen.
Elder Hakon Anderson from Kanosh,
Utah, who arrived in Copenhagen,
May 4, 1883, also accompanied the
emigrants; he returned on account
of poor health.

Among the emigrating Saints was Elder Hugo D. E. Peterson, who had spent about two and a half years in the mission office as writer for "Nordstjernan" and attending to other routine work required of him by his superiors. He had labored under President Niels Wilhelmsen for about eight months and nearly two years under Pres. Christian D. Fjeldsted.

The steamers "Pacific" and "Milo," after a rough voyage across the North Sea, arrived at Hull, England, on the 18th, whence the company went by train to Liverpool. Here it was joined by 171 British Saints and four returning missionaries and sailed on the 20th of June on the steamer "Nevada," which arrived in New York July 1st. The company proceeded westward by train the same day, and a part of the company arrived in Ogden July 7th, while the reminder arrived there next morning (July 8th). Those who desired to go farther south than Ogden arrived in Salt Lake City at noon July 8th. A little child of English parentage died in Omaha, and an old Swedish brother, Ola Rasmusson of Slimminge, Skåne, died soon after the arrival of the train in Salt Lake City.

A company of Icelandic Saints, consisting of 18 persons, including Eirik Olafsson, all destined for Spanish Fork, Utah, arrived in Liverpool, July 9, 1883, and continued the journey under the direction of John A. Sutton, on the 14th, per steamship "Wisconsin."

Another company of emigrating Scandinavian Saints (284 in number), the 64th company of emigrants from the Scandinavian Mission, left Copenhagen Aug. 24, 1883, on the steamer "Bravo." The following returning missionaries accompanied the emigrants: Hans A. Hansen (leader of the company), Hans Andersen,

Anders L. Andersen, Jens C. Fro Henrik C. Jensen, Frederik Peters and John N. Olson. In the morni of Aug. 27th the company arrived Hull, England, and proceeded then by rail to Liverpool. On the 29 the company, having embarked the steamer "Nevada," left the do and anchored in the River Merse Here the company was organized f the voyage with Elder Peter F. Gc as president. The company was nc composed of 264 British, 284 Scan navian and 106 Swiss and Germ Saints and 28 returning missionari There were also 120 other passenge on board. The steamer brought passengers safely to New York Se¡ 7, 1883, and the Saints were th transported west by rail to Ogd and Salt Lake City, arriving the Monday, Sept. 17, 1883, all wel

A company of 122 emigrati Saints and seven returning missio aries, bound for Utah (the 65th en grating company), sailed frc Copenhagen Oct. 19, 1883, on t steamer "Milo," in charge of Ha Jörgensen. The other returning El ers were: Peter S. Sherner, Cl Poulsen, Niels Larsen, Anders Jc son (from St. Charles, Idaho), Jä gen Daniel Olsen and John Wir After a stormy voyage across t North Sea, the company arrived la in the evening of the 22nd in Hu England, and the next day took tra for Liverpool. Here the emigra¡ were lodged in the "Temperan Hotel" until the 27th, when they e¡ barked on the steamer "Wisconsir together with some British Sair and sailed from Liverpool in t evening. After a rough voyage, caus by unfavorable and stormy weath the ship arrived safely with precious cargo in New York, N¡ 7th. On the following day (N¡ 8th), the journey westward was I gun on the railway and the compa¡ arrived safely and well in Ogden the evening of Nov. 14th. The following day at noon the south-bound train brought that portion of the company to Salt Lake City, whose destination was in that direction. Twenty emigrating S a i n t s, in charge of Elder Mikkael Andreas Faldmo, sailed from Christiania, Oct. 20, 1883, bound for Utah. Among he emigrants were Sister Anna K. G. Widtsoe,a widow, with her two children (John A. and Osborne J. P.).

MIKKAEL ANDREAS FALDMO,

orn Aug. 27, 1856, at Mosjön, Nordland, orway, is the son of Gabriel Sörensen Faldmo nd Beret Marie Andersen. He was baptized pril 17, 1881, ordained an Elder July 31, 1881, nd set apart to preside over the Frederikshald ranch. As a missionary he suffered considerable persecution, being arrested three times nd sentenced once to a bread and water diet. e was transferred to the west coast of Noray, in company with Elder Andrew Amundn, where, after baptizing several persons, e assisted in organizing a branch at Bergen. October, 1883, he emigrated to Utah in arge of a small company of Norwegian aints, including Sister Anna K. G. Widtsoe d her two sons. Bro. Faldmo made his me in Logan, Cache County, and on June 1884, was united in marriage to Hanna onstanse Jakobsen, who bore him ten chilen. In 1915-1917 he again filled a mission Norway and presided over the Trondhjem onference. At present (1927) he resides in lt Lake City.

lder Faldmo had labored over two ears as a missionary in Norway. is little company of Norwegian

Saints joined the larger company from Denmark and Sweden in England, and with them crossed the At-

ANNA KARINE GAARDEN WIDTSOE,

Who emigrated to Utah in 1883, was born June 4, 1849, on Titran, Island of Frojen, Thondhjem Amt, Norway. Her father, Peder O. Gaarden, was the chief or royal pilot at Titran; her mother, Beret Martha J. Haavig, was the daughter of a wealthy real estate owner. Anna received a liberal education and was married to John A. Widtsoe, a prominent educator, Dec. 29, 1870, but was left a widow with two children, Feb. 14, 1878. Soon afterwards she was engaged as a teacher at the Namsos industrial school. Becoming a convert to "Mormonism," she was baptized April 1, 1881, by Anthon L. Skanchy, and acted as counselor and secretary in the Relief Society of the Trondhjem Branch. Emigrating to Utah in 1883, she located at Logan, Cache County, Utah, where she acted as a counselor in the Logan First Ward Relief Society and held other positions of trust. Sister Widtsoe also labored in the interest of woman's suffrage and took an active part among the Scandinavian sisters in Utah. She died in Salt Lake City, July 11, 1919.

lantic on the S. S. "Wisconsin," which sailed from Liverpool Oct. 27, 1883. Apostle John Henry Smith, Pres. of the European Mission, accompanied by James Wrathall, arrived in Copenhagen, July 11, 1883, on a visit to Scandinavia. During their visit these brethren attended meetings in Copenhagen, Malmö, Stockholm and Christiania, and left Den-

mark for Stettin, Germany, July
30th. Pres. Smith's visit to Scandinavia was a source of great joy to
the Elders and Saints generally, who

listened with great attention to his
spirited and inspiring sermons.

In October, 1883, the Saints in
Malmö, Sweden, hired a new hall,
after which the meetings were better
attended in that city than they had
been before. At this time, Oct.
26, 38 native missionaries, besides the Elders from Zion, were engaged in preaching the gospel in
Scandinavia. Besides these, about
90 of the local brethren spent their
Sundays in going from house to
house to bear testimony to the truth
of the gospel. The distribution of

JOHN A. WIDTSOE,

Born Jan. 31, 1872, on the Island of Frojen,
Trondhjem Amt, Norway, was baptized April
3, 1884, by Anthon L. Skanchy; emigrated
to Utah with his mother and younger brother
in 1883; located in Logan, Cache County,
Utah; acted in various Church positions in the
Logan First Ward, and in Cache Stake; graduated from the Brigham Young College in 1891,
and from Harvard University, Cambridge,
Massachusetts, with the highest honors, in
1894; served as professor of chemistry in the
Utah Agricultural College in Logan in 1894-
1898; was ordained a Seventy and set apart
as a missionary and to study in Europe, August 5, 1898, traveled and studied on the continent of Europe until 1900; introduced the
gospel in Titran, Norway, and took the degrees of A. M. and Ph. D. from the University of Göttingen, Germany, in 1899. Upon
his return to Utah in 1900 he was made director of the Utah Agricultural College experiment station; became director of the department of agriculture in the Brigham Young
University in 1905-1907; president of the Utah
Agricultural College in 1907-1916; president
of the University of Utah in 1916-1921. During this time he served in a number of important church positions, including senior presidency of the 178th Quorum of Seventy, and
membership on the general board of the
Young Men's Mutual Improvement Association. He has written extensively, both in
behalf of the gospel and industrial education,
and reclamation, has served at various times
on reclamation commissions for the United
States government, the Dominion of Canada,
and various western states, and has held a
variety of important positions. He was chosen
a member of the Quorum of Twelve in 1921,
and in October, 1927, was called to preside
over the European Mission, succeeding Apost'e
James F. Talmage in that position.

OSBORNE J. P. WIDTSOE

Was born Dec. 12, 1877, in Namsos, Norway
emigrated with his mother and older brothe
to Utah 'in 1883; located in Logan, Cach
County, Utah, where he was baptized in 1886
served as a counselor in the Y. M. M. I. A
of the Logan First Ward, and as an activ
Sunday School worker. He graduated from
the Utah Agricultural College with the degre
of B. S. in 1897; was ordained a Sevent
and filled a mission to the Society Islands i
1897-1899. After his return home he a
tended Harvard University, where he too
the degree of M. A., and later became pres
dent of the L. D. S. University. In 1919 l
was ordained a Bishop and set apart t
preside over the Nineteenth Ward, Salt Lak
City, and later was made a member of tl
general board of Y. M. M. I. A. In 1915 l
became head of the English department
the University of Utah. Elder Widtsoe die
in Salt Lake City, March 14, 1920.

tracts was prosecuted as vigorously as circumstances would allow. The laws forbid the selling of pamphlets, and the enemies of the Saints were seeking to catch the missionaries in these acts of selling tracts, in order to cause them trouble; yet tracts and pamphlets to the amount of nearly 9000 kronor had been disposed of among the people. Some of the missionaries penetrated the dreary wilds of northern Sweden and even crossed the boundary line between Sweden and Russian Finland, leaving here and there a message of glad tidings in print, for the enlightenment of the people. About one thousand souls emigrated from Scandinavia to Utah in 1883, and money to the amount of 120,000 kroner had been sent by brethren in America to help emigrate their friends and relatives. Nearly all who could raise means enough to emigrate did so, and those who were left were very poor and scarcely able to do very much towards carrying the burden of the mission.

Elder Andrew Amundsen, who was laboring as a missionary in the western part of Norway, appealed in vain to the authorities of the city of Bergen for the privilege of holding meetings. He, however, commenced distributing tracts and endeavored to get the principles of the gospel before the people, who were in total ignorance of it, and also of the true character of the Saints, their only sources of information being the mendacious stories issued from the press and pulpit. To correct some of these statements, he wrote an article, giving facts in relation to the Saints and their history, but the editors refused to publish it. After a while he commenced holding meetings in a private house, but suspicion was aroused and the owner of the house was summoned. Not thinking any harm would result from it, this man answered all the questions that

1 8

were put to him, and the result was that Elder Amundsen was arrested for preaching and fined 85 kroner, which, according to the "Mormon" custom of paying such fines in that country, he settled by suffering himself to be lodged in prison for five days, not, however, before he had borne his testimony to the court officials. While in prison, he spent most of his time fasting and praying, and the jailor occasionally spent hours at a time listening to him explaining the principles of the gospel. After his imprisonment he held several meetings in the country districts, and the first out-door meetings, he thinks, that have been held in Norway. Previous to this no missionary work had been done in Bergen for 30 years.

In the year 1883, forty-four Utah Elders, assigned to labor in the Scandinavian Mission, arrived in Copenhagen, Denmark, in the following order: Hakon Anderson of Kanosh, Frederik Julius Christiansen of Mayfield, Lars M. Bood of Salt Lake City, Christian Nilsson of Spring City, Utah, Niels Larsen of Montpelier, Idaho, Andrew Andersen of Ephraim, Martin Jensen of Mantua, Jörgen Daniel Olsen of Fillmore, Thorwald A. Thoresen of Hyrum, Gustave L. Rosengren of Union Ward, Andrew Christensen of Fairview, Frederik Ludvigsen of Gunnison, Chas J. A. Lindquist and John Hyrum Anderson of Logan, Jörgen Hansen of Provo, Peter S. Sherner of Ogden, Charles W. Knudsen of Brigham City, Utah, Christian Nielsen of Portneuf, Idaho, Joseph Monson of Richmond, Hans Poulsen of Plain City, Samuel P. Nielsen of Smithfield, John P. Ipsen of Mantua. Lars Peter Jensen of Mayfield. and Emil Erickson of Spring City. Utah, arrived May 4th. Daniel K. Brown of Levan. Ole Sörensen of Fountain Green, Charles J. Christensen of

Ephraim, Utah, Niels Petersen of Bloomington, Idaho, Lars F. Swalberg of Gunnison, August Svenson of Spanish Fork, John Wink and

ANDREW CHRISTENSEN

Was born Dec. 16, 1839, at Skuldelev, Copenhagen amt, Denmark, the son of Christian and Karen Petersen, joined the Church in 1855, emigrated to Utah in 1860, crossed the Atlantic in the ship "William Tapscott" and the Plains in Reuben Eldredge's freight company. He was ordained a Seventy in 1861 and in 1862 he married Anna Rasmussen, who was born April 19, 1835, at Krokstad, Trondhjem amt, Norway, the daughter of Syver Rasmussen and Ingeborg Haldorsen. In 1883-1885 Elder Christensen filled a mission to Scandinavia, laboring in the Copenhagen Conference. He was ordained a High Priest in 1902 by John B. Maiben, and died Feb. 12, 1926, in Fairview, Sanpete County, Utah.

Martin Christoffersen of Salt Lake City, Utah, arrived June 5th. Anthon H. Lund of Ephraim (on his second mission), arrived Sept. 28th. Hans D. Pettersson of West Weber, Mons Monson of Moroni, Oley Oleson of Hooper, Albin C. Anderson of Moroni, August Valentine and Lars Larsen of Brigham City, and Ole Hansen of Smithfield, Utah, arrived Nov. 7th. Mads Frederik Theobald Christensen of Fairview, Andrew P. Renström, Andrew J. Anderson and Niels C. Mortensen of Huntsville, Utah, arrived Nov. 13th, 1883.

Hakon Anderson, Lars M. Bood, Chas J. A. Lindquist, Lars Frederik Swalberg, August Svenson, John Wink, Mons Monson and Andrew P. Renström were appointed to labor in the Stockholm Conference. Gustaf Larson Rosengren was appointed to labor in the Stockholm Conference and later to preside over the Göteborg Conference. Oley Oleson was appointed to labor in the Stockholm

CHARLES J. A. LINDQUIST

Missionary in 'Sweden, was born July 24, 1864, in Salt Lake City, Utah, the son of Niis Aaron Lindquist and Josephine C. Höglund. He was the oldest of eleven children and emigrated with his parents to Utah in 1863. Three years later the family moved to Logan. Cache County, and young Charles worked with his father making furniture and caskets. During his mission in Sweden (1883-1885) he presided in the Eskilstuna, Vestmanland and Dalarne branches. In Logan he labored in the Y. M. M. I. Associations, but moved to Ogden Jan. 12, 1887. In 1888 (Aug 16th) he married Amelia C. Ness, who bore him eight children, seven of whom are still living. His wife died April 3, 1914, and on May 12, 1915 he married Ada C. Theurer, who bore him three children. In 1903-1905 he filled a second mission to Sweden, presiding over the Stockholm Conference; he selected the site for a new mission house at No. 3 Svartens gatan, Stockholm; the chapel on the premises was completed and dedicated Oct. 22, 1904 by Pres. Heber J. Grant. The property, with improvements, cost about 200,000 kronor. In the Ogden Second Ward Elder Lindquist acted as a counselor to the late Bishop Robert Mc Quarrie for ten and a half years, and he is now (1927) a member of the Weber Stake High Council.

Conference and later to preside over said conference.

Frederik J. Christiansen, Niels Larsen, Martin Jensen, Charles W. Knudsen, Christian Nielsen, Lars Peter Jensen and Daniel K. Brown were appointed to labor in the Aalborg Conference. Frederik Ludvigsen, Peter S. Sherner, Ole Hansen and Niels Chr. Mortensen were appointed to labor in the Aarhus Conference. Ole Sörensen was appointed to labor in, and later to preside over the Aar-

ANDREW P. RENSTRÖM,

Born Dec. 30, 1857, at Viksta, Upsala län, Sweden, was baptized Nov. 14, 1872; emigrated to Utah in 1873 and located in Huntsville, Utah, where he still (1927) resides. In 1883-1885 he filled a mission to Sweden, laboring in the Eskilstuna Branch and later in the northern part of Sweden. Early in 1885 he visited Finland, held meetings with a few Saints there and finished his mission in Vestmanland and Dalarne. Returning to Huntsville, he married Caroline Petersen and acted as assistant superintendent of the Huntsville Sunday School in 1888-1889. He filled a second mission to Scandinavia in 1889-1891, laboring in the Stockholm Conference and later presiding over the Göteborg Conference. On July 31, 1898, he was set apart as first counselor to Bishop David McKay of Huntsville and appointed Bishop of that Ward in 1905. He was released from that positon after the death of his wife. In 1908 he filled a home mission in the Seventh Ward, Ogden. He filled a third mission to Sweden in 1923-1925.

hus Conference. Christian Nilsson and John H. Anderson were appointed to labor in the Skåne Conference. Hans D. Petterson was appointed to labor in the Skåne Conference, part of the time as president of said conference.

Andrew Andersen, Jörgen Daniel Olsen, Andrew Christensen, Niels Petersen, August Valentine (banished May 23, 1885) and Lars Larsen were appointed to labor in the Copenhagen Conference. Mads F. T. Christensen was appointed to labor in the Copenhagen Conference and later as a translator and writer at the mission office in Copenhagen. Jörgen Hansen was appointed to labor in the Copenhagen Conference as a traveling Elder and later as president of said conference. Thorwald A. Thoresen, Joseph Monson, Hans Poulsen, Charles John Christensen, Martin Christoffersen and John P. Ipsen were appointed to labor in the Christiania Conference. Elder Ipsen was banished from Christiania. Samuel P. Nielsen, Emil Erickson, Albin C. Anderson and Andrew J. Anderson were appointed to labor in the Göteborg Conference. Anthon H. Lund, on this his second mission, was appointed to preside over the Scandinavian Mission.

A monument in honor of the late President Niels Wilhelmsen was erected on the "Assistents Kirkegaard" in Copenhagen, Denmark, Dec. 24, 1883. All the Elders from Zion laboring in the Mission had contributed to the monument and a Brother A. J. Andersen of Aarhus had made the same. The monument was composed of a light Cremer marble.

CHAPTER 67 (1884)

Local Elders do splendid missionary work in Sweden—Difficulties with mobs at Veile, Denmark—Emigration to Zion continues—President John Henry Smith visits Scandinavia—Johan Blom persecuted in Finland—Arrival of 36 Elders from Zion.

Under date of Jan. 22, 1884, Elder Carl A. Ek, president of the Stockholm conference, reported that two brave young men had recently been sent to Vermland as missionaries, and that most of the branches of the conferences were presided over by Elders from Zion. The native sons exhibited a zeal which could not be excelled in spreading literature and bearing testimony to the truth. A young brother in Norrland had already sold books for 150 kronor, during the past three months. In Eskilstuna, the Saints held their meetings in the houses of the Saints. Elder Lars F. Swalberg, in Finland, had been sought after by the civil officers, but so far he had not been arrested. Brother August S. Hedberg, who had earned the reputation of being the champion tract distributor in Norrland, wrote from Hernösand as follows:

"I have visited a large sawmill called Sandviken. In this neighborhood I came nearly receiving a whipping from a baker who tried to hit me with a large brush, but I succeeded in getting away from him; a few minutes later, however, I met the inspector, who took all my books under his arm and made me follow him to the priest, where, he said, I should soon become acquainted with 'something different.' He carried a long whip which he swung in a threatening manner, while he uttered the most foul oaths and curses. He presented me to the priest as a messenger from the deepest hell and said if I did not immediately leave the place, he would call his men together, in which case he would not be responsible for the consequences. In the meantime the priest could do nothing with me and he gave me back my books. When I left the place, they let loose a big black dog, undoubtedly thinking it would attack me, but instead of doing so it walked away. You may believe, Bro. Ek, that the inhabitants in this northern country are a hard set, but I do not mind this; at some future day they will wish that they had not acted so cruelly toward one who traveled for the purpose of offering them the greatest gift of life."

When Elder Carl A. Ek delivered the Stockholm Conference to his suc-

cessor (Oley Oleson) in Octobe 1884, he reported that since hi arrival in Sweden, or during his a ministration of the Stockholm Co ference, 1568 meetings had bee

CARL AUGUST EK

A successful missionary, born July 10, 184 at Skokloster, Upsala län, Sweden, was ba tized April 23, 1871, ordained an Elder Oc 1, 1882, and sent out to preach the gospel a local missionary. In that capacity he pr sided over the Örebro Branch in 1873-187 and then over the Stockholm Branch unt 1878, when he emigrated to Utah, and locate in Logan, Cache County. In 1882-1884, l filled a mission to Sweden, laboring first a traveling Elder in and later as president the Stockholm Conference. Returning hon he had charge of a company of emigratir Saints. He was ordained a Seventy Nov. 1 1884, removed to Salt Lake City in 1895, whe he acted as Bishop of the Twenty-fifth Wa from 1902 to 1912. He died in Salt La City, Nov. 8, 1912.

held among strangers, and 417 per sons had been baptized, of whom 62 were baptized by himself.

In the year 1860, the island Gotland was first visited by Elde Truls A. Hallgren, who commence to circulate books and pamphle and preach the gospel, both in pr vate and public meetings, and o the 13th of January, 1861, the fir aptism by divine authority took lace on the island. In April, 1861, branch was organized on Gotland, ith six members. Between the years 860 and 1884, 378 men and women ere baptized on the island. Some f these emigrated to Zion, others ent the way of all flesh, but the Gotland Branch, in July, 1884, still ad 82 members.

In 1884, the Elders laboring in the Aarhus Conference, Denmark, met with considerable success. In Veile, where there was a branch of the Church with about one hundred members, a hall was rented for holding meetings. The mobocratic spirit, which caused the Elders to cease their public meetings the year before, was counteracted by the brethren who decided to protect themselves, as the civil authorities refused them protection. Agreeable to the saying that every man is a police officer in his own house, all persons upon whose faces were stamped "disturbers of the peace," were refused admittance to the meetings of the Saints. This stand on the part of Elders had the desired effect; after that, meetings could be held in peace.

Elder Daniel K. Brown, under date of June 2, 1884, reported that a number of people had joined the Church near the town of Lögstör, in Denmark. On a certain occasion, a number of normal students from Ranum, who had heard that a "Mormon" baptism was to take place, decided to witness the same, and after the baptism had been performed, they had planned to duck the "Mormon" priest under the water. But the Elders outwitted the students by selecting another place for the holy ordinance, and the students, after being exposed to a terrific rainstorm until 4 o'clock in the morning, returned to their homes, soaked to the skin, wiser, if hot better, men.

Elder Pauli E. B. Hammer, who had labored for some time as a missionary in Austria, but had been banished from that country, arrived in Copenhagen. June 4, 1884, he

DANIEL KNUD BROWN

Was born Jan. 17, 1860, in Pleasant Grove, Utah, where his father farmed for President Daniel H. Wells; later he moved to Nephi, Juab County, where in 1880 he married Sarah M. Knowles, who bore him seven children. He filled a mission to Scandinavia in 1883-1885, laboring in the Aalborg Conference, Denmark, and a second mission in 1896-1898. On the latter mission he labored first in the Aalborg Conference, Denmark, but, being banished from Denmark for preaching the gospel, he finished his mission in Norway. At home Elder Brown was an energetic Church worker and acted as president in a quorum of Seventy. He died at Nephi Sept. 27, 1905, leaving a wife and seven children, the youngest only four months old. His widow is still alive and resides in Nephi. Elder Brown was a successful missionary and a good speaker.

was appointed to labor in the Aarhus Conference.

In Norway, Elders Niels Chr. Skougaard and Peter Olaus Olsen were sentenced, May 30, by the Christiania municipal court to pay 40 kroner in fine and 25 kroner for costs of court for having performed the ordinance of baptism.

A large company of Saints emigrating to Utah (the 66th emigrant company from Scandinavia) left

Copenhagen, April 4, 1884, per steamer "Milo." It consisted of 87 souls, including 5 returning Elders, viz., Christian D. Fjeldsted (leader of the company), Peter Sundwall, John Anderson, Sören Madsen and Nils W. Anderson, the latter having been released by the First Presidency on account of the sickness of his wife at home.

On the same day (April 4th) a small company of Saints in charge of Elder Andrew Amundsen (who was now released from his second mission to Scandinavia) left Christiania and went direct to England, where the Norwegians joined the emigrating Saints from Denmark. The "Milo" arrived at Hull, England, April 7th, in the morning, and the same day the emigrants went by train to Liverpool, where all the Scandinavians, now numbering 95 souls, were joined to a company of 207 British emigrating Saints and 11 more returning missionaries. They all sailed from Liverpool, April 9th, on the steamer "Nevada," which arrived in New York on the 19th in the evening. The next day (April 20th) the emigrants were landed at Castle Garden and on Monday, April 21st, they left New York by train westward bound for Utah. On leaving Liverpool the whole company numbered 336 souls, of whom 17 were returning missionaries.

This was the first company of emigrating Saints which arrived in Utah from Europe in 1884; it arrived in Ogden, April 27th, and 85 of the company arrived in Salt Lake City the following day, after a successful and speedy journey from their native lands. The only mishap occurring on the journey worth mentioning was the fact that a four-year old boy from some unknown source got a bottle of whiskey of which he drank quite a quantity. This caused inflammation of the brain which resulted in the death of the child.

With the departure of Pres. Chr D. Fjeldsted, Elder Anthon H. Lund took charge of the Scandinavian Mission.

ANTHON H. LUND

Was born May 15, 1844, in Aalborg, Denmark; baptized by Jacob Julander May 15, 1856. At 16 years of age he was appointed president of the Aalborg Branch and traveled extensively as a local missionary in a number of branches until he emigrated to Utah in 1862. In 1864 he went to the Missouri River as a Church teamster after emigrants. In 1870 he married Sarah Ann Peterson, daughter of Canute Peterson, which marriage was blessed with seven sons and two daughters. He filled a mission to Scandinavia in 1871-1872, managed the Ephraim Co-op store ten years, presided over the Scandinavian Mission in 1884-1885, served twice in the Utah legislature, was an officer in the Sunday schools and a member of the High Council of the Sanpete Stake, also Stake clerk and vice president of the Manti Temple. In 1889 he was chosen as a member of the Council of Twelve Apostles; presided over the European Mission in 1893-1896, filled a special mission to Palestine in 1897-1898; acted as second counselor to Pres. Joseph F. Smith from 1901 to 1910 and as first counselor to Presidents Joseph F. Smith and Heber J. Grant from 1910 to 1921. He died in Salt Lake City March 2, 1921. President Lund was a lovable character, an educated man, a wise counselor and the most prominent Elder of the Church of Scandinavian birth.

A small company of emigrating Saints (71 souls) bound for Utah sailed from Copenhagen June 6, 1884, per steamer "Panther," which arrived safely in Hull, England; thence the emigrants proceeded by rail to Liverpool where they were joined by two other companies of Saints from Scandinavia. Of Elders from Zion returning with this company were the following: Jens Peter Jensen, who took charge of the company, Niels Rasmussen, John Capson, Jeppa Nilson, Nils Johnson and Peter Mikkelsen. Elder Mikkelsen, who had recently arrived in the Mission, returned home because of poor health.

Another small company of emigrating Saints bound for Utah sailed from Copenhagen, June 9, 1884, per steamer "Milo," while a small division from Norway (47 souls) in charge of Elder Halvor Olson, a returning missionary, went direct to England. The "Milo" arrived in Hull, Thursday, June 12th, and the emigrants at once proceeded to Liverpool by railway, joining the rest of the Scandinavians there who had crossed the North Sea in the "Panther," and many British Saints.

The whole company now numbered 531 souls, of whom 406 were Scandinavians, 100 British and 25 were returning missionaries. Among these were the following Scandinavian Elders: Johan B. Hesse, leader of the company, Peter Christensen, Niels P. Petersen, Lars H. Outzen, Christian J. Christiansen, Hans Poulsen, Jacob J. H. Jensen, Niels C. Schougaard, Peter Anderson, Mons Rosenlund, Jeppa Monson, Charles E. Anderson, Andrew H. Anderson, Thomas S. Lund and Waldemar Petersen. They all embarked on the steamer "Arizona" which sailed from Liverpool, Sunday morning, June 15th. After a pleasant and speedy voyage the mighty vessel arrived in New York on Monday, June

23rd, and the same day the passengers landed at Castle Garden. This was the third company of emigrating Saints from Europe in 1884; it arrived in Ogden and Salt Lake City, June 29th.

Still another company of emigrating Saints bound for Zion sailed from Copenhagen Aug. 25, 1884, on board the steamer "Panther." After a successful voyage on the North Sea, the emigrants arrived at Hull on Thursday, Aug. 28th, and the next day continued their journey by railroad to Liverpool, where a small company of Norwegian Saints, who had come direct from Norway (leaving Christiania Aug. 22nd), joined them, and all went on board the steamer "Wyoming," which sailed on the 30th. The whole company now numbered 496 souls, including 31 returning missionaries, 222 Scandinavian Saints, 193 British and 50 Swiss and German Saints. The ship arrived in New York Tuesday evening, Sept. 9th. The following morning the company landed at Castle Garden and late in the evening started westward by train from Jersey City. This was the season's fourth company of emigrating Saints from Europe. It arrived in Ogden and Salt Lake City, all well, Sept. 17th. Among the Utah Elders who returned with this company were the following from Scandinavia: Emil Andersen, Charles A. Tietjen, Andrew J. Hansen, Lars Peter Ovesen, Gustaf Anderson, Christian Larsen, James P. Olsen. Sören Pedersen, Sören Sörensen, Anders Anderson, Olaus Johnson Nordstrand and Peter P. Dyring. The latter was released because of poor health. Elders Nordstrand and Dyring accompanied the Norwegian Saints from Christiania to Liverpool.

A company of Saints, consisting of 66 emigrants and eight returning missionaries, viz., Carl August Ek, Andreas Peterson, Bengt M. Ravsten,

Charles Jensen, Frederik Julius Christiansen, August Svenson, Pauli E. B. Hammer and Hans Christensen, left Copenhagen, Oct. 17, 1884, bound for Utah. Elder Andreas Peterson, one of the returning Elders, gives the following account of the journey:

"Pres. Anthon H. Lund called Carl A. Ek to act as leader of the company. On the day of sailing the weather was very stormy and a contrary wind was blowing from the north. Hence, after running against the wind and waves for several hours, we had to cast anchor off Helsingör (Elsinore), where we remained until Saturday morning at 2 o'clock, when the wind ceased sufficiently for us to continue the voyage. In the afternoon we had a meeting of the Saints and in the evening we held a public meeting, at which a number of other passengers besides Saints were in attendance. On Monday (Oct. 20th) we arrived at Hull, England, at 7 p. m. The next morning we continued the journey by railroad to Liverpool, where we remained until Thursday, Oct. 23rd, when we went on board the steamer "City of Berlin." Here we were joined by eighteen emigrants and one returning missionary from Norway (Chr. H. Steffensen), which swelled our company to 84 emigrating Saints and nine returning Elders. We sailed from Liverpool at 12 o'clock noon. On Saturday, Oct. 25th, we were exposed to a very strong wind. The storm increased during the day and the night was still worse. About 12 o'clock midnight, six of the missionaries arose and united in prayer, asking the Lord to quiet the elements. Our prayers were answered, for the weather on Sunday morning was much better and we praised the Lord. On Sunday, Nov. 2nd, we arrived at New York, and in the evening of the same day we left New York by railroad train. During the next six days we enjoyed a pleasant journey over the fertile fields, plains, valleys and mountains of our beautiful America, and on Sunday, Nov. 9th, we arrived at Ogden, Utah, all happy and well."

Apostle John Henry Smith and Elder George C. Lambert arrived in Copenhagen, Aug. 5, 1884, on a visit to Scandinavia. After their return to England the following appeared as an editorial in the "Millennial Star:"

"We [President John Henry Smith and Elder George C. Lambert] recently enjoyed the privilege of paying a brief visit to the Scandinavian Mission and learning

APOSTLE JOHN HENRY SMITH,

Born Sept. 18, 1848, at Carbunca, near Kanesville, Pottawattamie County, Iowa; died Oct. 13, 1911, in Salt Lake City, Utah.

by observation and report of the progress of the work in Denmark and Sweden. We held meetings in Copenhagen, Aarhus, Aalborg, Göteborg and Malmö, thus visiting five out of the seven conferences of the mission, those of Stockholm and Christiania being alone excepted. Though laboring under the disadvantage of not being able to speak the language of the country, we were fortunate in having most excellent interpreters, generally Pres. Anthon H. Lund, to render what we said intelligible to those who did not understand English. And as for understanding the people, if their language was not always plain to us, there was no mistaking the spirit that animated the Saints when they met us, that caused their faces to beam with joy and prompted the hearty greeting. It was the same spirit that characterizes the Saints of God in every land. We met 24 of the Utah Elders who were engaged in the Scandinavian Mission, and found them enjoying the spirit of their calling and generally in good health. Not as many conversions are made now in that region as at some periods in the past, but this is from no fault of the Elders who are laboring there, for they are zealous and energetic in their efforts to bring the people to a knowledge of the truth. Scandinavia has been a very prolific field for the propagation of the gospel. It has yielded a large number of very good Saints,

ho are among the staunchest supporters
f the work of God at the present day."

Elders Smith and Lambert left
Copenhagen, returning to England,
Aug. 15, 1884.

Under date of July 18, 1884, a local
Elder, Johan Blom, wrote from Aminnefors, Finland, to the effect that
he had been summoned before the
authorities of the province, and after
trial was fined for having circulated
tracts and for having baptized two
people on a Sunday night, which the
court interpreted as breaking the
Sabbath. He was fined 597 marks,
besides costs of court, amounting to
913 marks, altogether 1510 marks.
Brother Blom writes:

"The costs of court will be paid by the
selling of my little furniture, and the fine
I must, through lack of means, atone for
by 28 days in prison on water and bread.
However, I was permitted to appeal the
case to the Senate within 60 days, reckon-
ing from June 30th. * * I am now waiting to see what the outcome will be. I am
at present engaged in laying out a garden
here at Aminnefors Bruk. The Saints here
are good and faithful and believe that
these prosecutions will result in good.
Some friends declare that the greater the
persecutions, the stronger their faith in the
gospel is established."

Under date of Nov. 22, 1884, Elder
August L. Hedberg wrote to Pres.
Anthon H. Lund from Åbo, Finland,
as follows:

"I arrived here in Åbo, Oct. 8, 1884,
safe and well, with my books and stayed
here eight days; sold some books and baptized two persons. On the 16th I traveled
to Helsingfors, where I also spent a few
days, sold books and baptized one person.
Incidentally I called on two priests and
offered my literature and spent several
hours in conversation with them. I was
successful in my discussion and afterwards
held a meeting, the first which had ever
been held in that place. Thence I went to
Sibbo, where some Saints and investigators
are living. I there held many good meetings and the people expressed a desire that
I should continue to preach to them. I
therefore held meetings every second day,
occasionally every day, and on one day I
held three meetings. For some time I

wondered how long Lucifer would permit
me to have such progress, but I did not
have to wonder very long, for one morning,
at 7 o'clock, I was visited by a parish
magistrate armed with a written order
from the Governor commanding me to
leave the neighborhood within three days.
The officer was accompanied by another
man as a witness. I paid no attention,
however, to this order, but continued to
hold meetings and baptized one person.
On the 9th of November, in the evening,
the officer called again, but on that occasion I was several miles away holding a
meeting at the home of one of our sisters.
I was afterwards informed that he had
visited a number of people, asking them
what I had taught them, and he was answered that I had taught them doctrines
contained in the Bible. The following day,
as early as possible, I was compelled to
leave the place, and went to Helsingfors.
Here I had to be very prudent, as the police
officers were after me. The newspapers
throughout the province were filled with
stories concerning me and four police officers got hold of my books, which I had
left with one of the Saints, and carried
them away with them, which caused the
editors much joy. * * While I stayed
there three days the officers sought in
vain for me twice, and then I thought I
had better leave, which I did and walked to
the residence of Brother Blom at Bilnas
Bruk, ten miles from Helsingfors. When the
baron heard that I intended to visit that
place, he caused such an uproar that
Brother Blom was not permitted to give me
shelter. Consequently, I had to find lodging with strangers. Brother Blom has suffered much for the gospel's sake and
still expects 28 days' imprisonment and
also several hundred marks fine, but he
is happy, nevertheless, although he had
to eat his Christmas meals in prison. He
has done much good for the spread of the
gospel here. I spent a couple of days there
and baptized two persons; several others
requested baptism. I held a meeting at the
home of a sister God, in the village of
Ajale. There I received a letter from Sister
Vorster of Helsingfors, in which she stated
that she had called at the police station
for my books, but was answered that they
could not be delivered, and that if they
got hold of me I would have to pay at
least 600 marks in fine, as it was abso-
lutely forbidden to sell "Mormon" literature in the city.

"Notwithstanding all the opposition I
have had, I am happy to be laboring for

the progress of the work of the Lord, and never in my life have I been more blessed than during my sojourn in Finland: yet I shall soon have to leave here in order to avoid punishment, for no mercy can be found among the Finns; yet I expect to visit Helsingfors and Sibbo once more, for there are some there who will receive the gospel and some of my effects are there. The officers will have to do with me what they like, for I know that my cause is right, and I hope that the Lord will continue to be with me. If he had not helped me, my circumstances would have been worse than they are. Tomorrow I expect to hold a meeting here (in Åbo) and I shall watch for the consequences."

Elder Hedberg departed from Finland after baptizing eight persons. A number of others were believers when he left. The mail department in Finland adopted the habit of opening the "Nordstjernan" packages and sending the empty wrappers to the Saints. On being remonstrated with, the post office officials explained that their orders were to let no "Mormon" papers enter Finland.

During the year 1884, 36 Elders were called to Scandinavia as missionaries from Zion. They arrived on the following dates: Waldemar Petersen of Salt Lake City (on his second mission), Christian F. Olsen of Hyrum, Ferdinand F. Hintze of Cottonwood, James Nielsen of Brigham City, Hans Christensen of Richfield, Peter Mikkelsen and Peter P. Dyring of Manti, James Olsen of Logan and Sören Christensen of Deseret, arrived on May 6th. Pauli E. B. Hammer of Salt Lake City, (who had been banished from Austria) arrived on June 4th (on · his second mission), Christian Anderson of Ogden, Jeppa Jeppsson of Brigham City, Thomas R. Schröder of Nephi, Mads P. Madsen of Ephraim, Niels C. Christensen of Levan, Nephi Anderson of Peterson, Utah, Matts S. Mattson of St. Charles, Idaho, Swen A. Wannberg of Salt Lake City, Peter W. Peterson of Smith-

field, Edward Hanson of Logan Christian Christiansen (on his secon mission) of Levan, Niels Hansen o Manti, Christian N. Lundsteen o Levan, and Carl Gustaf Anderson c Salt Lake City, Utah, arrived Nov 1st, Jas. H. Clinger of Provo, arrive Nov. 2nd. Rasmus Borgquist o Salt Lake City arrived Nov. 8th Andrew Olson of Gunnison, John J Johnson (Johanson) of Logan, Joha Peter Mortensen of Salt Lake City John A. Eliason and Anders Gusta Sandberg of Grantsville, Lars Tool son of Smithfield, Charles J. Ström berg, Peter M. Anderson and Augus K. Anderson of Grantsville arrive

CHARLES J. STRÖMBERG

Was born April 8, 1847, at Kyrkefalla, Skaraborgs län, Sweden, the son of John Fredrick Strömberg and Ulrika Julina Johnson; baptized Aug. 25, 1862, by John Felt; emigrated to Utah the same year; crossed the Plains by oxteam in Captain Joseph Horne's company; married Anna Dorothea Erickson, Jan. 10, 1876, which marriage was blessed with 13 children (9 boys and 4 girls), of whom 7 are still (1926) living. In 1876 he commenced a seven-years' mission among the Indians, and performed a mission to Sweden in 1884-1886, laboring in the Stockholm Conference, mostly on the island of Gotland and in Eskilstuna. Returning home he had charge of 400 emigrants to Hull, England. He was ordained a Seventy in 1884, by Joseph Young, and was president of a Seventies quorum for years. He has had two sons on missions; one, Noel L. Strömberg, labored in Sweden, in 1926.

ov. 18th, and Rasmus P. Marquard-
:n of Elsinore arrived Dec. 24th,
384.

Waldemar Petersen, Christian F.
)lsen, Peter Mikkelsen, Mads P.
Iadsen, and Peter W. Peterson, were
)pointed to labor in the Copenhagen
onference. Hans Christensen, Pauli
. B. Hammer, 'Niels C. Christensen,
ohn J. Johnson (Johanson) and
ohan P. Mortensen were appointed
) labor in the Aarhus Conference.
.hristian Christiansen was appointed
) labor in the Aarhus Conference,
,art of the time as president of said
onference. Rasmus P. Marquardsen
/as appointed to labor in the Aarhus
;onference and afterwards in the
nission office in Copenhagen. Sören
.hristensen and Christian N. Lund-
teen were appointed to labor in the
\alborg Conference. Elder Lund-
teen was subsequently banished
rom Denmark.

Peter P. Dyring, Christian Ander,
,on, Nephi Anderson and James H.
;linger were appointed to labor in
he Christiania Conference. Andrew
)lson and Charles John Strömberg
vere appointed to labor in the Stock-
iolm Conference. Edward Hanson
vas appointed to labor in the Stock-
iolm Conference and later as trans-
ator and writer in the mission
)ffice in Copenhagen. Jeppa Jepps-
;on, Matts S. Mattson, Rasmus Borg-
juist, Lars Toolson and Peter Mag-
ius Anderson were appointed to
labor in the Skåne Conference. Swen
A. Wannberg, Carl Gustaf Anderson,
John A. Eliason and Anders G. Sandberg were appointed to labor in the
Göteborg Conference. August K.
Anderson was appointed to labor as
traveling Elder and later as president
of the Göteborg Conference. Jens
Olsen and Thomas R. Schröder were
appointed to labor in the Aalborg
Conference and later in the Aarhus
Conference. Ferdinand F. Hintze,
James (Jens) Nielsen and Niels

Hansen were appointed to labor in
the Aalborg Conference.

CHAPTER 68 (1885)

Banishment of Elders from Denmark—Healing of the sick—Elders in Sweden summoned
to appear in court—President Daniel H. Wells
and Elder Chas. W. Penrose visit Scandinavia
—General condition of the mission.

The enforcement of the anti-polyg-
amy laws against the Latter-day
Saints in the United States had its
effects also in the Scandinavian
countries, especially after the U. S.
ambassadors and consuls abroad
had been instructed from Washington
not to extend any protection to American citizens who were engaged in
missionary work in the interest of
the "Mormons." The effect of this
was felt at once in Denmark, where
Latter-day Saint missionaries hitherto had enjoyed more liberty than in
either Sweden or Norway. The civil
authorities on the island of Bornholm
were the first to issue edicts of banishment against the Elders. Thus the
court at Rönne on May 23, 1885,
banished Elder August Valentine
from the island for having preached
"Mormonism." He was sent to
Copenhagen, where he was imprisoned five days, and then sent to Hull,
England. Brother John P. Ipsen,
who had labored as a missionary in
Norway, visited Bornholm for the
purpose of seeing some of his relatives and preach the gospel. He was
summoned into court at the same time
as Bro. Valentine, and was arrested,
but was given permission to remain
on the island, if he would promise
not to preach "Mormonism." Elder
Ipsen replied that he neither could,
nor would, make such a promise.
Bro. Valentine had appointed a meeting out in the country on Whitsuntide
Sunday, and Bro. Ipsen went to the
place appointed, and, at the request
of the owner of the house and others
present, he delivered a discourse on
the doctrines of Christ, proving his

assertions from the Bible. As there was religious liberty in Denmark, he did not imagine that it could be

AUGUST VALENTINE

Was born Aug. 27, 1837, on the island of Bornholm, Denmark, the son of Valentin Valentinsen. His parents were among the first converts to the gospel on the island of Bornho.m, being baptized in 1852, August was baptized soon afterwards and emigrated to Utah, with his parents' consent, leaving Copenhagen in December, 1852, in the so-called John E. Forsgren company, and located in Brigham City. Soon afterwards his parents arrived in Utah and the family passed through many vicissitudes and hardships of pioneer life. August received a common school education and when 22 years of age married Mary Houston who bore him eleven children. In 1883-1885 he filled a mission to Scandinavia, but was banished from Denmark for preaching the gospel. In 1885 he married Sophy Hansen Egesen who bore him six children. From 1892 to October, 1905, he acted as Bishop of the Brigham City Second Ward. In 1914 he removed with his family to Salt Lake City, where he labored in the Temple and where he died Jan. 11, 1916, as a faithful Latter-day Saint. Bishop Valentine held many positions of responsibility and trust in the community and was known as an honest, upright, public-spirited man who never shirked a duty; he was kind and considerate to his family.

otherwise on Bornholm, and did not surmise that the civil authorities would forbid Danish men and women to exercise their liberties as the constitution of the country guaranteed them. Yet, Bro. Ipsen was interrupted in his sermon and compelled

to close the meeting. He was the arrested and taken to Rönne, wher he was imprisoned till the followin day, when he was sentenced to tw days' imprisonment for havin preached Bible doctrines. After serv ing his time in prison, he was libera ted, but soon afterward he was agai summoned into court, where an orde was read to him, similar to the on that had been read to Bro. Valentin the week before. He was taken t Copenhagen and, after suffering tw days' imprisonment, he was trans ported to England.

Speaking about those cases o banishment, Pres. Anthon H. Lun wrote under date of May 28, 1885 the following:

"Here in Denmark we have been s secure, having religious liberty, that w have not considered the civil authoritie would do anything against us by the law It was therefore like a bomb in our cam when we heard, yesterday, that Bro. Niel Hansen had been banished from the coun try. We have heard for some time tha they wanted to drive the Elders from Den mark and we knew that something was brewing, as they had called the Elders up before the police courts, asking them a great many questions; but we had no idea that they could do anything of the kind. I went to see a lawyer about this, and he told me they could not do it, as there was no law against preaching, and he thought that Bro. Hansen should demand a trial. I telegraphed him to that effect and felt quite assured that we would gain the case. In the afternoon (yesterday) we had a still greater surprise. We received a letter from Bro. Valentine that he was confined in one of the cells in the courthouse here in this city (Copenhagen), expecting to be sent away from the country tonight. He had advertised to hold meetings on Bornholm and was then called up and told to leave forthwith, or they would send him away by force. He refused to go and five minutes after the appointed time two policemen came for him, and he was sent here to Copenhagen with orders that he should be sent to England. I called on the U. S. minister today and asked him the question, if American citizens could be banished from the country without a trial. He said: 'I believe they can; there is some law that gives them arbitrary power to expel foreigners.' He then told me that he had tried to help Mr. Frandson (the preacher who was in Utah about four years ago), but they had banished him anyhow. This Frandson had many influential friends, but they could not move the authorities. When I learned they had banished him, I wondered how long they would leave us alone. The minister promised, if we sent him a written statement and the party's citizenship papers, that he would go to the chief of the department of justice and see what could be done; but he had very little hopes. Our counsel had meanwhile been up to find out the grounds on which they banished Bro. Valentine, and found that it was not on account of religious belief, or preaching, but that they had construed, or rather ·contorted, a paragraph in the law concerning foreigners to be applicable to our missionaries. It was originally intended for socialists and political agitators, but the law being very arbitrary in its wording, the authorities can expel any foreigner who has not obtained the right to be supported, if they have occasion to believe that he may become obnoxious. Our counsel said there was nothing to do, as the judge who banished Bro. Valentine did it according to orders received from the attorney-general. Had the initiative come from the lower courts, we might have had some chance of fighting it, but as it came from the head, we had none. When I saw there was no chance to bring the case before the courts, I telegraphed for Bro. Niels Hansen to come to Copenhagen.

"Bro. Valentine left here tonight. He was taken on board by one of the police. It was with curious feelings I saw Bro. Valentine leave. He is the first one that my native land, always so law-revering, has banished from her shores for preaching the gospel of Christ. Where will it end? Brother Daniel K. Brown, who wishes to visit relatives in England before going home in June, went by the same steamer. Bro. Valentine will go to Liverpool to get orders from you what to do. If it meets your mind, he might be sent to Norway, where we are short of missionaries. He might labor in England, as he talks English better than Danish. He has been in this mission a little more than a year and a half."

Elder Niels Hansen, who had labored in the Frederikshavn Branch, arrived in Aalborg, May 27th, having been served with papers banishing him from the country. He was given permission to remain two days in Frederikshavn, two days in Aalborg and two days in Copenhagen. If he was not out of the country by the end of these days of grace, he was to be fined 180 kroner, or be imprisoned 30 days on bread and water.

When Elder Hansen arrived in Copenhagen, he was appointed to labor in Norway. A couple of brethren accompanied him to the court house in Copenhagen to let the police know that he had arrived. They were quite astonished when they opened the door and entered the hall to meet Elder John P. Ipsen, who had been led away to a cell to be kept in confinement until he could be sent out of the country. Bro. Ipsen had been released to return home, having served two years in the mission as a missionary, and he was simply on a visit to his friends on Bornholm when he was arrested.

Elder Ferdinand F. Hintze was called before the police court in Aalborg, Denmark, May 26, 1885, to give an account of himself and his fellow-missionaries in that city. He had been questioned by these officers once before. Later orders of banishment from Denmark were served on Elders F. F. Hintze and Christian Nielsen (Lundsteen) at Aalborg, June 8, 1885. Bro. Hintze, however, was permitted to stay in Aalborg until the 13th.

Elders Hintze and Lundsteen arrived in Copenhagen, June 14th, and as they appeared in court, Elder Lundsteen did not answer the questions put to him to the satisfaction of the officer in charge, and so he was placed in prison, where he was kept until the ship on which he was to leave Denmark left the following day. He was stripped of all his valuables and kept on prison fare. At night the prison officers ordered him to take off his clothes and go to bed; they took his clothes out of his room, and according to his saying "was treated like a dog." Bro. Lundsteen submitted to this treatment cheerfully, realizing that he only suffered for the gospel's sake, and that the treatment he received was unjust and unrighteous. Elder Hintze was turned loose, and finally permitted to visit his friends and relatives on Sjælland. To escape the results of banishment he was appointed to labor in Norway. Under date of June 19, 1885, Elder Hintze journalizes as follows: "This was the last day of grace for me. Today I was to leave my native land never more to return, but there will come another day when the servants of the Lord will be treated differently."

Bro. Hintze left Copenhagen for Norway June 19, 1885, where he had been appointed to labor and where he arrived after visiting friends and relatives in Sweden.

As a sample of how the Elders occasionally were mobbed in Denmark we quote the following from the pen of Elder Hintze:

"We came to Nibe (near Aalborg, Denmark) in a cold and severe northeastern blizzard, the snow blowing right into our faces; but as we had appointed a meeting in Nibe for that evening, we were determined to fill our appointment. At the appointed hour the hall was filled with a turbulent element, only a few decent people being seen among them. Seeing the kind of people who had come together, we decided to hold no meeting, as it was evident that the great majority of the people had come to kick up a row, and besides, we thought it blasphemy to ask the Lord to bless a drunken mob. As soon as it was announced that we would not hold a meeting, the mob began howling and whistling and clapping their hands, acting in a way which reminded me of the wild Indians of Western America. We donned our overcoats with the intention of taking a walk out in town, but we had no sooner started before the mob commenced to yell, curse and swear and threaten to baptize us in the fjord. We had scarcely reached the outer door when some of the mobbers crowded in upon us and compelled us to fall back in a corner of the room. There I stood silent, saying but little except when some of the rabble got too close to me. They, however, got hold of Brother Lauritzen and before I was aware he was beyond my reach. The main part of the mob, however, stayed by me, as it seemed that I was the particular object of their hatred. One cried out querying, 'Who was it that was pulled out?' 'The little one,' answered one of the mobbers. Then several shouted 'Out with the big one, as he must be the prophet; baptize him good and see that he gets completely under water.' A number of other threats were uttered, but some unseen power seemed to prevent them from hurting us. One strong fellow attempted to take hold of me, but he did not succeed in moving me from my position. In a little while, Bro. Lauritzen came; they had thrown him to the ground, but had not hurt him bodily, as some one out in the street had interfered, and had commenced boxing some of the mob, thus giving Bro. Lauritzen a chance to get away. In the meantime the landlord came around and succeeded in dividing the mob, and we found an opportunity to retire into a little side chamber until the mob dispersed. The mobbers seemed to be led by a sailor by the name of Petersen and his sons. A rope-maker named Foldager and others also seemed to be among the ring-leaders, while a Mr. Ole Graveson and his son, Bran, defended us most nobly, together with a Mr. Jörgen Hermansen and family. Altogether the outlook in the beginning was that we would be maltreated, but the Lord, by raising up friends, over-ruled it all for our good, and we got away without receiving a single scratch on our bodies. During the whole affair we were not the least frightened, and after it was all over, we felt to thank the Lord for our deliverance."

Cases of miraculous healings under the administration of the Elders were of very frequent occurrences in the Scandinavian Mission, though only a few instances have been referred to in detail in this history. Bro. Marcus Hermansen and wife (Marie Christine Hermansen), who were baptized in October, 1884, published their testimony to the world that their little son was subject to having fits every day, and often several times a day, and suffered so that they did not think the child could live, but that he has been healed by the power of God through the laying on of hands by Elders Christian Nielsen and Daniel K. Brown. After the administration the child was entirely free from these attacks and was perfectly well. The man was a miller, well known and highly respected.

During the winter of 1884-1885, the missionaries who labored in Namsos, Norway, baptized a family in which the wife had been a chronic invalid, but after her baptism she had not been sick a single day.

A man by the name of Martinsen, a sort of religious agitator, delivered lectures against the Mormons, uttering the grossest lies and slanders that could be imagined. In his lectures, he exhibited the kind of clothing used by the Saints in their temples.

Under date of May 28, 1885, Pres. Anthon H. Lund reported that some of the brethren in Norway had been treated to the dreaded diet, bread and water.

In Stockholm, Sweden, Pres. Oley Oleson was called up before the court to meet the charge of having preached after being warned by the church council not to do so. It was considered best for him not to meet the charge in person, but request leave to answer in writing. This threw the burden of proof upon the prosecuting attorney, who asked to have the case postponed until a later day. The police authorities had expected to get evidence from Bro. Oleson himself by asking him questions, but his answering by letter instead of appearing in court spoiled their calculations for the time being. A gentleman not in the Church offered to conduct the case, and while there was not much chance to escape trial,

it would postpone the time until Pres. Oleson's missionary term had expired, so that he could return home. After leaving the country, he would not care what the sentence might be.

When Bro. Oley Oleson was summoned to appear in court June 20th, the charge against him for teaching in the Sunday school was quashed, but Bro. N. Erickson, in whose name the Saints had hired a hall, was sentenced to a punishment for using the hall for Sunday school purposes. August Johanson was convicted for having taught children under 15 years of age the Latter-day Saint catechism, and Bro. Oleson for having preached, after having been forbidden to do so by the Church council.

On Tuesday, Sept. 22, 1885, Elders Francis M. Lyman, jun., and Geo. C. Naegle arrived in Copenhagen, Denmark, on a visit to Scandinavia. They spent several days in Copenhagen.

Pres. Daniel H. Wells, president of

DANIEL H. WELLS

Born Oct. 27, 1814, in Trenton, Oneida Co., New York, died March 24, 1891, in Salt Lake City, Utah.

the European Mission, and Elders Chas. W. Penrose and Melvin D. Wells of Salt Lake City, Utah, and George Osmond, of Bloomington, Idaho, arrived in Copenhagen, Sept. 26, 1885, on a visit to Scandinavia. These visiting brethren attended meetings in Malmö (Sweden), Christiania (Norway), Stockholm (Sweden), and at these places gave timely and good instructions to the Saints; their visit accomplished a great deal of good.

After the return of Pres. Daniel H. Wells to England, the following editorial from the pen of George Osmond was published in the "Millennial Star:"

"The aptitude of the Scandinavians to receive the gospel, and the important part taken by them in the great Latter-day work, are sufficient to make interesting any particulars relating to that mission, and therefore, during the recent visit of Pres. Wells and party, a few items were gathered for the information of our readers.

"The work of the Scandinavian Mission is moving slowly at the present time. The people, generally, manifest great indifference to religion of all kinds. Denmark appears to have been thoroughly warned by our Elders, who say that our tracts are to be found in nearly every house they visit. Nearly all the people they meet and converse with tell them they have relatives and friends in Utah. Of course, among the thousands who have gone up to Zion some have been disaffected, and the letters, which that class of people has sent home, seem to have enjoyed a much larger circulation than the letters sent by the faithful and contented Saints. It is possible, too, that they have been more industrious in writing.

"All religions are tolerated in Denmark with the rather vague condition that nothing immoral shall be taught. No out-door preaching is allowed in any part of Scandinavia. The correspondence columns of the *Star* have made our readers acquainted with the arbitrary "Foreigners' Law" of Denmark, by means of which any resident foreigners, who may become obnoxious to the government, can be summarily banished from the kingdom without trial or hearing. That such a law exists in autocratic Germany is not surprising, but it is an ugly

blot upon the free institutions of Denmark, and is so regarded even by some members of the government themselves, and probably nothing less than an intense fear of Socialists and dynamiters (for the law was professedly made for their benefit) could reconcile a liberty-loving people to such a law. Be that as it may, it has been taken advantage of by the hireling clergy, who have brought a great pressure to bear upon the government against our missionary Elders, in whose successful labors they see the overthrow of their man-made and un-inspired systems of religion. It is a singular fact that at a large religious convention, held some months ago, the representatives of the various sects could agree upon no matter of business nor doctrine that came up, until the subject of 'Mormonism' was broached, when all immediately united in the sentiment that 'the "Mormons" must go.' It is also said that American influence is at work inducing the Danish Government to turn the law against our Elders. When the mayor of Aalborg banished Elder Neve under the 'Foreigners' Law,' he asked how such an arbitrary course could be taken in a country where religious freedom was claimed to exist, against a man whose only offence consisted in preaching the gospel. The mayor candidly acknowledged the injustice of the act, but said his orders came from high officials and he believed that American influence had something to do with it. Six of our Elders have already been banished from Denmark under this law, which is justified by its supporters upon the theory that visiting foreigners are the guests of a nation, and government assume to say who shall be its guests, on the principle that a man has a right to say who shall visit his house.

"In Norway and Sweden all Christian dissenters are tolerated, but the Latter-day Saints are not recognized as a Christian sect. * * The consequence is that in Sweden and Norway the Saints have no right to preach or pray in meetings, administer the Sacrament or baptize. But the law in this matter is not strenuously enforced, and we find that the practice is far better than the theory. * *

"Stockholm, the capital of Sweden, and its environs present the best field at present for our missionaries, there being a flourishing branch in that city and a spirit of friendliness and enquiry among the people. In this conference is a fine corps of a dozen young, native missionary Elders.

"In Christiania, the capital of Norway

there is a fine branch of the Church, with a good choir. * * The Saints are blessed in the possession of a large, well-built house, which affords a suite of rooms for conference purposes, a commodious and well-fitted-up meeting hall, and several spare rooms which are rented out. At a critical time, when there seemed to be danger of the property passing from the possession of the Saints through debt, a little timely help from President Taylor carried them safely over the crisis.

"The Saints have suffered some persecutions in all these three Scandinavian countries, and many of our Elders have been imprisoned at various times. About three years ago, one of our young missionaries was arrested in Upsala, Sweden, and sentenced by the judge to seventeen days' imprisonment on bread and water. Three days after passing sentence the judge died. A short time after this a policeman was requested to arrest some 'Mormons.' He refused, remarking at the same time that they could spare no more judges.

"While it is certain that the lives of some of our brethren have been considerably shortened by exposure, ill-usage and imprisonment in Scandinavia, there has been but one who has suffered direct martyrdom for the Gospel's sake. This was about eight years ago, in the City of Aalborg, Denmark. A young man was quietly walking in the streets, when he was attacked by a ruffian who, without the slightest provocation, cursed him for being a 'Mormon' and stabbed him in the throat. The young brother died in a few days from the effects of the wound, and his murderer was sentenced to one year's imprisonment, which would be considered by some as rather a severe sentence, considering that his victim was only a 'Mormon.'

"While in Copenhagen, Pres. Wells and party visited the grave of Elder Niels Wilhelmsen, who died in that city, August 1, 1881, just at the close of his presidency of the Scandinavian Mission, an office which he honorably filled for about two years. His fellow-laborers in the missionary field erected a monument over his grave, which, though not grand nor pretentious in its style, is considered an exquisite piece of work, Elder Wilhelmsen had been a close personal friend of some of the party, and as we stood reverently by his grave, we recalled his pleasant, kindly manner and unfaltering devotion to the truth.

"The Scandinavian Saints cherish his

memory with great affection, and as President Lund traveled with us through the conferences he was occasionally addressed by the Saints as 'Brother Wilhelmsen,' and we learned that it was intended as the greatest compliment that could be offered him. We need hardly say that Brother Lund looked upon it in the same light.

"About five hundred baptisms have rewarded the labors of the Elders in Scandinavia so far this season, and we found the brethren full of faith and zeal, abounding in good works. At the various meetings attended by Pres. Wells and party, the Saints and strangers crowded the meeting houses and paid close attention to the remarks of the speakers. That the service of interpreters had to be called into requisition was a little drawback, but the excellent spirit that prevailed needed no interpreter."

CHAPTER 69 (1885)

Elder Nils C. Flygare succeeds Anthon H. Lund as president of the mission—Another large emigration—Forty Elders from Zion arrive in Scandinavia.

Elder Nils C. Flygare of Ogden, Utah, arrived in Copenhagen, Denmark, Oct. 14, 1885, having been appointed to succeed Pres. Anthon H. Lund in the presidency of the Scandinavian Mission. For several days after that, the outgoing and incoming president were busy balancing accounts and making the transfers. When Pres. Lund left with the emigrant company Oct. 19, 1885, Elder Flygare took charge of the mission.

The emigration of Saints to Zion from Scandinavia in 1885 was not quite as large as the previous year; but we notice the following comparison: The steamship "Milo" sailed from Copenhagen, April 2, 1885, with 73 Saints on board, including three returning Elders, bound for Utah. The returning Elders were Niels Petersen, Lars Peter Jensen and Niels C. Christensen. After a pleasant voyage across the North Sea, the company arrived in Hull, England, at 10 p. m. on the 5th. The following day the emigrants were joined by 10 emigrating Saints

19

from Norway, who had left Christiania on the 3rd, under the leadership of Hans Poulsen, and the same day the journey was continued to Liverpool, where the emigrants stoped at a hotel until April 11th, when they sailed from Liverpool on the ship "Wisconsin," together with other returning missionaries and emigrants from Great Britain. Elder Louis P. Lund was placed in charge of the company, which arrived in New York April 22nd, and in Salt Lake City, April 28th, 1885. During the voyage across the Atlantic the emigrants encountered stormy weather and also came in close contact with an iceberg.

A Company of emigrating Saints, 32 in number, sailed from Copenhagen, June 11, 1885, per steamship "Cato" in charge of Elders Lars F. Swalberg. Another company of Saints, 40 in number, sailed from Christiania, June 12, per steamship "Angelo," in charge of Elders Martin Christoffersen, Thorvald A. Thoresen and Joseph Monson. After a pleasant voyage, this company of emigrants arrived in Hull, England, on Sunday afternoon, June 14th, after 47 hours' voyage across the North Sea. They remained on board the ship until Monday morning, when they continued the journey to Liverpool by rail. Here they joined the company of Saints which had left Copenhagen the previous Thursday (June 11th).

A company of emigrating Saints, consisting of 273 Danish and Swedish emigrants, sailed from Copenhagen June 15, 1885, per steamer "Panther," which had been specially chartered for the purpose of bringing these emigrants to England. The company was placed in charge of Elder Jörgen Hansen. Other returning Elders were the following nine: Frederik Ludvigsen, Chas. J. A. Lindquist, John Hyrum Anderson, Samuel P. Nielsen, Emil Erickson, Ole Sören-

sen, Chas. J. Christensen, Ole Hansen and Chr. N. Lundsteen. The

JÖRGEN HANSEN

Leader of emigrant company, was born Aug. 1, 1852, in Haulykke, Lolland, Denmark, the son of Peter Hansen and Anne Danielsen, who joined the Church in April, 1857. Jörgen was baptized by his father May 13, 1865. With his parents he emigrated to Utah in 1866, crossing the Atlantic in the sailing vessel "Cavour" and the Plains in Captain Abner Lowry's company. His mother died on the steamboat going up the Missouri river, and his three brothers died on the plains. Bro. Hansen made his home in Provo, Utah, where he has lived ever since, and after being ordained to offices in the Priesthood became a member of the 34th Quorum of Seventy, Jan. 28, 1876. On May 13, 1877, he married Mary Nielsen; twelve children were born to them, five sons and seven daughters. In 1883-1885 Elder Hansen filled a mission to Scandinavia, where he presided over the Southwest Sjælland Branch and later over the Copenhagen Conference. Returning home in June, 1885, he had charge of a company of 541 emigrating Saints (including 335 Scandinavians) and thirty returning missionaries, crossing the Atlantic on the ship "Wisconsin." The company arrived in Salt Lake City July 7, 1885. Bro. Hansen was ordained a High Priest July 19, 1885, and set apart as first counselor to Bishop James W. Loveless of the Provo Second Ward; later, he served as second counselor to Bishop Myron Tanner of the Provo Third Ward. In 1885 (Oct. 9th) he married Alma Nielsen, who, after giving birth to a son died Sept. 27, 1886. He acted as a home missionary and president of a quorum of block teachers. In a civil capacity he has served as a member of the city council and as street supervisor of Provo City, deputy water-master, justice of the peace, etc. He also acted as superintendent of the Timpanogas Ward Sunday School for eleven years and is now secretary of the Timpanogas Ward High Priests' Quorum.

weather was fine and the best of order prevailed while the emigrants boarded the ship. Many friends and strangers had gathered on the wharf to witness the departure of the "Mormons." Just before the sailing of the vessel, Elder Christian Nielsen Lundsteen was brought on board by the police; he had been banished from the country, and when he arrived in Copenhagen the previous Sunday morning and reported himself at police headquarters, he was placed under arrest and kept a prisoner till the following afternoon. He did not feel downcast because of the unpleasant event, but rejoiced because he was counted worthy to suffer for the sake of Christ. The steamer "Panther" encountered stormy weather on the voyage from Copenhagen to Hull, especially in doubling Cape Skagen, where a delay of 12 hours was made necessary on account of the bad weather. Considerable seasickness prevailed as a matter of course. Early in the morning of June 19th, anchor was cast off Hull, but, owing to low water, the emigrants did not land till about noon. The same day an extra train was placed at their disposal and they left Hull at 12:30 p. m., and arrived in Liverpool in the evening, the train taking them direct to the Alexandria dock, whence their baggage was hauled to the steamship "Wisconsin," on which they went on board, together with quite a number of emigrating Saints from Great Britain. The whole company then consisted of 541 emigrating Saints and 30 returning Elders, under the direction of Jörgen Hansen.

On Thursday, Aug. 20, 1885, a company of emigrants, 93 in number, sailed from Copenhagen with the steamship "Cato" for Hull, bound for America, under the leadership of Elder Niels C. Mortensen. Three other Elders from Zion, returning home from missions, also went with this company, namely, Lars Larsen, Mons Monson and Andrew J. Anderson. After a successful voyage across the North Sea, during which the emigrants were treated with due courtesy by the ship's officers and crew, the emigrants arrived in Hull, Aug. 23rd. Thence they continued the journey by rail to Liverpool where they went on board the steamship "Wisconsin" August 28th, together with a number of British Saints and several returning missionaries. The company was organized with Elder J. W. Thornley as president and Niels C. Mortensen and Thomas Biesinger as his assistants. The ship sailed Aug. 29th and had a pleasant voyage across the Atlantic. During the voyage a child, two years old, died, belonging to Sister Margrethe Degelbleck from Germany. Sister Johanna Nyberg, after several days' sickness, also died on board Sept. 6th, and her remains were consigned to the watery grave on the 7th. Several meetings were held on board. The "Wisconsin" arrived in New York harbor in the evening of Sept. 8th and the following day, Sept. 9th, the emigrants landed at Castle Garden, New York. The same day, the journey was continued by rail westward. They arrived in Salt Lake City, Sept. 14th.

On Friday, Aug. 21st, a company of emigrating Saints, 38 in number, sailed from Christiania, Norway, with the steamship "Angelo" under the leadership of Elder Niels Hansen, a returning missionary. The company reached England in safety, where they joined the larger company of Scandinavian Saints which had left Copenhagen August 20th, and together with them they crossed the Atlantic in the ship "Wisconsin."

A company of emigrating Saints, 112 souls, and 8 returning Elders, sailed from Copenhagen, Denmark, in the evening of Oct. 15, 1885, per steamship "Bravo," under the leadership of M. Fred. T. Christensen, who had labored in the office of "Skandinaviens Stjerne." The following day (Oct 16th), the company was organized so as to hold prayer meetings morning and evening at three places on board. The weather during the voyage across the North Sea was exceptionally good and the company arrived in Hull, Sunday morning, Oct. 18th. Owing to low water the harbor was not reached until the afternoon and the emigrants spent another night on board. After landing Monday morning, Oct. 19th, and passing through the custom-house, the emigrants traveled by rail to Liverpool, where they stopped at a hotel until the afternoon of the 23rd, when they went on board the steamship "Nevada." The next morning (Oct. 24th) the company was organized by Pres. Daniel H. Wells and Charles W. Penrose, with Anthon H. Lund as leader and Christopher J. Arthur and Samuel R. Bennion as his counselors. There were 433 passengers on board of whom nearly 300 were Latter-day Saints, including 26 returning Elders. Pres. Lund appointed Elder M. Fred. T. Christensen to preside over the Scandinavian Saints with Hans D. Petterson and James Olsen as his assistants, and Edward Morgan to preside over the English Saints and Brother John R. Boshard over the German Saints. It was decided to hold prayer meetings at 7 'clock morning and evening, and that everything was to be quiet after 9 p. m., that all who desired to rest might do so.

The ship sailed from Liverpool Oct. 24, 1885, in the evening. The next day (Oct. 26th) there was considerable seasickness on board, as the sea was somewhat rough, but as the voyage proceeded the passengers, one after another, came to their meals and could spend their time on deck. The time on board was spent in different amusements, such as generally are engaged in on board ship. The pilot came on board Nov. 3rd and the following day (Nov. 4th) in the morning, the shores of Long Island were seen, and early in the afternoon the ship arrived at the quarantine station, where the emigrants were subjected to close examination by the doctors. The ship arrived in New York on Thursday, Nov. 5th, in the morning, at the Guion Dock where the luggage was examined by the customhouse officers. The emigrants were next taken to Castle Garden, where their goods were weighed, and later in the afternoon they were taken on a tender to Jersey City; the same night (Nov. 5th), they boarded the cars at Jersey City and traveled by rail via Philadelphia, Pittsburgh, Chicago and Omaha to Salt Lake City, where they arrived on Tuesday, Nov. 10th. Some of the emigrants, however, had left the company at Evanston, Wyoming, and some at Ogden, Utah.

Oley Oleson, Albin C. Anderson, Mads F. T. Christensen, Andrew P. Renström, James Olsen and Chr. Christiansen, all returning Elders, traveled with this company.

Besides the Elders who returned home with emigrant companies, the return of the following missionaries is noted: Some time in May, 1855, Elders Christian Nilson, Andrew Andersen, Andrew Christensen and Gustave L. Rosengren left Copenhagen, to return to their homes in Zion. Elders Daniel K. Brown and August Valentine left Copenhagen for their homes in America, May 28, 1885. Elders Martin Jensen, Charles W. Knudsen and Christen Nelson left Copenhagen, June 2, 1885, to return to their homes in Utah. John P. Ipsen left Copenhagen on the steamer "Milo" for Hull, England, June

4, 1885, on his return to America. Hans D. Petterson, left Copenhagen Nov. 15th, 1885, for his home in Zion.

In 1885, 50 Utah Elders were called as missionaries to Scandinavia, who arrived in Copenhagen as follows: August L. Hedberg of Salt Lake City, March 7th; Sören P. Neve of S. L. City (on his second mission) and John Felt of Huntsville, Utah,

SVEN-CARL NILSON

Was born Dec. 24, 1838, at Damstorp, Sallerups parish, Malmöhus län, Sweden. When 17 years old he moved to Copenhagen, Denmark, where he became a convert to the restored gospel and was baptized in 1863. In 1867, being ordained to the Priesthood, he was called to labor as a local missionary on the island of Sjælland, during which he presided over several branches of the Church. He married Maren Sophie Jörgensen and emigrated to Utah with a company of Saints which arrived in Salt Lake City Aug. 10, 1870. After residing in Logan two years he became a permanent settler of Richmond, Cache County, Utah, where he presided over the Scandinavian meetings from 1895 to 1917. In 1883, he was called to labor as a home missionary in the Cache Stake and in 1885-1887 he filled a mission to Scandinavia, presiding part of the time over the Aalborg conference, Denmark, and later labored as a missionary in the Skåne conference, Sweden. After returning home he continued his labors as a home missionary and acted as a president of the 39th quorum of Seventy. In 1914 he visited Scandinavia and traveled considerably in Sweden, Denmark and Norway. He is now a High Priest. For a number of years he has been a member of the Richmond City council and has also acted as sexton in Richmond. Although advanced in years, Elder Nilson is still active in Church affairs.

arrived April 17th; Ole Poulsen of Brigham City, Niels H. Jensen and Peter Mattson of Mt. Pleasant, and Hans J. Christiansen of Logan, Utah, arrived April 20th; Jens W. Jensen of Moroni, James Yorgason (Jorgenson) of Fountain Green, Jens Chr. Nielsen of Moroni, Utah, and Niels Jörgensen of Oxford, Idaho, arrived April 29th; Sören Thomsen of Bear River City, Nils A. Anderson of Spanish Fork, Anders P. Eliason of Logan, Sven Carl Nilsson of Richmond, Utah, Jens C. Nielsen of Gentile Valley, Idaho, Carl Frederik Carlson of Manti, Christian Nielsen and Nils P. Peterson of Pleasant Grove, Peter C. Jensen of Ephraim, Einar Erickson of Spanish Fork, James Petersen of Fillmore, Nils Anderson of West Jordan, Frederick N. Christiansen of Ephraim, John Hagman of Salt Lake City, Hans Chr.

NILS P. PETERSON

Was born in Bara, Skåne, Sweden, March 6, 1840, the son of Anders Petterson and Anna Öfgren. He was baptized in April, 1867, and emigrated to America in 1868, crossing the Atlantic in a sailing vessel. Many deaths occurred on this voyage owing to bad drinking water. Brother Peterson married Mathilde Holden, who bore him three children, namely, Nils, Frithiof and Hermes. In 1885-1887 he filled a mission to his native country, Sweden, and died at Pleasant Grove, Utah County, Utah, May 8, 1926.

Petersen of Logan, Sören Christoffersen of Manti, Utah, arrived May 4th; Jens Chr. Nielsen and Peter A.

SÖREN   CHRISTOFFERSEN

Born March 5, 1819, in Bodstrup, Sörbymagle parish, Sorö Amt, Denmark, embraced the Gospel and was baptized Dec. 8, 1851, by John E. Forsgren; presided over the Sönder-Overdrev Branch, Copenhagen Conference, two and one-half years; and when he, as a well-to-do farmer sold his property to emigrate to Zion in 1856, he assisted quite a number of poor Saints to emigrate with him. He located in Brigham City and removed to Sanpete County in 1858; filled a mission to Denmark in 1860-62, laboring in the Aarhus and the Skive conferences; participated in the Black Hawk war; filled another mission to Denmark in 1874-75, laboring as traveling Elder in the Copenhagen Conference; acted as a counselor to Bishop Hans Jensen, of Manti, several years; filled a third mission to Denmark in 1885 and died Dec. 29, 1894, after an active life in the Church and in the community.

Forsgren, of Brigham City, Utah, arrived June 24th; Johan L. Berg of Showlow, Arizona, arrived Aug. 19th; Elof Gustaf Erickson of Salt Lake City, Utah, arrived Sept. 23rd; Nils Chr. Flygare of Ogden, arrived Oct. 14th; Joseph Anderson of Fountain Green, Chas. Oscar Petersen of Fairview, Andrew L. Hyer of Lewiston, Erastus Anderson of Ephraim, Anton Anderson of Logan, Peter Anderson of Ephraim, Utah, Rasmus Rasmussen of Mink Creek, Idaho, Christen Frandsen of Ephraim, and Erick B. Ericksen of Mt.

Pleasant, Utah, arrived Nov. 3rd; Swen Ole Nilsson of Fairview, Niels Mikkelsen of Fountain Green, Victor Chas. Högsted of Harrisville, James J. Anderson of Fountain Green, Mouritz Mouritzen of Smithfield, Peter Olson of Moroni, Rudolph Ström of Mt. Pleasant, Nils Oscar Gyllenskog of Smithfield and Hemming Hansen of Spring City, Utah, arrived Dec. 1, 1885.

August L. Hedberg, John Felt,

NIELS MIKKELSEN

Was born Jan. 31, 1850, near Randers, Denmark, and performed military service in the Danish army as a dragoon from Jan. 15, 1872, to Sept. 28, 1873. From July, 1876, to November, 1879, he was in the service of Prime Minister Estrup, and while thus employed he became a convert to the restored gospel and was baptized June 8, 1879, at Randers. After being ordained to the Priesthood he labored as a local missionary from November, 1879, to June, 1881, and then emigrated to Zion, arriving in Salt Lake City in July, 1881. In 1881 (Aug. 10th) he married Dorothea Marie Nielsen, who was born at Öster Velling, Aug. 10, 1854, and emigrated to Utah in 1880. This marriage was blessed with two sons and two daughters. In 1885-1887 he filled a mission to Denmark and acted part of the time as president of the Aalborg conference. He filled a second mission to Scandinavia in 1903-1905, laboring principally in Aalborg, Aarhus, Veile and Randers. During these missions he baptized about twenty persons. Two of his brothers and one sister received the gospel and emigrated to Utah, settling in Fountain Green, Sanpete County. Brother Mikkelsen's wife and brothers have done temple work for about 600 persons.

Peter Adolph Forsgren, Joseph Anderson, and Rudolph Ström were appointed to labor in the Stockholm Conference. Sören Peter Neve (banished), Christian Nielsen, Peter Chr. Jensen, Christen Frandsen, Victor Chas. Högsted, and Mouritz Mouritzen were appointed to labor in the Aalborg Conference. Ole Poulsen, Niels Jörgensen, Jens Chr. Nielsen, Frederick N. Christiansen, Sören Christoffersen (on his third mission), Jens Chr. Nielsen, Johan L. Berg, Rasmus Rasmussen and Hemming Hansen were appointed to labor in the Copenhagen Conference. Niels H. Jensen, Nils A. Anderson, Carl Fred Carlson, Jens Petersen, Hans Chr. Petersen, Charles Oscar Petersen, Anton Anderson and Erick B. Ericksen were appointed to labor in the Christiania Conference. John Hagman, Sven Ola Nilsson and Nils O. Gyllenskog were appointed to labor in the Skåne Conference. Peter Mattson was appointed to labor in and afterwards as president of the Skåne Conference. Jens W. Jensen, Jens Chr. Nielsen (on his second mission), Sören Thomsen, Erastus Anderson and Peter Andersen were appointed to labor in the Aarhus Conference. Anders P. Eliason, Nils Peter Peterson, Nils Anderson, and Elof G. Erickson were appointed to labor in the Göteborg Conference.

Hans Jacob Christiansen (on this his second mission to\ Scandinavia) was appointed to labor in the Copenhagen Conference, and later to preside over the Christiania Conference. James Yorgason (on his second mission) was appointed to preside over the Göteborg and later over the Stockholm Conference. Sven Carl Nilsson was appointed to labor in the Copenhagen Conference and later to preside over the Aalborg Conference. Einar Erickson was appointed to labor in Iceland. Nils Chr. Flygare was called to preside over the Scandinavian Mission on this his second mission to Scandinavia.

Andrew L. Hyer was appointed to labor in Norway and afterwards (Dec. 17, 1886,) was called to England to labor. Niels Mikkelsen was appointed to labor in the Aarhus Conference, but labored in the Aalborg Conference, part of the time as conference president. Jens Jörgen Andersen was appointed to labor in the Aarhus Conference, Denmark, but was banished and finished his mission in the Skåne Conference, Sweden. Peter Olsen was appointed to labor in the Copenhagen Conference and afterwards in the Aarhus Conference.

CHAPTER 70 (1886)

Newspaper slanders—Johan Blom imprisoned in Finland—Emigrants to Zion leave in small companies—Arrival of 31 Elders from America.

Under date of March 9, 1886, Pres. Nils C. Flygare wrote the following:

"The newspapers have been very busy of late circulating anti-'Mormon' stuff against us. One of the leading papers of Copenhagen and a paper having a large circulation in the country, had a very severe article against us a couple of weeks ago, based upon Surveyor-General Dement's interview in America. This article set forth that the 'Mormon' Apostles had carried on for years a great land fraud, and had swindled the government and robbed the people of thousands of dollars; this, with other lies, spread like wildfire over the land. I wrote a lengthy and truthful answer to the article, showing up the falsehood of every statement made therein. I went to the editor of the paper with but a very faint hope of getting him to publish the article, but I was agreeably surprised when he began to make apologies for the article he had published against us, saying that it was not original, and offered to make any corrections I desired. I told him I had written an answer and that he would do an unpopular people a great justice in publishing it. I handed him the paper; he read it very carefully and said, 'Yes,

I will publish your answer in full.' I had a long talk with him on Utah matters, and he seemed to be quite interested in hearing our side of the question. The next day my article appeared in full with my signature to it, in a very prominent place in his paper, and without any comment. It has had a good effect. Nearly everybody was talking about the two articles, and gave him credit for being candid and truthful."

Early in the year 1886, Johan Blom, who had been living in Finland several years, was sent to prison for 28 days, on water and bread, for having performed baptisms. He appealed his case to the supreme court of Finland, but the sentence was confirmed with the expenses of the court added, which amounted to about 400 marks. This was very hard on him, as he was a poor man having a large family.

Under date of March 10, 1886, Elder Einar Erickson wrote from Westmanöen, Iceland, to the effect that there were 28 members of the Church in Iceland; that seven had been baptized during the past year (1885) and three; up to the date of writing, in 1886; three Saints had also emigrated to Zion.

A company of Saints emigrating to Zion (69 souls) and four returning Elders sailed from Copenhagen, April 8, 1886, for England. Elder Charles J. Strömberg was appointed leader of the company to England. The other returning Elders were: Jeppa Jeppsson, Thomas R. Schröder and Peter W. Peterson. After an uneventful voyage the emigrants arrived in England, whence the journey was continued to Liverpool by rail. Here the emigrants, together with other emigrating Saints from the British Isles, went on board the steamship "Nevada" April 16th. The following day (April 17th) the company was organized by Pres. Daniel H. Wells with Elder Edwin T. Woolley as leader and Charles J. Ström-

berg and James L. McMurrin as his assistants. During the voyage three meetings were held on board, one of them in the first-class cabin. The captain was exceedingly kind and obliging to the Saints, and the weather was pleasant, the wind being favorable, and the Saints had a good time, except that a few of them suffered a little with sea sickness. The ship arrived in New York, April 27th, and the Saints were landed at Castle Garden in the evening. The same day (April 27th) the company left New York and traveled by rail via Chicago and Omaha to Ogden, where they arrived safe and well early in the morning of May 4, 1886. The train on which they traveled was delayed 12 hours at Laramie, Wyoming, on account of a strike among the laborers. A similar tie-up occurred at Rawlings, Wyoming. The strikers permitted the train to go on, if the conductor would agree to go through without a brakeman, the strike being on this occasion among the brakemen of the road. The conductor, agreeing to do this, the journey was continued and finished without further molestation.

A small company of emigrating Saints, under the leadership of Elder James Nielsen, sailed from Christiania, Norway, April 9, 1886, for England, and after a safe voyage across the North Sea this company reached Liverpool in good condition and there joined the larger company of Scandinavian emigrants, which had sailed from Copenhagen, April 8th, and traveled with them across the Atlantic Ocean and the continent of America to Utah.

A small company of 17 emigrating Saints and two returning missionaries (Ferdinand F. Hintze and James H. Clinger) sailed from Christiania, Norway, June 18th, 1886, destined for the gathering places of the Saints in the Rocky Mountains. After a successful voyage across the North Sea, this company arrived in England, where they joined a large company of emigrating Saints, which sailed from Copenhagen, Denmark, June 21st.

A company of Saints, consisting of 290 emigrants and 11 returning missionaries, sailed from Copenhagen, Denmark, June 21, 1886, on the steamship "Otto," under the leadership of Christian F. Olsen. The other

CHRISTIAN FREDERIK OLSEN.

Missionary in Scandinavia, was born May 23, 1859, in Copenhagen, Denmark, the son of Frederik Olsen and Bolette Hendriksen. His parents having joined the Church in 1853, he was baptized when eight years old and emigrated to Utah in 1870. He completed his education in the University of Deseret, and the B. Y. College at Logan. In 1875 he located in Hyrum, Cache County, where his parents already resided. There he taught school and filled various positions in the Church and the city. In 1882 (Nov. 7th) he married Emrett Anderson. He filled a mission to Scandinavia in 1884-1886, presiding over the Copenhagen Branch and Conference part of the time. He baptized 43 persons on this mission. Elder Olsen has served 24 years as teacher in the Hyrum schools and two terms as senator in the Utah legislature; he has also acted as county assessor and a director of the Agricultural College. In 1890 (Oct. 20th) he married Mary Ann Unsworth, who died April 11, 1894. In 1900-1901 he filled another mission to Denmark, laboring in the Copenhagen Conference. In 1918 he was appointed county assessor in Cache County, and in 1905 · (June 7th) he married Hilda Christina Kjellberg, which marriage has been blessed with six children.

Elders from Zion who returned to Utah with this company were the following: Fred N. Christiansen, Mads P. Madsen, Johan Peter Mortensen, John Felt, Peter A. Forsgren, Rasmus Borgquist, Swen A. Wannberg, Elof Gustaf Erickson, Lars Toolson and Erastus Anderson.

The voyage across the North Sea was quite stormy, a brisk wind blowing against the ship most of the way; consequently, seasickness became quite general, yet good cheer prevailed among the emigrants, who were not seasick, and they passed the time singing songs of Zion and associating pleasantly together. Having safely arrived in the Humber River, the emigrants landed at Hull early Friday morning (June 25th) and continued the journey the same day by rail to Liverpool, where the emigrants boarded the steamship "Nevada," which sailed from Liverpool Saturday, June 26th. During the voyage across the Atlantic two children, belonging to Danish Saints, died and were consigned to a watery grave. As they had been sick almost from the beginning, their demise was not altogether unexpected. A little girl from Copenhagen died July 6th, of lung trouble and the same evening a lame sister (Andreasen) from Copenhagen, Denmark, was stricken with apoplexy, which ended her life. One of the stewardesses in the employ of the steamship company was also stricken with a fit of apoplexy and died on the 6th, and her remains, like the others, were lowered into the depths of the sea. Such mortality among Latter-day Saint emigrants was something very unusual in the history of the emigration of recent years. , Otherwise the condition among the Saints on board during the voyage was good. Union and peace prevailed and the Saints were willing to abide by the counsel given them by those in charge. A number of meetings were also held on board. The "Nevada" arrived in New York July 17. The railroad journey was commenced from Jersey City and at Philadelphia, 12 persons were added to the company, increasing the total number of the emigrants and returning Elders to 437 souls. Traveling via Chicago and Omaha, the company arrived in Ogden, Utah, Monday afternoon, July 10th, and those who were destined for the southern settlements reached Salt Lake City the same night. Elder Chr. F. Olsen proved himself an efficient leader.

A number of Saints (131 souls) emigrating to Zion sailed from Copenhagen, Aug. 12, 1886, per steamship "Bravo," in charge of five returning Elders, namely, August K. Anderson, Anders Gustaf Sandberg, Peter M. Anderson, Christian Nielsen and Nephi Anderson.

After a safe voyage across the North Sea, the emigrants arrived in Hull, England, Sunday, Aug. 15th, and thence traveled by rail to Liverpool, where they joined with other emigrants and returning missionaries from the British Isles. At Liverpool they went on board the steamship "Wyoming," which sailed from that port on Saturday, Aug. 21, in charge of Elder David Kunz, a returning Elder from the Swiss and German Mission. After a pleasant voyage, the company arrived in New York on the 31st. Forty-five of the emigrants were detained there by Commissioner Stephenson on pretended charges of pauperism, but finally all were permitted to continue their journey, except a woman and three children who were sent back to England. The rest of the company left New York Sept. 21, 1886, and traveled over the Baltimore and Ohio and the Denver and Rio Grande railroads to Utah, arriving safe and well in Salt Lake City, Sept. 27, 1886.

A small company of Saints, 13 in number, emigrating to Utah, sailed from Christiania, Norway, Aug. 13, 1886, per steamship for England, where they arrived in safety and were united for the journey across the Atlantic with the company of Scandinavian Saints which left Copenhagen, Denmark, August 12th.

A company of emigrating Saints, 103 persons, including eight returning missionaries, sailed from Copenhagen, Oct. 7, 1886, at 7 p. m. on the English steamship "Milo," Captain Leach, to begin their migration to Zion. Elder Edward Hansen was appointed leader of the company. The names of the other returning Elders were, Rasmus P. Marquardson, John A. Eliason, Carl Gustaf Anderson, John J. Johnson, Sven C. Nilsson, Anders Olson and Matts S. Mattson. After a safe passage across the North Sea, the emigrants arrived in Hull, England, on the 10th, and continued their journey by rail to Liverpool on the 11th of October. Here they went on board the steamship "British King," together with emigrants and returning Elders from other parts of the European Mission, and sailed from Liverpool Oct. 13th. The voyage across the Atlantic Ocean was stormy; consequently, nearly all the Saints suffered more or less from seasickness. Sister Karen Petersen of the Aalborg Conference met with a misfortune whilst standing in a door-way when a wave struck the door, slamming it with such force against her arm that one of the bones was fractured. Receiving the best attention, she recovered. On the 8th a little girl from Wales died and her body was consigned to a watery grave. The Saints, whilst on board, were divided into districts with Elders to preside over them and to call them to prayer morning and evening. On Sunday, Oct. 24th, a meeting was held on deck which cheered and comforted the Saints. The captain, officers and crew were very kind to the emigrants. The company arrived in Philadelphia Oct. 27th, in the morning, being the 5th company of Latter-day Saint emigrants of the year 1886, from Europe, but the first company to land in Philadelphia. Later, the same day on which they landed, the emigrants started westward and traveled by rail via Baltimore, Chicago and Omaha, arriving in Salt Lake City, Nov. 1, 1886.

A small company (13 persons) of emigrating Saints sailed from Christiania, Oct. 8, 1886, bound for Utah. After a safe voyage across the North Sea, this company reached England, where they joined the larger company of Scandinavian emigrants who had left Copenhagen Oct. 7th.

In 1886, 31 Elders from Utah, called on missions to Scandinavia, arrived in Copenhagen, Denmark: Jens Hansen of Spanish Fork, Utah (on his third mission), arrived Jan. 27th; Peter Chr. Geertsen of Huntsville, Utah (on his second mission), arrived March 20th; Martin Christensen of Manassa, Colo., and Louis J. Holther of Ogden, Utah, arrived May 4th; Peter Gustaf Hanson of Payson, Joseph Christenson of Gunnison, John Anderson of Fountain Green, Anders Gustaf Nygren of Grantsville, Andrew N. Michaelsen and Chr. Thomsen Balle of Mayfield, Abraham Johnson of Mt. Pleasant, August F. Westerberg of Logan, Pehr Håkanson of Hyrum, Carl Erickson of Manti, Albert Nephi Tollestrup of Gunnison, Utah, Svante J. Koeven - of Montpelier, Idaho, Christian Olsen of Weston, Idaho, and Nils Larson Högberg of Salt Lake City, Utah, arrived Sept. 28th. Karl H. P. Nordberg of Lewiston, Anthon L. Skanchy (on his second mission) and Nils P. Lindelöf (on his second mission), both of Logan, Utah, Charles R. Dorius of Ephraim,

Gustave Backman of Salt Lake City, and Christoffer O. Folkmann of Plain City, Utah, arrived Nov. 2nd; Christian D. Fjeldsted (on his third mission) of Logan, Ola Olson of Millville, Pehr Olof Pehrson of Logan, and Hans C. N. Hansen of Preston, Idaho, arrived Nov. 16th; Willard S. Hansen of Brigham City, and Jacob Hansen of Bear River City, Utah, arrived Nov. 23rd, and Christian L. Christensen of Salem, Utah, arrived Dec. 24th, 1886.

JOSEPH CHRISTENSON,

Chief Recorder of the Salt Lake Temple, was born April 19, 1865, at American Fork, Utah County, Utah, the son of John Christenson and Johanna Harling. He was baptized June 4, 1873, by James Hanson. In 1886-1888 he filled a successful mission to Scandinavia, laboring in Sweden. After his return home he labored as a home missionary in the Salt Lake Stake for several years. In 1893 he assisted Elder John Nicholson in preparing the records for the opening of the Salt Lake Temple and was appointed Temple Recorder April 30, 1916, succeeding Duncan D. McAllister. Bro. Christenson was ordained a High Priest Dec. 21, 1902, by Charles W. Penrose, and on Aug. 21, 1904, appointed Bishop of the Tenth Ward, Salt Lake City, which position he held until Feb., 1925. Elder Christenson has been connected with the Genealogical Society of Utah for several years, is a member of the board and the librarian. He is an efficient clerk and recorder and has gained the confidence and good will of his associates in the Temple and the Saints generally.

Jens Hansen and Albert Nephi Tollestrup were appointed to labor in the Aarhus Conference. Martin Christensen, Christian Thomsen Balle and Christian Larsen Christensen were appointed to labor in the Aalborg Conference. Louis J. Holther, Abraham Johnson, Carl Ericksen, Christian Olsen and Charles R. Dorius were appointed to labor in the Christiania Conference. Anthon L. Skanchy was appointed to preside over the Christiania Conference. Peter Gustaf Hanson, John Anderson, Svante J. Koeven and Nils Larson Högberg were appointed to labor in the Stockholm Conference. Joseph Christenson, Pehr Håkanson, Pehr Olof Pehrson and Ola Olson (second mission) were appointed to labor in the Skåne Conference. Anders Gustaf Nygren, August F. Westerberg and Gustave H. Backman were appointed to labor in the Göteborg Conference. Karl H. P. Nordberg was appointed to labor in the Göteborg and later in the Stockholm Conference. Andrew N. Michaelsen, Hans Chr. Nielsen Hansen, Willard Snow Hansen, and Jacob Hansen (on his second mission) were appointed to labor in the Copenhagen Conference. Peter Chr. Geertsen (on his second mission) was appointed to labor in the Aalborg Conference and later as translator and writer in the mission office in Copenhagen. Nils P. Lindelöf was appointed to labor in the Skåne and Göteborg conferences, on this his second mission to Scandinavia. Christoffer O. Folkmann (on his second mission) was appointed to labor in the Copenhagen and later in the Christiania Conference. Christian D. Fjeldsted was appointed to preside over the Scandinavian Mission on this his third mission to Scandinavia.

In a letter written by Pres. Nils C. Flygare, Dec. 1, 1886, the writer refers to some excellent meetings held in different parts of the mission, in which fair and impartial reports were given, in several instances, by the newspapers.

In the beginning of the year 1886, it seemed as if the Elders would not be permitted to do missionary work in Denmark, as the government had decided to banish the Elders. Although one more Elder was banished from Denmark in 1886, and several others had been arrested and brought before the police courts, they had been set at liberty, and then had continued their labors as missionaries. The authorities of the land, being well aware that the Saints were loyal and law-abiding people, who sustained the government and took no part in political agitation, became convinced that the banishment of "Mormon" missionaries was not in keeping with the general spirit of the country. The Latter-day Saints in Denmark were not found in drinking saloons or other places of bad repute; they were not brought before any court and convicted of crime, but were found to do what the gospel teaches, viz., be honest, sober, industrious, virtuous, and alltogether a God-fearing people. In Sweden in 1886, the prospect for increased missionary work was very good. The Elders were seldom interfered with and met but very little opposition. During the summer of 1886, the missionaries extended their labors further north than ever before, and some of the people were baptized on the borders of Lappland. New fields of labor were opened and in many places where the work had stood still for some time, new life was being infused and fresh starts made.

At this time, the "Skandinaviens Stjerne" in Denmark and Norway, and the "Nordstjernan" in Sweden, had a good circulation, many non-Mormons subscribing for those periodicals regularly. Books and pamphlets to the amount of nearly 3000 kronor were disposed of in Sweden, during the year 1886.

In Norway, the Elders had also extended their labors to the far north and new members had been added to the Church by baptism on the barren and inhospitable islands of the sea. The Elders met but very little opposition in Norway, yet Norway was, as it had been from the beginning, a very hard missionary field for the Elders, who had long distances to travel, and the people were, in some instances, rather inhospitable towards them. Pastor Mortensen, who had spent some time in Utah, still labored very hard in Christiania and other places to get the "Mormon" Elders forbidden to preach. He gave a number of lectures about Utah and its people, basing his false statements upon such literature as that of Stenhouse, Beadle and others, which, while sensational enough, was, in many instances, too coarse for decent people. He continued to illustrate his lectures with the exhibition of a so-called set of temple clothes, to the disgust of many people. However, his labors were in vain, for his lectures had the tendency to fill the Saints' hall with attentive listeners. The fair-minded people of Norway, after listening to his accusations, desired to hear the "Mormon" side of the question, as well as his.

CHAPTER 71 (1887)

Death of Elder Jesper Petersen—Apostle George Teasdale visits Scandinavia—Emigrants for America continue to leave in small companies—Arrival of 45 Elders from America.

Under date of Jan. 17, 1887, Elder Jens C. Nielsen reported that he had just returned from a pleasant visit to the island of Bornholm, and that he found 34 members, where eighteen months before there were only nineteen. Yet sixteen people had recently emigrated to Zion. Not long before, eleven persons were added to the Church by baptism on the island, mostly young people ranging from sixteen to thirty years.

To show the change of policy which of recent years had taken place in Sweden, we may say, that when some rough element disturbed a Latter-day Saint meeting at Malmö, in November, 1886, two of the ring-leaders were promptly arrested, brought into court and fined 100 kronor each; they also served a month's imprisonment each for breaking open the hall door.

Elder Jesper Petersen of Castle

JESPER PETERSEN,

Son of Rasmus Petersen and Ane Marie Hansen, was born June 6, 1847, at Moderup, Odense amt, Denmark. Becoming a convert to the gospel, he was baptized Nov. 16, 1860, and emigrated to Utah in 1866. Soon after his arrival in Utah he married Louise Jensen and located in Castle Valley, Emery County, Utah. In 1886-1887 he filled a mission to the Southern States and was then transferred to Scandinavia, arriving in Denmark April 26, 1887. He was appointed to labor in the Odense Branch of the Aarhus Conference. Toward the close of May his health began to fail and he died June 23, 1887, at Odense. Since his death the Saints of Odense have taken care of his grave in the Odense cemetery.

Dale, Emery County, Utah, who was laboring as a missionary on the island of Fyen, Denmark, died in Odense.

Elder Petersen arrived in Copenhagen April 26, 1886, and was assigned to labor on the island of Fyen. Previous to his arrival in Denmark he had filled a six months' mission in the Southern States (America). On his arrival in Denmark, he was apparently healthy and strong, but was soon afterwards attacked with the chills and fever, which continued to get worse until it terminated his earthly career. Brother Petersen left an interesting family in Zion. His remains were interred in the Odense cemetery, where his resting place has ever since been taken care of by local Saints.

Apostle George Teasdale, president of the European Mission, and Elder Robert S. Campbell of Logan, arrived in Copenhagen, July 30, 1887, on a visit to Scandinavia. They attended meetings in Copenhagen, Stockholm and Christiania, and, returning to England, they sailed from Christiania Aug. 12th.

Under date of Nov. 30, 1887, Elder Halder Johnson wrote from Sölfhöl, Iceland, that he had labored in that mission 18 months and had baptized 20 people, and that the membership on Iceland numbered 34, most of whom were very anxious to gather to Zion, but as nearly all of them were poor they could not expect to have their desires fulfilled without assistance. Bro. Johnson had appointed Tobias Tobiasen of Reykjavik to take charge of the Iceland Mission.

A company of emigrants (108 souls) and nine returning missionaries sailed in the steamship "Panther" from Copenhagen, April 7, 1887, bound for Utah, under the leadership of Elder Martin Christensen. The other returning Elders

were: August L. Hedberg, Ole Po[ ]sen, Niels H. Jensen, Sören Thoms[ ] Anders P. Eliason, Peter C. Jens[ ] Nils Anderson and John Hagma[ ]

After a safe voyage across t[ ] North Sea, the emigrants arrived [ ] Hull, where a small company [ ] emigrating Saints from Norway, w[ ] had sailed from Christiania on Ap[ ] 8, 1877, joined them. From Hu[ ] the emigrants proceeded by rail [ ] Liverpool on Monday, April 11th. T[ ] gether with a number of emigrati[ ] Saints and returning missionari[ ] from the British Mission they board[ ] the steamship "Nevada," which sail[ ] from Liverpool on Saturday, Ap[ ] 16th, in charge of Daniel P. Callist[ ] a returning missionary. The co[ ] pany arrived in New York, Ap[ ] 29th and in Salt Lake City, May 4[ ]

A small company of emigran[ ] (14 souls) sailed from Christian[ ] Norway, May 27, 1887, bound f[ ] Utah, under the direction of Carl [ ] Carlson, a returning Elder. Aft[ ] an ordinary passage across the Nor[ ] Sea, the little company arrived sa[ ] ly in England, where they joined [ ] larger company of emigrating Saint[ ] who sailed from Copenhagen, M[ ] 30th.

A larger company of emigrati[ ] Saints (138 in number) destined f[ ] the gathering places of the Saints [ ] America, sailed from Copenhage[ ] May 30, 1887, per steamship "Argo[ ] together with 11 Elders from Zi[ ] returning to their homes, namel[ ] Peter Mattson, Jens W. Jensen, Jam[ ] Yorgason, Jens C. Nielsen (of Ge[ ] tile Valley, Idaho), Niels Pet[ ] Petersen, Jens James Petersen, Ha[ ] Chr. Petersen, Jens Chr. Nielsen ([ ] Brigham City, Utah), Niels A. Ande[ ] son, Niels Jörgensen and Christi[ ] Thomsen Balle.

After a successful voyage, lasti[ ] two days and 11 hours (spendi[ ] two nights on the North Sea), t[ ] good ship "Argo" brought its pr[ ] cious cargo safely to Hull, England, June 1st. On the voyage the Saints assembled for prayer morning and night and the officers of the ship treated the emigrants with kindness. On their arrival in Liverpool they were at once taken on board the steamship "Wyoming," and on the 3rd of June the Norwegian Saints, who had already spent several days in Liverpool, went on board. The "Wyoming" sailed from Liverpool on Saturday, May 14th, having on board 159 Saints, including 14 returning Elders, in charge of Jens C. Nielsen. The voyage across the Atlantic was pleasant, though there were several days of windy weather causing some seasickness. The number of passengers was increased during the passage on the morning of June 11th, when Sister Ramström, from Stockholm, Sweden, gave birth to a daughter, to whom was given the name Oceana. The emigrants landed in New York, June 15th, whence they continued the voyage the same day in the afternoon on the fine steamship "Seneca" (of the Old Dominion Line), and after a pleasant passage along the American coast, they arrived in Norfolk, Virginia, on the 16th. From there the emigrants journeyed by rail to Salt Lake City, where they arrived June 3rd.

A company of emigrating Saints (88 souls) and nine returning Elders sailed from Copenhagen, Sept. 9th, 1887, per steamship "Bravo," under the leadership of Rasmus Rasmussen, for the gathering places of the Saints in America. The names of the other returning missionaries were: Charles Oscar Pedersen, Niels Mikkelsen, Victor Charles Högsted, Peter Olsen, Nils Oscar Gyllenskog, James Ottesen, Gustaf Blomquist and Simon P. Eggertsen. Without any accident or unpleasantness the emigrants arrived in Hull, England,

whence they traveled by rail to Liverpool, and there boarded the ship "Nevada," together with emigrating Saints and returning Elders from Great Britain, the whole company being in charge of Elder Joseph S. Wells, a returning Elder. The ship sailed from Liverpool Oct. 8th, and after an uneventful voyage arrived in New York on the 18th. Here the emigrants the following day (Oct. 19th) boarded another steamship on which they sailed to Norfolk, Virginia, whence they traveled by rail to Salt Lake City, Utah, arriving there October 25th.

A company of emigrating Saints destined for Utah (165 souls), together with eight returning missionaries, sailed from Copenhagen, Aug. 18, 1887, per steamship "Bravo" under the direction of Jens C. Nielsen, of Moroni, Utah, a returning Elder. The names of the other returning Elders were: Johan L. Berg, Joseph Anderson, Peter Anderson, Christian Frandsen, James J. Anderson, Mouritz Mouritzen and Hemming Hansen. The passage of this company of emigrants across the North Sea was pleasant in the early part of the voyage and the Saints frequently grouped on the deck singing hymns and enjoying themselves. On Friday evening a brisk wind sprung up which soon put the sea into an uproar, causing violent heavings of the vessel and universal seasickness among the passengers. However, on Sunday morning, Aug. 21st, the ship arrived in Hull, but owing to low water could not cross the bar until the evening. The steamship "Rolla" which had sailed from Christiania, Aug. 19th, with 32 emigrating Saints, in charge of Elder Anthon Anderson, arrived in Hull about the same time, and the two companies being united then constituted 198 Saints, besides nine returning missionaries. On Monday morning, Aug. 22nd, the emigrants passed through the custom house in Hull, and then continued the journey by rail to Liverpool, where they arrived in the afternoon of the same day and were taken to a hotel on Kent Square. In Liverpool the emigrants went on board the steamship "Wisconsin," together with emigrating Saints and returning Elders from the British Isles (about 400 souls in all), in charge of Elder John I. Hart, a returning Elder. The company, after a safe voyage across the Atlantic Ocean, arrived in New York, Aug. 27th. Thence the journey was continued to Salt Lake City, Utah.

In 1887, 45 Elders from Zion arrived in Copenhagen as missionaries to Scandinavia, in the following order: Jesper Petersen of Castle Dale, Utah, arrived April 26th; Jens Peter Meilstrup of Ephraim, on May 4th, and James Clove of Panguitch, on June 8th. John Peter Sörensen of Salt Lake City, Utah, Ephraim Mortensen of Sanford, Colorado, Gustaf W. Blomquist of Richfield, Frantz T. Grönberg of Salt Lake City, Hans Larsen of Woodland, Utah, James Ottesen of Ephraim, Colorado, Claus H. Karlson of Oakley, Idaho, Peter Nilson of Smithfield, Ole Olson of Lewiston, James Jens Thomsen of Brigham City, Christian J. Plowman of Smithfield, Simon P. Eggertsen and Lars E. Eggertsen of Provo, John Peter Toolson of Smithfield, Adolph Anderson of Logan, Mads Jörgensen of Provo, Hans J. Nielsen of Logan, Hans C. Sörensen of Orderville, Carl Eliason of Millville, Ola Jonson Nordberg of Logan and Carl B. Olsen of Brigham City, Utah, Jacob Madsen of Bloomington, Idaho, and Henrich Peter Jensen of Provo, Utah, arrived June 14th. Lars S. Andersen of Ephraim and Andrew Knudsen of Provo, Utah, arrived June 24th; Henry Jensen of Gentile Valley, Idaho, on July 5th, and John

Anderson Quist of Big Cottonwood, Utah, arrived July 19th; Carl C. A. Christensen of Ephraim and James Hansen, jun., of Brigham City, Utah, arrived Sept. 16th; and Jens C. A. Weibye of Manti, on Sept. 30th; John A. Hendricksen of Logan, Olof Jenson of Brigham City, Otto Julius Swenson of Plain City, Julius Johnson of Hyrum, Anders Mortenson of West Porterville, Jonas Östlund of Elsinore, Olaus T. Nilsson of Heber City, Ferdinand Jacobsen and Rasmus Larsen of Logan, Utah, arrived Nov. 8th; James Anderson of Spanish Fork, John Berg of Santaquin and Carl K. Hansen of Fairview, Utah, arrived Dec. 9th.

Jesper Petersen, Jens P. Meilstrup, John P. Sörensen, Simon P. Eggertsen, Lars E. Eggertsen, Hans J. Nielsen, Henrich P. Jensen, Ferdinand Jacobsen and Rasmus Larsen were appointed to labor in the Aarhus Conference. Lars Strib Andersen, on this his second mission, was appointed to preside over the Aarhus Conference, Denmark. Hans Larsen was appointed to labor in the Aarhus Conference and afterwards in the Copenhagen Conference. James Clove, Henry Jensen, James Hansen, jun., and James Anderson were appointed to labor in the Copenhagen Conference. Ephraim Mortensen was appointed to labor in the Copenhagen Conference, but finished his mission in England. Jens C. A. Weibye, on this his second mission, was appointed to preside over the Copenhagen Conference, Denmark. Gustaf Blomquist, Frantz T. Grönberg, Jonas Östlund and John Berg were appointed to labor in the Stockholm Conference. Adolph Anderson was also appointed to labor in the Stockholm Conference and afterwards as a translator and writer in the mission office in Copenhagen, Denmark. James Ottesen, Jens Thomsen, Christian J. Plowman,

Hans C. Sörensen, Carl K. Hansen, Mads Jörgensen and Jacob Madsen were appointed to labor in the Aalborg Conference; later Elders Jörgensen and Madsen acted as presidents of the Aalborg Conference. Claus H. Karlson, Ola Olson, Carl Eliason, Ola J. Nordberg, Otto J. Swenson, Olaus T. Nilsson and John Anderson Quist (on his second mission) were appointed to labor in the Göteborg Conference. Peter Nilsson (on a second mission), John P. Toolson and Anders Mortenson were appointed to labor in the Skåne Conference. Carl B. Olsen, Andrew Knudsen and Julius Johnson were appointed to labor in the Christiania Conference. John A. Hendricksen was appointed to labor in the Christiania Conference, but finished his mission in England. Olof Jenson was appointed to labor in the Christiania Conference, Norway, but later transferred to the Skåne Conference, Sweden. Carl C. A. Christensen (on his second mission) was appointed to labor as a translator and writer in the mission office in Copenhagen.

CHAPTER 72 (1888)

Four companies of emigrating Saints leave for Utah—Chr. D. Fjeldsted becomes president of the mission a second time—Twenty new Elders arrive from Zion.

Under date of Jan. 17, 1888, Pres. Nils C. Flygare reported that encouraging news from all parts of the mission were received at the mission office, and therefore, the Elders laboring in Scandinavia began the year 1888 with bright prospects.

The season's first emigrating company of Latter-day Saints from Scandinavia sailed from Copenhagen, May 24, 1888, with the steamship "Milo," under the leadership of Elder Peter C. Geertsen. The company numbered 102 souls, Danish and Swedish Saints. Six Elders from Zion, who had labored faithfully

20

and successfully in the Scandinavian Mission, returned to their homes with this company, namely: Peter C. Geertsen (who had labored as a writer for "Skandinaviens Stjerne"), Jens Hansen, Pehr Håkanson, Svante J. Koeven and Charles R. Dorius.

After a pleasant voyage the emigrants arrived at the harbor of Hull, England, on the 27th in the afternoon. They landed the following morning (May 28th) and proceeded by rail to Liverpool, where they, an hour after their arrival, were joined by a small company of emigrating Saints from Norway. The Norwegian contingent of the company (24 souls) sailed from Christiania, Norway, May 25, 1888, in charge of Louis J. Holther, who returned from a mission to Scandinavia. The little company had a safe passage across the North Sea to England.

Together with other emigrants and returning Elders from the British Mission, the Scandinavians went on board the steamship "Wisconsin," sailed from Liverpool, June 2nd, and, after a safe voyage, arrived in New York, June 13th. From New York the westward journey was continued and part of the company arrived in Salt Lake City, June 19th. One death occurred on the voyage, that of an infant daughter of a Swedish lady named Anderson. From New York the company proceeded by coast steamer to Norfolk, Virginia, on the 8th, and arrived in Salt Lake City, Aug. 15th, having traveled by rail from Norfolk, Virginia.

The third company of emigrating Saints from Scandinavia (62 souls from Denmark and Sweden) and five returning missionaries sailed from Copenhagen, Aug. 23, 1888, for Hull, England. The names of the five Elders were: Willard S. Hansen (leader of the company), Peter G. Hanson, August F. Westerberg, Nils L. Högberg and Jacob Hansen. On

Sunday, Aug. 26th, about noon, the company arrived in Hull harbor, and the following day (Aug. 27th) the emigrants landed and continued the journey by rail to Liverpool.

A small company of emigrating Saints (10 souls) sailed from Christiania, Norway, Aug. 24, 1888, in charge of Abraham Johnson, a returning Elder. After a successful voyage across the North Sea, this little company arrived safely in England and there joined the company which sailed from Copenhagen, Aug. 23rd. The amalgamated company sailed from Liverpool on board the steamship "Wyoming," on Saturday, September 1st, Elder Abraham Johnson in charge. After a pleasant voyage the company arrived in New York, Sept. 11th, and in Salt Lake City, Utah, Sept. 19th and 20th.

The fourth and last company of Saints who emigrated from Scandinavia in 1888, consisted of 102 souls, including seven returning Elders, and sailed from Copenhagen, Sept. 27, 1888. The names of the returning Elders were: Nils P. Lindelöf (leader of the company), Joseph Christenson, John Anderson, Albert Nephi Tollestrup, Gustave Backman, Hans C. N. Hansen and Hans J. Nielsen. After a safe voyage across the North Sea the emigrants arrived in Hull, England, and thence continued their journey by rail to Liverpool, where they, together with a small company from Norway (19 souls), boarded the ship "Wisconsin," which sailed from Liverpool, Oct. 6th, in charge of Elder Lindelöf. Part of the Norwegian company sailed from Christiania, Sept. 28, 1888, in charge of Carl Erikson and Christian Olsen. This little company had a safe voyage across the North Sea. After a safe voyage across the Atlantic the "Wisconsin" arrived in New York Oct. 15th. A family with two children was left in New York, because the

husband had diphtheria. The other emigrants boarded the ship "Roanoke" in New York and enjoyed a voyage along the American coast to Norfolk, Virginia, whence they traveled by railroad to Salt Lake City, where they arrived safe and well, Oct. 23, 1888.

Pres. Nils C. Flygare, after a successful mission in Scandinavia, left Copenhagen, Oct. 3, 1888, to return to his home in Utah, in charge of a company of emigrating Saints. Elder Christian D. Fjeldsted succeeded him as president of the mission.

The second company of Scandinavian Saints, who emigrated to Zion in 1888, sailed from Copenhagen, July 19, 1888, per steamship "Cato" in charge of Elder Christen L. Christensen, who, together with three other Elders from Zion (Anders Gustav Nygren, Andrew N. Michaelsen and Pehr Olof Pehrson), were returning home to Zion after successful missionary labors in Scandinavia. There were 113 souls in this company from Denmark and Sweden. The weather being good, only a very little seasickness was experienced by the emigrants. On Sunday forenoon (July 22nd) a meeting was held on deck with the captain's permission, and many of the 125 other passengers on board had the opportunity of listening to explanations of the first principles of the gospel by "Mormon" Elders for the first time in their lives. The captain and the crew were very kind to the emigrants. The ship reached Hull, England, that day (Sunday, July 22nd). The following day, the emigrants continued the journey by rail to Liverpool.

A small company of emigrating Saints from Norway sailed from Christiania July 20, 1888, in charge of Elders Hans J. Christiansen and Chr. O. Folkmann, who were returning to their homes, after having performed faithful missions. This company had a safe voyage across the North Sea to England, where they joined the emigrant company which left Copenhagen, Denmark, July 19th. At Liverpool the amalgamated company boarded the steamship "Wyoming" and sailed from that port, July 28th, in charge of Elder Hans J. Christiansen. After a pleasant voyage across the Atlantic, the emigrants landed in New York August 8th.

In 1888, 20 Elders from Zion, who were appointed to labor as missionaries in Scandinavia, arrived in Copenhagen, Denmark, in the following order: John Jacob Carlson of Pleasant Grove, Anders Johan Anderson of Santaquin, Utah, Ola Peterson of Bennington, Idaho, and Ludvig Ernström of Ogden, Utah, arrived May 4th; James Poulsen of Liberty, Idaho, arrived May 9th; John J. Nielsen of Brigham City, Mathias C. Lund of Plain City, Bengt Johnson, jun., of Provo, Gearsen S. Bastian of Washington, Ole Pedersen of Clarkston, Nils Anthon of Spanish Fork and Elof George Erickson of Grantsville, Utah, and Lars Peter Nielsen of Ovid, Idaho, arrived June 6th; Joseph Christoffer Kempe of Alpine, Arizona, arrived June 20th; Carl Edwin Peterson of Ogden, Hans C. Kofoed of Levan, Andrew K. Andersen and Erastus C. Willardsen of Ephraim, arrived October 30th; Frands Peter Petersen of Koosharem, arrived Nov. 13th, and Erik Hogan of Bountiful, Utah, arrived Dec. 3rd.

Elders John Jacob Carlson and Bengt Johnson, jun., were appointed to labor in the Skåne Conference. Anders Johan Anderson and Elof George Erickson in the Göteborg Conference, and Olof Peterson and Nils Anthon in the Stockholm Conference. Ludvig Ernström was appointed to labor in the Stockholm Conference and afterwards as president of said conference. Jens Poulsen and Mathias Chr. Lund were appointed to labor in the Copenhagen Conference. John J. Nielsen

NILS ANTHON,

Son of Johan Gustav Anthon and Hannah Pearson, was born Oct. 30, 1862, at Käflinge, Sweden; baptized June 8, 1882, and, emigrating to Utah, arrived in Spanish Fork July 16, 1882. He married Caroline Jörgensen Hansen in the Logan Temple Dec. 10, 1884. In 1888-1890 he filled a mission to Sweden, laboring in Stockholm, Gotland, Upsala and Eskilstuna; at Upsala he was fined 100 kronor for preaching the gospel. He filled a second mission to Scandinavia in 1900-1903, laboring in the Stockholm Conference and later as president of the said conference. Upon his return to America he had charge of an emigrant company of 200 souls. Being ordained a High Priest, he was set apart as first counselor to Bishop George Hales of the Spanish Fork Third Ward. He has been a resident of Salt Lake City since July, 1920.

and Carl Edwin Peterson were appointed to labor in the Copenhagen Conference, Denmark, and later in the Christiania Conference, Norway. Erastus Chr. Willardsen was appointed to labor in the Copenhagen Conference and later in the Aarhus Conference. Gearsen S. Bastian and Frands Peter Petersen were appointed to labor in the Aarhus Conference and Ole Petersen and Anders K. Anderson in the Aalborg Conference. Anders K. Anderson acted as president of the Aalborg Conference until his death which occurred Jan. 5, 1890. Lars P. Nielsen was appointed to labor in the Aalborg Conference, Denmark, and later in the Christiania ¦ Conference, Norway. Joseph C. Kempe, Hans Chr. Kofoed and Erik Hogan were appointed to labor in the Christiania Conference, Norway.

CHAPTER 73 (1889)

Mobbings on the island of Bornholm—Four companies of Saints leave for Utah—Arrival of 43 Elders from Zion.

Elders James Hansen and Erastus C. Willardsen were on trial on the island of Bornholm before the mayor of the city of Rönne, Feb. 5, 1889. Elder Hansen had labored about sixteen months on the island and through his diligence made a number of converts. During his absence from the island on a visit to Copenhagen, a Lutheran priest (Hasle) in Rönne published a scurrilous article in the newspaper of that city in which he slandered the Saints and their doctrines. As the success of the Elders had already caused uneasiness in certain circles, this article added additional fuel to the flames and excited the rude and somewhat ignorant population. Consequently, when Elder Hansen, accompanied by Elder Willardsen (who had been appointed to labor as a missionary on Bornholm with Brother Hansen) arrived in Rönne and held a meeting the same evening in their hired hall, a mob appeared, making hideous noises and sundry demonstrations in the presence of the 'pious priest', who seemed to sanction the disturbance. Strange to say, the following Sunday passed without any demonstration on the part of the mob, and the Saints held their meeting in peace as usual. But the next Sunday, Feb. 3rd, the police officers arrived and broke up the meeting. A certain man had, in the forenoon, apparent-

ly as a friend, invited the brethren to take supper with him, but the Elders were impressed not to accept the invitation, and later they found out that this was only a part of the plans of the mob laid for the purpose of bringing the brethren into their power, for a dozen or more men had gathered to inflict bodily violence upon the brethren, should they put in an appearance. While the mob thus waited to carry out their plans, the brethren, guided by the Spirit, chose a round-about road, in order to reach a certain place previously selected, where they administered the holy ordinance of baptism to three persons. The mob next sought after the brethren in their assembly hall, and gave vent to their hatred by breaking in the doors and some of the windows until they were at last dispersed by the assistance of the police. On Tuesday, Feb. 5th, the Elders, as stated, were called into court for a preliminary hearing, and on this occasion the mayor advised the brethren in all kindness to leave the island, which they did a few days later, after having baptized four other persons, agreeable to the Savior's admonition, "When they persecute you in one city, flee to another."

In the early part of 1889, the Lutheran priests in several districts in Sweden used their authority to forbid the Elders to preach, and in a couple of instances they were fined to the amount of 60 and 100 kronor, ($15 and $25) respectively. The latter was imposed on one of the native young men, about 18 years of age, and was based on the ground that he had, notwithstanding he was forbidden to preach in public, "offered extempore prayers in the 'Mormon' spirit."

A company of emigrating Saints (239 souls) sailed from Copenhagen, Denmark, May 30, 1889, in the evening per steamship "Milo," for Hull and Liverpool, England, on their way to America. Thirteen Elders from Zion, who, during the last two years, had labored as missionaries in Scandinavia, returned to their homes with this company of emigrants; their names follow: John P. Sörensen, Francis T. Grönberg, Claus H. Karlson, Peter Nilsson, Christian J. Plowman, Charles Carl Eliason, Carl B. Olsen, Jacob Maden, Lars S. Andersen, Henry Jensen, James Hanson, jun., Bengt Johnson, jun. (released on account of sickness), and Karl H. P. Nordberg. On Sunday, June 2nd, the emigrants arrived in Hull harbor, landed the following day (Monday) and continued their journey by rail to Liverpool. A smaller company of emigrants from Norway, under the leadership of John A. Hendricksen and Carl B. Olsen, sailed from Christiania May 1st, reached Hull Sunday evening, and joined the larger company from Copenhagen, in Liverpool, June 3rd. Together with a number of Swiss and German Saints the two companies of Scandinavians sailed from Liverpool in the ship "Wyoming" June 8, 1889, and after a pleasant voyage the company arrived in New York on the 9th. Thence the journey was continued to Salt Lake City, which was reached in safety June 26, 1889.

The second company of emigrating Saints from Scandinavia for this season, consisting of 150 souls, sailed from Copenhagen, Aug. 8, 1889, per steamship "Bravo," destined for the gathering place of the Saints in the Rocky Mountains. After a successful voyage across the North Sea, the company arrived in Hull, England, Sunday, Aug. 11th, all well. In the forenoon of that day, the Saints had held a meeting on the deck, by permission of the captain, and had altogether been treated very well by the ship's crew. The following day

(Aug. 12th), early in the morning, they landed and continued their journey by rail to Liverpool. While staying in Liverpool the emigrants secured lodgings at Hotel Svea.

A company of Norwegian Saints, numbering 22 souls, who sailed from Christiania, August 9th, in charge of Elder Olof Jensen, joined the larger company in England. The leadership of the amalgamated company was entrusted to Elder Jens C. A. Weibye with Mads Jörgensen and Andrew Knudsen as his assistants. Besides these three brethren there were 12 other returning missionaries, viz., Hans Larsen, Ole Olson, James Thomsen, John P. Toolsen, Hans C. Sörensen, Ola Jönson Nordberg, Henrik P. Jensen, Olof Jensen, Otto J. Swenson, Anders Mortensen, James Anderson and Ole Petersen. At Liverpool the Saints boarded the steamship "Wyoming" and sailed on the 17th. Altogether 191 emigrating Saints crossed the Atlantic in the steamship "Wyoming," which arrived in New York August 27th, in the morning. Thence the emigrants traveled by rail to Salt Lake City.

The third company of the season's Latter-day Saint emigration from Scandinavia (42 souls) sailed from Copenhagen, Sept. 12, 1889, per steamship "Milo," under the direction of Elder Rasmus Larsen. After a successful voyage over the North Sea the company arrived in Hull, whence they traveled by rail to Liverpool, where they went on board the steamship "Wyoming" and sailed from Liverpool, Sept. 22nd. A company of 16 souls from Norway, which sailed from Christiania Sept. 13th, joined the larger company in England, a local brother having had charge of the company from Norway. After an uneventful voyage across the Atlantic, the "Wyoming" arrived in New York, Oct. 1, 1889; the voyage had, however, been somewhat stormy.

From New York the voyage was continued by steamboat to Norfolk, Virginia, whence the emigrants proceeded westward by rail and arrived safely in Salt Lake City. The Utah Elders returning with this company were the following: Rasmus Larsen, John Berg and Lars E. Eggertsen. The 42 souls sailing from Copenhagen were emigrants from Denmark and Sweden and the 16 sailing from Christiania were emigrants from Norway.

Another company of Saints bound for Zion sailed from Copenhagen, Oct. 17, 1889, per steamship "Cameo" and arrived in Hull, Sunday morning, Oct. 20th. Some Norwegian Saints, under the leadership of Elder Anthon L. Skanchy, arrived in Hull the same day on a steamer, which laid to by the side of the "Cameo." On Monday morning, Oct. 21st, the emigrants landed and journeyed by rail to Liverpool where they were taken care of at Hotel Svea. In Liverpool the emigrants were joined by other Saints emigrating to Utah from Great Britain and Holland, and boarded the steamship "Wyoming," which sailed from Liverpool on Saturday, Oct. 26, 1889, with 161 Saints on board, namely: 116 from Scandinavia, 6 from Holland and 24 from Great Britain, besides 12 returning Elders and three returning visitors; the whole company was placed in charge of Anthon L. Skanchy. After a pleasant voyage, during which the weather was mild and pleasant most of the time, the ship reached New York harbor in the evening of Nov. 5th. The following day, the emigrants passed through quarantine and landed in New York. The emigrants re-embarked on the ship "Wyanoke" and sailed for Norfolk, Virginia, where they arrived Nov. 7th; thence they started westward by rail and traveled via Pueblo, Colorado, etc., to Salt Lake

City, where they arrived Nov. 13, safe and well. The names of the Elders from the Scandinavian Mission who returned with this company are as follows: Anthon L. Skanchy, Ola Olson, Carl C. A. Christensen, Julius Johnson, Olaus T. Nilson, Ferdinand Jacobsen, Carl K. Hansen, John J. Nielsen and Edmund Sanderson (on account of ill health).

In 1889, 43 Elders arrived in Copenhagen from Zion, as missionaries to Scandinavia, on the following dates: Jens Jensen of Salina, Utah, arrived Feb. 24th; Lars Chr. Johnson of Redmond, and Ole H. Berg of Provo, Utah, on March 26th; Alif Ericksen of Mt. Pleasant, August Severin Schow of Richmond, Niels Peter Madsen of Manti, Andrew Johnson (Jonson) of Union, Jonas Mattson of Salina, Carl Söderlund of East Mill Creek, Niels Nielsen of Salt Lake City, Lars K. Peterson of Huntsville, John Elof Johnson of Tooele City, Christian M. Jensen of Mantua, Edmund Sandersen of Gunnison, Sören P. Jensen of Ephraim, Lorentz Petersen of Hyrum, Utah, John Dahlquist of Oakley, Idaho, Lars Erik Larson of Richmond, John August Beckstrand of Meadow, Nils Nilson of Santaquin, Christian J. Mortensen of Salina and Christian Hermansen of Elsinore, Utah, arrived April 30th; Niels Frederiksen of Salem and Hans Peter Miller of Richfield arrived May 27th; and Erastus Kofoed of Mt. Pleasant on June 24th. Truls A. Hallgren of Ogden, James Petersen of South Jordan, Hans Martin Hansen of Fremont, Andrew P. Renström of Huntsville, Michael A. Hansen of Elsinore Boye P. B. Petersen of Castle Dale Oleen N. Stohl of Brigham City Andrew P. Anderson of Salt Lake City, Utah, and James Keller, jun., of Mink Creek, Idaho, arrived Aug 28th; Johan A. Hellström and Michael Nielsen of Richfield, Utah arrived Oct. 2nd. Frands Carl Michaelsen of Redmond, John Johnson of Provo, Ole Olson of Smithfield, and John Peter Olsen of Scipio, Utah, arrived Oct. 29th; Carl Edward Thor-

Hans Martin Hansen, Michael Nielsen and Johan Gustaf Jörgensen were

LORENTZ PETERSEN

Was born Feb. 15, 1857, in Valby, Sjælland, Denmark, the son of Hans Petersen and Doris Laurentsen. He emigrated with his parents to Utah in 1863, crossing the Atlantic on the ship "John J. Boyd," and the plains with ox teams in the company of Captain Young. He was baptized when eight years of age, and married Christine Nielsen in 1877, which union was blessed with nine children, six sons and three daughters. In 1890-1892 Bro. Petersen filled a mission to Denmark, during which he presided over the Copenhagen Conference. He acted as Bishop's counselor for twenty years, and has officiated in the Logan Temple about thirty years. Three of his sons have filled missions, one in England and two in the United States.

stensen and Hans Erickson of Logan, and Johan Gustaf Jörgensen of Koosharem, Utah, arrived Nov. 28th.

Jens Jensen, Sören Peter Jensen, Michael A. Hansen and Boye Peter B. Petersen were appointed to labor in the Aarhus Conference. Niels Frederiksen was appointed to labor in the Aarhus Conference and later in the Copenhagen Conference. Frands Carl Michaelsen was appointed to labor in the Aarhus Conference and later in the Aalborg Conference. Alif Ericksen, Erastus Kofoed (Kofford)

JOHAN GUSTAV JÖRGENSEN,

Son of Jens Jörgensen and Caroline Gustava Fredrikke Fjeldström, was born in Drammen, Norway, Jan. 25, 1837. The father was a sailor from Nötterö, near Tönsberg, and the mother a native of Drammen. The parents died while he was still a small child, and at the age of 15 he became an apprentice in the cooper shop of Erland Pedersen. While working there, he was attracted one evening by singing in the home of one Amund Dahle. Invited in, he attended the meeting and received a testimony that the people there assembled were the Saints of God. After three years of inquiry, he was baptized, Jan. 30, 1858. In November, 1859, he received a master's diploma as a cooper, and the following year he was sent on a mission to Kongsberg and the Drammen district, and from 1860 to 1863 he presided over the Stravanger Branch. He emigrated to Utah in 1863, crossing the ocean in the sailing vessel "John J. Boyd," married Mrs. Serine K. Staalesen at Florence, Neb., crossed the Plains with ox teams, and arrived in Salt Lake City Sept. 12, 1863; he located in Ephraim, Sanpete County. Elder Jörgensen was known as J. Gustav Jensen, until he and his wife entered the Endowment House, when he was counseled to take his father's surname. Of five children, there are now (1927) living: Enoch, at Sandy; Bertha J. Paulsen at Ephraim, and Heber, in Chicago, Ill. May 17, 1869, Bro. Jörgensen married Annette Matilda Iversen. Of fourteen children by this union six now are living: Joseph A., and Mary O. Nelson, at Richfield, Utah; Sam M., at Salina, Utah; Amanda J., in Oklahoma; Dr. James M., and Jennie J. Jones, in Salt Lake City. Bro. Jörgensen suffered trials and hardships incident to pioneer life by Indian depredations, etc. In 1878 he became a pioneer of Koosharem, Utah, and in 1889-1891 he filled a mission to Norway, laboring in Bergen and Christiania; after his return he moved to Salina, Utah, where he died, May 18, 1900.

appointed to labor in the Christiania Conference. Ole H. Berg was appointed to preside over the Christiania Conference. August S. Schow

OLEEN N. STOHL

Was born Feb. 19, 1865, at Sugar House Ward, Salt Lake County, Utah, the son of Ole N. Stohl and Christina Johnson. The family moved to Brigham City in 1866, where Oleen grew to manhood and took an active part in religious and civic affairs. In 1889-1891 he filled a successful mission to Sweden, laboring in the Christianstad Branch, Skåne Conference, and later in the Stockholm Conference. In 1892 (Sept. 7th) he married Sarah Peters, from which union three sons and three daughters were born. Bro. Stohl acted as president of the Boxelder Stake from May 29, 1905, until his death, which occurred Nov. 28, 1916. He was a success as a presiding officer and was universally beloved and respected by all who knew him.

was appointed to labor in the Christiania Conference and later in the Copenhagen Conference. Christian Hermansen was appointed to labor in the Christiania Conference, and later in the Aalborg Conference. John Johnson was appointed to labor in the Christiania Conference and later to preside over said Conference. Niels Peter Madsen and Christian M. Jensen were appointed to labor in the Aalborg Conference. Christian J. Mortensen was also appointed to labor in the Aalborg Conference, but

being banished from Denmark in October, 1889, he finished his mission in England. Andrew Johnson, Niels Nielsen, Lars K. Peterson, Nils Nilson, and Truls A. Hallgren (second mission) were appointed to labor in the Skåne Conference. Oleen Nilsson Stohl was appointed to labor in the Skåne, Göteborg and Stockholm conferences. Jonas Mattson, Carl Söderlund, Anders Peter Anderson and Hans Erickson were appointed to

CARL EDWARD THORSTENSEN

Was born March 6, 1863, in Christiania, Norway, baptized July 17, 1873, ordained to the Priesthood and sent out as a missionary when 16 years old. He was ordained an Elder at 17 and appointed superintendent of the Christiania Branch Sunday School and late president of the Y. M. M. I. A. in the Christiania Branch and clerk of the Norwegian Mission. After emigrating to Utah in 188 he was ordained a Seventy and located at Logan, Utah. In 1889-1891 he filled a mission to Scandinavia and acted as a translator in the office of the "Skandinaviens Stjerne," and during the last five months he also acted as president of the Copenhagen Conference. He acted as superintendent of the Logan Seventh Ward Sunday School for thirteen years and in February, 1899, he was set apart as a president of the 119th quorum of Seventy. Bro. Thorstensen died at Logan, March 11 1903.

labor in the Stockholm Conference. Andrew P. Renström (on his second mission) was appointed to labor in the Stockholm Conference and later in the Göteborg Conference. Johan August Hellström was appointed to labor in the Stockholm Conference and later as a writer and translator in the mission office in Copenhagen, Denmark. Lars Chr. Johnson was appointed to labor in the Copenhagen and later in the Aalborg Conference, Denmark. Edmund Sandersen, Lorentz Petersen, Hans Peter Miller, James Petersen, James M. Keller, jun., and John Olson were appointed to labor in the Copenhagen and later in the Aalborg Conference. Carl Edward Thorstensen was appointed to labor in the mission office in Copenhagen and later as president of the Copenhagen Conference. John Elof Johnson, John Dahlquist, Lars Erik Larson, John A. Beckstrand and Ola Olson were appointed to labor in the Göteborg Conference.

CHAPTER 74 (1890)

Death of Elders Andrew K. Andersen and John Anderson Quist—Four companies of Saints emigrate to Utah—Edward H. Anderson succeeds Chr. D. Fjeldsted as president of the mission—Arrival of 36 Elders.

Elder Andrew K. Andersen, president of the Aalborg Conference, died in Aalborg, Denmark, Jan. 5, 1890, of lung trouble, after only a few days' sickness. He was buried on the 12th in Hovlbjerg parish, Viborg Amt, Denmark, by the side of his parents. Brother Andersen was born Aug. 6, 1859, in Hovlbjerg parish, Viborg Amt, Denmark, and emigrated to Utah when quite young. He arrived in Denmark as a missionary to Scandinavia in October, 1888, and after laboring a short time as a traveling Elder in the Aarhus Conference, he was appointed to preside over the Aalborg Conference, Nov. 3, 1888, which position he held until his demise.

Elder John Anderson Quist, president of the Göteborg Conference, died at Vingåker, Sweden, March 13,

ANDREW K. ANDERSEN

Was born in Hovlbjerg parish, Viborg amt, Denmark, Aug. 6, 1859, baptized May 5, 1880, and emigrated to Utah about 1881, locating in Ephraim, Sanpete County. Here he was ordained a Seventy and became a member of the 47th quorum of Seventy. In 1888 he was called on a mission to Scandinavia, his wife accompanying him. After laboring one year as a traveling Elder in the Aarhus Conference, he presided over the Aalborg Conference until Jan. 5, 1890, when he died in Aalborg of pneumonia after only a few days' illness. He was buried at Hovlbjerg. Elder Andersen, who was called hence in the midst of a useful career, was beloved by all who knew him, both at home and abroad.

1890. He was one of the most successful and faithful Elders in the mission.

A company of emigrating Saints, consisting of 116 souls, and six returning missionaries, sailed from Copenhagen April 24, 1890, per steamship "Cameo" for Hull, England, bound for Utah, under the direction of Elder Adolph Anderson. The names of the other returning Elders were as follows: Gearsen S. Bastian, Ole Peterson, Nils Anthon, Elof G. Erickson and Mathias C. Lund. The voyage across the North Sea was successful, though considerable seasickness prevailed on the Saturday, which was stormy. Capt. Chambers treated the emigrants with kindness and consideration. The company arrived in Hull, England, on the 27th,

ANNA K. ANDERSEN,

Wife of Andrew K. Andersen, was born June 7, 1858, in Copenhagen, Denmark, married Andrew K. Andersen Oct. 14, 1879, accompanied her husband on a mission to Denmark in 1888-1890 and rendered efficient help in missionary labors until she became a widow. After burying her husband beside his father in his native village (Hovlbjerg) she returned to her home in Ephraim, Sanpete County, Utah, where she still resides. For a number of years Sister Andersen took an active part in the Primary Association in Ephraim, acting as counselor to the local president.

in the morning. A small company of emigrating Saints (29 souls) and two returning missionaries (Ludvig Ehrnström and Lars P. Nielsen) sailed from Christiania, Norway, Apr. 25, 1890, bound for Utah. After a somewhat stormy voyage across the North Sea this company arrived in Hull on the evening of the 27th, where they joined the larger company of Scandinavian emigrants who left Copenhagen on the 24th. On Monday morning (April 28th) the two emigrant companies traveled by rail to Liverpool, where lodging was secured for them at Hotel Svea. President George Teasdale organized the company with Adolph Anderson

as leader and Elders Ludvig Ehrnström and Gearsen S. Bastian as his assistants. On Friday evening, May 2nd, the emigrants went on board the steamship "Wyoming" and sailed from Liverpool the next day, May 3rd. A few hours after leaving the River Mersey, stormy weather set in, causing considerable sickness among the emigrants. After a quick voyage across the Atlantic, the "Wyoming" arrived in New York May 13th, whence the emigrants continued their journey to Utah.

The season's second company of emigrating Scandinavian Saints, con-

JOHN A. QUIST

Was born Dec. 9, 1845, near Kongelf, Bohus län, Sweden, baptized June 7, 1863, in Norrköping, and labored as a missionary about six years in Norway and Sweden before he emigrated to Utah in 1869. He located in Big Cottonwood, Salt Lake County. In 1877-1879 he filled a mission to his native land, laboring first as a traveling Elder and later as president of the Göteborg Conference. Returning home, he was leader of a company of emigrating Saints. He then labored with zeal as a home missionary in the Salt Lake Stake of Zion, was one of the presidents of the Second quorum of Seventy, etc. In 1887 he was called on a second mission to Scandinavia and the Göteborg Conference once more became his field of labor. While working diligently as a missionary he died, March 13, 1890, at Vingåker.

sisting of 158 souls and three returning missionaries, sailed from Copenhagen, Denmark, May 29, 1890, on
their way to Utah. The names of the
returning Elders were: John J. Carlson, who had labored in the Skåne
Conference (leader of the company),
James Poulsen from the Copenhagen
Conference and John Dahlquist from
the Göteborg Conference. This company had a safe voyage to Hull, England, and proceeded to Liverpool
where they embarked on the steamship "Wyoming" June 7, 1890, for
New York, where they arrived June
19th.

A small company of emigrating
Saints (12 souls) and Elder Erastus
C. Willardsen, returning from his
mission in Scandinavia, sailed from
Christiania, Norway, May 30, 1890,
destined for the gathering place of
the Saints in America. This little
company, after a safe voyage across
the North Sea, joined the larger company of Scandinavian emigrants in
Hull, England, June 2nd. The amalgamated company sailed from
Liverpool June 7, 1890, for New York
on the steamship "Wyoming" in
charge of Elder Erastus C. Willardsen. It arrived in New York June
9, 1890, whence the journey was
continued by rail to Utah.

The third of this season's emigrant
companies of Scandinavian Saints,
consisting of 107 souls and four returning missionaries, sailed from
Copenhagen, Denmark, Aug. 7, 1890,
under the leadership of Elder Jonas
Östlund, one of the returning Elders.
The other returning Elders were:
Anders Johan Anderson, Michael A.
Hansen and Andrew J. Aagaard.
After a safe voyage across the North
Sea, the company arrived in Hull
on the 10th. No sickness had prevailed among this company on the
voyage owing to fine weather. A
small company of emigrating Saints
(6 souls) sailed from Christiania,

Norway, Aug. 8, 1890, under the
leadership of Elder Joseph C. Kempe,
bound for Utah. After a safe voyage
across the North Sea, this little company of Norwegians arrived in Hull,
and were united with the larger company of emigrating Saints which had
left Copenhagen, on the 7th. On
Monday, August 11th, the emigrants
went by rail to Liverpool, where
they, on the 15th, went on board the
steamship "Wyoming" and sailed
from Liverpool on the 16th. After
an unusually pleasant voyage across
the Atlantic Ocean, during which
they were treated with kindness and
due consideration by the captain and
other officers of the vessel, they arrived in New York on August 26th.
Thence the journey was continued by
rail to Utah.

The season's fourth company of
emigrating Saints from the Scandinavian Mission, consisting of 133
souls, three returning missionaries
and Sister Anna Anderson, from
Utah, who had spent two years in
Denmark visiting relatives, sailed
from Copenhagen, Sept. 13th, 1890,
under the leadership of Elder Jens
Jensen, and Lars C. Johnson. A
small company of emigrating Saints
(23 souls) sailed from Christiania,
Norway, Sept. 12th, 1890, bound for
Utah, under the direction of Elder
Erik Hogan, a returning Elder. After
a successful voyage across the North
Sea, this company joined the emigrants who had left Copenhagen on
the 13th. The amalgamated company sailed from Liverpool Sept.
20th, per steamship "Wyoming,"
which arrived safely in New York,
whence the emigrants traveled by rail
to Utah.

Elder John U. Stucki, president of
the Swiss and German Mission, and
Elder Wm. B. Preston, jun., arrived
in Copenhagen, June 21, 1890, on a
visit to Denmark. They spent a very
pleasant time in Copenhagen and

vicinity, visiting Saints and places of interest.

President Chr. D. Fjeldsted, who had presided over the Scandinavian Mission since October, 1888, and Elder Carl E. Peterson, who had presided over the Copenhagen Conference, left Çopenhagen Sept. 29, 1890, for their homes in Utah, having performed efficient and faithful labors in the Scandinavian Mission. Elder Edward H. Anderson succeeded Chr. D. Fjeldsted as president of the mission.

In 1890, 36 Elders from Zion arrived in Copenhagen, as missionaries to Scandinavia, in the following order: Mads Nielsen of Spring City, Utah, arrived April 14th; H. W. Hanson of Salt Lake City, Lars L. Nilson of Provo, Utah, James C. Berthelsen of Sanford, Colorado, Rasmus Sörensen of Levan, and Andreas Jensen Aagaard of Fountain Green, Utah, arrived May 2nd; Ola Jenson of Peoa, Charles W. Olson of Grantsville, Lars Johan Henström of Logan, Laurentius Dahlquist of Salt Lake City and Joseph R. Olson of Grantsville, Utah, arrived May 23rd; Anders Sörensen Hyrup of Salt Lake City, Utah, June 27th, and Edward Berg and Lars Pehrson of Logan, August 23rd. Edward H. Anderson of Ogden, Jens N. Hansen and John O. Rosenkrantz of Logan, Utah, Christian H. Poulsen of Franklin, Idaho, Harold F. Liljenquist of Hyrum, Peter H. Sörensen, Jens H. Kofoed and Thor C. Nielsen of Brigham City, Michael Johnson of Hyrum, Pehr Cronquist of Logan, Andrew Hansen and Andrew G. Johnson of Pleasant Grove, and Pehr N. Pehrson of West Jordan, Utah, arrived Sept. 28th. Anton E. Christensen of Fountain Green, Peter Christensen, Niels J. Anderson and Jens Peter Petersen of Moroni, Peter Henry Hansen and Mads P. Sörensen of Mayfield, John H. Forsgren of Brigham City and

Nils Borgeson of Lewiston, Utah, arrived Oct. 28th, and Christian Meyer of Vermillion, Utah, on Nov. 14th, 1890.

Mads Nielsen, Jens N. Hansen, Harold F. Liljenquist, Jens H. Ko-

EDWARD H. ANDERSON

Was born Oct. 8, 1858, in Billeberga, Malmöhus län, Sweden, emigrated to Utah in 1864, was baptized July 1, 1869, resided in Mill Creek, Farmington and Huntsville successively, laboring alternately on the farm and attending schools. He graduated from the Normal department of the University of Deseret in 1877, was superintendent of public schools and taught school for several years in Weber County. He figured as a newspaper manager and editor in Ogden from 1879 to 1889, and served six years as city recorder, in 1894-1900; was a member of the fourth Utah legislature, and United States surveyor-general in 1901-1905. He was ordained an Elder in 1880 and married Jane S. Ballantyne in 1882. They have six sons and one daughter. He was ordained a High Priest in 1882, served the Weber Stake as superintendent of the Y. M. M. I. A. and High Counselor for several years. From 1888 to 1890 he edited the "Contributor" for Junius F. Wells. After arriving home from his mission field in Scandinavia, 1890-1892, he wrote "A Brief History of the Church", a "Life of Brigham Young", followed later by "Conduct", "Courage", "Character", "Spiritual Growth", "The Apostles of Jesus Christ", etc. He has been associate editor of the "Improvement Era" since June, 1899; clerk of the general conferences of the Church since September, 1916, and counselor in the Granite Stake presidency for a number of years.

oed, and Peter H. Hansen were appointed to labor in the Copenhagen Conference. Niels J. Andersen was appointed to labor in the Copen-

HAROLD FRIDTJOFF LILJENQUIST,

Son of Ola N. Liljenquist and Christine Jacobsen, was born Jan. 19, 1857, in Copenhagen, Denmark, emigrated with his parents to Utah in 1857, was baptized when about nine years old, and was raised and schooled in Hyrum, where he was also ordained to the Priesthood and took part in Church affairs from his early youth. He married Laurine Rasmussen Jan. 1, 1876, which marriage was blessed with eight sons, of whom five are still living. In 1890-1892 he filled a mission to Scandinavia, laboring in the Copenhagen Conference, Denmark, part of the time as conference president. Returning home he had charge of a company of emigrating Saints. At home he acted as president of the Y. M. M. I. A. for two years, and as assistant superintendent and superintendent of the Sunday School in the Hyrum Ward. When Hyrum was divided into three wards, he was chosen as Bishop of the First Ward, which position he held for twelve years. He has also served as county commissioner (one term), mayor of Hyrum (three terms), city councilman (seven terms), and has been an employee of the Amalgamated Sugar Company, as fieldman, for twenty-two years.

hagen and later in the Aarhus Conference. James C. Berthelsen, Rasmus Sörensen, Andreas J. Aagaard, Anders S. Hyrup, Christian H. Poulsen (who finished his mission in England), Peter H. Sörensen, Jens P. Petersen and Mads P. Sörensen were appointed to labor in the Aarhus

Conference. Christian Meyer was also appointed to labor in the Aarhus Conference, having labored a short time in Germany and Switzerland. Anders Hansen was appointed to labor in the Aalborg and later in the Copenhagen Conference. H. W. Hanson, Lars J. Henström, Joseph R. Olson, Lars Pehrson, Andrew G. Johnson and John H. Forsgren were appointed to labor in the Stockholm Conference. Lars L. Nilson was appointed to labor in the Stockholm and later in the Göteborg Conference. Ola Jenson, John O. Rosenkrantz, Pehr Cronquist, and Pehr N. Pehrson were appointed to labor in the Skåne Conference. Charles W. Olson, and Nils Borgeson were appointed to labor in the Göteborg Conference. Laurentius Dahlquist was appointed to labor in the Göteborg Conference and later as president of said conference. Edward Berg, Michael Johnson, Anthon E. Christensen and Peter Christensen were appointed to labor in the Christiania Conference. Thor C. Nielsen was appointed to labor in the Aalborg Conference.

CHAPTER 75 (1891)

Saints in Scandinavia study the English language—Apostle Brigham Young, jun., visits the Scandinavian countries—Saints in charge of returning Elders leave Scandinavia for Zion—Fifty-eight Elders arrive from America.

Elder Andrew P. Renström reported in January, 1891, that the meetings in the city of Göteborg, Sweden, were, at that time, better attended than for several years past. In Eskilstuna and vicinity the Elders had held a number of well attended meetings in country districts, but the local Lutheran priest had opposed them and presented some of the old threadbare accusations against the Prophet Joseph Smith and the Saints generally.

In January, 1891, a night school

for teaching the Danish Saints the English language was commenced in the Copenhagen Branch. The school was divided into three divisions and met every Monday evening. About this time also the Copenhagen Branch choir increased its membership until it became the largest choir in the mission. The success of the splendid meetings, which had recently been held in Copenhagen, was partly due to the excellent musical numbers rendered by this choir. In July a hall for holding meetings was rented in Slagelse on the island of Sjælland, Denmark.

Apostle Brigham Young, jun., president of the European Mission, and Elder John F. Squires of the Liverpool office, England, arrived in Copenhagen, April 25, 1891, on a missionary trip to Scandinavia. These brethren attended conference meetings in Copenhagen (Denmark), Christiania (Norway), Stockholm (Sweden), and public meetings also in other parts of the mission. The visiting brethren left Göteborg on their return to England May 20, 1891.

Under date of June 19, 1891, Elder Edward H. Anderson, president of the Scandinavian Mission, gives an interesting report of conference meetings which he attended in Copenhagen, Christiania, and Stockholm, in company with Apostle Brigham Young, jun., and also of other conference meetings which he later attended in Norrköping, Malmö, Aalborg and Aarhus. Pres. Anderson reported that the Elders in most parts of Sweden labored under the disadvantage of having too large a territory to travel in, with an insufficient number of laborers. In many districts of country the restored gospel had not recently been preached, but there were openings everywhere for the Elders to preach, though this generally had to be done by hiring

halls, which meant expenses that some of the Elders were not prepared to meet.

The name of the street in Copenhagen where the mission office had been located for many years, was changed in June, 1891, from Lorentzensgade to Sankt Pauls Gade.

The following Elders, who had been released from their labors in the Scandinavian Mission, left Copenhagen April 2, 1891, on their return to their homes in Zion: Frands Peter Petersen, Alif Ericksen, Jonas Mattson, Christian M. Jensen, Lorentz Petersen, Lars Erik Larson and Hans Martin Hansen (released early on account of sickness at home). These Elders sailed per steamship "Volo," accompanied by 43 emigrating Saints.

The following Elders, who had labored as missionaries in Scandinavia, left Copenhagen April 16, 1891, to return to their homes in Utah: Christian Hermansen, Erastus Kofoed, Truls A. Hallgren, John O. Rosenkrantz, Niels Nielsen and Lars K. Peterson. They were accompanied by 59 emigrating Saints.

On May 14, 1891, Elders Niels Frederiksen, Hans Peter Miller, Jens P. Petersen and James C. Berthelsen, who had labored as missionaries in Scandinavia, left Copenhagen for their homes in America, accompanied by 24 emigrating Saints.

A company of emigrating Saints (141 souls) sailed from Copenhagen, Denmark, May 28, 1891, bound for Utah; 41 of these were from the Skåne, 14 from the Göteborg, 66 from the Stockholm, 11 from the Aarhus and 9 from the Aalborg Conference. The following Elders who returned from missions accompanied the emigrants: Carl Söderlund, John A. Beckstrand, Nils Nilson, Andrew P. Renström and Boye B. P. Petersen.

In June, 1891, another company of emigrating Saints (42 souls), of whom 10 were from Norway, sailed from Copenhagen and Christiania, bound for Utah, accompanied by four returning Elders, namely, Ole H. Berg, John Elof Johnson, James M. Keller and Pehr Cronquist.

Elder Hans Eriksen, who had labored as a missionary in the Stockholm Conference, left Copenhagen Aug. 6, 1891, for his home in Zion, in charge of 34 emigrating Saints, namely, 13 from the Copenhagen, 12 from the Aarhus, 3 from the Aalborg, 2 from the Christiania, 2 from the Stockholm and 2 from the Göteborg Conference.

Elder Ola Olson, jun., who had labored as a missionary in the Göteborg Conference, left Copenhagen, Aug. 20, 1891, accompanied by 38 emigrating Saints, namely, 20 from the Copenhagen, 9 from the Göteborg, and 5 from the Stockholm Conference, also four others from different places.

Elder Andrew P. Anderson, who had presided over the Stockholm Conference, left Copenhagen Sept. 3, 1891, homeward bound, in charge of 52 emigrating Saints, namely, 24 from the Stockholm, 9 from the Copenhagen, 7 from the Aalborg and 1 from the Skåne Conference, and 11 others from different places.

A company of Saints (66 souls) left Copenhagen for Utah, Sept. 17, 1891, namely, 13 from the Copenhagen, 10 from the Stockholm, 3 from the Göteborg, 15 from the Aalborg and 25 from the Christiania Conference, in charge of Elders Oleen N. Stohl and Johan Gustav Jörgensen, who had labored faithfully in the Stockholm and Christiania conferences.

Elder Rasmus Sörensen and Hans Peter Olsen, who had labored as missionaries in Scandinavia, left Copenhagen, Oct. 1, 1891, bound for their homes in Utah. These Elders were accompanied by 47 emigrating

Saints, namely, 16 from the Copenhagen, 18 from the Aarhus, 2 from the Aalborg, 9 from the Stockholm and 2 from the Christiania Conference.

Besides the Elders whose return is mentioned in connection with the emigrating companies, the following Elders, who had labored as missionaries in Scandinavia, were released and returned home on the following dates: August S. Schow, from Copenhagen June 22; James Petersen, July 23rd; Pehr H. Pehrson, Oct. 20; Mads Nilson and John Johnson Oct. 29th; Frands Carl Michaelsen and Carl Edward Thorstensen, Nov. 9th, and Laurentius Dahlquist, Nov. 30th.

In 1891, 58 Elders from Zion arrived in Copenhagen, to labor as missionaries in Scandinavia. They arrived on the following dates: Fred Lundberg, Carl Nyman and Joseph A. Anderson of Logan, Jacob Jörgensen and Theodor Gyllenskog of Smithfield, Anders Hanson of West Jordan, Anders Anderson of Providence, Johan Svenson of Salt Lake City, Utah, Olof Requel Olson of Oxford, and Martinus Nielsen of Ovid, Idaho, arrived March 21st; John Lawrence (Larsson) and Jacob Broman (Anderson) of Salt Lake City, James Erickson of West Bountiful, Peder C. Christensen and Joseph Christiansen of Mayfield, Andrew Olson of Beaver, Hans Peter Olsen of Fountain Green, and Lars F. Johnson of Bear River City, Utah, arrived May 1st; Nils Matts Nilson of Sandy on May 10th; and Nils Peter Larsen, of Pleasant Grove, July 20th. Adolph Madsen of Brigham City, Hans Andreas Pedersen, August Westerberg and Mouritz Mouritzen of Logan, Carl G. Anderson and Niels J. Henricksen of Salt Lake City, Joseph Jeppson of Millville, Lars C. Möller and Andrew Pedersen of Newton, Utah, and Hans C. Hansen of Mink Creek, Idaho, arrived Sept.

18th. Christian Nephi Anderson and James Nielsen, jun., of Brigham City, Peter Berthelsen Green of Plain City, Christian Peter Larsen of

OLOF R. OLSON

Was born at Österåker, Södermanland, Sweden, July 16, 1859, was baptized May 11, 1879, and labored as a missionary in Vestervik, Småland, from Sept. 1, 1880, till 1882, when, in the month of June, he accompanied his parents and brothers and sisters to Utah. Bro. Olof R. Olson filled a mission to Sweden in 1891-1892 and presided over the Vingåker Branch until the fall conference in 1891. He was then sent to the Vestervik Branch and was released in June, 1892, to proceed home on account of the severe illness of his wife. He now (1927) resides at Oxford, Idaho.

Manti, Jens P. Andreasen of Eden, Brynte Anderson of Ogden, Martin Nielsen of Levan, Anders Jensen of Gunnison, Utah, Joseph A. Folkman of Gentile Valley, Ole Olsen of Iona, and John A. Cederlund of Montpelier, Idaho, and Sören C. Sörensen of Mesa, Arizona, arrived Sept. 19th, and John Anderson of Salina, Utah, on Sept. 29th; Adolph Martin Nielsen and Andrew M. Israelsen of Hyrum, Charles Ludvig Olsen of Payson, John A. Anderson of Huntsville, Anthony Christensen of Oak City, Utah, Andrew Jepsen of Mink Creek, Idaho, Olof Monson of Pleasant Grove and Ole Sörensen, jun., of

Fountain Green, Utah, arrived Nov 1st, and Gustav W. Söderberg o Ephraim and John Christensen o Gunnison, Utah, on Nov. 9th. Pete Trulson Rundquist of West Jordan Pehr A. Björklund and Hermar Knudsen of Provo, Utah, arrived Dec. 12th, and Christian Magnusor of South Cottonwood and Erik P Lindquist of Salt Lake City, Utah, on Dec. 18th.

Jacob Jörgensen, Hans Peter Olsen, Hans Chr. Hansen, Lars C. Möller, Peter B. Green, Sören Chr. Sörensen, Andreas Jepsen, and Gustaf W. Söderberg were appointed to labor in the Aarhus Conference. Martinus

MOURITZ MOURITZEN

Was born at Svendstrup, Aalborg amt, Denmark, April 2, 1857, the son of Peter Christian Mouritzen and Inger Jörgensen, was baptized at Aalborg, Jan. 3, 1877, by Anders Frederiksen, and called to labor as a missionary in the Aalborg and Sæby branches. In 1878 he presided over the Thisted Branch and while laboring in Thyland, he and N. C. Larsen were arrested for preaching but were liberated the next day. Being honorably released from his mission, he emigrated to Utah and arrived in Salt Lake City July 29, 1880; he settled first in Manti and later in Logan. In 1881 (Oct. 27) he married Jensine Jensen. Being ordained a High Priest Nov. 3, 1890, he was appointed second counselor to Bishop Christian J. Larsen of the Logan Seventh Ward. Bro. Mouritzen performed a mission to Denmark in 1891-1893, laboring in the Aalborg Conference, part of the time as president. He still (1927) resides in Logan, Utah.

Nielsen, Peder C. Christensen (second mission,) Niels Peter Larsen, James Nielsen, jun., Anders Jensen, and Anthony Christensen were appointed to labor in the Aalborg Conference. Mouritz Mouritzen was also appointed to labor in the Aalborg Conference, and later as president of said conference. Lars F. Johnson was appointed to labor in the Copenhagen and Aalborg conferences, and later as president of the Aalborg Conference. Andrew Pedersen, and Jens P. Andreasen were appointed to labor in the Copenhagen Conference. Niels J. Henricksen was also appointed to labor in the Copenhagen Conference, but being banished from Denmark, he was called to preside over the Skåne Conference, Sweden. Chr. P. Larsen was appointed to labor in the Copenhagen Conference, part of the time as president of said conference. Martin Nielsen was appointed to labor in the Copenhagen Conference and later in the Aarhus Conference. Adolph M. Nielsen was appointed to labor in the Copenhagen Conference, and later in the Christiania Conference. Ole Sörensen, jun., was appointed to labor in the Copenhagen Conference, but being banished from Denmark, he finished his mission in the Christiania Conference. Carl Nyman, Joseph A. Anderson, John Lawrence (Larsson,) Jacob Broman (Anderson), John A. Cederlund, John Anderson, Christian Magnuson and Erik P. Lindquist were appointed to labor in the Stockholm Conference, Sweden. Johan Svenson, Anders Olson, Nils Matts Nilson, Joseph Jeppson, Olof Monson and Anders Hanson (2nd mission) were appointed to labor in the Skåne Conference. Frederik Lundberg was appointed to labor in the Skåne Conference and later presided over the Stockholm Conference. Peter T. Rundquist was appointed to labor

21

in the Skåne Conference, a part of the time as conference president. Pehr Anderson Björklund was appointed to labor in the Skåne Con-

NIELS JACOB HENRICKSEN

Was born Oct. 1, 1858, at Raabylille, Möen, Denmark; baptized Feb. 11, 1879, by Carl Jensen; labored as a missionary on Sjælland until 1881 when he emigrated to Utah. In 1891 he was ordained a Seventy by Pres. C. D. Fjeldsted and called on a mission to Denmark; he presided over the Öernes Branch until he was banished from the country. He then went to Skåne, where he first labored as a traveling Elder, and later as conference president. In 1903 he was again called to labor in Scandinavia and presided over the Copenhagen Conference till 1906, when he returned home. From 1911 till 1924 he labored among the Scandinavians in Granite Stake, first as counselor to Elder C. M. Nielsen and then as president of the Scandinavian meetings. From March, 1925, to September, 1927, he presided over the Danish L. D. S. meetings in Salt Lake City.

ference, and while faithfully discharging his duties died August 28, 1893, in Helsingborg.

Olof R. Olson, Anders Anderson, Theodor Gyllenskog, Carl Gustaf Anderson (second mission), August Westerberg (second mission), and John Christensen were appointed to labor in the Göteborg Conference. James Erickson, Adolph Madsen, Hans A. Pedersen, Chr. N. Anderson, Joseph A. Folkmann, Brynte Anderson, Ole Olsen, John A. Anderson and Herman Knudsen were appointed to labor in the Christiania Conference. Andrew M. Israelsen was also appointed to labor in the Christiania Conference; later he became conference president. Charles L. Olsen was appointed to labor as a writer and translator at the mission office in Copenhagen, Denmark. Joseph Christiansen was appointed to preside over the Aarhus Conference and later as president of the Scandinavian Mission, succeeding Elder Edward H. Anderson.

CHAPTER 76 (1892)

Unsuccessful attempt at preaching the gospel in Schleswig—Missionary experiences within the Arctic Circle—Progress of the work in Sweden—More Elders banished from Denmark—Elder Joseph Christiansen succeeds Edward H. Anderson as president of the Mission—Fifty-nine Elders arrive from Utah.

In January, 1892, Elder Lars C. Möller went into Schleswig from Fredericia, Denmark, to commence missionary labors among the Danes in North Schleswig, which province, though belonging to Germany, had been added to the Aarhus Conference, most of the inhabitants there being Danes. Elder Möller walked to Christianfeld, a little city about two miles across the national boundary line into Schleswig, where he commenced his missionary labors, but finding no one willing to show him hospitality, he put up at a hotel for the night, where he witnessed much wickedness, a number of the guests being drunk. On the 22nd of January he walked to Haderslev, where he found a few people who seemed willing to receive his testimony, but as he again had to stop over night at a hotel. and was short

of money, he soon returned t Fredericia in Denmark.

In Norway, the Elders continue their missionary labors with ur abated zeal, and with considerabl success. Elder Hans A. Pederse and other Elders had recently visite Örkedalen, near Trondhjem, but th Lutheran priests in that locality in terfered and prevented them fror hiring a hall for holding meetings

In Hedemarken, Bergen, Trond hjem and other places in Norway th Elders met with considerable suc cess. Elder John A. Anderson visit ed Langesund, Kragerö, Arendal an Mosby, and held successful meeting in these towns as well as in some o. the country districts. In one of these meetings, where Elder Anderson ex plained that faith alone was insuf ficient for complete salvation, on of those present remarked that a mar who would advocate such a doctrine ought to be whipped and banishec from the country. In Frederikstad a Brother Hansen had just erected a fine two-story building, the upper story of which had been built for a meeting hall, which he rented to the Saints for holding meetings. The first meeting in this new hall was held Sunday, April 17th. Elder James Ericksen, together with the local brother (Hansen), had made great sacrifices and had labored faithfully to secure such a commodious place for holding meetings.

In Christiania, Pastor Mortensen lectured against the "Mormons," and the brethren inserted in a newspaper an advertisement in which they promised to answer the questions, "Was Joseph Smith a deceiver?" and "Is the Book of Mormon false?" The meeting, which was held May 30, 1892, was crowded, the hall being filled to overflowing with hearers, and among those present was the pastor whom the brethren invited to the stand; he, however, refused to come. The Elders who spoke were filled with the Spirit of the Lord and all present listened with rapt attention.

In June, Elder Ole Sörensen, jun., and A. E. Christensen held an open air meeting in Guldbrandsdalen, in which they preached to 300 people.

Late in the year 1892, missionary labors were re-opened by Elders John L. Johnson and James Erickson in Aalesund, Norway, where the restored gospel had not been preached for about thirty years. The two Elders arrived there Dec. 24, 1891, and attended a Lutheran meeting on Sunday, Dec. 25th. As the preachers got into a discussion among themselves about certain passages in the Bible, the Elders asked for permission to say a few words, which was granted. When the people found out that the brethren were "Mormons," a newspaper article was published warning the people against the Elders, who were forbidden by the police to preach. Soon a rumor was circulated that the Elders were going to hold a meeting in the evening of Nov. 1st, and a number of men and boys prepared themselves to break up the meeting and mob the Elders. A police officer came up and asked the brethren if they were going to hold a meeting. They answered in the negative and tried to find out his intentions, but did not succeed. In the evening another man came up and asked them the same question, when the Elders began to think that something was wrong. However, they entertained their visitor by explaining the principles of the gospel to him. Soon he got uneasy and went out; then all at once a war yell was heard and a shower of rocks was sent against the house. The mob then rushed up the stairs and threw the door open, when 50 men and boys rushed into the room. Elder Johnson arose and addressed

them, explaining to them the principles he taught, and suggested to them that if they thought the "Mormons" were in error, they should endeavor to convince them in a Christian way with love and good will and the Bible for their guide, and not with violence. Elder Erickson then gave them good counsel and answered several questions satisfactorily to them. The mild influence of the Spirit overcame their wrath, so that they did not molest the Elders.

Elder Hans A. Pedersen wrote from Tromsö, Norway, under date of Dec. 27, 1892, that he and Elder Gustaf A. Iversen had arrived safely and well in Tromsö, after a tiresome and unpleasant voyage of 7½ days from Trondhjem. On their arrival at Tromsö they succeeded in hiring a couple of rooms, one of which was large enough to hold meetings in, and the few Saints in that far-off part of Norway endeavored to make the Elders as comfortable as possible. As soon as it became known that the "Mormons" had entered the town, some interest was aroused and many of the inhabitants came to the meetings which the Elders commenced to hold soon after their arrival, and at the time of writing, meetings were being held three times a week. Brother Pedersen writes:

"For those who are not used to it, it seems strange to live in a place where the lamps must burn continuously, not only in the night, but also in the daytime. It is strange indeed to see the moon beam both day and night, while the sun in the summer season shines both night and day. At this time of the year (December) we see no sun, nor will it shine again for a month to come; hence it is not very pleasant in this northern part of Norway. The most interesting feature of nature here is the northern lights ('aurora borealis'), which every evening, when the weather is clear, sends its golden rays in different colors far beyond the zenith. It is certainly a grand sight, especially for those who have not seen it before. Of late the weather has been very cold, and during the past two or three days much snow has fallen and a cold winter seems to be approaching. Perhaps we have no reason to expect anything else in a place lying so near the north pole and the icy Arctic Ocean. I cannot say how large this branch is, as it reaches many miles southward and as far north as any human being may be pleased to travel. There are quite a number of inhabitants occupying the various islands and hamlets, and consequently there will be work for many missionaries, but it is very expensive for one to sojourn here, as the cost of food, especially in the winter, is very high. Everything is much dearer here than in districts farther south. Here are many of the descendants of Adam who have never heard the true gospel of Christ, but are bound in the chains of false traditions and ignorance. It is strange enough that wherever we go, the people have heard lying stories about the Latter-day Saints, but scarcely a word of truth."

In Sundswall, Sweden, the Elders advertised in the newspapers quite extensively, which had the effect that their meetings were well attended by strangers every Sabbath. In Karlskrona, the Elders hired a hall in which well attended meetings were held regularly. Recently 20 persons had been added to the Church by baptism in that part of Sweden. On several occasions, in the neighborhood of Jönköping, the Elders had been shown the door, after being promised lodgings for the night, as soon as the householders learned they were "Mormons." Several successful meetings were held in the home of a rich farmer in the Vesterås Branch. The large room in which the Elders held forth was filled with attentive listeners. In the summer of 1892, Pres. Carl G. Anderson visited the various branches and localities in the Göteborg Conference and held many meetings, some of which were attended by several hundred people. Bro. Anderson was invited to speak at a Good Templars' Feast, which was held in the forests near Göteborg. He spoke

an hour, and at the close of the meeting he answered a number of questions which seemed to temper the prejudice which had existed against the "Mormons."

At Osby, near Christianstad, Skåne, 21 persons were added to the Church by baptism; among whom were a school teacher and his family.

In Copenhagen, Denmark, the excellent branch choir, under the direction of Carl Löhdefinck, did splendid work in making the meetings in the Danish capital interesting. The English school, divided into four classes, which was held every Monday evening, proved a success, and many of the pupils had already become quite proficient in the English language.

On the island of Bornholm, the Elders met with some success during the year 1892, but while meeting houses on the island were numerous and were placed at the disposal of all so-called Christian preachers, the "Mormon" Elders had so far been denied the privilege of preaching in any of them.

In Jutland, Denmark, the headquarters of the Horsens Branch had been moved to Fredericia because of the enmity which had been manifested against the "Mormons." In Fredericia the people seemed to be more interested in the message of the Elders.

In the city of Odense and vicinity, on the island of Fyen, the Elders met with considerable success. Elder Peter Sörensen had recently hired a hall in the town of Assens, where meetings were held regularly. The Elders had hired a hall in Randers capable of seating 150 persons. In the little city of Skive, Jutland, where the gospel had not been preached for thirty years, the reappearance of "Mormon" Elders caused considerable interest, as a new generation had grown up since the Elders had labored there before. Pres. Joseph Christiansen visited Skive Feb. 21, 1892, on which occasion he dedicated the hall which had been hired there and advertised regular meetings for Thursday evenings and Sundays at 2 and 7 p. m. The first meeting held after that was so well attended that the hall was incapable of holding them all. On the 26th of Feb. the Elders visited a sister who had been baptized about three years previously, and who, through sickness, had kept her bed over two months. At her request she was administered to by the Elders and was miraculously healed. The same day she arose from her bed of affliction, enabled to perform her domestic duties.

In the spring of 1892, Elders N. J. Henricksen and Ole Sörensen, jun., were banished from Denmark by order of the police authorities. These brethren had succeeded in holding a number of meetings and in baptizing several persons on the islands of Falster and Möen. This annoyed the Lutheran priests, who complained to the civil authorities and asked that the "Mormon" Elders should be designated as "dangerous foreigners with false and misleading doctrines." Elders Henricksen and Sörensen were therefore brought before the authorities, who gave them two weeks to get out of the country. At Hilleröd and Tolstrup, north of Copenhagen, the Elders were mobbed. On a Saturday evening, at Tolstrup, the brethren were threatened, the lamps put out and the windows broken. After receiving some severe knocks, the Elders finally escaped by the assistance of a friend, leaving the mob to fight amongst themselves. The crowd was led by a priest. It seems that nothing but the power of God saved the Elders from severe injury.

In both places there were quite a number of respectable people who were disgusted with the proceedings of the mob, and the Elders received opportunities to bear their testimonies, notwithstanding the tumult. The two Elders banished from Denmark were sent to finish their missions, Elder Henricksen in Sweden, where he presided over the Skåne Conference, and Elder Sörensen in Norway.

In Hjörring, Jutland, the hall which had been used by the Elders for meeting purposes proved to be too small to accommodate the people who attended the meetings; hence a larger hall was secured.

The day for emigrating to Zion in large companies from Scandinavia had passed, and those who did emigrate left their native lands in small numbers, usually in care of returning Elders. Four emigrating Saints left Copenhagen, Jan. 14, 1892, bound for Utah.

On April 28, 1892, Elder Charles W. Olson, who had labored in the Göteborg Conference, Lars Johan Henström, who had labored in the Stockholm Conference since May, 1890, and Niels J. Andersen left Copenhagen to return to their homes in Utah. These Elders were accompanied by 21 emigrating Saints. Eight emigrating Saints who left Christiania, Norway, April 29th, joined the Copenhagen company in England.

On May 12, 1892, the following Elders, who had labored faithfully as missionaries in the Scandinavian Mission, left Copenhagen, to return to their homes in Zion: Lars L. Nilson of Provo, Utah, Anders S. Hyrup of Salt Lake City, Andrew Hanson of West Jordan and Niels Peter Larsen of Pleasant Grove, Utah. The latter had filled a genealogical mission. In charge of these Elders was a company of 64 emigrating Saints, namely, 8 from the Copenhagen, 12 from the Skåne, 7 from the Aalborg, 2 from the Copenhagen, 20 from the Göteborg and 15 from the Stockholm Conference. On May 13, 1892, three emigrating Saints left Christiania, Norway, to join the company in England which had left Copenhagen on the 12th inst.

On June 9, 1892, Elder Anders Hansen, of Pleasant Grove, Utah, and Olof Requel Olson of Oxford, Idaho, who had labored as missionaries in Scandinavia, left Copenhagen on their return home, having been honorably released. These Elders had charge of a company of 74 emigrating Saints, namely, 10 from the Göteborg, 8 from the Aalborg, 11 from the Aarhus, 24 from the Copenhagen and 21 from the Stockholm Conference.

On July 14, 1892, Elder Lars Pehrson, who had labored in the Stockholm Conference since August, 1890, left Copenhagen, returning to his home in Logan, Utah. He had charge of a company of 12 emigrating Saints.

A company of emigrating Saints (39 souls) left Copenhagen, Aug. 4, 1892, to emigrate to Zion; of these 12 were from the Copenhagen, 4 from the Stockholm, 11 from the Göteborg, 10 from the Aarhus and 2 from the Skåne Conference. Elder Peter H. Sörensen, who had labored in the Aarhus Conference, and Peter Henry Hansen, who had labored in the Copenhagen Conference, returned home with this company.

On Aug. 18, 1892, a company of 49 emigrating Saints left Copenhagen in charge of Elders Harold F. Liljenquist and Nils Börgeson. Of the emigrating Saints 28 were from the Stockholm, 3 from the Skåne, 14 from the Göteborg, 2 from the Copenhagen and 2 from the Aalborg Conference. On the 19th, 15 emigrating

Saints left Christiania, Norway, f⟨ Utah. They joined the Copenhage⟨ company in England.

On Sept. 1, 1892, Elder Andre⟨ G. Johnson, who had labored in t⟨ Stockholm and Göteborg conferenc⟨ since September, 1890, Elder Ant⟨ E. Christensen and Peter Christense⟨ who had labored in Norway sin⟨ October, 1890, left Copenhagen, r⟨ turning to their homes in Utah, ⟨ charge of a company of 15 emigra⟨ ing Saints, namely, 1 from the Stoc⟨ holm, 6 from the Aarhus, 2 fro⟨ the Aalborg and 6 from the Götebo⟨ Conference.

Elder Edward H. Anderson, wh⟨ had presided over the Scandinavia⟨ Mission, Christian Meyer, who ha⟨ labored in the Aarhus Conferenc⟨ and Peter Mortensen, who had l⟨ bored in the Copenhagen Conferenc⟨ left Copenhagen, homeward boun⟨ Sept. 22nd, 1892, in charge of ⟨ company of 21 emigrating Sain⟨ from Scandinavia. Five emigratin⟨ Saints from Norway joined this con⟨ pany in England. Elder Anders⟨ had presided over the mission sin⟨ Sept. 29, 1890, and his administr⟨ tion represented ability, energy an⟨ good leadership. He was succeed⟨ in the presidency of the mission b⟨ Elder Joseph Christiansen, who f⟨ some time had presided over t⟨ Aarhus Conference.

A small company of emigratin⟨ Saints (28 souls) left Copenhage⟨ Oct. 27th, 1892, in charge of Elde⟨ Peter C. Christensen, Martinus Nie⟨ sen and Andrew Olson, returnin⟨ Utah Elders. Of the emigrants, ⟨ were from the Stockholm, 2 fro⟨ the Göteborg, 8 from the Aalbor⟨ and 12 from the Aarhus Conferenc⟨

Besides the Elders mentioned ⟨ connection with companies of em⟨ grating Saints, the following bret⟨ ren from Zion who had labored ⟨ missionaries to Scandinavia, to⟨ their departure, returning home ⟨

e following dates: Jens C. Hansen, eb. 4th, Mads P. Sörensen, Ole nson and John A. Hellström, March

aries in Scandinavia, arrived in Copenhagen, Denmark, as follows: August Carlson of Ogden and Levi Pehrson of Peoa, Utah, arrived Feb. 19th; Rasmus Rasmussen of Mt. Pleasant, German Rasmussen of Ephraim, William Jacob Backman of Salt Lake City, Utah, John Andrew Larson,

JOSEPH CHRISTIANSEN,

resident of the Scandinavian Mission in 92-1893, was born Aug. 17, 1854, in Salt ake City, Utah, the son of Niels C. and atherine Christiansen. He was baptized when ght years old at Ephraim, Sanpete County, d ordained an Elder in January, 1876. On n. 31, 1876, he married Hannah M. Peter- n and removed to Mayfield (Sanpete County), tah, being one of the pioneer settlers of that ace, and during the following years utilized s best energies and ability in the interest of e new settlement. He was manager of the ayfield Co-op store from 1881 to 1890, and perintendent of the Mayfield Sabbath school om 1878 to 1891. In 1888 he was ordained High Priest and acted as second counselor Bishop Ole C. Olsen. In 1891-1893 he filled mission to Scandinavia, presiding fifteen onths over the Aarhus Conference, Den- ark, and for nearly a year was president of e Scandinavian Mission. Elder Christiansen ed at Mayfield, March 6, 1895.

AUGUST CARLSON

Was born April 4, 1861, in Öttum, Skaraborgs län, Sweden, and baptized Dec. 28, 1878, by C. J. Janson. He was ordained a Teacher, April 5, 1879, and an Elder, Oct. 8, 1879. He labored as a missionary in Vesterås and Dalarne from 1879 to 1881 and received wonderful manifestations of the power of God. He emigrated to Utah in August, 1881, locating in Ogden In 1892-1894 he performed a mission to Sweden and labored six months as a writer for the "Nordstjernan," and about 21 months as president of the Stockholm Conference. In 1905 he was again called on a mission to Sweden, laboring for three months in Örebro and the remaining time as president over Stockholm Conference. He was accompanied by his family. He had an audience with King Oscar of Sweden, and, as president of Stockholm Conference, introduced Pres. Heber J. Grant to the king. Bro. Carlson moved to Salt Lake City in 1908 and in 1916 was ordained a High Priest and set apart as a counselor in the bishopric of the Nineteenth Ward, which position he held until the Ward was divided in 1925, when he became a member of the Capitol Hill Ward, where he still (1927) resides.

1st, Joseph Reuben Olson, April 4th, Edward Berg, July 1st, Thor . Nielsen and Michael Johnson, Aug. 8th, and John H. Forsgren, Jacob . Anderson and Charles P. Okernd, Oct. 13th.

In 1892, 59 Elders from Zion, who ad been called to labor as mission-

Peter Simon Jensen and Thomas Spongberg of Preston, Idaho, arrived

Mar. 15th, and Martin Andersen of Richfield, Utah, on March 19th; Peter M. Jensen of Huntsville, Peter Mortensen of Salt Lake City, and Gustaf W. Carlson of Salem, Utah, arrived Apr. 29; Adolf Z. Fjellström and George Wm. Lindquist of Logan, and George William Johnson of West Bountiful, Utah, April 30th; Michael O. Nash of Salem, Utah, May 11th; Gustaf A. Iverson of Ephraim, Carl A. Lundell of Benjamin, Gustaf Lindahl, Andrew J. Wahlquist and Gustaf Albert Anderson of Salt Lake City, Utah, and John Edward Mattson of Burton, Idaho, arrived May 27th. Nils Benson of Spring City, Peter Nielsen, Johan A. Johnson (Johanson) and Andrew Larsen of Monroe, Charles Perry Okerlund of Loa, August Malmquist of Vermillion, Amel Burnett Jensen and John Jensen of Richfield, Louis Söderberg of Elsinore, Hans Peter Jörgensen of Fountain Green, John W. Dehlin of Mt. Pleasant and Andreas Johansen of Hyrum, Utah, arrived June 6th; Adam L. Petersen, Peter C. Geertsen, jun., and Nephi H. Nielsen of Huntsville, James Andersen and John Johnson (Johansen) of Logan, Carl A. Carlquist, Ludvig S. Hanson and John L. Johnson of Salt Lake City, Utah, arrived June 20th; Charles John Wahlquist of Charleston, Utah, arrived Aug. 29th; Lars P. C. Nielsen of Mantua, and Peter Jenson of West Jordan, Utah, arrived Oct. 11th; Carl M. Levorsen of Draper, John J. Plowman and Peter Hansen of Smithfield, Nils Monson of Pleasant Grove, Utah, Frederik C. Olsen of Preston, Idaho, John W. Winterrose and Erick Erickson of Heber City, Utah, arrived Nov. 5th; Christian Wm. Sörensen, Joseph Johansen and Anders C. Olsen of Mt. Pleasant, Anton Nielsen of Huntington, Christian Hansen of Ephraim, and Andrew G. Bolander of Ogden, Utah, arrived Nov. 12th,

and Charles Sörensen of Hyrum, Utah, Dec. 13th, 1892.

Rasmus Rasmussen, Martin Andersen, Peter M. Jensen, John Johnson

CHRISTIAN W. SÖRENSEN,

Son of Christian and Christine Sörensen, was born in Mt. Pleasant, Sanpete County, Utah, Nov. 1, 1863; educated in the public schools and Brigham Young Academy; taught school in Mt. Pleasant for fourteen years and filled a mission in the Manti Temple in 1889-1890. He performed a mission to Scandinavia in 1892-1894, presiding over the Aarhus Conference, Denmark. When the North Sanpete Stake was organized in 1900, he was appointed a member of the High Council; later he acted as second counselor to Stake President C. N. Lund, and held this position until the Stake presidency was re-organized in 1914. Bro. Sörensen has served as city recorder, assessor and collector, councilman, member of the House of Representatives, member of the district school board, and has followed the business of banking and farming. In April, 1886, he married Dina A. Hansen, who died Sept. 27, 1888; they had two children. On June 24, 1891, he married Eva Madsen, of Manti; they have three children. Bro. Sörensen still (1927) resides in Mt. Pleasant, Utah.

(Johansen), John J. Plowman and Anton Nielsen were appointed to labor in the Aarhus Conference. German Rasmussen was also appointed to labor in the Aarhus Conference and also in Schleswig, as he spoke the German language. Peter Christian Geertsen, jun., was appointed to labor in the Aarhus Conference and later in the Aalborg Conference. Christian Wm. Sörensen was appointed to

bor in the Aarhus Conference, part
f the time as conference president.
Jephi H. Nielsen, Carl M. Levor-
en, Frederik Chr. Olsen and Chris-

CHARLES SÖRENSEN
(Original name, Carl B. Larsen),

Missionary to Scandinavia in 1892-1894, was
born March 25, 1860, in Odense, Denmark, emigrated with his widowed mother to Utah in
1866, crossing the Atlantic in the ship "Kenil-
orth," and after residing one year in Brig-
am City, the family located permanently in
Hyrum, Cache County, where Bro. Sörensen
as baptized, educated in part, grew to manhood and was ordained successively a Teacher,
Priest, and Elder. He married Alice Unsworth
in 1882, who bore him eight children. In
1892-1894 he filled a mission to Scandinavia,
where he labored in the Copenhagen Confernce, Denmark, and later as president of
the Skåne Conerence, Sweden. At home
he has acted as a M. I. A. officer and assistant
uperintendent of a Ward Sunday school, and
lled two home missions in the Hyrum Stake.
In a civil capacity he has served in the Hyrum
ity council. As occupations, he has followed
ailroad contracting, farming, stock raising,
nd real estate business.

an Hansen were appointed to labor
n the Aalborg Conference. Michael
. Nash was also appointed to labor
n the Aalborg Conference and later
n the Christiania Conference, Nor-
vay.

Peter Mortensen, Lars P. C. Niel-
en, Peter Hansen and Anders Chr.
Olsen were appointed to labor in the
Copenhagen Conference. Peter Niel-
en was appointed to labor in the

Copenhagen Conference, and later
in the Christiania Conference. Hans
P. Jörgensen, James Andersen and
Joseph Johansen were appointed to
labor in the Copenhagen Conference
and later in the Aarhus Conference.
Adam L. Petersen was appointed to
labor in the Copenhagen Conference;
later he was called to act as conference president. Charles Sörensen
was appointed to labor in the Copenhagen Conference and later in the
Skåne Conference. John A. Larson,
Thomas Spongberg, Gustaf W. Carlson, Adolph Z. Fjellström, Carl A.
Lundell, Gustaf Lindahl, August
Malmquist, Amel B. Jensen, Louis
Söderberg and Erick Erickson were
appointed to labor in the Stockholm
Conference. August Carlson was
also appointed to labor in the Stockholm Conference, and later as conference president. George Wm. Lindquist was appointed to labor in the
Stockholm Conference. John Jensen
was appointed to labor in the Stockholm Conference, but was sent to the
Skåne Conference because of trouble
and was finally released.

Levi Pehrson, George Wm. Johnson, Charles P. Okerlund, Ludvig S.
Hanson, Peter Jenson and Nils Monson were appointed to labor in the
Skåne Conference. John W. Dehlin
was appointed to labor in the Skåne
and later in the Stockholm Conference. Anders G. Bolander was appointed to labor in the Skåne Conference and later in the Göteborg Conference. Peter S. Jensen, Wm. J. Backman, John E. Mattson, Nils Benson,
Johan A. Johanson (Johnson) and
John W. Winterrose were appointed
to labor in the Göteborg Conference.
Andrew J. Wahlquist was also appointed to labor in the Göteborg Conference, part of the time as president
of said conference. Carl A. Carlquist
was appointed to labor in the Göteborg Conference; later he was chosen

as president of said conference and still later as president of the Scandinavian Mission. Gustaf A. Iverson,

ADAM LIND PETERSEN.

A prominent Elder and missionary, was born March 2, 1870, in Huntsville, Weber County, Utah, the son of Sören L. Petersen and Anna E. Nielsen. He was baptized in 1878 by Samuel S. Hammond, ordained a Seventy in 1892 by Abraham H. Cannon, and ordained a High Priest in 1907 by David O. McKay. He served as a member of the Stake Sunday School Board (Weber Stake) from 1887 to 1890, presided over the Y. M. M. I. A. of the Huntsville Ward from 1888 to 1891, filled a mission to Scandinavia in 1892-1894, acting part of the time as president of the Copenhagen Conference, Denmark; filled a special M. I. A. mission to the San Juan Stake of Zion in 1898, and filled a second mission to Scandinavia in 1902-1904, presiding over the Aarhus Conference, Denmark, at which time the Aarhus L. D. S. Church property was purchased. After his return from that mission he was chosen as a member of the Weber Stake Sunday School Board in 1906 and a member of the High Council in the Ogden Stake in November, 1907. Afterwards he was appointed to preside over the Scandinavian meetings in the three Stakes in Weber County. Bro. Petersen has also served as justice of the peace in Huntsville precinct and city, and later in the Eden precinct. He served as chief clerk of the House of Representatives in 1917 and secretary of the Senate of the Utah Legislature in 1919. In 1917 he filled a short mission to the Eastern States, being assigned especially to Washington, D. C., and for three months he served as reading clerk in Congress, a position with which no other Utah man ever before was honored. Bro. Petersen moved with his family to Salt Lake City in 1919 and is now a resident of the Eleventh Ward. In 1888 (Nov. 8th) Bro. Petersen married Anna M. Petersen, the daughter of Christian Petersen and Emma Backman, in the Logan Temple. This marriage has been blessed with nine children. Bro. Petersen is now (1927) manager of the Associated Newspapers.

Andrew Larsen, Andreas Johansen and John L. Johnson were appointed to labor in the Christiania Conference. Gustaf A. Anderson was appointed to labor in the office at Copenhagen and afterwards was sent to labor in the Göteborg Conference, but was released on account of trouble (June 7, 1893).

Charles J. Wahlquist was appointed to labor in the Stockholm Conference and later as a translator and writer for "Nordstjernan" at the mission office in Copenhagen.

CHAPTER 77 (1893)

Elder Carl A. Carlquist succeeds Joseph Christiansen in the presidency of the mission—Elder Amel B. Jensen crossed the Torneå River from Sweden to Russia and distributed tracts—Death of Elder Pehr A. Björklund in Sweden—A branch of the Church organized in Esbjerg, Denmark—Visit of Anthon H. Lund, president of the European Mission—Arrival of 45 Elders from Zion.

Elder Joseph Christiansen, soon after he had succeeded Edward H. Anderson as president of the Scandinavian Mission, made a tour of most of the conferences in Denmark, Sweden and Norway, so as to acquaint himself with the affairs of the mission. He speaks in his report of two Elders who had been appointed to labor in Haderslev and other places in Schleswig. They worked there for awhile, but as their influence grew and fears were entertained by the civil authorities that some of the citizens would join the Saints, the Elders were ordered to leave the country within 24 hours.

In Sweden, the work progressed. A new meeting hall had been hired in the Halmstad Branch, and a new branch was organized with headquarters in Kalmar on the Baltic coast. The Elders were also extending their labors into new fields along the Bay of Bothnia.

Elder Joseph Christiansen, who had

presided over the Scandinavian Mission since Aug. 26, 1892, left Copenhagen for his home in Mayfield, Utah, May 11, 1893. He had been a successful mission president and had gained the love and respect of both Saints and strangers. His successor, Elder Carl A. Carlquist of Salt Lake City, Utah, had acted as president of the Göteborg Conference for several months.

In the summer of 1893, Elder Amel B. Jensen and his missionary companion labored in the northern part of Sweden. When they arrived at Haparanda, Bro. Jensen and his companion separated, and dividing the towns between them, appointed a place to meet at a later date. Bro. Jensen, having finished his labors sooner than he expected, and seeing a town on the further side of the river Torneå, crossed a bridge and entered the town. His success was phenomenal; he sold books in nearly every house into which he entered, where his language was understood, and was well received by the people. When he was ready to go back, he made the discovery that he had unknowingly entered the Czar's dominion. The wonder is that he was allowed to cross the bridge which separates Sweden from Russian Finland, as the officers were usually very alert, and had they met him, they undoubtedly would have confiscated his books and tracts. He says that "he hit the right moment to go over and did it innocently, as he did not know that he was doing anything unlawful; he acknowledged the hand of the Lord in the incident."

On Monday, Aug. 28, 1893, Elder Pehr Anderson Björklund, who labored as a missionary in the Skåne Conference, Sweden, died at Helsingborg. He had suffered from rupture for several years, and according to the advice of doctors he underwent an operation on Aug. 27th, which seemingly resulted in his death. Bro. Björklund was born Jan. 30, 1833, in Önnestad parish, Christianstads län, Sweden, was baptized July 7, 1879,

CARL ARVID CARLQUIST

Was born near Venersborg, Sweden, Jan. 8, 1857. His mother accepted the gospel in Trollhättan, Sweden, when he was a child, and Carl A. was baptized when eleven years of age. He was ordained a Priest when 17 years old and sent on a mission. At the age of 18 he was ordained an Elder and afterwards labored in the Göteborg Conference for three years. Emigrating to Utah, he arrived in Salt Lake City July 15, 1877, and on Sept. 3rd of the same year he married Hulda Augusta Nathalia Östergren, with whom he had been acquainted in Sweden. He engaged in the furniture business under the firm name of Sörensen & Carlquist, and continued this until the spring of 1892, when he was called on a mission to Scandinavia, during which he labored in the Göteborg Conference and later as president of the Scandinavian Mission. After his return home in the summer of 1894 he became a leading figure among the Scandinavians, both in business and social affairs. In 1910-1912 he filled a mission to Sweden, presiding first over the Göteborg and later over the Stockholm Conference; he also visited all the conferences of the mission, answering anti-Mormon agitators who were traveling through Sweden at government expense. Together with two other Elders he obtained an audience with King Gustaf of Sweden. In 1912 he acted as a counselor in the bishopric of the Fifth Ward, Salt Lake City, and on Sept. 8, 1917, he succeeded Jesse R. Pettit as Bishop of said Ward, which position he still (1927) holds.

emigrated to Utah in 1880, and located in Provo, where he resided until called on his mission.

A new branch of the Church was organized at Esbjerg, Denmark, Nov. 15, 1893. Esbjerg is a new city located on the western coast of Denmark, on the shores of the North Sea. From the fact that it has a mixed population which had come from nearly all the surrounding countries, and that the town from consisting of only a few houses located on sand-banks 25 years before, had, in that short time, sprung up to be a modern city with about 8000 inhabitants, it was nicknamed the "San Francisco of Denmark." The reasons for this phenomenal growth were that a harbor situated southwest of the little town, at the foot of the sand-hills, and the railroads that connect with the lines of steamers that ply the North Sea, principally between Denmark and England, had been finished. This harbor has the advantage over all the other harbors in Denmark that it never freezes, no matter how hard the winter. After the branch was organized in Esbjerg, a nice little hall was rented in the center of the town, where public meetings were held twice on Sundays and also on Thursday nights. A well-attended Sunday School was organized about the same time, and there is still a flourishing little branch of the Church in Esbjerg, which in 1893 had about 7,000 inhabitants.

In the fall of 1893, the Elders rented a fine hall in Drammen, Norway, in which two or three meetings were held every week. A good choir under the direction of Elder Anton Olson did much to make the meetings interesting.

Elder Anthon H. Lund, president of the European Mission, arrived in Copenhagen, Sept. 25, 1893, on a visit from England. He visited Aarhus, Aalborg, Stockholm, Christiania and many other places, attending conferences and a number of special meetings. Being able to speak the Scandinavian language Pres. Lund exercised great influence by addressing the many congregations of Saints and strangers throughout the mission. After finishing his tour of the mission, he left Copenhagen Oct. 20, 1893, returning to England

During the year 1893, a number of Saints emigrated to Zion in small companies, like the preceding years. Thus 11 emigrating Saints left Copenhagen, April 27, in charge of Anders Jensen, a returning Elder. Another company consisting of 32 emigrating Saints left Copenhagen, May 4th in charge of Andrew Pedersen, of Newton, Utah, who had labored as a missionary in the Copenhagen Conference, Denmark. A large company of emigrating Saints (100 souls) left Copenhagen, June 8th in charge of Lars Chr. Möller, Jens P. Andreasen, and Lars P. C. Nielsen returning Elders who had labored in the Aarhus and Copenhagen Conferences. Elder Hans C. Hansen of Mink Creek, Idaho, who had presided over the Aarhus Conference, left Copenhagen July 6, 1893, returning to his home. He also was accompanied by a small company of emigrating Saints, which on their arrival in England was augmented by a few Saints from Norway, the whole company then numbering 35 souls. Besides Elder Hansen two other missionaries returned home with this company, namely, Joseph A. Folkman and Brynte Anderson, who had labored in Norway. Another company of emigrating Saints (71 souls) left Copenhagen, Aug. 10, 1893 in charge of the following returning Elders: Mouritz Mouritzen, Niels J. Henricksen, Peter Berthelsen Green, Ole Olsen, Sören C. Sörensen, John A. Cederlund, Gustaf A. Anderson and August W. Carlson and wife (visitors). Elders Martin Nielsen, Christian Peter Larson, Ole Sörensen, jun., Wm. Backman, Hans A. Pedersen and Chr. Nephi Anderson left Copenhagen, Sept. 7, 1893, returning to their homes in Zion. They were accompanied by 24 emigrating Saints. On Friday, Oct. 6th, Elders James Nielsen, jun., Christian Hansen and John Anderson left Copenhagen, returning to their homes in Utah, accompanied by 35 emigrating Saints. About the same time, Adolph M. Nielsen, John A. Anderson and Andrew M. Israelsen, who had labored as missionaries in Norway, left Christiania for their homes in Utah. They joined the Copenhagen company in England.

A small company of emigrating Saints (21 souls) left Copenhagen, Nov. 16th, en route for Utah, accompanied by the following returning Elders: Anthony Christensen, Christian Magnuson and Anders P. Stenblom. About the same time Herman Knudsen, who had labored in Norway, sailed from Christiania, Norway, homeward bound.

Besides the Elders mentioned in connection with companies of emigrants, the following brethren from Zion, who had labored as missionaries in Scandinavia, took their departure, returning home on the following dates: Carl Nyman, Feb. 1st; Fred Lundberg, Jacob Jörgensen, Anders Anderson, Theodor Gyllenskog, John Swenson and Adolph Madsen, Feb. 22nd; Joseph A. Anderson, Feb. 26th; Lars F. Johnson, March 9th; John Lawrence, James Erickson, Niels M. Nielsen, August Westerberg, Andrew Jepsen and Gustaf W. Söderberg, Mar. 30th; Joseph Christiansen, May 11th; Carl J. Anderson, Apr. 13th; and John Jensen, Dec. 14th.

In 1893, 45 Elders from Zion were called to labor as missionaries in Scandinavia; they arrived in Copenhagen on the following dates: Anders P. Stenblom of Hunter, Utah, Feb. 2; Törkel Evan Törkelsen of Salt

PETER CHRISTIAN RASMUSSEN

Was born June 7, 1857, at Grönfeld, Randers amt, Denmark, was baptized April 9, 1882, and emigrated to Utah in 1883, locating at Draper, Salt Lake County. Filling a mission to Scandinavia in 1893-1895, he labored eighteen months in Norway and later a few months in Denmark. After his return home he was ordained a High Priest and acted as counselor in the bishopric of the Draper Ward. In 1910-1912 he filled a second mission to Scandinavia, presiding over the Christiania Conference, Norway, twenty months and later presiding over the Aarhus Conference, Denmark. Returning home, he circumnavigated the globe together with Elder Andrew Jenson. In September, 1914, he succeeded his brother, Sören Rasmussen, as Bishop of the Draper Ward, which position he held until 1919, when he located at Midvale, where he is now (1927) carrying on an extensive mercantile business. His wife, Mette Marie Jensen, whom he married in August, 1880, bore him eighteen children, seven of whom are alive and all faithful members of the Church.

Lake City, Mar. 11; Nils Mattson of St. Charles, Idaho, March 17th; Christen Petersen of Ferron, Hans J. Zobell of Lake View, Hans A. Thomsen of Juarez, Mexico, David Holmgren of Bear River City, John F. Lundquist of Snowflake, Arizona,

Theodor Peterson of Logan, Nils Sandberg of St. George, Carl P. Anderson of Clarkston, Andrew N. Kongstrup of Loa, John Hektor Peterson of Fremont, Christian G. Christensen of Richmond, Ole Ole-

LARS PETER CHRISTIANSEN

Was born Dec. 25, 1857, at Gjerlev, Sorö amt, Sjælland, Denmark, the son of Peter and Anna Christiansen. He was baptized March 15, 1863, by Niels C. Edlefsen, and emigrated with his parents to Utah in 1863. The family located in Hyrum, where young Lars Peter became a Church worker in his early youth. As a Seventy, filled a mission to Scandinavia in 1893-1895, laboring in the Copenhagen Conference, Denmark. He acted as Bishop of Mount Sterling Ward, Cache County, Utah, from 1903 to 1906.

sen of Mantua, and Carl Johan Gustafson of Providence, May 7th; Hans Peter Hansen of Hyrum, Peter C. Rasmussen of Draper, Abraham Jörgen Hansen of Spanish Fork, Lars P. Christiansen of Hyrum, Chr. P. Hald of Ephraim, Jacob Larsen of Paradise, Martin M. Hansen of Bluff Dale, and John Anderson of Salt Lake City, Utah, May 22nd; August J. Höglund of Salt Lake City and Hans J. Christiansen of Logan, May 31st; Charles J. Christensen and James C. Frost, jun., of Ephraim, June 9th; Hanmer Magleby of Monroe, Utah, and Frantz M. Winters

of Montpelier, Idaho, July 19th; James A. Hansen of Newton, Utah, Sept. 18th; William Sörensen and Peter Chr. Petersen of Glenwood, Charles F. Rytting of Grantsville, James Christensen of Brigham, and Lorenz Ockander of Santaquin, Oct. 13th; Niels A. Nielsen of Nephi, Utah, Oct. 6th; Lars Severin Christenson of Lyman, Idaho, Nov. 13th; Nils M. Jenson of Union and Gustaf Johanson of South Cottonwood, Nov. 26th; John A. Olson of Salem, Hans

CHARLES JOHN CHRISTENSEN,

The eldest son of Carl C. A. Christensen an Eliza Rosella Haarby, was born at Fairview Sanpete County, Utah, March 21, 1861. H says his "humble pioneer birthplace was a ce lar, eight by ten feet, roof and floor of tl mother earth." When he was only ten da old his parents moved to Mt. Pleasant on a count of Indian trouble at Fairview. For number of years he taught school, and the engaged in farming and stock-raising. Whi filling a mission in Scandinavia, in 1883-188 he labored in Norway. In 1886 he marri Maria Elizabeth Frost. When on a seco mission to Scandinavia in 1893-1895 he p sided over the Copenhagen Conference mo than a year. In 1910 he went on a short m sion to Southern Utah; in 1916 his son S mour was called to take a mission to Englar In 1918 Bro. Christensen moved to Salt La City, became a member of the Capitol H Ward and received a call to labor as a m sionary, which he gladly accepted.

Andersen of Levan, Chr. F. B. Lybbert of Vernal, Utah, Charles H. Hogensen and Ole Swenson of Montpelier, Idaho, Dec. 27th.

Anders P. Stenblom, David Holmgren, John F. Lundquist, Carl J. Gustafson, John Anderson, Lorenz Ockander and Gustaf Johanson were appointed to labor in the Stockholm Conference, Sweden. Nils Mattson, Nils Sandberg and Nils M. Jenson were appointed to labor in the Skåne Conference, Sweden. Törkel E. Törkelsen, Abraham J. Hansen, Hanmer Magleby, James A. Hansen, James Christensen, Charles H. Hogensen and Ole Swenson were appointed to labor in the Christiania Conference. Peter Chr. Rasmussen was appointed to labor in the Chris-

HANMER MAGLEBY,

who filled a good mission to Scandinavia in 93-1895, was born Feb. 24, 1867, at Milton, organ County, Utah, the son of Hans Olsen agleby and Gertrud Marie Christensen, received a good education, which he finished h four years' studies at the Brigham Young ademy at Provo, Utah. Soon after returnhome from his mission, however, he died, ., 3, 1896, at Monroe, Utah County, Utah. was a good and exemplary young man.

tiania Conference, but finished his mission in the Aarhus Conference. Hans J. Christiansen (third mission) was appointed to preside over the Christiania Conference, Norway. Charles J. Christensen (second mission) was appointed to labor in the Christiania Conference and later presided over the Copenhagen Conference. James C. Frost, jun., was appointed to labor in the Christiania Conference and later in the Aalborg Conference. Chr. Petersen, Hans J. Zobell, Chr. G. Christensen, Ole Olesen and Lars P. Christiansen were appointed to labor in the Copenhagen Conference. Hans A. Thomsen, Andrew N. Kongstrup, Jacob Larsen, William Sörensen and Hans Andersen were appointed to labor in the Aarhus Conference. Hans Peter Hansen was appointed to labor in the Aarhus Conference and later as president of the Aalborg Conference. Niels Andrew Nielsen was appointed to labor in the Aarhus Conference, having previously spent some months as a missionary in England.

Theodor Peterson, Christian P. Hald, Martin M. Hansen and Frantz Martin Winters were appointed to labor in the Aalborg Conference. Peter Chr. Petersen was appointed to labor in the Aalborg Conference, part of the time as president of said conference. Chr. F. B. Lybbert was appointed to labor in the Aalborg Conference, having previously labored in Holland. Carl P. Anderson, John H. Peterson, Charles F. Rytting and Lars S. Christenson were appointed to labor in the Göteborg Conference, Sweden. August J. Höglund was appointed to labor in the Göteborg Conference, part of the time as conference president. John A. Olson was appointed to labor in the mission office in Copenhagen as a writer and translator. He also led the Copenhagen Branch choir.

During the year 664 persons were added to the Church by baptism in the Scandinavian Mission.

CHAPTER 78 (1894)

Elder Peter Sundwall becomes president of the mission—More small companies of Saints leave for Utah—Swedish newspapers comment on "Mormonism"—Sixty-four Elders arrive from America.

Elder Carl A. Carlquist, who had presided over the Scandinavian Mission since May, 1893, left Copenhagen, Denmark, April 11, 1894, for his home in Salt Lake City, Utah, accompanied by other returning Elders. Elder Carlquist, who was succeeded in the presidency of the mission by Elder Peter Sundwall, had been a zealous and successful mission president. Being a good speaker and a splendid reasoner, and possessing a pronounced personality, his influence was felt wherever he traveled and associated with the people.

During the year 1894 a number of Saints emigrated to Zion in small companies. Thus 13 emigrating Saints bound for Utah sailed from Copenhagen April 5, 1894, accompanied by the following Elders from Zion, who had labored as missionaries in the Scandinavian Mission: Erik P. Lindquist and Gustaf Lindahl of Salt Lake City, Rasmus Rasmussen of Mt. Pleasant, German Rasmussen of Ephraim, Martin Andersen of Richfield, Gustaf W. Carlson and Michael O. Nash of Salem, Geo. Wm. Johnson of West Bountiful, Geo. Wm. Lindquist of Logan, Johan A. Johnson of Monroe and Nephi H. Nielsen of Huntsville, Utah. This company of missionaries and emigrants traveled by steamer to Hull, thence by railroad to Liverpool, England, thence across the Atlantic in the steamship "Arizona," together with a few returning missionaries and emigrating Saints

from the British and Swiss and German missions. After a pleasant voyage, the "Arizona" arrived in New York April 23rd, and thence the emigrants traveled by rail to Salt Lake City, where they arrived April 28th, 1894.

Another company of emigrating

PETER SUNDWALL

Was born June 11, 1848, at Aspås, Jemtlands län, Sweden, embraced the gospel and was baptized Feb. 27, 1866. After being ordained to the Priesthood he performed missionary labors in different branches of the Stockholm Conference, commencing in the fall of 1867, when he was sent to Gotland; afterwards he labored in Sundsvall, Östersund, Eskilstuna and Stockholm. He emigrated to Utah in 1872 and made his home in Fairview, Sanpete County. While filling a mission to Scandinavia in 1881-1883 he labored in the mission office in Copenhagen as business manager. He filled a second mission to Scandinavia in 1894-1896, presiding over the Scandinavian Mission. In 1908-1910 he filled a third mission to Scandinavia, this time presiding over the Swedish Mission. At home, Bro. Sundwall always took an active part in any calling assigned to him in a Church capacity, being always faithful at his post of duty. He also occupied many positions of prominence in the community and filled office under the government, the county and the city, being a successful business man. For several years he was mayor of Fairview and also served as a member of the High Council of the North Sanpete Stake. He died at Holladay, Utah, July 17, 1925. Among the many Elders that the Scandinavian Mission has produced, Elder Sundwall ranks among the most able and faithful workers in the Lord's vineyard.

Saints (24 souls) sailed from Copenhagen May 3, 1894, accompanied by the following Elders from Zion, who had performed successful missionary labors in the Scandinavian Mission: August Carlson of Ogden, Utah, who had presided over the Stockholm Conference, John A. Larson and Peter S. Jensen of Preston, Idaho, Peter M. Jensen and Peter C. Geertsen, jun., of Huntsville, Utah, Andrew J. Wahlquist of Salt Lake City, who had presided over the Göteborg Conference, Nils Benson of Spring City and Adam L. Petersen of Huntsville, who had presided over the Copenhagen Conference.

Another company of emigrating Saints, consisting of 53 souls, left Copenhagen for Utah June 7, 1894, accompanied by the following returning Elders: Thomas Spongberg of Preston, Idaho, Adolf Z. Fjellström of Logan, Utah, Carl A. Lunell of Benjamin, Utah, John Edward Mattson of Burton, Idaho, Peter Nielson, sen., of Monroe, Utah, and Louis Söderberg of Elsinore, Utah.

Another company of emigrating Saints (44 souls) left Copenhagen, Denmark, July 19, 1894, accompanied by the following Elders, who had performed missionary labors in Scandinavia: Amel Burnett Jensen of Richfield, Hans Peter Jörgensen of Fountain Green, John W. Dehlin of Mt. Pleasant, James Andersen and John Johnson of Logan, and Ludvig Hansen of Salt Lake City.

Elders Gustaf A. Iverson, Andreas Johansen and Carl M. Levorsen, having been honorably released from their missions in Scandinavia, sailed from Christiania, Norway, July 20, per steamer "Scotland" en route for their homes in Zion, accompanied by 6 emigrating Saints.

Accompaning 15 emigrating Saints, Elders John W. Winterrose and Erick Erickson of Heber, Utah, left Copenhagen, for Utah, Aug. 16th, 1894.
22

Peter Jenson of West Jordan left about the same time.

A company of 31 emigrating Saints left Copenhagen Sept. 20, 1894, in charge of Elder Charles J. Wahlquist. In this company were also Elders Nils Monson, Peter Hansen, Fred C. Olsen and Törkel Evan Törkelsen, who had performed faithful missionary labors in Scandinavia. The little company traveled by steamer to Leith, Scotland, thence by rail to Glasgow, and crossed the Atlantic in the ship "City of Rome" together with Elders and emigrating Saints from England, Elder Wahlquist being in charge of the company to Utah.

Elders John J. Plowman of Smithfield, Anton Nielsen of Huntington, and Andrew C. Olsen of Mt. Pleasant, Utah, left Copenhagen, Oct. 25, 1894, to return to their respective homes, after filling honorable missions in Scandinavia. They were accompanied by 23 emigrating Saints bound for Zion.

Elder Andrew J. Bolander of Logan, Charles Sörensen of Hyrum (who had presided over the Skåne Conference, Sweden), and Rasmus M. Larsen of Basalt, Idaho, left Copenhagen Nov 8, 1894, to return to their homes in Zion, accompanied by a company of 8 emigrating Saints. They traveled via Glasgow, Scotland, and crossed the Atlantic in the steamship "Furnesia."

Besides the Elders mentioned in connection with companies of emigrating Saints, the following brethren from Zion, who had labored as missionaries in Scandinavia, took their departure, returning home on the following dates: Charles L. Olsen and Peter T. Rundquist, Jan. 4th; John Christensen and Levi Pearson (Pehrson), Feb. 22nd; Christian F. B. Lybbert, April 17th; John L. Johnson, Andrew Larsen and Peter Nielsen, sen., June 1st; Hans J. Zobell, June 13th; Chr. Wm. Sörensen and Joseph Johansen, Oct. 16th.

An influential newspaper (Handels och Sjöfarts-Tidning), published in Göteborg, Sweden, devoted a column of closely printed matter to the "Mormons" in Sweden. It gave a detailed statement of the statistical condition of the mission, and then added: "It would be unjust to judge the labors and influence of the 'Mormons' in Scandinavia, and especially in Sweden, by the number of those only who have been baptized into that Church and who are members of that organization. One must also take into consideration that the Mormon Elders are showing much zeal and energy as distributors of tracts, though they seldom appear as speakers before large congregations. Notwithstanding that during the winter they find it difficult to hire halls, Elder August J. Höglund succeeded in securing the opportunity of preaching the Christmas sermon last year (1893) in the large and commodious hall of the Good Templars in Norrköping before an audience of about 350; also in the Good Templars hall in Motala this man preached March 4th to 500 people. A similar attempt on the hall of that order in Kalmar miscarried, but even the Good Templars hall in Sundsvall, the Labor Union Hall in Vesterås and the E. and V.'s hall in Eskilstuna have been opened to the Mormon Elders. During the summer the worry as to a hall in which to preach disappears, because then it is possible to hold meetings in the open air, sometimes to as many as 700 and 800 listeners, as, for instance, at the factory of Sandviken."

The same paper continues its comments as follows:

"As a sample of the perseverance and power of the Mormon Elders to gain access to those of different beliefs may be cited the following as related by one of the

Elders who, with his companion, recently returned from a trip through Härjedalen When the Elders on Saturday had arrived at Öfver-Högdals parish, they commenced to sell books and tracts. The following Sunday they sought to find a member of the school-board, but he had gone to a place where the people of that vicinity were in the habit of congregating for the purpose of hearing a sermon read to them out of a "Postilla," or a selection of sermons. The Mormon Apostles went to the same place. The leader at the meeting was just in the act of reading an explanation of the prophecy of Isaiah about an ensign that was to be raised up among the heathen. The contents of the sermon seemed familiar to the Elders: they opened their ears and soon found to their pleasant surprise that it was a tract very familiar to the 'Mormons,' the title of which is the Voice of Warning, which they had sold the day before."

In 1894, 64 Elders from Zion called to labor as missionaries in Scandinavia, arrived in Copenhagen Denmark, on the following dates Jonathan F. Petersen and Andrew Eskildsen of Mantua, and James Larsen of Logan, Utah, Jan. 7th; Ezra E Nielsen and Hans B. Nielsen of Hyrum, Utah, Jan. 8th; Asmus Jörgensen of Glendale, Utah, on Jan. 13th Rasmus Rasmussen and Martin Olson of Millville, and Peter C. Jensen or Bear River City, Utah, Jan. 30th William Buckholt of Nephi, James Larsen of Mapleton, and Christian P. Thomsen of Levan, Utah, Feb 3rd; Nils R. Lindahl of Union, Alfred G. Söderberg of West Jordan Charles Lindell of Sandy, Carl A Sundström of Union and Sören Peter sen of Spanish Fork, Utah, Feb 18th; Herman H. Sundström of Sandy, Hyrum Petersen of Spring City, Niels P. Nielsen and Joseph F Anderson of Ephraim, Joseph Berge sen of Lewiston, Wm. Isaac Sörensen of Mendon and Christian P. Larsen of Gunnison, Utah, March 23rd Peter Sundwall of Fairview, Utah March 30th; Peter Nelson of Harris ville and Peter Swenson of Sugar

House, Utah, Mar. 31st; Heber C. Christensen of Richfield and Louis C. Larsen of Fairview, Utah, April 2nd; Sören C. Sörensen and Lars (Louis) Madsen of Manti, Henry Hans Danielsen and James J. Larsen of Richmond, Anders P. Fillerup of Lake View, Carl Johan Wiberg of Sandy, John A. Carlson of Logan, Michael Sörensen of Salt Lake City, Erick Gillen of South Cottonwood and Erik Christensen of Ephraim, Utah,

May 6th; Nils Anthon Pehrson of Logan, Rasmus M. Larsen of Basalt, Idaho, John A. Jenson of Cedar City, Carl Hansen of Spring City, Carl A. Johnson (Johanson) of Huntsville,

HYRUM PETERSEN

Was born May 14, 1859, in Little Cottonwood, Salt Lake County, Utah, the son of Jens Petersen and Christine Johnson, who emigrated to Utah in 1856 or 1857. Bro. Hyrum was baptized when eight years old. In 1882 (March 23rd) he married Emma Scofield, who was born July 16, 1860, at Lehi, Utah. In 1884-1886 he filled a mission to Scandinavia, laboring eighteen months in Hjörring and six months in Thisted, Aalborg Conference, Denmark. He has been a resident of Spring City for many years and is a devoted member of the Church.

HERMAN H. SUNDSTRÖM

Was born Feb. 15, 1860, in Stockholm, Sweden, and baptized in Copenhagen, Denmark, Feb. 15, 1880, by Elder Andrew Jenson; was ordained a Deacon, April 14, 1880, by Niels Wilhelmsen and sent on a mission in the Stockholm Conference; labored in the Örebro Branch till Oct. 8, 1881, and then in Upsala; was arrested April 21, 1882, and sent in chains to the prison, where he was incarcerated nineteen days and then tried on various charges, but was set free. His accuser died afterwards in an insane asylum. The sheriff died a miserable death, tormented by his own conscience. On May 14, 1882, Bro. Sundström was sent to Gotland, where he labored till Oct. 14, 1883, when he was sent to Eskilstuna; May 28, 1884, he was released to emigrate. He had baptized 55 persons, sold books to the value of 642 kronor, and traveled on foot about ten thousand miles. Arriving in Salt Lake City June 29, 1884, he engaged in church activities and was ordained a Seventy Aug. 31, 1890. In 1894-1896 he filled a mission to Sweden, labored in Upsala, Örebro, Westmanland, Uppland and Ekilstuna; baptized twenty-seven converts, traveled on foot 3,500 miles, sold many books, etc., during a period of two and one-half years. Arrived home in Salt Lake City May 8, 1896, where he still resides.

and Carl A. Lundgren of Mayfield, Utah. May 11th; Nils Forsberg of Salt Lake City, June 30th; Bengt M. Ravsten of Clarkston and Niels A. Mörck of Salt Lake City, Aug. 6th; Peter Jensen of Mantua, Carl E. Cederström and Hans S. Rasmussen of Salt Lake City, and Christopher Iverson of Ephraim, Oct. 1st; Math. Anderson of Sterling, Gustaf Johnson of Gunnison, Anders Chr. Jensen of Hyrum, Michael Schow of Mantua, Peter August Nordquist of Ogden and Peter O. Hansen, jun., of Paradise, Nov. 4th; Louis J. Holther, jun., of Ogden, and Nephi Anderson of Gunnison, Utah, Nov.

24th; George S. Backman of Salt Lake City, Dec. 8th; Jens P. Jensen of Draper, Utah, William Georgesen

ANDERS PETER FILLERUP,

Born May 30, 1831, at Pannerup, Aarhus amt, Denmark, the son of Peter Jakob Fillerup and Karen Rasmussen, was baptized about 1861 by Sören Petersen; arrived in Utah in October, 1867, with ox teams; settled in Provo, and took up farming. In 1867 he married Caroline Rasmussen of Salt Lake City, daughter of Rasmus and Jensine Rasmussen of Wibye, Denmark, who bore him nine children, namely, Caroline Rasmine, Amalia Petronelle, Andrew Peter, Carl Richard, Erastus Kruse, Zenos Kimberly, Albert Frederick, Loftus, Alexander, and Rosena Eleanora Andrea. The family home is at Vineyard, Utah County, Utah. Elder Fillerup performed a mission to Denmark in 1894-1896, and died July 12, 1912, as a High Priest.

of Weston, Idaho, and Bengt Peterson of Heber, Utah, Dec. 17th.

Jonathan F. Petersen, Rasmus Rasmussen, James Larsen, Niels P. Nielsen, James J. Larsen, Erik Christensen and William Georgesen were appointed to labor in the Copenhagen Conference. Peter Jensen was also appointed to labor in the Copenhagen Conference, part of the time as president of said Conference. Andrew Eskildsen, Peter C. Jensen, William I. Sörensen, Louis Chr. Larsen, Lars (Louis) Madsen, Anders P. Fillerup, Michael Sörensen, Ras-

mus M. Larsen and Hans S. Rasmus sen were appointed to labor in th Aarhus Conference. William Buck holt was also appointed to labor i: the Aarhus Conference, part of th time as conference president.

Chr. P. Thomsen, Hyrum Petersei Chr. P. Larsen, Sören Chr. Sörense and Jens P. Jensen were appointe to labor in the Aalborg Conferenc Sören Petersen and Anders Chr. Je

JOHN AUGUST CARLSON

Was born June 28, 1859, at Lannaskede socke Jönköpings län, Sweden; and was baptiz June 8, 1885, at Jönköping, by Elder A. Anderson; he emigrated to Utah the same yea He returned to his native land to perform mission in the year 1894, laboring in Götebo and Vingåker, and received an honorable r lease to return home in 1897. Bro. Carls married Anna Lundström in 1886; both parer and the ten children born to them are all li ing and are active in Church work. The fa ily home is in Logan, Utah.

sen were also appointed to labor i the Aalborg Conference, part of th time as conference presidents. Har B. Nielsen, Asmus Jörgensen, Alfre G. Söderberg, Carl A. Sundströi Herman H. Sundström, Carl Wiberg, Nils A. Pehrson, Carl Augu Johanson (Johnson), Math. Anders and Peter A. Nordquist were a ointed to labor in the Stockholm Conference. Erick Gillen was also

ANTHON PEHRSON

Was born in Wrå, Kronobergs län, Sweden, Jan. 17, 1869, the son of Johan Salomon Pehrson and Kristine Nilsson, and was baptized in Halmstad, Sweden, in November, 1886, by Elder Aug. Westerberg. He emigrated to Utah in 1888, was ordained a Seventy by Pres. B. H. Roberts in 1894, and performed home missionary labors in Salt Lake and Logan Stakes. In 1896 he married Johanna Håkanson, from Stockholm. Bro. Pehrson filled a mission to Sweden in 1894-1896 (27 months) and baptized 42 converts; left for a second mission to Sweden in October, 1907, when he presided over the Sundsvall Conference for nine months; returned home in March, 1910, and has been a member of the Scandinavian presidency for nine years. In 1923 he was called to take a third mission to Sweden and presided over the Stockholm Conference; he baptized seventeen converts on this mission. Bro. Pehrson still resides at Logan, Utah.

appointed to labor in the Stockholm Conference, part of the time as conference president. Nils R. Lindahl was appointed to preside over the Stockholm Conference; this was his second mission to Scandinavia. James Larsen, Martin Olsen, Peter Nilson, Carl August Lundgren and Bengt Peterson were appointed to labor in the Skåne Conference. Bengt M. Ravsten (second mission) was appointed to preside over the Skåne Conference.

Ezra E. Nielsen, Peter Swenson, John A. Carlson, John A. Jenson,

Carl E. Cederström, Gustaf Johnson and George S. Backman were appointed to labor in the Göteborg Conference. Charles Lindell was also appointed to labor in the Göteborg Conference and later in the Skåne Conference. Joseph Bergesen, Heber Chr. Christensen, Henry H. Danielsen, Carl Hansen, Christopher Iverson, Peter O. Hansen, jun., Louis J. Holther (second mission) and Nephi Anderson were appointed to labor in the Christiania Conference. Michael Schow was appointed to labor in the Christiania Conference and afterwards in the Aalborg Conference. Niels A. Mörck was appointed to labor in the Christiania Conference, and later in

HANS SEVERIN RASMUSSEN

Was born at Aalsrode, Randers amt, Denmark, March 26, 1864, the son of Hans P. Rasmussen and Christine Marie Sörensen, and was baptized April 15, 1883, by Elder Jens M. Christensen. He emigrated to Utah and arrived in Salt Lake City July 7, 1885; moved to Pleasant Grove, where he married Ellen Svenson, Dec. 9, 1885, and moved to Salt Lake City a year later. In 1894-1896 he filled a mission to Denmark, where he presided over the Grenaa Branch for a time and then labored as traveling Elder in the Aarhus Conference. For years he engaged in business in Salt Lake, Draper and Pleasant Grove, and at present (1927) is proprietor and manager of the American Fork Bottling Works. He has been active in civic affairs as city councilman, president and director of the Chamber of Commerce, and is very much respected in the community.

the Copenhagen Conference. Joseph P. Anderson was appointed to labor in the Christiania Conference and later in the Aarhus Conference. Peter Sundwall (second mission) was appointed to preside over the Scandinavian Mission. Nils Forsberg was appointed to labor as a writer and translator in the mission office in Copenhagen, Denmark.

CHAPTER 79 (1895)

A Lutheran priest opposes "Mormonism"— Marvelous cases of healing—Elder August Joel Höglund in Russia—Missionaries in the extreme northern part of Norway—Returning Elders lead small companies of Saints to Zion— Arrival of 48 more Elders from America.

In the later part of 1894, Elder Joseph P. Anderson and William Sörensen were appointed to open up a new field of labor on the west coast of Jutland, Denmark. A family of Saints had just moved into that locality, which gave the Elders an opportunity for preaching the gospel there. A well-attended meeting was held, after which the Elders remained conversing with inquirers until past midnight. The next evening the Elders again spoke to a packed house, and so many people became interested in the doctrines advocated by the Elders, that they remained to converse until a very late hour of the night. Six weeks later the Elders returned to the same neighborhood, and soon learned that the power of evil had been at work during their absence. A Lutheran priest had been sent to the place to warn the people against the "Mormons," trying to prove that they were false prophets, and he advised his hearers not to open their doors for the Elders. Yet the seed which had been sown by them did not all fall upon stony ground, but, on the request of many, the Elders returned and held meetings again. The clergyman's efforts against them made the people all the more anxious to hear them, and

when the Elders arrived at the home of Brother Knudsen they were agreeably surprised to find many smiling faces awaiting them. Four successful meetings were held and people came from afar to hear them. At the close of one of the meetings a man arose from the audience and said in substance: "I lift up my voice against the false 'Mormon' priests and their devilish doctrines. I can take the Bible and prove to you all that every word they have uttered here this evening is without foundation." The speaker then cited the first three verses of the Revelation of John, 14th chapter, to which Elder Anderson had alluded in his talk. The priest remarked that he belonged to the 144,000 that would stand upon Mount Zion with the Lamb of God and called God to witness that the "Mormon" Elders were liars and deceivers, and if they were not so, he asked the Almighty to inflict upon him all sorts of torture, as, for instance, cut him up in pieces, grind him into powder, run red hot irons into his flesh and burn him into ashes. At this point, he turned white as the new-fallen snow and, quivering and trembling, he fell to his seat. The Bible was immediately handed to him, but he refused to open it. After a few remarks in defense of the Elders, another gentleman stepped forward and said, "My friends, I belong to no sect, but can bear my testimony that what these Mormons have said is the truth and they have proved their doctrines from the Bible." Another said: "I have learned more in hearing these Mormon Elders one night than I have learned all my life going to hear all my priests." The result of all this was, that many became investigators of the gospel and soon some asked for baptism. The meetings of the Elders, after that, were well attended by both strangers and Saints.

Under date of Feb. 5, 1895, Elder David Holmgren reported from Upsala, Sweden, that he had gathered the genealogy of faithful members of the Church who had died without the privilege of emigrating to Zion, in order that their names might be sent to headquarters, so that their work might be done for them in the Temples. This illustrious example was soon followed by other Elders in the Scandinavian Mission, and it finally resulted in a general movement throughout all the missions of the Church to gather the genealogies of faithful Saints for that purpose.

Marvelous cases of healing were frequently reported by the Elders in the Scandinavian Mission, in fulfilment of the promise: "These signs shall follow them that believe." Thus President Peter Sundwall, under date of April 4th, reports that a certain child, who was suffering with pain and had for several days been unable to walk, was brought to the hall (in which the Saints held meetings) by one of the sisters, who asked the Elders to administer to the child, saying that she had told its parents that the child would be healed if the Elders would anoint it with oil and pray for it. The Elders administered to the child, and it was taken home well, being able to walk and ask for something to eat. The parents attended the meetings of the Saints afterwards and testified to the healing of their child; later they embraced the gospel and felt happy in the knowledge which they had received. The father of the child had for years been engaged as a preacher in a free church of Lutherans, but after his baptism into the true Church, he became very diligent in trying to show his old friends the principles of the gospel as they had been revealed anew from heaven.

As a sample of diligent missionary labor, it may be stated here that Elder August J. Höglund, president of the Göteborg Conference, early in 1895 made an extensive tour through his conference, during which he visited Sköfde, where a new branch of the Church had been organized in the fall of 1893, Kyrkofalla, where he held three meetings, Kinnekulle, where four meetings were held, Tidaholm, where three meetings were held in a large hired hall, Hjo, Vadstena, Motala, Örebro (where the Saints still occupied the same hall which they used twenty years before), Vingåker, Vestervik, Norrköping, etc. During his visit, which covered a period of twelve weeks, Elder Höglund held 66 meetings, assisted by other Elders.

In the summer of 1895, Elder August J. Höglund visited St. Petersburg, Russia, where he was made welcome in the home of J. M. Lindelöf, who was investigating the gospel. Mr. Lindelöf and his wife, after lengthy gospel conversations, asked for baptism. Hence, on Tuesday, June 11, 1895, Mr. Lindelöf hired a boat and traveled for several miles with his wife and Elder Höglund to a somewhat secluded spot on the river Neva, where the Elder baptized Mr. Lindelöf and his wife and confirmed them members of the Church. Mr. Lindelöf was a goldsmith by profession and was born in Finland, but had resided in Russia 16 years. He spoke the Russian and Swedish languages, and was well acquainted with the Scandinavian population of St. Petersburg. Elder Höglund spent a very pleasant time with the new converts in St. Petersburg, which city he left June 21st, after having ordained Brother Lindelöf an Elder and instructed him in the duties of the Priesthood. Elder Höglund blessed three children belonging to the Lindelöf family, partook of the

Sacrament, and separated from the family with feelings of love and happiness. Before returning to Sweden, Elder Höglund also visited Helsingfors, Åbo, Poja, Jakobstad and other places in Finland.

In 1895, Elder Heber C. Christensen and Nephi Anderson held a number of meetings at Tromsö, Norway, where they hired the Good Templars Hall, and their meetings were well attended. They also visited Vadsö, one of the most northern cities of Norway, where they hired a hall and held a meeting. The announcement of this meeting caused considerable excitement in that little town, and more people gathered than could be accommodated in the little hall. The two Elders were gone on their northern trip eight weeks, during which they held 10 meetings, visited 194 families, had 108 gospel conversations, and sold and distributed many books and pamphlets.

Elder John A. Olson, in writing from Copenhagen, June 10, 1895, praises the Danish climate in the following:

"We have here dreary, long winters, with lots of rough, cold weather, dampness, fog, etc., but when the long summer months begin to stretch out and nature is coming out in holiday attire, a person cannot help forgetting the hardships of winter to a certain extent.

"The northern summer is almost a paradise on earth, especially to one who lives with his eyes open to the beauties of nature so sublime and grand; with his ears open to the thrills of the skylark, the charming tones of the nightingale and other singing birds. If a person is ever so lost to all these pleasing impressions, he cannot help to inhale the invigorating summer breezes, and his olfactory organs cannot resist enjoying the sweet aroma that in reality flows from flora's fascinating bosom. I say in reality, for a good many of the earth's inhabitants must be contented with only reading about it, and imagine themselves surrounded with such things.

"The long, mild days, not too hot, makes a fellow that isn't used to it feel somewhat lost; for instance, we can read a newspaper by daylight after 10 o'clock in the night, while up to that late hour you will hear hundreds of happy children playing in the streets, having their hours of recreation and romping. The parks and boulevards are filled with promenaders till after midnight, small groups of men and women are seen seated on the many comfortable benches in the parks; the large sound (Öresund) is in view, and hundreds of pleasure boats are seen crossing each other's wake in all directions and the huge steamers with half speed are gliding out and in on the busy sound."

Elder Anthon H. Lund, president of the European Mission, and George C. Naegle, president of the Swiss and German Mission, and wife arrived in Copenhagen, on a visit to Scandinavia, Sept. 6, 1895. Pres. Naegle and wife only remained in Copenhagen four days, when he returned to his field of labor in Germany, while Pres. Lund visited Aarhus and Aalborg in Denmark, Christiania in Norway, Eskilstuna, Stockholm, Vingåker, Göteborg and other places in Sweden, attending meetings and conferences and giving timely instructions to the Elders. Pres. Lund left Copenhagen Oct. 8th for Holland.

In Scandinavia, as well as in other missions, the Elders in their administrations frequently came in contact with evil spirits and were asked to administer to persons who were possessed of these. Elder Joseph P. Anderson relates an instance of this kind which occurred in a village called Tylstrup, not far from Aarhus, Denmark. A young woman, who had been subject to fits ever since she was six years old was growing gradually worse, and as soon as she began to investigate the gospel, it seemed that the devil commenced his work, for she then not only had cramps but seemed to be possessed of evil spirits. From the 20th of November to the 14th of December, when the Elders arrived, she had spells every day and some days two or three times. Just as the

Elders were approaching the house, they met the girl's father, who felt very much concerned about his daughter, who had just had a bad attack which so affected him that he fainted at the sight of it. The parents wanted the girl baptized the same night, but the Elders did not think it wise. Elder Anderson, however, talked with the father about the promises of the Lord through the administration of the ordinance of laying on of hands for healing the sick. The Elders united with the family in calling upon God to heal the girl from her terrible affliction. They administered to her, and from the 15th of December, 1895, to the date of writing (Feb. 1, 1896) she was entirely well without the slightest appearance of the disease. She was, at the time of writing, happy and praised the Lord for her recovery. The incident caused quite an excitement in that part of the country.

The emigration of Latter-day Saints to Utah in small companies from the Scandinavian countries was continued in 1895. Whenever Elders returned from their missions they were usually accompanied by a few emigrants, who wended their way to Zion. Thus it is recorded that on April 25th, 1895, a company of six emigrating Saints, accompanied by Elder Nils Mattson of St. Charles, Idaho, Andrew N. Kongstrup of Loa, John H. Peterson of Fremont, Christian G. Christensen of Richmond, and Jacob Larsen of Paradise, Utah, left Copenhagen, Denmark, for Zion.

A company of 21 emigrating Saints, accompanied by Elders Nils Sandberg of St. George, Christen Petersen of Ferron, Carl P. Anderson of Clarkston, Ole Olesen of Mantua, Hans P. Hansen of Hyrum and Charles J. Christensen of Ephraim, Utah, left Copenhagen, May 2, 1895, for Utah.

A company of 45 emigrating Saints bound for Utah, accompanied by the following Elders who had filled missions in Scandinavia, left Copenhagen, May 30, 1895: Hans A. Thomsen of Juarez, Mexico, Peter C. Rasmussen of Draper, Abraham J. Hansen of Spanish Fork, Lars P. Christiansen of Hyrum, Christian P. Hald of Ephraim, Utah, Frantz M. Winters of Montpelier, Idaho, and Martin M. Hansen of Bluff Dale, Utah.

A company of 23 emigrants, six of whom were not members of the Church, left Copenhagen, July 25, 1895, accompanied by Elders David Holmgren of Bear River City, Utah. John F. Lundquist of Snowflake, Arizona, Theodor Peterson of Logan, Jens P. Jensen of Draper and Bengt Peterson of Heber, Utah, (the two latter released on account of sickness). This company sailed from Copenhagen as passengers on the little steamer "Thorsö," arrived at Leith, Scotland, on the 28th, and continued by rail to Glasgow on the 29th. Here they went on board the steamer "Furnesia," August 1st, together with 17 emigrating Saints from Norway, accompanied by Hans J. Christiansen, who had sailed from Christiania July 26th. Besides these Saints and returning Elders, 12 emigrating Saints from Great Britain, and seven returning Elders and two visiting sisters sailed on the "Furnesia." The whole company consisting of 67 souls, under the leadership of Elder Hans J. Christiansen, landed in New York August 11th, and arrived in Salt Lake City, Utah, August 17, 1895.

Another company of emigrating Saints (18 souls), bound for Utah, left Copenhagen, August 29th, accompanied by the following returning Elders: August J. Höglund of Salt Lake City, who had presided over the Göteborg Conference, James

Andrew Hansen of Newton, William Sörensen of Glenwood, Gustaf Johnson of Gunnison and Mrs. Anna K. Bartlett of Vernal, Utah, the latter having visited relatives and friends in Denmark.

A small company of Saints, (21 souls) emigrating to Utah, left Copenhagen, Oct. 3rd, accompanied by the following returning Elders: Charles Frederik Rytting, of Grantsville, James Christensen of Brigham, Lorenz Ockander of Santaquin, Rasmus Rasmussen of Millville, and Peter Nilson of Harrisville, Utah. Elder Peter Christian Petersen of Glenwood, Utah, James C. Frost of Ephraim and Niels A. Nielsen of Nephi, Utah, sailed from Copenhagen, Denmark, Oct. 17, 1895, returning to their homes in Utah, after performing successful missionary labors in Scandinavia.

Another company of emigrating Saints (31 souls) sailed from Copenhagen, Nov. 14, 1895, accompanied by the following Elders who were returning to their homes in Zion, after performing good missions in Scandinavia: John A. Olson of Salem, Utah, Lars Severin Christenson of Lyman, Idaho, Hans Andersen of Levan, Andrew Eskildsen of Mantua, Hans Benjamin Nielsen of Hyrum, Carl August Sundström of Union, and Elias Jensen (a visitor) of Brigham City. Elder Charles H. Hogensen of Montpelier, Idaho, and Hanmer Magleby of Monroe, Utah, accompanied by three emigrating Saints, joined the Copenhagen Company in England. They had left Christiania Nov. 15, 1895.

Niels M. Jenson of Union, Asmus Jörgensen of Glendale, and James Larsen of Mapleton, Utah, who had labored as missionaries in Scandinavia, left Copenhagen Dec. 12, 1895, returning to their homes in Utah. They were accompanied by three emigrating Saints.

Besides the Elders mentioned in connection with companies of emigrating Saints, the following brethren from Zion who had labored as missionaries in Scandinavia, took their departure, returning home on the following dates: Peter O. Hansen, jun., March 8th, and Chr. P. Thomsen, July 4th.

In 1895, 48 Elders from Zion, called to labor as missionaries in Scandinavia, arrived in Copenhagen, Denmark, in the following order: Peter Andersen, Hyrum Daniel Jensen and Carl Johan Rehnström of Ogden, Theodore Tobiason of Salt Lake City, Canute Peter Hanson of Ephraim, Lorenzo O. Skanchy of Logan, Utah, and Abel Erickson of Albion, Idaho, arrived March 7th; Edward A. Olsen of Ogden, Utah, arrived April 22nd; Lars Erik Danielson and Erik Peter Erickson of Smithfield, Alonzo Blair Irvine of Logan, Utah, Peter Magnusson of Mesa, Arizona, John Lorenz Hallbom of Heber, Nephi Anderson of Vernon, Utah, Julius Johnson of Preston, Idaho, and Andrew Chr. Fjeldsted of Gunnison, Utah, arrived May 5th; Anders Björkman of Salt Lake City, and Ole Anderson of Pleasant Grove, Utah, arrived June 21st; Nephi Peter Anderson of Brigham City, Matthias Knudsen of Lehi and Lars Wilhelm Hendrikson of South Cottonwood, Utah, arrived July 21st; Peder A. Pedersen of Salem, Nils Frederik Alberg and Lars Gustaf Larson of Murray, Johan Fredrick Jonason and John Fred. Appelquist of Salt Lake City, and Joseph Y. Larsen of Holliday, Utah, arrived Sept. 22nd; Peder C. Christensen of Mayfield, Andrew Anderberg of Provo, Thomas Gundersen of Mill Creek, Edward Gundersen of Cottonwood, Carl Axel Ahlquist of Sugar House, Peter Ernström of Ogden, Johan L. G. Johnson and Martin E. Christophersen of Salt Lake

City, Utah, arrived Nov. 4th; Morten C. Mortensen of Bear River City, Jens Jörgensen of Draper, Utah, Andrew Johnson of Ovid, Idaho, Knud H. Fridal of Bear River City, Niels Chr. Sörensen of Central, James

JOHN L. HALLBOM

Was born in Wamlingbo, Gotland, Sweden, Sept. 18, 1859; joined the Church in 1878, in Stockholm; emigrated to Utah in 1882, and located in Heber City, where he was ordained to the various offices of the Priesthood. He filled a mission to Sweden in 1895-1897, labored first in Stockholm and later in Norrland, with Sundsvall as headquarters; presided in that branch for a year; in 1896 he took a short mission to Gotland in the interest of Church history, then labored in Eskilstuna until the spring of 1897, when he was honorably released. Bro. Hallbom also filled a three-months' mission in Millard County, Utah, in the interests of the Mutual Improvement Association, and also became a member of the High Council of that Stake. He moved to Salt Lake City in the spring of 1906, where he still (1927) resides.

Chr. Jensen of Glenwood, Olof Erik Olson and Christian Johansen of Mt. Pleasant, Utah, arrived Nov. 17th; Jacob Fikstad of Manti, Utah, Dec. 2nd; Carl W. Erikson of Springville, Frederik J. C. Danielsen of Fairview, John D. Amundsen of South Cottonwood and Emanuel F. Lennberg of Union, Utah, arrived Dec. 10, 1895.

Abel Erickson, Erik P. Erikson, Nephi Anderson, Lars W. Hendrik-

son, Johan F. Jonason and John D. Amundsen, were appointed to labor in the Göteborg Conference. Olof Erik Olson was appointed to labor in the Göteborg and later in the Stockholm Conference. Theodore Tobiason was appointed to labor in the Göteborg Conference, most of the time as conference president. Carl J. Rehnström, Lars Erik Danielson, John L. Hallbom, Anders Björkman, Nils F. Ahlberg, John F. Appelquist, Lars G. Larson, Peter Ernström, Carl W. Erikson and Emanuel F. Lennberg were appointed to labor in the Stockholm Con-

JOHN F. APPLEQUIST,

Second son of Johan Erik Applequist and Frederikka Hammar, was born June 24, 1862, in Danmark Parish, Upsala län, Sweden, and reared as a Lutheran. Having heard the gospel preached by the Latter-day Saints, he decided to cast his lot with that people, and emigrated to Utah in 1886, where he was baptized Feb. 1, 1887, and ordained an Elder Aug. 8, 1887. He married Ottilia J. S. Höglund, Aug. 12, 1887, but lost his wife by death Sept. 13, 1887. He labored as a teacher in the Thirteenth Ward, Salt Lake City, in 1893-1895; was ordained a Seventy by J. Golden Kimball, Aug. 30, 1895, and filled a mission to Sweden in 1895-1897, laboring in the Stockholm Conference, principally in the Örebro, Vesterås and Upsala branches. After his return to Utah he married Anna S. Krantz, Jan. 12, 1899; was ordained a High Priest by Sylvester Q. Cannon Feb. 4, 1906; labored as a teacher in the Sixth Ward about ten years, and in 1910 moved to the Second Ward of the Liberty Stake.

ference. Alonzo Blair Irvine was also appointed to labor in the Stockholm Conference, but later he presided over the Skåne Conference. Carl A. Ahlquist was appointed to preside over the Stockholm Conference. Peter Magnusson and Andrew Anderberg were appointed to labor in the Skåne Conference. Canute P. Hanson, Niels Chr. Sörensen and Christian Johansen were appointed to labor in the Aalborg Conference. Andrew Chr. Fjeldsted and James Chr. Jensen were also appointed to labor in the Aalborg Conference, part of the time as conference presidents.

Ole Anderson, Jens Jörgensen, and Frederik J. C. Danielsen were appointed to labor in the Aarhus Conference. Morten Chr. Mortensen and Knud H. Fridal were appointed to labor in the Aarhus and Copenhagen conferences, Elder Mortensen most of the time as president of the Aarhus Conference. Hyrum D. Jensen, Lorenzo O. Skanchy, Edward A. Olsen, Julius Johnson, Matthias Knudsen, Peder A. Pedersen, Thomas Gundersen, Edward Gundersen, Johan L. G. Johnson and Jacob Fikstad were appointed to labor in the Christiania Conference. Martin E. Christophersen was also appointed to labor in the Christiania Conference, part of the time as conference president. Peter Andersen (2nd mission) was appointed to preside over the Christiania Conference.

Joseph Y. Larsen was appointed to labor in the Copenhagen Conference, but being banished, he finished his mission in the Skåne Conference, Sweden. Peder Chr. Pedersen and Andrew Johnson were appointed to labor in the Copenhagen Conference, Denmark.

Nephi Peter Anderson (Niels Petersen) was appointed to labor as writer and translator in the mission office in Copenhagen, Denmark.

CHAPTER 80 (1896)

Early in 1896 Elder Peter Ernström, who labored as a missionary in Sweden, visited, among other places, the town of Borgvik, in Värmland, where about three hundred laborers were employed in some large iron works. A liberal-minded workman furnished Elder Ernström with lodgings. Elder Ernström visited this man at his work, and his fellow-workers were informed that he was a "Mormon priest" 'and,' said his friend, 'You should only hear him and you would soon acknowledge that he understands the plan of salvation far better than the parish priest, and he carries a lot of tracts with him which he sells very cheap." At the request of the workmen, Elder Ernström took some tracts with him to the works and distributed a large number of them. The men read these tracts during their lunch hour, and Elder Ernström visited them when they had stopped work for dinner and spoke to them about the gospel. They desired that he should hold a meeting on the place, but this seemed impossible, as the superintendent himself was the local preacher, and seemed displeased with Elder Ernström's efforts, and forbade the workmen to open their houses for holding meetings. This prohibition, however, seemed to sharpen the curiosity of the men still more, and they wished the Elder to address them, even if it had to be done on the highway. At last it was decided that he should lecture in the dining hall the following Sunday at 1 o'clock p. m. A great number of people assembled at that hour, but ust as Elder Ernström was getting ready to go to the meeting, the parish priest and council arrived at the house where he was staying and the following conversation took place between the priest, the Elder and the man of the house:

Priest: "Does the Mormon pastor stay here?"

The man: "Yes, there he is."

The priest, addressing Elder Ernström, then said: "I forbid you to preach here and lead the people astray with false doctrine."

Elder: "I don't preach anything but what you can find in this book, the Bible" (which Elder Ernström held in his hand).

Priest: "Yes, the Mormon Bible."

Elder: "No, it is no Mormon Bible. Look at the title page: 'The Bible printed at Stockholm in 1894'."

Priest: "Yes, you preach a little out of the Bible, in order to seduce young girls, then you take them to Utah and make them your concubines and slaves."

Elder: "What do you know about Utah? You have never been there."

Priest: "I have read it in the papers. Have you ever been in Utah?"

Elder: "Yes, sir, I have been there 3 years."

Priest: "I forbid you to preach, as I do not know who you are. Let me see your papers."

Elder: "With pleasure. Here are my citizenship papers."

Priest: "Why, you haven't even got Swedish papers."

Elder: "They are not needed. American papers are sufficient for American citizens."

Priest: "If you sell and scatter your tracts here, I will send a constable after you, and you will be taken away from here."

Elder: "All right, it will be pleasant to go over the road in a wagon, for it was very hard to get here; I

had to travel 30 miles on foot, and I will be very thankful to have a team take me away."

Priest: "You needn't joke about it, you may find that I am in earnest, for the parish council has met and determined to send a constable after you."

Elder: "I am not afraid of the parish council, nor the priest. I have done nothing wrong, but it is now as in the days of the Savior, when the priests and scribes set themselves against Jesus and his Apostles. Those who preach for hire have always been the most bitter opposers of the truth."

Priest: "Do you not have a salary?"

Elder: "No, sir, and I have even paid my fare to this country and I expect to remain here for about two years, and will meet all expenses connected with my stay."

Priest: "Are you a Mormon or Latter-day Saint?"

Elder: "I am, sir, and what reason have you to hinder me from preaching?"

Priest: "It is reason enough that a man is a Mormon and has come from Utah."

Elder: "If it is enough to condemn a man because he is from Utah, then it is now like it was in the days of Christ when the people said that no good could come from Nazareth, and so they rejected Jesus because he was a Nazarene. If you, Mr. Priest, will permit me, I will visit you tomorrow and I will make this agreement with you: I will abandon my faith in the Latter-day Saints doctrine, if you can prove to me that it is false; but, on the contrary, if I can prove that the doctrine you preach is composed of the commandments of men, then you will be just as willing to give up your faith in it."

Priest: "I will talk no more with you, and I will not permit you to enter my house; and I again forbid you to tract and preach in this parish."

The priest then went away, after Elder Ernström had informed him that he would preach the gospel when and where he had an opportunity to do so without asking his permission. He then went to the meeting and found over two hundred people waiting for him. He apologized for being late and explained the reason why he had not come at the time appointed. Then he delivered a comprehensive and spirited gospel sermon, and closed by advising the people to examine the doctrines he advocated for themselves, in order to prove or disprove their harmony with the doctrines of Christ and his Apostles. The people paid the strictest attention and bought nearly all Elder Ernström's books and tracts. They invited him to come again, and said that if they had ever heard the truth spoken, then it was the testimony which they had heard him bear concerning the gospel of Christ.

Elder Anders Björkman, who was laboring as a missionary in the Stockholm Conference, Sweden, died suddenly, August 19, 1896, while engaged with some friends at manual labor in the harvest field. A burial lot was purchased in the pretty graveyard belonging to Gustafs Församling, where the remains of Elder Björkman, clothed in temple robes and placed in a beautiful casket, were interred Aug. 25, 1896, in the presence of four Elders from Zion, a number of local Saints and several friends.

Elder Anders Björkman was born in Björklinge, Upland, Sweden, Jan. 22, 1838; embraced the gospel May 18, 1864, in Upsala, Sweden, being the first man in that city to embrace the restored gospel. He emigrated to Utah in 1869 and located in Salt

Lake City. Having been called on a mission to Scandinavia, he arrived in Copenhagen June 29, 1895, and was appointed to labor in the Stockholm Conference. At the time of his demise, he acted as president of the Sölfvarbo Branch in Dalarne.

In August, 1896, Elder Alonzo B. Irvine, who labored in the Skåne Conference, visited St. Petersburg, Russia, where he met Brother Lindelöf, the local brother who had been baptized by Elder Höglund about a year before. He received a hearty welcome by this family of Saints, which constituted the whole membership of the Church in Russia at that time. After spending a week at St. Petersburg, Elder Irvine returned to Sweden by way of Helsingfors, Åbo, Jacobstad and other places in Finland, visiting a few scattered Saints who were residents of that country.

Elder Peter Sundwall, who had presided over the Scandinavian Mission since April, 1894, left Copenhagen June 11, 1896, leaving the mission in charge of Elder Christian N. Lund from Mt. Pleasant, Utah. Elder Sundwall's administration had been a most successful one. Being a man of wisdom, sound judgment and exemplary in all his habits, he had great influence with Elders, local Saints and the people generally who came into his presence, and he left the mission in a prosperous condition.

Going home he was accompanied by the following Elders, who also returned from missions in Scandinavia: Heber C. Christensen of Richfield, Johan Carl Wiberg of Sandy, and Nils Anthon Pehrson of Logan, Utah, and also by 20 emigrating Saints.

Elder Daniel K. Brown, who labored in the Aalborg Conference, Denmark, as a successful missionary, held a well-attended meeting in the village of Nörretranders in June, 1896. The people gave good atten tion, but just before the close of the meeting, Mr. Tömmerup, the parish priest, put in an appearance, loaded with some literature. At the close

CHRISTIAN N. LUND

Was born Jan. 13, 1846, at Seest, Ribe amt, Denmark, the son of Lauritz Nielsen Lund and Fredrikka Jensen, and was baptized March 21, 1858, by Hans P. Iversen. He labored as a missionary in the Fredericia Conference from Nov. 7, 1865, to June 1, 1868, when he emigrated to Utah. He married Petra Antonia Marie Jensen, of Odense, Oct. 9, 1869, and settled in Mt. Pleasant, Sanpete County. In 1879-1880 he filled a mission to the Northwestern States. His first wife having died in 1882, he married Anna Nielsen, also of Odense, Denmark, in October, 1884. In 1889 and 1894, Elder Lund served in the Territorial Legislature, became a president of the sixty-sixth quorum of Seventy and later, being ordained a High Priest, he acted as counselor to Bishop William S. Seeley of Mount Pleasant, whom he succeeded as Bishop, Jan. 10, 1888. In 1896-1898 he filled a mission to Europe, presiding over the Scandinavian Mission. When the North Sanpete Stake was organized Dec. 9, 1900, he was chosen its president, which position he held until Sept. 12, 1914. Elder Lund died at Mount Pleasant, May 7, 1921.

of the meeting he tried to prove to the people by quoting extracts from Orson Pratt's works that the "Mormons" were heathens and worshiped many gods. The Elders were prepared to answer him and the outcome resulted in their favor. This made the priest so angry that he fairly raved and bolted out of the hall,

swearing vengeance on the Elders. On the 15th of June, Daniel K. Brown was notified to appear at the police station in Aalborg to answer to the awful crime of having preached the gospel. He had a private hearing before the chief of police and another limb of the law and, like Paul before Agrippa, he pleaded his own case. The officials treated Elder Brown courteously, and he was finally informed that he was at liberty to go. Later, however, he was arrested in Aalborg on account of his missionary activities and after a brief examination, during which he was denied the privilege of defending himself, he was banished from Denmark, Aug. 1, 1896. On the following day (August 2nd) he was taken by a police officer to the German boundary. In consequence of this trouble, Brother Brown's field of labor was changed from Denmark to Norway.

Elder Andrew Jenson, who was making a missionary tour of all the Latter-day Saint missions throughout the world in the interests of Church history, arrived in Copenhagen, Sept 9, 1896, accompanied by his wife, Emma H. Jenson. The same evening he preached to a large congregation of Saints and strangers at the branch hall, Krystalgade 24, Copenhagen. The next day, Elder Rulon S. Wells, president of the European Mission, arrived in Copenhagen from Germany to make a tour of the Scandinavian Mission. Later the same day Pres. Wells, Christian N. Lund (president of the Scandinavian Mission), Elder Andrew Jenson and wife, and Elder Enoch Jörgensen sailed from Copenhagen for Christiania, Norway, where they attended a conference, which was held on the 12th and 13th of September. On Friday, Sept. 18th, the party left Christiania for Stockholm, Sweden, where another conference was held on Saturday and Sunday, Sept. 19th and 20th. Leaving Elder Jenson in Stockholm to complete his historical labors, Presidents Wells and Lund left that city Sept. 23rd by train for Göteborg on their way to Copenhagen. Elder Jenson spent several days in Stockholm culling historical data from the records, and on the 27th traveled about one hundred miles to Vingåker, where interesting and successful meetings were held. Next, Elder Jenson visited Göteborg, where he attended to historical labors and then crossed the Cattegat, to Denmark, where he visited his birthplace and former missionary field of labor. He then returned to Copenhagen and later attended a conference in Göteborg. Still later, in company with Pres. Chr. N. Lund, he attended conferences in Aalborg and Aarhus, and preached in many other places in Denmark, while he, at the same time, was gathering data for Church history and collecting a number of old records which he subsequently shipped to the Historian's Office in Salt Lake City. After also visiting the Skåne Conference, Sweden, he finished his historical labors in the Scandinavian Mission, and after celebrating the 46th anniversary of his birth on Dec. 11th, he left Copenhagen, Dec. 14, 1896, for the Swiss and German Mission.

A number of Elders, who had labored faithfully as missionaries in Scandinavia, returned to their homes in Zion during the year 1896, most of them being accompanied by emigrating Saints. Thus Elders Jonathan F. Petersen of Mantua, Peter C. Jensen of Bear River City, Hyrum Petersen of Spring City, Joseph P. Anderson of Ephraim and Andrew P. Fillerup of Lakeview, Utah, left Copenhagen, March 5th, 1896, returning to their mountain homes, accompanied by only one emigrating Saint.

Ten emigrating Saints left Copenhagen for Utah, April 2, 1896, accompanied by the following Elders from Zion, who had labored with diligence in the Scandinavian Mission: James Larsen of Logan, Ezra E. Nielsen of Hyrum, Nils R. Lindahl of Union, Charles Lindell of Sandy, Niels Peter Nielsen of Ephraim and Christen P. Larsen of Gunnison, Utah.

Elder Herman H. Sundström of Sandy, James J. Larsen of Richmond, and Carl Hansen of Spring City, Utah, left Copenhagen May 14, 1896, to return to their homes in Zion after performing successful missionary labors in Scandinavia. They were accompanied by two emigrating Saints. About the same time, Elder H. H. Danielsen of Richmond, Utah, left Christiania, Norway, after being honorably released from his missionary labors there, to return to his home in Zion. He was accompanied by a small company of emigrating Saints.

A company of 28 emigrating Saints left Copenhagen for Utah, May 28, 1896, accompanied by Elder Peter Swenson of Sugar House, and Carl August Johnson of Huntsville, Utah, both returning Elders.

Another company of 20 emigrating Saints left Copenhagen July 16 1896, accompanied by Elders John A. Carlson of Logan, Math. Anderson of Stirling, and Canute Peter Hansen of Ephraim, Utah, returning Elders. On the same day. Elder Louis J. Holther, sen., who had labored as a missionary in Norway, left Christiania, homeward bound.

Another company of emigrating Saints (16 souls) left Copenhagen emigrating to Utah, in charge of the following Elders who returned to their homes in Zion: Michael Sörensen and Hans Severin Rasmussen of

Salt Lake City, Erick Gillen, of South Cottonwood, Bengt Mathias Ravsten of Clarkston and Peter Jensen of Mantua, Utah.

A company of Saints numbering 57 souls, including the following named returning Elders, left Copenhagen, Oct. 8, 1896, for Utah: Andrew C. Jensen, leader of the company, William Georgesen, Michael Schow, Jörgen Jörgensen, Carl J. Rehnström, George S. Backman, Carl Edwin Cederström and Peter August Nordquist. Emma H. Jenson, wife of Elder Andrew Jenson, left with the same company. Three other Elders (Julius Johnson, Niels A. Mörck and Nephi Anderson) and six emigrating Saints from Norway joined the Copenhagen company in Scotland. The company sailed on the steamship "Thursa" for Scotland on their way to America.

On Nov. 28, 1896, Elder Christoffer Iverson of Ephraim, Utah, left Christiania, Norway, accompanied by ten emigrating Saints on their way to Utah.

Besides the Elders mentioned in connection with companies of emigrating Saints, the following brethren from Zion who had labored as missionaries in Scandinavia, took their departure, returning home on the following dates: Martin Olson, William Buckholt, Joseph Bergesen and Ole Swenson, Jan. 23rd; Alfred G. Söderberg, Sören Petersen, Louis C. Larsen, Sören C. Sörensen, Louis Madsen, Erik Christensen, Wm. Isaac Sörensen, Carl August Lundgren, April 23rd, and Hyrum C. Christensen, Nov. 1st.

In 1896. 68 Elders from Utah, called to labor as missionaries in Scandinavia, arrived in Copenhagen, Denmark, as follows: Christian Madsen of Mt. Pleasant, and Nels Alma Nelson of Bear River City, Utah, arrived Feb. 17th; Jens. L. Nielsen of

23

Ephraim, Johan Chr. Christoffersen of Richmond, Jens Nielsen of Huntsville, and Niels C. Chistiansen of West Weber, Utah, arrived Feb. 18th; Jens Jörgen Jensen of Provo and Peter Lars Petersen of Ogden, Utah, arrived March 23rd; Daniel K. Brown of Nephi, Sören S. Christensen of Sandy, Ole Jensen of Manti, Utah, and Andrew A. Björn of Mink Creek, Idaho, arrived April 14; Peter P. Siggard, of Brigham City, Anton P. N. Peterson of Scipio, and Thomas Halvorsen of

JOHN C. CHRISTOFFERSEN,

Born at Nörre Tornby, Hjörring amt, Denmark, Sept. 2, 1854; joined the Church by baptism, April 1, 1880 (his wife being baptized the same day); emigrated to Utah in 1880 and settled in Richmond, Cache County; was ordained an Elder and appointed a Ward teacher soon after his arrival; ordained a Seventy in 1884. He filled a mission to Scandinavia in 1896-1897, laboring in the Randers and Esbjerg branches, Aarhus Conference. At home he also labored as a missionary. When filling another mission to Scandinavia in 1908-1909 he labored in the Aarhus Conference, over which he presided. A son of Brother Christoffersen, Christian, died in the mission field at Silkeborg, Denmark, Aug. 23, 1901, and about the same time two of his children passed away in Utah. It was a hard trial, but Bro. Christoffersen had learned to acknowledge the hand of the Lord in all things.

Spanish Fork, Utah, arrived April 21st; Henry Wing of Provo, George A. Sanders of Murray, Christian Johnson of Thurber, and Charles A. Thomsen of Oasis, Utah, arrived April 26th; Isak Carlson of Pleasant Grove, Utah, Hyrum C. Christensen of Manassa, Colorado, John E. Halvorson and John D. Hagman of Salt Lake City, Utah, arrived May 11th, and Christian Poulsen of Orangeville, Utah, May 18th. Peter Christensen of Emery and August Edward Rose of Richville, Utah, arrived May 25th; Christian N. Lund, George Christensen and Christian Wm. Anderson of Mt. Pleasant, James F. Iversen and Andrew A. Peterson of Salt Lake City, Peter Olsen, Jörgen Jörgensen and John Peterson of Ephraim, Niels Peter Nielsen of Elsinore, and Niels Christian Nielsen of Pleasant Grove, Utah, arrived June 1st, and Joseph H. Jenson of Union, and August Robert Lundin of Salt Lake City, Utah, June 16th; Christian Knudsen of Lehi, Albert F. Young and Ephraim Björklund of Salt Lake City, Utah, arrived June 29th; and Ole H. Peterson of Fairview, Charles Magnus Olson of Park Valley and Marius Mikkelsen of Spanish Fork, Utah, August 9th; Christian N. Lundsteen of Levan, Hans Christian Hansen of Salt Lake City, Geo. A. Christensen and James Chr. Breinholt of Redmond, and Jens N. Beck of Ephraim, Utah, arrived August 24th; Enoch Jörgensen of Ephraim, Utah, August 31st, and Niels S. Christoffersen of Brigham City, Sept. 29th; Carl Johan Fargergren, Johan L. Cherling and William Anderson of Salt Lake City, Utah, and Hyrum Nielson of Holliday, Utah, arrived Oct. 13th, and Severin Norman Lee of Brigham City, Utah, on Nov. 2nd; Kjeld Peter Jensen of Fountain Green, and Hans Peter Nielsen of Salt Lake City, Utah, ar-

rived Nov. 10th; Peter Erickson of Salt Lake City, and Peter Gustaf Hanson of Payson, Utah, arrived Nov. 16th; George August Miller-

CHRISTIAN KNUDSEN,

Son of Guldbrand Knudsen and Marie Andersen, was born at Stubberud, Ringsaker, Hedemarken, Norway, Sept. 24, 1856, graduated from the public schools at the age of 14, and emigrated to Utah with his parents, one brother and one sister the next year; crossed the Atlantic in Anthon H. Lund's company, which arrived in Salt Lake July 17, 1872. The family located at Lehi, where Christian was baptized Aug. 30, 1873, by Mons Anderson. On Nov. 14, 1879, he married Sarah L. Ottensen (daughter of Hans Ottesen and Johanne Christensen) in St. George Temple; they had ten children. Bro. Knudsen filled a mission to Norway in 1896-1898, laboring in Stavanger, Eidsvold and Tromsö. He was ordained a High Priest March 28, 1909, by Stephen L. Chipman; has been active in the Church as a Ward teacher, home missionary and member of building committees for the Utah Stake and the Lehi Tabernacles. Bro. and Sister Knudsen are still residents of Lehi, Utah.

berg of Union, Dykes Willard Sörensen of Ephraim, John Alfred Anderson of East Jordan, Hans Törkild Petersen of Smithfield, and Andrew Dahlsrud of Salina, Utah, arrived Nov. 21st; Lars Jensen Halling jun., of Grover, Wyoming, Eskild Eskildsen of Mink Creek, Idaho, and Henry Martin Pearson (Pehrson) of Sandy, Utah, on Dec. 27th, 1896.

Christian Madsen, Jens Nielsen

Sören S. Christensen, Ole Jensen, George A. Christensen, Niels S. Christoffersen and Kjeld P. Jensen, were appointed to labor in the

ENOCH JÖRGENSEN,

High Counselor in the Jordan Stake, is the eldest son of Johan G. Jörgensen and Serine K. Staalesen, born in Ephraim, Utah, Feb. 26, 1867; shared the hardships of pioneer life, particularly in the settlement of Grass Valley; worked for eight years in the summertime in the Jörgensen dairy at Fish Lake; assisted the government surveyors around the lake; wrote letters to the "Deseret News" (signed "Wilderness"), which created a sentiment for state fish and game laws; graduated from the Brigham Young Academy, and served as principal of the Wasatch Stake Academy, Heber, Utah, for many years. In 1908, Bro. Jörgensen organized the Jordan High School at Sandy, and ten years afterwards he was appointed principal of the Jordan Latter-day Saints Seminary; in 1914 he graduated from the University of Utah with the degree of Bachelor of Sciences. In 1888 he married Anna M. Berg of Provo; of their twelve children, these are still living: E. Berg, Henry C., Ruth, and Juanita. Bro. Jörgensen was ordained a Seventy, June 17, 1896, by Jonathan G. Kimball, and set apart for missionary labors, first in Chicago, then in Denmark; presided over the Copenhagen Conference the last year of his mission, and conducted a large company of emigrants to Utah.

Copenhagen Conference. Jens J. Jensen was also appointed to labor in the Copenhagen Conference, but being banished, he finished his mission in the Skåne Conference, Sweden. George Christensen was appointed to labor as president of the Copen-

hagen Conference, Denmark, as writer and translator for "Skandinaviens Stjerne," in the mission office in Copenhagen, and finally succeeded Christian N. Lund as president of the Scandinavian Mission. Enoch Jörgensen was appointed to labor in the Copenhagen Conference, having labored for some time in Chicago, Ill., before arriving in Scandinavia. Later he presided over the Copenhagen Conference.

Nels A. Nelson, Jens L. Nielsen, Christian Johnson, Peter Christensen, Jörgen Jörgensen, Niels P. Nielsen, Christian N. Lundsteen (second mission) and Jens N. Beck were appointed to labor in the Aalborg Conference. Hyrum Nielson was also ap-

NIELS S. CHRISTOFFERSEN,

Born July 14, 1861, in Aasö, Glumsö parish, Præstö amt, Denmark, and baptized Aug. 18, 1872, by Elder J. J. Nielsen, and emigrated to Utah with his parents in 1873, arriving in Brigham City July 24. In 1884 (April 24) he married Anna Sörensen; they had ten children, five of whom are still living. Bro. Christoffersen performed a mission to Denmark in 1896-1898, laboring in the Copenhagen conference. Returning home he was given charge of a company of forty emigrants and ten elders from Copenhagen to Utah. He is a fruit grower and has three sons in the same occupation, in Brigham City.

pointed to labor in the Aalborg and later in the Aarhus Conference. Daniel K. Brown (second mission)

ANDREW DAHLSRUD

Was born Feb. 20, 1858, in Sande, Jarlsberg amt, Norway, joined the Church at Drammen, May 7, 1881, and emigrated to Utah in 1883. He lived five years at Ephraim, Sanpete County, and then moved to Salina. He filled a mission to Norway in 1896-1898, laboring in the Arendal, Aalesund and Christiania branches. In 1915 he was called a second time to labor in Norway. He left Salt Lake in company with Elder Edward Strömness, and labored this time in Christiania and Bergen. In the latter conference he presided twenty-two months. He is still a resident of Salina, Sevier County, Utah.

was appointed to labor in the Aalborg Conference, but being banished from there he finished his mission in the Christiania Conference, Norway.

Johan Chr. Christoffersen, Niels Chr. Christiansen (from the Turkish Mission), Peter Lars Petersen, Peter P. Siggard, Henry Wing, Hyrum C. Christensen, James Chr. Breinholt, Dykes W. Sörensen and Hans T. Petersen were appointed to labor in the Aarhus Conference. Andrew A. Björn and Hans P. Nielsen were also appointed to labor in the Aarhus Conference and later as conference

presidents. James F. Iversen was appointed to labor in the Aarhus, Aalborg and Copenhagen conferences. Marius Mikkelsen (Morris Mickelson) was appointed to labor in the Aarhus Conference, Denmark, having previously labored in Chicago, Illinois. John E. Halvorson, Ephraim Björklund, Carl J. Fagergren, Johan L. Cherling, George A. Millerberg and John A. Anderson were appointed to labor in the Stockholm Conference. Anton P. N. Peterson was appointed to labor in the Stockholm Conference, and later as a writer and translator for "Nordstjernan" in the mission office at Copenhagen, Denmark, and finished his labors as president of the Stockholm Conference. Albert F. Young was appointed to labor in the Stockholm Conference, but he finished his mission in England.

Thomas Halvorsen, Isak Carlson, John D. Hagman, Chr. Wm. Anderson, Andrew A. Peterson and Peter Erickson were appointed to labor in the Skåne Conference, Sweden. Peter G. Hanson (second mission) was called to preside over the Skåne Conference, Sweden. George A. Sanders and Severin N. Lee were appointed to labor in the Skåne and later in the Stockholm Conference. August Ed. Rose, Joseph H. Jenson and William Anderson were appointed to labor in the Göteborg Conference, Sweden. August R. Lundin was also appointed to labor in the Göteborg and later in the Stockholm Conference. Charles M. Olson was appointed to labor in the Göteborg Conference and later in the Skåne Conference. Henry M. Pearson (Pehrson) was appointed to labor in the Göteborg Conference, part of the time as conference president. He had labored for six months previously in Chicago, Ill.

Charles A. Thomsen, Christian

Poulsen, Peter Olsen, John Peterson, Christian Knudsen, Ole H. Peterson, Hans Chr. Hansen, Andrew Dahlsrud, Lars J. Halling, jun., and Eskild Eskildsen were appointed to labor in the Christiania Conference. Niels Chr. Nielsen was also appointed to labor in the Christiania Conference, Norway, but later in the Aalborg Conference, Denmark.

CHAPTER 81 (1897)

A lone family of Swedish Saints in St. Petersburg, Russia—Elder Janne M. Sjödahl presents the king of Sweden with a copy of the Book of Mormon—Saints emigrate to Utah in charge of returning Elders—President Rulon S. Wells again visits Scandinavia—Arrival of 94 Elders from America.

Elder George Christensen, in reporting conditions in Scandinavia under date of March 16, 1897, laments the fact that Saints who had emigrated from their native lands to Utah were neglecting corresponding with their friends whom they had left in the old countries, and in doing this would often break solemn promises given to friends and relatives to the effect that after their arrival in Utah, they would write and explain conditions as they found them existing among the Saints in the mountains. This neglect had caused a great deal of dissatisfaction and had led in many instances to unpleasant surmisings in regard to the fate of their friends who had gathered to Zion. Also returning missionaries were blamed for not keeping their promises in regard to writing to the friends they had made on their missions, and to the Saints, whose hospitality they had partaken of while laboring in the Lord's vineyard.

The work of the Lord made good progress in Norway in 1897. The Norwegian Mission at that time consisted of ten branches each presided over by an Elder from Utah, who was assisted by one or more of the other Utah Elders. The branch head-quarters were at Christiania, Drammen, Bergen, Frederikstad, Trondhjem, Aalesund, Arendal, Frederikshald, Eidsvold and Tromsö. By a system adopted, every town, hamlet and fishing village along the coast and fjords, as well as inland cities, towns and "gaarde" could be reached. The president of the conference made it a rule to visit every branch of the Church between the semi-annual conferences, thereby keeping in touch with the requirements of each. In April, 1897, twenty energetic Utah Elders "were preaching the doctrines of Christ and searching for the blood of Israel in old Norway." The headquarters of the Norwegian Mission, or Christiania Conference, was at Christiania, where the Church owned its own building, which, at that time, was the largest and most commodious building owned by the Latter-day Saints in Europe.

In July, 1897, Elders Carl A. Ahlquist and Norman Lee visited Russia, Finland, and northern Sweden. First they went to St. Petersburg in Russia, and visited with the Swedish family, Lindelöf, who had joined the Church two years before and had been quite alone in that big city ever since. This lone family of Saints enjoyed the visit of the Elders very much, and after administering comfort and cheer to the family, the two Elders, after spending about six days in St. Petersburg, went to Helsingfors, Finland, and after visiting several other places in Finland and northern Sweden, they returned to Stockholm.

Elder Janne M. Sjödahl, who had been appointed by the First Presidency of the Church on a special mission to Sweden to present a copy de luxe of the Book of Mormon to King Oscar II, arrived in Stockholm Sept. 6, 1897. He had left Salt Lake City, Aug. 14, 1897. On

Wednesday, Sept 22nd, His Majesty granted a special audience to Elder Sjödahl, who presented the King with a beautifully bound copy of the Book of Mormon, which seemed to

JANNE M. SJÖDAHL,

Born in Karlshamn, Sweden, Nov. 29, 1853; emigrated to Utah and joined the Church in Manti, Sanpete County, in 1886; performed a special mission to Sweden in 1897; was connected with the editorial department of the "Deseret News" from 1890 to 1914; edited the "Milennial Star" from 1914 to 1919; is now directing editor of the Associated Newspapers—"Bikuben," "Utah Posten," "Salt Lake City Beobachter" and "De Utah-Nederlander."

please His Majesty. Elder Sjödahl also brought greetings from His Majesty's former subjects in far-off Utah.

Elder Sjödahl writes the following:

"I was ushered into the august presence of His Majesty, the King, and found myself alone with him in the audience hall. The next moment the king's hand was extended toward me and I reverently grasped it, saying, 'Your Majesty, I have come from Utah, one of the western States of the North American Union, to express to you, on behalf of the Swedes and Norwegians there, our most respectful homage and congratulations. We, too, in the far West, pray the Almighty to grant to your

Majesty a long life for the benefit of the brother nations.'

"The King's handsome face beamed as he listened to this little bit of oratorical effort.

"'Have the Norwegians there also sent you?' he said.

"'Yes, your Majesty.'

"'Are you a Swede or a Norwegian?' was the next question.

"'I am a Swede by birth, your Majesty.'

"'How long have you been in America?'

"'A little over eleven years.'

"'Well, well, please tell my countrymen, Swedes and Norwegians, in your State Utah, that I sincerely thank them for the handsome present they have given me. I wish them success in their far-away home.'

"The Jubilee gift from Utah was accompanied by the following address, signed by the First Presidency of the Church:

"'To Whom These Presents May Come, Greeting:

"'Elder J. M. Sjödahl, the bearer of this letter, is a gentleman of education and distinction, a Swede by birth, who has traveled extensively in the Orient as well as in Europe and America. His present residence is in Salt Lake City, Utah, where he is well and favorably known, and highly esteemed by all who know him.

"'Elder Sjödahl has been selected by his fellow-countrymen, natives of Sweden and

BOOK OF MORMON
Presented by Janne M. Sjödahl to King Oscar II of Sweden.

Norway, a large body of whom reside in and are citizens of the State of Utah, to proceed to the court of their Majesties, King Oscar II and Queen Sophia, on the occasion of the 25th anniversary of their ascension to the throne, for the purpose of presenting in their name and behalf, to their majesties a casket, made of Utah onyx, containing a copy of the Book of

Mormon as an expression of the high esteem, affection and love which the Scandinavians in this intermountain region entertain for their majesties, with the hope and earnest desire that their majesties will live to witness many happy returns of this most auspicious event.

"'And we ourselves, though not of the Scandinavian race, do most heartily join our Scandinavian friends and fellow-citizens in desiring long life, peace, prosperity and happiness for their majesties, King Oscar II and Queen Sophia of Sweden and Norway.

"'(Signed) Wilford Woodruff,
George Q. Cannon,
Joseph F. Smith.'"

The following missionaries from Zion, who had filled different positions in the Scandinavian Mission, left Copenhagen, Apr. 1, 1897, to return to their homes in Zion: Peter Andersen, Edward A. Olsen and Hyrum D. Jensen of Ogden, Utah, Abel Erickson of Albion, Idaho, Lorenzo O. Skanchy of Logan, and Lars E. Danielson of Smithfield, Utah, Peter Magnusson of Mesa, Arizona, Andrew C. Fjeldsted of Gunnison, Peter C. Christensen of Mayfield, Alonzo B. Irvine of Logan and Theodore Tobiason of Salt Lake City, Utah.

This company of missionaries and a few emigrating Saints went by steamer to Scotland, and on April 8th they went on board the ocean steamer "Circassia" and sailed down the River Clyde. The next day 150 Irish emigrants were taken on board at Moville, Ireland. The company of Saints on board consisted of 16 missionaries and 59 emigrants. The voyage across the Atlantic was a very stormy one. Elder Peter C. Christensen writes under date of April 23, 1897, on board the "Circassia" as follows:

"We have had heavy sea most of the time since we commenced our voyage, and in the night between the 9th and 10th inst., fire broke out in the ship. With much labor the crew succeeded in putting out the fire,

but we had exceedingly stormy weather until the evening of the 16th inst., when the screw axle broke with a terrific noise. Four of us returning Elders in the first cabin and eight in the second cabin united in sincere and earnest prayer that the Lord would preserve us. We all took our turns in praying, and when we were through, the storm ceased, and we all acknowledged the hand of the Lord in answer to our prayers. During the eight days in which the storm raged the ship seemed to be more under than over the water and some of the crew said it was the worst storm they had ever experienced. As a matter of course, much sea-sickness prevailed among the passengers, but after the weather settled, the Saints on board enjoyed themselves in singing the songs of Zion and in arranging concerts and other entertainments. The ship arrived in New York April 27th."

The following named Elders, who had labored in the Scandinavian Mission, left Copenhagen, Sept. 30, 1897, returning to their homes in Zion: Peter A. Pedersen, Nils F. Ahlberg, Lars G. Larson, Johan F. Jonason, Joseph Y. Larsen, John F. Appelquist, Andrew Anderberg, Thomas Gundersen, Edward Gundersen, Johan L. G. Johnson, Peter Ernström, Jens Jörgensen, Morten Chr. Mortensen, Andrew Johnson, Knud H. Fridal, Niels Chr. Sörensen, James Chr. Jensen, Olof E. Olson, Chr. Johansen, Sören S. Christensen, Ole Jensen, Henry Wing, Albert F. Young, Kjeld P. Jensen and Janne M. Sjödahl. Elder Andrew Johnson, who returned with this company, wrote the following account of the journey to America:

"I herewith send you a short statement of the last company of Saints and returning missionaries of which I was chosen to be the leader. We left Copenhagen on Sept. 30th and came to Leith in Scotland in the evening of the 3rd of October. The next morning we went through the custom-house and landed in Glasgow about noon. Here we met some Saints and returning missionaries from Norway. The total number of our company was then 47 emigrants and 25 missionaries. We left Glasgow in the evening of Oct. 7th. On the 8th we passed Ireland, where the boat stopped, and we got a party of Irish emigrants on board. We were then about 275 emigrants on the ship. It was a little crowded, but all has gone well and the crew on board treated us well. We arrived in New York Oct. 18th, all well, but I am sorry to say that two of our Saints were not allowed to come along with us. We offered to sign papers for them, but this offer was not accepted. I then telegraphed to their folks in Salt Lake City, asking them to send them the necessary papers, and the emigration agents promised to do all they could to get them through. Our journey from New York to Salt Lake City was uneventful. I left the company at Granger, Wyoming, and placed them in charge of Elder Janne M. Sjödahl."

In August and September, 1897, President Rulon S. Wells and his counselor, Joseph W. McMurrin, visited the different conferences in the Scandinavian Mission. Thus they attended conferences in Stockholm, Christiania, Göteborg. Malmö, Aalborg and Aarhus, and gave timely instructions to Elders and Saints, as well as preaching the gospel to strangers who attended the meetings. Presidents Wells and McMurrin left Aarhus, Denmark, for Germany, Holland and Belgium, Oct. 11, 1897, on their way to England.

Under date of Oct. 26, 1897, Elders Jacob Fikstad and Ole H. Peterson, who labored as missionaries in Norway, related an instance when Hans Emanuel Hansen, a ten-year-old boy, had been miraculously healed. The boy's eyes were in a very critical condition, so much so that the doctors thought he would go blind, but, on request, the Elders administered to the lad, who was healed almost instantly. He was able to attend school, and his teacher and all who saw him were astonished to learn that he had been healed by the power of God.

The following Elders, who had labored in Scandinavia, left Copen-hagen July 29, 1897, to return to their homes in Utah: Nephi Anderson of Vernon, Utah, Nephi P. Anderson of Brigham City, Lars Wm. Hendrikson of South Cottonwood, Andrew H. Larson of Washington and James F. Fjeldsted of Gunnison, Utah. These Elders crossed the Atlantic in the steamship "Furnesia," together with returning missionaries and emigrating Saints (51 persons) who sailed from Glasgow, Scotland.

John D. Amundsen of South Cottonwood, Carl W. Erikson of Springville, Christian Madsen of Mt. Pleasant, Nels A. Nelson of Bear River City, Jens L. Nielsen of Ephraim, Johan C. Christoffersen of Richmond, Jens Nielsen of Huntsville, Isaac Carlson of Pleasant Grove, and Christian W. Anderson of Mt. Pleasant, left Copenhagen for Utah, Nov. 11.

Elder Martin E. Christoffersen and Jacob Fikstad, who had labored as missionaries in Norway, sailed from Christiania, Nov. 12th, 1897, accompanied by four emigrating Saints bound for Utah.

Besides the Elders mentioned in connection with companies of emigrating Saints, the following brethren from Zion, who had labored as missionaries in Scandinavia, took their departure, returning home on the following dates: Alonzo B. Irvine, April 1st; Jens J. Jensen, May 26th; Erik P. Erikson, John L. Hallbom, Ole Anderson, Matthias Knudsen, Frederik J. C. Danielsen, Niels C. Christiansen, Jens N. Beck, Eskild Eskildsen, May 27th; Nephi Anderson, Nephi Peter Anderson, Lars Wm. Hendrikson, Andrew H. Larsen and James Fred. Fjeldsted, July 29th; John E. Halverson, Aug. 19th; Carl J. Rehnström, Oct. 8th; Charles (Carl) W. Erikson, Chr. Madsen, Chr. Wm. Anderson, John D. Amundsen, Nels Alma Nelson, Jens

L. Nielsen, Johan Chr. Christoffersen, Jens Nielsen, Peter L. Petersen, Isaac Carlson and Poul Poulsen, Nov. 11th; Carl Axel Ahlquist, Nov. 18th, and Emanuel F. Lennberg, Dec. 2nd.

In 1897, 94 Elders from Zion, called to labor as missionaries in Scandinavia, arrived in Copenhagen, Denmark, as follows: Hyrum Hogan of Bountiful, Utah, arrived Feb. 9th, and Peter Mogensen of Mt. Pleasant, Utah, Feb 10th; Gustaf A. Brandt of Salina, Aaron Lundberg, Ephraim Mikkelsen and Wm. Otto Hanson of Logan, Utah, arrived March 13th, and Mouritz F. A. Peterson of Murray, on April 9th; George M. Smoot and Martin Williamson of Lake View, Utah, arrived April 17th, and Andrew Johnson, Andrew Anderson and Rangvald Carlson of Union, Anton Anderson of Oasis and Olaus Johnson of South Cottonwood, Utah, arrived April 26th; James (Jens) N. Sörensen and Andrew H. Larson of Washington, Niels F. Swalberg and James F. Fjeldsted of Gunnison, Utah, arrived May 14th, and John W. Larson, Albert Peterson, Carl O. Johnson and Carl A. A. Augustson of Murray, Utah, Peter S. Olson of Mink Creek, Idaho, Carl G. Johanson of Sandy and Nils Jenson of Brigham City, Utah, on May 16th; Canute W. Peterson of Ephraim, and Louis M. Christiansen of Spring City, Utah, arrived on June 28th; Poul Poulsen of Ephraim, and Erick W. Edvaldson of West Weber, Utah, arrived July 4th, and Daniel P. Jensen of Elsinore, and Hyrum Olsen of Salt Lake City, Utah, on Aug. 7th; Christian T. Nielsen and Christian M. Mickelsen of Redmond, Utah, arrived Aug. 8th; and Rudolph V. Larson of Smithfield, and Jens Christensen of Spring City, Utah, on July 30th; John Felt, jun., and Joseph L. Petersen of Huntsville, Utah, arrived Aug. 22nd, and Christian S. Sören-

sen and Christian F. Schade of Huntsville, Utah, and Hyrum Jensen of Brigham City, Utah, Aug. 24th; John E. Groberg of Farr West, Joseph T. Torgersen of Ogden, and John P. Löfgren of Lynn, Utah, arrived on Aug. 28th, and Ole Jensen of Star Valley, Wyoming, and Janne M. Sjödahl of Salt Lake City, Utah, Sept. 5th; John Erick Carlson of Spanish Fork, and Albert A. Capson of East Mill Creek, arrived Sept. 12, and Albert S. Erickson of Grantsville, Sept. 27th; Carl Chr. Garff of Ogden, Gideon E. Olson, jun., of Paradise, Andrew B. Jensen of Eden, Erastus L. Ottesen of Spanish Fork, and Hans Chr. Hansen of Lake View, Utah, arrived on Oct. 9th; Alfred Hanson and Charles Chr. Jensen of Logan, Utah, James N. Skousen of Colonia Juarez, Mexico, Nephi J. Valentine of Brigham City, Jens N. Hansen of Showlow, Arizona, John E. Bolstad of Ogden, Hyrum J. Hansen of Bear River City, and Parley P. Jenson of Salt Lake City, arrived on Nov. 1st; Lauritz Lauritzen of Glenwood, Christian Pedersen, jun., of Holliday, James (Jöns) Jenson (Jönson) of Millville, Ole A. Okerlund of Lyman, Utah, Peter J. Sandberg of Weston, Idaho, Gustaf A. Anderson and Jens F. Fugal (Fugl) of Pleasant Grove, and Axel Olsen of Salt Lake City, Utah, arrived Nov. 7th; John Johnson, jun., of Prospect, Idaho, David Blomquist of La Belle, Idaho, George D. Hanson of Providence, and Christian P. Hald of Ephraim, Utah, arrived Nov. 14th; Dan Nephi Wilhelmsen of St. Charles, Idaho, Louis E. Erickson of Montpelier, Idaho, Axel L. Holmgren of Ogden, Utah, James Jenson, jun., of Grover, Wyoming, and Peter S. Nielsen of Nephi, Utah, arrived Dec. 5th; Rasmus Chr. Peterson, jun., of Mink Creek, Idaho, Hyrum Nielsen of Preston, Idaho, Chas. Fred John Carlson of Ovid, Idaho, John Peter

Anderson of Ogden, Adolph F.
Elggren of Hooper, Utah, Paul P.
Christensen of Liberty, Idaho, Jens
Larsen and Arnold L. Nelson of

NEPHI J. VALENTINE,

Born at Brigham City, Utah, Nov. 15, 1867, the
son of Valentin Valentinsen and Hannah Benson. His father was born near Rönne, Bornholm, May 24, 1813, and was baptized in October, 1852, among the first to accept "Mormonism" on the island, and came to Brigham
City, Utah, in 1854, where he died Sept. 26,
1877. His mother, Hannah Benson, was born
near Landskrona, Sweden, June 13, 1840, and
was the first in her family to join the Church.
She came to Utah in 1863, where she died
Sept. 29, 1918. Nephi J. was ordained to the
lesser Priesthood when a boy, became a Sunday
school teacher at 16, was ordained an Elder
at 20, and later a Seventy and then a High
Priest; served as Bishop's counselor in the
Second Ward, Brigham City, seventeen years,
and on March 31, 1922, was made Bishop of
that ward, which position he still (1927) holds.
He married Sarah B. Merrell, Jan. 4, 1888,
who died Aug. 28, 1895. To this union came
Merrell, Eustace, Elva, Fenley and Frost. He
married Ottoiina, Bengtson, March 7, 1900, to
which union was added Edith, Grace, Ruth,
Erma, Wilma, Thelma and Lee. Bro. Valentine left Utah Oct. 9, 1897, for a mission to
Sweden, where he labored in the Lund, Helsingborg and Malmö branches, Skåne Conference; returned home Dec. 15, 1899, since
which time he has been engaged in religious
activities and has also held positions of civil
trust.

Cleveland, Idaho, Sören C. Christensen of Moroni, Isaac Peter Peterson of Hooper, Joseph Jensen of
Levan, Michael P. Ipson of Wilson,
Utah, and Rasmus Nilson of Weston,

Idaho, arrived Dec. 11th, and
Zacharias W. Israelsen of Hyrum,
Ole Chr. Jensen of Mayfield, Utah,
and Christen Christensen of Swan
Lake, Idaho, Dec. 25, 1897.

Hyrum Hogan, George M. Smoot,
Martin Williamson, Olaus Johnson
(2nd mission), Joseph T. Torgersen,
John E. Bolstad, Axel Olsen, James
Jenson, jun., Hyrum Nielsen, John
Peter Anderson and Zacharias W.
Israelsen were appointed to labor
in the Christiania Conference, Norway. Canute W. Peterson was also
appointed to labor in the Christiania
Conference, part of the time as conference president. Louis M. Christiansen was appointed to labor in
the Christiania Conference, and later

JAMES JENSON

Was born April 10, 1866, at Svedala, Malmöhus län, Sweden; emigrated to Utah in 1884
and located at Millville, Cache County; was
baptized in 1887 by John King. He married
Christina Anderson of Millville, Feb. 13, 1889;
they had three children. Being called to perform a mission in Sweden, he left Salt Lake
City Oct. 14, 1897, labored in the Göteborg
and Skåne conferences, and returned home Nov.
15, 1899. His wife died July 11, 1900, and
in 1901 he married Emma Olson, daughter of
Ole Olson of Millville. Bro. Jenson has always been active in the Church and has been
a Bishop in Millville for twelve years.

in the Aalborg Conference, part of the time as conference president. Hyrum Olsen, Paul P. Christensen and Jens Larsen were appointed to labor in the Christiania Conference, and later in the Copenhagen Con-

PETER J. SANDBERG,

Born June 1, 1852, in Christianstad län, Sweden, was baptized Aug. 27, 1873, ordained a Teacher Nov. 10, 1873, and called to the local ministry; was ordained a Priest in February, 1874, and an Elder May 31, 1874. He labored as a missionary in the Skåne Conference for three years and emigrated to Utah in 1877, locating in Weston, Idaho, in 1882. He was ordained a Seventy Oct. 5, 1885, and in March, 1886, was arrested by United States deputy marshals on the charge of having resisted the officers when they raided Weston in search of polygamists in November, 1885, and sentenced to pay a fine of $75.00. He filled a mission to Sweden 1897-1899, laboring in the Skåne Conference and later presiding over the Stockholm Conference. In 1907-1909 he filled a second mission to Sweden. For some time he acted as a president of the Eighty-eighth Quorum of Seventy, was a worker in the Salt Lake Temple four years and died April 24, 1921.

ference. Christian F. Schade was appointed to labor in the Christiania Conference, and later in the Aarhus Conference. Hyrum Jensen was appointed to labor in the Christiania Conference, and later presided over the Bergen Conference.

Peter Mogensen, James F. Fjeldsted, Ole Jensen, Gideon E. Olson,

jun., Andrew B. Jensen, Charles Chr. Jensen, Jens N. Hansen and George D. Hanson were appointed to labor in the Copenhagen Conference. Nils Jenson was also appointed to labor in the Copenhagen Conference, part of the time as conference president. Christian T. Nielsen and Christian S. Sörensen were appointed to labor in the Copenhagen Conference, and later in the Aarhus Conference. Hans Chr. Hansen was appointed to labor in the Copenhagen Conference, and later in the Christiania Conference.

Poul Poulsen, Erastus L. Ottesen, Hyrum J. Hansen, Jens P. Fugal (Fugl), Chr. P. Hald and Sören Chr. Christensen were appointed to labor in the Aalborg Conference. Ephraim Mikkelsen and Parley P. Jenson were appointed to labor in the Aalborg Conference and later in the Christiania Conference. Jens Christensen (second mission) was also appointed to labor in the Aalborg Conference, part of the time as conference president. Joseph Jensen was appointed to labor in the Aalborg Conference and later in the Copenhagen Conference.

Anton Anderson, James N. Sörensen, Christian M. Mickelson, Joseph L. Petersen, Lauritz Lauritzen, Christian Pedersen, jun., Dan N. Wilhelmsen, Peter S. Nielsen, Rasmus Chr. Peterson, jun., Ole Chr. Jensen, and Christen Christensen were appointed to labor in the Aarhus Conference, Denmark. Daniel P. Jensen was also appointed to labor in the Aarhus Conference, but later in the Aalborg Conference. James N. Skousen was appointed to labor in the Aarhus Conference, and later in Norway. William O. Hanson, Rangvald Carlson, Andrew H. Larson, Carl G. Johanson, Carl O. Johnson, Erick W. Edvaldson, John Felt, jun., John E. Carlson, Albert A. Capson, Carl Chr. Garff and Michael P. Ipson were appointed to labor in the Stockholm

Conference. Gustaf A. Brandt and Carl A. A. Augustson were appointed to labor in the Stockholm Conference, and later as writers and

CARL OSCAR JOHNSON,

Born March 2, 1865, in Asker, Örebro län, Sweden, was baptized April 20, 1888, in Almunge, Uppland; was ordained to the Priesthood and called into the local ministry, laboring in Sundsvall and Sölfvarbo branches. He emigrated to Utah in 1891 and located in Murray, Salt Lake County. In 1897-1899 he filled a mission to Sweden, laboring in Stockholm Branch for seven months and as president of the Upsala and Sundsvall branches the balance of the time; he baptized thirty-eight souls while on this mission. In 1907 he moved to Shelley, Idaho, and filled a second mission to Sweden in 1912-1914, presiding over the Morgongåva Branch three months, over the Sundsvall Conference nine months, and over the Stockholm Conference twenty months. He now acts as one of the presidents of the 106th quorum of Seventy.

translators for "Nordstjernan" at the mission office in Copenhagen, Denmark. Elder Augustson also labored in the Göteborg Conference.

Aaron Lundberg, Mouritz F. A. Peterson, Peter S. Olson, Rudolph V. Larson, Ole A. Okerlund, John Johnson, jun., Louis E. Erickson, Charles F. J. Carlson, Adolph F. Elggren and Isaac P. Peterson were appointed to labor in the Göteborg Conference, Sweden. Andrew Ander-

son (second mission) was also appointed to labor in the Göteborg Conference, but later he presided over the Skåne Conference. John W. Larson was also appointed to labor in the Göteborg Conference, part of the time as conference president. John E. Groberg, John P. Löfgren, David Blomquist and Axel L. Holmgren were appointed to labor in the Göteborg Conference and later in the Stockholm Conference. Albert Svante Erickson was appointed to labor in the Göteborg Conference, after having labored in Germany for about two years. James Jenson (Jöns Jönson) was appointed to labor in the Göteborg Conference and later in the Skåne Conference.

Niels F. Swalberg, Alfred Hanson, Nephi J. Valentine, Arnold L. Nelson and Rasmus Nilson were appointed to labor in the Skåne Conference. Andrew Johnson, Albert Peterson and Peter J. Sandberg were appointed to labor in the Skåne Conference and later in the Stockholm Conference. Gustaf A. Anderson was appointed to labor in the Skåne and later in the Göteborg Conference.

CHAPTER 82 (1898)

Elder George Christensen becomes president of the mission—Death of Elders Joseph H. Jenson and Albert Petterson in Sweden and Ole Chr. Jensen in Denmark—Elder Andreas Peterson succeeds George Christensen as president of the mission—Arrival of 87 Elders from Zion.

On Feb. 2, 1898, a beautiful monument was erected on the grave of Elder Anders Björkman, who died in Sölfvarbo, Sweden, Aug. 19, 1896. The monument, which stands in the pretty cemetery belonging to "Gustafs Församling," is of dark grey granite, 6 feet high, 21 inches wide and weighing about 1,100 pounds. It has the following inscription upon the face in Swedish: "Anders Björkman, född den 22 Januari. 1838; död den 19 Augusti, 1896.

Ett minne rest till honom af tro-
fasta bröder." The monument, which
cost 110 kronor, was erected by Elders from Zion who labored in the
Scandinavian Mission.

Elder Joseph H. Jenson of Union,
Utah, who labored as a missionary
in Sweden, died March 8, 1898, at
Göteborg. Elder Jenson was born
in South Cottonwood, Salt Lake
County, Utah, Oct. 22, 1870, and
arrived in Copenhagen on his mission June 16, 1896. He was appointed to labor in the Göteborg
Conference and did excellent missionary work in Jönköping, Halmstad, Trollhättan and Vestervik. The
remains of Elder Jenson were interred in the Sanna churchyard at
Göteborg.

Elder Christian N. Lund, who had
presided over the Scandinavian Mission since July 5, 1896, left Copenhagen, May 19, 1898, for his home
in America. Pres. Lund had made
an execellent record while on his
mission and had gained the love and
respect of the Elders and Saints
generally in the whole mission. In
December, 1900, he was made president of the North Sanpete Stake of
Zion. Elder George Christensen succeeded Elder C. N. Lund as president
of the mission.

Elder Ole Christian Jensen, a Utah
Elder laboring in the Aarhus Conference, died at Randers, Denmark,
May 30, 1898, of pneumonia. Elder
Jensen was born in Ringköbing,
Denmark, May 7, 1830, and was 67
years of age at the time of his demise. He was an energetic and
faithful Elder.

A company of emigrating Saints,
numbering 41 souls, left Copenhagen,
April 21, 1898, emigrating to Utah.
They were accompanied by six re-
turning Elders, viz., Peter Chris-
tensen of Emery, August E. Rose of
Richville, Peter Olsen and Enoch
Jörgensen of Ephraim, Andrew An-

thon Peterson of Salt Lake City and
Niels Iversen of Bear River City,
Utah. In Scotland, they were joined
by four other returning Elders and
four Scotch emigrants. They crossed
the Atlantic in the steamship

GEORGE CHRISTENSEN

Was born in Aarhus, Denmark, Feb. 24, 1866,
emigrated to Utah with his parents in June,
1873, locating first in Brigham City, and later
(1874) in Mount Pleasant, Sanpete County.
He was appointed Stake superintendent of Sunday schools for Sanpete Stake Nov. 12, 1893,
ordained a Seventy Aug. 6, 1884, by Jens
Hansen, and a High Priest Nov. 13, 1893, by
Apostle John Henry Smith. Bro. Christensen
attended the Brigham Young Academy two
years and graduated from that institution as
No. 1 in his class in June, 1889; served as
principal of the Latter-day Saints Seminary
at Mount Pleasant three years and principal of
the Sanpete Stake Academy for one year. In
1896-1898 he filled a mission to Scandinavia,
labored successively as traveling Elder in the
Copenhagen Branch, president of the Copenhagen Conference, translator for "Skandinaviens Stjerne" and president of the Scandinavian Mission. In October, 1902, he married
Frances Elizabeth Ellison; three children
blessed this union. Bro. Christensen served
as principal of the commercial department of
the Snow College at Ephraim from 1904 to
1909. He has practiced law since 1904, when
he was admitted to practice before the Supreme
Court of Utah and the District and Circuit
Courts of the United States. Bro. Christensen
was elected and served as county attorney of
Sanpete County for two terms and in 1916 was
elected judge of the Seventh Judicial District of the State of Utah. He was again
elected to this office in 1922 and 1924 and is
at present occupying that position. He moved
to Manti in 1918 and to Price, Carbon County,
in 1921, where he now (1927) resides.

"Furnesia," which sailed from Glasgow, Scotland, April 20th, and arrived in New York after a somewhat stormy voyáge.

Another company of emigrating Saints (17 souls) sailed from Norway, April 29, 1898, accompanied by Elders Daniel K. Brown and Peter Olsen, returning missionaries. Besides the Elders whose returns are mentioned in connection with the emigration companies, the following brethren, who had labored as missionaries in Scandinavia, were released and returned home on the following dates: Albert S. Erickson, Jan. 12th; Chr. Poulsen and Chr. Johnson, Feb. 17th; John Peterson and Chas., A. Thomsen, May 6th'; John D. Hagman, James F. Iversen, Niels P. Nielsen, Henry M. Pearson (Pehrson), Peter Mogensen and Jens J. Jensen, May 26th; George A. Sanders, Niels Chr. Nielsen, Chr. Knudsen and Marius Mikkelsen, June 13th; Ephraim Björklund and Peter Erickson, June 16th; August R. Lundin, Ole H., Peterson, Charles M. Olson, Chr. N. Lundsten, George A. Christensen, James Chr. Breinholt, Niels S. Christoffersen, Hans Chr. Hansen and Bengt T. Bengtson, July 28th; Jens Christensen, Aug. 4th; Hyrum Nielsen, Sept. 1st; Severin N. Lee, Sept. 19th; Carl J. Fagergren, John L. Cherling, Hans P. Nielsen, Geo. A. Millerberg, John A. Anderson, Hans T. Petersen and Anton Anderson, Oct. 6th; Andrew Dahlsrud and Ephraim Mikkelsen, Oct. 14th; Wm. Anderson, Dykes W. Sörensen and John W. Larson, Oct. 17th'; Peter G. Hanson and Olaus Johnson Nordstrand, Nov. 10th; Peter Lars Petersen and Isaac Carlson, Nov. 11th; Lars J. Halling, jun., Nov. 24th; Andrew A. Björn, Peter P. Siggard, Anton P. N. Peterson and Thomas Halvorsen, Apr. 28th.

Elder George Christensen, who had presided over the Scandinavian Mission since May 19, 1898, lef Copenhagen, Sept. 19, 1898, on hi

ANDREAS PETERSON

Was born June 23, 1849, at Håbol, Dahl land, Sweden, the son of Pehr and Christin Janson. He went to Norway in 1871, whei he became a convert to "Mormonism," ar was baptized May 25, 1872, by Niels Isakse After being ordained to the Priesthood, I labored as a missionary four years, and ba tized sixty souls. He emigrated to America 1877, and after a short sojourn in Spri City, Sanpete County, Utah, he located pe manently in Logan, Jan. 8, 1878. In 187 (July 25th) he married Inga Overn, whic union has been blessed with five sons and for daughters. In 1883-1884 he filled a very su cessful mission in Scandinavia, laboring in tl Stockholm Conference. He walked 3,2 miles, held 190 meetings with strangers, ar baptized forty-two persons. He was ordaine a High Priest March 3, 1887, by Bishop Geor O. Pitkin, and was set apart as a memb of the High Council in the Cache Stake, whic position he held for thirty-three years. In 189 he was elected a member of the Logan cit council and served in that capacity two year He also served as a member of the school boa from 1891 to 1894. In 1898-1901 he filled a other mission to Scandinavia, this time president of the Scandinavian Mission. Aft his release he made a tour of the Orient(inclu ing Palestine, Africa, Italy, France, Switze land, etc.). In 1910-1912 he filled still anoth mission to Scandinavia, this time presidir over the Swedish Mission. During this mi sion he traveled 34,625 miles, attended 5 meetings and visited Russia and Finland. Sin 1920, Elder Peterson has acted as preside of the High Priests' Quorum in the Cacl Stake. He is a man of ability, a good speake and a zealous Church worker. Three of h sons have also filled successful missions, tw to Scandinavia and one to the Eastern State Bro. Peterson has also labored as ordinan worker in Logan Temple four years.

eturn to Utah. Elder Christensen had endeared himself to the Scandinavian Mission because of his affable manners and devotion to the cause of the Lord. Before presiding over the mission he had acted as president of the Copenhagen Conference and later as a translator for "Skandinaviens Stjerne." Elder Andreas Peterson succeeded him in the presidency of the Scandinavian Mission.

Elder Albert Peterson of Murray, Utah, who labored as a missionary in Sweden, died at Upsala, Dec. 30, 898. Elder Peterson was born March 7, 1872, in Wittinge, Uppland, Sweden, was baptized March 9, 1882, and emigrated to Utah in 1891. Being called on a mission, he arrived in Copenhagen, Denmark, May 6, 1897, having left his newlywedded wife in Utah. He first labored in the Blekinge Branch of the Skåne Conference and later in the Stockholm Conference. Dressed in temple robes, his remains were interred June 11, 1899, in the South Cottonwood cemetery, Salt Lake County, Utah.

In 1898, 87 Elders from Zion as missionaries to Scandinavia arrived in Copenhagen as follows: Niels Chr. Iversen of Bear River City, Henry F. Fernström of Salt Lake City, and Arnt Johanson of Logan, Utah, arrived Feb. 13th; John H. Harlan of Heber City, Charles John B. Bohman of Monroe, and John A. Christensen of Salt Lake City, Utah, Feb. 26th, and Albert John Johnson of Ogden, Utah, on March 2nd; Peter Henning Madsen of Manti, Julius H. Hansen of Lago, Idaho, and Swen Wm. Hall of Logan, Utah, arrived March 29th, and Niels L. Anderson of Richfield, Utah, Emil Fetterborg of Preston, Idaho, Albert I. Bergman of Salt Lake City, Gustaf A. Anderson of East Jordan, Hans P. Jensen and Lauritz Edward Larsen (Lauritzen) of Salem, Idaho,

on April 24th; Noah L. Pond of Pocatello, Idaho, Charles Erick Forsberg of Salt Lake City, Severin Swenson of Mt. Pleasant, Erick A. Modeen of Gunnison, Bengt Troed Bengtson of Salt Lake City, Andrew G. Erickson and Peter Hansen of Heber City, Utah, arrived April 30th; Jacob Christensen and Jonas Johanson (Johnson) of Big Cottonwood, Andrew M. Anderson of Sigurd, Torben J. Torbensen of Snowville, John H. Quist of Brinton, Nils Monson of East Jordan, Utah, and Niels C. Christiansen of Lyman, Idaho, arrived May 16th; Jacob N. Olson of Vernal, Christian Steffensen of Salt Lake City, Joseph M. Nelson of Mantua, Thomas P. Jensen of Elsinore, Frederick Jensen Holst and Louis O. Dorius of Ephraim, Utah, arrived May 30th, and Alexander J. Nielson of Salt Lake City, John H. Anderson of American Fork, and Parley Anderson of Koosharem Utah, arrived July 4th; Gustaf Johnson of Mill Creek, Martin Jensen of Redmond, and John J. Peterson of Salt Lake City, arrived July 31st; Niels J. Torkelsen of Salt Lake City, Utah, and August Wm. Ossman of Rigby, Idaho, arrived Aug. 14th, and Jeppa Monson of St. Charles, Idaho, arrived Aug. 28th; Andrew Peterson of Wanship, Rasmus A. Rasmussen of Ferron and Hans H. Pedersen of Salt Lake City, Utah, arrived Sept. 3rd; Andreas Peterson of Logan, Mads F. T. Christensen of Fairview. Peter Petersen of Brigham City, Elof Nilson of Elsinore, and Hans K. Hansen of Bear River City, arrived Sept. 9th, and George Albert Torgeson of Logan and Ole Petersen of Grover, Wyoming, Sept. 20th; Morten Jensen of Richfield, John W. Larson of Collinston, Swen Johan Nielson of Centerfield, and Adolph Bergen of West Jordan, Utah, arrived Oct. 1st, and Ola Olson of Millville, Sören Rasmussen of Draper, and Thorvald S. Jensen of Salt Lake City, Utah, arrived Oct. 10th; Peter Jensen and Alexander A. Larsen of Mantua, and August H. Erickson of Salt Lake City, Utah, arrived Oct. 15th, and Joseph Christoffersen of Burlington, Wyoming, George A. Peterson of Salt Lake City, Christian Canutson of Elsinore, Nils P. Anderson of Logan, and Mathias Erickson of Salina, Utah, arrived Nov. 12th; Christian Olson of Brigham City,

James P. Christensen of Bear River City, Hans C. Christensen of Emery, and Julius C. Andersen of Provo, Utah, arrived Nov. 15th; Severin

JULIUS C. ANDERSEN

Was born in Copenhagen, Denmark, April 25, 1877, the son of Knud Andersen and Johanne C. Juul, who were all baptized in Copenhagen, in 1888, and emigrating to Utah in 1889, located at Provo, Utah, where Julius continued his studies at the B. Y. University. After finishing a commercial course in that institution he became a member of the firm of Decker and Co., where he remained for twelve years. For the past eighteen years he has been president and manager of the Utah Abstract Company at Provo. In 1898-1900, Bro. Andersen filled a mission to Scandinavia, laboring at Vordingborg for the first part of his mission, and later in Copenhagen. At home he has served as Ward clerk for 18 years, and in the presidency of a quorum of Seventy for 14 years (the latter five years thereof as senior president of the 34th quorum). He is now a High Priest. On May 26, 1897, he married Esther L. Poulter of Ogden; they are the parents of seven children, five of whom are living.

Nielsen of Mill Creek, Utah, Johan A. Blomquist of La Belle, Idaho, Johan Axel Pehrson (Pearson) of Rexburg, Idaho, James C. Poulsen of Graham, Arizona, August Mineer of St. Johns, Arizona, John C. Nielsen of Hyrum, Charles D. Ahlström of Tropic, and Oluf Larson of Randolph, Utah, arrived Dec. 1st; Niels Nielsen of Morgan City, and James Thomson of Brigham City, Utah, ar-

MATHIAS ERICKSON,

Born at Tierp, Upsala län, Sweden, Aug. 27, 1862, the son of Erick Erickson and Johanna Pehrson; was baptized April 6, 1884, by J. A. Schelin; emigrated to Utah in 1885 and located at Salina. He left Salt Lake City Oct. 22, 1898, for a mission to Sweden, labored in Eskilstuna and Upsala; organized a branch in Gefle in 1900 (fifty years after the first baptisms there by John E. Forsgren), and was honorably released in December, 1900. In 1911-1913 he filled a second mission to Sweden and was again assigned to the Gefle and the Stockholm conferences; presided later over the Sundsvall Conference. Elder Erickson accompanied the body of Elder Gustav T. Anderson (who died in Luleå, Dec. 11, 1913) to Cardston, Canada, and arrived in Salina Feb. 19, 1914. Bro. Erickson left for a third mission to Sweden in November, 1920, and presided over the Gefle Conference, where twenty-three were baptized as the fruit of his labors. Bro. Erickson has been in the Scandinavian presidency in North Sevier Stake for twenty-five years, and presided the last twelve years.

ived Dec. 4th; and Raynor Ness of Salt Lake City, Olof Olson of Millville, and Christian Busath of Salt Lake City, Utah, arrived Dec. 19, 1898.

Niels Chr. Iversen, Peter H. Madsen, Julius H. Hansen, Peter Hansen, Torben J. Torbensen, Alexander J. Nielson and Julius C. Andersen were appointed to labor in the Copenhagen Conference. Jacob Christensen was also appointed to labor in the Copenhagen Conference, part of the time as conference president. Thomas P. Jensen was appointed to labor in the Copenhagen Conference and later in the Aalborg Conference. He was banished for preaching. John J. Peterson, Rasmus A. Rasmussen, Peter Petersen, Thorvald S. Jensen, Niels L. Anderson and Louis O. Dorius were appointed to labor in the Copenhagen and Aarhus conferences.

John A. Christensen (excommunicated, Aug. 10, 1899), Hans P. Jensen, Niels C. Christiansen, Joseph M. Nelson (Nielson), Fred. J. Holst, Martin Jensen, Ole Petersen, Swen . Nielson, Peter Jensen, Christian Olson and James C. Poulsen were appointed to labor in the Aalborg Conference. James Thomson (second mission) was also appointed to labor in the Aalborg and later to preside over the Copenhagen Conference. Christian Steffensen, Sören Rasmussen, Alexander A. Larsen, George A. Peterson, Christian Canutson, James P. Christensen, Severin Nielsen and Niels Nielsen were appointed to labor in the Aarhus Conference. Andrew Petersen was also appointed to labor in the Aarhus Conference, part of the time as conference president. Morten Jensen was appointed to labor in the Aarhus Conference and later as president of the Aalborg Conference. Erick A. Modeen, Andrew G. Erickson, Nels (Nils) Monson, Jacob N. Olson, Adolph Bergen, Mathias Erickson and Johan A. Blomquist were appointed to labor in the Stockholm Conference. Henry F. Fernström was also appointed to labor in the Stockholm Conference, but later transferred to the mission office in Copenhagen, Denmark. Andrew M. Anderson was appointed to labor in the Stockholm Conference, part of the time as conference president. John H. Carlan, Swen Wm. Hall, John H. Anderson and Charles D. Ahlström were appointed to labor in the Stockholm and Skåne conferences. Charles John E. Bohman, Gustaf A. Anderson and Gustaf Johnson were appointed to labor in the Stockholm and Göteborg conferences.

Arnt Johanson, Emil Petterborg, Lauritz E. Lauritzen, Severin Swenson, Jonas Johanson, Parley Anderson, Hans H. Pedersen, George A. Torgeson. Joseph Christoffersen, Nils P. Anderson, Hans C. Christensen, John C. Nielsen, Oluf Larson, Raynor Ness and Christian Busath were appointed to labor in the Christiania Conference. Niels J. Torkelsen was appointed to labor in the Christiania Conference, and later in the Copenhagen Conference.

Noah L. Pond. Charles E. Forsberg, John H. Quist, August Wm. Ossman, John W. Larson and August H. Erickson were appointed to labor in the Göteborg Conference. Albert J. Johnson and Albert H. Bergman were appointed to labor in the Skåne and Göteborg conferences. Elder Bergman was later appointed to the office in Copenhagen, Denmark.

Bengt T. Bengtson, Jeppa Monson (second mission), Elof Nilson, Johan A Pehrson, August Mineer and Olof Olson were appointed to labor in the Skåne Conference. Ola Olson was also appointed to labor in the Skåne Conference, part of the time as conference president; this was his third mission. Andreas Peterson

24

(second mission) acted as president of the Scandinavian Mission. Mads F. T. Christensen (second mission) was appointed to labor in the mission office in Copenhagen. Hans K. Hansen visited relatives in Denmark and did some missionary labors.

CHAPTER 83 (1899)

Pres. Platte D. Lyman visits Scandinavia—Returning Elders and emigrating Saints journey to America in small companies—Arrival of 77 Elders from America.

Elder Platte D. Lyman, president of the European Mission, arrived in Aarhus, Denmark, March 24, 1899, on a visit to Scandinavia. Accompanied by Andreas Peterson, president of the Scandinavian Mission, he first attended a conference in Aarhus, afterwards one in Aalborg, and later one in Copenhagen. On April 15th, Presidents Lyman and Peterson crossed Öresund to Sweden and attended conferences in Malmö, Göteborg and Stockholm successively. Thence they proceeded to Christiania, Norway, where they held conferences on May 6th and 7th. On this occasion, the Christiania Conference, which hitherto had embraced all of Norway, was divided into three conferences, viz., Christiania, over which Canute W. Peterson was continued as president, Bergen, with Hyrum Jensen as president, and Trondhjem, with Niels P. Nielsen as president. The Christiania Conference, after this division, consisted of six branches of the Church, viz., Christiania, Drammen, Frederikstad, Frederikshald, Arendal and Laurvik. The Bergen Conference consisted of the Bergen, Stavanger and Aalesund branches, and the Trondhjem Conference of the Trondhjem Branch and scattered members.

During this visit of the president of the European Mission to Scandinavia much good was done and new life infused into the missionaries and

Saints, resulting in renewed efforts on the part of Elders and Saints to spread the principles of truth more than ever before among the inhabitants of Scandinavia. Elder Lyman left Copenhagen May 11, 1898, for the Swiss and German Mission.

During the summer of 1899, Elder Christopher Jensen Kempe and Joseph Christoffersen, his missionary companion, held a number of well attended meetings (some of them in the open air) in Stavanger and vicinity, causing considerable awakening among the people in regard to the principles of "Mormonism." Opposition on the part of Lutheran priests only served to arouse the people to further investigation, and the rather exciting experience which the Elders had gave a fresh impetus to the work of the Lord in that part of Norway. For some time, Elder Kempe and his companion held from five to ten meetings a week.

On the 17th of August, 1899, a fire broke out in an upper room of the building in which the mission office was located in St. Paulsgade No. 14 Copenhagen. Among the property destroyed were all of the unbound books and many tracts belonging to the mission. Had the stock of books not been partly covered by insurance this fire would have proved a serious loss to the Church. The newspapers of Copenhagen, in describing the fire, had occasion to draw attention to the "Mormon Propaganda" in Denmark, and one of the leading papers "Politiken," in its issue of Aug. 23, 1899, commented very favorably upon the missionary work carried on by the Latter-day Saints. It happened that the editor of that paper had visited Utah, where a most favorable impression had been made upon him, and, being a fair-minded man he endeavored to tell the truth about the "Mormons."

In 1899, the Elders met with con

siderable success in Sweden; thus, for instance, the conference headquarters at Göteborg, where Charles E. Forsberg presided over the conference, was moved into a most elegant hall, which had a seating capacity of about two hundred people.

A company of emigrants left Copenhagen for Utah, April 20, 1899, accompanied by two returning Elders, viz., Mouritz F. A. Peterson of Murray, Utah, who had labored in the Göteborg Conference, and Peter S. Olson, of Mink Creek, who had labored in the Göteborg Conference.

A company of emigrating Saints (30 in number) sailed from Copenhagen, May 4, 1899, bound for Utah, accompanied by Elder Andrew Anderson, who had presided over the Skåne Conference, and Jens Niels Hansen, who had labored in the Copenhagen Conference. This company crossed the North Sea in the steamer "Berlin" and arrived at Leith, Scotland, May 8th. Boarding the steamer "Ethiopia" they sailed from Glasgow, Scotland, May 11, 1899, and reached Salt Lake City, June 10, 1899.

Another small company of emigrants sailed from Copenhagen, June 26, 1899, accompanied by Christian T. Nielsen and Chr. M. Mickelsen of Redmond, Utah, returning Elders. They arrived in Salt Lake City, July 18, 1899, after a successful journey on sea and on land.

Another company of emigrating Saints, bound for Utah, left Copenhagen, Aug. 31, 1899, in charge of Elder Daniel Peter Jensen of Elsinore, Utah, who, after a successful mission in Scandinavia, returned to his home in America.

Besides the Elders mentioned in connection with companies of emigrating Saints, the following brethren from Zion, who had labored as missionaries in Scandinavia, took their departure, returning home on the following dates: Gustaf A. Brandt, Jan. 23rd; George M. Smoot, Mar. 3rd; Martin Williamson and Rangvald Carlson, Mar. 17th; Chr. S. Sörensen and Andrew B. Jensen, Apr. 13th; Aaron Lundberg, Wm. Otto Hanson, Andrew Johnson, Carl G. Johnson, Carl Oskar Johnson, John E. Carlson and Hans Chr. Hansen, May 18th; Carl A. A. Augustson, Nils Jenson and Louis M. Christiansen, June 12th, and Canute W. Peterson and Niels F. Swalberg, June 20th; Jos. L. Petersen, Ole Jensen, Rasmus Chr. Petersen, jun., and Chr. Christensen, July 20th; Rudolph V. Larson, Aug. 4th; James N. Skousen, Sept. 11th; Alfred Hanson and Jens Larsen, Oct. 12th; Erick W. Edvaldson, Hyrum Olsen, Albert A. Capson, Adolph F. Elggren and John Felt, jun., Oct. 5th; John E. Bolstad, Axel Olsen and Chr. F. Schade, Oct. 6th; Arnold L. Nelson, Oct. 19th; John E. Groberg, John P. Löfgren, Peter J. Sandberg, David Blomquist, Joseph Jensen and Swen Wm. Hall, Nov. 6th; Jöns Jönson (James Jenson), Nov. 19th; Chas. Chr. Jensen, Nephi Valentine and Geo. D. Hanson, Nov. 20th; Carl Chr. Garff, Ole A. Okerlund, Gustaf A. Anderson, John Johnson, jun., Louis E. Erickson, Hyrum Nielsen, Isaac P. Peterson and Rasmus Nilson, Nov. 23rd; Gideon E. Olson, jun., Nov. 30; Jonas Johanson, John P. Anderson, Lauritz Lauritzen, Chr. Pedersen, jun., Peter S. Nielsen, Sören C. Christensen, Niels C. Christiansen and Geo. A. Peterson, Dec. 4th.

In 1899, 77 Elders from Zion, called to labor as missionaries in Scandinavia, arrived in Copenhagen, Denmark, as follows: Carl R. Erickson of Ogden, Utah, arrived Jan. 5th; Mads P. Andersen of Salt Lake City and James Peter Olsen of Brigham City, Utah, Jan. 23rd, and John Peterson of Ovid, Idaho, Feb. 11th;

Christoffer J. Kempe of Concho, Arizona, and Jens Christiansen of Elsinore, Utah, arrived March 4th, and John Persson of Payson and Niels P. Nielson of Pocatello, Idaho, March 16th; Noah A. Larson of College, Carl Oscar Winkler of Salt Lake City, Peter Andrew Sörensen of Mendon, and Alfred Anderson of Cedar Fort, Utah, arrived April 24th; Peter Frost of Benson, Emil Anderson of Logan, Utah, and Lewis Kimber

JAMES L. JENSON

Born Aug. 21, 1853, in Östra Torp, Malmöhus län, Sweden, the son of Lars Jönsson and Ingrid Anderson; was baptized May 1, 1866 by E. S. Greko; emigrated to Utah in 1866 crossing the Atlantic in the "Humboldt" (sailing vessel), and the Plains in Peter Nebeker's company, which arrived in Salt Lake City in the fall of that year. He married Bertha Maria Carlsson, June 15, 1874, was ordained an Elder on that date by Samuel H. Smith, labored as a missionary in the Northwestern States from April 18, 1881, to Dec. 9, 1882, and performed temple work for one year. On May 5, 1899, he left for a mission to Sweden, where he labored in Halmstad and Göteborg. He returned home, Aug. 5, 1901, and was appointed second counselor in the High Priests' quorum, Aug. 26, 1901, an became president of the High Priests' quorum of the Hyrum Stake in 1911. He is the father of 13 children and has been a resident of Hyrum, Utah, for 42 years.

ELDER EMIL ANDERSON

Of the Scandinavian presidency, Logan, Utah, was born, July 1, 1861, at Frederikshavn, Denmark; joined the Church in 1878, was called in 1879 to labor in the Aalborg Conference; emigrated to Utah in 1880; sent for his parents later and located in Logan, where he has resided ever since. In 1899 he labored in the Swedish Mission; returned in June, 1901; while in the Göteborg Conference, he baptized 19. In 1923-1925, he labored as a missionary in Denmark; presided over the Copenhagen Conference and baptized 27 souls as a result of his labors.

Anderson of Salem, Idaho, arrived May 7th; Michael Johnson of College Ward, Hans Andreas Pedersen of Logan, Thomas A. Fredericksen of Sugar House, Christian Johnson of Ashley, Oke O. Oberg (Öberg) of East Jordan, John Johnson of Benjamin, Ola Larson of Logan and Christen Christensen of Hyrum, Utah, ar-

rived May 13th and Jacob M. Laurit zen of Richfield, Christian Sörensen of Mendon, Christian Nielsen of Sa lina and James L. Jenson of Hyrum Utah, arrived May 29th; Richard Chr

Miller of Castle Dale, Knut Albert Anderson of Richmond, Casper Andreasen of Bear River City and Andrew C. Pehrson of Lehi, Utah arrived June 7th; Lars Petersen of Hyrum, and Emil Erickson of South Cottonwood, Utah, arrived June 20th Charles Chr. Rönnow of Panaca

Nevada, arrived June 27th; Peter N. Garff of Draper, Niels Frederiken of Vernon, Utah, Anton Henry Jenson of Preston, Idaho, and Alex. I. Oblad of Salt Lake City, Utah,

RICHARD C. MILLER (MÖLLER)

Son of Niels C. Möller and Petrea F. Holm, was born Nov. 14, 1854, at Aalborg, Denmark; was baptized Feb 7, 1877, by John E. Christiansen; performed military service for seven months, and labored as a missionary in Vendsyssel during the winter of 1877. He emigrated to Utah in the fall of 1878, and located in Salt Lake City. He moved to Castle Dale, Emery Co., in 1884, and went on a mission to Denmark in 1889, and labored in the Aarhus Conference for 12 months; presided over the Aalborg Conference for 10 months. He was called on another mission in 1910; presided over the Aalborg Conference for 20 months, and over the Copenhagen Conference for 7 months. In the Castle Dale bishopric he acted as first counselor for about five years; has been Ward Clerk for six years. He served as county treasurer for three terms, and has been a justice of the peace the last 12 years.

rrived Aug. 13th, and Johan Peter Mortensen and Jennie C. Mortensen of Salt Lake City, Hans Peter Jensen of Mapleton, Carl Edward Söderlund of East Mill Creek, Ahnar Oskar Larson of Millville and Asa Herman Farley of Ogden, Utah, arrived Aug. 27th; Joseph J. Cannon of Cannon Ward, Salt Lake City, arrived Sept. 28th and Herman F. F. Thorup of Salt Lake City and Sweny J. Nilson of Pleasant Grove,

Utah, arrived Oct. 16th; Henry W. Berg of Provo, Joseph L. Olson of Santaquin, Niels Jacobsen of Newton, and Charles Albert Halvorsen of Ogden, Utah, arrived Nov. 7th and Anders F. Ahlander of Provo, Niels (Nels) Peter Hansen of Mantua, Charles Leroy Anderson, jun., of Grantsville, Utah, and Niels P. H. Roholt of Mink Creek, Idaho, arrived Nov. 20th; William Olson

ANDERS FREDERIK AHLANDER

Was born Sept. 13, 1856, at Krokstad, Bohus län, Sweden, the son of Jonas Ahlander and Britta M. Jakobson. He was baptized March 10, 1877, by Andreas Peterson; emigrated to Utah 1886, and in 1895, became a permanent resident of Provo, where he was ordained a Seventy, Oct. 27, 1899; the same year he was called to fill a mission to Scandinavia, labored in Christiania Conference, Norway, and returned home in 1901. Bro. Ahlander has always been an active member in the Church, has been president of an Elders quorum, senior president of the 156th quorum of Seventy, and was ordained a High Priest in 1906. In 1879, he married Karin Johanson, who bore him four children. After his wife's death he married Ludovica A. Hermansen, who has borne him seven children. Brother Ahlander is a carriage maker and blacksmith by trade.

and Olof Rosenlöf of Mt. Pleasant, Wilford E. Anderson of Salem, Peter Victor Bunderson of Emery Niels Peter Johnson of Logan and Oluf Johnson of Brigham City, Utah, arrived Nov. 30th and Wrol Chr.

Olsen of Iona, Idaho, Christian J. Plowman and Niels O. Gyllenskog of Smithfield, Utah, Dec. 7th; Joseph N. Stohl of Brigham City, Charles A.

WILLIAM OLSON

Was born June 31, 1853, on the island of Bornholm, Denmark, the son of John Olson and Sofia Maria Skrevelius; was baptized in March, 1866; emigrated to Utah with his parents the same year, crossing the Atlantic in the sailing ship "Kenilworth" and the Plains in Captain Joseph S. Rawlins' company. The family located at Mount Pleasant and in 1876, Bro. Olson married Sara Jane Tidwell, who was born at Pleasant Grove, Utah, July 11, 1857. In 1899-1902, he filled a mission to Sweden, where he labored in the Skåne Conference. He also served as Bishop's counselor for 17 years, as city councilor and held other positions of responsibility. Bro. and Sister Olson have five children: William Arthur, Berkley, Guy Randolph, Theodor and Mary Estelle.

Larson of Ogden, Carl Larson of Sandy, Albert Swenson of Spanish Fork, Niels M. Jacobson of Murray, Utah, Hans Chr. Hansen and Carl E. Wallgren of Mink Creek, Idaho, Christian Christensen of Molen, Alfred Erickson and August Sjöström of Logan, Martin Jenson of Sandy, Enoch C. Lybbert of Vernal, and Parley P. Anderson of Parley's Park, Utah, arrived Dec. 10th, 1899.

Carl R. Erickson, Knut A. Ander-

son, Andrew C. Pehrson, Emil Erickson, Carl Edward Söderlund, Asa H. Farley, Joseph L. Olson, Joseph N. Stohl, Charles A. Larson and Albert Swenson were appointed to labor in the Stockholm Conference. John Johnson and Joseph J. Cannon were also appointed to labor in the Stockholm Conference, part of the time as conference presidents. Elder Cannon finished his mission at the Liverpool office in England. Charles L. Anderson, jun., was appointed to labor in the Stockholm Conference, but was called to preside over the

CARL LARSON

Born at Gårdstånga, Malmöhus län, Sweden, Jan. 28, 1871, the son of Hans Larson and Hanna Johanson, was baptized April 23, 1884, by Elder James Olson of Mt. Pleasant; emigrated to Utah with his parents the same year; filled a mission to Sweden in 1899-1901, laboring in Göteborg, Jönköping and Halmstad, finishing in the Skåne Conference; baptized quite a number of converts. He has labored as a home missionary in Jordan Stake; was ordained a Seventy, Nov. 17, 1899, by Elder Geo. Teasdale; was set apart as one of the presidents of the 93rd Quorum of Seventy, in August, 1923; became first counselor to Pres. A. P. Nielsen of the Scandinavian organization, and its president, Dec. 12, 1923; married Elma Söderman and became the father of twelve children, ten of whom are still living; carried the mail between Sandy and Alta, a mining town, for many years; has served in the city council two terms and filled other responsible positions in the county. Since 1884, he has been living on his farm at Sandy, Salt Lake County.

newly organized Sundsvall Conference.

John Persson, Oke O. Oberg (Öberg), Ola Larson, Ahnar Oskar

JOSEPH N. STOHL

Born December 21, 1875, in Brigham City, Utah, a son of Ole N. Stohl and Christina Johnson, was engaged ecclesiastically in Box Elder Stake until November 17, 1899, at which time he left for a mission to Sweden, laboring in the Stockholm Conference, and returned to Brigham City July 3, 1902. He married Orpha V. Hunsaker, June 22, 1904, and has been blessed with seven daughters. Bro. Stohl has served on Sunday School Stake boards, as superintendent of Sunday schools and as a member of the Box Elder Stake presidency for nine and one-half years. In business he has been connected with and held prominent positions in the Stohl Furniture Company, First National Bank of Brigham, Examiner of Securities for the Middlesex Banking Company, and is now (1927) Examiner of Securities and Manager of the Mortgage Loan Department of the Beneficial Life Insurance Company.

Larson, Swenny (Swen) J. Nilson, William Olson and Martin Jenson were appointed to labor in the Skåne Conference. Peter V. Bunderson was also appointed to labor in the Skåne Conference, part of the time as conference president. Niels O. Gyllen-

skog (second mission) was appointed to labor in the Stockholm and Skåne conferences.

Christoffer J. Kempe, Noah A. Larson, Peter A. Sörensen, Christian Johnson, Henry W. Berg, Charles A. Halverson, Anders F. Ahlander, Wilford E. Anderson and Vrol (Wrol) Chr. Olsen were appointed to labor in the Christiania Conference, Norway. Niels P. Nielson was appointed to labor in the Christiania, later in the Copenhagen and still later to preside over the Trondhjem Conference. Hans A. Pedersen (second mission) was appointed to labor in the Christiania Conference, most of the time as conference president. Mads P. Andersen, John Peterson, Jens Christiansen, Hans P. Jensen, Niels Jacobsen, Niels P. Johnson and Christian Christensen were appointed to labor in the Aalborg Conference.

James P. Olsen, Peter Frost, Christen Christensen, Casper Andreasen, Johan P. Mortensen (second mission), Niels P. Hansen, Hans Chr. Hansen, Parley P. Anderson and Lars Christoffersen were appointed to labor in the Aarhus Conference. Richard Chr. Miller was appointed to labor in the Aarhus and Aalborg conferences, part of the time as president of the Aalborg Conference. Jennie C. Mortensen was appointed to labor in the Aarhus and Copenhagen conferences, Denmark. Herman F. F. Thorup (second mission) was appointed to labor in the Aarhus Conference, part of the time as conference president.

Carl O. Winkler, Alfred Anderson, Emil Anderson, Olof Rosenlöf, Carl E. Wallgren, Alfred Erickson and August Sjöström were appointed to labor in the Göteborg Conference. James L. Jenson was also appointed to labor in the Göteborg Conference, part of the time as conference president. Lewis K. Anderson and Carl

Larson were appointed to labor in the Göteborg Conference and later in the Skåne Conference. Alex. H. Oblad was appointed to labor in the Göteborg and Stockholm conferences. Jacob M. Lauritzen and Enoch C. Lybbert were appointed to labor in the Trondhjem Conference. Michael Johnson (second mission), Thomas A. Fredericksen and Christian Nielsen were appointed to labor in the Trondhjem and Christiania conferences. Anton H. Jenson and Peter N. Garff were appointed to labor in the Bergen Conference, the latter part of the time as conference president. Christian Sörensen, Lars Petersen, Niels Frederiksen, Niels P. H. Roholt, Oluf Johnson, Chr. J. Plowman (second mission) and Niels M. Jacobson were appointed to labor in the Copenhagen Conference. Charles Chr. Rönnow was appointed to labor in the Copenhagen Conference, and later in the Trondhjem Conference, a part of the time as president of the latter conference.

CHAPTER 84 (1900)

Elders Charles C. Rönnow and Thos. P. Jensen are banished from Denmark—Death of Elder Henry W. Berg in Norway—Ninety-nine Elders from Zion arrive in Scandinavia—Strength of the mission at the close of the century.

Elder Ferdinand F. Hintze, returning from a mission to Turkey, arrived in Copenhagen on his way to America, Jan. 4, 1900. He gave an interesting report of his mission to Turkey, attended a number of meetings in Copenhagen and vicinity and then continued his journey to England.

Under date of Jan. 18th, Elder Parley P. Jenson, who labored as a missionary in Norway, related an instance in Drammen, where a young woman had accepted the true gospel of Christ, but was very much opposed in her so doing by an aunt, who was a very devout member of the Methodist Church, and thought that her special mission was "to convert her niece back to the fold of the Christian world." At first the good woman thought the task would be quite easy. Taking the Bible as her weapon

PARLEY PETER JENSON

Son of Andrew Jenson and Kjersten Marie Pedersen, was born Aug. 26, 1878, in Pleasant Grove, Utah County, Utah, and is now (1927) a resident of Salt Lake City, Utah.

she felt fully confident that victory would crown her effort, and therefore boldly attacked the faith of her "Mormon" niece. Time and time again, she asserted that "Mormons" were not Christians, but soon her arguments were turned against herself by the "Mormon" niece, who in each case was able to prove and make plain that while perhaps "Mormonism" was not Christian doctrine when defined and measured by the popular orthodox definition, yet was in perfect harmony with Bible teachings. The aunt, after having pursued this course for some time, concluded that she must adopt other means of attack, and, therefore, said that even though "Mormonism" was biblical, it was nevertheless beneath the dignity of any respectable member of society to be a "Mormon." The young Latter-day Saint was then confronted by those who were learned in the Scriptures, and they tried to show her the error of her ways, but, in spite of their much learning and knowledge, met with no better success than the aunt. By and by, the aunt plainly saw that some entirely new methods must be adopted, and so she inaugurated a rigid house dicipline. She forced her niece to remain at home, not allowing her any liberty that might enable her to visit "Mormon" meetings. All the friends of the family who were acquainted with the "dreadful history" of "Mormonism" were next invited to call at the house, and, with all the emotion they possessed, they related the horrible bloody tales that are alleged to have been connected with the "Mormon" Church, including the story of destroying angels, the Mountain Meadows affair, etc. This mode of warfare proved just as ineffective as the first. One day, however, when the "Mormon" Elders were visiting at the home of a friend living near by, the young sister also happened to call at the same place. They, of course, gave her all the encouragement they could and assured her that all would be for the best. When her aunt learned that her niece had met and conversed with the Elders, notwithstanding all her precaution, a climax was reached. The storm burst forth in a fury worthy of a better cause. The old lady accused her niece of having met the Elders by appointment, though the meeting was purely accidental. The aunt threatened that should the Elders ever attempt to visit her house,

she would show them the door so quick that it would astonish them. Just one week from that day not one, but four "Mormon" Elders spent the afternoon and evening at the home of that lady by special invitation. They were not only received kindly but treated with hospitality. When evening came and the Elders prepared to take their departure, the kind aunt insisted that they should remain for the evening meal. They did so, when to their total surprise their hostess invited them to hold a public service in her home that night and she would invite the neighbors to attend. A real good and well-attended meeting was held, and among those present there were many pronounced enemies. The Lord, however, blessed his young servants, and they were enabled to bear strong testimonies to the people, who listened with marked attention. A number of other meetings were held, as many of the neighbors opened their doors to the Elders to preach in private houses.

In January, 1900, an attempt was made to banish some of the Elders from Denmark, and Pres, Andreas Peterson and Elder Jacob Christensen called upon the American minister in Copenhagen, asking him to intercede with the Danish government in behalf of Elders Charles Christian Rönnow and Thomas P. Jensen, who were about to be banished from the island of Bornholm, where they had labored as missionaries. The efforts of the American minister were without avail and the two Elders named were finally banished from Denmark.

Brother Jensen soon afterwards left for his home in Utah, while Elder Rönnow's field of labor was changed from Denmark to Norway.

Elder Henry W. Berg, who labored as a missionary in Norway, died Feb. 21, 1900, in Christiania, of consumption. Elder Berg was born August 8, 1878, in Provo, Utah, the son of Ole H. Berg. He was called

HENRY W. BERG
Born Aug. 8, 1878; died Feb. 21, 1900.

on a mission in the fall of 1899, and on his arrival at mission headquarters was appointed to labor in Norway. While engaged in the ministry in the province of Hedemarken, he contracted a severe cold which settled on his lungs and turned into consumption. His body was shipped home and was interred in the Provo cemetery April 2, 1900.

Elder Jacob M. Lauritzen, who had been appointed to labor as a missionary in the northern part of Norway, wrote from Tromsö, March 6, 1900, as follows:

"I reached here on the 4th of July last year, and had I not been permitted to view the gradual change of conditions as I proceeded northward, I could easily have been convinced that I was on another planet, so marvelous were the changes, both in earth beneath and heaven above. The sun shone continuously, its course being one continual round in the heavens. At noon it would reach its highest point as well as its greatest brilliancy, while at midnight it sank low in the north, looking dim and dreamy. How often I have stood upon the beach watching the restless waves, one by one, come rolling in, each bathed in the glory of this golden light! Accustomed to darkness as the time for rest, I could not sleep, but wandered about, waiting for night which never came, at least, not while I longed for it. In September we had a short period of time during which the days and nights were nearly equal, but soon the days began to shorten rapidly and the nights were correspondingly lengthened. Slowly but surely we were made to realize that the shades of the long and dreary Arctic night were hovering about. Each day the sun sank lower and lower in the south and finally disappeared entirely. For about three months we were left to wander by the light of the stars and the silvery moon. How wonderful for a boy reared under our western sunny skies to eat his dinner day by day by the light of a lamp. I cannot describe my feelings, but I can assure the reader that the experience was unique and novel, and that I heartily enjoyed it. My health was good, although the last month or so I began to feel that the darkness was getting a little oppressive, and now that it is all over, and the sun has returned, I realize that my appetite and ambitions have perceptibly improved."

Elder James L. McMurrin, counselor in the presidency of the European Mission, arrived in Copenhagen, March 24, 1900. Accompanied by Pres. Andreas Peterson and other Elders he attended conferences in Aarhus, Copenhagen, Aalborg, Malmö, Göteborg, Stockholm and Christiania. Meetings were also held by the visiting brethren in some of the other large branches in the mission, and much encouragement was given to the Elders and Saints at these meetings. Elder McMurrin left Copenhagen for Germany, May 25, 1900.

In July, 1900, Pres. Andreas Peterson visited the northern provinces of Sweden, going as far north as Gellivare, Lappland, where, from Mount Dunderet, he had the opportunity of seeing the midnight sun. He held well-attended meeting in the Good Templars' Hall, and, being the only missionary, it became his privilege to sing, pray and preach. After the meeting he received several invitations to visit the people. During his ten days' trip to that part of Sweden he held ten meetings.

In the latter part of 1900, Elder Andreas Peterson, by invitation, delivered an address to an audience of about four hundred people, at a Good Templar meeting in Copenhagen, at which he had an opportunity of explaining the life of the Latter-day Saints in Utah. His theme was the economic and religious conditions in Utah, the training of children, and the Word of Wisdom as revealed to the Prophet Joseph Smith. The lecture took well with most of the people, and Elder Peterson was subsequently invited to deliver similar lectures before other societies.

During the year 1900, the migration of Scandinavian Saints to Utah continued in small companies, sometimes only a few persons, who generally traveled in care of some of the returning Elders. Thus a few emigrants left Christiania July 20, 1900, in charge of Elder Louis J. Holther, who had labored as a missionary in Norway.

John Hannibal Carlan of Heber City, Gustaf Adolf Anderson of East Jordan, John Henrick Anderson of American Fork, Niels Johan Torkelsen of Salt Lake City and Ola Olson of Millville, Utah, left Copenhagen July 23, 1900, to return to their respective homes in Zion, having labored as missionaries in Scandinavia.

A small company of emigrating Saints, in charge of Elder Mads Frederick T. Christensen, who had labored as a translator and writer for "Skandinaviens Stjerne," left Copenhagen Aug. 27, 1900. Five other Elders from Zion and one mis-

sionary sister returned to America in the same company, viz., Peter Petersen of Brigham City, Swen Johan Nielson of Centerfield, Sören Rasmussen of Draper, James Peter Christensen of Bear River City and Sister Jennie C. Mortensen of Salt Lake City, Utah, and Joseph Christoffersen of Burlington, Wyoming. The company sailed from Esbjerg Aug. 28th.

Another company of emigrating Saints (8 souls) sailed from Christiania, Norway, Oct 12, 1900, bound for Utah, in charge of Hans Henry Pedersen, who was returning from a mission to Norway.

Still another company of emigrants and returning missionaries left Copenhagen Nov. 26, 1900. Following are the names of the missionaries: Rasmus A. Rasmussen of Ferron, Morten Jensen of Richfield, Christian Canutson and Jens Christiansen of Elsinore, Julius C. Andersen of Provo, Charles D. Ahlström of Tropic, Oluf Larson of Randolph, Niels Nielsen of Morgan City, Lars Petersen of Hyrum, Anders Gustaf Lundström of Logan, Olof Rosenlöf of Mt. Pleasant, Utah, and John A. Pearson of Rexburg, Idaho. This company of returning missionaries and emigrants traveled by rail and steamboat to Esbjerg, thence across the North Sea to Grimsby, England, and thence by railroad to Liverpool. Together with other emigrants and returning Elders from the British Isles, the whole company, consisting of 52 souls, including 20 returning Elders, sailed from Liverpool, Nov. 29, 1900, per steamer "Commonwealth." Of returning Elders 7 were from England, 1 from Germany and 12 from Scandinavia. The emigrants consisted of 19 persons from Scandinavia, 7 from England and 6 from Germany.

Besides the Elders mentioned in connection with companies of emi-

grating Saints, the following breth-
ren from Zion, who had labored as
missionaries in Scandinavia, took
their departure, returning home on
the following dates: Erastus L. Otte-
sen, Hyrum J. Hansen and James P.
Olsen, Jan. 11th; Joseph T. Torge-
son, Jan. 12th; Axel L. Holmgren,
Chas. F. J. Carlson, Michael P. Ipson
and Henry F. Fernström, Jan. 25th;
Mads P. Andersen, Jan. 26th; Julius
H. Hansen, Niels L. Anderson and
Chr. Christensen, Feb. 15th; Hans P.
Jensen and Arnt Johnson, Mar. 1st;
Paul P. Christensen and Chr. Olson,
Mar. 5th; Jacob N. Olson, Mar. 8th;
James Jenson, jun., Jacob Christen-
sen, Thos. P. Jensen, Parley Ander-
son, John J. Peterson and Hans C.
Christensen, Apr. 12th; Jens P. Fugal
and Hyrum Jensen, April 15th;
Parley P. Jenson, May 26th;
Lauritz Ed. Larsen, Emil Petter-
borg and Severin Swenson, June
15th; Zacharias W. Israelsen, Noah
L. Pond, Peter Hansen, Torben
J. Torbensen, Chr. Steffensen, Jos.
M. Nielsen, Louis O. Dorius, Ole
Petersen, Severin Nielsen, James C.
Poulsen and Johan P. Mortensen,
June 18th; John H. Quist, Nils Mon-
son, Gustaf Johnson, Jeppa Monson
and Lars P. Nielsen, July 2nd, Chas.
E. Forsberg and Alex. J. Nielson,
July 9th; Albert H. Bergman, Aug.
6th; Albert J. Johnson, Andrew
Petersen, Alex. A. Larsen and Lars
Nielsen, Aug. 13th; Elof Nilson,
Aug. 31st; Erick A. Modeen, An-
drew G. Erickson and Adolph
Bergen, Oct. 15th; Chas. J. E. Boh-
man, Martin Jensen and August Wm.
Ossman, Oct. 22nd; Andrew M.
Anderson, August H. Erickson,
Mathias Erickson, August Mineer and
Chr. Busath, Nov. 19th; Hans K.
Hansen, Nov. 21st; Thorvald S. Jen-
sen, Johan A. Blomquist and Olof
Olson, Dec. 17th.

In 1900, 99 Elders from Zion ar-

rived in Copenhagen, Denmark, as
missionaries to Scandinavia, as fol-
lows: Lars Christoffersen of Salina
and Christian Jacobsen of Ephraim,
Utah, arrived January 2nd; Anders
G. Lundström of Logan, Johannes
Frederik Petersen of Salt Lake City,
Chris N. Christensen of Brigham
City, Utah, and James Peter Chris-
tensen of Preston, Idaho, arrived
Feb. 8th, and Christian Petersen of
Price, Utah, arrived March 13th;
Sven Wm. Nilson of Fairview and
Carl Alfred Carlson of Salt Lake
City, Utah, arrived March 27th;
Louis J. Holther of Ogden, Albert
John Knudson of Provo, Hyrum Al-
fred Christenson of Salt Lake City,
Axel Ferdinand Andreason of Vine-
yard, James P. Fugal of Pleasant
Grove, Utah, and Erastus Skouson of
Alpine, Arizona, arrived April 14th;
Lars Peter Nielsen, James Peter
Johnson and Parley Peterson of Ovid,
Idaho, Joseph Felt and Nils Löf-
gren of Huntsville, Albin Christen-
sen and Joseph A. Halvorsen of Salt
Lake City, Utah, Jarvis Daniel Jen-
sen of Chesterfield, Idaho, and Olof
I. Pedersen of Logan, Utah, arrived
April 27th; John Christensen of
Preston, Idaho, arrived May 1st, and
Willard A. Christopherson of Salt
Lake City, Lars Nielsen of Leam-
ington, Christian Wm. Christoffersen
of Richmond and Frederick Wm.
Christensen of Ephraim, Utah, May
6th; Jens Jensen of Leamington and
Oliver Christiansen (Dalby) of Le-
van, Utah, arrived June 3rd; Anders
Nilson of Franklin, Idaho, Eli J.
Bell of Rexburg, Idaho, Christian F.
Olsen of Hyrum, Carl A. Mattsson of
Salina, Utah, and Jens C. Nielsen
of Rockland, Idaho, arrived July
29th, and Ambrey Nowell and Carl
H. Carlquist of Salt Lake City, Utah,
arrived Aug. 6th; Lorenzo W. Ander-
son of Brigham City, Christian C.
Bindrup, jun., of College Ward, and
Peter L. Quist of Salt Lake City,

Utah, arrived Aug. 12th, and Peter Sundwall, jun., of Fairview, Utah, arrived Aug. 14th; Charles J. Olson of Elsinore, Milton H. Knudsen of Provo, Carl Nielsen of Salt Lake

JUDGE OLIVER C. DALBY

Of Salt Lake City, was born at Levan, Juab Co., Utah, Nov. 11, 1871, the son of Christian Christiansen Dalby and Anna Marie Jensen, early converts in Denmark. On Jan. 1, 1896, Elder Dalby married Frances Francom and was blessed with five children, all still living; filled a mission to Denmark in 1900-1902, laboring in Slagelse, Holbæk and Nykjöbing on Falster, and also presided over the Copenhagen Branch. In 1902 he taught school; served as superintendent of Juab County schools, and principal of Nephi City schools in 1904-1905; moved to Rexburg, Idaho, and became instructor in the Ricks Academy; ordained Bishop of Rexburg First Ward in 1907; served as probate judge in Fremont County one term and as county attorney in Madison County. In 1914 he moved to Brigham City; in 1917 was appointed assistant attorney-general of Utah and served four years; is now a Salt Lake City judge, filling the unexpired term of the late Judge Pratt.

City, Emil Johan Ross Isakson of Peoa, Christian H. Christiansen of Centerfield, Utah, and Peter W. Erikson of Dublan, Mexico, arrived Aug. 26th, and Christian P. Christensen of Richfield arrived Sept. 3rd; Carl Hugo Carlson and Axel Robert Larson of Salt Lake City, Utah, arrived Sept. 9th; Gustaf Waldemar Teudt of Salt Lake City, Joseph Nelson of Mantua, Martin

Luther Lee of Brigham City, Willard R. Skanchy of Logan, Carl Madsen of Riverton and Bengt P. Textorius of Holden, Utah, arrived Sept. 22nd, and Hans O. Young of Park City, Utah, arrived Oct. 17th; Niels C. Rasmussen of Salina, Utah, Johan Hansen Berg of Basalt, Idaho, Andrew P. Christoffersen of Lehi, Ole Emanuel Olsen, jun., of Provo, Nephi M. Nielson and Sören C. Christensen of Levan, Utah, John P. Jensen of St. Charles, Idaho, Albert E. Johnson, James Johnson and Andrew D. Mortensen of Preston, Idaho, Nephi Charles Wahlström of Laketown, Utah, Anthon Frederick Andreason of Eden and Peter Jensen of Para-

A. ROBERT LARSON

Who was born June 23, 1878, at Trollhättan, Elfsborgs län, Sweden, the son of John C. and Alida Hanson, joined the Church in 1892, and emigrated to Salt Lake City the same spring; moved to Sugar House; learned the trade of a blacksmith of his father, and worked as such in Utah and California. He filled a mission to Sweden in 1900-1903, laboring in Norrköping, Jönköping and Göteborg; in 1905 (April 24th) he married Alma Johnson, and moved to Sandy. This marriage was blessed with four children, namely, Golden R., Delmos R., Marvin J., and Iver C. Bro. Larson now acts as second counselor to Bishop James P. Jensen of the Sandy 2nd Ward. He was appointed postmaster by President Wilson and held that position for seven years; was fire chief for ten years; councilman two terms; has been deputy sheriff, city marshal, water superintendent, etc.

dise, Utah, Jens C. Petersen of
Colonia Juarez, Mexico, Gustaf W.
Forsberg of Salt Lake City and
Hyrum J. Hanson of Brigham City,
Utah, arrived Oct 28th; Hans J.
Zobell of Provo, Utah, Hans P. Chris-
tiansen of Moreland, Idaho, Wilford

GUSTAF W. FORSBERG
Born at Horndal, Dalarne, Sweden, Aug. 7,
1879; emigrated to Utah with his father, mother
and two sisters in May, arriving in Salt
Lake, June 24, 1891; was baptized March 2,
1893, by Elder David L. Murdock and was
ordained a High Priest by Pres. Joseph F.
Smith, after having previously been a Deacon,
Priest, Elder and Seventy. In 1900-1903, Bro.
Forsberg filled a mission to Scandinavia, labor-
ing in Eskilstuna, Dalarne, Gefle, Vermland
and Stockholm. He has been superintendent
of the Sunday School in the 22nd Ward, Salt
Lake Stake, and assistant to the late Elder
Osborne J. P. Widtsoe in the Sunday School
Board of that Stake; also second counselor to
Bishop Beesley of the 22nd Ward. Bro. Fors-
berg has also acted as second counselor to
Axel B. C. Ohlson, and as first counselor to
C. O. Johnson in the presidency of the
Swedish L. D. S. meetings in Salt Lake City,
and from 1925 to 1927 was president of said
meetings. He is the father of six children.

Moses Christensen of Goshen, and
Peter W. Nielsen of Logan, Utah, ar-
rived Nov. 12th, and James C. Lar-
sen of Bench, Uintah, Wyoming, ar-
rived Nov. 22nd; Andrew Swensen
of Mt. Pleasant, Emil Anderson, Niels
Chr. Mortensen, jun., and Angus
E. Berlin of Huntsville Andrew A.
Jenson of Herriman, Utah, Jens C.
L. Breinholt of Colonia Juarez,

Mexico, Mikkel C. Stenhus of Pleas-
ant Grove, John Henry Rose of Rich-
ville, Andrew C. Sörensen and Johan
Jensen of Salt Lake City, Peter Chris-
tensen of Elsinore, Erik Olson of
Smithfield, Nils Anthon of Spanish
Fork, Christian Cyrus Larsen of May-
field and Daniel Peter Thuesen of
Provo, Utah, arrived Nov. 27th;
Ernest F. Jörgensen of Draper, Utah,
arrived Dec. 21st, and Martin P.
Thomsen and Ole Anderson of
Grover, Wyoming, Sören P. Neve,
jun., of Salt Lake City, and Abraham
F. Sörenson of Leamington, Utah,
arrived Dec. 24, 1900.

James P. Christensen, Lars P.
Nielsen (2nd mission), James P.
Johnson, Lars Nielsen, Oliver Christiansen (Dalby), Christian F. Olsen
(second mission), Niels C. Rasmussen, Anthon F. Andreason, Wilford
M. Christensen and Andrew C. Sörensen were appointed to labor in the
Copenhagen Conference, Denmark.
Johannes F. Petersen and Hans J.
Zobell were appointed to labor in
the Aarhus and Copenhagen conferences. Lorenzo W. Anderson was
appointed to labor in the Copenhagen Conference, and later appointed to Iceland.

Lars Christoffersen, Christian
Jacobsen, John Christensen, Chr.
Wm. Christoffersen, Christian H.
Christiansen, Sören C. Christensen.
Albert E. Johnson, Andrew D. Mor-
tensen, Hans P. Christiansen, Peter
W. Nielsen, Jens C. L. Breinholt and
Daniel P. Thuesen were appointed to
labor in the Aarhus Conference.
Jens Chr. Petersen was also appoint-
ed to labor in the Aarhus Conference
and later he acted as conference
president.

Chris N. Christensen, Christian
Petersen. Axel F. Andreason, Jens
Chr. Nielsen, Christian P. Christen-
sen, Carl Madsen, Nephi M. Nielson,
James C. Larsen, Mikkel C. Stenhus
and Christian C. Larsen were appoint-

ed to labor in the Aalborg Conference. James Johnson was also appointed to labor in the Aalborg Conference, part of the time as conference president. Jens Jensen was appointed to labor in the Aalborg Conference and later as writer for the "Skandinaviens Stjerne" at the mission office in Copenhagen. Peter Christensen (on a 2nd mission) was appointed to labor in the Aalborg Conference and later presided over the Copenhagen Conference. Joseph Felt, Gustaf W. Teudt, Martin L. Lee, Gustaf W. Forsberg, Erik Olson, Angus E. Berlin and Ole Anderson were appointed to labor in the Stockholm Conference. Carl Alfred Carlson was also appointed to labor in the Stockholm Conference but later called to labor as a writer and translator for "Nordstjernan" at the mission office in Copenhagen. Carl A. Mattsson, Peter W. Erikson, Nephi C. Wahlström and Abraham F. Sörenson were appointed to labor in the Stockholm and afterwards in the Sundsvall conferences. Nils Anthon (on a second mission) and Peter Sundwall, jun., were appointed to labor in the Stockholm Conference. Elder Anthon later acted as conference president.

Sven Wm. Nilson, Emil J. R. Isakson, Bengt P. Textorius and Andrew Peter Christoffersen were appointed to labor in the Skåne Conference. Anders G. Lundström and Emil Anderson were also appointed to labor in the Skåne, but later transferred to the Göteborg Conference, Sweden. Hyrum A. Christenson, Albin Christensen, Anders Nilson, Carl H. Carlquist, Peter L. Quist, Carl H. Carlson, Axel R. Larson, John P. Jensen, Hyrum J. Hanson and John H. Rose were appointed to labor in the Göteborg Conference. Nils Löfgren was also appointed to labor in the Göteborg Conference, and later as conference president.

Louis J. Holther (second mission), Albert J. Knudson, Joseph A. Halvorsen, Olof I. Pedersen, Carl Nielsen, Ole E. Olsen, jun., Andrew Swensen, Johan Jensen, Martin P. Thomsen and Sören P. Neve, jun., were appointed to labor in the Christiania Conference. Willard A. Christophersen and Hans O. Young were also appointed to labor in the Christiania Conference, part of the time as conference presidents.

Joseph Nelson, Johan H. Berg, Andrew A. Jenson, Niels Chr. Mortensen, jun., and Ernest F. Jörgensen were appointed to labor in the Bergen Conference. Peter Jensen was also appointed to labor in the Bergen Conference; he afterwards became conference president. James P. Fugal was appointed to labor in the Bergen and later in the Aalborg Conference, Denmark. Erastus Skouson was appointed to labor in the Bergen and later in the Aarhus Conference. Frederick Wm. Christensen was appointed to labor in the Bergen and later in the Christiania Conference. Eli J. Bell was appointed to labor in the Bergen Conference and later in the Copenhagen Conference, Denmark.

Jarvis D. Jensen, Ambrey Nowell. Charles J. Olson and Milton H. Knudsen were appointed to labor in the Trondhjem Conference. Parley Peterson and Chr. C. Bindrup, jun., were appointed to labor in the Trondhjem and later in the Aalborg Conference. Willard R. Skanchy was appointed to labor in the Trondhjem, and later in the Christiania Conference.

At the close of the century (Dec. 31, 1900) the Scandinavian Mission consisted of 60 organized branches grouped into nine conferences. Of these conferences, 3 (Copenhagen, Aarhus and Aalborg) were in Denmark, 3 (Stockholm, Göteborg and Skåne) in Sweden and 3 (Christiania,

Bergen and Trondhjem) in Norway. Of Elders from Zion there were 165. The local membership of the mission was 4,535, including 268 Elder, 163 Priests, 143 Teachers and 71 Deacons.

CHAPTER 85 (1901)

The new century presents changed conditions in missionary work—Arrival and departure of missionaries.

During the year 1901 the Elders from Zion continued their labors as faithful messengers of the truth to the people in Scandinavia, but conditions had changed very materially since the mission was commenced, fifty years before. Though Elders from Zion first introduced the gospel into Scandinavia, it was not long before a number of intelligent, local brethren among the newly-made converts were ordained to the Priesthood and sent out to preach in different localities. Under their faithful labors, the mission soon became successful and many branches of the Church were raised up. In due course of time, some of these local Elders (many of whom spent from three to ten years in the missionary field) emigrated to Zion, and, after receiving their blessings at the headquarters of the Church, they were sent back to their native lands to continue their missionary labors. This infused additional life and activity in the three Scandinavian countries, and a flourishing period lasting a number of years was realized, during which thousands of new converts were made. These in due course of time emigrated to the gathering places of the Saints in America, in large organized companies. But as the Elders from Zion increased in numbers in the mission, the native Elders became less numerous, and at the beginning of the new century the Elders from Zion were doing nearly all the missionary work, while only a very few of the local Elders (that is, those who had never been in America) were engaged in missionary labors. Many of the American Elders were either sons or grandsons of the earlier missionaries who had embraced the gospel in Scandinavia, and had emigrated to Zion, where they had raised their families. Though the majority of the young Elders from America, who labored in Scandinavia at the beginning of the century, were born of Scandinavian parents in America, most of them were unable to speak the languages of Sweden, Denmark and Norway, and during the first year or so of their missionary activities they were capable of doing but very little except studying languages, and when they finally, somewhat prepared, commenced missionary work in earnest, they were still unacquainted with the customs and habits of the people, and were in many instances unable to approach them in the effectual way that their sires had done; in several cases they even failed to understand or appreciate the characteristics of the people among whom they were laboring. On the other hand, the natives were at a loss in many instances to understand the young men with their American training and methods of procedure. The consequence of all this was that the progress of the work was not what it had been in earlier days; nor were the number of people baptized up to the record made, for instance, during the sixties.

Another thing, which somewhat curtailed the Elders in their operations in the beginning of the new century, was the great change which had taken place among the people in Scandinavia regarding hospitality. In earlier days it was quite possible for the Elders to travel almost without purse or scrip, especially the Elders from Zion, who as a rule were made welcome in the homes of the peasants, many of whom were glad to entertain men who had traveled or who had had unusual experience in foreign lands. Such men were almost everywhere treated to the best the peasantry had in the shape of lodgings and meals, and very seldom were these Elders requested to pay for entertainments. In 1901, it was quite different; many visitors from America and other countries had taught the Scandinavian people that they might just as well receive pay for what they spent on travelers, as to keep them gratis, and the Elders were therefore often treated the same as regular tourists, except among their own co-religionists, or friends and investigators.

At the beginning of the new century, the first thing an Elder did after his arrival in the mission field was usually to secure a place of lodging, and make arrangements for having regular meals. Besides, there were only a few Saints left in the mission who were able to extend hospitality to the Elders, as the more well-to-do converts had long ago emigrated to Zion.

But notwithstanding all this the statistical reports of the mission continued to show a gradual increase to the Church in baptisms, and the Elders were not discouraged. If they did not succeed in making many converts or in baptizing great numbers, like their predecessors, their missionary training and experiences were of great benefit to themselves, and their testimonies in regard to the truth of the restored gospel and the divinity of the mission of Joseph Smith were continually made stronger. Most of the old branches of the Church (some of which dated back almost to the beginning of the mission) were kept alive, and halls were rented in the principal cities of all three Scandinavian countries, while

numerous cottage meetings were held in the country districts.

In 1901, 57 Elders from Zion arrived in Copenhagen, Denmark, to labor as missionaries in Scandinavia, as follows: John L. Christiansen of Logan, and Peter G. Lundell of Benjamin, Utah, arrived Feb. 12th; John N. Erickson of Mt. Pleasant, Jacob S. Bastian of Loa and Charles O. Larson of Fairview, Utah, arrived Feb. 25th; Julius B. Christensen of Manti, Hans C. Larsen of Mayfield, James M. Peterson of Richfield, and Hans Hansen of Manila Ward, Utah, arrived March 25th; Christian D. Fjeldsted and Anthon L. Skanchy of Logan, and Rasmus Rasmussen of Wellsville, Utah, arrived April 22nd; Peter C. Sörensen and Frederick N. Christiansen of Ephraim, Christian N. Christensen of Castle Gate, and James M. Peterson of Castle Dale, Octavius F. Gudmundson of Springville, Rudolph A. Christensen of Bear River City, Victor E. Johnson of Richmond, Joseph H. Jensen of Monroe and Rasmus Rasmussen of Logan, Utah, arrived May 5th, and Hans R. Hansen of Loa, Hyrum B. Madsen of Ephraim, and Frederik Hansen of Bear River City, Utah, arrived May 20th; David A. Thomsen of Ephraim and Andreas E. Anderson of Murray, Utah, and Niels L. Larson of Afton, Wyoming, arrived June 3rd; Alexander Elquist of Grantsville, and Jörgen S. Jörgensen of Ephraim, Utah, arrived June 17th; Sören Anderson and James S. Jensen of Centerfield, James Monsen of Mt. Pleasant, Andrew L. Thorpe of Ephraim, Charles Olson of Millville, and Christian M. Nikolaisen of Bear River City, Utah, arrived June 30th; Hans Peter Poulsen of Plain City and Arthur Halverson of Marriott, Utah, arrived July 16th; Arvid E. Anderson of West Weber, Utah, arrived Aug.

25

27th; Gustave A. Mossberg of Salt Lake City, and George W. Okerlund of Loa, Utah, arrived Sept. 21st; Carl E. Johnson of Salina, Winfred A. Fjeldsted of Centerfield, Ole Olson of Lewiston, Utah, and Nelson J. Hemmert of Thayne, Wyoming, arrived Oct. 20th; Ezra P. Jensen and Frederick G. Nielsen of Brigham City, Ola Hansen of Bear River City, Utah, Heber Hansen and Julia T. Hansen, his wife, of Freedom, Wyo., arrived Nov. 3rd; Walter Hazen Eardley of Salt Lake City, arrived Nov. 15th; Hans P. Bergen and Levi S. Andersen of Brigham City, and Peter Alma Westmann of Richfield, Utah, arrived Nov. 18th; James C. Jensen of Spanish Fork, Christian Hansen, jun., of Deweyville, Lars P. Nielsen of Brigham City, Utah, and Adolph S. Jensen of Afton, Star Valley, Wyoming, arrived Dec. 17th.

John L. Christiansen, Octavius F. Gudmundson, Nelson J. Hemmert, Heber Hansen, Julia T. Hansen and W. Hazen Eardley were appointed to labor in the Christiania Conference. Peter G. Lundell, Rudolph A. Christensen, Victor E. Johnson, Joseph H. Jensen, Andreas E. Anderson, Arvid E. Anderson, George W. Okerlund, Carl E. Johnson, Hans P. Bergen and Levi S. Andersen were appointed to labor in the Stockholm Conference. John N. Erickson, Charles Olson and Adolph S. Jensen were appointed to labor in the Skåne Conference. Jacob S. Bastian, Julius B. Christensen, Rasmus Rasmussen, David A. Thomsen, Andrew L. Thorpe, Christian M. Nikolaisen, Frederick G. Nielsen and James C. Jensen were appointed to labor in the Copenhagen Conference. Charles O. Larson, Hans C. Larsen, James M. Peterson, Rasmus Rasmussen, Fred. N. Christiansen, James Monsen, Arthur Halverson, Ezra P. Jensen and Ola Hansen were appointed

to labor in the Trondhjem Conference. Hans Hansen, Christian N. Christensen, Hans R. Hansen, Jörgen S. Jörgensen, and James S. Jensen were appointed to labor in the Aarhus Conference. Peter C. Sörensen, James M. Peterson, Hyrum B. Madsen, Winfred A. Fjeldsted and Lars P. Nielsen were appointed to labor in the Aalborg Conference. Frederik Hansen, Sören Anderson and Hans Peter Poulsen were appointed to labor in the Bergen Conference. Niels L. Larson, Alexander Elquist, Gustave A. Mossberg, Ole Olson, Peter A. Westmann and Christian Hansen, jun., were appointed to labor in the Göteborg Conference.

Anthon L. Skanchy succeeded Andreas Peterson as president of the Scandinavian Mission April 29, 1901, when Elder Peterson, in company with Charles L. Anderson, jun., left Copenhagen to make a visit to the Orient, including Palestine. Elder Peterson had presided over the mission since October, 1898, and his administration had throughout been crowned with success.

During the year 1901, Apostle Francis M. Lyman, president of the European Mission, visited Scandinavia. He attended conferences in Aarhus, Aalborg, Copenhagen, Malmö, Göteborg, Christiania, Bergen, Trondhjem and Stockholm, in the order named, and gave fatherly instructions to the Elders, besides preaching spirited gospel sermons to both Saints and strangers, with the assistance of translators.

During the year Christian D. Fjeldsted, one of the seven presidents of Seventies, also visited Scandinavia, for the purpose of assisting President Anthon L. Skanchy in purchasing real estate in Copenhagen, on which the Church could erect a mission office and assembly hall. Property at No. 11 Korsgade was secured in that part of Copenhagen known as Nörrebro.

CHAPTER 86 (1902)

Visit of President Francis M. Lyman—Dedication of a mission home in Copenhagen—Andrew Jenson's special mission—A new edition of the Book of Mormon—Discussion with Lutheran priests at Nykjöbing on Falster—More Elders arrive.

The year 1902 will always be known as the season in which the Scandinavian Mission secured a home owned by the Church, and a hall in which meetings and Sunday schools could be held, without renting from outsiders as heretofore. The dedication of the new mission house at Korsgade No. 11, Nörrebro, Copenhagen, Denmark, took place on Friday, July 4, 1902. One hundred and twenty-two Elders from Zion attended the dedicatory services, among whom were Apostle Francis M. Lyman, president of the European

APOSTLE FRANCIS MARION LYMAN
Was born Jan. 12, 1840, at Goodhope, McDonough Co., Ill., the son of Amasa M. Lyman and Louisa Maria Tanner. He died in Salt Lake City, Nov. 18, 1916.

Mission, Christian D. Fjeldsted, of the Council of Seventies, Anthon L. Skanchy, president of the Scandinavian Mission, Andrew Jenson, on a special mission to Scandinavia, Hugh J. Cannon, president of the German Mission, and Levi Edgar

Young, president of the Swiss Mission. Besides the many Elders laboring in the different conferences of the Scandinavian Mission, there were present also several missionaries from the German Mission. Never before in the history of the Scandinavian Mission had so many Elders from Zion been together in the lands of the North.

President Anthon L. Skanchy presided in the dedicatory meeting. The well-trained Copenhagen Branch choir, under the direction of Carl H. Löhdefinck, rendered excellent musical numbers. Pres. Skanchy gave a short history of the erection of the building. Pres. Lyman offered the dedicatory prayer and Elder Andrew Jenson delivered a speech appropriate for the occasion. During the two following days, Saturday and Sunday, July 5th and 6th, Priesthood meetings and well-attended and spirited public meetings were held in the new hall, at which Presidents Lyman and Fjeldsted and many others gave timely instructions and preached the gospel with power. Elder Andrew Jenson acted as translator for the English-speaking brethren.

The new mission house consists of a fine three-story building, erected in Gothic style, with a touch of American architecture in some of its details. The outside walls are thick and solid, built of burned brick, while some of the less important partition walls consist of lumber and plastering on wires. The timber or woodwork used for floors and woodwork in general is principally good and well-seasoned Swedish lumber. The painting and finishing was done by some of the best mechanics in Copenhagen. The roof is covered with Bornholm slate. The main building is about 80 feet long and 45 feet wide, outside measurement. In the basement there are, besides corridors, a kitchen, with two pantries, a dining room, two store-rooms and a baptismal font surrounded by

Headquarters of the Scandinavian Mission from 1857 to 1902. No. 14, Loventzensgade (later St. Paulsgade), Copenhagen, Denmark.

the whole upper story; it measures about 75 feet in length, about 40 feet in width, and is about 24 feet high from floor to ceiling. On the stand, which is build in the northwest end of the hall, there is room for the acting Priesthood and the choir. In the gallery, which is built on the opposite end of the hall, there is room for 75 people. Altogether the hall has a seating capacity for 500 persons, and in case of necessity, at least 700 people could be accommodated in the assembly hall. A winding stairway leads up from the floor below to the rear of the stand. The two side buildings, each of which

Headquarters of the Scandinavian Mission since 1902. No. 11 Korsgade, Nörrebro, Copenhagen, Denmark.

brass railings, two dressing-rooms (one for gentlemen and one for ladies), and a furnace-room in which a fine, modern furnace was built sufficient to give heat to the two lower stories. "Stuen," or the second or main floor, contains: (a) A smaller assembly hall 20x40 feet, which is used for Priesthood meetings and smaller gatherings. (b) Three larger rooms which are used respectively by the mission president, the writers for "Skandinaviens Stjerne" and "Nordstjernan," and for the president of the Copenhagen Conference. (c) Four bedrooms.

The large assembly room occupies

ANTON LORENTZEN SKANCHY

Born Sept. 17, 1839, at Trondhjem, Norway; was baptized Jan. 16, 1861, by T. Tönnessen; labored as a missionary in Norway about five years most successfully, part of the time in the Norwegian provinces beyond the Arctic circle, and part of the time as president of the Christiania Branch. Elder Skanchy subsequently filled three important missions to Scandinavia, one in 1879-1881, another in 1886-1889, and still another in 1901-1904. On the last mission he presided over the Scandinavian Mission and superintended the erection of a mission home and meeting hall in the city of Copenhagen, Denmark, in 1902. Elder Skanchy died April 19, 1914, in Logan, Cache County, Utah. For several years he had acted as Bishop of the Sixth Ward of Logan.

is 16x20 feet, are used exclusively for stairways. These are artistically and solidly built and easy to ascend. The railings do, as to excellence of workmanship and taste, compare favorably with any of the kind in the city of Copenhagen. The builder, Mr. E. Lytthaus Petersen, ranked as one of the best builders and contractors in the country. President Anthon L. Skanchy, who had had many years' experience as a builder and contractor in Utah, was the architect of the building, the erection of which cost about 50,000 kroner. The sum of 60,000 kroner was paid for the ground which was partly occupied by some old tenement houses, but with room enough in the rear to erect the mission house away from the street.

Elder Andrew Jenson, being called on a special mission to Scandinavia to assist in publishing a new edition of the Book of Mormon in the Danish language, arrived in Copenhagen May 31, 1902. Soon after his arrival, he, together with Chr. D. Fjeldsted, hired a room in the 5th story of St. Paulsgade No. 5, in which they immediately commenced their labors in connection with the revision, printing and publishing of the Book of Mormon, Elder Fjeldsted assisting in the proof-reading. An edition of 3000 copies was printed. The first sheets of the same were published in June, 1902

During their sojourn in Scandinavia, Elders Fjeldsted and Jenson visited a number of the conferences in the mission and did considerable preaching, both to Saints and strangers, with apparent good effects.

In September, 1902, Elder Jenson was requested to visit Nykjöbing on Falster to attend a special meeting at which opposition had been planned on the part of the Lutheran clergy. Among those who on that occasion came to oppose the work of the Lord

was the Rev. Leyenbak, Bishop of the Lolland-Falster diocese, a Pastor Kemp of Nykjöbing and a Pastor Bryant of Voggerlöse. The Elders who labored in that part of Denmark had been made to understand that they would be permitted to conduct the meetings as they liked, and occupy the time in presenting doctrines taught by Latter-day Saints, but they soon learned that the local Lutheran priests were to have entire control with the intention of giving the "Mormons" a sound thrashing, if possible, and subject them to such humiliation that they would be ashamed to show their faces again in Nykjöbing. Before the exercises began, the bishop, in a stentorian voice, and with much assumed dignity, remarked that no singing or praying would be permitted, as they (the Lutherans) could not condescend to worship together with "Mormons." Then Pastor Kemp opened the ball by speaking half an hour in a most bitter and abusive strain, in which he recounted some of the blackest and most abusive lies found in anti-Mormon literature, and he also endeavored by twists and turns to make some of the doctrines of the Latter-day Saints appear ridiculous to the minds of the people. Elder Jenson, who was permitted to reply, writes:

"I realized that the people had been much worked up in their feelings by listening to what Pastor Kemp had said and that giving us a fair hearing was not a part of the program. But feeling confident that the Lord would not desert us, I mounted the platform and commenced my speech about as follows: 'My honored countrymen, ladies and gentlemen. Though I am a son of Denmark, I realize that I stand among you here as a stranger in a strange land, as I have been a resident of America for many years, but, believing that the chivalry and fairness which characterized our forefathers in past ages has been transmitted to their children, I appeal to you, the intelligent citizens of Nykjöbing, to listen attentively to what

I have to say. I may not possess such unlimited knowledge of the 'Mormon' people, and their doctrines and history, as the pastor who has preceded me, judging from his bold assertions, but it is nevertheless a fact that I have spent 36 years among the 'Mormons' in Utah; that I have visited every nook and corner of the land which they occupy, and that I have spent 25 years of my life in studying and writing the history of the 'Mormons'; and while these facts may not, with some people, weigh much against the statements made, yet they are certainly worthy of your consideration.'

"The effects of these few remarks were more than I expected. The people at once seemed deeply impressed and settled down to listen as quietly as any congregation I have ever addressed, while I talked to them about an hour concerning the history of the Latter-day Saints, the true character of Joseph Smith, the doctrines of the Church, and the general character of the message we declare to the world, and also of the fruits of 'Mormonism.' With the exception of one of the priests (Mr. Brandt), who jumped about like a madman, talking to the bishop and his brother priests and making notes, not a soul made the least sign of uneasiness while I spoke. When I was through, I gave the people an opportunity to ask questions. A couple of such were propounded, which I answered, and, there being no more, I stepped down from the platform.

"The bishop, an elderly man with a clean-shaven face, then arose and began to murmur something about blasphemy, and proceeded to relate something about having attended a Mormon meeting many years before, in which something was said about healing the sick by the power of God. Before a fair-minded American audience, the bishop would have become an object of ridicule for relating such silly stuff; as it was, his remarks did not find general favor with the people, and so the great Reverend, the highest ecclesiastical authority of the Lutheran Church on the islands of Lolland-Falster, withdrew, as he seemingly felt ashamed of himself.

"Pastor Brandt next mounted the rostrum and began reading from his notes, but while doing so he shook like an aspen leaf with wrath and nervous excitement, and twice as he appealed to me to sanction certain things which he said, I had the opportunity of assuring the people that he had no knowledge whatsoever of the subjects he was talking about. He certainly made a most miserable failure of his attempt to expose us, and so Pastor Kemp, who had made the opening speech stepped forward to discuss some of the points he had forgotten before.

"When he was through, I stepped forward to make answer, but a Mr. Larsen asked for the floor and in his remarks he objected to 'Mormonism' because he said it was based upon licentiousness and because negroes were not admitted into the Mormon Church.

"It now became my turn to speak a second time, and it turned out to be the closing speech of the meeting, though such an ending was certainly not intended by our opponents. But after I had answered the questions last propounded, I was prompted to close by saying that I now would submit the case as it had been presented by my four opponents and myself to the people, so that they might have an opportunity to judge for themselves. The little trick succeeded, for when I sat down the people arose before the presiding pastor could give them a parting shot and quitely left the building while they were still under my influence.

"Several gentlemen present then gathered around me and congratulated me on my success and said that, while they did not endorse the Mormon religion, they were immensely pleased with the answers I had given to the questions propounded, as well as my entire lecture. The Elders left the hall well pleased with the outcome, considering that it was not our meeting, but that we were, throughout the entire proceedings, at the mercy of our opponents."

Before leaving Scandinavia, on this special mission, Elder Jenson gave two illustrated lectures on "Mormon" history. When he left Copenhagen for England, Dec. 11, 1902, he wrote:

"This being the 52nd anniversary of my birthday, I received several congratulations by mail and otherwise from friends, and also visited a number of Saints to say good-bye, and finally paid my last visit to the heart of Copenhagen. During the day I received a number of presents, among which a copy of the new Danish edition of the Book of Mormon. It certainly is a fine book, undoubtedly the best printed and most carefully prepared of any of our Church works ever published in the Scandinavian Mission. I thank the Lord that my mission has been a success. I also feel thankful indeed that the Lord has blessed my humble efforts so that I have gained the hearts of those who have listened to my testimony, as I have done a great deal of preaching since I first arrived in Copenhagen, and have rejoiced at being able to present the gospel of Christ by the power and demonstration of the Holy Spirit. I shall never forget the good time I have had while on this mission, and the many good people I have learned to love and who in turn seem to have become attached to me.

"About 7 o'clock p. m. I took leave of the mission house and Brother Fjeldsted; the rest of the personnel of the office accompanied me to the railway station, where nearly half of the members of the Copenhagen Branch had gathered to see me off. What an outburst of good and tender feelings! The sisters almost covered me with flowers, gave me sweets and fruits to carry away with me and placed portraits and presents into my hands as they said goodbye. I have scarcely before been the object of so much attention and good feelings in taking leave of a group of Saints and friends. I could scarcely satisfy their handshaking propensities. Again and again, some of them would press my hand, saying some words which they had previously forgotten. At last the train pulled out, and the last I saw of the Elders and Saints was their hands waving hats and handkerchiefs."

In 1902, 83 Elders from Zion arrived in Copenhagen, Denmark, as missionaries to Scandinavia, as follows: Niels L. Monson of Manila, Stephen A. Christensen of Levan, and Jens C. Jensen of Provo Bench, Utah, arrived Jan. 30th; Moroni K. Petersen and Ole Sonne of Logan, Arthur H. Sconberg of Salt Lake City, Hyrum A. Anderson of Lehi, Joseph B. Jeppesen of Mantua, Utah, Charles P. Swensen of Blackfoot, Idaho, Sören Oluf Thompson of Hyrum, Julius Christensen of Moroni, Alfred Johnson of Fountain Green, and Niels Larsen of Vineyard, Utah, arrived Feb. 18th; Arthur W. Morrison of Richfield, Joseph H. Olsen of College, and Brigham Nielsen of Perry, Utah, arrived March 21st; Carl G. Youngberg of Lyman, Wyoming, Hyrum Selander and

Carl A. Schurler of Salt Lake City, Utah, arrived March 31st; Gustave A. Anderson of Providence, Charles G. Johnson of Lindon, David

ALFRED JOHNSON

Was born in Hamnared parish, Halland, Sweden. Dec. 17, 1857. In 1878, he went to Aalborg, Denmark; was baptized in the spring of 1880; labored as a local missionary in 1882 and 1883, in the Aalborg Conference, and emigrated to Utah in 1883. On Aug. 29, 1885, he married Mette Marie Jensen (a widow with two children), by whom he had three children; the youngest of these, Ernest J. Johnson, is now (1927) Bishop of the Fountain Green Ward, Sanpete Co. Elder Alfred Johnson filled a mission to Sweden in 1902-1903 and labored in the Skåne Conference. He is now (1927) a High Priest and counselor in the locale Scandinavian organization.

Lee of Farr West, Utah, and Charles W. Larsen of Salem, Idaho, arrived April 22nd; Niels Erickson of Salem, Clarence S. Nelson of Ogden, Peter M. Jensen of Huntsville, and Frederick E. Mitchell of Clinton, Utah, arrived May 5th, and Alma G. Jacobson of Logan and Niels A. Thomson of Ephraim, Utah, on May 18th; Christian D. Fjeldsted of Logan, Andrew Jenson of Salt Lake City and Hans O. Young of Park City, Utah, arrived May 31st; Elias S. Larsen of Cove, and Niels

J. Nelson of Brigham City, Utah, arrived June 16th, and Martin W. Mangelsen of Levan, Utah, arrived July 14th; Finn H. Berg of Ammon,

ARTHUR WILLIAM MORRISON

Born at Richfield, Utah, March 21, 1881, the son of William Morrison and Anna Maria Hanson, was baptized by Elder William G. C. Morrison, April 1, 1889. In 1902-1904, he filled a mission to Sweden, laboring first in Eskilstuna, then in Gefle, for one year, the last six months as president of the branch; later he presided over the Gotland Branch for six months, and completed his mission in the Eskilstuna Branch. On Nov. 9, 1904, he married Esther E. Elggren in the Salt Lake Temple, and have had the following children: Arthur Wendell, Adrian Lorenzo (deceased), Frances Elggren, Clarence Wilbur, Geneveve Esther, Anna Marie, Frederick William, Marjorie Ruth, Reed Elggren, and Charles Grant (the last two twins). Bro. Morrison, after laboring in various quorums of the Priesthood, was ordained a High Priest and Bishop, Jan. 17, 1920, by Apostle George F. Richards, and set apart to preside over the Stockton Ward as its first Bishop. He was a member of the 14th State Legislature of Utah in 1921 from Tooele, and is at present (1927) a member of the Belvedere Ward, Salt Lake City.

Idaho, Niels P. Nielsen, jun., of Logan, Joseph Mortensen and James Peter Olsen of Brigham City, Utah, Christen Jensen of Mesquite, Nevada, Niels C. Thompson of St. Johns, Arizona, and Lorentz Pehrson of West Jordan, Utah. arrived July 15th, and Joseph W. Poulsen of

Richfield, Utah, on July 27th; Adam L. Petersen of Huntsville, Oluff Petersen of Brigham City, Otto J. Poulsen of Timpanogos, Andrew Iverson of Salem and Joachim C. Anderson of Moroni, Utah, arrived August 16th, and William Martinson of Grant, Idaho, and Gustaf Leonard Ohlson of Sandy, Utah, arrived Aug. 25th; Waldemar Jensen of Goshen, Utah, arrived Sept. 20th; Emanuel Martin Olsen of West Jordan and Niels Peter Sörensen of Moroni, Utah, arrived Oct. 4th; Jens Chr. Westergaard of Baker City, Oregon, Peter J. Nordquist of Ogden, and John Peter Johnson of Spring City, Utah, arrived Oct. 20th; Hans

JOSEPH HENRY OLSEN

The third Bishop of College Ward, Cache Co., Utah, was born at Brigham City, Utah, Oct. 13, 1867, the son of Jens Olsen and Marie Petersen, and baptized in August, 1876. He married Else Jensen of Logan, Nov. 4, 1896; they have ten children, nine of whom are living. In 1902-1904, he filled a mission to Denmark, laboring for 21 months in the Aarhus Conference and presiding for nine months over the Randers Branch. He was later transferred to the Aalborg Conference. In May, 1905, Bro. Olsen was ordained a High Priest and set apart as second counselor to Bishop C. O. Dunn of the College Ward, Cache Co., Utah, and on July 20, 1918, he was set apart as Bishop of the College Ward, which position he still (1927) holds. He has also served as school trustee, and as deputy assessor of Cache County; in 1922 he was elected county commissioner.

. Christiansen of Logan, Joel Milton Poulsen of Richfield, Peter L. Anderson of Mt. Pleasant, Joseph F. Quist, John M. Thorup, George A. Knudsen, Alma E. Rasmussen and Axel L.

GUSTAV L. OHLSON

Son of Anders Erick Ohlson and Johanna Elisabeth Larson, was born Sept. 28, 1875, at Sjöholm, Sorunda, Sweden; was baptized April 4, 1890, by Niels Anthon. Emigrating to Utah, he arrived in Salt Lake City, July 1, 1893, and located in Sandy. He filled a mission to Sweden in 1902-1904, laboring in Eskilstuna, and presided in Stockholm. Returning home, he took charge of a company of Saints (33 souls) from Liverpool, arriving in Salt Lake City, Nov. 20th. In 1905 (Jan 11th), he married Esther Elleonora Södergren; they had five children: Elis Leonard, Alice Elleonora, Gordon Gustave, Martin Rudolf and Sylvia Katrina; two (Alice and Gordon) are still living. Elder Ohson has been active in. Church work; he has also served as councilman in Sandy, been a member of the various quorums of the Priesthood and was ordained a Seventy, Nov. 16, 1919, by James P. Jensen.

Fikstad of Salt Lake City, Alfred B. Helquist of Koosharem, Amer E. Hansen of Brigham City, Niels P. Andersen of Elsinore, Utah, and John T. Johnson of Weston, Idaho, arrived Nov. 1st; Joseph Ulrich Peterson of Salt Lake City, John Ephraim Swenson of Murray, Anders Anderson of Huntsville, Henry E. Heilesen of Glenwood, Niels Peter Jeppesen, jun., of Mantua, Otto J. Monson of Richmond. Utah, Lars

Peter Christensen of Preston, and Hans Rasmussen of Mink Creek, Idaho, arrived November 17th; Ole H. Anderson of Hyrum, Lars P. Larsen of Cleveland, Franklin O. Hales of Milburn, Don C. Sörensen of Ephraim, James C. Johnson of Logan, Hans J. Hansen of Richfield, Utah, and Oluf E. Anderson of Salem, Idaho, arrived Dec. 16th. Niels L. Monson, Sören O. Thompson and Alfred Johnson were appointed to labor in the Skåne Con-

JENS CHRISTENSEN WESTERGAARD

The son of Christen Jensen Thulstrup and Karen Jensen Westergaard, was born at Lee, Viborg amt, Denmark, March 4, 1858, and baptized in Copenhagen in 1886. He began military training at the age of 18, was discharged two years later as a corporal; became a coachman for the Honorable Estrup, premier and minister of finance of Denmark. Later he became manager of Clausholm, and lived the last four years before he emigrated at Halling, between Aarhus and Randers. He joined the Church and emigrated to Utah in 1886. For 15 years he was car inspector and air-brake expert for the Southern Pacific Railroad. Bro. Westergaard filled a mission to Denmark and Norway in 1902-1904, laboring in Bergen, Stavanger and Haugesund, Norway, one year, and later in Aarhus and Randers, Denmark. In Viborg, Denmark, he found records of ancestors and relatives in the archives back to the year 1613. After his return from this mission, Elder Westergaard presided for several years over the branch of the Church at Portland, Oregon, a position he had held for some time previous to going to Scandinavia, he being the first president of the Portland Branch. Bro. Westergaard is still a resident of Portland.

ference. Stephen A. Christensen, Clarence S. Nelson, Frederick E. Mitchell, Niels J. Nelson, Oluff Petersen, Waldemar Jensen, Lars Peter Christensen and Don C. Sörensen were appointed to labor in the Aalborg Conference. James Peter Olsen, Peter L. Anderson, Alfred B. Helquist and Joseph U. Peterson were appointed to labor in the Sundsvall Conference. Jens C. Jensen, Joseph H. Olsen, Brigham Nielsen, David Lee, Niels Erickson, Joseph W. Poulsen, Adam L. Petersen, Niels P. Sörensen, Niels P.

JAMES C. JOHNSON

The son of Mr. and Mrs. Christian Johansen Degnsgaard, was born at Höjslev, Viborg amt, Denmark, Sept. 16, 1853; joined the Church by baptism, June 10, 1875, and emigrated the same year, crossing the Atlantic in the steamship "Idaho." He filled a mission to Denmark in 1902-1904, laboring in the Aarhus Conference, and is now (1927) a resident of Logan, Utah.

Andersen, Henry E. Heilesen and James C. Johnson were appointed to labor in the Aarhus Conference.

Moroni K. Petersen, Hyrum A. Anderson, Elias S. Larsen, George A. Knudsen and Hans J. Hansen were appointed to labor in the

Trondhjem Conference. Arthur H. Sconberg, Arthur W. Morrison, Hyrum Selander, Carl A. Schurler, Alma G. Jacobson, Gustaf L. Ohlson, Emanuel M. Olsen, Peter J. Nordquist, Joseph F. Quist, Franklin O. Hales and Oluf E. Anderson were appointed to labor in the Stockholm Conference.

Joseph B. Jeppesen, Niels Larsen, Martin W. Mangelsen, Christen Jensen, Niels C. Thompson, Jens Chr. Westergaard, Amer E. Hansen, Axel L. Fikstad, Niels Peter Jeppesen, jun., and Otto J. Monson were appointed to labor in the Bergen Conference. Charles P. Swensen, Carl G. Youngberg, Charles G. Johnson, Otto J. Poulsen and John Peter Johnson were appointed to labor in the Göteborg Conference. Ole Sonne, Julius Christensen, Charles W. Larsen, Finn H. Berg, Niels P. Nielsen, jun., Joseph Mortensen, Andrew Iverson, John M. Thorup, John Ephraim Swenson and Hans O. Young were appointed to labor in the Christiania Conference.

Gustave A. Anderson, Lorentz Pehrson, William Martinson and John T. Johnson were appointed to labor in the Skåne Conference. Peter M. Jensen, Joachim C. Anderson, Hans J. Christiansen, Niels A. Thomson, Joel M. Poulsen, Alma E. Rasmussen, Anders Anderson, Hans Rasmussen, Ole H. Anderson and Lars P. Larsen were appointed to labor in the Copenhagen Conference.

CHAPTER 87 (1903)

Erection and dedication of a new mission home in Christiania, Norway—A large gathering of Utah people—More Elders arrive from America.

The mission house which was erected in Christiania, Norway, in 1871, served the purpose for which it was erected for many years, but at length the ground upon which it stood seemed to give way and the building became unsafe; hence, it was taken down in 1902 and a new Latter-day Saint meeting house erected on the same ground in 1903. This house was dedicated July 24,

The new conference house in Christiania, built and dedicated in 1903.

1903, on which occasion 159 Elders and visitors from Zion were present, including Apostles Francis M. Lyman, president of the European Mission, Chr. D. Fjeldsted of the Seventies, Anthon L. Skanchy, president of the Scandinavina Mission, Willard T. Cannon, president of the Netherlands Mission, and Levi Edgar Young, president of the Swiss Mission. Besides nearly all the missionaries from Zion laboring in the Scandinavian Mission, 18 Elders were present from the German Mission, 16 from the British Mission, 1 from the Netherlands Mission, and 21 visitors from Utah.

As early as Wednesday, July 22nd, the Elders and other visitors began to arrive from different parts of the country, and on Thursday evening, July 23rd, the Christiania Branch choir, consisting of 52 members, gave a most successful concert. President Anthon L. Skanchy made a neat little speech, in which he explained that the Church had appropriated 18,500 kroner towards the erection of the new mission house and that the Norwegian Saints, both in Zion and in Norway, had donated freely towards the erection of the new building. Prof. Evan Stephens of Salt Lake City, the leader of the Tabernacle Choir, bore the expenses of the beautiful decorations in the hall. Apostle Francis M. Lyman offered the dedicatory prayer. A number of telegrams of congratulations were read, among which was a cablegram signed by Pres. Anthon H. Lund, Assistant Historian Andrew Jenson and Patriarch C. C. A. Christensen at Salt Lake City.

A general conference was held in connection with the dedication of the meeting house on the following Saturday and Sunday, July 25th and 26th. A number of interesting Priesthood meetings were also held.

In 1903, 106 Elders from Zion arrived in Copenhagen, Denmark, as missionaries to Scandinavia, as follows: Joseph E. Jörgensen of Vernon, John V. Johnson of Lindon, Peter C. Carlston of Fairview, Utah, Louis E. Johnson of Snowflake, Hans Hansen, jun., of Pinetop, Arizona, and Oley Oleson of Hooper, Utah, arrived Jan. 7th, and Christian Olsen, jun., of Elwood, Utah, arrived Jan. 13th; David R. Wheelwright of Brigham City and Niels Sandberg, jun., of St. George, Utah, arrived Feb. 26th; William E. Racker of Lehi, Utah, Nels K. Nelson of Rockland, Idaho, John Högsted of Salem, Idaho, Louis Thomson of Pleasant Grove, J. David Larson, of Salt Lake City, John A. Erickson of Grantsville, and Peter Ingemanson of Murray, Utah, arrived March 19th; John Martin Leu (Lew) and Carl Albin Krantz of Salt Lake City, Utah, Wm. A. Wahlquist and Niels R. Petersen of Oakley, Idaho, C. Julius Petersen of Albion, Henry C. Christensen of Lago, Idaho, Hans H. Hansen of Hyrum, and John A. Johnson of Richmond, Utah, arrived April 22nd; Charles J. A. Lindquist of Ogden, Charles J. Erickson, Niels

Madsen and Hyrum C. Sandberg of
Salt Lake City, Utah, Martin L.
Okleberry of Island, Idaho, Peter

JOHN VICTOR JOHNSON

Son of Andrew Gustave Johnson and Charlotta Christine Anderson, was born July 3,
1880, at Pleasant Grove, Utah. His boyhood
was spent on his father's farm and after being
baptized at the age of eight years, he was
ordained to the various offices in the Priesthood. He attended the district school, spent
two winters at the Brigham Young Academy
at Provo, and was active in the auxiliary organizations in the Lindon Ward. In 1902-
1905, he filled a mission to Scandinavia,
being assigned to labor in the Sundsvall Conference, Sweden. In July, 1903, he attended
the dedication of the L. D. S. Chapel at
Christiania, Norway, and spent twenty-three
months of his mission in the "Land of the
Midnight Sun"; also four months in Oskars-
hamn, Sweden. In October, 1904, he attended
the dedication of the Mission Home at Stockholm, Sweden, and during his mission had the
privilege of baptizing three people. December
20, 1905, he married Jennie Walker; seven
children have been born to them.

W. Harrison of Osmond, Wyoming,
Rupert Peter Olsen and Peter W.
Knudson of Brigham City, Utah, arrived May 16th, and Joseph Fagergren of Salt Lake City, Andrew Johnson of Heber City, Hans Sörensen,
jun., of College Ward, Hyrum P.
Nökleby and George Turville Larsen of Ogden, Edward A. Gustavesen

of Holliday, Sören J. Nielsen o:
South Jordan, Utah, Nils A. Hanson
of Preston, Idaho, and Erastus Wil
lard Mortensen of Dublan, Mexico
arrived May 25th; Ferdinand F
Hintze, jun., of Salt Lake City, Utah
arrived June 3rd; Albert Hagen of
Mammoth, David F. Fredericksen
Nis C. Christiansen and Herman F.
F. Thorup of Salt Lake City, Herman
H. Danielsen of Lewiston, Rozilla K
Petersen of Brigham City, Utah
Svante J. Koeven of Montpelier
Idaho, and Joseph Anderson of
Ammon, Idaho, arrived June 15th,
and Andrew L. Larsen of Matthews
ville, Arizona, Peter Taney Petersen
of Mink Creek, Idaho, Djalmar E.
Lund of Salt Lake City, Christian
Fonnesbeck, of Logan, Mouritz

AUGUST ERICKSON

Born Dec. 30, 1872, at Tierp parish, Uppland, Sweden, the son of Erick Erickson and
Johanna Pehrson, was baptized March 15,
1889, and called to labor as a missionary in
the Stockholm Conference. He emigrated to
Utah in 1892. In 1903-1905, he filled a mission
to Sweden, presiding over the Sundsvall Conference the entire time. In 1917, he was
ordained as Bishop to preside in Salina, Sevier
Co. Bro. Erickson has held other responsible
positions in the Church. He is active in the
community and prominent in mercantile business.

Chas. Petersen of Mt. Pleasant, John Peterson of Huntsville, Jos. M. Nielson and George A. Jörgensen of Ephraim, Utah, on June 22nd;

CARL FREDRIK KRANTZ

Born in Alsike, Uppland, Sweden, April 18, 849, son of Jan Erik Janson and his wife, Maria Margreta Henriksdotter; served many ears as a non-commissioned officer in the Swedish army. After a long search for truth, e at length heard the gospel and it appealed o him. He was baptized January 1, 1888, by Elder P. G. Hanson of Payson, and confirmed by Elder G. F. Brodd; came to Utah on the th of December, 1900, and returned three ears later to his native land on a mission; did missionary work in the Eskilstuna and Upsala branches, and helped, as a carpented, to finish the L. D. S. Mission headquarters in Stockholm. During his absence his wife, Sophia C. Holmbom, died, and upon his return he married Clara Schader. His robust health became broken down with asthma, and he passed away in Salt Lake City, April 17, 1924.

Gustave Thomasson of Logan, Niels Mikkelsen of Draper, Jens Jensen f Leamington, Sören C. B. Sörensen of Manti, Anna K. G. Widtsoe and Petroline J. P. Gaarden of Salt Lake City, Utah, arrived July 13th, and Thorvald Hansen of Ephraim arrived July 23rd; August Erickson and Emeal Nielsen of Salina, Carl F. Krantz of Salt Lake City. Claudie D. Michaelson of Mayfield, Niels Mikkelsen Thorup of Fountain Green, and Hans S. Larsen of Brigham City, Utah, arrived July 27th;

John A. Hendricksen of Logan, Utah, arrived Aug. 15th; Niels J. Henricksen of Salt Lake City, Utah, and Lars P. Jensen of Ovid, Idaho, arrived Aug. 19th, and Jens Peter Nielsen and Louis O. Keller of Mink Creek, Idaho, Heber A. Anderson and Parley P. Petersen of Redmond, Utah, Julius C. Beck of Alpine City, and Stephen M. Peterson of Moroni, Utah, arrived Aug. 24th; Wilford Olsen of Weston, Idaho, arrived Sept. 9th; Ole H. Olsen of Santaquin and John Spande of Logan, Utah, arrived Sept. 21st; Ernest L. Swalberg of Gunnison, arrived Oct.

DJALMAR E. LUND

Son of Rasmus Hansen Lund and Petrine Jensen, was born May 4, 1882, in Söllestad, Lolland, Denmark; emigrated to Utah with his parents, arriving in Salt Lake City, Sept. 3, 1893. He was baptized Oct. 3, 1893, by John T. Thorup in Salt Lake City; confirmed Oct. 5th, by Jos. McMurrin, and sealed to his parents in April, 1895. He moved to Pleasant Grove in 1897; was secretary of the Deacons' quorum, and moved to Salt Lake City (Ninth Ward) in 1901. In 1903-1905, he filled a mission to Scandinavia, laboring in the Aarhus Conference, Denmark, under the direction of Adam L. Petersen and Hans Christian Hansen; presided over the Otter Branch and then over the Odense Branch. Before leaving for his mission, on May 27, 1903, he married Aagot M. Randby in the Salt Lake Temple. He located in the 24th Ward, Salt Lake Stake, in 1909; was ordained a Seventy Nov. 24, 1919, and set apart as one of the presidents of the 30th Quorum, September 5, 1926; the same year he was appointed a member of the Temple Committee of the 24th Ward.

5th; Hans C. Hansen of Fillmore, Iver A. Alme of Logan, Oscar Andersen of Peterson, Christian A. Hansen of Richfield, and Sören Marinus

CARL ALBIN KRANTZ

Was born in Håbo-Tibble, Uppland, Sweden, Sept. 16, 1871, the son of Carl F. Krantz and Sophia C. Holmbom. He heard the gospel in Knifsta, Uppland, in 1887, through Elder P. G. Hanson of Payson; was baptized in Stockholm, May 7, 1888, by Elder G. F. Brodd (Broady), and confirmed by Elder Karl H. P. Nordberg; labored as district teacher, secretary of the Mutual, and Sunday school teacher in Stockholm during 1889-1890, and performed a missionary labor in 1891-1893, laboring in the Sundsvall, Eskilstuna and Upsala branches. He emigrated to Utah in the fall of 1893, arriving in Salt Lake City, Dec. 4, 1893. In 1897, he married Gerda C. Höglund, and as an Elder from Zion he filled a mission to Scandinavia in 1903-1905, laboring in the mission office of Copenhagen as a writer for "Nordstjernan." After his return to Utah, Elder Krantz was assistant editor of "Utah-Posten" in 1909-1923, and counselor to D. B. Jones in South Cottonwood Branch Y. M. M. I. A. (Murray). He labored in the Fifth and Sixth Wards in Salt Lake City, at various times, as teacher, choir-manager, class-leader in Mutual, special missionary, presiding teacher, assistant superintendent of Sunday schools, etc., and member of the council of the 23rd Quorum of Seventy.

Petersen of Newton, Utah, arrived Nov. 2nd, and Hans Julius Yool of Ogden, Utah, on Nov. 6th; Ezra A. Valentine of Brigham City, Elmer Johnson of Salt Lake City, Hans Lauritz Rasmussen and Peter M. Peterson of Spring City, Hans Benjamin Nielsen of Hyrum, Utah, and

Carl J. Lundgren of Lund, Idaho, arrived Nov. 20th; Erick C. Henrichse of Provo, John J. Plowman of Smith field, John P. Jeppesen of Bea River City, Utah, and Peter I Christensen of Mink Creek, Idaho arrived Nov 28th; Lehi Jensen c Redmond, Niels C. Christensen c Brigham City, Christian R. Rasmus sen of Parley's Park, Charles J. Ar derson of Grantsville, Utah, Jame P. Nielsen of Sublette, Idaho, an

CARL JOHAN LUNDGREN

Born May 16, 1855, in Horn, Skarabor, län, Sweden, was baptized Nov. 2, 1873. 1866, a messenger came to the home of Broth Lundgren's parents and preached the restor gospel, predicting also that Carl J., who w then 11 years old, would become a missionar Being ordained to the Priesthood, he w called into the mission field in May, 1873, met with considerable success in Eskilstun He was particularly blessed with the spi of healing and many sick were restored health under his administration. In 1875, was sent to Örebro, and in 1876 called preside in Eskilstuna. In 1877, he was a pointed to preside over the Gotland Branc and in 1879, to preside in Vesterås. Aft laboring six years as a missionary, he w released with permission to marry and em grate to Utah. He was ordained a Sevent June 28, 1890. As an Elder from Zion filled a mission to Scandinavia in 1903-190 laboring in the Göteborg and Stockholm cc ferences. He was ordained a High Prie May 17, 1908, and a Patriarch in the Ida Stake, Feb. 29, 1920; he is now (1927) resident of Lund, Idaho.

George Petersen of Salem, Idaho, rrived Dec. 24th.

Joseph E. Jörgensen, Albert Hagen, David F. Fredericksen, Joseph Anderson, Sören C. B. Sörensen, Anna K. W. Widtsoe, Petroline J. P. Gaarden, Claudie D. Michaelson, Louis O. Keller, Parley P. Petersen, Wilford Olsen, Ole H. Olsen, Oscar Anderen, Hans Julius Yool, Hans Benjamin Nielsen and Peter M. Peterson were called to labor in the Trondhjem Conference.

John V. Johnson, John M. Leu Lew), Charles J. Erickson, Peter V. Harrison, Andrew Johnson, Edward A. Gustavesen, Svante J. Loeven and Ezra Anthony Valentine

ERIK CHRISTIAN HENRICHSEN

Born Dec. 30, 1847, in Veile, Denmark, joined the Church at the age of 20 years; was ordained a Deacon, March 8, 1868; later a Priest and an Elder, and labored as a local missionary. He performed a mission in Norway under the name of Christian Grönbeck, laboring in Frederikstad and Drammen. Bro. Henrichsen emigrated in 1871 and located in Provo. On July 22, 1872, he married Albine Ensine Pauline Jensen; they had 11 children. In 1903-1906, he filled a mission to Norway, laboring principally in the Bergen Conference. Later he was ordained a Seventy and became the senior president of the 134th Quorum of Seventy; was ordained a High Priest in 1920, and set apart as Stake president of the Scandinavian meetings, which position he held until October, 1927. He still resides in Provo, where he is proprietor of the Provo Pottery.

were appointed to labor in the Sundsvall Conference. Peter C. Carlston, Christian Olsen, jun., Peter W. Knudson, Hyrum P. Nökleby, George T. Larsen, Herman H. Danielsen, Herman F. F. Thorup, George A. Jörgensen, Thorvald Hansen, John A. Hendricksen, Christian R. Rasmussen and James P. Nielsen were appointed to labor in Christiania Conference.

Louis E. Johnson, William E. Racker, Nels K. Nelson, Erastus W. Mortensen, Nis C. Christiansen, Djalmar E. Lund, Christian Fonnesbeck, Niels Mikkelsen and John P. Jeppesen were appointed to labor in the Aarhus Conference.

Hans Hansen, jun., Niels Madsen, Rupert P. Olsen, Hans Sörensen, jun., Rozilla K. Petersen, Emeal Nielsen, Niels M. Thorup, Julius C. Beck, Sören M. Petersen and John J. Plowman were appointed to labor in the Aalborg Conference.

Oley Oleson, Charles J. A. Lindquist, August Erickson, Carl F. Krantz, Elmer Johnson, Peter B. Christensen, Charles J. Anderson and George Petersen were appointed to labor in the Stockholm Conference.

David R. Wheelwright, John Högsted, Louis Thomson, Ferdinand F. Hintze, jun., Hans S. Larsen, Niels J. Henricksen, Lars P. Jensen, Jens Peter Nielsen, Hans C. Hansen, Hans Lauritz Rasmussen, Lehi Jensen and Niels C. Christensen were appointed to labor in the Copenhagen Conference.

Niels Sandberg, jun., Peter Ingemanson, Hans H. Hansen, Martin L. Okleberry, Hyrum C. Sandberg, Nils A. Hanson, Andrew L. Larsen and Ernest L. Swalberg were appointed to labor in the Skåne Conference.

J. David Larson, John A. Erickson, Wm. A. Wahlquist, C. Julius Petersen, Niels R. Petersen, Joseph Fagergren, John Peterson, Joseph M. Nielson, Gustave Thomasson and Carl J. Lundgren were appointed to labor in the Göteborg Conference. Henry C. Christensen, John A. Johnson, Sören J. Nielsen, Peter T. Petersen, Mouritz C. Petersen, Heber A. Anderson, Stephen M. Peterson, John Spande, Iver A. Alme, Christian A. Hansen and Erick C. Henrichsen were appointed to labor in the Bergen Conference.

Carl Albin Krantz was appointed to labor in the mission office in Copenhagen.

Jens Jensen came to Scandinavia on a genealogical mission.

CHAPTER 88 (1904)

A new edition of "Joseph Smith's Levnetslöb" in the Danish-Norwegian language—Visit of President Heber J. Grant—Dedication of a mission house in Stockholm, Sweden.

In August, 1904, Apostle Heber J. Grant, president of the European Mission, visited Scandinavia, accompanied by his wife, Emily W. Grant, and two daughters, Edith and Grace. Pres. Grant attended conferences in Göteborg, Christiania, Bergen, Trondhjem, Sundsvall and Malmö.

Elder Andrew Jenson, assistant Church historian, arrived in Copenhagen Sept. 21, 1904, on another special mission to Scandinavia, being called to assist in publishing a new edition of the history of Joseph Smith (Joseph Smith's Levnetslöb) in the Danish-Norwegian language. The first edition of this historical work was printed in Salt Lake City in 1879, but as the whole of that edition had been sold long ago, and only a few copies had reached the Scandinavian countries, the Church authorities considered it advisable to publish a second edition. The manuscript had been carefully revised by Pres. Anthon H. Lund and Andrew Jenson, and the latter now brought the same to Denmark to have it published in book form in Copenhagen. Upon

his arrival, Elder Jenson received a hearty welcome from President Fjeldsted and Skanchy, and the same room in the Mission House which

APOSTLE HEBER J. GRANT

Born Nov. 22, 1856, in Salt Lake City, Utah, the son of Jedediah M. Grant and Rachel Ridgeway Ivins.

he had occupied on his former special mission was again placed at his disposal. Elder Jenson commenced his literary work immediately and before the end of the year the book was issued from the press. It is a neat volume containing 650 pages and the edition consisted of 3000 copies.

Pres. Heber J. Grant arrived in Copenhagen from Liverpool on another visit to Scandinavia, Oct. 20 1904. On the same day he, accompanied by Elders Chr. D. Fjeldsted and Andrew Jenson, left Copenhagen crossed the Sound (Öresund) on steamer to Malmö and thence continued by rail to Stockholm, where the party arrived the following day (Oct. 21st). In the evening a fine concert was given by the Stockholm choir. On Saturday (Oct. 22nd about seventy Elders from Zion, and about six hundred local Saints gathered in the new hall in Stockholm, among whom were Pres. Heber J. Grant, Anthon L. Skanchy, Chr. D. Fjeldsted and Andrew Jenson. The dedicatory services commenced at 8:30 p. m. After the opening exercises, Pres. Anthon L. Skanchy made a few remarks, after which Pres. Grant offered the dedicatory prayer. Telegrams of congratulations were read. On this occasion the stand was occupied by about 40 members of the Stockholm Branch choir, of which all the female members were dressed in white, while the gentlemen wore dark suits. With

HEADQUARTERS OF THE SWEDISH MISSION

The property known as Svartensgatan No. 3, Stockholm, Sweden, purchased and partly rebuilt, with additions, in 1904.

Elder G. Leonard Ohlson as chorister, the splendid singing of this choir did much to make the services throughout a success.

The regular semi-annual conference of the Stockholm Conference was held in the new hall on Sunday, Oct. 23rd. The forenoon meeting was mostly devoted to a Sunday school program, at which Elder

26

Grant also spoke, with Elder Gustaf L. Ohlson as translator. The afternoon meeting was addressed by the several conference presidents and Elder Andrew Jenson. The principal speaker in the evening meeting was President Grant with Elder Carl A. Krantz as translator. Pres. Anthon L. Skanchy also spoke, and the hymn "A Poor Wayfaring Man of Grief," translated into Swedish, was most excellently rendered by one of the Swedish sisters. The spirit of God was poured out in rich measure in all the meetings.

The following day (Oct. 24th) two Priesthood meetings were held in Stockholm, at which 67 Elders, including two local missionaries, spoke briefly, as did also Pres. Chr. D. Fjeldsted, Andrew Jenson and Anthon L. Skanchy. Pres. Grant occupied about two hours, speaking in a most instructive and interesting manner. After the afternoon meeting, Pres. Grant set Chr. D. Fjeldsted apart to succeed Anthon L. Skanchy as president of the Scandinavian Mission.

During this special mission in Scandinavia, Elder Andrew Jenson delivered a number of lectures on Church history and otherwise preached in many other meetings as well as conferences. Thus on Sunday, Nov. 27th, he lectured on his travels around the world in the little city of Stege on the island of Möen, Denmark, and finished by describing conditions among the Latter-day Saints in Utah. About 150 attentive listeners attended the lecture. Among those who greeted Elder Jenson at the close of the meeting was a man who had heard him speak about 23 years before at Nakskov on the Island of Lolland, and remarked that he had never forgotten what he had heard on that occasion, and that he was now, together with his family, investigating "Mormonism" with a

view to joining the Church. It was
an illustration of the Scriptural
saying: "Bread cast upon the waters
shall return after many days."
President Anthon L. Skanchy, who
had presided over the Scandinavian
Mission about 3½ years, left Copenhagen Dec. 6, 1904, to return to his
home in Zion, leaving Christian D.
Fjeldsted in charge of the mission
the third time.

In 1904, 92 Elders from Zion ar-
rived in Copenhagen, Denmark, as
missionaries to Scandinavia, as fol-
lows: Nephi J. Hansen of Brigham
City, Owen W. Halverson of Ogden,
Niels E. Jensen of Fountain Green,
Lars Persson of Logan, Utah, and
Robert Draper of Franklin, Idaho,
arrived on Feb. 19th, and John S.
Johnson of Wilson, Martin Wilford
Poulson of Pleasant Grove, Hans M.
Gabrielsen, jun., of Logan, and
Joseph G. Nielson of Manti, Utah,
on March 16th. Andrew Lorenzo
Andreason of Mink Creek, Idaho,
Charles H. Norberg of Salt Lake
City, George C. Sörensen of Mt.
Pleasant, Utah, Lars P. C. Nielsen
of Ammon, Idaho, Daniel Anderson
of Moroni, James C. Jensen of Ches-
ter, Christian P. Larsen of Center-
field, Sören P. Sörensen of Ben-
jamin, Oscar Junius Barrett of
Mendon, Nicolai Jörgensen of Hy-
rum and Jens P. Jensen Ostrup of
Logan, Utah, arrived April 14th, and
Louis Anderson of Richmond, Wil-
ford J. Knudsen of Provo, Jasper P.
Petersen of Castle Dale, Utah, Niels
Evensen of Mancos, Colorado, L.
Anthon Louritzen of Newton, Bernhardt (Bernard) Newreen of Scofield, Henry H. Hintze of Big Cottonwood, Utah, Hans Chr. Hansen of
Mink Creek, Idaho, George M. M.
Jörgensen of Levan, and Adolph
Z. Fjellström of Logan, Utah, ar-
rived May 14th; Andrew F. Sundberg
and Jeppa Nilsson of Pleasant Grove,
Utah, A. Henry Monson and Alvin

O. Peterson of St. Charles, Idaho,
Gustave H. Anderson of Sandy, Ole
Andersen and Andrew Eliason, jun.,
of Logan, Gilbert Torgersen and
Peter Jensen (genealogist) of Ogden,
Utah, and Lauritz M. Christensen of
Pocatello, Idaho, arrived June 15th.
Andrew O. Ingelström of Basalt, Ida-

MARTIN WILFORD POULSON

Was born Nov. 21, 1884, at Pleasant Grove,
Utah, the sixth in a family of seven children
of Niels Poulson and Maria Wahlström. His
parents joined the Church in Helsingborg,
Sweden, July 11, 1881, and emigrated to Utah.
Bro. Poulson filled a mission to Sweden from
February, 1904, to June, 1906, where he
labored in the Christianstad, Malmö and Helsingborg branches of the Skåne Conference.
April 24, 1907, he married Estelle Mecham of
Provo, Utah; they have six children. From
1913 to 1917, Bro. Poulson served as president
of the Third Quorum of Elders in the Utah
Stake, and from 1917 to 1920, he was superintendent of religion classes in the same stake.
He graduated from Pleasant Grove public
schools in 1902; was a public school teacher in
1908-1909; graduated from the Normal Department, B. Y. University, in 1910; took A.
B. degree at B. Y. University in 1914; took
M. A. degree in the University of Utah in 1919;
was a graduate student at the University of
Chicago two and one half years; vice president
of the Library Department, N. E. A. in 1920-
1921; president of Utah Library Association in
1922; elected to membership in the Utah
Academy of Science, Phi Delta Kappa national
professional fraternity, and the American Association for the Advancement of Science.
He has held the following appointments on the
Brigham Young University faculty; instructor,
1910-1916; assistant professor of education,
1916-1919; associate professor, 1919-1922, and
professor of psychology, 1922. He has been
a resident of Provo, Utah, since 1907.

ho, Joseph L. Petersen, Carl E. A. Peterson and John Felt, jun., of Huntsville, Lars L. Olson, jun., of

NILS EVENSEN

Born June 14, 1858, at Rinsager, Hedemarken, Norway, was baptized June 2, 1873, by Carl Ericksen. He was ordained a Teacher, June 22, 1875, and labored among the Saints; was ordained a Priest, Aug. 15, 1876, and an Elder, Sept. 29, 1879. He presided in the Arendal Branch until May, 1880, when he was called to Denmark and labored in West and South Sjælland until July, 1882, when he emigrated to Utah. He married Margrethe Hansen, Feb. 1, 1883, in the Endowment House, Salt Lake City, and was ordained a Seventy, Jan. 8, 1884. He moved to San Juan County, New Mexico, in June, 1890, and later to Mancos, Colorado. In 1904-1906, he filled a mission to Norway, where he labored in Röraas Branch, then presided over the Trondhjem Conference for eighteen months, where he was arrested twice for baptizing and administering the Sacrament. Bro. Evensen was set apart as a president of the 125th Quorum of Seventy, July 29, 1906, and, being ordained a High Priest, Aug. 4, 1907, was set apart as first counselor in the bishopric of the Kline Ward, Colorado. He moved to Durango and was called to preside over that branch in 1913, which position he still (1927) holds.

Mammoth, and Alfred M. Nelson of Ogden, Utah, arrived July 13th, and Erick Eliason of Murray, Utah, Hyrum Larsen of Vernon, Idaho, and Joseph S. Hansen of Mink Creek, Idaho, arrived on Sept. 7th. Andrew Jenson of Salt Lake City and James

R. Petersen of South Jordan, Utah, arrived Sept. 21st, and Olaf E. Jörgensen of Scofield, Harvig A. Oakeson of South Jordan, Utah, Frederick W. Christensen of Holbrook and Emil S. V. Erickson of Pocatello, Idaho, Oct. 5th. Ephraim Peterson and Hans Chr. Nielsen of Mink Creek, Idaho, Carl V. Rex Pehrson of American Fork, Per Gustave Peterson of Murray, and Anthon E. Samuelson of Wilford, Utah, arrived Oct. 26th, and Niels Didricksen of Brigham City and Sören Nielsen of Manti on Nov. 2nd. Carl O. Johnson of Salt Lake City, Jens Carlson of Ogden, Anton J. T. Sörensen of Milford, Emil Christoffersen of Elsinore, Albert L. Zobell of Provo, Utah, and James J. Nelson of Glendale, Idaho, arrived Nov. 9th. James

ANDREW O. INGELSTRÖM

Born in Ystad, Sweden, Oct. 10, 1853; emigrated in 1879, and settled in Basalt, Idaho. He left his home for a mission to Sweden, June 20, 1904; visited on the road the Temple grounds at Independence, Mo.; sailed from Boston and landed in Liverpool, July 9th; arrived in Copenhagen, July 13th, and was met by President Anthon L. Skanchy and C. D. Fjeldsted; was sent to Sweden, to preside over the Skåne Conference, to succeed Pres. James P. Olson; traveled extensively in the conference, bearing his testimony to thousands of Saints and investigators. Being honorably released, he arrived home Dec. 11, 1906. He still (1927) resides at Basalt, Idaho.

Erickson of Ogden, Lars K. Larsen of Hyrum, Lars J. Carlson of Logan, Alfred Pehrson and Jens P. L. Breinholt of Ephraim, James P. Schow and Charles A. O. Ramsin of Lehi, Carl P. Anderson of Clarkston, Niels A. Petersen and Hyrum C. Christensen of Elwood, Nephi Peterson of View, Utah, Peter M. Christiansen of Mink Creek, Idaho, Abel Johnson of Sandy, Julius Nielsen of Honeyville, Niels Christian Simonsen, Orson J. Olson and Lars H. Larsen of Brigham City, Carl W. Jacob-

sen and Enoch Gillen of South Cottonwood, Niels L. Lund of May-

LARS JOHN CARLSON

Born at Yxtorp, Sweden, Jan. 26, 1853, was baptized and confirmed, July 6, 1879, and received a testimony of the divinity of the mission of Joseph Smith. He was called to labor as a missionary and ordained a Priest, Oct. 8, 1879, by Lars M. Olson, at Stockholm, and sent to Örebro; was ordained an Elder by John A. Johnson, Feb. 2, 1880, and transferred to Finland. In October, 1880, he was transferred to Sundsvall, and in May, 1881, to Gotland, then, in October, 1881, to Avesta, Dalarne; was honorably released in June, 1882. He traveled without purse or scrip. In July, 1882, he emigrated to Utah. As an Elder from Zion he filled a mission to Sweden, from November, 1904, to November 1906, presiding first in Dalarne and then in Örebro. He always depended on the guidance of the Spirit of God in his labors. He is at present (1927) a resident of Logan, Utah.

CARL OSCAR JOHNSON

Born in Ystad, Skåne, Sweden, Dec. 13, 1859, the son of Jöns Larson and Anna Nilson, was baptized and confirmed by James Yorgason, Aug. 14, 1882. He labored as a missionary in Malmö for some time; emigrated to Utah, arriving in Salt Lake City, Sept. 17, 1884, and labored as a stone cutter on the Salt Lake Temple for nearly six years. Bro. Johnson married Elna Gustaveson, Aug. 15, 1885, and became the father of four boys and six girls. He filled a mission to Sweden in 1904-1906, laboring as a counselor and as president of the Swedish L. D. S. meetings in Ensign Stake for 15 years, and from March, 1925, to October, 1927, he acted as first counselor to Elder Frederik F. Samuelsen, president of the Scandinavian religious meetings in Salt Lake City.

field, Utah, James C. Jensen of Hibbard, Idaho, Daniel Jensen of Spring City, and Ida Sofia Peterson of Huntsville, Utah, arrived Dec. 14th, and Herman A. Andelin of Cedar City, Utah, on Dec. 20th.

Robert Draper, Alvin O. Peterson, Gustave H. Anderson, Carl E. A. Peterson, Alfred M. Nelson, Anthon E. Samuelson, Nephi Peterson, Abel Johnson and Enoch Gillen were appointed to labor in the Sundsvall Conference.

Nephi J. Hansen, Nicolai Jörgensen, Wilford J. Knudsen, Niels Even-

NIELS A. PETERSEN

Born Aug. 1, 1854, in Sundbylille, Frederiksborg amt, Denmark, the son of Anders Petersen and Johanne Kristine Hansen, was baptized Aug. 28, 1880, by Hans J. Christiansen, confirmed by Elder Hans Funk, and ordained successively a Teacher, Elder, Seventy and High Priest. Bro. Petersen married Johanne Larsen in 1877, at Hjorlunde, Denmark; they were sealed in the Salt Lake Endowment House, Nov. 17, 1881; had nine children, namely: Mary Johanne, Andrew Peter, Niels, Lars Nephi, Joseph, Johanna, William, Alma, and Oloff. Bro. Petersen married Amalia Larsen Nov. 17, 1881; he had 11 children by her, namely: Lars Charley, Margaret Amelia, Mina Christina, Alice Celina, Vego Leonard, Oscar Erastus, Aaron Lewis, Einer Benjamin, Royal Theodore, Ernest Sylvester, and Melvin Ezra. Bro. Petersen filled a mission to Denmark, in 1904-1907, and died Nov. 22, 1921, at Elwood, Box Elder County, Utah.

sen, Lars L. Olson, jun., Olaf E. Jörgensen, Ephraim Peterson, Niels Didricksen, Sören Nielsen, Niels L. Lund and James C. Jensen were appointed to labor in the Trondhjem Conference.

Owen W. Halverson, Hans M. Gabrielsen, jun., Joseph G. Nielson, Daniel Anderson, Ole Andersen, Gilbert Torgersen, Jens Carlson,

Anton J. T. Sörensen, James Erickson and Lars K. Larsen were appointed to labor in the Christiania Conference.

Niels E. Jensen, Joseph L. Petersen, Hyrum Larsen, Emil Christoffersen, Hyrum C. Christensen and Julius Nielsen were appointed to labor in the Bergen Conference.

Lars Persson, John S. Johnson, Charles H. Norberg, Adolph Z. Fjellström, John Felt, jun., Carl O. Johnson, Lars J. Carlson and Charles A. O. Ramsin were appointed to labor in the Stockholm Conference.

Martin W. Poulson, Louis Anderson, Jeppa Nilsson, A. Henry Monson, Andrew O. Ingelström, Harvig A. Oakeson, Karl V. Rex Pehrson and Alfred Pehrson were appointed to labor in the Skåne Conference.

George C. Sörensen, Christian P. Larsen, Jens P. Jensen Ostrup, L. Anthon Lauritzen, Joseph S. Hansen, James R. Petersen, Frederick W. Christensen, James J. Nelson N. Christian Simonsen, Orson J. Olson and Lars H. Larsen were appointed to labor in the Aalborg Conference.

Andrew L. Andreason, James C. Jensen, Sören P. Sörensen, Jasper P. Petersen, Hans Chr. Hansen, George M. M. Jörgensen, Hans Chr. Nielsen, Jens P. L. Breinholt, Carl W. Jacobsen and Daniel Jensen were appointed to labor in the Aarhus Conference.

Lars P. C. Nielsen, Henry H. Hintze, Lauritz M. Christensen, Peter Jensen, Albert L. Zobell, James P. Schow, Niels A. Petersen, Peter M. Christiansen and Ida S. Petersen were appointed to labor in the Copenhagen Conference.

Oscar J. Barrett, Bernhardt Newreen, Andrew F. Sundberg, Andrew Eliason, jun., Erick T. Eliason, Emil S. V. Erickson, Per Gustave Peterson, Carl P. Anderson and Herman A. Andelin were appointed to labor in the Göteborg Conference.

CHAPTER 89 (1905)

Elder Andrew Jenson faces opposition on the part of the Lutheran clergy—The Scandinavian Mission divided—Sweden is made a separate mission.

A number of Saints in Copenhagen, who had become known as the Utah colony on account of having spent some time in Utah, and others who were born in America, held a reunion in Copenhagen, Jan. 3, 1905. There were 15 of them present, viz., Chr. D. Fjeldsted, Andrew Jenson, Hans J. Christiansen, Niels J. Henricksen, David R. Wheelwright and wife, Thor C. Nielsen with wife and two children, Carl A. Krantz, George A. Knudsen, Niels G. Christensen, Miss Christine Fyhn and Mary K. Jörgensen.

Before Elder Jenson left Copenhagen to return to his home in Zion, he visited his birthplace in Jutland and held a significant disussion with Pastor H. O. Fremodt-Möller, who had lived in the United States as a Lutheran priest and since his return to Denmark had held a number of anti-Mormon meetings in churches and halls in which he had made all kinds of false statements about the Saints and their religion, and he was imported from Aarhus to do up the "Mormons" in great style. The discussion took place in Nibe, and Elder Jenson succeeded in putting important facts before the people in regard to Utah and her people, so that the discussion ended in victory for the Elders. It was estimated that about 1200 people were present and that many others could not obtain admission. The Elders felt truly thankful and expressed their gratitude to their Heavenly Father in prayer after the meeting.

After this discussion in Nibe, Elder Andrew Jenson preached in Aarhus and Veile on his way to Germany, but while in Veile he received an "official" notification

that Fremodt-Möller would hold a public meeting in the large K. F. U. M. Hall the following Friday evening, to which he invited the "Mormon" leaders. After reading the challenge, the Elders of the Aarhus Conference, who were visiting Veile, persuaded Elder Jenson to return with them to Aarhus and help them out in that meeting. He responded reluctantly, as he felt that his duties called him to Germany. Consequently Elder Jenson, accompanied by the other Utah Elders who were with him, returned as far as the city of Horsens that day and there learned that Fremodt-Möller was holding forth against the "Mormons" in a large hall. The Elders, arriving early, obtained good seats and soon the large hall was filled to suffocation, about 2000 persons being present. After some introductory remarks by a vile and bitter anti-Mormon priest, Fremodt-Möller harangued for an hour, telling all kinds of stories, and devoted much of his time to attacking Elder Jenson on account of what had taken place in Nibe and Aarhus. He endeavored to be fair in some of his statements, particularly those relating to the industry of the "Mormons" in Utah. As soon as he was through, Elder Jenson asked for permission to speak. This being granted, he held the attention of the people for three quarters of an hour, speaking with much freedom in the face of gall and bitterness, for he had scarcely a friend in the immense congregation, save the few Saints and the Elders who were accompanying him. Elder Jenson writes: "Praise be to Almighty God who stood by his servant and enabled him to defend the Prophet of God and the religion of the Savior with courage in the face of such opposition. Other speakers followed, and as might be expected, exasperated as they were at the de-

fense of my people, they continued
their abuse and vilifications and
warnings, and flatly refused me the
floor or the pulpit again, not even
permitting me to ask a simple question, but I shall be much mistaken if
many who were present at that meeting did not return to their homes
with serious thoughts on 'Mormonism.' "

From Horsens, Elder Jenson and
his companions returned by train to
Aarhus, where a number of Elders
and many local Saints attended the
meeting held in the K. F. U. M.
hall on Klostergade. They occupied
seats which had been reserved for
them in front of the pulpit. Shortly, the large hall was filled to over-
flowing, until nearly 2000 people
were present, and every avenue and
passage was crowded to its utmost
capacity. Pastor Fremodt-Möller
came early, and so did a dozen other
clergymen, besides newspaper men
and many other prominent citizens.
Precisely at 8 o'clock p. m. Mr.
Fremodt-Möller stepped forth, and,
after singing and a very short prayer,
he spoke 55 minutes, telling all kinds
of yarns, some of which were partly
true and others entirely false. He
seemed to feel the influence of the
Elders and Saints who were present,
and some of his main points fell flat
on the ears of his hearers. He certainly did not reap the applause that
had been given him the night before
in Horsens. After he was through,
he gave the floor to a Mr. Möller,
a school-teacher, who acted very fair
and permitted Elder Jenson to occupy as much time as that which the
pastor had used. Elder Jenson writes:

"The Lord be praised for that opportunity. Under the influence of the Spirit
of God, I spoke as I had seldom spoken
before in the defense of truth and the
work of God. From my notes which I
had made while the pastor was speaking,
I took up, item after item, the accusations which had been brought out against
us, and either refuted or explained them,
and I soon learned that I had many friends
in the congregation. I was not interrupted at all and my mind seemed unusually clear on all the points handled.
Thus ended the first act; then other
speakers asked for the floor, and among
those who then came out as 'reserve force'
were Pastor Monk, a priest of the Aarhus
cathedral, Pastor Lyngby, priest at the
St. Paul Church in Aarhus, Mr. Beck, a
missionary of the 'Indremission,' and
one or two others; also Fremodt-Möller
spoke again twice. I was granted the
privilege of answering every speaker, and
that kept me continuously at the front,
having to go up to and from the pulpit
again and again. It was one of the opportunities of my life, and while I was
abused and insulted in various ways, I was
pleased with the privilege of meeting the
attacks of my opponents, and I firmly believe that good will come out of the discussion. The Elders and Saints were
jubilant and flocked around me with
smiling faces at the close of the meeting,
which was dismissed just before midnight.
A large number of Saints followed us to
the conference house where they, unwilling to scatter, remained until about
1 o'clock in the morning."

About noon the following day,
Elder Jenson took leave of his
brethren and the Saints in Aarhus and
started once more for Germany.

For some time the advisability of
dividing the Scandinavian Mission
had been under consideration by the
First Presidency of the Church, but
the plan did not assume practical
shape until 1905, when it was decided to separate Sweden from Denmark and Norway and organize the
Swedish part of the mission into a
separate mission with Peter Mattson,
of Mount Pleasant, Utah, as its
president, and to retain Denmark
and Norway under the old name of
the Scandinavian Mission. Elder
Jens M. Christensen of Salt Lake
City, who had arrived in Denmark
several months before, and had already visited the different conferences in Denmark and Norway, in
company with Pres. Chr. D. Fjeld-

sted, was appointed president. This change went into effect July 1, 1905.

During the first six months of 1905, before the mission was divided, 51 Elders from Zion arrived in Copenhagen, Denmark, as missionaries to Scandinavia, as follows: Andrew M. Nelson, Hyrum L. Johnson and Hans Knudsen of Brigham City, Daniel N. Sörensen, jun., of

HYRUM D. NIELSEN

Of Hunter, Utah, was born Sept. 3, 1886, in Hunter, Salt Lake County, Utah. His father, Rasmus Nielsen, drove stock across the Plains in 1865. His mother, A. Charlotte Nielsen, arrived in Utah in 1874. Brother Hiram D. Nielsen left on a mission to Sweden, Dec. 28, 1904; he labored in Upsaa a, Dalarne and Stockholm. After being honorably released, he returned home April 11, 1907. In 1910 he married Augusta, the daughter of John Ek, of Pleasant Green, Utah.

Salt Lake City, Hyrum D. Nielsen of Hunter, Utah, Jens L. Sörensen of Blackfoot and Hans H. Hansen of Preston, Idaho, arrived Jan. 19th. Oscar S. Boeker of Salt Lake City, Andrew J. Anderson of Lehi, Carl Oscar Turnquist of Ogden, Niels Wm. Knudsen of Provo, and Ole Peter Peterson of Grover, Utah, arrived Feb. 1st, and Anders Frederiksen of Manti and N. Chr. M. Andersen of Salt Lake City, Utah, on March

11th. Carl O. V. Piersun of Sandy, Utah, and Charles Andersen of Independence, Idaho, arrived March 29th. Victor E. Madsen and David O. Stohl of Brigham City, Orson Poulsen of Ephraim, Anders P. Nielsen of Granger, Gustave A. Seequist of Murray, Christian Jensen (Miller) of Hyrum, Jeppe Jeppensen and Jens M. Christensen of Salt Lake City, and Swen Swenson of Pleasant Grove, Utah, arrived April 12th. Joseph E. Kjær, Willard R. Smith and George C. Smith of Salt Lake City, Cyrus Jensen of Lewiston, Oliver Hanson of Logan, Orson H. Peterson of Newton, Leo B. Clawson of Providence, Gustave Anderson of Yost, Nephi H. Nielsen of Monroe, Utah, Nephi Rasmussen of Lyman, Wyoming, Niels C. Christensen of Archer, Idaho, Joseph P. Fernelius and Heber A. Fernelius of Uintah, Utah, arrived May 10th. Mads Frederick Theobald Christensen of Fairview, Jared Nordgran of Monroe, Carl J. Larson and Fritz M. Jensen of Salt Lake City, Christian P. Christensen of Spring City, Samuel Petersen of Kanesville, Alvin J. Jacobsen of Moroni and Martinus Nielsen of Centerfield, Utah, John Erickson of Fish Haven, Idaho, Gustave H. Johnson of Idaho Falls, Idaho, and Bennie Ravsten of Clarkston, Utah, arrived June 7th. Heber A. Knudsen of Provo, and Peter Mattson of Mt. Pleasant. Utah, arrived June 14th.

Andrew M. Nelson, Daniel N. Sörensen, jun., Hans Knudsen and Heber A. Knudsen were appointed to labor in the Christiania Conference. Jens L. Sörensen, Joseph E. Kjær, Nephi H. Nielsen, Nephi Rassmussen and Christian P. Christensen were appointed to labor in the Bergen Conference.

Hans H. Hansen, Anders P. Nielsen, Jeppe Jeppesen and Alvin J. Jacobsen were appointed to labor in the Aarhus Conference. Hyrum L.

Johnson, Ole Peter Peterson, Victor E. Madsen and Carl J. Larson were appointed to labor in the Copenhagen Conference.   ,

Hyrum D. Nielsen, David O. Stohl and Gustave A. Seequist were appointed to labor in the Stockholm Conference. Oscar S. Boeker, Andrew J. Anderson, Carl O. V. Pierson, and Bennie Ravsten were appointed to labor in the Skåne Conference.

C. Oscar Turnquist, Jared Nordgran and Gustave H. Johnson were

ANDREW RASMUS ANDERSEN

Born March 9, 1844, in Veddum, Denmark, the son of Jens Andersen and Katrine Rasmussen, was baptized March 13, 1861, labored as a local missionary and organized a branch of the Church. Emigrating with his parents, he and his mother reached Utah in 1862, but his father died while crossing the North Sea. They located in Ephraim, Sanpete County, where Elder Andersen married Mary Ann Petersen Jan. 7, 1863; six children were born to them; eight children were also born by his marriage with Nielsine M. Andersen. He took an active part in the Black Hawk war in 1865-1867 and moved to Lehi, Utah County, in 1870. On his mission to Denmark in 1874-1875 he presided over the Aarhus Conference. From June 10, 1877, to Sept. 21, 1879, he acted as counselor to Bishop David Evans of Lehi and later to Bishop Thomas R. Cutler. On Jan. 24, 1904, he was called to be a member of the High Council of the Alpine Stake and from April 30, 1911, till his death (which occurred July 10, 1919, at Lehi) he acted as president of the High Priests' Quorum of said stake.

appointed to labor in the Göteborg Conference.

John Erickson, Fritz M. Jensen, Niels Wm. Knudsen, Willard R. Smith, Cyrus Jensen, Orson H. Peterson, Niels C. Christensen, Samuel Petersen, Martinus Nielsen and John Erickson were appointed to labor in the Trondhjem Conference.

Anders Frederiksen, N. Chr. M. Andresen, Charles Andersen, Orson Poulsen and Christian Jensen were appointed to labor in the Aalborg Conference.

George C. Smith, Oliver Hanson, Leo B. Clawson, Gustave Anderson, Joseph P. Fernelius and Heber A. Fernelius were appointed to labor in the Sundswall Conference.

At the time of the division, the Scandinavian Mission consisted of 10 conferences and 63 organized branches of the Church. Of these, 3 conferences and 17 branches were in Denmark, 4 conferences and 28

WILLIAM WALLACE CLUFF

Born March 8, 1832, in Willoughby, Geauga Co., Ohio, came to Utah in 1850, filled a mission to Hawaii in 1854-1857, filled another mission to Hawaii (in 1864) and two missions to Scandinavia (1861-1863 and 1870-1871, presided for many years over the Summit Sake of Zion and died in Salt Lake City, Utah, Aug. 21, 1915.

branches in Sweden, and 3 conferences and 18 branches in Norway. As no half-yearly statistical reports were made out in 1905, we can only take the annual report of the mission for 1904 and state that on Dec. 31, 1904, the total local membership of the Scandinavian Mission was 4,398 souls, including 245 Elders, 127 Priests, 160 Teachers, and 55 Deacons. Of these, 1,089 souls (including 59 Elders, 32 Priests, 39 Teachers and 15 Deacons) were in Denmark, 2,181 souls (including 143 Elders, 67 Priests, 73 Teachers and 30 Deacons) were in Sweden, and 1,128 souls (including 43 Elders, 28 Priests, 48 Teachers and 10 Deacons) were in Norway.

From 1850 to 1905 the Scandinavian Mission embraced Denmark, Sweden and Norway, but from 1905 to 1920, it consisted of Denmark and Norway only and in this history, during these 15 years, it is called the Danish-Norwegian Mission. With the separation of Denmark and Norway in 1920 this mission ceased to exist, and the three countries, originally included in the Scandinavian Mission then became the Swedish Mission, the Danish Mission, and the Norwegian Mission, respectively. Following is a complete list of the presidents of the Scandinavian Mission:

1. Erastus Snow, 1850-1852.
2. John E. Forsgren, 1852.
3. Willard Snow, 1852-1853.
4. John Van Cott, 1853-1856.
5. Hector C. Haight, 1856-1858.

6. Carl Widerborg, 1858-1860.
7. John Van Cott (2nd term) 1860-1862.
8. Jesse N. Smith, 1862-1864.
9. Samuel L. Sprague, pro tem., 1864.
10. Carl Widerborg (2nd term), 1864-1868.
11. Jesse N. Smith (2nd term), 1868-1870.
12. William W. Cluff, 1870-1871.
13. Canute Peterson, 1871-1873.
14. Chr. G. Larsen, 1873-1875.
15. Nils C. Flygare, 1875-1876.
16. Ola N. Liljenquist, 1876-1877.
17. August W. Carlson, pro tem., 1877-1878.
18. Nils C. Flygare (2nd term), 1878-1879.
19. Niels Wilhelmsen, 1879-1881.
20. Andrew Jenson, pro tem., 1881.
21. Christian D. Fjeldsted, 1881-1884.
22. Anthon H. Lund, 1884-1885.
23. Nils C. Flygare (3rd term), 1885-1888.
24. Christian D. Fjeldsted (2nd term), 1888-1890.
25. Edward H. Anderson, 1890-1892.
26. Joseph Christiansen, 1892-1893.
27. Carl A. Carlquist, 1893-1894.
28. Peter Sundwall, 1894-1896.
29. Christian N. Lund, 1896-1898.
30. George Christensen, 1898.
31. Andreas Peterson, 1898-1901.
32. Anthon L. Skanchy, 1901-1904.
33. Christian D. Fjeldsted (3rd term), 1904-1905.

History of the Danish-Norwegian Mission

CHAPTER 1 (1905-1908)

Jens M. Christensen's administration.—Arrival of Elders from Zion—Sören Rasmussen presides—Death of Oliver A. Hansen.

The history of the Danish-Norwegian Mission commences with July 1, 1905, when Sweden became a separate mission, and after that date Denmark and Norway were continued officially for 14 years and 9 months under the old name (Scandinavian Mission), but in this history it is called the Danish-Norwegian Mission, of which Elder Jens Möller Christensen of Salt Lake City, Utah, was the first president. On

JENS MÖLLER CHRISTENSEN

Son of Christen Andersen and Ane Margrete Jensen, was born at Hornstrup, Denmark, Jan. 8, 1846. At an early age he became doubtful of the truth of the teachings of the Lutheran church and suffered persecutions at the in-

July 1, 1905, after the transfer of 60 Elders to the Swedish Mission, only 113 Elders from Zion were left to continue missionary labors in Denmark and Norway, but during the last six months of the year 1905, thirty-nine (39) Elders from America arrived in Denmark and Norway, as follows:

Ole J. Larsen of Ogden, Utah, arrived July 5th. Thor C. Nielsen of Montpelier, Idaho, arrived July 10th. Niels C. Jensen of Spring City, and Andrew Stephensen of Holden, Utah, arrived July 19th. Albert Richard Petersen o f Richfield, Charles L. Edman of Salina, Christian L. Gregersen of Elsinore, John A. Israelsen of Hyrum, and Niels P. Andersen of Manti, Utah, arrived Aug. 2nd. Niels P. Nielsen and Anna Otte of Logan, Utah, arrived Sept. 6th. Christian Mortensen and Franklin Mortensen of South Jor-

stigation of his school teachers. After meeting some L. D. S. missionaries, he joined the Church by baptism, May 31, 1864, was called to do missionary work in the Fredericia Conference and given charge of the Fredericia Branch; later he labored in Aarhus Conference and presided over the Randers Branch. He emigrated to Utah with his young wife in 1867 and located at Moroni, Sanpete County. In 1881-1883, he filled a mission to Denmark, presiding over the Aarhus Conference. He labored as a home missionary in Milburn, Sanpete Co., in 1891. In 1893, he moved to Salt Lake City, and on Sept. 11, 1899, was called to the Northern States Mission. On March 21, 1905, he was called to take charge of the Scandinavian Mission, returning home in 1907. At home Brother Christensen has filled positions as Sunday School superintendent, High counselor, Bishop's counselor, etc., and at the time of his death he served in the presidency of the High Priest's Quorum of Salt Lake Stake. He served as mayor of Moroni three times and has been a miner, sheep-raiser, farmer, merchant, etc. He was the father of fifteen children, of whom eight survived him, viz., Alfred and Lorenzo of his first marriage, and John F., Harvey M., Pearl L., Vera L., Sadie and Anna of a later marriage. Brother Christensen died in Salt Lake City, Jan. 7, 1915.

dan, and Lola E. Jörgensen of Hyde Park, Utah, arrived Oct. 4th. Joseph Stephensen of Levan, James P. Christensen of Salem, Elmer Hans Jörgensen of Benson, Christian Mortensen of Cleveland, Sören L. Larsen of Spring City, James Andersen of Levan, Peter E. Andersen of Provo and Charles P. Andersen of Elsinore, Utah, Adolph M. Nielsen of

Shelley, Idaho, and Francis Jensen of Mt. Pleasant, Utah, arrived Nov. 1st. Hans P. Folkersen of Salt Lake City, Lewis E. Hemmingsen of South Jordan, Martin Nielsen and Lorenzo Eggertz of Logan, Christian F. Petersen of Moroni, Thomas Nielsen of Elsinore, Joseph Petersen of Richfield, Niels L. Petersen and Charles C. Nielsen of Redmond, Utah, Edw. C. Ekman of Erda, Utah, and Niels Jensen of Independence, Idaho, arrived Nov. 29th. Peter Jörgen Petersen of Brigham City, Andres Peter Jacobsen of Nephi, Orson Magleby of Monroe, and Willard N. Petersen of Spanish Fork, Utah, arrived Dec. 20th.

During the last six months of the

JOHN A. ISRAELSON

A prominent Elder in the Church of Norwegian parentage, was born March 23, 1886, at Hyrum, Cache County, Utah, the son of Andrew M. Israelson and Boletta Wilson. John A. was the firstborn of five children, was educated in the public schools and the Brigham Young College, and Agricultural College, Logan, and was appointed postmaster at Hyrum in 1911, and again in 1922. He has served as chief of the State Dairy and Food Department, president of the Utah Jersey Cattle Club, secretary and president of the Hyrum Chamber of Commerce, and vice-president of the Utah Postmasters' Association. Since June, 1926, he has acted as president of the Utah branch of the National League of District Postmasters. From his early youth he has been engaged in Church activities and filled a mission to Norway in 1905-1907. At home he has labored as a Sunday School teacher and superintendent, and also as president of Y. M. M. I. A. He was appointed second counselor to Joseph B. White, president of the Hyrum Stake, in July, 1920. In 1908 (Dec. 23rd) he married Eliza Jane Dunn, daughter of Bishop Chas. O. Dunn and Jane Welch, in the Logan Temple. Having no children of their own, they have adopted a boy (J. Howard) and a girl (Clara May).

NIELS PETER ANDERSEN

A missionary Elder, was born Nov. 9, 1866, at Sönderhaa, Thisted amt, Denmark, the son of Martin Ogaard and Jensine Birgitte Andersen. He emigrated to Utah with his parents in June, 1881, arrived in Manti July 20th, and was baptized July 6, 1882, by Bishop William T. Reid. On April 3, 1888, he married Caroline M. Madsen of Manti; they had five children, four now living. Being ordained a Seventy Feb. 15, 1905, Brother Andersen went on a mission to Denmark, labored in the Aalborg Conference, helped to finish the meeting house in Aalborg and returned home in July, 1907. He was called on a second mission to Scandinavia in 1925, but returned home after four months, because of sickness. His wife passed away June 28, 1917. Brother Andersen is still living at Manti, Utah.

year 1905, a number of Utah Elders were released to return to their homes; hence the official statistical report of Dec. 30, 1905, states that 67 Elders and two missionary sisters from Zion were on that date laboring in Denmark, and 59 Elders and two missionary sisters in Norway. At that time also the total membership of the Church in Denmark was 1,135 (including 53 Elders, 27 Priests, 35 Teachers and 18 Deacons), and in

Norway 1,213 (including 41 Elders, 40 Priests, 43 Teachers and 16 Deacons). During the year 1905, 173 persons were added to the Church by baptism in Denmark and 132 in Norway. There were 3 conferences and 17 organized branches of the Church in Denmark, and 3 conferences and 18 organized branches in Norway, at the close of the year 1905.

In 1906 missionaries from Zion arrived in the Danish-Norwegian Mission on the following dates:

John A. Olsen of Salem, Alfred C. Nielsen of Draper, Jens A. Ander-

HANS PETER FOLKERSEN

A veteran Elder in the Church, was born July 28, 1858, in Haldagergaarde, Fuglebjerg, Denmark, the son of Folker Christensen and Inger Hansen. In 1874, his father and one sister joined the Church, the latter being healed of rheumatism under the administration of the Elders. Hans Peter was baptized Jan. 13, 1879, by Lars Peter Andersen; ordained a Priest and sent to Bornholm as a missionary; was ordained an Elder Jan. 4, 1880, and appointed to labor in the south part of Sjælland that summer, and then again sent to Bornholm. He left Copenhagen for America July 28, 1882, preached on board the ship and was contradicted by a clergyman; arrived at his brother's home in Michigan, Aug. 12th, and arrived in Salt Lake City in December, 1882. Brother Folkersen married Anna Anderson, April 4, 1883, and Caroline G. Madsen, March 6, 1886, and was ordained a Seventy in 1889. He filled a mission to Denmark in 1905-1907, laboring in the Copenhagen Conference. For several years he presided over the Scandinavian meetings in the Liberty Stake, Salt Lake City, and was ordained a High Priest in 1912. Brother Folkersen is still (1927) a resident of Salt Lake City.

PETER JÖRGEN PETERSEN

Was born March 25, 1858, in Kikhaven, Frederiksborg amt, Denmark. His mother, Anne Katrine Petersen, died in Denmark in 1859 and in 1860 his father emigrated to Utah, together with his little son. They crossed the Atlantic in the ship "William Tapscott" and the Plains with a handcart company, arriving in Salt Lake City in the fall of 1860. Peter Jörgen received his early education in Mantua, Box Elder Co., and later settled in Brigham City. On Aug. 19, 1891, he was united in marriage to Ellen Larsen, who became the mother of four children, namely, Stella, Sylvia, Franklin J. and Norman R. In 1905-1907 Brother Petersen filled a mission to Denmark, laboring in the Copenhagen Conference, part of the time as president of the Northeast Sjælland Branch. Brother Petersen died at the family residence at Brigham City, April 27, 1924. His daughter, Sylvia, with her husband, W. Lamont Glover of Brigham City, filled a two-years' mission to Japan, and his son, Norman R. Petersen is at present (1927) filling a mission to Denmark.

sen of Harrisville, and Hans G. Johnson of Deweyville, Utah, Jacob Petersen of Mink Creek, Idaho, and Richard Andersen of Mantua, Utah, arrived Jan. 27th. Alfred Hansen of Salt Lake City, Utah, and Lawrence C. Wall of Lyman, Wyoming, arrived March 3rd. Charles J. Olsen of Levan, Nicolai Andersen of Salt Lake City, Utah, and Olaf F. Olsen of Grace, Idaho, arrived April 7th. Peter Borup of Eureka, William L. Larsen of Newton, George W. Kofoed of Levan, Peter M. Andersen of Bear River City, James R. Olsen of Manti, and Willard R. Lund of Plain City, Utah, Mathias J. Benson of Moreland, and Jacob L. Hartvigsen of Downey, Idaho, arrived May 9th. Joseph E. Michelsen, Rasmus Rasmussen, and Sören Rasmussen of Draper,

Newman J. Beck and Charles O. Hansen of Centerfield, Christian Andersen of Green River and Andrew L. Andersen of Huntington, Utah, and Hans F. Jensen of Idaho Falls, Peter M. Frandsen of Iona, Hans Sörensen of Independence, Peter Petersen of Bench, and Nicolai C. Miller of Trenton, Idaho, and Hans Peter Jensen of Mapleton, Utah, arrived May 23rd. Lars P. Thomsen of Ferron, Hyrum M. Christensen of Salt Lake City and James E. Frandsen of Redmond, Utah, arrived June 20th. Ingeborg Olesen of Brigham City, Utah, arrived July 18th. Louis C. Jensen of Grover, and David Peterson of Lyman, Wyoming, and Hyrum J. Jensen of Salt Lake City and Christian O. Thomson of Hyrum, Utah, arrived

CHRISTEN O. THOMSEN

An active Elder in the Church, was born March 8, 1862, at Öland, Denmark, the son of Ole Thomsen and Mette Katrine Bertelsen; emigrated to America in 1881, and to Utah in 1882, where he joined the Church and located at Hyrum, Cache County. He married Annie C. Johnsen in the Logan Temple, Jan. 5, 1887; they had seven children;¹ the wife died Aug. 17, 1909. Brother Thomsen filled a mission to Denmark in 1906-1908, laboring in Aalborg and vicinity. On Oct. 11, 1911, he married Clara C. Sventzer, filled several positions of trust and was a great lover of music.   He died at Hyrum, Sept. 24, 1926.

HANS PETER OLSEN, JUNIOR

Was born May 3, 1872, at Fountain Green, Sanpete Co., Utah, the son of Hans Peter Olsen and Ellen R. Aagaard; his father joined the Church June 28, 1853 and performed missionary work before emigrating to Utah in 1858. Hans Peter, junior, was baptized when eight years old and took his part in Church activities. In 1892 (Feb. 14th) he married Inger Andersen, who died in 1902, leaving two sons. In 1904 Brother Olsen married Minnie Livingstone, who bore him two sons. In 1905-1908 Brother Olsen filled a mission to Denmark, laboring in the Aarhus Conference. At present (1927) he is senior president of the 49th Quorum of Seventy. He has always made his home at Fountain Green.

July 25th. John J. Piepgrass of Raymond, Canada, Christian Johnson and Hans Peter Olsen, junior, of Fountain Green, Utah, Hosea Berg and Julia A. Berg of Tilden, and Lauritz P. Henricksen of Parker, Idaho, and Carl M. Nielsen of Logan, Utah, arrived Aug. 15th. Hyrum J. Amundsen and Hugo C. A. Peterson of Salt Lake City, and Orson W. Gunderson of Winder Ward,

CARL MAGNUS NILSSON

Was born Oct. 17, 1852, in Helsingborg, Malmöhus län, Sweden, the son of Jöns Nilsson and Ingrid Monson, who were among the first converts to the restored gospel in Helsingborg, being baptized in the spring of 1853 and confirmed at the first conference of the Church held in Sweden in the barn of Johan Capson at Lund. In June, 1853, Carl Magnus was blessed at that meeting, being six months old. His parents moved to Copenhagen in 1854, where Carl was baptized Sept. 26, 1861. Soon afterwards he was ordained a Priest and labored as a local missionary in the Copenhagen Conference in 1870-1874. Emigrating to Utah, he arrived in Salt Lake City, July 15, 1874, and became associated with the United Order in Brigham City. Soon afterwards he married Anna Laurine Jensen from Copenhagen, which marriage was blessed with seven children. In 1882 he filled a mission among the Indians at Washakie, Utah. He acted as presiding Elder of the Greenville Branch in Cache Valley, and when the branch was organized as a ward he served as first counselor to the Bishop, being ordained a High Priest May 9, 1892, by Moses Thatcher. In 1906-1908 he filled a mission to Scandinavia, laboring in the Aarhus Conference, Denmark. For several years Brother Nilsson has been a resident of Logan.

Utah, and William A. Peterson of Victor, Idaho, arrived Sept. 12th. John Eskildson of Coveville, Franklin T. Nelson of Redmond, Haakon E. Aamodt of Murray, Knud H. Fridal, junior, and Elias Andersen of Elwood, John L. Larsen of Newton, James Jensen of Wales, and J. Andrew Olsen of Centerfield, Utah, Peter Marion Mortensen of Sanford, Colorado, and Peter A. Petersen of Mink Creek, and Joseph Christensen of Preston, Idaho, arrived Nov. 7th. Alma Benson of Newton, Charles Jensen and Thorwald Erastus Christensen of Redmond, Peter Mortensen of Elwood, Rasmus Johnson of Emery, Niels P. Petersen of Ephraim, Alma Jensen of Bear River City, Niels C. Christensen, junior, and Lars Anderson of Salt Lake City, Lorentz Petersen of Hyrum, Ole Eliasen Olsen of Provo, Niels P. Andersen, junior, of Brigham City, Niels J. Nielsen of Riverton, and Hans O. Sörensen of Leamington, Utah, Hyrum Larsen of Georgetown, and Nephi Christensen of Blackfoot, Idaho, and Lars J. Halling, junior, of Grover, Wyoming, arrived Dec. 19th.

Sister Julia A. Berg, who together with her husband, Hosea Berg, arrived in Copenhagen, Aug. 15, 1906, and was appointed to labor in the Christiania Conference died of typhoid fever, Nov. 21, 1906, in a hospital at Frederikstad, Norway. She was 37 years old, and resided in Tilden, Idaho. Her remains were prepared and shipped to Idaho, accompanied by her husband, who was released from his mission in Norway for that purpose.

In 1907, a building lot was purchased by the Church in the City of Aalborg, Denmark, on which a chapel and conference house was built that year. It consists of a two-story red-brick structure, with a basement. The building is 63 feet long and 34 feet wide, outside measurements; the

walls are 25 feet and the tower 45
feet high. The basement, in which
the walls and floor are built of ce-
ment, is used for bathing and laun-

LATTER-DAY SAINTS CHAPEL
Erected in Aalborg, Denmark, in 1907.

dry purposes and for storage. The
first story above the basement contains dwelling apartments, including
the conference office, a small meeting hall, kitchen and closets; also a
baptismal font with adjoining dressing-rooms. The second story is occupied by the main auditorium,
which has a seating capacity of three
hundred. The chapel was built under the supervision of Elder Hyrum
J. Jensen of Salt Lake City, Utah,
and was dedicated July 7, 1907, by
Apostle Charles W· Penrose, presi-
ent of the European Mission, who
came over from England on a visit
to Scandinavia, on the occasion of
the dedication.

The following missionaries from
Zion (84 in number) arrived in the
Danish-Norwegian Mission during
the year 1907:

Anton Jensen of Weston, Idaho,
and Hyrum Hansen of Spanish Fork,
Morten C. Jensen of Richfield, and
Joseph H. Hansen and Henry O. Ol-

sen of Brigham City, and James P.
Rasmussen of Millville, Utah, ar-
rived Jan. 30th. Niels J. Larsen of
Salt Lake City, Utah, arrived March
6th. Alma B. Larsen of Salem, Ida-
ho, arrived April 10th. Willard E.
Steffensen of Inverury, Albert E.
Delange and Charles Martinsen of
Koosharem, Carl Berg of Castle Dale,
Robert Anderson, Paul K. Nielsen
and August H. Knebelau of Salt
Lake City, Lars S· Christensen of
Hyde Park, Jens C. Jensen of Spring
City, James B. Christiansen and Hen-

HYRUM JULIUS JENSEN

A well known business man, was born in
Salt Lake City, March 13, 1869, the first of
six children. The father, Sören Jensen, was
born at Hvirring, Denmark, and arrived in
Salt Lake City in 1857, having crossed the
Plains with a handcart company. The mother
crossed the Plains by ox team and arrived in
Salt Lake City in 1867. She was born at
Gylling, Jutland. In 1906-1908 Hyrum filled
a mission to Denmark, presided over the Aalborg Branch 11 months and over the Aalborg
Conference 14 months . He supervised the
erection of the L. D. S. chapel at Aalborg in
1907. At home he has labored as a home missionary, and now acts as a counselor in the
presidency of the High Priests' quorum of
the Granite Stake. From 1924 to 1927 he was
second counselor to Pres. Niels J. Henricksen
in the presidency of the Danish meetings in
Salt Lake City. Brother Jensen is a successful contractor and builder, and the owner of
large real estate interests in Salt Lake City
and vicinity.

ry J. Nelson of Spanish Fork and Niels Jensen of Providence, Utah, Enoch E. Christoffersen of Le Grande, Oregon, and Orson Peter Heilesen of Burton, James M. Keller of Mink Creek, and Otto E. Johnson and Rolf C. Wald of Preston, Idaho, arrived May 20th. Frederick Jörgensen of Ephraim and Nephi W. Hansen of Draper, Utah, arrived June 19th. Henry Danielsen of Hyrum, Utah, arrived July 17th. George W. Christophersen of Salt Lake City, Henry O. Poulsen, Niels N. Busk and Orson F. Christensen of Richfield, and Andrew H. Andersen of Fountain Green, Utah, Peter H. Wes-

tenskow of Imbler, Oregon, and Niels P. Nielsen, junior, of Pocatello, and Wrol Chr. Olsen of Iona, Idaho, arrived Aug. 12th. Charles O. Petersen and Wilford A. Jörgensen of Logan, Frank C. Torkelson, Axel Christian Nielsen and Jens Peter Meilstrup of Salt Lake City, Peter A. Nielsen of Draper and James Brown of Monroe, Utah, arrived Sept. 7th. John G. Hansen, Andrew W. Jensen of Salt Lake City, Joseph S. Baird of Brigham City, Jens Chr. Nielsen of Levan, Ernest James Nielsen and Jacob Petersen of Murray, Edward A. Olsen, junior, of Ogden, Niels C. Madsen of Summit, and Sören Christiansen of Richfield, Utah, Henry M. Bohne of Aetna, Canada, and George Arthur Nielsen of Mink Creek, Idaho, arrived Oct. 6th. Peter

JOSEPH W. PETERSON

Son of John A. Peterson and Marie Hansen, was born at Logan, Cache Co., Utah, Feb. 6, 1877. The family located in Smithfield in 1882, which has been their home ever since. Brother Peterson received his education in the Smithfield public schools and in the Brigham Young College, and taught school in Cache County for several years, principally at Smithfield. He married Laura C. Merrill, Sept. 3, 1902, by which union three sons and four daughters were born. Brother Peterson filled a mission to Scandinavia in 1907-1909, laboring in the Copenhagen Conference. He was ordained a High Priest March 23, 1913, served as Ward clerk for some years in the Smithfield First Ward and later called to act in the same capacity in the Smithfield Second Ward, which position he still holds. He served as city recorder in 1912-1913, and 1920-1926. At the present time he is editor of the "Smithfield Sentinel."

JENS CHRISTIAN PEDERSEN

Was born Sept. 24, 1865, in Aasted parish, Hjörring amt, Jutland, Denmark, the son of Christian Petersen and Katrine Christensen. He was baptized May 15, 1887, by Elder Victor C. Högsted, emigrated to Utah the same year and located in Spring City, where he still resides. Brother Petersen filled a mission to Scandinavia in 1907-1909, laboring in the Bergen Conference, Norway, and in the Aalborg Conference, Denmark. In 1913 (Jan. 15th) he married Martha Olufine Gabrielsen, formely of Stavanger, Norway; they have seven children (three boys and four girls). Brother Petersen now holds the office of High Priest.

27

R. Petersen, junior, of Ferron, Jörgen Madsen of Manti, Ben. D. Jensen of Chesterfield, Utah, Lester F. Nielsen of Shelley, Idaho, and Kleam Poulsen of Liberty, Idaho, arrived Oct. 23rd. Carl C. Nielsen of Mink Creek, Idaho, Joseph H. Johnson of Salem, Alfred E. Sörensen and Carl Norman Skanchy of Logan, Abraham O· Jacobsen of Murray, Utah, George Gorgeson of Weston, Idaho, Simon Christensen of Richfield, Ja-

cob J. H. Jensen of Fountain Green, Jens C. Christensen of Provo, Utah, Peter P. Skriver of Aetna, Canada, Joseph W. Petersen of Smithfield, Joseph M. Olsen of Spanish Fork, Utah, James A. Johnson of Rexburg, Idaho, Sören Rasmus Nielsen of Manti, Jens Christian Pedersen of Spring City, Joseph P. Johansen of Mt. Pleasant, and Hans Christian Hansen of Tooele, Utah, arrived Nov. 20th, and Christian C. Johnson and Oliver A. Hansen of Bear River City, George Sidney Schow of Lehi, Anton R. Christensen of Ogden, Ole C.

SÖREN RASMUSSEN

Second president of the Danish-Norwegian Mission, was born April 26, 1865, in Grönfeld, Randers amt, Denmark, the son of Rasmus Rasmussen and Bertha Marie Petersen, and baptized June 9, 1885, by Elder Rasmus P. Marquardsen, emigrated to Utah the same year and located in Draper, Salt Lake County. He was ordained successively to the offices of Teacher and Elder, the latter ordination taking place in the fall of 1885, at which time he also married Anna Boline Andersen. In 1898-1900 he filled a mission to Denmark, laboring in the Aarhus Conference. In 1906-1909 he filled another mission to Scandinavia and presided over the Christiania Conference about sixteen months, after which he succeeded Elder Jens M. Christensen as president of the Danish-Norwegian Mission. After his return from this mission he was called to preside as Bishop of the Draper Ward. Being released from that position in August, 1914, he acted as first counselor in the presidency of the Jordan Stake, and in May, 1919, upon the release of President William D. Kuhre, Elder Rasmussen was chosen and set apart as president of the Jordan Stake, a position which he held for eight years. He is a prominent figure among the Scandinavian Saints, always taking an active part in their gatherings.

NIELS PETERSEN

Son of Niels A. Petersen and Johanne Larsen, was born Dec. 11, 1882, in Big Cottonwood, Salt Lake County, Utah. He held successively the offices of Deacon, Teacher and Priest, and was ordained an Elder Aug. 11, 1907, by J. A. Jörgensen. Leaving Salt Lake City, Dec. 29, 1907, for a mission to Denmark, he labored in the Aalborg Conference, mostly at Hadsund, Hobro, Lögstor and Aalborg; he returned home May 15, 1910. Brother Petersen was teacher of a Sunday school theological class in 1910-1920, and counselor in a quorum of Elders in 1914-1920. He moved to Roseworth, Twin Falls Stake, Idaho, in 1920, and acted as first counselor in the Bishopric there from August, 1922, to December, 1925. He married Ingeborg Olsen in the Salt Lake Temple, March 22, 1911. They have four daughters (Ruth, Esther, Oda and Rozella) and are still (1927) living at Roseworth, Idaho.

Larsen of Redmond, Niels P. Jeppesen of Mantua and Hans Mikkelsen of Hyrum, Utah, arrived Dec. 21st.

Elder Sören Rasmussen, who had presided over the Christiania Conference, Norway, and who had been appointed by the First Presidency of the Church to succeed Jens M. Christensen as president of the Danish-Norwegian Mission, proceeded to Copenhagen, and took charge of the mission, Nov. 8, 1907. Elder Christensen had presided over the mission about two years and six months; he was successful and conscientious in his administration.

Sixty-eight missionaries from Zion arrived in the Danish-Norwegian Mission during the year 1908, as follows:

David O. Nielsen of Hyrum, Moses P. Jörgensen and James J. Larsen of

OLUF JOSVA ANDERSEN

A veteran Elder in the Church, was born in Christiania, Norway, April 4, 1849, was baptized August 25, 1865, by Elder John Larsen and by him ordained an Elder Nov. 6, 1867. By vocation Elder Andersen was a school teacher and held a government permit. By appointment of Pres. Carl Widerborg, he acted as conference secretary in Christiania in 1868-1869; was later called to labor as a traveling Elder in the northern and western parts of Norway and afterwards presided over the Frederikstad and Frederikshald branches. He emigrated to Utah in 1874 and located at Ephraim, Sanpete, County, but later moved to Emery County, where he was appointed Stake clerk by Pres. C. G. Larsen and first counselor to Bishop Henning Olsen of the Castle Dale Ward. In November, 1891, Elder Andersen was called by Pres. Anthon H. Lund to edit "Bikuben," a weekly paper, published in Salt Lake City in the Danish-Norwegian language. He acted in this position until September, 1895. In 1908-1912 he filled a special mission to Scandinavia, being set apart by Pres. Joseph F. Smith to labor as associate editor and translator of "Skandinaviens Stjerne" at Copenhagen. Elder Oluf J. Andersen is one of the most gifted, energetic and faithful men who joined the Church in Scandinavia. He has held many important positions both in the Church and in the State of Utah. He is now (1927) a resident of Castle Dale, Emery County, Utah, possesses a pleasant and agreeable personality, and is popular among the people.

ORSON A. J. GARFF

Born March 2, 1885, at Draper, Utah, is the son of Peter N. Garff and Antomine Sörensen. His parents and grandparents emigrated to Utah in 1856, crossing the Plains in a hand-cart company. Bro. Orson filled a mission to Denmark in 1908-1910, laboring in Odense, Esbjerg and Aarhus, part of the time acting as secretary of the Aarhus Conference, and had the privilege of baptizing five converts during this mission. He married Bodel M. Lyngby of Logan, April 6, 1911; they have five children: Ruth L., Marjorie L., Dorothy L., O. Reed and Betty Lou. His wife died Nov. 9, 1926. Elder Garff acted as counselor to Bishop Sören Rasmussen of Draper three years. Moving to Logan in 1916 he was set apart as counselor to Bishop James R. Thomas of the Logan 11th Ward, which position he still occupies. Bro. Garff is active in scout work, is a member of the Rotary Club and of the Chamber of Commerce at Logan, and is engaged in mercantile business.

Logan, Alfred Axel Johansen and Isak A. Jensen of Brigham City, Niels Petersen of Elwood, James R. Ware of Monroe and Orson A. J. Garff of Draper, Utah, arrived Jan. 16th. John H. Berg, of Basalt, Ingvard G. Henriksen of Egin and James O. Petersen of Shelley, Idaho, arrived Feb. 22nd. Niels Iversen of Fillmore, Utah, arrived March 7th. Oluf J. Andersen of Castle Dale, Utah, arrived April 2nd. Jens Edward Rasmussen of Elba, Idaho, Hyrum W. Hansen of College Ward, Utah, Lauritz M. Sörensen of Lovell, Wyoming, and John M. Jensen of Aetna, Canada, arrived April 29th. Carl Kjær and Ole Gulbrandsen of Salt Lake City, Jens C. Hansen of Axtell, Wilford H. Wilde of Brigham City, Carl Marius D. Simonsen

of Gunnison, Aurelius Thoresen, Christian H. Johnson and Hans C. Johnson of Logan, James C. Christensen of Chester, David L. Christiansen of Hyrum, Erastus Johnson of Richmond and Sören Andersen of Centerfield, Utah, arrived May 13th. Ferdinand A. Petersen of Rigby, Idaho, Joseph S. Nielsen and Peter Rasmussen of Salt Lake City, Oliver M. Munk of Logan, Karl J. Knudsen of Provo, Heber J. H a n s e n of Benjamin, Utah, and Hans C. Hansen of Weston, Idaho, arrived June 17th. Jens. D. Nielsen of Manti and Herman F. Hansen of Salt Lake City, Utah, arrived July 15th. Peter Edward Parry Mackelprang of

OLE GULBRANDSEN

Missionary in Norway, was born Feb. 5, 1873, at Frederikstad, Norway, the son of O.e Gulbrandsen and Anna Marie Halvorsen. He emigrated to Salt Lake City, Utah, in May, 1886, and was ordained an Elder by John H. Burton Feb. 13, 1899. On March 15, 1899, he married Halvorine O. Halvorsen in the Salt Lake Temple. Brother Gulbrandsen filled a mission to Norway in 1908-1910, laboring in the Christiania Conference. On his return home, he was selected second counselor to Pres. John Lawrence of the Scandinavian meetings in Salt Lake City, and later became the president of said meetings held in the Assembly Hall. He is at present superintendent of the 34th Ward Sunday school and engineer of the Church buildings on the Temple Block and vicinity.

HYRUM W. HANSEN

A missionary, was born in Providence, Utah, Jan. 20, 1866, the son of Mads Hansen of Vemmelev, Denmark, and was baptized July 2, 1885. On February 10, 1897, he married Emma Jensen of Hyrum, Utah, and is the father of seven children, six of whom at the present writing (1926) are living. Brother Hansen filled a mission to Denmark in 1908-1910, laboring in the Aarhus Conference, mostly in the Esbjerg, Randers and Odense branches. He acted as superintendent in the College Ward Sunday school for a number of years.

Cedar City, John C. Christoffersen of Richmond and Ruedora C. Jörgensen of Logan, Utah, arrived Aug. 12th. Franklin J. D. Jensen of Provo, Utah, arrived Aug. 15th. Torkel E. Torkelsen of Salt Lake City, arrived Sept. 9th. James Jensen of Garland, Charles H. Sörensen and Carl H. L. Jensen of Salt Lake City, Utah, arrived Oct. 7th. Donizett D. Hansen of Provo, Lorenzo Petersen of Fairview, Utah, Hans C. Hansen of Salem, Idaho, Joseph C. Christensen of Mt. Pleasant, Henry O. Hansen of Smithfield, Niels J. Larsen of Salt Lake City, Edward W. Jensen of Mantua and Hans P. Andersen of Hyrum, Utah, Leroy P. Skousen of

Colonia Juares and Niels Larsen of Dublan, Mexico, and Hyrum Nielsen of Preston, Idaho, arrived Nov. 4th. Louis M. Breinholt of Redmond, James C. Johnson, junior, and James C. Sörensen of Logan, Carl Christensen of Salem, Lars C. Larsen of Mapleton, William D. Norman of Provo, Oscar D. Jensen of Preston, Lars Fredrikson of Weston and Levi Seversen of Coltman, Idaho, arrived Dec. 12th, and James

DAVID L. CHRISTIANSEN

Who labored as a missionary in Norway and Denmark in 1908-1910, was born Oct. 17, 1886, in Hyrum, Cache Co., Utah, the son of Lars Peter Christiansen and Amy L. Shaw. He was baptized and ordained to the Priesthood when quite young and on his arrival in Copenhagen was appointed to labor in the Trondhjem Conference, Norway. In answer to prayer he learned to read and converse in the Norwegian language in a remarkably short time, and during the beautiful summer in the Land of the Midnight Sun he and his missionary companions tracted all the numerous small islands around Narvik. They held many meetings and organized the most northern L. D. S. Sunday school in the world. Elder Christiansen writes: "During the summer months we baptized four new members and during the long, dark winter months, when the sun did not show its face for three months, we spent the time holding meetings and tracting the little city of Narvik, which town will always bring back very dear memories as long as I live. I thank my Heavenly Father for the privilege I had to fill that mission, for I obtained a testimony and a schooling which could not have been obtained in any other way." Elder Christiansen finished his mission in the Copenhagen Conference, Denmark, and is now (1927) a resident of Ogden, Utah.

CHRISTIAN H. JOHNSON

Was born in Logan, Utah, Jan. 2, 1883, the son of Jacob C. Johnson and Bertholine Madsen, the former being born at Degnsgaard, near Viborg, and the latter at Hammel, Denmark. They joined the Church in Denmark; Bro. Johnson emigrated to Utah and three and a half years later sent for his intended wife and they were married in the Endowment House, Salt Lake City. Their son, Christian H. Johnson, the subject of this sketch, filled a mission to Denmark in 1908-1910, laboring in Veile, Odense and Silkeborg. On Jan. 31, 1912, he married Lillie Maud Pauli; they have three children, Pauli, Hilman and Vewene. Bro. Johnson is secretary of a quorum of Elders.

C. Peterson of Boulder and Albert A. Smith of Victor, Idaho, arrived Dec. 23rd.

Oliver A. Hansen, of Tremonton, Box Elder County, Utah, who was laboring as a missionary in Norway, was released because of sickness and started for home in November, 1908, but died en route in Chicago, Nov. 29, 1908.

ERASTUS JOHNSON

A successful missionary, was born April 18, 1883, in Richmond, Cache Co., Utah, the son of Niels Johnson and Margaret Rasmussen, and was baptized Aug. 6, 1891, by Elder Alonzo D. Merrill. In 1908-1910, Elder Johnson filled a mission to Norway, presiding part of the time over the Aalesund Branch and later over the Bergen Conference; he baptized nineteen persons. After his return to Utah he was chosen second counselor in the Scandinavian presidency in Richmond and a board member in the Y. M. M. I. A. of the Benson Stake; he was ordained a Seventy May 3, 1912, by Clarence L Funk. Brother Johnson married Nellie Maria Merrill, daughter of Apostle Marriner W. Merrill; they have had seven children, four of whom are now (1927) living. In 1920-1922 Brother Johnson filled another mission to Norway. Foreign travel presented many difficulties at this time, but at length he got his passport visaed in Copenhagen, Norway, after which he presided over the Trondhjem Conference seventeen months. He baptized sixteen converts and returned home in December, 1922. On April 12, 1925, he was set apart as one of the presidents of the 39th quorum of Seventy by Pres. J. Golden Kimball. Elder Johnson is still (1927) a resident of Richmond and a faithful Elder in the Church.

CHAPTER 2. (1909-1911)

Death of Elder Charles Martinsen—Andrew Jenson's administration—Visits of Presidents Anthon H. Lund and Charles W. Penrose— Beyond the Artic Circle—Visit of Apostle Rudger Clawson—President Joseph F. Smith and Bishop Charles W. Nibley visit Scandinavia—Illustrated lectures.

Elder Charles Martinsen, who was laboring as a missionary in Norway, died in Stavanger, Jan. 12, 1909.

Elder Andrew Jenson succeeded Sören Rasmussen as president of the Danish-Norwegian Mission, Feb. 15, 1909, having been called and set apart by the First Presidency for that position. President Rasmussen had presided over the mission with dignity and success about 14 months and left the affairs of the mission in good condition.

President Anthon H. Lund, wife and daughter, Apostle Charles W. Penrose and wife, and Emma H. Jenson, wife of Andrew Jenson, and daughter Eva, arrived in Denmark,

JAMES D. NIELSEN

A missionary, was born July 10, 1852, at Viuf, Veile amt, Denmark, emigrated to Utah and was baptized at Manti, Sanpete County in 1884. He performed a mission to Denmark in 1908-1909, where he labored in the Aarhus Conference. In 1911 (July 26th) Brother Nielsen married Mrs. Anna Hendriksen, who had five children, three sons and two daughters, by a previous marriage.

on a visit to Scandinavia. On their arrival in Fredericia, July 3, 1909, they were joined by Pres. Andrew Jenson and his daughter, Eleonore, and the party traveled to Aarhus the same day, where they celebrated American Independence Day, July 4th, by participating in an American banquet, in connection with the Exposition, which, at that time, was being held at Aarhus. After holding a number of meetings in Aarhus and Randers, the whole company proceeded to Aalborg, President Lund's native city, where interesting and well-attended meetings were held on July 7th. The people of Aalborg seemed to be delighted in

hearing the voice of one of their countrymen, who had spent so many years in America, and had gained renown, not only among his countrymen, but in the community at large. From Aalborg, the company continued their journey by rail to Frederikshavn and by steamer to Göteborg, Sweden, whence they went by rail to Christiania, Norway, where they arrived on the 10th and

LARS FREDRICKSON

Was born Aug. 30, 1857, in Denmark, the son of Ferdinand Fredriksen and Sine Marie Larsen Möller. With his mother and two brothers he emigrated to Utah in 1865, crossing the Atlantic Ocean in the sailing ship "B. S. Kimball" and the Plains with a freight train, walking every step of the way. The father who had emigrated the previous year met them in Salt Lake City and took them to Logan, where they made their home until 1868, when they moved to Weston, Idaho. Here Bro. Fredrickson engaged in farming and later owned one of the finest farms in the locality, equipped with fine stock and the latest farming appliances. In 1876 he married Stine Jensen Skellet; to them were born nine children, five boys and four girls. In 1908-1910 he filled a mission to Denmark, laboring in the Aalborg Conference twenty months, when he was released on account of the illness of his wife. Sister Fredrickson continued in poor health until she died at the sanitarium at Lava Hot Springs, Idaho, Oct. 18, 1915. On Nov. 27, 1919, Elder Fredrickson married Amanda Loland, a native of Norway. The following year he and his wife made a trip to Denmark and Norway to gather genealogy; they were away more than a year and since their return have resided in Logan, where they are engaged in doing work in the Temple for the redemption of their dead.

WILLIAM DOUGLAS NORMAN

Son of George William and Inger S. Norman, was born in Bergen, Norway, Oct. 5, 1882, joined the Church there, being baptized Nov. 23, 1896, Elder Hyrum Jensen officiating. He emigrated to Utah in the fall of 1901 and settled at Provo. On June 1, 1904, he married Catherine Jensen, of Provo, in the Salt Lake Temple. In 1908-1911 he filled a mission to the Scandinavian countries, being set apart for this mission by Apostle John Henry Smith. He labored with success in the Bergen and Aarhus conferences and after his return home was set apart as second counselor in the Scandinavian presidency in Provo. He was ordained a High Priest April 27, 1923, and appointed second counselor to Bishop Alfred W. Harding of the Pioneer Ward, Provo. Brother Norman is at the head of the Interior Decoration Department of the Dixon-Taylor-Russell Company of Provo.

OLIVER A. HANSEN

Who died while filling a mission abroad,
was born Oct. 29, 1886, in Bear River City,
Boxelder County, Utah, the son of Peter M.
Hansen and Hannah M. Andersen. He was
baptized Nov. 1, 1894, ordained to the Priesthood and called on a mission to Scandinavia
in 1907, and was appointed to labor in Norway.
His health failing, he was honorably released
and started for home, but died en route, passing away in Chicago, Ill., Nov. 8, 1908. He
was a good young man, unmarried, and highly respected by all who knew him.

APOSTLE CHARLES W. PENROSE

President of the European Mission, was born
Feb. 4, 1832, at Camberwell, London, England.
He died in Salt Lake City, Utah, May 16,
1925,, as first counselor to President Heber
J. Grant. Elder Penrose was one of the ablest
expounders of the gospel known in the Church
and one of its most successful missionaries.

CHARLES MARTINSEN

Who died while filling a mission in Scandinavia, was born July 11, 1865, in Norway,
the son of Peter Martinsen and Toline Christensen. He was baptized when ten years of age
and became an earnest and efficient Church
worker in the Röken Branch before he emigrated to America. Emigrating to Utah he
located in Koosharem, Sevier County, where
he was ordained a Seventy and called on a
mission, in April, 1907, to Scandinavia. While
laboring faithfully as a missionary in Norway
he was stricken with appendicitis, underwent
an operation and died Jan. 12, 1909, in Stavanger. His remains were shipped home for
burial. Elder Martinsen was an exemplary
man, unmarried, and well respected both at
home and abroad.

ANDREW JENSON

Assistant Church Historian, born Dec. 11,
1850, in Torslev parish, Hjørring amt, Denmark, presided over the Danish-Norwegian
(Scandinavian) Mission in 1909-1912. (See
page 215.)

spent a couple of days holding meetings and visiting. Leaving most of the visitors in Christiania, Presidents Lund, Penrose and Jenson went by rail over the mountains to Bergen, on the west coast of Norway, where they arrived July 13th, held interesting meetings with the Elders and Saints, and then returned on the 15th to Christiania. Here Pres. Lund, wife and daughter left the party and traveled by rail to Stockholm to hold meetings, while Apostle Penrose and wife and Andrew Jenson and wife and two daughters, traveled by railroad July 17th to Trondhjem, where meetings were held, and places of interest visited.

Taking an affectionate leave of the Elders and Saints in Trondhjem, the visitors took passage on a steamer on which they sailed up the coast of Norway about eight hundred miles to the city of Vardö, beyond Nordkap, and within the Artic Circle. Here a most excellent meeting was held July 23, 1909, at the close of which the clouds, which had hung heavily upon the mountains and coast of Norway for several days, lifted, and a most pleasing and perfect sight of the midnight sun was revealed. At that time, two Elders, Heber J. Hansen and Karl J. Knudsen, labored in Vardö, and there was only one local member of the Church, but the people who attended the meeting at Vardö received and greeted the visitors as if they had been so many Saints, and when the meeting was over the multitude followed the departing visitors to the harbor and further to the breakwater, where they were last seen waving their hats and handkerchiefs until the ship was far out in the ocean.

On their return journey, President Penrose and party celebrated Pioneer Day (July 24th) at Hammerfest, the northernmost city in the

JAMES OLSEN

Of College Ward, Logan, is the eldest son of James Olsen and Maria Petersen, and was born Dec. 22, 1862, at Brigham City, Utah, where he also was baptized at the age of eight years. On Jan. 5, 1887, he married Alice Helena Hansen; they have ten children, seven of whom are still living. In 1909-1911 Bro. Olsen filled a mission to Denmark, laboring in the Aalborg Conference. He has been a resident of the College Ward, near Logan, since 1880, when he located there with his father's family.

CHARLES W. PENROSE AND
ANDREW JENSON

President Charles W. Penrose preaching, with Andrew Jenson as translator.

world. They sang the Pioneer song, climbed the mountain to enter the northernmost forest in the world, and, continuing the voyage southward, soon reached Narvik, the northernmost railway station in the world, whence they crossed the mountains into Sweden, visiting on the way Gillivare, and Luleå, on the border of Finland, where they stopped over night. Thence they traveled southward through Lappland, passing through the heavy, woodland of Sweden, near the shores of the By of Bothnia, and after a long and somewhat interesting railway journey they arrived in Stockholm July 29th. Here they were greeted by Peter Sundwall, president of the Swedish mission, and other Elders and local Saints, who made the visit of their traveling friends very pleasant. After holding several meetings in Stockholm, the party traveled southward by rail through Sweden to Malmö, and thence crossed Öresund to Copenhagen, Denmark, where Pres. Penrose and party joined President Lund and family August 1st. Good and well-attended meetings were held in Copenhagen on Sunday and Monday, Aug. 1st and 2nd. Pres. Lund and family left Copenhagen for Germany Aug. 2nd, but Elder Penrose and wife stopped another day in Copenhagen, taking in the sights, and then left for England, via Germany, Aug. 3rd.

In 1909, 58 missionaries from Zion arrived in the Danish-Norwegian Mission on the following dates:

OLE J. SITTERUD

A veteran Elder of the Church, was born Oct. 17, 1848, at Odalen, Norway, and married Karen O. Ihler Jan. 2, 1872; they had nine children. Becoming converts to the gospel in 1875, they emigrated to Utah in 1876, settled at Lehi, moved to Fountain Green in April, 1877, and to Emery County in June, 1884, where Brother Sitterud and others became the founders of Orangeville. He held the position of Ward teacher for 25 years, was superintendent of the Sunday school for eleven years and was for years a president of the 91st quorum of Seventy. In 1909-1911 he filled a mission to Norway, laboring in the Bergen Conference, over which he was appointed president, Oct. 31, 1909. Elder Sitterud was elected county clerk and recorder for Emery County in 1894, re-elected twice and has held other positions of civic importance. He still (1927) resides in Orangeville.

ARCHIBALD CHRISTENSEN

A missionary, was born in Fairview, Sanpete Co., Utah, June 28, 1886, the son of Albert Christensen and Agnes J. Anderson, and performed a mission to Norway in 1909-1911, laboring in the Christiania and Trondhjem conferences. He married Pearl Pritchett of Fairview, June 17, 1908.

Andrew Amundson of Salt Lake City, Utah, arrived Jan. 1st. James Larsen of Mapleton, Utah, arrived Jan. 30th. Andrew Jenson of Salt Lake City, Utah, arrived Feb. 11th. James Olsen of College Ward, and Henry J. Amundsen of Salt Lake City, Utah, arrived March 3rd. Erastus J. Christiansen of Mayfield, Utah, arrived April 15th. Holger M. Larsen of Salt Lake City, Christian Fredricksen of Centerfield, Archibald Christensen of Fairview, Leo M. Greenhalgh of Scofield, James M.

Jensen and Orrin P. Hansen of Logan, and John E. Larsen of Bingham, Utah, arrived May 1st. Andrew P. Nielsen of Cleveland and Andrew H. C. Ottesen of Salem, Utah, Nephi Hansen of Darby, Idaho, Joseph K. Nichols of American Fork, Reed J. Knudsen of Provo, Utah, and Ole Petersen Jensen of Burton, Idaho. arrived June 5th. Niels E. Larsen, James A. Stevenson and Alvin Edward Olson of Salt Lake City, Jo-

CHRISTIAN ANDERSEN

A missionary, is the son of Anders Christensen and Maren Pedersdatter, and was born Sept. 23, 1864, in Rodsted, Aalborg amt, Denmark; baptized May 1, 1882, by Elder Sören C. Petersen at Aalborg; emigrated to Utah in 1884, arriving in Salt Lake City in November, and located in Monroe, Sevier County, the following summer. In 1898, he married Ida M. Williams, daughter of James V. Williams (the youngest member of the Mormon Battalion); they have two sons, Ernest V. and Anders K. Linden. In 1909, Brother Andersen was called on a mission to Scandinavia; he arrived in Copenhagen Aug. 4th and was assigned to the Aalborg Conference. Being honorably released in 1911, he returned home in the summer of that year. He was ordained a Seventy and set apart as one of the presidents of the 41st Quorum of Seventy; later he was ordained a High Priest by Elder James L. Staples of the South Sevier Stake presidency. He still (1927) resides at Monroe.

GEORGE WILLIAM THULIN

A missionary, was born March 16, 1870, in Christiania, Norway, the son of Johan Martinus Thulin and Gunda Olsen, was blessed by the Elders in 1871, baptized June 26, 1882, by his brother Martin Thulin, ordained to the various offices in the lesser Priesthood in his native country and emigrated to Utah in 1889, where he was ordained an Elder Aug. 7, 1899, by Stephen Chandler, and a Seventy Jan. 8, 1912, by Pres. B. H. Roberts. In 1909-1911 he filled a mission to Norway, laboring in the Bergen and Christiania conferences; he baptized thirteen persons while on this mission. After his return home he was appointed by Pres. Nephi L. Marris as second counselor in the presidency of the Scandinavian meetings, held weekly, in the Assembly Hall, which position he held for threee years. He has devoted nearly ten years to Temple work, having been baptized as proxy for 19,000 souls. As a resident of Salt Lake City, Elder Thulin is now (1927) filling a second mission to Norway.

seph C. Skougaard of Manti, Christian Jensen of Goshen, Ole J. Sitterud of Orangeville, and Albert Norman Hagen of Mammoth, Utah, Hyrum Petersen of Samaria, Idaho, and Peter Martin Petersen and Niels Peter Jensen of Preston, Nevada, arrived June 26th. Christian Andersen of Monroe, Jens Lyman Nielsen of Bluff, and Carl Evin Wilberg of Castle Dale, Utah, arrived Aug. 4th. George Wm. Thulin of Salt Lake City, Utah, and Andrew Larsen of Sterling, Canada, arrived Sept. 8th. Andrew Funk and N. Claudius Holst of Brigham City, Erastus P. Rasmussen of Castle Dale, Lorenzo Jensen of Mantua, Axel L. Fikstad, junior, of Salt Lake City, Utah, and Junius M. Sörensen of Lago, Idaho, arrived Oct. 27th. James P. C. Christensen and Jonathan W. Anderson of Brigham City, James G. Christensen of Hyrum and Anton Cramer of Cleveland, Utah, and Lorenzo Swenson and Victor Mouritzen of Montpelier, Idaho, arrived Nov. 27th. Lee Ross Christensen and Hyrum Smith Andersen of Fairview, Utah, Peter A. C. Pedersen of Bear River City, Hans J. Mortensen, junior, of Parowan, Joseph A. Christiansen of Mayfield, Hilmar M. Nelson of Pleasant Grove, Sören Edward Sörensen of East Garland, Carl E. Nielson of Axtell, Utah, Peter Johnson of Bench, David H. Larsen of Ashton and Niels A. O. Nielsen of Independence, Idaho, and Erastus Larsen of Lyman, Wyoming, arrived Dec. 5th.

The eightieth anniversary of the organization of the Church was remembered in the Danish-Norwegian Mission by the holding of special meetings in the different branches on the 6th of April, 1910.

Apostle Rudger Clawson, president of the European Mission, arrived, in Esbjerg, Denmark, June 28, 1910, on a visit to Scandinavia.

Accompanied by Pres. Andrew Jenson they visited Copenhagen, Christiania, Bergen, Stockholm, Göteborg, Aalborg, Aarhus, etc., holding spe-

APOSTLE RUDGER CLAWSON

President of the European Mission, was born in Salt Lake City, Utah, March 12, 1857, the son of Hiram B. Clawson and Margaret Gay Judd.

cial meetings and conferences in all these places. Pres. Clawson left Copenhagen for Germany, July 19, 1910.

President Joseph F. Smith, wife and son, and Presiding Bishop Charles W. Nibley, wife and two daughters, arrived in Copenhagen on a visit to Scandinavia July 27, 1910. Accompanied by Pres. Andrew Jenson, who also acted as interpreter and guide for the party, visits were made to several places in Denmark and Norway, and meetings were held in Copenhagen, Christiania and Stockholm. The Elders from Zion and the local Saints, as well as many friends, were delighted to bid President Smith and Bishop Nibley welcome to the lands of the North. It was the first time that a President of the Church and Presiding Bishop of he Church visited the Scandinavian countries· Though Pres. Smith's health was not the best, he delivered excellent discourses which comforted and cheered the Saints, and left a good impression on all who heard them. The newspapers of Denmark and Norway published friendly re-

tian Nielsen of Salem, Utah, arrived Feb. 26th. Leonard B. Christensen of Richfield and Carl P. Lind of Salt Lake City, Utah, arrived April 2nd.

JOSEPH F. SMITH

Sixth president of the Church of Jesus Christ of Latter-day Saints, was born Nov. 13, 1838, at Far West, Caldwell County, Missouri, the son of Hyrum Smith, the Patriarch (martyred with his brother the Prophet Joseph Smith), and Mary Fielding. Pres. Smith died in Salt Lake City, Utah, Nov. 19, 1918.

CHARLES WILSON NIBLEY

Presiding Bishop of the Church, born Feb. 5, 1849, at Hunterfield, Scotland, son of James Nibley and Jean Wilson. He was the first presiding Bishop of the Church to visit the Scandinavian countries.

ports of the meetings held. Elder Jenson acted as interpreter for the visiting brethren and sisters. Fifty-one Elders from Zion attended a special meeting held in Copenhagen in the evening of Aug. 2nd. The following day, Aug. 3rd, President Smith and Bishop Nibley and their families left Copenhagen for Germany.

Seventy-two Elders from Zion arrived in the Danish-Norwegian Mission during the year 1910. Following are their names and dates of arrival:

Andrew W. Munk of Benson and Andrew M. Andersen of Brigham City, Utah, arrived Jan. 8th. Alma L. Petersen of Huntsville and Chris-

President Joseph F. Smith addressing the Saints in Scandinavia, with Andrew Jenson as translator.

James C. Hansen of Lehi, Oliver S. Olsen of Provo, John H. Evensen and P. Waldemar Nielsen of Salt Lake City, Jonathan C. Jensen of Bear

CARL P. LIND

Was born Oct. 9, 1877, in Gran, Hadeland, Norway; was baptized Jan. 6, 1899, by C. F. Schade; was ordained a Teacher April 28, 1899, a Priest Sept. 4, 1900, and an Elder Sept. 3, 1901. He emigrated to Utah in 1902, and on Sept. 19, 1906, married Ragnhild Christoffersen. He was ordained a Seventy Nov. 29, 1909. In 1910-1912 he filled a mission to Norway, laboring in the Tönsberg and Christiansand branches of the Christiania Conference. In November, 1920, he was set apart as one of the presidents of the 204th Quorum of Seventy. He has acted as secretary and treasurer of the L. D. S. Norwegian organization of Salt Lake City and vicinity since April 2, 1925, and is at present a resident of the Wells Ward, Grant, Stake, Salt Lake City.

River City, James R. Paystrup of Levan, John W. Madsen of Lake View and Christen Christensen of Pleasant Grove, Utah, arrived May 7th. Andrew C. Andersen and William H. Petersen of Manti, Niels Ira Nelson and Stephen H. Chipman of American Fork, Leonard Larsen and William Henry Squires of Hyrum, Erik Ludvigsen, junior, of Sterling, Anthon Wilford Nielsen of Huntsville and Ole Carl Olsen of Ogden, Utah, and Carl Christian Jensen of Alberta, Canada, arrived May 25th. Peter Christian Rasmussen of Draper,

Richard Christian Möller of Cast Dale, Andrew Jensen of Centerfiel Michael Hansen of Loa, George A bert Petersen and James V. Lars of Mt. Pleasant, Thomas L. Thoms of Ephriam and Hyrum Domgaa of Fayette, Utah, and Charles Je sen of Burton, Idaho, arrived Ju 8th. Johannes Halvorsen of Sa Lake City and Peter C. Lundgreen Monroe, Utah, arrived June 22n Anton J. T. Sörensen of Salt La City, Utah, arrived July 3rd. Lew A. Thomas of Lewiston, Ernest Ant Jensen of Preston, and Christian Mo tensen of Salem, Idaho, and Georg S. Sanders of Salt Lake City, Uta

JOHN HENRY EVENSON

A missionary, was born Feb. 3, 1886, Huntsville, Utah, the son of Johan Evens and Oline Amundsen. In 1889, the fami moved to Murray, Salt Lake County, whe the father died shortly afterwards. In Apr 1910, Brother Evenson left for a mission Norway, laboring most of the two and on half years in the Trondhjem Conference. C his release in September, 1912, he visited h mother's relatives in Hedemarken. Tw years after his return to Utah he marri Lina M. Knudsen of Bergen, Norway, who he had met and baptized in Trondhjem whi on his mission. Six children are the frui of this union. Brother Evenson is active an officer in the Central Park Ward, Gra Stake.

rrived July 6th. Jacob B. Johnson f Lawrence and Haldor Johnson of leveland, Utah, arrived July 16th. ohn Elmer Larsen of Taber, Can-

PAUL OLUF STRÖMNESS

Born Aug. 18, 1857, in Dikemark, Asker arish, Norway, son of Even Jacobsen Ström- ess and Petra Antoinette Christensen, was aptized Dec. 9, 1882, in Christiania, and emi- rated to Utah in 1883. He married Antonette horstensen in the Logan Temple Aug. 13, 885. In 1910-1912 he filled a mission to orway, laboring in the Christiania Confer- nce, principally in the capital. He and his ife reside in Winder Ward, Salt Lake Coun- y, Utah.

ida, and Hans Sanders of Salt Lake City, Utah, arrived Aug. 4th. Chris. en M. Christensen of Provo, Helmar 'aul Andersen of Ogden, and Peter Iulbert Jensen of Pocatello, Idaho, rrived Sept. 15th. John R. Nielsen, unior, of Manti, and A. Woodruff 5örensen of Draper, arrived Oct. 2th. Henry A. Björkman of New- on, Lars Jensen of Mapleton, Aaron '. Christiansen of Mayfield, Victor). Nelson of Ferron, Jacob W. Ol- en of Vernal, Paul Oluf E. Ström- ess of Park City, Utah, and Charles C. Sörensen of Ovid, Idaho, arrived)ct. 26th. Christian M. Jensen of Mantua, Peter Hansen of Redmond, Walter E. Fridal of Elwood, Herman

Christensen of Levan, Jacob Jensen of Brigham City, and Norman K. Amundsen of Salt Lake City, Utah, arrived Nov. 9th. Peter A. Andrea- sen of Smithfield, Ferdinand C. Sö- rensen of Spring City, Utah, and John E. Christensen of Central, Ida- ho, arrived Nov. 23rd. Frederick C. Mickelson and James Andersen of Shelley, Idaho, John Berntsen and Lawrence C. Monson of Salt Lake City, Olof Anderson of Lynne and Arthur L. Olsen of Logan, Utah, ar- rived Dec. 14th, and Lyman W. Poul- sen of Richfield, Utah, and James Christensen of Weston, Idaho, ar- rived Dec. 21st.

During the year Pres. Andrew Jen. son traveled extensively in Denmark and Norway, attending conferences

HERMAN O. CHRISTENSEN

Born March 20, 1887, at Levan, Juab Coun- ty, Utah, is the son of Stephen C. and Annie Christensen. His father was one of the early settlers of Levan. Brother Herman O. Chris- tensen filled a mission to Scandinavia in 1910- 1913, laboring in the Christiania Conference, Norway. He married Ann Memel Taylor, April 29, 1914, and is at present (1927) as- sistant Sunday school superintendent at Levan; he has held responsible positions in several Church organizations.

and special meetings, and also gave fifty-two illustrated lectures in some of the principal cities in Denmark and Norway.

During the year 410 persons were

FERDINAND C. SÖRENSEN

Born at Ephraim, Utah, Feb. 26, 1870, the son of Frederik C. Sörensen and Petrine Pedersen. For two years previous to emigrating to Utah in 1853, the father (Frederick C. Sörensen) had been prominent as a missionary, and in 1865-1867 filled a mission to Denmark, as one of the early missionaries from Zion. Ferdinand C. Sörensen was baptized when eight years old and was faithful to his duties in the Church. He married Botilda C. Malmgren, Jan. 14, 1891; they had two daughters. His wife died Jan. 3, 1896. On October 19, 1898, he married Maria Larsen of Spring City; they have three children. In October, 1907, Brother Sörensen was ordained a Seventy in the 80th quorum and appointed one of the presidents of said quorum in March, 1910, by Apostle Rudger Clawson. In 1910-1912 Brother Sörensen filled a mission to Scandinavia, laboring in the Christiania Conference, mostly in Drammen, Frederikstad and Arendal. At present (1927) he resides at Spring City, Utah.

added to the Church by baptism, which represented more baptisms in Denmark and Norway than in any other single year for nearly a quarter of a century.

On June 7, 1911, Rudger Clawson's family and three others arrived in Esbjerg on a visit to Scandinavia. Andrew Jenson accompanied them in

their travels. They crossed the Cattegat from Frederikshavn, Denmark, to Göteborg, Sweden, whence they took a most interesting canal route to Stockholm. Thence they traveled to the far North by rail, via Boden, to give them an opportunity to see the midnight sun. Via Gellivare, Kiruna, etc., in Swedish Lappland, and crossing the mountains to Narvik in Norway, the party had the privilege of seeing the midnight sun. From Narvik, where they arrived June 14th, they took steamer down the Norwegian coast to Trondhjem, whence they traveled by rail via Christiania, Göteborg, Helsingborg, etc., to Copenhagen, where they arrived June 20th.

Several anti-Mormon agitators delivered lectures in different parts of Denmark in the summer of 1911. President Jenson, assisted by Oluf J. Andersen and others, debated with them in Copenhagen, June 21, 1911, in the presence of newspaper representatives and quite a number of Lutheran priests. The largest hall in Copenhagen had been hired by the agitators, in which droll accusations were hurled against the Latter-day Saints, but the brethren were given no opportunity to meet their opponents before the general public. The discussion referred to took place after the larger meeting, and ended with perfect satisfaction on the part of the brethren. For the first time in the history of the Scandinavian Mission, the Danish press came out in defense of the "Mormons," as against their accusers, and Hans Peter Freece, a certain person, who took the leading part in maligning the Saints, was advised by the most influential newspaper of Copenhagen to pack his valise and return to America, or to some other country, where perhaps he would find more willing ears to listen to his stories, than in Denmark, where the people were fair-minded and were not particularly interested in lies.

During the year President Andrew Jenson continued his illustrated lectures with good effect until he had visited nearly every city in Denmark, and some of the principal towns in Norway. The lectures were, as a rule, well received, and it was afterwards learned that many who had never heard the doctrines of the Latter-day Saints advocated before, nor heard the fruits of "Mormonism" explained, were impressed to such an extent that it resulted in their conversion. Altogether Elder Jenson delivered 78 illustrated lectures on this mission.

In August, 1911, Pres. Andrew Jenson, accompainied by Elder Alma L. Petersen, made a visit to Iceland, traveling by steamer via Scotland and the Faroe Islands. It was the first time that a president of the Scandinavian Mission had visited Iceland, Jacob B. Johnson and Haldor Johnson, the two Elders from Utah, who at that time were laboring as missionaries in Iceland, were delighted to receive a visit from mission headquarters in Denmark, and the visting brethren in turn enjoyed their visit with the few Saints in Iceland, and also in taking in the sights of the country, as they visited the historical Thingvalla, where the courts of Iceland met centuries ago, the famous geysers, and enjoyed a perfect view of the famous volcano, Hekla. Pres. Jenson and Elder Petersen left Copenhagen for Iceland Aug. 3rd and returned to Copenhagen Aug. 29, 1911. They delivered illustrated lectures in Reykjavik and on board the ship which carried them to and from Iceland preached the gospel to their fellow-passengers and enjoyed the trip throughout.

The following missionaries from

Zion arrived in the Danish-Norwegian Mission during the year 1911 on the dates given:

Carl M. Gjettrup of Driggs, Ida-

H. HARRY MADSEN

Was born Oct. 20, 1885, in Salt Lake City, the son of Peter Wilhelm Madsen and Elise Christine Larsen (formerly of Denmark), was baptized Oct. 1, 1894, by Henry Coulam, confirmed Oct. 4, 1894, by Joseph H. Felt and was active in the Deacons' quorum of the Eleventh Ward, Salt Lake City. He was ordained an Elder Sept. 17, 1911, by Harold Eriksen in the Murray First Ward and a Seventy, Nov. 13, 1921, by Leonidas Fisher in the Richards Ward, Salt Lake City. On Sept. 27, 1911, he married Dora Godfrey (daughter of James Godfrey and Fanny Jones of Murray, Salt Lake County) in the Salt Lake Temple; this marriage has been blessed with one daughter, Elise Christine Larsen Madsen (born Feb. 23, 1915, and baptized in the Richards Ward May 26, 1923). Bro. Madsen was set apart for a mission to Scandinavia Nov. 14, 1911, by Charles H. Hart and labored thirty-three months in the Aarhus Conference, where he organized the Svendborg Branch and later presided over the Odense Branch. Through his efforts many were brought into the Church. After his return home Elder Madsen acted as president of an Elders' quorum and five years was chairman of the Richards Ward amusement committee. He also organized a series of Scandinavian charity balls, the proceeds from which were distributed among the needy of the Scandinavian race in Salt Lake City. He is favorably known for his kindness and generosity—standing ever ready to help in any worthy cause. He is also prominent in social and business circles, and its secretary of the P. W. Madsen Investment Company and secretary and manager of the P. W. Madsen Furniture Company of Salt Lake City.

28

ho, Andrew M. Jensen and James H. Christiansen of Centerfield, Utah, arrived Feb. 12th. Anders C. Pedersen of Benson, and John A. Larsen of Logan, Utah, arrived March 16th. Ether Frederiksen of Sanford, Colorado, and Wyman Nielsen of Salt Lake City and Christian Dausel of Elsinore, Utah, arrived April 12th. Andrew A. Kruse and Richard W. Christensen of Salt Lake City, Orson Chr. Nielsen of Salina, Sören Andersen of Inverury, Utah, and James Hansen of Taber, Canada, arrived May 10th. Conrad Earl Ahnder of Hyrum, Utah, arrived May 27th. Hulda Garff Mickelson, of Shelley, Idaho, arrived May 31st. Hilbert K. Andersen of Salt Lake City, Utah, arrived July 19th. Andrew E. Lauritzen of Moroni, Utah, arrived Aug. 16th. Thomas Peter Jensen of Glenwood, Alfred C. Larsen of Provo, Erastus Madsen of Elsinore, George Jensen of Oasis, L. Walter Johnson of Moroni and Kathinka Andersen of Castle Dale, Utah, and Hyrum D. Jensen of Preston, Idaho, arrived Sept. 27th. August A. H. Knebelau and Leroy L. Larsen of Salt Lake City, and Mikkel A. Mikkelsen of Fountain Green, Utah, arrived Oct. 25th. Neeley Löfgren Hansen of Brigham City, Utah, arrived Nov. 9th. Christian O. Jensen and H. Harry Madsen of Salt Lake City, Parley Heber Johnson of Spanish Fork, Jonas Verner Nielsen of Hyrum, and Jens Marius Jensen of Manti, Utah, arrived Dec. 7th. George D. Petersen and Andrew Hintze Hansen of Salem, Idaho, Ezra Peter Jensen of Garland, and Norman H. Anderson of Uintah, Utah, arrived Dec. 20th. Carl Johan Olavesen of Menan, Idaho, Carl Louis Albrechtsen of Emery, Simon Christensen, junior, of Richfield, and Robert H. Sörensen of Salt Lake City, Utah, arrived Dec. 27th.

CHAPTER 3 (1912-1920)

Martin Christoffersen presides—Apostle Hyrum M. Smith visits Scandinavia—Hans J. Christiansen succeeds to the presidency of the mission—The Elders ;from Zion return to America—Local Elders are called into presiding positions.

In the spring of 1912, President Andrew Jenson made his farewell tour through Denmark and Norway, holding conferences and other meetings in different localities. In most

MARTIN CHRISTOFFERSEN

Fourth president of the Danish-Norwegian Mission, was born in Lommedalen, Borum, Norway, April 13, 1850; joined the Church in May, 1865; was called into the local missionary field in May, 1870, and called to take charge of the Frederikstad Branch, where he labored for fifteen months with good success. While there he was arrested and imprisoned for baptizing. He emigrated to Utah in 1871. Arriving in Salt Lake City, he was employed by D. F. Walker Esq., as a gardener. Brother Christoffersen filled a mission to Scandinavia in 1883-1885; took charge of the Drammen branch for seven months, after which he presided over the Christiania Conference. At home he acted as a counselor to Anders W. Winberg and later to J. M. Sjödahl in the presidency of the Scandinavian meetings in Salt Lake City. In the fall of 1893 he was elected county commissioner for Salt Lake County. When the Granite Stake was organized, Brother Christoffersen was ordained a High Priest and set apart as a High Counselor. He presided over the Danish-Norwegian Mission in 1912-1914, and over the Norwegian Mission in 1925-1927. Soon after his return from his last mission, he died in Salt Lake City, Aug. 24, 1927.

of these he was accompanied by Elder Martin Christoffersen, who had arrived in Copenhagen April 4, 1912, to succeed to the presidency of the mission. While on this last visit to Bergen, Pres. Jenson succeeded in completing, in behalf of the Church, the purchase of a fine property known as "Jury-Lokalet," or No. 44 Kong Oskarsgade, into which the headquarters of the Bergen Conference was moved. The first meeting was held in the newly acquired property April 18, 1912. The large auditorium had a seating capacity of about five hundred, and was truly a great improvement compared with the dingy and uncomfortable quarters which the Saints had occupied in Bergen for many years. The purchase price of "Jury-Lokalet" was 50,000 kroner, and a few months later the property could be sold for twice that amount. Besides the large auditorium, the building afforded good accommodations for the Elders as Conference headquarters. The property was centrally located, though situated at the foot of a high mountain, but it faced one of the main thoroughfares of Bergen. The building was dedicated April 21, 1912, by Pres. Andrew Jenson, in connection with the holding of a semi-annual conference.

The main building on the property purchased was a two-story rock structure. Besides the large hall in the first story, there were several smaller rooms and a number of closets. On the second floor there were three other good-sized rooms and a long corridor. In the attic there were also three rooms. There were several sheds and outhouses in the rear of the main buildiny. "Jury-Lokalet" was without doubt one of the best properties purchased by the Church in Scandinavia up to that time. The premises were owned by a temperance society, "Total Afholdsforeningen," which sold the same to the Latter-day Saints much against the will of the Lutheran clergy in Bergen.

Elder Martin Christoffersen succeeded Andrew Jenson as president of the Danish-Norwegian Mission, May 15, 1912. On that date, Elder Jenson, together with Peter C. Rasmussen of Draper, Utah, left Copenhagen for their homes in Utah, after witnessing the proclaiming of Christian X as King of Denmark, they crossed Öresund to Malmö, Sweden; thence they traveled by rail to Stockholm; thence by steamer via Helsingsfors, Finland, to St. Petersburg, Russia; thence by railroad via Moscow, Penza, the Ural Mountains, and through Siberia, to Vladivostok; thence by steamer to Tsuruga, Japan; thence by railroad across the island of Japan to Yokohama and Tokio, where a short stop was made to cull data from the records of the Japanese Mission, which had been opened eleven years before by President Heber J. Grant and others. Meeting with Pres. Elbert D. Thomas and other Elders in Japan, and taking in the sights of Tokio and Yokohama, was most enjoyable to the two traveling Elders, who took steamer at Yokohama June 16, 1912, and proceeded across the Pacific Ocean via Hawaii to San Francisco, Cal. On reaching his home in Salt Lake City July 18, 1912, from this mission, Elder Jenson had circumnavigated the globe twice.

The following missionaries from Zion arrived in the Danish-Norwegian Mission during the year 1912:

Peter H. Sörensen of Brigham City, James Christian Bolander of Shelley, Idaho, Joseph E. Jensen of Groveland, Idaho, Stanley A. Rasmussen of Draper, Olof Wilford Pedersen of Logan, Alfred Denstad, Franklin Madsen, Ole Andersen Wold, Johannes Frederik Petersen and Agda A. C. J. Petersen of Salt Lake City, Utah, and James A. Jensen of Taber, Canada, arrived Feb. 11th. Martin Christoffersen, Sister Jannet Christoffersen, Alvin R. Christoffersen, Iver Charles M. Nielsen and Maggie L. Nielsen of Salt Lake City, Utah, arrived March 31st. Johannes S.

IVER CARL MAGNUS NIELSEN

A diligent Church worker, was born Jan. 26, 1856, at Christiania, Norway, the son of Christoffer and Maren Sophie Nielsen. He was baptized March 10, 1872, performed missionary labors locally at the age of sixteen, and, before emigrating to Utah in 1876, he had presided over the Arendal and Odalen branches. He located in the Sevier Stake, where he acted as a home missionary and later acted in the same capacity for five years in the Salt Lake Stake. In 1883-1884, he filled a mission to the Northwestern States; on his return he clerked in a store and studied law at the University of Utah, being admitted to the bar as an attorney-at-law in 1895. From 1888 to 1896 he served as a member of the executive committee of the People's Party in Salt Lake City. He served as a justice of the peace in Salt Lake City for five years. In 1912 he filled a mission to Norway, presiding over the Christiania Conference, and in returning home had charge of a company of emigrating Saints from England. In January, 1916, he was appointed judge of the Juvenile Court in the Third Judicial District of Utah in which position he served two years, when he returned to his profession as attorney-at-law. At the time of his departure for the Scandinavian Mission he presided over the Scandinavian meetings in the Granite Stake, the Scandinavian Missionary Society and also over a Scandinavian political club.

Hansen of Salt Lake City, and James Hamilton Martin of Ogden, Utah, arrived April 24th. Anton Marius Jensen of Taber, Canada, and Sören Marius Sörensen of Koosharem, Utah, arrived May 9th. Charles F. Petersen of Preston, Idaho, arrived May 22nd. John Johanneson of Raymond, Canada, and Louis C. Jacobsen of Salt Lake City, Utah, arrived June 5th. Adolph Petersen of Manti, Daniel Lemont Jensen of Spring City, Eric Adolph Cramer of Huntsville, Utah, Joseph S. Pehrson of Haden, Idaho, Peter W. Kjær, of Salt Lake City, Utah, and Jesse Hans Nielsen of Lincoln, Idaho, arrived July 3rd. Alfred E. Pedersen of Salt Lake City, Utah, arrived Aug. 14th. Isak A. Jensen of Brigham City, and Hans

DANIEL LEMONT JENSEN

Is a son of Daniel Jensen and Margaret Alice Blaine of Spring City, Sanpete County, Utah, where Daniel was born August 7, 1893. He was baptized on his birthday, when eight years old. In June, 1912, he was called to perform a mission to Norway and labored his entire time in the Christiania Conference. He was honorably released and returned home in October, 1914. On the 27th of March, 1915, he married Lafern Allred of Spring City, and is now (1927) a Seventy in the 80th quorum.

Peder Wamsal of Draper, Utah, arrived Sept. 25th. Otto N. Smith of Centerville, Utah, arrived Nov. 8th. Sterling D. Madsen of Brigham City, Utah, arrived Nov. 9th. Alma M. Sörensen of Salt Lake City, Utah, Thomas Wm. Jensen of Manassa, Colorado, Oscar Arnold Jeppesen of Mantua, Norman Hans Salvesen of Hyrum, Niels Hansen of Murray, Utah, and Joseph E. Jensen of Idaho Falls, Idaho, arrived Nov. 20th. Ezra M. Nielsen of Moroni, Utah, Lars William Larsen of Taber, Canada, Knud Terkelsen of Mt. Pleasant, and John W. Christensen of Bear River City, Utah, arrived Dec. 4th.

Forty-five missionaries from Zion arrived in the Danish-Norwegian Mission during the year 1913:

Earl R. Sörensen of Axtell, Wilford L. Breinholt of Ephraim, J. Archie Christensen of Brigham City, Erastus H. Petersen of Manti, Jens Jensen of Leamington, Utah, and Thorvald Hemmert of Blackfoot, Idaho, arrived Jan. 1st. Joseph J. Christiansen of Emery, Lawrence Hansen of Bear River City, Andrew Amundsen and Jens P. C. Egelund of Salt Lake City, Utah, arrived Feb. 1st. Virgil Andrew Fjeld of Lehi, Utah, arrived March 12th. Joseph N. Busath of Salt Lake Ciyt, Utah, arrived April 9th. Hans Johansen of Sandy, Utah, arrived April 24th. Daniel C. Jensen of Salt Lake City, Erastus P. Petersen of Levan and Harold F. Hansen of Perry, Utah, arrived May 8th. Charles Landvig Olsen of Ephraim, Christian P. Christensen of Brigham and Nephi L. Williams of Castle Dale Utah, arrived July 2nd. Einar Erickson and Elias W. Erickson of Cleveland, Utah, arrived July 11th. Heber S. Nielsen of Salt Lake City, Utah, arrived Aug. 1st. William Jensen of Brigham City, Heber Johnson, Abel M. Paulson and August V. Nielsen of Salt Lake City, and Ole Andersen of Pleasant Grove, Utah, arrived Aug. 2nd. Willard R. Jensen of Centerfield, Edwin J. Jensen of Ephraim and Martin G. Hansen and Alexander Carlsen of Ogden, Utah, arrived Oct. 4th. P. Eugene Johansen and Ernest E. Jensen of Castle Dale, Utah, arrived Nov. 1st. Ernest E. Nielsen of Hunter, Melvin C. Olsen of Brigham City and Kenneth N. Schow of Milford, Utah, arrived Nov. 15th. Alvin D. Stocker of Clearfield, Bernard W. Nash of Salem, David Leroy Olsen of Logan, Utah, and Hyrum W. Jeppsen of Mink Creek, and James F. Peterson of Preston, Idaho, arrived Nov. 29th. Andrew L. Knaphus of Central, Howard M. Andreasen of Elwood, James C. Jensen of Provo, Utah, and Christian W. Andersen of Shelley, Idaho, arrived Dec. 24th.

ERASTUS P. PETERSEN

Bishop of Levan Ward, was born at Levan, Juab Co., Utah, May 17, 1889, the son of Erick Peterson and Anna Sörensen; was educated in Levan and the Brigham Young University. He has been active in Church and community affairs and performed a mission to Denmark in 1913-1915, laboring in the Aalborg Conference. When most of the missionaries were called home on account of the war, in 1914, he was one of the eight who remained. He married Olga Christiansen, Sept. 15, 1915; they have three children (Lamont, Lillian and Marjorie).

In 1914, the Elders from Zion succeeded in securing a property in
Trondhjem for meeting and conference purposes. The new home was
dedicated Feb. 8, 1914, by Pres. Martin Christoffersen. It was located
on Gamle Kongevei.

Elder Hans J. Christiansen succeeded Martin Christoffersen as
president of the Danish-Norwegian
Mission May 8, 1914. This was Elder Christiansen's fifth mission to
Scandinavia and it became his privilege to pilot the mission throughout

the trying and distressing World war
period.

Apostle Hyrum M. Smith, President of the European Mission, arrived
in Aarhus, Denmark, on a visit to

APOSTLE HYRUM M. SMITH

President of the European Mission, was
born March 21, 1872, in Salt Lake City, Utah,
the son of President Joseph F. Smith and
Edna Lambson. He died Jan. 23, 1918, in
Salt Lake City.

HANS J. CHRISTIANSEN

Fifth President of the Scandinavian Mission, was born Jan. 9, 1848, at St. Jörgens-
bjerg, near Roskilde, Denmark, the son of
Christian Hansen and Margrethe Jacobsen.
He was baptized Dec. 26, 1871, in Copenhagen
and emigrated to Utah, together with 396
other emigrants, in 1872, crossing the Atlantic
in the steamship "Nevada." He located in
Salt Lake City and later was a resident of
Logan, Cache Co. Elder Christiansen spent
most of his life in the missionary field, having
filled five missions to Scandinavia (1879-1882,
1885-1888, 1893-1895, 1902-1905 and 1914-
1919). On his last mission he presided over
the Danish-Norwegian Mission. Brother Christiansen died in Salt Lake City, May 27, 1923,
survived by his wife (Inger Marie Larsen),
two sons and two daughters.

Scandinavia, June 13, 1914. Accompanied by Pres. Hans J. Christiansen, he attended meetings in
Aarhus, Aalborg, Christiania, Bergen, Trondhjem, etc. While Pres.
Smith was making this tour of the
mission, as well as the Swedish Mission, he left his family in Denmark
as the guests of Thomas S. Hermansen, who, while not a member of the
Church, had for many years been
very kind and hospitable to the Elders. He was a man of means and always delighted in associating with his
English-speaking visitors, as he himself had spent some time in America
and understood the English language.
His wife was a faithful member of
the Church.

The following missionaries from Zion arrived in the Danish-Norwegian Mission during the year 1914: James Larsen, junior, of Thatcher, Idaho, and Alma M. Andreasen of Hyrum, Utah, arrived Jan. 31st. Joseph O. Christensen of Sugar City, Idaho, and Christian M. Sörensen of Koosharem, Utah, arrived March 4th. Levi J. Andersen of Hyrum, Utah, arrived April 4th. Charles W. Jensen of Moroni, Utah, arrived April 11th. Lydia R. Jensen of Moroni, Wilford R. Jensen of Manassa, Colorado, Denmark Jensen of Brigham City, Poul C. Petersen of Glenwood, Ernst M. Ernsten of Loa, Hans

NIELS FREDERIK HAAHR NIELSEN
GREEN

Was born Jan. 28, 1863, at Ölgod, Ribe amt, Denmark. He obtained a liberal education, and graduated as a school-teacher in 1883. Becoming a convert to "Mormonism" in Copenhagen, he was baptized Feb. 2, 1885; was ordained to the Priesthood and became an active member of the Copenhagen Branch; emigrating to Utah in 1893, he located in Ogden. He filled a mission to Denmark in 1914-1920, laboring as writer and translator at the mission office for "Skandinaviens Stjerne" in connection with general missionary work. He has written and translated extensively for "Bikuben" and "Skandinaviens Stjerne," and has composed a number of hymns to well-known melodies. His literary ability is well-known among the Scandinavian Saints. Since his return to Utah he has acted as secretary in the Danish meetings in Salt Lake City, where he now (1927) resides.

J. Christiansen, Fred S. Hess and Christian Petersen, junior, of Salt Lake City, Utah, arrived April 29th. Jens Hagbert Andersen of Ogden, Utah, Andrew Jensen of Cowley, Wyoming, Joseph J. Kjær of Salt Lake City, James C. Nielsen, of Newton, and Cornelius O. Petersen of Fielding, Utah, arrived May 13th. Peter M. Lundgren of Monroe, Heber Lauritzen of Hyrum, and Olaf Anderson of Richfield, Utah, arrived June 6th. Jörgen P. E. Rasmussen of Ephraim, James A. Hansen and B. Everett Wilhelmsen of Salt Lake City, and Grover C. Jensen of Brigham City, Utah, arrived July 8th, and Niels F. Green of Ogden, Utah, arrived Oct. 20th.

According to instructions from the authorities of the Church, most of the Elders from Zion left their fields of labor in the different countries in Europe on account of the World war. Seventy such Elders left the Danish-Norwegian Mission in 1914 to return to their homes in Zion or to labor in the United States. Hence, at the close of the year 1914 there were only 18 Elders from Zion laboring in the Danish-Norwegian Mission.

Owing to certain influences and opposition on the part of the Lutheran clergy in Bergen, Norway, the brethren sold "Jury-Lokalet" (which had been purchased by Andrew Jenson in 1912), at a good profit, and so the brethren purchased another property in Bergen known as "Store Markevei" No. 36. But as those premises were not satisfactory, or suitable, for meeting purposes, the brethren exchanged the "Markevei" property for another place at "Vaskerelvsgade" No. 1, where the meetings are still (1927) held.

In 1915, the labors of the Elders in Denmark and Norway were rewarded by 90 additions to the

Church by baptism, viz., 37 in Denmark and 53 in Norway. At the close of the year, 17 Elders from Zion were laboring as missionaries in Denmark and Norway.

The following missionaries from Zion arrived in the Danish-Norwegian Mission during the year 1915: Adolph M. Nielsen of Shelley, Idaho, and Mikkael Andreas Faldmo of Salt Lake City, Utah, arrived April 24th. Edward E. Strömness of Salt Lake City and Andrew Dahlsrud of Salina, Utah, arrived June 2nd.

Moroni P. Stærk of Spanish Fork, Utah, arrived July 17th. Andrew Mollerup of Salt Lake City, Utah, arrived Aug. 7th. Christen Sörensen of Georgetown, Idaho, Hans C. Petersen of Logan and August Jensen of Ogden, Utah, and Robert J. Bischoff of Lowell, Wyoming, arrived Oct. 29th, and Orvill H. Larsen of Brigham City, Grover E. Christensen of Hyrum, and Christian P. Sörensen of Salt Lake City, Utah, arrived Dec. 12th.

Thirteen missionaries from Zion arrived in the Danish-Norwegian Mission during the year 1916, namely:

Fred Henry Hesse of Blackfoot,

EDWARD E. STRÖMNESS

Who labored in the Danish-Norwegian Mission in 1915-1917, was born Aug. 21, 1865, in Asker, Norway, son of Even Jakobsen Strömness and Petra Antoinette Christensen. Brother Strömness learned the trade of a wheelwright, and, becoming a convert to "Mormonism," was baptized at the age of 16 years and emigrated to Utah in 1885. In 1887 (Sept. 29th) he married Laura Marie Johansen of Hurum, Norway, and resided successively in Salt Lake City, Wanship and Park City. In the latter place he took an active part in the affairs of the Church, but moved back to Salt Lake City in 1905. He left a wife and ten children when he responded to a call to go on a mission to his native land in 1915, where he labored for more than two years in the Christiania and Bergen conferences. In Salt Lake City Elder Strömness acted for several years as a counselor to Hans P. Folkersen in the presidency of the Scandinavian meetings of the Liberty Stake, and later presided over the Norwegian L. D. S. organization of Salt Lake City. Elder Strömness is at present engaged in the automobile business.

ANDREW MOLLERUP

Was born Nov. 8, 1861, in Skjödstrup, Randers amt, Denmark, baptized in Copenhagen Jan. 8, 1884, ordained to the lesser Priesthood in February, 1884, and emigrated to Utah in the fall of that year. In 1886 (Nov. 10th) he married Amanda Elida Öfgren in the Logan Temple. For two years he acted as second counselor in the presidency of the 10th Quorum of Elders in the Salt Lake Stake, was ordained a Seventy by Seymour B. Young in 1909 and a High Priest July 30, 1911, by Edward T. Ashton. In 1915-1918 he filled a mission to Denmark, laboring for thirty-two months in the Aarhus Conference. He filled a second mission to Denmark in 1923-1925 and after presiding over the Hjörring Branch of the Aalborg Conference for ten months, he labored as a traveling Elder in the whole conference. He now (1927) resides in Salt Lake City.

Idaho, and Erastus L. Ottesen of Spanish Fork, Utah, arrived March 23rd. Cephus E. Andersen of Garland, Utah, arrived May 4th. Nephi Andersen of Salt Lake City, Utah, arrived July 13th. Carl H. Löhdefinck of Provo, and Peter R. Johansen of Salt Lake City, Utah, arrived Nov. 13th. Peter Hansen of Vernon, and Fred L. Petersen of Tremonton, Utah, Ammon Martin Poulsen of Woodville, Idaho, and Jens Thomsen of Ephraim and Hyrum P. Nökleby of Ogden, Utah, arrived Dec. 8th, and Arvell L. McKay of Ogden and John J. Plowman of Smithfield, Utah, arrived Dec. 25th.

Besides the Elders from Zion, a number of local Elders were called into the missionary service in Denmark and Norway, who rendered the Elders from America efficient help.

During the year 1916, as well as during previous years, Pres. Hans J. Christiansen traveled considerably in Denmark and Norway, attending conferences, holding meetings and counseling with the Elders laboring under his jurisdiction. It was the war period, during which the people of the Scandinavian countries were distressed in many ways and conditions very much unsettled; hence the few Elders from Zion laboring in the mission at that time were kept busy endeavoring to preach the gospel of peace in the midst of war, and comfort and encourage the Saints. During the year, 56 persons were added to the Church in Denmark, and 36 in Norway.

No Elders from Zion arrived in the Danish-Norwegian Mission in 1917, and at the close of the year only 13 Elders from America were laboring in Denmark and 10 in Norway. The statistical report shows 126 baptisms during the year, namely, 59 in Denmark and 67 in Norway.

No Elders arrived from Zion in 1918, and as the majority of the Elders who had labored in the mission were permitted to return to their homes after long and faithful labors in the mission, only four Elders from Zion were left to labor as missionaries in Denmark, and the same number in Norway. The local brethren showed great efficiency in

FREDERIK FERDINAND SAMUELSEN

Was born April 12, 1865, in Copenhagen Denmark, and moved to Aarhus in 1889. In 1890 he married Marie Mariane Jensen, from Roskilde; they have five children: Julie, Ella, Wilford, Kaj and Ove Emil. Becoming converts to the gospel, Brother Samuelsen and his wife were baptized Dec. 21, 1892. Brother Samuelsen graduated with high honors as a mechanic in his native country, receiving a silver medal for efficiency and a stipend to enable him to travel. He was a member of the Aarhus city council in 1900-1919, director of a Working-men's Savings Bank, etc., was elected a member of the Danish Rigsdag (parliament) in 1906 and re-elected several times with increasing majority in spite of Lutheran opposition. He was not ashamed of his religion and testified, whenever occasion offered, to the truth of the restored gospel; he presided over the Aarhus Conference in 1918-1919. Accompanied by his wife and two sons, he emigrated to Utah in 1919, two daughters having previously emigrated. On April 11, 1920, he was ordained a High Priest and from March, 1925, to October, 1927, he presided over the Scandinavian meetings held weekly in the Assembly Hall, in Salt Lake City.

their labors. Elder Frederik F. Samuelsen, a local Elder, who had served for many years as a member of the Danish Rigsdag (parliament) succeeded Carl H. Löhdefinck, a Utah

of a sufficient number of American Elders to occupy important presiding positions, Oluf K. Karlsen was called to preside over the Bergen and Eyolf R. Larsen over the Trondhjem

CHRISTIAN PETER SÖRENSEN

Was born June 22, 1860, in Aalborg, Denmark, the son of Andreas Julius Sörensen and Fredericka Carolina Elizabeth Hinckel. He was baptized March 12, 1882, by Jens Peter Jensen, and emigrated to America in 1883, locating in Logan, Cache County, Utah, July 8, 1883. In 1915-1918 he filled his first mission to Scandinavia, laboring in the Aalborg Conference; filled a second mission in 1919-1920, during which he presided over the Aalborg Conference. In 1922-1924 he filled a third mission to Scandinavia, again presiding over the Aalborg Conference. He is still a resident of Salt Lake City, Utah, and is the father of thirteen children of whom seven are living.

Elder, as president of the Aarhus Conference.

During the year 1918, 107 baptisms took place in the Danish-Norwegian Mission, namely, 41 in Denmark and 66 in Norway.

Christian Peter Sörensen of Salt Lake City, Utah, who arrived Oct. 3rd, and Carl E. Peterson of Ogden, Utah, who arrived Nov 6th, were the only Elders from Zion who arrived that year to labor in the Danish-Norwegian Mission. In the absence

MARTINE CHRISTINA ELIZABETH JENSEN SÖRENSEN

Wife of Christian Peter Sörensen, was born Nov. 19, 1857, in Vaddum parish Vendsyssel, Denmark, daughter of Sören Peter Jensen and Maren Christine Petersen. She accompanied her husband on his third mission to Scandinavia in 1922-1924, and did considerable missionary labor in Aalborg.

Conference. They were both good and energetic local Elders and made excellent presiding officers.

In December, 1919, Elder Carl E Peterson, of Logan, Utah, succeeded Elder Hans J. Christiansen as president of the Danish-Norwegian Mission. Bro. Christiansen had presided since May 9, 1914, (about 5½ years) and his administration covered the war period, during which condition were indeed hard and trying in the Scandinavian countries, and the number of missionaries so very few compared with former years.

Early in 1920, the authorities of the Church divided the Danish-Nor wegian Mission, so that Denmark constituted a separate mission called the Danish Mission, and Norway another mission named the Norwegian Mission. Carl E. Peterson, who had presided over the Danish-Norwegian Mission, was appointed president of the Danish Mission, and August S. Schow president of the Norwegian Mission. This change went into effect April 1, 1920. At that time, three Elders from Zion, namely, Carl E. Peterson, Niels F. Green and Chr. Peter Sörensen, labored in Denmark and one (Hyrum Parley Nökleby) in Norway. A number of local Elders assisted in the missionary work.

Following is a list of the presidents of the Danish-Norwegian Mission, during the 15 years of its existence:

1. Jens M. Christensen, 1905-1907.

2. Sören Rasmussen, 1907-1909.

3. Andrew Jenson (Historian). 1909-1912.

4. Martin Christoffersen, 1912-1914.

5. Hans J. Christiansen, 1914-1919.

6. Carl E. Peterson, 1919-1920.

History of the Swedish Mission

CHAPTER 1 (1905-1909)

Peter Mattson's administration—Arrival of missionaries—Peter Sundwall presides—Visits of Presidents Anthon H. Lund and Charles W. Penrose.

Upon Elder Peter Mattson of Mt. Pleasant, Sanpete County, Utah, fell the honor to become the first president of the Swedish Mission. Being chosen and set apart by the First

PETER MATTSON

First president of the Swedish Mission, was born March 3, 1851, at Herslöf Malmöhus län, Sweden, and died March 1, 1919, at Mount Pleasant, Sanpete Co., Utah.

Presidency of the Church to that position, he arrived in Copenhagen, Denmark, June 13, 1905, and a few days later arrived in Stockholm, Sweden, which was to be the headquarters of the newly-established mission, with offices in the recently erected large and commodious Church edifice at Svartensgatan 3, on which property a beautiful, roomy and modern chapel had been erected. The chapel had been dedicated the

previous year by Pres. Heber J. Grant, in the presence of seventy-one Elders from Zion.

With the beginning of the Swedish Mission, fifty-six missionaries from Zion, who were already laboring in Sweden, were transferred from the Scandinavian to the new Swedish Mission, and during the last six months of the year, thirty-two new Elders arrived, who had been called by proper authority in Zion, to labor in Sweden. Some of the older Elders returned home during the year. At the time of its organization the Swedish Mission consisted of four conferences, namely, Stockholm, Göteborg, Skåne and Sundsvall, but a new conference was organized Oct. 24, 1905, namely, the Norrköping, which was created by dividing the Göteborg Conference, or taking from that conference the Norrköping, Vingåker, Vestervik and Kalmar branches to form the new conference, while the Göteborg, Sköfde, Jönköping, Borås and Vermland branches were retained in the Göteborg Conference. Elder Carl P. Anderson was appointed president of the new conference.

In September, 1905, Peter Mattson made a trip to St. Petersburg, Russia, that country, together with Finland, being a part of the Swedish Mission. His principal object in visiting Russia was to call upon the few Saints who resided in that country and who seldom enjoyed the association of a missionary from Zion.

The one hundreth anniversary of the Prophet Joseph Smith's birth (Dec. 23rd) was celebrated by the Saints in most of the branches of the Swedish Mission by the holding of divine services.

At the close of the year 1905 the Swedish Mission had a total baptized membership of 2,058, including 138 Elders, 65 Priests, 71 Teachers and 30 Deacons. The five conferences contained 28 branches of the Church, and 64 Elders from Zion were laboring in the different conferences at the close of the year.

Among the Elders who were transferred from the Scandinavian to the Swedish Mission was Swen Swenson, who had labored as translator and writer for "Nordstjernan" in Copenhagen, Denmark, but as the office of said periodical was moved to Stockholm, Elder Swenson was appointed to continue the same labors there at the headquarters of the new mission.

The following missionaries from Zion arrived in the Swedish Mission during the last six months of the year 1905, to vit.:

Peter Mattson of Mt. Pleasant, Utah, arrived June 13th. August Carlson of Ogden, Utah, arrived July 6th. John O. Löfgren of Mt. Pleasant, Utah, arrived July 13th. Charles G. Dahlquist of Provo, Utah, arrived July 22nd. Axel A. Nylander of Ogden, Utah, arrived Aug. 9th. Jöns Petter Jönsson of Logan and Arvil T. Forsgren of Brigham, Utah, arrived Sept. 16th. Gustaf A. Höglund of Salt Lake City, Utah, arrived Oct. 13th. Joseph Carlson of Logan and Aaron L. Quist and August A. Nordvall of Salt Lake City, Utah, arrived Nov. 4th, and Carl E. Nelson of Greenville, Hyrum Felt of Huntsville, Emil Elm of Bear River City, and Gustaf Peterson of Smithfield, Utah, arrived Dec. 2nd.

During the year 1906, forty Elders arrived from Zion to do missionary work in Sweden, as follows:

Peter Johnson of Salt Lake City and Andrew F. Anderson of Grantsville, Utah, arrived Jan. 29th. August W. Rytting and Elias A. Monson of

Salt Lake City, and Alma A. Minew of East Jordan, and N. Andrew Peterson, Mrs. John Felt and Mrs. Carl E. Peterson of Huntsville, Utah, arrived May 11th. Conrad K. E. Erick-

SWEN SWENSON

Son of Swen and Kerstin Olson, was born in the parish of Ifvetofta, Christianstad län, Sweden, Jan. 4, 1850. He received a good education, graduated with honors from the University of Lund in 1875 and attended a seminary for teachers in Skåne in 1882-1883. In 1873 he married Thilda Pehrson, daughter of Pehr Poulson and Maria Sophia Hennig; ten children were born to them. Elder Swenson taught school for fifteen years. Becoming a convert to the gospel, he and his family were baptized June 5, 1892, and in April, 1895, he was called to Copenhagen to labor as a writer for "Nordstjernan." In 1896 he emigrated and joined his family, who, one by one, as opportunity offered, had preceded him to Utah and were located in Pleasant Grove, Utah Co. In 1905 he was called on a mission to Scandinavia to write again for "Nordstjernan." On the division of the Scandinavian Mission in 1905 the office of the magazine was moved to Stockholm, the headquarters of the new mission. Elder Swenson returned home in 1908, but in November, 1911, he was, for the third time called to edit "Nordstjernan," in Stockholm, succeeding his son, D. A. Swenson, in that position. While in Sweden he also translated the "Pearl of Great Price" into the Swedish language and returned home in January, 1916. Soon afterwards he became almost blind, but partially regained his sight and again went to Stockholm as writer for "Nordstjernan." He was, however, released in January, 1920, on account of failing eyesight. After his return from this last mission he devoted himself to Temple work and lived to have ordinances performed for every name on his record. The last two years of his life were spent in total blindness. Brother Swenson died in Salt Lake City, Aug. 21, 1925.

son of Salt Lake City, John E. Anderson and August M. Nelson of Sandy, and Reed T. Johnson of Provo, Utah, and Henry Swenson of Afton, Wyoming, arrived May 27th. John Anderson of Logan, Utah, arrived June 20th. John W. Johnson and John A. Runswick of Salt Lake City, Utah, arrived June 21st. Gustaf William Jenson of East Jordan, Charles U. Erickson of Wilson, and John O. Peterson of Logan, Utah, arrived July 28th. Ernst J. Sjöstrand of Salt Lake City, Utah, arrived Aug. 7th. Thomas Spongberg of Preston, Idaho, arrived Aug. 13th. William N. Lee of Brigham City, Utah, arrived Aug. 20th. Pehr G. Peterson

of Cardston, Canada, arrived Sept. 12th. Carl W. Roos of Bedford, Wyoming, and Joseph H. Anderson

JOHN AXEL RUNSWICK

Was born March 23, 1876, in Attmar parish, near Sundsvall, Sweden, the son of Anders M. Runswick. He was baptized April 27, 1887, the same day as his father, his mother having joined the Church in February the same year. He emigrated to America in 1890, lived first in Arizona and then in California, and arrived in Salt Lake City, Utah, Oct. 16, 1898. On May 15, 1901, he married Emma M. Frederikson in the Salt Lake Temple, and they have been blessed with four children. On May 30, 1906, he left for a mission to Sweden, where he labored in Upsala and Eskilstuna, and baptized sixteen converts. On March 25, 1925, he was set apart as second counselor to Elder Gustaf W. Forsberg, president of the Swedish L. D. S. meetings in Salt Lake City, and acted in that capacity until 1927.

JOHN E. ANDERSON

Son of John Hyrum Anderson and Anna Charlotta Eliason, was born Dec. 3, 1886, at Logan, Utah, where he attended the Brigham Young College. In 1906-1908 he filled a mission to Sweden, laboring in the Stockholm Conference, and in the Örebro and Eskilstuna branches, where he made a number of converts. In 1909 (March 17th) he married Coila Montrose in the Logan Temple; three children were born to them, namely, John Montrose, Coila Luella and Naomi La Priel. Being ordained a High Priest by Apostle Orson F. Whitney, Brother Anderson served for eight years in the bishopric of the River Heights Ward and is at present (1927) a member of the Logan Stake Sunday School Board. He is also engaged in the mercantile business and is well known and respected in Cache Valley.

of Pocatello, Idaho, arrived Sept. 25th. Neils P. Swenson of West Jordan, Utah, arrived Oct. 10th. Carl O. Peterson of Franklin, Idaho, Hjalmar Landgren of Fairview, Brigham Monson of Richmond, Carl G. Carlson of Union and Leonard Olson of Smithfield, Utah, arrived Nov. 8th. Frank Wm. Olend of Fort Bridger, and Joseph Wall, junior, of Lyman, Wyoming, Armand F. Rundquist of West Jordan, Horace W. Egan of Richmond, Isaac Peter Thunell of Salt Lake City, and Axel W. Borgström of Thatcher, Utah, arrived Dec. 21st.

A Lutheran priest who was also a member of the Swedish riksdag (parliament) by name of Per Pehrsson, in Österby, Dannemora, wrote an article in the "Upsala Nya Tidning" of

ERNST J. SJÖSTRAND (SEASTRAND)

Was born in Skåne, Sweden, Feb. 27, 1880, baptized in Copenhagen, Oct. 5, 1900, by Elder Lorenzo Anderson of Brigham City, and emigrated to America in May, 1902. He remained in New York about two years and then, coming West, resided in Salt Lake City 22 months. In 1906-1908 he filled a mission to Sweden, laboring 29 months in Malmö, Halmstad and Christianstad. Returning home he arrived in Salt Lake City Oct. 6, 1908. In January, 1909, he moved to American Fork, where he established a tailoring business. He married Myrtle Robinson of American Fork and they have six children (two sons and four daughters). Brother Sjöstrand has been engaged in Church work ever since he became a member of the Church, has acted as Sunday school superintendent and ward clerk, and is at present (1927) counselor to Bishop James T. Gardner of the American Fork First Ward.

Sept. 28, 1906, against the Latter-day Saints, in which he attacked and misrepresented their teachings and the Prophet Joseph Smith, and in so doing employed the tactics usually adopted by the slanderers of the "Mormon" people by repeating some of the worn-out fables concerning them. This write-up was re-printed in some of the other newspapers in Sweden. Elder John A. Rundswick tried to get the paper mentioned to

publish an answer to the priest's fulmination, but the request was denied. "Utah-Posten," the Church publication printed in Salt Lake City, Utah, however, met the attack in a splendid article repudiating the claims in Pastor Pehrsson's attack and annihilated his extravagent statements.

The statistics of the Swedish Mission for the year 1906 showed 91 baptisms during the year, and also that 76 members of the Church had emigrated to Zion.

In 1907 "Nordstjernan," the Church periodical, reproduced from "Stockholmstidningen" one of Stock-

BRIGHAM MONSON

Son of Christian H. and Ellen Monson, was born in Richmond, Utah, Aug. 30, 1877, and baptized Oct. 1, 1885. He has held many offices in the different organizations of the Church and was ordained to the Melchizedek Priesthood Nov. 7, 1897. He married Matilda Anderson in the Logan Temple, Nov. 7, 1900. In 1906-1909 he filled a mission to Sweden, laboring in the Sundsvall and Stockholm conferences. While in Stockholm, being an accomplished musician, he took charge of the musical organizations there, organized a male chorus, translated hymns, etc. He also did a great deal of tracting and visiting among Saints and investigators. Brother Monson was enabled to compile genealogies of his father and mother, and since his return home has performed a considerable amount of Temple work. In a civil capacity he has been a justice of the peace, city councilman, mayor, choir leader, etc. Elder Monson holds the Swedish people in high regard.

holm's large daily newspapers, an
article relating to an "unusual circumstance in life's happenings," in
which the writer remarked with

ARMAND FRITHIOF RUNDQUIST

Of West Jordan, Salt Lake Co., Utah, was
born Jan. 31, 1878, in Salt Lake City, Utah,
the son of Peter F. Rundquist and Bengta
Jönson. When three years old, he, with his
parents, moved to West Jordan. He has been
active in Church work, both Stake and Ward,
and filled a mission to Sweden in 1906-1909,
presiding over the Sundsvall and Norrköping
conferences. On Feb. 17, 1909, he married
Karin Nilsson of Köla parish, Vermland, Sweden. Brother Rundquist is at this writing
(1927) superintendent of the Sunday school
at West Jordan and senior president of the
95th Quorum of Seventy. He is a farmer by
occupation.

some satisfaction that a golden wedding celebration had taken place at
Hyde Park, Utah, in the family of
Absalom Woolf, who had married
two wives on the same day. Usually
such an occurrence would be ridiculed in Swedish newspapers, but, in
this instance, the paper named took
delight in stating that the lives of the
bridegroom and his two brides had
been happy and congenial from the
very beginning.

The Elders carried on their work
of bringing the gospel message to
the people in the Swedish Mission
during the year 1907, and their efforts were crowned with success.

About 160,000 homes were visited by
the missionaries, who had held more
than 24,000 gospel conversations,
showing that less than one-seventh of
the homes thus visited had opened
their doors for the Lord's embassa-
dors. However, the labors of the
Elders were rewarded by 124 new
converts, while 104 persons had emigrated to Zion.

Thirty-one missionaries from Zion
arrived in the Swedish Mission during the year 1907 as follows:

Victor E. Krantz of Salt Lake City,
Utah, arrived Feb. 3rd. Alfred F.
Anderson of Grover, Wyoming, ar-
rived Feb. 5th. Lester L. Hansen of

VICTOR E. KRANTZ

Was born in Håbo-Tibble, Uppland, Sweden,
Oct. 29, 1882, the son of Carl F. Krantz and
Sophia C. Holmbom. Becoming a convert to the
restored gospel, he was baptized in the fall
of 1893 by his brother Carl A. Krantz and
confirmed by Elder Thomas Spongberg. With
his parents Brother Krantz emigrated to Utah,
in 1900. He filled a mission to Sweden in
1907-1909, laboring in the Sundsvall, Luleå and
Gefle branches, and edited "Nordstjernan"
from July, 1908, to July, 1909. In the year
1916 he married Kerstin Schader, who fell a
victim to the influenza epidemic of 1919, leav-
in a year old son. In the spring of 1924 Elder
Krantz married Esther Sanders. He has always been active in Ward activities, and when
business took him to Montana and Chicago,
he assisted the missionaries in those places.
In many ways he has also given a helping
hand to the Swedish L. D. S. organizations of
Salt Lake City, where he now resides.

Brigham City, arrived Feb. 26th. Nelson W. Anderson of Mt. Pleasant, and James Eugene Holladay of Salt Lake City, Utah, arrived March 9th. Emil J. Jacobson of Provo, Utah, arrived April 15th. Andrew G. Johnson of Pleasant Grove, Andrew F. Jensen of Mayfield, Peter James Sandberg of Salt Lake City, A. Wilhart Schade and Joseph Peterson of Huntsville, and William C. Jenson of Fremont, Utah, arrived May 22nd. Victor Liljenquist of Rexburg and Andrew Anderson of Lund, Idaho, arrived June 19th. A. George Lavin of Salt Lake City, Utah, arrived July 5th. Nephi Peterson of Mink Creek, Idaho, arrived July 20th. Gustave Wm. Gunnarson of Ogden, Utah, arrived Sept. 10th. Joseph Wm. John-

LAWRENCE M. MONSON

A missionary, was born Oct. 2, 1887, at Pleasant Grove. Utah, the son of Mons Monson and Lydia S. Broberg; baptized when eight years old; was educated in the public schools and high school in his home town, and the B. Y. U. of Provo. He was called in September, 1907, to perform a mission in Sweden, where he labored seventeen months in the Norrköping Conference, presiding over the Vestervik and Halmstad branches, Skåne Conference. He spent 31 months in the mission field. On July 30, 1913, he married Mary Smith from Snowflake, Arizona. Brother Monson acted as counselor to Bishop John Miller in Holbrook Ward, Arizona, for about two years, and has always been active in the various organizations of the Church.
29

son of Ogden and Lawrence Mons Monson of Pleasant Grove, Utah, arrived Oct. 8th. Oliver H. Nielsen of Millville, Utah, arrived Oct. 26th. Nils H. Hallström of Rexburg, Idaho, Rudolph Nels Holm of Salt Lake City, Lars John Larson and Nils E. Benson of Vernon, Ernest Johnson of Richmond, Servis Jenson of Richfield, Anthon Pehrson of Logan and David W. Woodard of Elsinore, Utah, arrived Nov. 20th, and Otto A. Johnson of South Bountiful, Lester Petersen of Mapleton, Utah, and Lars Anderson of Lund, Idaho, arrived Dec. 23rd.

The members of the Woman's Relief Society of the Vingåker Branch (Norrköping Conference), through means raised by subscriptions, honored one of their departed sisters, in the summer of 1908, by raising a monument over her grave in the Vingåker cemetery. It was Sister Brita Persson, the first person who embraced the gospel in Vingåker. She had labored zealously to promote the work of the Lord for twenty-seven years, and many received through her efforts a testimony of the truth of the restored gospel. Sister Persson was born in Vingåker Dec. 28, 1827, and died there Dec. 29, 1904; she was baptized in the spring of 1877.

Two stalwart Swedish Church veterans were this year called to another sphere of action; one of these was Nils C. Flygare, who had presided over the Scandinavian Mission three times; he died in Ogden, Utah, Feb. 19, 1908, sixty-seven years old. The other was Peter A. Forsgren, the first man baptized in Sweden by divine authority, who died in Brigham City, March 1, 1908, aged 81 years.

Pres. Peter Mattson, after having presided over the Swedish Mission for nearly three years, was honor-

ably released and left for his home
in Utah, April 27, 1908, accompanied by his wife. He was succeeded
in the presidency of the mission by
Elder Peter Sundwall.

During the year the missionaries
in Sweden visited nearly 169,000
homes of strangers; they could report 27,000 gospel conversations and
121 baptisms. Seventy members of
the Church had emigrated to Zion
during the year.

The following missionaries from
Zion arrived in the Swedish Mission
during the year 1908, on the dates
given:

Peter Sundwall of Fairview, Utah,
arrived April 3rd. John N. Beck-

ström of Spanish Fork, William O.
Beckström of Lake Shore, Martin H.
Hallström of Mt. Pleasant, John A.

MARTIN HANSSON HALLSTRÖM

Was born Jan. 27, 1859, in the parish of
Söfde, Malmöhus, län, Sweden, the son of
Hans Pehrson. He emigrated in May, 1885,
to Minnesota, and in June, 1888, to Utah,
where he was baptized Sept. 17, 1888, at Sandy.
In July, 1890, he married Maria Lindberg, in
the Manti Temple, and lived in Mt. Pleasant,
Sanpete Co., from 1890 to 1920. Called to
do missionary work in Sweden, he left Salt
Lake City, April 10, 1908, and was assigned to
Malmö, and later to preside in Helsingborg,
with Aaron Pehrson from Smithfield, Utah, as
companion; still later he was again assigned
to Malmö, where his brother Johan Holmquist
and four children joined the Church. Brother
Hallström baptized eight persons and returned
to Salt Lake City June 5, 1910. He was ordained a High Priest March 13, 1920, by Orson F. Whitney.

JOHN NILS BECKSTRÖM

Son of Håkan Beckström and Fredrika
Eleanora Baer, was born June 4, 1851, in
Malmö, Sweden; came to Utah with his parents in 1863, having crossed the ocean in the
sailing vessel "John J. Boyd," and the Plains
in John R. Murdock's company. He was baptized about 1873. On April 5, 1875, he married Mary Christine Hansen in the Endowment House, Salt Lake City, Utah; she was
born in Spanish Fork, July 18, 1858, daughter
of Jens and Karen P. Hansen. They were
blessed with twelve children. Elder Beckström performed successful missionary work
in Sweden in 1908-1910. He is a member of
the High Priests' quorum of Spanish Fork
and follows the occupation of farmer and stock
raiser.

Durrell and Erick Joseph Erickson of
Murray, Utah, and Charles P. Anderson of St. Johns, Arizona, arrived April 30th. John O. Erickson
of Sandy, Utah, arrived May 2nd.
Ephraim Adamson of Richmond, Alma Monson of Pleasant Grove, and
Allan Clawson of Hyrum, Utah, arrived May 15th. Clarence P. Larson
of West Weber, Utah, arrived June
19th. Charles A. Lindström of Santaquin, Utah, and Emil W. Weed of
Raymond, Canada, arrived July 15th.

Willard Hendricks of Lewiston, Aaron A. Pehrson of Millville, and Carl A. Dahlquist of Provo, Utah, arrived Aug. 14th. Ernest Lindquist of Ogden, Utah, arrived Sept. 11th. Gideon N. Hulterström of Salt Lake City, Utah, and George L. Olson of Osmond, Wyoming, arrived Oct.

10th. Wilford Martensen of Spring City, Peter A. Erickson of Koosharem, Niels Fugal of Pleasant Grove, Gustave Felt of Huntsville, Nils J. Sandberg of Brighton and John Anderson, Gustave Waldemar Teudt and Emma S. Teudt of Salt Lake City, Utah, arrived Nov. 7th, and Albert Capson of East Mill Creek, Gustaf E. Oscarson and Martin S. Christiansen of Pleasant Grove, George F. Erickson of Grantsville, and Holger Nilson of Cleveland, Utah, arrived Dec. 14th.

CHARLES PETER ANDERSON

A prominent Elder in the Church, was born at Ledsjö, Skaraborg län, Sweden, Jan. 2, 1856, the fourth son of Per Anderson and Maria Catherina Larson; arrived in Utah Oct. 22, 1866, with his mother, a brother (Claus) and a sister (Hilda), having crossed the Atlantic in the ship "Cavour" and the Plains in Capt. Abner Lowry's company. Many of the emigrants that year died of cholera. Charles was baptized at Mount Pleasant, Sanpete Co., Nov. 4, 1866, by C. C. Rowe, and located in Grantsville, Tooele Co., in 1868. He married Anna Louisa Anderson Oct. 3, 1877; became a member of the Tooele Stake Y. M. M. I. A. superintendency; also of the Grantsville city council. In April, 1884, he was called to go to St. Johns, Arizona, where a Stake was organized July 23, 1887, and he there became a member of the High Council, having been ordained a High Priest by Francis M. Lyman. On Oct. 6, 1892, he was ordained a Bishop and set apart to preside over the St. Johns Ward by Anthon H. Lund. He held this office for 13 years. In October, 1905, he was appointed first counselor to Stake President David K. Udall. On March 30, 1908, he left for Sweden; was assigned to the Göteborg Conference by Pres. Peter Sundwall and made conference president Jan. 1, 1909. He returned to St. Johns June 16, 1910, where he still (1927) resides.

ERICK JOSEPH ERICKSON

Was born Dec. 22, 1878, in Vingåker, Södermanland, Sweden, was baptized Feb. 24, 1898, in Österåker by Elder Frederick Petterson, emigrated to Utah in April of the same year and settled in Salt Lake City. In 1908-1910 he presided over the Vesterås branch for eighteen months, and over the Norrköping Conference until released. At home he has presided over an Elders' quorum and also over a Y. M. M. I. A. On Nov 18, 1922, he left Salt Lake City, accompanied by his wife and children, on a second mission to Sweden. He was called to preside over the Norrköping Conference, and after being honorably released, returned home in 1924. While in the mission field Elder Erickson distributed about 30,000 tracts, sold about 3,000 books and baptized 32 persons. He is engaged in mercantile business in Salt Lake City.

The Elders of the Church, always on the alert to bring the message of salvation to their fellow-men, meet with many obstacles, both serious and

CHARLES A. LINDSTRÖM

Was born April 19, 1862, in Skarkind, Östergötland, Sweden, the son of Anders Fredrick Lindström and Beata Charlotta Carlsdotter; was baptized by Nils R. Lindahl and confirmed by R. Berntzon, July 9, 1882. Brother Lindström labored as a missionary in Vestervik, Sweden, from May 15, 1883, till the spring of 1884, when he emigrated to Utah and settled in Santaquin, Utah Co. On Jan. 14, 1885, he married Hannah C. Anderson; they were blessed with seven children. Brother Lindström was ordained a Seventy by Jacob Gates, June 11, 1891, and called to perform a mission in Sweden, June 26, 1908, where he presided in Vingåker. Being honorably released Aug. 10, 1910, he arrived home Sept. 2, 1910. He was set apart as one of the presidents of the 15th Quorum of Seventy Nov. 23, 1919, and ordained a High Priest March 8, 1925.

amusing. They do not usually temporize at the edicts of petty officials, but take steps to find out the real reason why they are hindered and opposed in their labor of l o v e for mankind, and as many or most of them were born and reared in America, where they have breathed the air of freedom and religious liberty, they do not hesitate to contend for their rights, while they at the same time endeavor to maintain a respectful demeanor. As an

example we may state that Elders Lewis Jensen, Wilford Martensen and John O. Peterson had arranged and advertised to hold a meeting in the City of Östersund, in the north of Sweden, one day in July, 1909, and had for that purpose secured the Good Templars' Hall. Arriving at the hour set for the appointed meeting, the Elders found the door locked, and no one connected with the organization from whom the hall had been rented could be found to open the door for two hundred persons waiting to be admitted. It soon leaked out that the city's chief of po-

GUSTAVE EMIL OSCARSON

A missionary, was born in Södermanland, Sweden, June 8, 1862; baptized April 28, 1889; emigrated to Utah in May, 1890, and settled in Murray. He married Johanna Akerlind in the Manti Temple, Nov. 25, 1891; moved to Pleasant Grove, in 1896, where his wife died Nov. 16, 1902; later he married her sister, Minnie Akerlind in the Salt Lake Temple. Brother Oscarson was set apart for a mission to Sweden Nov. 19, 1908, arrived in Stockholm, Dec. 14, 1908; labored there two years, baptized thirteen converts, including his mother and brother, and returned home Dec. 25, 1910. He was set apart in March, 1915, as first counselor to the Bishop of the Pleasant Grove First Ward, which position he still (1927) holds. He has been chairman of the genealogical committee of the Ward for some years. Brother Oscarson is the father of eleven children, ten of whom are still living. He is a fruit-grower by occupation.

lice, under threats of prosecution, had forbidden the Good Templars to open the doors of their hall to the "Mormons," and through fear of the powers that be the managing directors kept themselves under cover, and so the meeting was called off, to the dissatisfaction, if not to the disgust, of the people who had gathered. The following morning, Elder Peter-

BISHOP MARTIN S. CHRISTIANSEN

Was born at Pleasant Grove, Utah, Oct. 13, 1884, the son of pioneer parents, studied electrical engineering in his youth. In 1908-1910 he filled a mission to Sweden, his mother's native land, laboring in Stockholm and Norrköping. He married Hedve Johnson, June 14, 1914, in the Salt Lake Temple; they have five children. In July, 1913, he became identified with the Utah Power and Light Company and is now foreman at one of their large power stations. On March 22, 1923, he was appointed Bishop of the Pleasant Grove Third Ward, which position he still holds. He is also president of the Pleasant Grove Chamber of Commerce.

son went in search of the police chief ("polismästaren"), whom he found, and asked the reason for the arbitrary action of the police the previous evening. The police official evaded the question in an offensive manner, and when the Elder demanded as an American citizen to be civilly treated and to be informed why the doors had been closed against him, his as-

sociates and hundreds of friends, the official said that his position permitted him to do as he pleased. The Elder said be would be glad to have that particular paragraph in the Swedish law which gave a chief of police such extraordinary power pointed out to him; and if the chief failed to find such a paragraph in the law, said Elder Peterson, then he and his associates would hold a meeting the following Sunday evening. The Elders did so, having for that occasion rented the Labor Union's Hall, which was not closed, although the police had forbidden its occupation by the "Mormons."

At the summer conference held at Stockholm on Sunday, June 25, 1909, the Elders and Saints enjoyed the presence as well as the teachings and encouragements of Pres. Anthon H. Lund, who was visiting the Scandinavian countries. On this occasion words of cheer and encouragement were given, and the Stockholm Branch choir, under the able leadership of Elder Gustave W. Teudt, rendered some beautiful numbers. On the Thursday following (July 29th) Pres. Charles W. Penrose and wife, and Historian Andrew Jenson, wife and daughters, arrived in Stockholm, returning south from their visit to Nordkap to view the midnight sun. A Priesthood meeting was held, as well as a public meeting in the chapel, where the visiting brethren addressed large audiences. Forty-nine missionaries from Zion were in attendance.

In August, 1909, the mission received from the Swedish Missionary Society in Salt Lake City, Utah, a sum of money to pay for subscriptions in behalf of those who were so short of means that they could not afford to subscribe for "Nordstjernan," the mission periodical.

A writer to "Enköpingsposten"

complained a b o u t "M o r m o n Apostles" forcing their way into the houses with Bibles in their hands, trying to induce young women to trek to Utah, and presented other anti-Mormon tirades and falsehoods. It

ERICK AUGUST STENQUIST

Was born May 23, 1880, in Stora Malm parish, Södermanland, Sweden, son of Carl A. Stenquist and Carolina Augusta Anderson; was baptized Aug. 24, 1888, by Elder Ola Olson of Lewiston, Utah; emigrated to Utah in 1898, and located in Murray; moved to Draper four years afterwards. He left his home Jan. 9, 1909, for a mission to Sweden; labored seventeen months in Örebro and presided in Upsala nine months; was honorably released and returned home July 20, 1911; he moved to Bear River Valley the same year. On March 25, 1914, he married Maria Elizabeth Sedell, formerly of Vesterås, Sweden. Brother Stenquist has been identified with the Bishopric in the Bear River Ward (Boxelder Stake) for three years, and has held other important positions in the Church.

showed that the writer was simply ruminating English newspaper verbiage. "Utah-Posten" took the writer in hand and showed up his false stories in good shape.

During the year 1909, the missionaries laboring in the Swedish Mission visited more than 167,000 homes, and held some 24,000 gospel conversations. Their labors and activities resulted in bringing 140 new

members into the Church by baptism while 80 members emigrated to Zion Twenty-eight Elders from Zion arrived in the Swedish Mission during this year as follows:

Andrew Gustav Erickson of Heber Frank Ravsten of Clarkston, Eric A. Stenquist of Draper, Nelphe Swenson of Harrisville, and Willard Jenson of Bear River City, Utah, arrived Feb. 2nd. James Monson of St. Charles, Idaho, and David E Quist of Claresholm, Canada, arrived April 19th. Conrad Joseph

DAN ARTHUR SWENSON

Son of Swen Swenson and Thilda Pehrson was born in Ousby, Christianstad län, Sweden Nov. 8, 1880; was baptized June 6, 1892, by John Swenson. He emigrated to Utah in 1894 and later attended the Utah Agricultural College, from which institution he graduated in 1915 with the degree of B. S. He filled a mission to Sweden in 1909-1911, laboring in the Gotland Branch fourteen months; after that he was called to Malmö to act as clerk of the Skåne Conference. There he led the choir and was superintendent of the Sunday school He was transferred to mission headquarters at Stockholm in 1911 to edit and translate for "Nordstjernan," and returned home in January 1912. Brother Swenson married Anna Margareta Elizabeth Hellberg, formerly of Eskilstuna, Sweden, Aug. 21, 1912, who bore him seven children (three sons and four daughters) In 1913, Brother Swenson was appointed as sistant professor in woodwork at the Agricultural College at Logan, which position he still holds. He is a president of the 128th quorum of Seventy, and resides at Logan, Utah.

'all and Carl A. Johnson of Salt ake City, Utah, arrived May 1st. oni C. Ahlquist of Salt Lake City, tah, arrived June 3rd. Andrew C. jörk and Dan A. Swenson of Salt ake City, Utah, and Peter Fritchuf wenson of Twin Falls and Joseph .. Christofferson of Rexburg, Ida- o, arrived June 6th. Albin Edward ohnson and Hyrum E. Hanson of

Utah, and Gustave E. Olson of Glencoe, Idaho, arrived Dec. 5th.

Elder Niels R. Holm and companion, who were laboring in Jemtland län, reported in the early part

JAMES MONSON

Was born Oct. 2, 1874, in St. Charles, Bear ake Co., Idaho, the son of Jeppa Monson and elli Maria Swenson. He was baptized July 9, 1883, by Elder Martin Jacobson and or- ained a Seventy Dec. 11, 1911, by Pres. oseph W. McMurrin. Brother Monson per- ormed a mission to Sweden in 1909-1911, la- oring in the Norrköping and Skåne confer- nces. He is a resident of Smithfield, Utah.

CARL JOHAN JOHNSON

Was born July 2, 1850, in Brevik, Skaraborg län, Sweden; baptized March 28, 1872, and emigrated to America in 1873 on the S. S. "Nevada." He located at Grantsville, Tooele County, where he lived for seven years. He married Anna Sofia Johnson; to them were born eight children. In 1876, Brother Johnson, who is a plasterer by trade, was called to work on the St. George Temple for six months. In 1880, he moved to Pleasant Grove. In 1909-1911 he filled a mission to Sweden, laboring in Sköfde, Göteborg Conference, for nearly two years. His wife died in 1919.

ogan, and Hildur M. Wikström of alt Lake City, Utah, arrived June 9th. Mary Sundwall of Fairview, Jtah, arrived July 2nd. Eric J. sakson of Ogden, Utah, arrived Aug. th. Charles J. Johanson of Lindon, Jtah, arrived Oct. 26th. John I. Ben- on of Spring City, Utah, arrived Nov. 28th. Alfred Erickson, Amos C. Nilson and Edwin Erickson of Smithfield, and Heber F. Johnson of Richmond, Gustave Larson of Gar- and, Clarence E. Johnson of Tooele,

of the year 1910, that many in that part of Sweden were investigating the truth, and that some of those who had been, and were yet, opposed to the work of the Lord had changed their opinion about the Saints, acknowledging that whatever evil report had been circulated about the Latter-day Saints, honest people were bound to admit that the "Mormons" were clean in their habits and polite and courteous in their conduct.

CHAPTER 2 (1910-1913)

Pres. Rudger Clawson visits Sweden—Visit of Pres. Joseph F. Smith and Bishop Charles W. Nibley—Successful labors of Elders—Elder Andreas Peterson presides—Audience with King Gustaf V.—Death of Emil C. Thedell, Nephi R. Olson and Gustaf P. Anderson— A. Theodore Johnson presides—Theodore Tobison succeeds to the presidency of the mission.

A special conference of the Swedish Mission, held in Stockholm July 10, 1910, was attended by Apostle Rudger Clawson, president of the European Mission, Historian Andrew Jenson and forty-five other Elders from Zion. The meetings were well attended by both Saints and strangers who not only enjoyed the preaching but the beautiful singing. On the Saturday evening, the Stockholm Branch choir gave a splendid free concert in the chapel.

Later in July President Joseph F. Smith, accompanied by his wife and son Franklin, Presiding Bishop Charles W. Nibley, wife and two daughters, and Historian Andrew Jenson visited Sweden. The coming of these Church officials was made known only a few days previous to their arrival by telegram, but the prospect of being visited by the President of the Church and Presiding Bishop called for hasty preparations. Willing and busy hands were soon engaged in renewing the decorations in the new chapel; and fresh flowers and foliage and hundreds of yards of wreaths greeted the eye everywhere in the beautiful edifice. During the meetings, which were thoroughly enjoyed by all who attended, many instructions and much counsel were imparted by the distinguished visitors. President Smith refuted the story about the Latter-day Saint Elders in Sweden or anywhere else trying to influence the Saints to hasten emigration to Utah. While in Stockholm, the visiting brethren were chosen as American representatives of the International Peace Congress,

which at this time was held in Stockholm.

Elder Amos C. Nilson reported that the priests and police in Luleå had tried to hinder the missionaries in their activities, and that Elder Cederlund and companion had lately been under arrest, being apprehended while out tracting, and taken to the police station, where they were subjected to a close examination by the officers, who made frequent use of the telephone while questioning the Elders, whose answers were recorded. The brethren were finally set at liberty.

In 1910 more than 158,000 houses were visited by the Elders in the Swedish Mission, who held 23,500 gospel conversations, and baptized 173 new members. Ninety-two persons emigrated to Utah during the year.

Fifty-one Elders from Zion arrived in the Swedish Mission within the year 1910, as follows:

Anders A. Carlson of Alta, Wyoming, and Anders Pehrson of American Fork, Utah, arrived Jan. 10th. Clarence N. Pearson of West Jordan, Utah, arrived Feb. 26th. Alvin Westenskow of Imbler, Oregon, and Andrew F. Gutke and Carl A. Carlquist of Salt Lake City, Utah, arrived April 3rd. John A. Omansen of Spring City, Fredrik Anderson of Hyde Park, Nels Erik Swenson of Ephraim, and Harold Cederlund, Victor Peterson and Alonzo Lindquist of Logan, Albert L a r s o n of Murray and Nephi N. Valentine of Brigham City, Utah, arrived May 7th. Bengt Johnson, junior, of Provo and Joseph N. Larson of Hyrum, Utah, arrived June 1st. Jonas Anderson of Lyman, Wyoming, Clements H. Jensen of Salem, and Arthur C. Davidson of Driggs, Idaho, arrived June 9th. John A. Cederlund of Springville, Utah, arrived June

14th. John E. Anderson of Richmond, Utah, Olof P. Johanson of Archer and Peter Lavern Madsen of Rigby,

NEPHI MERRELL VALENTINE

Was born Oct. 28, 1889, at Brigham City, Utah, son of Nephi J. Valentine and Sarah B. Merrell; set apart as a missionary by Elder Anthony W. Ivins April 11, 1910, and left the next day for Sweden, where he labored in Helsingborg, Halmstad and Karlskrona. Honorably released from his mission, he left Malmö, Sweden, May 1, 1912, visiting continental Europe and Great Britain before returning home. He did missionary work in London, England, from February, 1919, to July, 1919. He has attended the University of Utah, the Georgetown University, and the Washington College of Law, in Washington, D. C., where he received the degree of Doctor of Law. He was admitted to practice before the courts of the District of Columbia in 1921, and before the State and Federal courts for the State of Utah in 1922. He served in France during the World War, and represented the U. S. Government as a law student at Lincoln's Inn, London, at the conclusion of the war. Brother Valentine married Hilda Mason June 13, 1919, from which union two children have been born (Barbara and Elaine). From early youth he has always been active in religious and civic affairs.

Idaho, arrived June 24th. Arthur O. Nielson of Mt. Pleasant, Utah, arrived July 9th. George H. Sörensen of Parker, Idaho, arrived Aug. 5th. Andreas Peterson of Logan, Emil C. Thedell of Ogden, Andrew Theodore Johnson of Vernal, Herbert P. An-

derson of Salt Lake City, and Clarence M. Englestead of Mt. Carmel, Utah, arrived Sept. 16th. Carl E. Nilson of Tooele, Peter Nelson of Provo and George C. Mitchell of Hooper, Utah, arrived Oct. 13th. Edward S. Carlson of Manti, Utah, and William Ray Larsen of Robin and John N. Johnson, junior, of Rexburg, Idaho, arrived Oct. 29th. Niels R. Erickson of Logan, Elias P. Forsgren of Brigham City, Reuben T. Dahlquist of Salt Lake City and

OLUF P. JOHANSON

Bishop of Archer Ward, Fremont Stake, Idaho, was born May 24, 1862, at Valiby, Elfsborg län, Sweden, the son of Johannes Swenson and Christina Person; baptized Aug. 10, 1882, by Andrew Eliason; ordained a High Priest Dec. 24, 1899, by John Henry Smith and labored as a missionary in Trollhättan, Sweden, in 1883-1884. He emigrated to Logan, Cache Co., Utah, in 1884; settled at Lyman, Idaho, in 1885, and bought a house and stable and squatter's rights on 260 acres of land for $50. He married Johanna Louisa Ridderbjelke, Sept. 10, 1886; they had two children, Minnie J. and Carl J. Johanson. Brother Johanson filled a mission to Sweden in 1910-1912, laboring in the Göteborg and Sundsvall conferences; presided in Göteborg part of the time; was appointed Bishop of Archer Ward in 1912, while in Sweden. He has served as counselor to two Bishops, been school trustee and director of canal companies, and has seen a wonderful transformation of the country from barrenness to fertility and prosperity.

Carl O. Peterson of Murray, Utah, arrived Nov. 12th. John F. Rosdahl of Central and Erik W. Olson of Oxford, Idaho, arrived Nov. 25th. Peter O. Peterson, Carl O. Youngberg and Gustaf E. Sjöberg of Salt Lake City, and John Wm. Anderson, Otto Johnson and John Perry Erickson of Grantsville, and Carl J. Olson of Logan, Utah, arrived Dec. 16th. John P. Pehrson of Sandy and James J. Dahl of Midvale Utah, arrived Dec. 23rd.

In November, 1910, Andreas Peterson succeeded Peter Sundwall as president of the Swedish Mission. Elder Sundwall had been a successful president.

On Feb. 28, 1911, President Andreas Peterson and Elders Carl A. Carlquist and Dan A. Swenson had an audience with King Gustaf V, and delivered to him a memoranda from a number of Utah people of Swedish decent, in which they set forth the misleading and untruthful statements made in a petition from the "Augustana" (Lutheran) ministers in America, in an effort which they made to have the "Mormon" Elders banished from Sweden. The three Elders were courteously received by the King, who accepted their memorial, listened to their allegations, asked questions, and expressed his willingness to receive whatever literature the Elders might be pleased to furnish him, setting forth the teachings and doctrines of the Latter-day Saints. The King intimated to the Elders that he might change his views in regard to the doctrines of the Saints after he had perused their books, which he promised to read.

Elder Emil C. Thedell of Ogden, Utah, who arrived in Stockholm, Sept. 16, 1910, died in the mission field July 18, 1911. His remains were sent home in care of Elder Joseph A. Christofferson. Brother Thedell was survived by his young wife, an aged mother and other relatives; his death was mourned by the Saints, in whose midst he had labored, and by his missionary companions.

One of Stockholm's large dailies, "Morgonbladet," was liberal enough to print a rejoinder on Aug. 12, 1911, signed by Elders Andreas Peterson, Carl A. Carlquist, A. Theodore Johnson and Dan A. Swenson, against a slanderous article written by a former Utah pastor, P. A. Äslev, which had appeared in said paper a short time before.

Twenty-two missionaries from Zion arrived in the Swedish Mission in 1911, as follows:

John C. Sederholm of Brigham City, and Henry G. Lundell of Benjamin, Utah, arrived Feb. 13th. Ludvig M. Larsen of American Fork, Utah, arrived April 14th. Joseph N. Anderson of Grover, and Nephi Robert Olson of Lovell, Wyoming, arrived July 18th. Charles A. Monson of Richmond, and G. Albin Schelin of Ogden, Utah, arrived Aug. 16th. Henry P. Booke of Provo, and Eben R. T. Blomquist of Salt Lake City, Utah, arrived Sept. 27th. Henry M. Carlson of Spanish Fork, Utah, arrived Oct. 26th. Oscar M. Olson of Salt Lake City, Frans Oscar Dahl of Farmington, Utah, and Edward Bergquist of Mink Creek, Idaho, arrived Nov. 10th. Roice B. Nelson of Cedar City, Utah, arrived Nov. 15th. Swen Swenson and Birger E. Lundevall of Salt Lake City, and Wallace E. Malmström of Midvale, Utah, arrived Dec. 8th. Mathias Erickson of Salina, Charles A. Kim of Sandy, Carl J. Carlson of Richmond, and Carl W. Jonsson of Logan, Utah, arrived Dec. 23rd. Henry P. Jensen of West Jordan, Utah, arrived Dec. 29th.

Sunday, Jan. 28, 1912, was observed by the Saints in the Swedish Mission as a day of fasting and prayer.

Elder Nephi Robert Olson of Lo-

EBEN R. T. BLOMQUIST

Was born at Christianstad, Sweden, Sept. 19, 1890, the son of Johan Alfred Blomquist and Carolina Sophia K. Johanson. He graduated from the common school at Sölvesborg at the age of eleven; received a diploma with high honors as a barber and "frisör" at Malmö; was baptized and confirmed by Elder Alfred M. Nelson of Tooele, Utah, June 6, 1906; emigrated to Utah and arrived in Salt Lake City, Oct. 3, 1908. Brother Blomquist was called on a mission to Sweden in September, 1911, labored in the Örebro and Upsala branches, presided over the Norrköping and Skåne conferences, and was honorably released Dec. 1, 1913. He managed the Blomquist Brothers Paint Co.'s store at American Fork; organized the Eben R. T. Blomquist Realty Company in Salt Lake City, and became manager of the Western Casualty Company. In 1914, he married Ethel E. Johnson, who was born Dec. 31, 1891, in Sandy. They have four children, namely, Russel E., Wayne T., Lavon and Melvin R.

vell, Wyoming, died in the Swedish Mission Feb. 13, 1912. He arrived in Malmö, July 18, 1911, and was appointed to labor in the Skåne Conference. He was zealous in distributing books and tracts, and was beloved by the Saints and his associates. His body was properly dressed and prepared for shipment

to his former home. Elder Gustaf E. Olson from Glencoe, Idaho, accompanied the remains.

The claim having been made that Utah missionaries in Sweden were acting as secret emigrant agents, and therefore ought to be expelled from the country, Elder Andreas Peterson and Einar Johanson sent a communication, accompanied by circular letters and other appropriate data, to the civil department of the Swedish Government denying the allegations mentioned and showing the true character and movements of the missionaries of the Church. Prof. Torild Arnoldson of the Utah University faculty, who was visiting Sweden (his native land), published in "Aftontid-

BIRGER EMANUEL LUNDEVALL

Was born July 31, 1888, at Upsala, Sweden, the son of Anders Lundevall and Charlotte Jung, was baptized June 18, 1897, and emigrated to Utah in 1903. He located first in Bear Lake Valley, but moved to Salt Lake City in 1905, where he was ordained an Elder by Herbert Gedge, Sept. 11, 1911. Brother Lundevall married Amy Blomquist Nov. 10, 1911, and was called to fill a mission to Sweden a few days afterwards; labored in Upsala, Eskilstuna and Vesterås (Stockholm Conference) and was later called to preside over the Göteborg Conference, returning home in November, 1913. In 1917 (March 4th) he was ordained a Seventy by Pres. J. Golden Kimball and has held responsible positions in Ward organizations. He still (1927) resides in Salt Lake City.

ningen" of August 15, 1912, a statement setting forth his observations of the people and the conditions in Utah studied by him during the eight years he had been a teacher in the State University. He claimed that polygamy was not practiced in Utah any more, and that white slavery in connection with the emigration to Utah, was, in his opinion, without any foundation whatsoever.

Elder Andreas Peterson, after having presided over the Swedish Mission upwards of two years, was released in October, 1912, with permission to return to his home in Zion after a successful mission. He was succeeded in the presidency of the mission by Elder A. Theodore Johnson.

Only eleven Elders arrived from Zion during the year 1912 to do missionary work in the Swedish Mission. Their names and arrivals follow:

Swen S. Örström of Annes and Carl O. Johnson of Shelley, Idaho, arrived Feb. 14th. John H. Johnson of Salt Lake City, Utah, arrived May 10th. Frederick Thunell and Carl E. Cederström of Salt Lake City, Utah, arrived May 24th. Henry Moray of Salt Lake City, Utah, arrived July 11th. Olof Monson of Pleasant Grove, Utah, arrived Aug. 14th. John A. Olson of Murray, Utah, arrived Sept. 26th. Hans Johanson of Crescent, and Ernest E. Monson of Richmond, Utah, arrived Nov. 14th, and Peter G. L. Fernelius of Uintah, Utah, arrived Dec. 5th.

"Stockholms-Tidningen," one of the largest daily newspapers in Sweden, published in its issue of Jan. 18, 1913, some statements made by Prof. Gunnar Anderson, before the Swedish Association for Anthropology and Geography, in Stockholm. The professor, a member of said association, praised the Utah people,

which he said ranked very high in regard to ethics, and credit for the exalted culture that had grown up in what was formerly a wild American desert was due to the indomitable energy of its colonizers. His own visit and that of other scientists to Salt Lake City had shown the greatness of Brigham Young as a pioneer and organizer.

President Ezra Taft Benson of the Europeon Mission, accompanied by Pres. Martin Christoffersen and Elder Jesse Nielson visited Stockholm in June, 1913. Well-attended meetings were held in the Stockholm chapel on Sunday June 22nd, when twenty-five missionaries laboring in the Stockholm and Sundsvall conferences were in attendance. Mission President A. Theodore Johnson afterwards accompanied Pres. Benson to Norrköping, Göteborg and Malmö, where profitable meetings were held, and where the Elders laboring in these conferences received good counsel and instructions.

President A. Theodore Johnson was honorably released from the presidency of the Swedish Mission in October, 1913. He had presided about one year, and was succeeded by Theodore Tobiason of Salt Lake City as president.

Another of Sweden's newspapers, "Smålänningen" of Oct. 4, 1913, published an article in defense of the Latter-day Saints, and in condemnation of the (as the paper states) "nasty and infamous persecution by the Swedish priests that is now going on against the religious society called Latter-day Saints." Especially did he hold up to view "the shameful treatment accorded the Swedish-American Mormon preacher [Frans O. Dahl], who now is serving twenty-two days in the penitentiary at Jönköping, to satisfy the judgment of a two hundred kronor fine, for breach against a certain ordinance prohibiting the practice of religious teachings." "These heretical burnings, started by the priests

THEODORE TOBIASON

President of the Swedish Mission, was born March 2, 1864, emigrated to Utah with his mother in 1871 and located in Salt Lake City. In 1887-1889 he filled a mission to the Northwestern States, and in February, 1895, he left for his first mission to Sweden. He presided over the Göteborg Conference until he was released in 1897. Being called to preside over the Swedish Mission, he left Salt Lake City Aug. 21, 1913, and returned May 21, 1916. During this mission he visited St. Petersburg, Russia. In 1919 he was called a second time to preside over the Swedish Mission. He left home June 28, 1919, presided 18 months, and left Sweden Dec. 10, 1920, to make a visit home, but was denied the privilege of returning again by the Swedish government. While in Sweden, he defended the Church in the Swedish Riksdag, when the Saints were being misrepresented by Pastor Aslev. For a number of years Brother Tobiason was an ordinance worker in the Salt Lake Temple.

and righteous preachers, are a disgrace to the country," he concludes, "and even the Mormons are entitled to free, religious exercise," etc.

Elder Gustaf P. Anderson of Taylorville, Alberta, Canada, died in the City of Luleå from appendicitis. He arrived in Stockholm Feb. 2, 1913, as a missionary to Sweden, and was appointed to labor in the Sunds-

vall Conference. He had spent his time intermittently in the Hernösand and Luleå branches, where he had distributed much literature, and left his testimony wherever opportunity had presented itself; he was a zealous worker. His remains were properly clothed and shipped to America, accompanied by Elder Mathias Erickson of Salina, Utah.

During the year 1913, the missionaries visited 158,261 strangers' houses, and held 18,412 gospel conversations, outside of the regular meetings in chapels and in private houses. Fifty-three persons were added to the Church by baptism, and forty-one members had emigrated to Zion.

Forty-six Elders arrived from Zion in 1913 to labor in the Swedish Mission as follows:

Jens Rosenquist Nelson of Pleasant Grove and David Larson of Garland, Utah, arrived Jan. 2nd. Hyrum Peter Sörensen of Salt Lake City, Utah, Lars Willard Nelson of Mink Creek and Olof Angus Olson of Oxford, Idaho, and Gustave Theodore Anderson of Taylorville, Canada, arrived Feb. 2nd. Emil Andrew Neilson and Otto Alfred Harrison of Afton, Wyoming, and Alma Aquilla Olson of Richmond, and Victor Eugene Erickson of Sandy, Utah, arrived March 14th. Adolf W. Sander of Richmond, Utah, arrived April 10th. John Watcher Hillström of Brigham City, John Hallman of Cedar City, Joseph E. Lindberg and Erb M. Johnson of Tooele, John Peterson of Spring City, Utah, and Lars W. Hendrickson of Kirtland, New Mexico, arrived May 10th. Lorenzo A. Oakeson of South Jordan, Jacob P. Lambert of Salt Lake City and Walter Turnquist of Ogden, Utah, Carrie Olson of Lovell, Wyoming, and Axel R. Carlson of Arimo and Charles A. Fjellström of Independence, Idaho, arrived June 5th. Nephi Nordgran of Monroe, Utah, and Bert Bunderson and Chester O. Tranström of St. Charles, Idaho, arrived July 4th. Hans Erik Peterson of Sterling, Alberta, Canada, Lawrence Raymond Nelson of Provo and A. Edwin Blomquist of Salt Lake City, Utah, arrived Aug. 2nd. Matt Anderson of Sterling, Utah, arrived Aug. 7th. Theodore Tobiason of Salt Lake City, Utah, arrived Sept. 17th. Erick W. Larson and Eric Henry Erickson of Ogden, Utah, arrived Oct. 6th. Nils A. Hanson of Thatcher and Peter Swenson, of Twin Falls, Idaho, J. Alma Janson of Gunnison, J. Edwin Söderquist of Ferron and Erik Wilhelm Johanson of Salt Lake City, Utah, arrived Nov. 4th. Homer Holmgren of Brigham City, and Walter A. Peterson of Salt Lake City, Utah, arrived Nov. 18th. William A. Shuldberg of Winder, Carl O. Hanson of Turner, L. Albin Erickson of Mink Creek and Arland L. A. Davidson of Parker, Idaho, and August G. Omer of Salt Lake City, Utah, arrived Dec. 2nd, and Henry R. Selin and Francis G. Lundell of Benjamin, Utah, arrived Dec. 26th.

CHAPTER 3 (1914-1920)

Arrival of American Elders—Anders P. Anderson presides over the mission—The publication of "Nordstjernan" temporarily suspended—Theodore Tobiason again presides.

The following missionaries from Zion arrived in the Swedish Mission during the year 1914: Olof LeRoy Olson of Oxford, Idaho, and Hyrum Danielson of Knight, Wyoming, arrived Feb. 13th. Erick W. Nyberg of Logan and John A. Carlson of Salt Lake City, Utah, arrived March 7th. Elick J. Sörensen of Bear River City, Utah, arrived April 8th. Floyd Weed of Salt Lake City

and Nephi E. Swenson of Spanish Fork, Utah, and Peter Magnusson o Mesa, Arizona, arrived May 1st John Olin Ockerman of Benjamin Hilmar Erickson of Ogden, Ru dolph A. Peterson of Provo, Utah and August E. Hedin of Pocatello Idaho, arrived June 7th, and Josep August Carlson of Salt Lake City Utah, arrived July 9th.

A proposition had been made i the Swedish riksdag (parliament) t petition His Majesty, the King, t have the "Mormon" Elders, who wer called "Mormon" agents, banishe from Sweden. The question wa called up in that august assembly and after lengthy arguments pro. an con., the vote was taken on Augus 12th, and decided by a great majorit in favor of the "Mormons." Pres Theodore Tobiason was permitted t present the Latter-day Saints' side o the question and was listened to wit marked respect and attention by th members of the riksdag.

An unexpected and discouragin order was received at mission head quarters from the authorities in th European Mission at Liverpool to re lease, with a few exceptions, the mis sionaries from Zion in the Swedis Mission to return to America, read to embark in Liverpool on Oct. 14th This was sad news to the local Saint throughout the mission, who realize what it meant to be left on their ow resources, and be bereft of their be friends and counselors. Thirty-seve missionaries were consequently re leased at once, most of them to con tinue their missionary labors in th United States. The effects of this de parture of American Elders was soo felt throughout the mission, for the had worked diligently, and befor their departure 132,430 homes o strangers had been visited, 20,59 gospel conversations had been hel and 86 persons had been added to the Church by baptism.

During the year 1914, several local brethren and sisters were rendering the Elders from Zion efficient help in promulgating the truth among their country-people. Among them were Oscar F. Bergström, who was released early in the year, after having spent nearly two years in the field; Adolf Zettergren, who had labored in the Stockholm Conference, Claes Person, who had labored in the Skåne Conference, Sister Clara Lundberg, a gifted young woman residing in Malmö, who was called to assist in the editing of "Nordstjernan," and Sisters Edith Landberg of Gefle and Gerda Elvira Börsch of Eskilstuna, who both were called to assist in the missionary work in the Stockholm Conference. Sister Lundberg is still (1927) furnishing "Nordstjernan" with valuable contributions in the way of poetry, original articles and translations. She would, no doubt, years ago, have gathered with the Saints in Zion, but her love and duty in behalf of her invalid mother, under whose watch-care Sister Clara from her childhood was brought up in the teachings and faith of the gospel, kept her in her native country.

The few missionaries from Zion who labored in the Swedish Mission during the year 1915 visited over thirty-one thousand homes of strangers, held nearly six thousand gospel conversations, and added sixty-seven souls to the membership of the Church by baptism.

The following missionaries from Zion arrived in the Swedish Mission during the year 1915: Anders P. Anderson, George A. Anderson, Peter Anderson, Svante Alfred Erikson and Werner L. Strömberg of Salt Lake City, Utah, arrived July 17th. Carl G. Johnson of Sandy, Utah, arrived Aug. 7th. Carl T. Peterson of Logan,

Utah, arrived Oct. 23rd. Oscar W. Söderberg of Salt Lake City and Ephraim Lundberg of Logan, Utah, arrived Dec. 11th, and Carl A. Erickson of Archer, Idaho, arrived Dec. 23rd.

In May, 1916, Pres. Theodore Tobiason was honorably released from presiding over the Swedish Mission, which had made good head-

SVANTE ALFRED ERIKSON

Was born at Trehörna, Skaraborg län, Sweden, Sept. 26, 1875, the son of Erik Erikson and Christine Anderson, was baptized June 2, 1895, by Anders Björk at Trollhättan, Sweden. He emigrated to Utah in 1896, was ordained an Elder Oct. 8, 1890, by A. C. Sörensen and a Seventy March 26, 1906, by John W. Boud. In 1906 (Oct. 24th) Elder Erikson married Beda Amalia Lindbeck. In 1915-1918 he filled a mission to Sweden, laboring thirty months in the Göteborg Conference, president pro tem. for some time. Brother Erikson resides in Salt Lake City, faithful to his duties in the Church.

way during his presidency, considering the few Elders he had to assist him in the good work of preaching the gospel. That which among his activities stands out most prominently, is perhaps his defense of his people before the Swedish riksdag.

Elder Anders P. Anderson, a missionary from Utah, had been called by the Presidency of the Church to succeed Elder Tobiason, who left Stockholm May 29, 1915, for his home in Salt Lake City. The usual summer conference was held in the Swedish Mission in the beginning of July in Stockholm, conducted by Pres. Anders P. Anderson. Many splendid meetings were held and good counsels and instructions given.

During the year 1916 nearly 58,-000 homes of strangers were visited by the missionaries, who by such visits had held about 7,000 gospel conversations. The Church membership had been increased by 85 baptisms.

The following missionaries from Zion arrived in the Swedish Mission during the year 1916: Samuel P. Nilson of Smithfield, Utah, and John

JOHN WILFORD CARLSON

Son of John August Carlson, was born May 11, 1892, at Logan, Utah; graduated from the Brigham Young College in 1911 and with B. S. in Agriculture from the Utah Agricultural College in 1922. He filled a mission to Sweden during the war years from 1916 to 1919, laboring in Norrköping and Vingåker. At present (1927) he is a member of the staff of the Utah Agricultural Experiment Station, with headquarters at Fort Duchesne, Utah.

Johnson of Rigby, Idaho, arrived Feb. 16th. Joseph A. Johanson of Rexburg, Idaho, and John W. Carlson of Logan, Utah, arrived May 8th. Nephi Harold Dahlström of Idaho Falls, Idaho, arrived July 13th. Arthur Eugene Peterson of Salt Lake City, arrived Nov. 1st. Lawrence Frithiof Lind of Lynne, and Charles Spenar Broderick of Roosevelt, Utah, arrived Nov. 4th. Arthur J. Anderson of Sandy, Utah, arrived Dec. 8th, and August W. Lundström of Salt Lake City, Utah, arrived Dec. 24th.

A summer conference was held in Stockholm in July, 1917, in which all the missionaries laboring in the Swedish Mission, 23 in number, took part. As usual, many interesting and spirited meetings were held.

Elder Arthur J. Anderson, who had been arrested and for four weeks incarcerated in a prison in Göteborg for preaching the gospel, was finally restored to liberty.

An excellent record was made during the year 1917 by the Elders laboring in the Swedish Mission. They visited over 109,000 strangers' homes, held nearly 10,000 gospel conversations and distributed some 169,000 books, pamphlets and tracts. There were added to the Church membership by baptism during the year, 83 souls. No Elders from Zion arrived in 1917.

"Nordstjernan," the Swedish Mission organ, commenced in 1877, was temporarily discontinued with its second number in June, 1918. No particular reason or explanations were given for such action by those to whom the Saints looked for light in the matter, except a simple announcement to subscribers, stating that "because of unforeseen circumstances, "Nordstjernan" would for the time being cease publication. The discontinuance of the only periodical in Sweden which advocated the cause of the Latter-day Saints caused great disappointment, both among Saints and strangers. The periodical had been published for nearly forty-two years, and had, during that period, done an excellent missionary work, both in the mission fields and, to some extent also, among the Saints and strangers in America.

At the beginning of the year 1918, there were fifteen missionaries, all told, laboring in the Swedish Mission. Of this number three were released to return home during the year, which left only twelve missionaries to carry on the work, and as no Elders from Zion arrived in 1918, it devolved upon this little band of laborers to look after the welfare of the mission in five conferences.

The statistics of the first five months of this year show that the missionaries during that time visited 31,220 homes of strangers, and held 2,803 gospel conversations, baptized 18 souls, and distributed upwards of 51,000 books and tracts.

Elder Theodore Tobiason arrived in Sweden, July 22, 1919, having been called to preside the second time over the mission. He came to succeed President Anders P. Anderson. In his company were also a few other Elders who came to swell the small number of missionaries, who, during the past two years, had carried on missionary work in Sweden to the best of their ability.

Pres. Tobiason's first concern after his arrival was to re-commence the publication of the mission's organ, "Nordstjernan," which had been suspended over a year. Thus the first number of its forty-third volume was issued from the press Oct. 1, 1919. This number contained the newly-arrived mission president's greeting

30

to the Saints, and the retiring president's valedictory, besides other interesting reading matter. Arrangements were next made for the holding of the fall conferences in the five conferences of the mission. These conference meetings were usually well attended and were much enjoyed by the Elders, local Saints and friends.

"Nordstjernan" announced that the sisters in the Norrköping Branch met weekly and occupied their time in sewing while one of their number would read extracts from "Nordstjer-nan" and "Utah-Posten"; the sisters made contributions with which to assist the local Elders who had been called to labor in the missionary field.

Axel E. Johnson of Burley, Idaho, who arrived June 5th, and Theodore Tobiason, Swen Swenson and Oscar W. Söderberg of Salt Lake City. Utah, and Jonas Östlund of Sterling, Alta, Canada, who arrived July 22nd, were the only Elders from Zion who arrived in Sweden in 1919.

In the spring of the year 1920, the Saints in the Göteborg Conference enjoyed the privilege of holding conference in their chapel at St. Pauli-gatan 15, Göteborg. This property had lately been purchased and recon-structed by the Church. The building contained one large and one small hall for meeting purposes, branch and conference offices, apartments for the missionaries, and also apartments for renting purposes, so as to make the building self-support-ing. Dedicatory services were held on Saturday, April 17, 1920, that being the first session of the regular conference. Pres. Theodore Tobiason officiated. The main hall was decorated for the occasion with green boughs, flowers, and Swedish and American flags.

A summer conference of the Swedish Mission was held in Stockholm, July 4th, attended by Apostle George Albert Smith, president of the European Mission, his son George Albert, jun., Junius F. Wells, assistant editor of the "Millennial Star," Pres. Theodore Tobiason and a number of other Utah and local Elders, besides Saints and strangers. Two excellent meetings were held.

The few missionaries from Zion who labored in Sweden during the year 1920 visited as many as 13,502 h o m e s of strangers, and held 2,156 gospel conversations. They distributed 33,930 books and tracts,

and 48 souls were added to the Church by baptism.

In December, 1920, Pres. Theodore Tobiason left Sweden, intending to make a short visit to his home in Utah, leaving the mission-secretary, Oscar W. Söderberg, to look after the interests of the mission during his absence. Elder Tobiason, who could not get his pass visaed by the Swedish consul at New York, was unable to return to Sweden.

The following missionaries from Zion arrived in the Swedish Mission during the year 1920: Gideon N. Hulterström and Signe L. Hulterström of Salt Lake City, Utah, arrived Sept. 8th. James H. Olson of Sandy, Utah, arrived Nov. 3rd. Mathias Erickson of Salina, Utah, and Olof J. Hokanson of Grover, Wyoming, arrived Nov. 30th, and August A. Forsberg of Riverside, Utah, arrived Dec. 29th.

OSCAR W. SÖDERBERG

Of Salt Lake City, Utah, was born in Göteborg, Sweden, May 26, 1855; learned the painter's trade and established a business in Göteborg in April, 1877. He married Emma Karolina Erikson April 14, 1878; joined the Church Nov. 11, 1894, and emigrated to Utah, arriving in Salt Lake City, April 3, 1903. In 1915 he was called to assist Pres. Theodore Tobiason to edit "Nordstjernan," and arrived in Stockholm Dec. 11, 1915; labored in this calling and as instructor of the choir until August, 1917, when he was called home. He was again called on a mission to Sweden June 21, 1919, and labored as mission secretary and writer for "Nordstjernan." When Pres. Tobiason left for home in December, 1920, Brother Söderberg was left in temporary charge of the mission. In July, 1921, Elder Isaac P. Thunell was appointed mission president, and at the end of that year Elder Söderberg returned home.

CHAPTER 4 (1921-1924)

Elder Issaac P. Thunell presides—Gideon N. Hulterström in charge—Hugo D. E. Peterson's administration—Death of Ernst George Hedberg—Visits of Apostles Reed Smoot, David O. McKay and John A. Widtsoe—Trouble with the Swedish Government regarding the landing of Elders.

The following missionaries from Zion arrived in the Swedish Mission during the year 1921: Olof Wilford Monson of Pleasant Grove, Utah, arrived Jan. 10th. Joseph H. Monson of Huntsville, Utah, arrived Feb. 18th. Isaac P. Thunell and Adolph Söderberg of Salt Lake City, Utah, arrived March 1st. Johan H. Holmquist of Salt Lake City, Utah, arrived March 8th. Andrew P. Anderson of Taylor, and Nils S. Blad of Murray, Utah, arrived March 11th. Carl A. Lundell of Spanish Fork and Elon Keding of Salt Lake City, Utah, arrived March 28th. Fred. Thedell of Ogden, Utah, arrived May 31st. Josephine Holmquist and Carl Simon

Fors of Salt Lake City, Utah, arrived June 29th. Anna L. Peterson of Salt Lake City, Utah, arrived July 4th. Charles Anderson of Seattle, Washington, arrived Aug. 8th. Victor Edward Blomquist of Salt Lake City, Utah, arrived Aug. 9th. Morris C. Johnson and Nathaniel Johanson of

ISAAC P. THUNELL

dency to succeed Elder Theodore Tobiason as president.

The death of Pres. Anthon H. Lund, March 2, 1921, in Salt Lake

President of the Swedish Mission, is the son of John Fredrik and Erika C. Thunell, and was born in Stockholm, Sweden, May 2, 1886. The same year the family emigrated to Utah, settling in Fountain Green, later in Manti, and Gunnison, Utah, and located in Salt Lake City in 1903. When the Waterloo Ward was organized in 1905, Brother Thunell was called to labor in the Sunday school. In 1906-1909 he filled a mission to Sweden, laboring in Malmö and Upsala, and later presided over the Eskilstuna Branch. He baptized twenty persons. After residing in Waterloo Ward and Salt Lake City many years, working actively in the choir and Sunday school, he moved to Sugar House Ward, where he acted as first counselor in the presidency of the Y. M. M. I. A,; later he became superintendent of the Ward Sunday school. Elder Thunell filled a second mission to Sweden in 1921-1922, and acted first as secretary of the Swedish Mission, and on July 24, 1921, was called to preside over the said mission, which position he held until Nov. 10, 1922, when he was honorably released to return home. The Swedish Mission prospered, both spiritually and financially under his administration. Although there were only 19 Elders in the field, 70 persons where baptized in 1921, and 87 in 1922. Upon returning home he became a member of the Wasatch Ward and labored there as a special missionary, and as second assistant superintendent of the Sunday school. On June 15, 1924, he succeeded Marvin O. Ashton as Bishop of the Wasatch Ward, which position he held until November, 1927. In October, 1927, he was installed as president of the Scandinavian meetings in Salt Lake City. On April 5, 1911, Bro. Thunell married Hildegard V. Ohlson in the Salt Lake Temple. They have five children, three boys and two girls.

JOHAN HANSON HOLMQUIST

Was born Feb. 26, 1856, in Söfde parish, Skåne, Sweden, the son of Hans Person and Hanna Nilsson. He served for some time in the Swedish Army; was baptized in Malmö, April 10, 1910, by John P. Person, and called by Pres. Theodor A. Johnson to labor as a missionary in the Hernösand branch, at Kramfors. For two years and a half he remained there and then presided for six months in Gefle; twenty-three persons joined the Church through his intstrumentality. Emigrating to Utah he arrived in Salt Lake City, May 29, 1916. As an Elder from Zion, Brother Holmquist filled a mission to Sweden in 1921-1923, laboring in Vingåker, Malmö and Göteborg, and in Norrköping as conference president. While on this mission he baptized twenty-three persons. His wife, Josefina Matilda Holmquist, born in Harpinge parish, Sweden, Sept. 22, 1869, accompanied her husband on his mission, and labored in Halland and Malmö, Göteborg and Norrköping. Brother Holmquist resides in Salt Lake City at present (1927).

Salt Lake City, Utah, arrived Nov. 23rd.

Elder Isaac P. Thunell took charge of the mission, July 24, 1921, having been appointed by the First Presi-

City, Utah, caused considerable sadness among the Saints in Sweden. Brother Lund had been a father to the Scandinavian people for many years and was much beloved by all who knew him.

CARL SIMON FORS

Was born in Veckholm, near Upsala, Sweden, Feb. 6, 1884, the son of Johan Axel Fors and Margreta Kristina Blom; married Sofia Elizabeth Edling, Dec. 5, 1908, and was baptized May 1, 1910, by Emil W. Weed and confirmed by Peter Sundwall. He arrived, with his wife, in Salt Lake City, June 5, 1911. Being called to perform a mission, he left for Sweden June 9, 1921; labored in Stockholm and Gefle till October, 1921; was then called to preside over the Dalarne branch, and in April, 1922, to preside over the Stockholm Conference. In November of that year he was called to assist in editing "Nordstjernan," and being released June 20th. he arrived home July 9, 1923. On March 8, 1924, he lost his wife in an automobile accident, and was left with four children. On March 12, 1925, he married Elsa Johanna Oscarson of Pleasant Grove.

During the year 1921, Elders Carl A. Lundell, Nils S. Blad and August A. Forsberg were banished from Sweden for preaching the gospel. Other Elders, including Pres. Thunell, were threatened with banishment by the Swedish authorities, but, by the providence of the Almighty and the assistance of the American Embassy in Stockholm, and of Senator Reed Smoot in Washington, D.

C., they were permitted to remain and finish their missions.

Only two missionaries from Zion arrived in the Swedish Mission during the year 1922, namely, Joseph E. Erickson and Joseph W. Höglund of Salt Lake City, Utah; they arrived Dec. 6th.

A special three days' conference was held in Stockholm, commencing July 22, 1922. It was attended by missionaries, local Saints and friends from all parts of the mission. Pres. Isaac P. Thunell presided, and good reports were given by the presiding Elders. A Priesthood meeting was also held, in which confidence and

VICTOR EDWARD BLOMQUIST

Of Salt Lake City, Utah, was born Nov. 13, 1851, in the parish of Vagnhärad, Nyköping län, Sweden; was baptized June 25, 1896, and emigrated to Salt Lake City, Utah, in 1909. In 1921-1923 he filled a mission to Sweden, laboring in the Stockholm Conference. Elder Blomquist says that when 14 years old he went out on the ice to fish, when he and his companions heard wonderful music and saw in the sky a supernatural being, who came from the east and went westward. He had an instrument on which he played sweet harmonies. The vision made an indelible impression on his mind, and he began searching for truth, which he, after many years, found in the Church.

good will was expressed by the Elders for one another and for the presiding brethren. The mission president imparted timely counsel and instruction to his co-laborers. The beautiful singing by the Stockholm Branch choir was appreciated by all

ström and his wife had labored in Sweden as missionaries since their arrival, Sept. 8, 1920.

Elder Hugo D. E. Peterson, who had been called and set apart by the First Presidency of the Church in Salt Lake City, Utah, on May 23,

MORRIS C. JOHNSON

Was born Aug. 20, 1885, in Dalarne, Sweden, the son of Carl E. and Sofia Johnson; joined the Church by baptism March 4, 1894. and in 1904 emigrated to Utah with his parents and six brothers and sisters. In May, 1921, Brother Johnson was called to do missionary work in England, labored in London for seven months, and then proceeded to Sweden, where he presided in Norrköping and Gefle for twenty months, and returned home in August, 1923. In 1924 (May 21st) he married Ingeborg Petterson, a native of Sweden, who died April 4, 1927. Brother Johnson is engaged in the manufacture of sheet iron in Salt Lake City.

INGEBORG PETTERSON JOHNSON

Wife of Morris C. Johnson, was born Oct. 4, 1890, in Bockebacken, Blekinge, Sweden, the daughter of Johan Petterson and Carolina Anderson, and baptized Aug. 10, 1901. She came to Utah in 1903, and labored diligently to assist other members of her family to emigrate. From April, 1919, to December, 1920, she filled a mission to the Central States and on May 21, 1924, was married to Morris C. Johnson in the Salt Lake Temple. She died April 4, 1927, survived by her husband and infant son.

present and helped to make the gathering a success.

Elder Isaac P. Thunell, who during sixteen months had presided over the Swedish Mission, was honorably released Nov. 10, 1922. Before his departure for his home in Utah (by request of Pres. Heber J. Grant), he appointed Elder Gideon N. Hulterström to succeed him in the presidency of the mission. Elder Hulter-

1923, to preside over the Swedish Mission, arrived in Stockholm, June 16, 1923, to succeed Elder Gideon N. Hulterström, who had presided over the mission eight months. Brother Peterson was accompanied by his wife (Axeline M.) and his daughter (Mildred L.), who had also been set apart for missions to Sweden. Elder Peterson took charge of the mission in July, 1923.

Elder Ernst George Hedberg, a young missionary, died in Göteborg,

July 12, 1923, and was buried in that city July 17th. Elder Hedberg was a son of Conference President August A. Hedberg. Memorial services were

on his way to Norway to make a short visit among the relatives of his departed mother. Apostles McKay and Widtsoe spoke in the Sunday school and also in the evening meeting, being listened to with rapt attention. Several of the Stockholm daily newspapers published favorable interviews with Senator Smoot, who, with his traveling companions, left Stockholm July 25th for Norway.

Apostle McKay, who was president of the European Mission, returned to Stockholm from Norway, Saturday, July 28th, and held a successful con-

NATANAEL JOHANSON

Was born Nov. 18, 1865, in Holta, Bohus län, Sweden; was baptized March 11, 1891, by Elder L. Dahlquist. Emigrating to Utah, he arrived in Salt Lake City, April 28, 1905, together with his wife, Anna Fredrika Olson; eleven children were the fruit of their marriage. Brother Johanson performed a mission to Sweden in 1921-1923, laboring in the Göteborg, Norrköping and Stockholm conferences, presiding part of the time in the Vingåker and Vesterås branches. His wife died Feb. 22, and on Aug. 15th, following, he married Sofia Flood. He has been active in ecclesiastical work and has held the High Priesthood since Jan. 9, 1916. His son, Erik, now departed, filled a mission in Sweden and the United States in 1913-1915.

held in the Latter-day Saints chapel in Göteborg, at which Presidents Hulterström and Peterson and Elder Morris C. Johnson made appropriate remarks.

The Elders and Saints in Stockholm enjoyed a pleasant visit from Apostles Reed Smoot, David O. McKay and John A. Widtsoe, July 22, 1923. Senator Smoot was on a tour in Europe in the interests of the American Government and was now

JOSEPH WILFORD HÖGLUND

Son of August Joel Höglund and Anna M. Swenson, was born Feb. 24, 1901, at Salt Lake City, Utah. He was baptized July 3, 1909, ordained a Deacon at the age of thirteen years and then a Teacher (acting as president of his quorum); later he was ordained successively to the offices of Priest, Elder and Seventy. In 1922-1925 he filled a mission to Sweden and was called to labor in the Gefle Conference. After acting as branch president and conference secretary for about a year, he was called to labor in the Göteborg Conference and to preside in the Jönköping branch. After his return home Elder Höglund acted as a home missionary. In April, 1926, he moved with his wife to Los Angeles, California, where he now lives.

ference session with the Elders laboring in the Swedish Mission and the local Saints from many parts of Sweden. A number of well attended meetings were held in the Saints' chapel in Stockholm, and, as usual, the excellent singing and instrumental music rendered gladdened the hearts of all present. Pres. McKay left Stockholm on Sunday evening, July 29th.

Pres. Peterson, wife and daughter,

GIDEON NICANOR HULTERSTRÖM

President of the Swedish Mission, was born Oct. 31, 1885, at Vintrosa, Sanna, Örebro, Sweden, son of Johan Hulterström and Adler Sophie Videstrand. He was baptized June 30, 1894, ordained a Deacon April 1, 1900, and called to do missionary labor, such as to distribute Church literature, etc. Emigrating to America in 1902, he arrived in Salt Lake City, Utah, Sept. 10th. He received a good education and business training, first in Sweden and later in Salt Lake City. In 1908 (Aug. 26th) he married Signe Victoria Lindskog. In 1908-1911 he filled a mission to Sweden, laboring in Eskilstuna and Vesterås branches; returning home he was leader of a small company of emigrants and some returning missionaries. In 1920-1923 he filled another three years' mission to Sweden, this time accompanied by his wife who had also been called to fill a mission in Sweden. During this mission he acted as president of the Stockholm Conference; later as mission secretary and still later as president of the Swedish Mission. After his return home he labored as a home missionary in the Ensign Stake of Zion and on March 25, 1925, he was called to act as first counselor to Gustave W. Forsberg in the presidency of the Swedish meetings in Salt Lake City. He held this position until Aug. 17, 1927. In October, 1927, he was called on a third mission to Sweden, this time to succeed Andrew Johnson as president of the mission.

SIGNE VICTORIA LINDSKOG
HULTERSTRÖM

Wife of Gideon N. Hulterström, was born Nov. 29, 1887, at Flodafors, Floda parish, Sweden, emigrated to Utah and arrived in Bear River City Sept. 22, 1901. Two years later she went to Salt Lake City, where she attended the L. D. S. Business College, having previous to this graduated from the public schools in Sweden. On January 5, 1907, she was baptized, and on Aug. 26, 1908, she was married to Gideon N. Hulterström, in the Salt Lake Temple. For two years she labored as a Primary teacher and as a teacher in the Relief Society in the Twenty-ninth Ward, Salt Lake City. In 1920-1923 she filled a three years' mission to Sweden, together with her husband, laboring in Eskilstuna, Upsala, Vesterås and Stockholm. During the latter part of her mission she presided over the relief societies of the Swedish Mission. After her return home she labored as a home missionary in the Ensign Stake.

made a short visit to the city of Visby, Gotland, in August, 1923, and held a meeting with the few Saints residing there. He also, in company with Elder and Sister Gideon N. Hul-

terström, held successful meetings in
Vesterås, and other parts of Sweden.
Pres. Peterson was accompanied to
some of the branches by Elders Algot
Johnson, Charles Anderson and
others, and before the year ended,
Pres. Peterson was kept busy writing

answers to scurrilous newspaper articles, and pleading with the American legation to take steps toward
securing permission for several
American Elders, who were detained
in Copenhagen, to enter Sweden.
These Elders had been refused visaes

HUGO DANIEL EDWARD PETERSON, AXELINE MANUELLA PETERSON AND
MILDRED LOUISA PETERSON.

Hugo D. E. Peterson, president of the Swedish Mission, has since his arrival in Zion
in the summer of 1883 been steadily engaged
in Church work. He married Axeline M.
Nielsen, May 23, 1884, in the Endowment
House, Salt Lake City. In this union he and
his wife have been blessed with nine children:
Hugo C. A., Alma Sophia, Walter A., Francis (Frank) E., Norma, Viola, Ella, Earl L.,
and Mildred L., all living. Brother Peterson
was ordained a Seventy, Feb. 23, 1885, and
is at present (1927) a president of the Fourth
Quorum of Seventy. In the early part of 1884
he entered the "Deseret News" office as a com-
positor, and was the first linotype operator on
that daily, when it installed typesetting ma-
chines. He was choir leader in the Scandinavian meetings in Salt Lake City for about
25 years. On Jan. 26, 1906, he was set apart
as the first president of the Swedish meetings
in the Ensign Stake, holding that position for
ten years; he has also presided over the Swedish Missionary Society. In 1909 he was appointed by the First Presidency to compile
and publish Zions Sånger, in the Swedish, and
Zions Sange, in the Danish-Norwegian language,
words and music. In June, 1914, he was
called to take charge of Utah-Posten,
a Swedish weekly publication, which he,
with Elder C. A. Krantz as assistant, edited and published until May, 1923, when he
was called to preside over the Swedish Mission, and while there, in addition to his many
duties, he edited the Nordstjernan. Since his
return from this his second mission, he has
taken up former labors in his home ward, the
21st, and, together with his wife, is working
in the Temple. He spent about three years as

a missionary among the non-"Mormon" population in Ensign Stake, about three years administering to the sick in the hospitals, etc.,
and holds now a position in the Church Historian's office. Two sons have filled foreign
missions, and one son was in the late war. (See
page 253.)

Axeline M. Peterson, wife of Hugo D. E.
Peterson, was born Dec. 10, 1865, in Copenhagen, Denmark, daughter of Hakon and Sophia
Nielsen, and was baptized Oct. 12, 1881. In
childhood she was a member of the Sunday
school, and in her youth took part in the activities of the auxiliary organizations of the
Copenhagen branch, as teacher in the Sunday
school, secretary of the Y. L. M. I. A. and
member of the choir, being thus active until she
emigrated to Zion in 1884. Sister Peterson
has been a worker among the Scandinavians,
and in the Relief Society of the 21st Ward,
Salt Lake City. In 1923-1925 she accompanied her husband as a missionary to Sweden.
She acted as president of the Relief Societies
in the Swedish Mission, and also as president
of the Relief Society of the Stockholm branch.

Mildred L. Peterson, born Aug. 28, 1908,
was baptized when eight years old. Although
young in years, she carried out her part in
the missionary labors assigned to her, which
were mostly centered in the Stockholm
branch, where she acted as organist in all the
organizations, and besides played violin solos
in private and public gatherings at concerts,
funerals, etc. She organized two English
classes, which she taught once a week, and
since her return home has finished a course
in the L. D. S. Business College.

to their passports by the Swedish consuls in Chicago, New York and Copenhagen.

The Sacrament was administered for the first time in the Sunday school in Stockholm, Nov. 11, 1923, this being a new custom, which was shortly afterwards introduced in some of the other branches of the Church in Sweden. Sets of individual Sacramental services were received for that purpose from Basel, Switzerland. Exercises similar to those carried out in the Sunday schools of Zion were introduced on this oc-

casion in Stockholm. Elder C. Albin Jonsson and Sisters Mildred Peterson and Karin Weijland furnished orchestral music.

The following missionaries from Zion arrived in the Swedish Mission during the year 1923: Axel R. Boström of Salt Lake City, Utah, arrived March 20th. Hjalmar A. Sjödin and Stellan H. Thedell of Salt Lake City, Utah, arrived April 24th. Peter Anderson of Roosevelt, Utah, arrived May 22nd. Johannes Erikson of Murray, Utah, arrived June 12th. Hugo D. E. Peterson, Axeline M. Peterson and Mildred Louisa Peterson and Per Nilson of Salt Lake

AXEL R. BOSTRÖM

Was born in Frändefors parish, Elfsborg län, Sweden, Jan. 26, 1886, the son of Erik J. Larsson and Sofia A. Olsson. Emigrating to Utah, he arrived in Salt Lake City in September, 1907; was baptized July 2, 1910, by Nephi Y. Schofield, and confirmed July 3rd by Gustav Fryekberg, and was ordained an Elder April 1, 1912, by Bishop Francis B. Platt. On April 3, 1912, he married Edla Maria Anderson, daughter of August Person and Sofia Christine Fihn; was ordained a Seventy Dec. 14, 1920, by Seymour B. Young, and on March 2, 1923, set apart by Melvin J. Ballard for a mission to Sweden. He labored in the Skåne Conference from March 30, 1923, till July 28, 1923, and after that presided over the Stockholm Conference till Feb. 23, 1924, and over the Skåne Conference till Feb. 28, 1925, when he was released to return home.

JOHANNES ERIKSON

Son of Erik Nilson and Anna Lisa Larsson, was born in Hysna, Elfsborg län, Sweden, Sept. 6, 1886. He was baptized March 21 1893, by Elder August Westerberg, confirmed by Elder C. G. Anderson and was ordained an Elder Sept. 5, 1897, by Elder H. M. Pehrson. Brother Erikson emigrated from Sweden Feb. 13, 1911. After he arrived in Salt Lake City, he married Carolina Emelia Gustafson in the Salt Lake Temple, Aug. 18, 1915. He went back to Sweden and performed a mission during the years 1923-1925, laboring in the Göteborg and Norrköping conferences, part of the time as president of the latter conference. Brother Erikson resides at present (1927) in the Grant Ward, Cottonwood Stake.

City, Utah, arrived June 16th. Andrew P. Renström of Salt Lake City, Utah, and Victor E. Lindquist of

PER NILSSON

Was born April 27, 1868, in Bunkeflo parish, Malmöhus län, Sweden. Together with his wife and daughter, he was baptized March 2, 1908, in Copenhagen, Denmark, by Pres. Sören Rasmussen. With his family he emigrated to Utah in 1910, and located in Salt Lake City. In 1923-1925 he filled a mission to his native country, laboring in the Skåne Conference with diligence and success. Elder Nilsson is still (1927) a resident of Salt Lake City.

Lewisville, Idaho, arrived July 3rd. C. Albin Jonsson of Salt Lake City, Utah, arrived July 5th. Gustave E. Johnson and Karen O. Johnson of Salt Lake City, Utah, arrived July 11th. Anthon Pehrson of Logan, Utah, arrived Sept. 27th. Eric Holmgren of Logan, Utah, arrived Oct. 31st, and Einar I. Applequist and Henry C. Krantz of Salt Lake City, Utah, arrived Nov. 27th.

In 1924, several Elders and missionaries who had been set apart for the Swedish Mission had, at different times since the previous fall, arrived in Copenhagen, Denmark, where they unwillingly had "stranded," the Swedish consuls in America and in Copenhagen having refused to sign their passports. One of these Elders,

Darcey U. Wright of Murray, was at length, through the interceding by the American legation at Stockholm, permitted to enter Sweden, Jan. 23rd, and was assigned to the Göteborg Conference. Pres. Peterson, who had made several visits to the legation in behalf of the Elders who had been refused entrance to Sweden, felt much encouraged by the untiring efforts exhibited by Ambassador Bliss, Secretary Meier and his assistant, to secure a permanent ruling by the Swedish government in favor of American Elders landing in Sweden without hindrance or annoyance.

GUSTAVE E. JOHNSON

Who filled a mission to Sweden and Norway in 1923-1925, was born Feb. 13, 1869, on the island of Gotland, Sweden, emigrated to Utah and was baptized Oct. 31, 1908, in Salt Lake City, where he also was ordained to the Priesthood and presided over the Ninth Quorum of Elders in the Pioneer Stake in 1914-1918. He acted as secretary of the Cannon Ward Genealogical Society in 1920-1923.

Karen O. Johnson, wife of Gustave E. Johnson, was born June 27, 1877, in Norway, and baptized in Trondhjem May 1, 1901. She emigrated to Utah in 1907 and among her activities in the Church she acted as a teacher in a Ward Relief Society, was supervisor of a religion class, primary and parents' class teacher, etc. She accompanied her husband on a mission to Sweden and Norway in 1923-1925.

Elder Vance O. Lind arrived in the Swedish Mission, Feb. 27, 1924, by way of Christiania, Norway, where he secured the Swedish consul's signature to his passport. He was assigned to the Gefle Conference.

On March 5th, Elder John A. Anderson and wife, of Hooper, Utah, who were among those detained in Copenhagen, at length had their passports signed and were permitted to enter Sweden. They arrived at the Stockholm headquarters March 9th, and were assigned to labor in Vesterås, Stockholm Conference.

Elder Allan O. Johnson, another of the Elders who had been detained in Copenhagen, also received permission to enter Sweden, after his passport had been visaed.

Very unusual innovations and change of heart were this year exhibited by some of the state church

HENRY CLARENCE KRANTZ

Was born in Salt Lake City, Utah, June 18, 1903 (son of Carl A. Krantz and Gerda C. Höglund), attended the public schools in his home town, and learned the printer's trade. He held the various offices in the Aaronic Priesthood, and was early ordained an Elder, serving as secretary and class leader in the quorum in the Fifth Ward. He also labored as a teacher in the Sunday school and as choir leader. In November, 1923, he left for a mission to Sweden, where he first labored in the city of Göteborg. In the fall of 1924 he took charge of the choir in Stockholm, and the following spring he was called to preside over the Stockholm Conference. As an item of special interest may be mentioned that he, as far as is known, was the first Elder of the third generation of a Swedish family in the Church to be sent from Zion to labor for the spreading of the gospel in Sweden—his grandfather and father having filled similar missions.

EINER ISADORE APPLEQUIST

Son of John F. Applequist and Anna Krantz, was born Oct. 19, 1901, in Salt Lake City, Utah, and baptized in November, 1919. He followed the trade of a linotype operator at the "Deseret News." He was ordained an Elder by Milan I. Tilberry, May 30, 1920 and on Nov. 6, 1923, was set apart by Elder Charles H. Hart for a mission to Sweden, being, on his mother's side the third generation to bear witness to the inhabitants of that land that God has spoken to earth in these latter days. His father also had preceded him as a missionary to Sweden. Elder Applequist presided for some time in Gefle and then had charge of the Stockholm branch. He returned to his home in Salt Lake City Dec. 31, 1925.

ministers towards the Latter-day Saints, when on several occasions the Stockholm Branch choir and musicians were privileged to participate in funeral exercises. Hitherto the Swedish clergy were the only ones authorized to officiate in such cases. It was, therefore, quite a novelty to hear the "Mormon" choir sing in the state cemetery chapels and to witness the chapel organist playing "Mormon" tunes, and that the priest even requested another of "your beautiful hymns." It also became quite common for "Mormon" Elders to dedicate the grave of their own Church members after the other ceremonies were over. Occasionally the Lutheran priests would remain and listen to the dedicatory prayer and admit to the Elders that the services were beautiful. Sister Mildred Peterson, daughter of the president, played violin solos on several such occasions, and the choir sang in several of the Stockholm hospitals on certain holidays.

A communication from the American Legation's secretary, Mr. Cord Meier, was received by Pres. Peterson, June 12th. It read: "With reference to our previous conversations concerning the Swedish restrictions for the entry of missionaries of the Church of Jesus Christ of Latter-day Saints, I beg to inform you that this legation has recently been informed by the Royal Swedish Minister for Foreign Affairs, that in the future the same regulations for obtaining a visa for entering Sweden will apply to persons belonging to the Mormon Church the same as to other foreigners." It may here be stated that up to this writing (1927) the Swedish Government has conscientiously adhered to this ruling as regards Latter-day Saint Elders, none of whom have since been refused entrance.

Elder Oscar Söderquist was the next to leave Copenhagen and permitted to enter Sweden.

Pres. David O. McKay and his wife, Sister Emma Ray McKay, arrived in Stockholm, July 12, 1924, to participate in the summer conference, which was held the following two days; it was an occasion of joy and happiness to all present. Three spirited meetings were held on the

Sunday, and an impressive Priesthood meeting was held on Monday forenoon, lasting 5½ hours; other good public meetings were held in the evening and the following day.

Presidents McKay and Peterson had a very pleasant interview with Secretary Cord Meier of the American Legation, on Wednesday, July 16th. From Stockholm President and Sister McKay took their departure for Germany, July 17th.

Elder Allan O. Johnson, whose case had been under consideration for some time by the Swedish authorities, he having applied for the visa of his passport, was refused his request and banished. He left Stockholm for Copenhagen, Oct. 6th, to finish his mission in Great Britain.

OSKAR SANDER

Of Salt Lake City, Utah, was born Dec. 29, 1881, at Malmö, Sweden, the son of Lars Nilson Sander and Beata Nilsson. He joined the Church when a young man and emigrated to Utah in 1901. In 1920 (Dec. 1st) he married Signe Linea Johnson of Salt Lake City. Brother Sander was called to perform a mission to Sweden in 1924, leaving Salt Lake City Jan. 25th; was called to preside over the Gefle Conference, where he labored for a year; later he presided over the Skåne Conference; was honorably released Feb. 20, 1926, and arrived in Salt Lake City, March 10th. Elder Sander is an earnest worker in the Church and at present (1927) a member of the 18th Ward, Salt Lake City.

Under the energetic labors of Elders Joseph W. Höglund and Darcey

DAVID CLARENCE CARLSON

Son of August Carlson and Caroline Theb.om, was born in Ogden, Utah, Aug. 14, 1901, presided successively over a quorum of Deacons and an Elders' quorum in the 19th Ward, Salt Lake City. In 1924, he was called to take a mission to Sweden, where he was appointed secretary of the mission and superintendent of the Sunday school in the Stockholm branch. He returned to Utah, May 15, 1926.

U. Wright, the Jönköping Branch of the Göteborg Conference, after having been closed for a number of years, was re-opened in the fall of 1924, and on Nov. 29th and 30th, special meetings were held in a new hall just remodeled and opened there for meeting purposes. Pres. Hugo D. E. Peterson and Elders August A. Hedberg, Darcey U. Wright and Gustave Johnson addressed the large congregations.

Illustrated lectures were given during December in the Stockholm chapel by Pres. Peterson, about two hundred new slides having been re-

ceived from home. The lecture and pictures were greatly enjoyed by both Saints and strangers. Similar lectures were subsequently delivered in Göteborg and Malmö.

During the year many special meetings were held in the different parts of the mission by Pres. Peterson, who was sometimes accompanied by his wife and daughter, and assisted by the mission-secretary, David C. Carlson, Conference Presidents Anthon Pehrson, Oskar Sander, August A. Hedberg and others. These meetings were highly enjoyed by Saints and friends, who did not often receive visits from the Elders, there not being missionaries enough in Sweden at this time to make regular visits everywhere. It was also

JOHN J. MALMSTRÖM

A faithful member of the Church, was born July 5, 1867, in Malmö, Sweden; was baptized April 11, 1887, and ordained an Elder in May, 1893, by Elder Niels J. Henricksen. In 1894 (Mar. 24th) he married Esther Ljungttröm, and emigrated to Utah in June, 1899. Mrs. Malmtröm died April 11, 1921, and in 1924-1927 Elder Malmström filled a mission to Sweden, during which he labored in the Skåne Conference, over which he presided nine months. He returned home June 10, 1927. Bro. Malmström lost a son in the late world war.

quite a novelty with some people to hear and see ladies from Utah.

The following missionaries from Zion arrived in the Swedish Mission during the year 1924: Oskar Sander of Salt Lake City, Utah, arrived Feb. 18th. Vance O. Lind of Lynn, Utah, arrived Feb. 27th. John A. Anderson and Sigrid A. Anderson of Hooper, Utah, arrived March 9th. Darcey U. Wright of Murray, Utah, arrived March 20th. Allan O. Johnson of Shelley, Idaho, arrived March 26th. Gustave Johnson of Salt Lake City, Utah, arrived April 8th. Paul Carl Holm of Idaho Falls, Idaho, arrived April 28th. David Clarence Carlson of Salt Lake City, Utah, arrived April 29th. Gustave A. Seequist and Gunnar W. Lindberg of Salt Lake City, Utah, arrived May 7th. Oscar E. Söderquist of Ferron, Utah, arrived July 4th. Arthur J. Fagergren of Salt Lake City, Utah, arrived Oct. 5th, and John J. Malmström of Salt Lake City, and Knut T. Borg of Sandy, Utah, arrived Dec. 8th.

CHAPTER 5 (1925-1926)

Opinion of Archbishop Nathan Söderblom— John H. Anderson presides—Apostle James E. Talmage visits Sweden—Presidents of the Swedish Mission—Skåne Conference—Stockholm Conference—Göteborg Conference—Norrköping Conference—Sundsvall Conference— Gefle Conference.

"Aftonbladet" and "Stiftstidningen," both semi-religious daily news-papers published in Göteborg, and edited by ministers of the Lutheran Church, published in the beginning of 1925 articles of an anti-Mormon nature. Copies of both these papers fell into the hands of Pres. Hugo D. E. Peterson, who wrote an answer to them, which the papers named were liberal enough to publish in their columns. In his answer to the misrepresentations made against the Latter-day Saints, Brother Peterson expressed a doubt that the broad-minded and tolerant arch-

bishop, Honorable Nathan Söderblom, would permit his subordinates to bring false accusations and misrepresentations against any religious body, and fearing that some one might poison the archbishop's mind by perverting the motive why his name was mentioned in connection with the article, Bro. Peterson sent a copy of his answer to the archbishop, together with an explanation. In due time, Archbishop Söderblom sent Pres. Peterson a note, acknowledging the receipt of his article. And this is what the head of the Lutheran Church in Sweden said:

"Dear Mr. Peterson: Everybody knows that in the Mormon Church are found members who have inherited that form of religion from fathers and mothers, and who are most estimable people. But my study of the rise and history of the Mormon Church makes it impossible for me to count it in with the Christian Church. Besides, the Mormon Church in its own records refuse such a consideration and judge the Christian Church in a manner that is incompatible with the gospel. On your letter-head we read: the 'Swedish Mission.' We beg to be excused from being considered and treated as a mission field. Every similar propaganda cannot be reconciled with the fundamental principles of the evangelical church.
With highest regard,
Nathan Söderblom."

The answer to the newspaper articles can be found in "Nordstjernan," volume 49, pp. 56-60.

In March, 1925, Apostle James E. Talmage, president of the European Mission, arrived in Sweden on a visit. He was met by Pres. Peterson at Malmö, whence the journey was continued to Göteborg and Stockholm. In all three cities, successful and profitable public and Priesthood meetings were held, in which Pres. Talmage presented the principles of the gospel in a plain and forcible manner and imparted counsel and advice to the missionaries laboring in the mission.

On March 10, 1925, an ecclesiastical court, composed of fellow-missionaries laboring in the Stockholm, Norrköping and Gefle conferences, convened at the mission headquarters in Stockholm to try Elder Gunnar W. Lindberg of Salt Lake City, who, on several occasions, had been derelict in his duties, and disobedient to his superiors in the Priesthood. His case was throughly considered, and he was excommunicated from the Church. Mr. Lindberg is still (1927) residing in Sweden.

In June, 1925, Pres. Peterson, accompanied by Elder Vance O. Lind, visited a number of scattered Saints in the northernmost parts of Sweden —a part of the Gefle Conference. This visit was thoroughly enjoyed by the visitors themselves as well as the local Saints and their friends. A hall was hired in the city of Hernösand, where the Saints could hold regular meetings. For several years meetings had been held in private homes. Meetings were also held in other parts of the mission, where Elders were not available.

On July 24th, Pres. Peterson and wife, and Elders Henry C. Krantz and Einar I. Applequist, attended a public reception tendered by Ambassador and Mrs. Bliss, at their palatial residence on "Djurgården" in Stockholm, which was greatly enjoyed by the Utah missionaries.

Elder Hugo D. E. Peterson, who for some 27 months had successfully presided over the Swedish Mission, left Stockholm Sept. 5, 1925, on his return home, accompanied by his wife and daughter. The affairs of the mission were turned over to Elder John H. Anderson of Logan, Utah, who had been appointed successor to Brother Peterson in the presidency of the Swedish Mission. Several farewell entertainments were tendered the departing missionaries by

the several Church organizations in Stockholm, attended not only by local Saints but also by many from distant places outside of Stockholm. Felicitous telegrams and letters were received from many who could not be present, and the number of gifts received testified of the universal love entertained by the local Saints towards their departing friends and fellow-workers. As the president and his family bade farewell to their devoted friends, tears flowed freely, especially when the Stockholm choir sang their last farewell as the train pulled out of the railroad station, Sept. 5, 1925.

JOHN HYRUM ANDERSON

President of the Swedish Mission in 1925-1927, was born in Logan, Cache County, Utah, Sept. 24, 1864, the son of Johannes Anderson and Johanna ◄Olson. His parents emigrated from Viarp, Sweden, to Logan in 1859, crossing the Plains with two yoke of oxen. Brother Anderson filled a mission to Sweden in 1883-1885, laboring in the Skåne Conference. He married Anna Charlotta Eliason, Nov. 18, 1885, has always been a faithful worker in the Church, labored in the Logan Temple for eight years, presided over the Scandinavian organization in Cache Stake for ten years, served as Bishop in the Mendon Ward in 1900-1903 and as Bishop of the Logan Fourth Ward in 1913-1919. He is now a member of the Logan Stake High Council. Brother Anderson is an active and enterprising business man and has served as mayor of Logan. He has had four sons and one daughter in the mission field.

Pres. John H. Anderson who arrived in Stockholm August 12, 1925, was shortly afterwards busily engaged in the mission and its affairs. His first attention was directed to the holding of fall conferences in Gefle, Norrköping, Göteborg, Malmö and Stockholm in the order named.

The news of the death of Elder Swen Swenson in Salt Lake City, August 21, 1925, caused sadness among many of the Saints in Sweden. Brother Swenson had spent altogether ten years and a half as writer and translator for "Nordstjernan," the mission periodical, and was loved and respected by all who knew him.

The following missionaries from Zion arrived in the Swedish Mission during the year 1925: Andrew Johnson of Murray, Utah, arrived Jan. 5th. Rudolph Albert Anderson of Malad City, Idaho, and George Albert Hazelgren of Murray, Utah, arrived Feb. 12th. Alma Gustave Jacobson, jun., of Salt Lake City, Utah, arrived April 6th. Eric N. Larson of Ogden, and M. Foss Smith of Snowflake, Arizona, arrived May 13th. Gustave E. Anderson of Central, Idaho, and Franklin G. Forsberg and Joseph Douglas Swenson of Salt Lake City, Utah, arrived July 14th. John H. Anderson of Logan, Utah, arrived Aug. 12th. John Conrad Berglund of Price and Carl A. Hanson of Cornish, Utah, arrived Sept. 21st. Carl Axel Söderberg and Harold Sörensen of Salt Lake City, and John Strömberg of Eureka, Utah, arrived Oct. 26th, and Willard O. Olson and Wilford O. Peterson of Murray, Milford Harold Jenson and Lionel E. Danielson of Smithfield, Utah, arrived in December.

The old Swedish custom of meeting for devotional exercises early Christmas morning and arrange watch parties on New Years Eve to see the old year out and the new year in, has been followed also by the Latter-day Saints, both in the mother country and in their new homes in their adopted country. Thus in the several branches throughout the Swedish Mission such watch parties were arranged at the close of the year 1925, and a musical program given between the hours of 10 p. m. and 12 o'clock midnight.

The Elders looked forward toward a good year in which to carry on their missionary labors. The spring conferences were held as usual.

CARL AXEL SÖDERBERG

Was born Aug. 2, 1873, in Stockholm, Sweden, baptized May 30, 1895, ordained an Elder Jan. 22, 1897, and emigrated to Utah Aug. 20, 1897. He married Pauline M. Karlström, June 15, 1898; their children are: Adolph, Rupert, Vera, Inez, Stella M., Raymond A., and Ruby P. Brother Söderberg has been active as a teacher and superintendent in Sunday school, and in various offices in the Church; was ordained a Seventy in 1912, and labored as a home missionary in the Liberty Stake in 1924. By avocation he is a machinist, and was instructor in mechanics in the University of Utah in 1910-1918; went to Chile, South America for the Braden Copper Company in 1918-1919. In 1925-1927 he filled a mission to Sweden. His little daughter, Ruby, was killed in an accident in Liberty Park, Salt Lake City, July 4, 1923, and his faithful wife passed away March 29, 1924.

Pres. James E. Talmage and Sister May Booth Talmage arrived in Göteborg July 16, 1926, and held an in-

ANDREW JOHNSON

President of the Swedish Mission, was born Aug. 9, 1871, in Hägglinge, Malmöhus län Skåne, Sweden. He emigrated to America in 1892, lived in Nebraska a few months and then came to Utah. He married Ellen Anderson in 1897 and made his home in Murray, Salt Lake County. Brother Johnson was baptized in March, 1917, was faithful in the discharge of his duties and after being ordained to offices in the Priesthood, was called in 1925 to fill a mission to Sweden, where he labored in the Skåne Conference for a time and was then called to Stockholm to edit "Nordstjernan." In November, 1926, he succeeded Elder John H. Anderson as president of the Swedish Mission. Previous to going on his mission Elder Johnson presided over the Scandinavian organization of the Murray Second Ward.

teresting meetings there the same day, attended by Elders and Saints in that conference. The following day (July 17th) the visitors proceeded to Stockholm, where the meetings were held in the large and beautifully decorated hall, attended by the Elders laboring in the Stockholm, Norrköping and Gefle conferences. This visit by Pres. Talmage was much enjoyed by both Saints and strangers. A donation of 100 kronor was received by "Nordstjernan" from the

estate of the late Peter Sundwall, of Fairview, Utah, who had served four terms as a missionary in the Scandinavian countries. On account of failing health, Pres. John H. Anderson, who had presided over the Swedish Mission since August 21, 1925, was honorably released and started for his home in Utah in November, 1926. His successor was Elder Andrew Johnson of Murray, Utah. Pres. Anderson was a successful leader, a good executive and a wise counselor; his abrupt departure was much regretted by the missionaies and local Saints.

The following missionaries from Zion arrived in the Swedish Mission during the year 1926: Knut A. J. and Anna E. P. Brandt of Portland, Oregon, arrived in January. Joseph S. Thelin of Orton, Alberta, Canada, arrived in May. Edwin S. Pearson of Salt Lake City, Emil G. Thedell of Park City, and Wilford F. Peterson of Murray, Utah, arrived in August. Carl Oscar Olson of Midvale, and Claude N. Monson of Salt Lake City, Utah, arrived in October. Noel L. Strömberg of Grantsville, Utah, arrived in November, and Heber J. Olson of Virginia and Clyde R. Gustavson of Preston, Idaho, arrived Dec. 20th.

The members of the Eskilstuna Branch, where there has been no organization for several years and no general public meetings held, were made happy in 1926 by the securing of a hall in which to hold public gatherings. Sister Signe Östby, president of the Branch Relief Society, had for several years through her energetic efforts, and at her own expense, been able to hold the members together, and it was with her assistance that the Elders, after some searching, were fortunate to secure the hall, which was duly dedicated on Sept. 12, 1926. The dedicatory prayer was offered by Conference

31

President Carl A. Söderberg. On this occasion the Eskilstuna branch was reorganized with Elder Arthur J. Fagergren as president. At the close of the year 1926, the Swedish Mission consisted of five conferences (or districts, as each subdivision of a mission is now designated). They were Gefle (formerly Sundsvall), Göteborg, Norrköping, Skåne (or Malmö) and Stockholm. These conferences were subdivided into 23 branches, some of which were presided over by local Elders, while a few were left without any organization at all, there being no one available to take charge of them. Thirty-one Elders and one missionary sister from Zion were laboring in the mission at the end of the year. Of native Elders there were 122, and also 50 Priests, 33 Teachers, 33 Deacons and 1,336 lay-members, making a total of 1,674 people, exclusive of children under eight years of age.

The number of souls baptized does not always act as a barometer of missionary activities. The Elders sometimes labor for months, and even years, without seeing any results from their own efforts, and return home without carrying any sheaves with them, proving the truth of the saying of Paul: "Paul have planted, Apollos watered; but God gave the increase." Yet 62 persons were baptized during the year, and 21 persons emigrated. At the end of the year 1926, Elder Gustave E. Anderson presided over the Gefle, Elder Erick W. Larson over the Göteborg, Elder John J. Malmström over the Skåne (or Malmö), Elder Lionel E. Danielson over the Norrköping, and Elder Carl A. Söderberg over the Stockholm Conference. Elder Andrew Johnson was president of the mission. These brethren, with their little corps of assistant Elders, were determined to use their best efforts in spreading the

light of the glorious gospel, even into the farthermost corners of this mission, the Lord being their helper. The outlook for finding yet many souls of the House of Israel in this land of the Far North were very promising.

LLOYD OLEEN STOHL

Of Salt Lake City, was born Aug. 12, 1906, at Brigham City, Utah, the son of Oleen N. and Sarah Peters Stohl; left home Jan. 16, 1927, for the Swedish Mission, and is now (November, 1927) laboring in the same field, where his father and grandfather labored years ago.

Following s a list of the presidents of the Swedish Mission from 1905 to 1926:

1. Peter Mattson, from May, 1905, to May, 1908.
2. Peter Sundvall, May, 1908-November, 1910.
3. Andreas Peterson, November, 1910-November, 1912.
4. A. Theodore Johnson, November, 1912-October, 1913.
5. Theodore Tobiason, October, 1913-June, 1916.
6. Anders (Andrew) P. Anderson, June, 1916-August, 1919.
7. Theodore Tobiason (2nd term), August, 1919-August, 1921.

* Oscar W. Söderberg, pro tem. December, 1920-August, 1921.
8. Isaac P. Thunell, August, 1921-November, 1922.
9. Gideon N. Hulterström, November, 1922-July, 1923.
10. Hugo D. E. Peterson, July, 1923-August, 1925.
11. John H. Anderson, August, 1925-November, 1926.
12. Andrew Johnson, November, 1926.

SKÅNE CONFERENCE

Skåne Conference (sometimes called Malmö Conference) was organized June 26, 1853. It contains the extreme southern provinces of Sweden, and its northern boundaries have been changed several times. Following is a complete list of the Elders who have presided over the Skåne Conference:

1. Hans Lundblad*, 1853-1854.
2. Nils Nilson*, 1854-1856.
3. Nils B. Ädler*, 1856-1858.
4. Johan Fagerberg*, 1858-1861.
5. Nils Rosengren*, 1861-1863.
6. Swen Nilson*, 1863-1865.
7. Swen J. Jonasson*, 1865-1866.
8. Johan Fagerberg (2nd term), 1866-1867.
9. Peter T. Nyström*, 1867-1869.
10. John Holmberg, 1869-1871.
11. Paul Dehlin, 1871-1873.
12. Nils Anderson, 1873-1875.
13. Carl Johan Gustafson, 1875-1876.
14. Swen Nilson (2nd term) 1876-1877.
15. Ola Olson, 1877-1878.
16. Jöns Anderson, 1878-1879.
17. John A. Halvorson, 1879-1881.
18. Nils B. Ädler (2nd term), 1881.
19. Martin Jakobson, 1881-1882.
20. James Yorgason, 1882-1883.
21. Carl A. Tietjen, 1883-1884.
22. Hans D. Petterson, 1884-1885.
23. Peter Mattson, 1885-1887.

24. Ola Olson (2nd term), 1887-1889.
25. Truls A. Hallgren, 1889-1891.
26. Frederik Lundberg, 1891.
27. John Svenson, 1891-1893.
28. Niels J. Henricksen, 1893.
29. Peter T. Rundquist, 1893-1894.
30. Charles Sörensen, 1894.
31. Bengt M. Ravsten, 1894-1896.
32. Alonzo B. Irvine, 1896-1897.
33. Peter Gustaf Hanson, 1897-1898.
34. Andrew Anderson, 1898-1899.
35. Ola Olson (3rd term), 1899-1900.
36. Anders G. Lundström, 1900.
37. Peter V. Bunderson, 1900-1902.
38. John N. Erikson, 1902-1903.
39. Sören O. Thompson, 1903-1904.
40. Anders O. Ingelström, 1904-1906.
41. J. P. Jönson, 1906-1907.
42. Peter J. Sandberg, 1907-1909.
43. Albert Capson, 1909-1910.
44. Bengt Johnson, jun., 1910-1913.
45. John P. Pehrson, 1913.
46. Joseph N. Anderson, 1913.
47. Eben R. T. Blomquist, 1913.
48. Olof Monson, 1913-1914.
49. John A. Carlson, 1914-1916.
50. Samuel P. Nilsson, 1916-1919.
51. Axel E. Johnson, 1919-1920.
52. James H. Olson (pro tem.), 1920-1921.
53. Olof W. Monson, 1921-1922.
54. Adolph Söderberg, 1922-1923.
55. Algot Johnson*, 1923-1924.
56. Axel R. Boström, 1924-1925.
57. Oskar Sander, 1925-1926.
58. Axel W. Fors*, 1926.
59. David C. Carlson, 1926.
60. John J. Malmström, 1926.

STOCKHOLM CONFERENCE

The Stockholm Conference was organized in the latter part of 1854, and was up to the year 1905 a part of the Scandivavian Mission. In 1905 it became a conference in the Swedish Mission. Following is an

*Local Elders.

unbroken list of the Elders who have presided over the Stockholm Conference from the beginning:

1. Åke Jönsson*, 1854-1856.
2. Christian A. Madsen*, 1856.
3. Lars Nilsson*, 1856-1858.
4. Gustaf A. Ohlson*, 1858-1860.
5. Carl Johan Sundbäck (Gyllenswan)*, 1860-1861.
6. Nils C. Flygare*, 1861-1864.
7. C. L. Erickson*, 1864.
8. George W. Gee, 1864-1865.
9. P. O. Holmgren*, 1865.
10. Magnus Cederström*, 1865-1866.
11. Lars Peter Edholm, 1866.
12. Johan B. Hesse, 1866-1868.
13. Ole C. Olsen, 1868-1869.
14. E. Peterson, 1869-1872.
15. Mathias B. Nilsson, 1872-1874.
16. John F. Oblad, 1874.
17. John C. Anderson, 1874.
18. Nils C. Flygare (2nd term), 1874-1875.
19. John C. Anderson (2nd term), 1875-1876.
20. Erik F. Branting, 1876-1877.
21. Alfred Hanson, 1877-1878.
22. John Larsson, 1878-1879.
23. Lars M. Olson, 1879-1881.
24. Rasmus Berntzon, 1881-1882.
25. Nils R. Lindahl, 1882-1883.
26. Carl A. Ek, 1883-1884.
27. Ola Olson, 1884-1885.
28. James Yorgason, 1885-1887.
29. Karl H. P. Nordberg, 1887-1889.
30. Ludvig Ehrnström, 1889-1890.
31. Anders P. Anderson, 1890-1891.
32. Fred. Lundberg, 1891-1893.
33. August Carlson, 1893-1894.
34. Nils R. Lindahl (2nd term), 1894-1895.
35. Erick Gillen, 1895-1896.
36. Carl A. Ahlquist, 1896-1897.
37. Anton P. N. Peterson, 1897-1898.
38. Peter J. Sandberg, 1898-1899.
39. Andrew M. Anderson, 1899-1900.
40. John Johnson, 1900-1901.
41. Joseph J. Cannon, 1901-1902.

42. Nils Anthon, 1902-1903.
43. Carl J. A. Lindquist, 1903-1905.
44. John Felt, jun., 1905-1906.
45. August Carlson (2nd term), 1906-1907.
46. Charles V. Erickson, 1907-1908.
47. Emil W. Weed, 1908-1911.
48. Carl Arvid Carlquist, 1911-1913.
49. Carl O. Johnson, 1913-1914.
50. Ernest E. Monson, 1914-1915.
51. Erick W. Larson, 1915.
52. Theodore Tobiason, 1915-1916.
53. Andrew (Anders) P. Anderson, 1916-1919.
54. Theodore Tobiason, 1919-1920.
55. Gideon N. Hulterström, 1920-1922.
56. Elon Keding, 1922-1923.
57. Hugo D. E. Peterson (pro tem.), 1923.
58. Axel R. Boström, 1923-1924.
59. Anthon Pehrson, 1924-1925.
60. Arthur Fagergren, 1925.
61. Henry C. Krantz, 1925.
62. C. Axel Söderberg, 1925-1926.

———
*Local Elders.

GÖTEBORG CONFERENCE

The Göteborg Conference was organized Sept. 5, 1857, but in 1870 it was amalgamated with the Norrköping Conference, and was after that for a couple of years known as the Jönköping Conference. In 1872 the office was moved from Jönköping to Göteborg, when the conference again became known as the Göteborg Conference, which name it has retained ever since. It was from its first organization up to 1905 a part of the Scandinavian Mission, but in the year named it became a conference in the Swedish Mission. Following is a list of the Elders who have presided over the Göteborg Conference (those marked with a * are local Elders):

1. Mathias B. Nilsson*, from 1857-1859.

2. Rasmus Berntzon*, 1859-1861.
3. Anders Pontus Söderborg, 1861-1864.
4. John C. Sandberg*, 1864-1865.
5. J. Larson*, 1865-1866.
6. Fred C. Anderson, 1866.
7. Johan P. Wretberg, 1866-1867.
8. Christoffer O. Folkmann, 1867-1868.
9. Samuel Peterson, 1868-1870.
10. John Ehrngren, 1870-1871.
11. Anders Chr. Grue, 1871-1872.
12. Nils P. Lindelöf, 1872-1874.
13. Samuel Johnson, 1874-1875.
14. August Thomasson (pro tem.), 1875.
15. John C. Sandberg (2nd term), 1875-1877.
16. Ingwald C. Thoresen, 1877-1878.
17. John Anderson Quist, 1878-1879.
18. Charles L. Anderson, 1879-1880.
19. Ole Nilsson Stohl, 1880-1881.
20. Anders G. Johnson, 1881-1882.
21. Andrew Eliason, 1882-1883.
22. Bengt M. Ravsten, 1883-1884.
23. Gustaf L. Rosengren, 1884-1885.
24. August K. Anderson, 1885-1886.
25. Nils Peter Peterson, 1886-1887.
26. Nils Peter Lindelöf (2nd term), 1887-1888.
27. John A. Quist (2nd term), 1888-1890.
28. Andrew P. Renström, 1890-1891.
29. Laurentius Dahlquist, 1891-1892.
30. Carl G. Anderson, 1892-1893.
31. Carl Arvid Carlquist, 1893.
32. Andrew J. Wahlquist, 1893-1894.
33. A. Joel Höglund, 1894-1895.
34. Theodore Tobiason, 1895-1897.
35. Henry M. Pearson, 1897-1898.
36. John Werner Larson, 1898.
37. Chas. E. Forsberg, 1898-1900.
38. James L. Jenson, 1900-1901.
39. Nils Löfgren, 1901-1902.
40. Hyrum J. Hanson, 1902-1903.
41. Carl G. Youngberg, 1903-1904.
42. Andrew Eliason, jun., 1904-1906.
43. George C. Smith, 1906-1907.
44. Thomas Spongberg, 1907-1908.

45. Armand F. Rundquist, 1908-1909.
46. Chas. P. Anderson, 1909-1910.
47. Carl A. Carlquist (2nd term), 1910-1911.
48. Olof P. Johanson, 1911-1912.
49. Peter O. Peterson, 1912-1913.
50. Birger E. Lundevall, 1913.
51. Nephi Nordgran, 1913-1915.
52. Emil A. Nielson, 1915.
53. Svante A. Erikson (pro tem.), 1915-1916.
54. Carl T. Peterson, 1916-1917.
55. Svante A. Erikson (pro tem.), 1917.
56. Nephi H. Dahlström (pro tem.), 1917-1919.
57. August A. Hedberg* (pro tem.), 1919-1921.
58. Carl A. Lundell, 1921.
59. August A. Hedberg* (2nd term), 1921-1926.
60. Erick W. Larson, 1926.

NORRKÖPING CONFERENCE

Norrköping Conference was organized May 12, 1858, it having been part of the Stockholm Conference. In 1870 the Norrköping Conference was amalgamated with the Göteborg Conference under the name of the Jönköping Conference, but two years later the name was again changed to Göteborg Conference. Up to the year 1905, this conference was part of the Scandinavian Mission, but in that year it became a conference in the Swedish Mission. Following are the names of the Elders who have presided over the Norrköping Conference (those marked * are local Elders):
1. Ole Nilsson Stohl*,
2. Lars Nilsson*, 1862-1864.
3. C. F. Rundquist*, 1864-1866.
4. Gustaf A. Ohlson, 1866-1867.
5. Adolph W. Nilson, 1867-1868.
6. George K. Riis, 1868-1869.
7. Erik Johan Pehrson, 1869-1870.
As before observed, this conference was discontinued in 1870, when

its membership was added to the Jönköping (later Göteborg) Conference. On October 24, 1905, the Norrköping Conference was reorganized, with headquarters at Norrköping, as in earlier days, and became a part of the Swedish Mission, and the following brethren have since acted as conference presidents:

8. Carl P. Anderson, from 1905 to 1906.
9. August A. Nordvall, 1906-1907.
10. Nils H. Hallström, 1907-1909.
11. Joseph E. Erickson, 1909-1910.
12. Andrew G. Erickson, 1910-1911.
13. Anders Alfred Carlson, 1911.
14. Albin Edward Johnson, 1911-1912.
15. Carl Joel Olson, 1912.
16. Eben R. T. Blomquist, 1912-1913.
17. L. W. Hendrickson, 1913-1915.
18. Theodore Tobiason, 1915.
19. Peter Anderson, 1915-1917.
20. Carl T. Peterson, 1917-1918.
21. John W. Carlson (pro tem.), 1918-1919.
22. Lawrence Lind, 1919-1920.
23. C. J. Samuelson (pro tem.), 1920-1921.
24. Nils S. Blad, 1921.
25. Johan H. Holmquist, 1921-1923.
26. Jos. E. Erickson (2nd term), 1923-1924.
27. Johannes Erikson, 1924-1925.
28. Gustaf A. Seequist, 1925-1926.
29. Lionel Danielson, 1926.

SUNDSVALL CONFERENCE

The Sundsvall Conference was organized in June, 1859. From April, 1865, it had a president in common with that of the Stockholm Conference, of which it soon afterwards became a part, and has also been known as the Norrland Conference. The Sundsvall Conference was re-established in 1902, but the name of Sundsvall Conference was on April 16, 1921, changed to Gefle Conference with the city of Gefle

as its headquarters. The following Elders have presided over the Sundsvall Conference:

1. Carl Erik Lindholm, from 1859 to 1861.
2. Anders Svedlund, 1861-1864.
3. Magnus Cederström, 1864-1865.

Since the re-establishment of the Sundsvall Conference May 19, 1902, the following Elders have been its presidents; those whose names are attached with a * were local Elders:

4. Charles L. Anderson, 1902.
5. Andrew E. Anderson, 1902-1903.
6. James P. Olson, 1903-1904.
7. August Erickson, 1904-1905.
8. Carl E. Peterson, 1905.
9. August Erickson, 1905.
10. Carl E. Peterson, 1905-1906.
11. Gustaf A. Höglund, 1906-1907.
12. Armand F. Rundquist, 1907-1908.
13. A. W. Schade, 1908-1909.
14. Anthon Pehrson, 1909-1910.
15. William O. Beckström, 1910.
16. Frederick Anderson, 1910-1912.
17. John W. Anderson, 1912-1913.
18. Mathias Erickson, 1913-1914.
19. N. A. Hanson, 1914-1915.
20. Anders P. Anderson, 1915-1916.
21. Johan H. Holmquist*, 1916.
22. John Johnson, 1916-1918.
23. Joseph A. Johanson, 1918.
24. Jonas Östlund, 1918-1920.
25. Joel Erickson* (pro tem.), 1920.
26. Mathias Erickson, 1920-1921.

GEFLE CONFERENCE

As before stated, the name of the Sundsvall Conference was changed to Gefle Conference, when the first named conference became extinct. The following Elders have been its presidents:

1. Mathias Erickson, 1921-1922.
2. Morris C. Johnson, 1922-1923.
3. Charles Anderson, 1923-1924.
4. Oskar Sander, 1924-1925.
5. Vance O. Lind, 1925-1926.
6. Knut T. Borg, 1926.
7. Gustave E. Anderson, 1926.

History of the Danish Mission

CHAPTER 1 (1920-1926)

Carl E. Peterson's administration—John S. Hansen presides—Joseph L. Petersen's presidency—Arrival of Elders—List of conference presidents in Denmark, namely, Copenhagen, 1851-1926; Fredericia, 1851-1868; Aalborg, 1851-1926; Bornholm, 1852-1864; Lolland, 1852-1868; Fyen, 1855-1864; Aarhus, 1857-1926; Skive, 1857-1864; Öernes, 1864-1868; Odense, 1871-1872.

The Danish Mission, at its commencement in April, 1920, consisted of three conferences, namely, the

Copenhagen Conference, with Carl E. Peterson as president, the Aarhus Conference, with Lauritz Larsen (a

WILLIAM PETERSEN

Son of Niels A. Petersen and Johanne Larsen, was born Feb. 22, 1891, at Draper, Salt Lake Co., Utah, baptized June 4, 1899, ordained successively a Deacon, Teacher and Priest, and an Elder March 16, 1913, by Niels Petersen. After being ordained a Seventy Dec. 4, 1920, by Seymour B. Young, Elder Petersen left on a mission to Denmark, Dec. 8th. He labored in the Aarhus Conference until released Oct. 26, 1922, and arrived home Nov. 12th of that year. As a boy he served as Sunday school librarian, was a Ward teacher for many years and a home missionary in the Bear River Stake. On June 9, 1926, he married Mary L. Wagstaff in the Logan Temple and now (1926) resides at Elwood, Utah.

JOHN H. JÖRGENSON

Son of Hans Jörgensen and Karen Marie Hendriksen, was born Sept. 18, 1867, at Eden, Utah, and was baptized and confirmed July 30, 1876, by David McKay. From his early youth he was the main support of the family, owing to his father's poor health. When fifteen years of age he was healed by the power of God when suffering from a broken leg and other injuries, as the result of an accident. His father died Jan. 28, 1882, and his mother March 10, 1907. On March 20, 1889, Brother Jörgenson married Ella Rozina Allen; they have had ten children, eight of whom are still (1927) living. Brother Jörgensen filled a mission to Denmark from February, 1921, to October, 1922, laboring in the Aalborg Conference, part of the time as president. He was ordained a High Priest March 23, 1924, by Asael Farr and resides at Huntsville, Weber County, Utah.

local Elder) as president, and the Aalborg Conference, with Christian P. Sörensen as president. The total local membership in the mission was (on Dec. 31, 1919), 1,400, including 73 Elders, 49 Priests, 47 Teachers and 45 Deacons. Carl E. Peterson was the first president of the Danish Mission.

Only three missionaries from

Zion arrived in the Danish Mission during the year 1920, namely, Jens I. Larsen of Preston, Idaho, who arrived May 23rd; Hans C. Hansen of Tremonton, Utah, who arrived Nov. 3rd, and William Petersen of Tremonton, Utah, who arrived December 29th.

In July, 1920, Apostle George Albert Smith, president of the European Mission, and Elder Junius F. Wells from the Liverpool office,

APOSTLE GEORGE ALBERT SMITH

President of the European Mission, was born April 4, 1870, in Salt Lake City, Utah, the son of John Henry Smith and Sarah Farr.

visited Denmark. They arrived in Copenhagen from Sweden July 8th, attended meetings in Copenhagen, Aarhus and Aalborg, and gladdened the hearts of the Elders and local Saints by their timely advice and good counsel. They left Copenhagen for Germany July 15th.

Six missionaries from Zion arrived in the Danish Mission during the year 1921, namely, Thorleif Jacobsen of Weston, Idaho, who arrived Feb. 21st; John H. Jörgensen of Huntsville, Utah, who arrived March 8th;

Niels Sörensen of Perry, Utah, who arrived May 4th; Carl Madsen of Riverton, Utah, who arrived July 26th; Christian M. Nicolaisen of Tremonton, Utah, who arrived Aug. 10th, and Owen Paulsen of Levan, Utah, who arrived Nov. 23rd.

JOHN S. HANSEN

Second president of the Danish Mission, was born Sept. 6, 1877, at Copenhagen, Denmark, the son of Sören Hansen and Christine Andersen. He was baptized April 5, 1889, ordained successively to the offices of Deacon, Teacher and Priest, and labored as a district teacher and as assistant superintendent of the Y. M. M. L. A. in Copenhagen. In 1898 he emigrated to Utah and in 1900 (June 15th) he married Anna C V. Jensen, who was born on the same day as her husband (Sept. 6, 1877). Brother Hansen was ordained an Elder and later (Jan. 15, 1912) a Seventy, becoming one of the presidents of the 140th quorum of Seventy. In 1912-1914 he filled a mission to Denmark, laboring as writer and translator for "Skandinaviens Stjerne." After his return, he became editor of "Bikuben" and has also translated a number of books into the Danish language, including the "Life of Brigham Young." "Journal of Wilford Woodruff," etc. On April 21, 1921, Brother Hansen was ordained a High Priest by Frank Y. Taylor and set apart as second counselor to Bishop Stayner Richards of the Highland Park Ward, holding this position until he, in the spring of 1923, was called by the First Presidency of the Church to preside over the Danish Mission. Arriving in Copenhagen April 23, 1923, in response to this call, he took charge of the mission May 1st and served with fidelity as president until Feb. 15, 1926, when he was succeeded by Joseph L. Petersen. Brother Hansen was now (1927) a counselor in the presidency of the Scandinavian meetings in Salt Lake City, and otherwise active in Church affairs.

Three missionaries from Zion arrived in the Danish Mission during the year 1922; they were Paul L. Gregersen of Pocatello, Idaho, who arrived Jan. 28th, and Christian P. Sörensen (on a second mission) and Martine Sörensen of Salt Lake City, Utah, who arrived Sept. 5th.

The following missionaries from Zion (17 in number) arrived in the Danish Mission during the year 1923 as follows: N. Peter Christensen of Salt Lake City, Utah, arrived Feb. 9th. Emil Andersen of Logan, Utah,

arrived March 21st. John S. Hansen of Salt Lake City, Utah, arrived April 23rd. Fay L. Courtz of Salt Lake City, Utah, arrived June 12th. An-

CHRISTEN LARSEN

Was born Feb. 8, 1859, in Jyderup, Holbœk amt, Denmark; married Karen Marie Olsen in 1889, who bore him ten children, six of whom are still living. Becoming a convert to "Mormonism" he was baptized in 1891 and emigrated to Utah in 1893. He located at Huntsville, later in Ogden and still later in Salt Lake City. Filling a mission to Denmark in 1923-1925, he presided over the Aalborg Conference.

drew Mollerup of Salt Lake City, Utah, arrived July 3rd. Kaj E. C. Jörgensen of Storrs, Utah, arrived July 6th. Anna J. Hansen and Bryan L. Petersen of Salt Lake City, and Aage Jensen Falslev of Benson, Utah, arrived July 24th. Julius Bruun of Salt Lake City and Darcey U. Wright of Murray, Utah, arrived Sept. 25th. Christen Larsen and Anthon H. Lund of Salt Lake City, and Hans N. Ögaard of Brigham City, Utah, arrived Nov. 27th. Peter Petersen and Herschel S. Lund of Salt Lake City arrived Dec. 16th, and Orson W. Jensen of Sandy, Utah, arrived Dec. 18th.

BRYAN L. PETERSEN

Son of Adam L. and Anna M. Petersen, was born at Huntsville, Weber Co., Utah, Jan. 11, 1901. Being called to the Danish Mission from the Eleventh Ward of Salt Lake City, he arrived in Copenhagen July 23, 1923. He was appointed secretary of Aarhus Conference Oct. 25, 1923, and president of the same conference Jan. 11, 1925, and was honorably released Oct. 24, 1925. After returning home he worked in various organizations of the Eleventh Ward, Salt Lake City, and is now (1927) working in the capacity of second assistant superintendent in the Sunday school of that Ward, and in the presidency of an Elders' quorum.

Elder John S. Hansen succeeded Carl E. Peterson as president of the Danish Mission May 1, 1923. Fifteen missionaries from Zion ar-

WALTER M. NIELSEN

Son of Niels Christian Nielsen and Amalie Reher, was born in Aarhus, Denmark, July 31, 1898. He was baptized Jan. 27, 1910, and emigrated to Utah with his parents in 1914, locating at Logan. He filled a mission to Denmark in 1924-1925, arriving at his field of labor Feb. 27, 1924. While there he labored in the Aarhus Conference for some time, as presiding Elder in Odense nine months; later he was traveling Elder in the Copenhagen Conference four months. Being honorably released in November, 1925, he arrived in Salt Lake City Dec. 5, 1925, where he still (1927) resides.

rived in the Danish Mission during the year 1924, namely: Harvey Martin Larsen of Ogden and Oscar Söderquist of Ferron, Utah, who ar. rived Feb. 13th; Walter M. Nielsen of Logan, Utah, who arrived Feb. 27th; Allan Oscar Johnson of Shelley, Idaho, who arrived Feb. 28th; Oliver C. Petersen of Gunnison, Leonel Rasmussen of Midvale, Edward H. Sörensen of Salt Lake City, and Truman O. Nielsen of Brigham City, Utah, who arrived March 21st; Wallace P. Winkler of Salt Lake City, Utah, who arrived April 8th; Niels Anders Pehrson of Kaysville, Utah,

who arrived May 6th; Waldemar L. Jensen of Salt Lake City, and Theodore Kilts and Claude A. Malan of Ogden, Utah, who arrived June 18th; Amos B. C. Jensen of Yost, Utah, who arrived July 17th, and Eugene F. Erickson of Murray, Utah, who arrived Dec. 8th.

Eleven missionaries from Zion arrived in the Danish Mission during the year 1925, namely: Heber J. Christiansen of Monroe, Utah, and

RASMUS MICHELSEN

A missionary to Denmark, was born Oct. 14, 1862, at Sleth, near Aarhus, Denmark, the son of Rasmus and Karen Marie Michelsen. He became a convert to "Mormonism" in his earliest youth, was baptized in Aarhus Nov. 18, 1887, emigrated to Utah in July, 1880, and two years later married Julia Caroline Bond, which union has been blessed with nine children, five of whom are still alive. Two of their sons served in France during the war, and one of them was killed in the battle at Chateau Thierry. He lived for a number of years in the 3rd Ward Salt Lake City. In 1925-1927 he filled a mission to Denmark, arriving in Copenhagen Feb. 11, 1925. He labored in the Aarhus Conference and presided in the Esbjerg Branch from August, 1925, to April, 1926, after which he presided over the Aarhus Conference. For many years Elder Michelsen has been employed as a traveling salesman in Utah and Idaho. He has always been an active and faithful Church worker, has musical talent and has served many years as chorister and organist.

Hugo D. Jörgensen of Rigby, Idaho, who arrived Feb. 10th; Rasmus Michelsen and Charles A. Larsen of Salt Lake City, and Egert M. Larsen

FRANK ANDERSON VAN COTT

A missionary in Denmark in 1925-1927, is a son of Frank V. Van Cott and Annie Anderson (and a grandson of the late John Van Cott). He was born Feb. 20, 1906, in Salt Lake City, Utah, and baptized Feb. 28, 1914; was ordained a Deacon Jan. 27, 1918, a Teacher Feb. 6, 1921, a Priest Jan. 19, 1925, and an Elder March 1, 1925. On his mission he labored principally in Randers, Aarhus and Copenhagen, always taking the lead in singing, mostly as chorister; also giving musical concerts. Elder Van Cott received a good education in his youth and has always been an active Church worker.

of Sandy, Utah, who arrived March 1st; J. Howard Fjeldsted of Garland, Utah, who arrived June 8th; Niels P. Andersen of Manti, Frank A. Van Cott of Salt Lake City, Norman L. Petersen of Brigham City, Utah, and William Georgeson of Preston, Idaho, who arrived July 10th, and Hans Andersen of Levan, Utah, who arrived Sept. 21st.

The following missionaries from Zion arrived in the Danish Mission during the year 1926, on the dates

given: Peter Adolf Nielsen of American Fork, Utah, and Sören W. Hansen of Mink Creek, Idaho, arrived Jan. 21st. Joseph L. Petersen and Ida S. Petersen of Huntsville, Holger O. Petersen of Salt Lake City, and N. Halvor Madsen of Provo, Utah, arrived Feb. 10th. Alfred L. Sörensen of Claresholm, Alberta, Canada, and Achton C. Jensen of Smithfield, Utah, arrived March 2nd. Niels Jörgen Larsen of Logan, and George Philip N. Jensen of Salt Lake City, Utah, arrived March 23rd. Karl

PETER ADOLF NIELSEN

Was born at Rosenholm, Randers amt, Denmark, March, 19, 1870, the son of Jens Peter Nielsen and Ane Rasmussen. The mother died Nov. 4, 1881. Through a housekeeper "Mormonism" became known in the home, and the boy, 14 years old, was baptized July 5, 1884. He was ordained a Teacher June 6, 1886, a Priest Oct. 27, 1889, and an Elder Nov. 9, 1889, and labored in Aalborg, Hjörring and Frederikshaven as a local missionary. In October, 1891, he emigrated to Utah, crossing the ocean in the S. S. "Nevada." While on board the ship, Oct. 16, 1891, he married Ane Marie Jensen from Aarhus. They arrived in Salt Lake City Oct. 29, 1891, after which Brother Nielsen was ordained a Seventy and became one of the presidents of the 67th quorum at American Fork, in which place he acted as city judge from Jan. 2, 1912, to Jan. 4, 1916, and as precinct judge from Jan. 1, 1917 to Jan. 1, 1921. In January, 1926, he was called on a mission to Scandinavia, where he labored in the Aarhus and Aalborg conferences. He has been a resident of American Fork, Utah County, Utah, since 1900.

Mons Juul Thomsen of Magna, and Peter S. Christiansen and Wilhelmine J. Christiansen of Salt Lake City, Utah, arrived May 22nd. Niels P. Rasmussen of Burley, Idaho, arrived June 10th. Clifton E. Henrichsen of Provo, Utah, arrived July 13th. Christian Dausel of Elsinore, and Richard Thomas Andersen of Salt Lake City, Utah, arrived Sept. 14th. Hyrum Domgaard of Clarion, Utah, arrived from Norway Oct. 22nd. Anders Peter Andersen of Burley, Idaho, arrived Oct. 26th. Clarence

Brown Jacobs and Aage Kjölby of Salt Lake City, Utah, arrived Nov. 19th, and Eugene Lyman Petersen of Salt Lake City, Utah, arrived Dec. 19th.

Elder Joseph L. Petersen succeeded John S. Hansen as president of the Danish Mission Feb. 15, 1926.

At the close of 1926, the Danish Mission was (as it had been many years) divided into three conferences, namely, Copenhagen (Nils E. Larsen, president), Aarhus (Rasmus Michelsen, president), and Aalborg Con-

JOSEPH LIND PETERSEN

Third president of the Danish Mission, was born in Huntsville, Utah, July 15, 1876, the son of Sören L. and Louisa Petersen. Practically all his life so far has been spent in Huntsville, where he is engaged in the mercantile business. He has occupied different positions of trust in Church and civic affairs and served as Bishop of the Huntsville Ward from 1916 to 1926. He also served as president of the town board in 1923-1925 and was re-elected for another term at the fall election of 1925. During his term of office he was instrumental in securing for the town a modern water system. He was also one of the directors of the First National Bank of Ogden. Brother Petersen has filled three missions to Denmark, the first in 1897-1899, the second in 1904-1906 (when he presided over the Aarhus Conference part of the time) and the third in 1926, when he was called to preside over the Danish Mission, which position he still (1927) occupies.

IDA A. PETERSEN

Wife of President Joseph L. Petersen, was born in Huntsville, Utah, Jan. 24, 1880, daughter of Gustav Anderson and Mary Christina Johnson. She was married to Elder Petersen in the Salt Lake Temple May 21, 1902, and is at present filling a mission together with her husband in Denmark, acting as president of the Danish Mission Relief Societies, and in other ways assisting in missonary work.

ference (Egert M. Larsen, president). Thirty-two Elders from Zion were laboring in the mission, and the total baptized membership was 1,535, including 74 Elders, 35 Priests, 42 Teachers and 20 Deacons.

Of the Elders from Zion laboring

in the Aarhus Conference at the close of 1926, six were doing missionary

PETER S. CHRISTIANSEN

Son of Sören Christiansen and Ane Kirstine Andreasen, was born Feb. 26, 1861, in Aarslev, Aarhns amt, Denmark. He learned lithography and founded his own printing office in 1885. Becoming a convert to the gospel, he was baptized Jan. 4, 1891, at Aarhus by F. C. Michelsen, from Redmond, Utah, and labored diligently in the Church at Aarhus for twenty-two years. He took an active part in obtaining for the branch its real estate and managed the property for several years. In 1913, Brother Christiansen sold his business and emigrated to Utah with his family. They made their home in Huntsville, Weber Co., but later moved to Salt Lake City, where he became associated with "Bikuben," first with the business management and later with the editorial department. In the spring of 1926 he was called to Denmark to edit "Skandinaviens Stjerne" and, in company with his wife, left Salt Lake City May 4, 1926. They are still (1927) laboring in the Danish Mission.

work in Schleswig, namely, Hyrum Domgaard and Achton C. Jensen with headquarters in Åbenraa, Charles A. Larsen and Alfred L. Sörensen with headquarters in Sönderborg, and Wm. Georgeson and Sören W. Hansen with headquarters in Haderslev.

COPENHAGEN CONFERENCE

The Copenhagen Conference was organized at a general conference of

the Scandinavian Mission, held Nov. 16, 1851, and included the islands of

WILHELMINE JENSEN CHRISTIANSEN

Wife of Peter S. Christiansen, was born April 10, 1870, at Roskilde, Denmark, and baptized in Aarhus July 22, 1892, by Elder Peter S. Christiansen, to whom she was married Nov. 4, 1892. She was active in the Sunday school and Relief Society, presiding over the latter organization for some years. She accompanied her husband and two children to Utah, and in 1926 was called to accompany him to Copenhagen, where she is still (1927) laboring as a missionary.

Sjælland, Lolland, Falster, Möen, Bornholm and a number of smaller islands; but on August 14, 1852, the dimensions of the conference were diminished by the organization of other conferences (Bornholm and Lolland), so that it only included the large island of Sjælland and a number of smaller islands, as a separate conference was organized on Bornholm, and the Saints on Lolland and Falster were also organized into a separate conference. In the beginning of 1864, the Bornholm Conference was discontinued and the membership added to the Copenhagen Conference, and when the Öernes

(Islands) Conference was discontinued in the summer of 1870, the

EUGENE LYMAN PETERSEN

Was born Sept. 11, 1906, in Weber County, Utah, the son of Adam L. Petersen and Anna M. Petersen. He was baptized Sept. 11, 1914, by his father and worked in the presidencies of the Deacons' and Teachers' quorums of the Eleventh Ward, Ensign Stake. In 1926-1927 he served as a missionary in Denmark, laboring in the Aalborg Conference until Sept. 16, 1927, when he was honorably released on account of ill health.

Copenhagen Conference was enlarged to its original dimensions and to what it now (1927) is.

Following is a list of the presidents of the Copenhagen Conference:

1. John E. Forsgren, 1851-1852.
2. Peter O. Hansen, 1852-1853.
3. Christian J. Larsen, 1853.
4. Ola N. Liljenquist, 1853-1857.
5. Lars Eriksen, 1857-1859.
6. Niels Wilhelmsen, 1859-1861.
7. P. Wilhelm Poulsen, 1861-1863.
8. Niels C. Edlefsen, 1863-1864.

9. Hans Christian Högsted, 1864-1865.
10. Frederik R. E. Bertelsen, 1865-1866.
11. Niels Nielsen, 1866. He was the first Elder from Zion who presided over the conference.
12. Frederik C. Sörensen, 1866-1867.
13. Christian H. Halvorsen, 1867-1869.
14. Carl Larsen, 1869-1870.
15. Peter F. Madsen, 1870-1873.
16. Peter C. Carstensen, 1873-1874.
17. Knud Petersen, 1874-1876.
18. Sören P. Neve, 1876-1878.

KARL MONS JUUL THOMSEN

Son of Karl J. Thomsen and Johanna Andersen, was born in Provo, Utah, March 14, 1902, baptized March 2, 1912, ordained successively to the offices of Deacon, Teacher, Priest and Elder and was ordained a Seventy by Rulon S. Wells April 1, 1926. In his youth Elder Thomsen was educated in the public schools of Utah County and at the Lehi High school. In 1919 he moved to Magna, where he went to work for the Utah Copper company, holding various positions of trust, including that of photographer. He has also been a diligent worker in the Church, was Stake secretary of Religion Classes in the Alpine Stake, and acted in the superintendency of the Y. M. M. I. A. and the Sunday school of the Magna Ward, Oquirrh Stake. Being called to fill a mission to Denmark, Elder Thomsen left Salt Lake City May 4, 1926, and upon his arrival in Denmark was appointed to labor in the Aalborg Conference; later he was transferred to the Aarhus Conference, where he is still (1927) laboring.

19. Otto Edward Wilhelm Thorwald Christensen, 1878-1879.
20. Carl C. Asmussen, 1879-1880.
21. Hans Funk, 1880-1881.
22. Hans J. Christiansen, 1881-1882.
23. Hans Olsen Magleby, 1882-1883.
24. Emil Andersen, 1883-1884.
25. Jörgen Hansen, 1884-1885.
26. Christian F. Olsen, 1885-1887.
27. Willard S. Hansen, 1887-1888.
28. Jens C. A. Weibye, 1888-1889.
29. Carl E. Peterson, 1889-1890.
30. August S. Schow, 1890.
31. Carl E. Thorstensen, 1890-1891.
32. Harold F. Liljenquist, 1891-1893.
33. Christen P. Larsen, 1893.
34. Adam Lind Petersen, 1893-1894.
35. Charles J. Christensen, 1894-1895.
36. Peter Jensen, 1895-1896.
37. George Christensen, 1896-1897.
38. Enoch Jörgensen, 1897-1898.
39. Nils Jensen, 1898-1899.
40. Jacob Christensen, 1899-1900.
41. James Thomson, 1900-1901.
42. Peter Christensen, 1901-1902.
43. Hans J. Christiansen (2nd term), 1902-1905.
44. Niels J. Henrichsen, 1905-1906.
45. Niels L. Lund, 1906-1907.
46. Lorentz Petersen, 1907-1909.
47. James J. Larsen, 1909-1910.
48. Hans Mikkelsen, 1910.
49. Carl Kjær, 1910.
50. Anton J. T. Sörensen, 1910-1911.
51. Oluf J. Andersen, 1911-1912.
52. Richard C. Miller, 1912.
53. Henry A. Björkman, 1912-1913.
54. Neeley L. Hansen, 1913.
55. Jesse H. Nielsen, 1913-1914.
56. Denmark Jensen, 1914.
57. Joseph J. Kjær, 1914-1915.
58. Hans J. Christiansen (3rd term), 1915.
59. Carl E. Peterson, pro tem.
60. Jens I. Larsen, pro tem.
61. Hans C. Hansen, 1922.
62. Carl E. Peterson, pro tem, 1922-1923.

63. Emil Andersen, 1923-1925.
64. Julius Bruun, 1925.
65. Valdemar L. Jensen, 1925-1926.
66. Niels J. Larsen, 1926-1927.

FREDERICIA CONFERENCE

The Fredericia Conference was organized at a general council meeting held Nov. 15, 1851, in Copenhagen, Denmark, and consisted of the southern part of Jutland as far north as Randers and also included the islands of Fyen, Langeland, and a number of smaller islands. In 1852, the branch of Schleswig was added. When the Aarhus Conference was organized in the summer of 1857, the Fredericia Conference lost its northern branches, and on April 13, 1868, the conference was entirely dissolved and added to the Aarhus Conference. Following is a list of the conference presidents who presided continuously from the beginning:

1. Christian J. Larsen, from 1851 to 1852.
2. Niels Mikkelsen, 1852.
3. Anders Andersen, 1852-1853.
4. Jens Jörgensen, 1853-1857.
5. Christoffer O. Folkmann, 1857-1858.
6. Peter Nielsen, 1858-1861.
7. Johan P. R. Johansen, 1861-1863.
8. Jens Christian Olsen, 1863-1864.
9. Gustaf Pegau, 1864.
10. Wilhelm F. O. Behrman, 1864-1865.
11. Jens M. Christensen, pro tem., 1865.
12. Frederick C. Sörensen (the first president from Zion), 1866.
13. Sören Iversen, 1866-1867.
14. Anders Larsen, 1867-1868.

AALBORG CONFERENCE

The Aalborg Conference was organized at a general conference of the Scandinavian Mission, held Nov. 16, 1851, and consisted of the northern half of the Jutland peninsula; but when the Vendsyssel Conference was organized Aug. 14, 1852, and the Aarhus and Skive conferences were organized in the summer of 1857, the boundaries of the Aalborg Conference were changed. About New Year, 1864, the Skive Conference was discontinued and its former membership partly added to the Aalborg Conference, while all of Vendsyssel was added to the Aalborg Conference in 1868. Since that time the Aalborg Conference has consisted of all that part of North Jutland which lies north of the Limfjord, as well as the islands in said fjord and also the so-called Himmerland, which extends south as far as Hobro and the Mariager Fjord. Following is a complete list of the presidents of the Aalborg Conference:

1. Christian Christiansen, from 1851 to 1852.
2. Johannes Larsen, 1852-1856.
3. Christian D. Fjeldsted, 1856-1858.
4. Johan F. Klingbæk, 1858-1859.
5. Hans Jensen, 1859-1860.
6. Rasmus Nielsen, 1860-1861.
7. Lauritz Larsen, 1861-1862.
8. Niels C. Edlefsen, 1862-1863.
9. Sören Jensen, 1863-1865.
10. Jens Thomsen, 1865.
11. Hans Jensen Hals, 1865-1867. He was the first Elder from Zion who presided over the conference.
12. Christian D. Fjeldsted (2nd term), 1867-1868.
13. Jens Johansen, 1868-1869. He became president when the Vendsyssel Conference was added.
14. Jens Jensen, 1869-1870.
15. Jacob H. Jensen, 1870-1872.
16. Peter Christian Christensen, 1872-1874.
17. Christoffer S. Winge, 1874.
18. Peter O. Hansen, 1874-1875.
19. Mads Christensen, 1875-1876.
20. Knud H. Bruun, 1876-1877.
21. Niels Mortensen (Petersen), 1877-1878.
22. Jens Christensen, 1878-1879.
23. Niels P. Rasmussen, 1879-1880.
24. Simon Christensen, 1880-1882.
25. Lars Peter Christensen, 1882-1883.
26. Sören Sörensen, 1883-1884.
27. Ferdinand F. Hintze, 1884-1885.
28. Sören P. Neve, 1885.
29. Sven C. Nilson, 1885.
30. Niels Mikkelsen, 1885-1887.
31. Mads Jörgensen, 1887-1889.
32. Charles K. Hansen, 1889.
33. Andrew K. Andersen, 1889-1890.
34. Christian N. Jensen, 1890-1891.
35. Frantz Carl Mikkelsen, 1891.
36. Lars F. Johnson, 1891-1893.
37. Hans Peter Hansen, 1893-1895.
38. Peter C. Christensen (2nd term), 1895.
39. Sören C. Petersen, 1895-1896.
40. Andrew C. Jensen, 1896.
41. Andrew C. Fjeldsted, 1896-1897.
42. Jens Christensen (2nd term), 1897-1898.
43. Louis M. Christiansen, 1898-1899.
44. Morten Jensen, 1899-1901.
45. Richard C. Miller, 1901.
46. James Johnson, 1901-1903.
47. Lars P. Christensen (2nd term), 1903-1904.
48. John J. Plowman, 1904-1905.
49. Jens P. L. Breinholt 1905-1906.
50. Charles C. Nielsen, 1906-1907.
51. Hyrum J. Jensen, 1907-1908.
52. Isaac A. Jensen, 1908-1909.
53. James A. Johnson, 1909-1910.
54. James Jensen, 1910.
55. Richard C. Miller (2nd term), 1910-1912.
56. Christen M. Jensen, 1912-1913.
57. James C. Bolander, 1913.
58. John F. Petersen, 1913.
59. William Jensen, 1913-1915.
60. Peter M. Lundgren, 1915.

61. Moroni P. Stærk, 1915-1917.
62. Carl H. Löhdefinck, 1917-1918.
63. Grover E. Christensen, 1918-1919.
64. Jens Thomsen, 1919.
65. Christian Peter Sörensen, 1919-1920.
66. Waldemar Garlick (local), 1920-1921.
67. John H. Jörgensen, 1921-1922.
68. Christian Peter Sörensen (2nd term), 1922-1924.
69. Chr. Larsen, 1924-1925.
70. Amos B. C. Jensen, 1925-1926.
71. Egert M. Larsen, 1926-1927.

BORNHOLM CONFERENCE

The Bornholm Conference was organized at a general council meeting held in Copenhagen, Denmark, Aug. 14, 1852. It included the island of Bornholm which previously had belonged to the Copenhagen Conference, on to which conference the island of Bornholm was again added when the Bornholm Conference was disorganized in the beginning of 1864. Since that time the Saints on the island of Bornholm have constituted a branch of the Copenhagen Conference. Following is a list of the presidents of the Bornholm Conference:
1. Ole Svendsen, from 1852 to 1853.
2. Christen G. Larsen, 1853.
3. Hans Peter Olsen, 1853.
4. Christen G. Larsen (2nd term), 1853-1857.
5. Hans Jensen, 1857-1858.
6. Mads Andersen, 1858-1862.
7. Peter C. Nielsen, 1862-1864.

LOLLAND CONFERENCE

The Lolland Conference was organized at a general conference of the Scandinavian Mission held in Copenhagen, Denmark, Aug. 14, 1852. It consisted of the islands of Lolland,

Falster, Möen and other smaller islands. About New Year, 1864, this conference was amalgamated with the Fyen Conference and was thereafter known by the name of Öernes (Islands) Conference until the summer of 1870, when that part of the Öernes Conference which originally was the Lolland Conference was added to the Copenhagen Conference, to which it still belongs as a branch known as the Lolland-Falster Branch. Following is a list of the presidents of the Lolland Conference:
1. Johan Svenson, from 1852 to 1855.
2. Jens Jensen, 1855-1857.
3. Mads Jörgensen, 1857-1858.
4. Hans M. Nissen, 1858-1859.
5. Jens Hansen, 1859-1864.

VENDSYSSEL CONFERENCE

The Vendsyssel Conference was organized at a general conference held in Copenhagen, Denmark, Aug. 14, 1852, and consisted of the Saints residing in the province of Vendsyssel, or the Hjörring amt, which from the beginning has been a most fruitful field for the Latter-day Saint missionaries. Prior to the large emigration in 1862, there were about seven hundred members of the Church in the conference, though at that time the boundaries of the conference had been changed so that the southern part of Vendsyssel belonged to the Aalborg Conference. No province in America or Europe has, in comparison to its area and number of inhabitants, yielded so much good material to the Church as has the little province of Vendsyssel. In 1868 (May 20th), the Vendsyssel Conference was dissolved and its membership added to the Aalborg Conference. Following is a list of the presidents of the Vendsyssel Conference:

1. Niels Christian Schow, in 1852.
2. Lauritz Larsen, from 1852 to 1857.
3. Peter A. Fjeldsted, 1857-1859.
4. Jens C. A. Weibye, 1859-1862.
5. Hans Christian Högsted, 1862-1864.
6. Lars Larsen, 1864-1866.
7. Morten Lund,* 1866.
8. Hans Hansen, 1866-1867.
9. Otto Anton Thomsen, 1867.
10. Jens Johansen,* 1867-1868.

---

*Elders from Zion.

FYEN CONFERENCE

The Fyen Conference, which consisted of the islands of Fyen and Langeland, and about 30 smaller islands, was organized at a general conference of the Scandinavian Mis. sion held in Copenhagen, Dec. 30, 1855. About New Year, 1864, the conference was amalgamated with the Lolland Conference under the name of Öernes (Islands) Conference. Following are the names of the presidents of the Fyen Conference:

1. Peder Nielsen, from 1855 to 1856.
2. Sören Peter Guhl, 1856-1859.
3. Christian P. Rönnow, 1859-1862.
4. Peter C. Carstensen, 1862-1864.

AARHUS CONFERENCE

The Aarhus Conference was organized at a conference meeting held at Veile, July 5, 1857, by taking the Randers district with 30 members from the Aalborg Conference and the Aarhus and Silkeborg districts with 105 members from the Fredericia Conference. In 1868, all of the Fredericia Conference was added to the Aarhus Conference, and in 1870, also the Fyen part of the Öernes Conference. Besides this the Saints in Schleswig, later a part of Germany, has belonged occasionally to the Aar.

hus Conference, which, in point of area, is the largest conference in Denmark. For a long time the gospel gained splendid ground in the Aarhus Conference, and for a number of years more persons were added to the Church in that conference than in any other conference in Scandinavia. Following is an unbroken chain of presidents of the Aarhus Conference. Those marked with a star are local Elders:

1. Lars Christian Geertsen,* 1857-1861.
2. Peter Christian Geertsen,* 1861-1864.
3. Hans Jörgensen,* 1864-1866.
4. Andrew Nielsen, 1866-1867. (He was the first Elder from Zion who presided over the conference.
5. Hans Jensen Hals, 1867.
6. Lauritz Larsen, 1867-1869.
7. John H. Hougaard, 1869-1870.
8. Peter Madsen, 1870-1871.
9. Christen Madsen, 1871-1872.
10. Christian F. Schade, 1872-1874.
11. Peter C. Geertsen (2nd term), 1874-1875.
12. Andrew R. Anderson, 1875-1876.
13. Christian Jensen, 1876-1877.
14. Sören Jensen, 1877.
15. Jens Christian Nielsen, 1877-1879.
16. Rasmus Nielsen, 1879.
17. Lars Svendsen, 1879-1880.
18. Christen Jensen, 1880-1881.
19. Jens Iver Jensen, 1881-1882.
20. Jens M. Christensen, 1882-1883.
21. Johan B. Hesse, 1883-1884.
22. Ole Sörensen, 1884-1885.
23. Christian Christiansen, 1885.
24. John G. Johnson, 1885-1886.
25. Jens C. Nielsen (2nd term), 1886-1887.
26. Lars S. Andersen, 1887.
27. Jens Jensen, 1887-1890.
28. Niels Frederiksen, 1890-1891.
29. Joseph Christiansen, 1891-1892.
30. Martin Nielsen, 1892-1893.

31. Christian W. Sörensen, 1893-1894.
32. Theodor Petersen, 1894-1895.
33. William Buckholt, 1895-1896.
34. Morten C. Mortensen, 1896-1897.
35. Andrew A. Björn, 1897-1898.
36. Hans Peter Nielsen, 1898.
37. Andrew Petersen, 1898-1900.
38. Herman F. F. Thorup, 1900-1901.
39. James C. Petersen, 1901-1903.
40. Adam L. Petersen, 1903-1904.
41. Hans Christian Hansen, 1904-1906.
42. Joseph L. Petersen, 1906.
43. Anders P. Nielsen, 1906-1907.
44. Charles Jensen, 1907-1909.
45. Andrew H. Anderson, 1909.
46. John C. Christoffersen, 1909.
47. Isaac A. Jensen, 1909-1910.
48. Niels J. Larsen, 1910-1911.
49. Andrew Funk, 1911.
50. Alma L. Petersen, 1911-1912.
51. Peter C. Rasmussen, 1912.
52. Peter H. Sörensen, 1912-1914.
53. Wilford L. Breinholt, 1914-1915.
54. Peter M. Lundgren, 1915-1916.
55. Christen Sörensen, 1916-1918.
56. Carl H. Löhdefinck, 1918.
57. Frederik F. Samuelsen,* 1918-1919.
58. Lauritz Larsen,* 1919-1921.
59. Niels Sörensen, 1921.
60. Lauritz Larsen* (2nd term), 1921-1922.
61. Paul L. Gregersen, 1922-1923.
62. Julius Bruun, 1923-1925.
63. Bryan L. Petersen, 1925-1926.
64. Rasmus Mickelsen, 1926-1927.

SKIVE CONFERENCE

The Skive Conference, consisting of a western district of the central part of North Jutland, was organized in the summer of 1857, from portions of the Fredericia and Aalborg conferences. Thyland and Salling were the principal districts of country within the boundaries of the con-

ference, which existed only about seven years, as it was disorganized in the beginning of 1864, when that part of the same lying north of the Limfjord with the small islands in said fjord were added to the Aalborg Conference, while that part lying south of the Limfjord became a part of the Aarhus Conference. Following are the names of the presidents of the Skive Conference:

1. Lars Jacobsen, from 1857 to 1858.
2. Hans Jensen, 1858-1859.
3. Rasmus Nielsen, 1859.
4. Aron G. Ömann, 1859-1861.
5. Hans C. Hansen, 1861-1862.
6. Christoffer S. Winge, 1862-1863.
7. Sven J. Jonasson, 1863-1864.

ÖERNES CONFERENCE

The Öernes (Islands) Conference was organized early in 1864, by the amalgamation of the Fyen and the Lolland conferences, and existed for about six years, or until 1870, when it was disorganized. On that occasion the islands of Fyen and Langeland and a number of smaller islands were added to the Aarhus Conference, while the islands of Lolland, Falster, Möen and some smaller islands became a part of the Copenhagen Conference. The following Elders presided over the Öernes Conference:

1. Sven J. Jonasson, from 1864 to 1865.
2. Ole H. Berg, 1865.
3. Peter Hansen, 1865-1868.
4. Morten Mortensen, 1868-1870.

ODENSE CONFERENCE

The Odense Conference was organized about Jan. 1, 1871, from branches formerly belonging to the Aarhus Conference. It contained the islands of Fyen and Langeland and some of the smaller islands belonging to Denmark, and also the Saints residing in Schleswig and Holstein, but the conference ony existed one and a half years, when it was dissolved and the Saints comprising it were transferred back to the Aarhus Conference. Following are the names of the presidents of the Odense Conference:

1. Niels P. Edlefsen, 1871.
2. Niels P. Petersen, 1871-1872.

The student of Church history, or the reader of this history of the Scandinavian Mission, is kindly requested to study carefully the statistics found in pages 533, 534, 535, and 536. The tabulations on these four pages will, perhaps, better than anything else illustrate the growth and success of the Latter-day Saint missions in Denmark, Sweden and Norway, in their various details. And when, at some future day, these statistics shall be compared with those of the missions of the Church in other parts of the world, it will be seen that of all such missions established among non-English speaking peoples the Scandinavian Mission, so far, stands at the head of the list. The work was first commenced in Denmark whence it spread to Sweden and Norway, and the statistics referred to will by comparison also show the fruits of the missionary work in the three countries separately.

History of the Norwegian Mission

CHAPTER 1 (1920-1926)

August S. Schow's administration—Albert Richard Peterson presides—Martin Christoffersen's presidency—Lorenzo W. Andersen succeeds to the presidency—Arrival of Elders—Mission presidents—Christiania Conference—Bergen Conference—Trondhjem Conference.

August S. Schow of Richmond, Utah, was the first president of the Norwegian Mission, being called by the First Presidency and set apart for

AUGUST S. SCHOW

First president of the Norwegian Mission, was born June 7, 1857, near Christiania, Norway, the son of Hans Olsen Schow and Marie Andersen. He graduated from the common schools at the age of 14. While learning the trade of a carpenter, he became acquainted with the Latter-day Saints and was baptized Feb. 1, 1875, by Elder Peter Anderson. Soon afterwards he was called to do missionary work under the direction of Elder Andreas Peterson, of the Drammen Branch. On April 22, 1876, he was called to take charge of the Stavanger and Arendal branches and latei labored as a traveling Elder in Trondhjem. In 1880 he emigrated to Utah, making his home in Richmond, Cache County. In 1889-1891 he filled a mission to Scandinavia, laboring first in Drammen and Trondhjem, and later as president of the Copenhagen Conference. On March 4, 1920, he was set apart by Pres. Heber J. Grant to preside over the Norwegian Mission and returned home in July, 1923. Brother Schow has served two terms in the city council at Richmond, two terms as chairman of the town school board and has been elected mayor of the city four times.

that position when it was decided to divide the Danish-Norwegian Mission into two distinct missions. Elder Schow arrived in Christiania, Norway, March 21, 1920, received the mission accounts April 1, 1920, from Carl E. Peterson, who had acted as the last president of the Danish-Norwegian Mission.

At that time, Hyrum Parley Nökleby, who presided over the Christiania Conference, was the only missionary from Zion who labored in Norway, with the exception of Herman F. Hansen of Idaho, who had arrived in Norway some time before on a visit. He was set apart to do missionary work April 5, 1921, but was not successful in his labors.

When the Norwegian Mission came into existence in April, 1920, Oluf K. Karlsen, a local Elder, presided over the Bergen Conference, and Eyolf R. Larsen (later known as Arveseth), another local Elder, presided over the Trondhjem Conference. Heber J. Gustafsen, also a local Elder, who had acted as secretary of the Christiania Conference, was made the first secretary of the new mission.

Sverre Jensen, another local Elder, was set apart to do missionary labors in the Bergen Conference April 23, 1920. Hilmar Björndal, also a local Elder, was set apart May 3, 1920, to do missionary work in the Bergen Conference. He labored mostly in Stavanger. Augusta K. Olsen, an intelligent local sister, was set apart July 10, 1920, to do missionary work in the Drammen and Arendal branches.

Hans Heggen, of Meeteetsee, Wyoming, arrived from America Nov.

2, 1920. He labored in the Bergen Conference.

In June, 1920, Apostle George Albert Smith and Elder Junius F. Wells visited Norway. They arrived in Bergen from England June 24th, held meetings in Bergen, Christiania and Trondhjem, and left the latter place for Sweden July 1st.

Sister Caroline Martinusen who arrived in Norway on a visit, Jan 5, 1921, was called into the missionary field, and labored in Christiania, most of the time as mission-secretary, succeeding Heber J. Gustafsen in that position. She was a faithful missionary, and was released May 8, 1923, to return to her home in Zion.

Elder Erastus Johnson of Richmond, Utah, arrived on his second mission to Norway, Jan. 11, 1921, and was assigned to the Bergen Conference, but as the civil authorities in Norway at that time objected to the presence of "Mormon" missionaries in the country, Elder Johnson was banished successively from Bergen, Stavanger, Haugesund, Aalesund and Christiansund. He finally arrived in Trondhjem, where he, through the friendship of a Mr. Sverre A. Christiansen, an influential business man of Trondhjem, was permitted to stay in that city unmolested, and was then appointed president of the Trondhjem Conference.

Hyrum M. Norseth of Ogden, Utah, arrived Feb. 11, 1921, and was appointed to labor in Arendal and Drammen.

George W. Widsten of Salt Lake City, Utah, arrived March 21, 1921. He labored first in Drammen and later in Trondhjem, where he presided.

With the beginning of 1922, the publication of a new mission organ, called "Morgenstjernen," was commenced by Pres. August S. Schow in Christiania, in the interests of the Norwegian Mission. It was a sixteen-page periodical of the same size as "Skandinaviens Stjerne," and was published semi-monthly for four years. A local brother, Rennhart Olsen, of some literary ability, assisted in the editorial department; he was succeeded later by Carl M. Hagberg, an Elder of literary attainments who had spent some time in Utah. Bro. Hagberg acted as assistant editor until the paper ceased publication at the close of 1925. Altogether, 96 numbers of "Morgenstjernen" were published, and it was discontinued through lack of a sufficient number of subscribers, after which "Skandinaviens Stjerne," published in Copenhagen, Denmark, again became the Church organ for both the Danish and Norwegian missions.

During the year, Sister Sigrid M. Holtan of Salt Lake City, Utah, arrived in Norway as a visitor. Soon after her arrival, she was called into the missionary field and labored successfully in Christiania, until her return to Utah in January, 1924.

Elder Albert Richard Peterson of Storrs (now Spring Canyon), Carbon Co., Utah, who had been called to succeed August S. Schow as president of the Norwegian Mission, arrived in Christiania, April 9, 1923, accompanied by his wife (Margaret M. Peterson) and daughter. When President Schow left Christiania June 9, 1923, for his home in Utah, Brother Peterson succeeded him in the presidency of the mission. His wife, afterwards, was appointed president of the Relief Societies in Norway; the daughter also rendered aid in the missionary work.

Elder Axel A. Nylander of Ogden, Utah, arrived in Christiania, to gather genealogy, and was called into the missionary field, June 16, 1923. He labored as president of the Christiania Branch until Aug. 21, 1924, when he left for his home in Utah. His wife, Borghild L. Nylander, joined her husband in Norway, Aug. 31, 1923, and labored as a missionary in the Christiania Branch until released, Aug. 21, 1924.

In July, 1923, Apostles Reed Smoot, David O. McKay and John A. Widtsoe visited Norway. Brother Smoot came especially to visit the relatives of his departed mother, near

Reed Smoot and to visit his native land, Norway.

Ernest A. Jörgensen of Salt Lake City, Utah, arrived in Norway, Oct. 29, 1923. He labored as mission secretary until January, 1926.

Ole Hansen of Menan, Idaho, arrived in Norway, Dec. 14, 1923. He labored as branch president in Bergen, and later in Trondhjem until he returned home in October, 1925.

AXEL ANDERSON NYLANDER

Was born Jan. 24, 1878, in Skillingmark parish, Vermland, Sweden. At the age of 13 he moved to Christiania, Norway, and learned the tailoring trade. He was baptized and confirmed April 23, 1894, by Hans J. Christiansen, emigrated to Utah in November, 1899, and has lived successively in Logan, Ogden and Salt Lake City. In 1905-1907 he filled a mission to Sweden, laboring in the Göteborg and Stockholm conferences; led the choir in the Stockholm Branch eighteen months, and labored one year and a half in Vermland. In 1922, he went to Norway to gather genealogy, was called into the mission field while there, and presided over the Christiania Branch. In 1923, in Christiania, he was joined by his wife, Borghild Lerdal Nylander, and his daughter, Ruth Lillian Nylander.

Frederikstad. He also had an audience with King Haakon, at the royal castle in Christiania. David O. McKay visited Norway in the capacity of his position as president of the European Mission. Elder Widtsoe came as a companion to

BORGHILD LERDAL NYLANDER

Of Salt Lake City, Utah, was born May 11, 1884, in Christiania, Norway, of parents in the Church; baptized when nine years old by Hans J. Christiansen; emigrated to Utah in December, 1907; was married to Elder Axel A. Nylander, Feb. 5, 1908, in the Salt Lake Temple; filled a mission with her husband to Norway in 1923-1924, and assisted in translating for "Morgenstjernen." Sister Nylander has been a choir member, both in Norway and in Utah, and took an active part in the Christiania Branch Relief Society.

RUTH LILLIAN NYLANDER

Was born April 1, 1910, and accompanied her parents on their mission in 1923-1924.

Michael O. Fröisland, of Salt Lake City, Utah, arrived in Norway in August, 1923, as a visitor, and was appointed to do missionary work in Bergen Conference. He died in Stavanger, Dec. 12, 1923, of pneumonia. His remains were shipped to his home in Utah.

Olaf Haakon Vogeler, a local Elder, was set apart Jan. 21, 1924, to labor in the Bergen Conference. James Leland Anderson of Salem,

ALBERT RICHARD PETERSON

Second president of the Norwegian Mission, was born Sept. 8, 1882, at Richfield, Sevier Co., Utah, son of Ole Petersen and Julie Marie Hansen. He was baptized March 2, 1892, ordained a Deacon Jan. 4, 1898, ordained a Teacher April 19, 1903, and ordained an Elder May 2, 1905. In 1905-1907 he filled a mission to Norway and in 1908 (May 20th) he married Margaret May Berntsen. After being ordained a High Priest, Aug. 9, 1914, by Heber J. Grant, he acted as second counselor to Bishop Victor D. Nielsen of Ferron, Emery Co., Utah, for two years, after which he moved to Storrs, Carbon County, where he acted as president of the Storrs Ward Y. M. M. I. A., as Sunday school superintendent and as Ward clerk, and from 1919 to 1923 he acted as Bishop of the Storrs Ward. In 1923-1926 he filled another mission to Norway and presided over the Norwegian Mission. He left Norway Jan. 27, 1926, delivering the affairs of the mission into the hands of Martin Christoffersen. After his return home Elder Peterson again located at Ferron.

MARGARET M. BERNTSEN PETERSON

Wife of Pres. Albert Richard Peterson, was born Dec. 21, 1888, in Hanksville, Wayne Co., Utah, daughter of A. Berntsen and Caroline Thomson. She accompanied her husband on his mission in 1923-1926, and while in Norway she took charge of the mission home in Christiania, presided over the Relief Societies in the Norwegian Mission and visited all of the branches in the mission, doing missionary work.

CARRIE MARGARET PETERSON

Daughter of Albert Richard Peterson and Margaret May Berntsen was born Nov. 6, 1912, in Helper, Utah, accompanied her parents to Norway, attended the district school in Christiania, becoming very efficient in the Norwegian language. She bore her testimony in all the branches and assisted the missionaries in tracting.

Idaho, arrived in Norway, Feb. 25, 1924. He labored as president of the

APOSTLE REED SMOOT

Was born Jan. 10, 1862, at Salt Lake City, Utah, the son of Abraham O. Smoot and Anna Kirstine Mouritsen, is prominent in ecclesiastical, political and business circles. He has represented the State of Utah in the U. S. Senate at Washington, D. C., since 1903.

APOSTLE DAVID O. M'KAY

Born Sept. 8, 1873, in Huntsville, Utah, son of Bishop David McKay and Jennette Evans.

Drammen Branch, later in the Trondhjem Conference, and still later as

APOSTLE JOHN A. WIDTSOE

Was born Jan. 31, 1872, on the island of Froen, Trondhjem amt, Norway, the son of John A. Widtsoe and Anna C. Gaarden. (See page 272.)

president of the Bergen Conference, until he was released, April 4, 1926.

Erling Björn Halvorsen, Harold M. Helgesen, Ivar M. Flöisand and William Björndal, local brethren, were set apart July 3, 1924, to labor in the Bergen Conference as missionaries.

Frans Olsen of Salt Lake City, and his wife, Karen Olsen, arrived in Norway as missionaries, July 18, 1924. Brother Olsen labored as presiding Elder in Christiania, Bergen and Larvik, until released in September, 1926, assisted by his wife.

Willard F. Larsen (Arveseth), a local Elder, was set apart July 21, 1924, to labor in the Christiania Conference. Gustave Elmer Johnson of Salt Lake City, Utah, and his wife, Karen Olsen Johnson, arrived in Norway, July 27, 1924, from the Swedish Mission; they labored in Trondhjem.

Anthon H. Lund of Salt Lake City, Utah, who had labored for some time as a missionary in Denmark, arrived in Norway, Sept. 20, 1924, and labored in the Drammen Branch.

Charles E. Peterson of Thatcher, Boxelder County, Utah, arrived in Norway, Oct. 4, 1924, and was appointed to labor in Trondhjem.

Gustav Adolph Erickson, a local Elder, was set apart to labor as a missionary in Norway, Jan. 8, 1925. He labored part of the time in the Arendal and Drammen branches, and was released on account of sickness, June 1, 1926.

Sister Borghild E. Nielsen, a local sister, was set apart Jan. 27, 1925, to labor as a missionary. After spending one year in Drammen, she acted as mission-secretary until she emigrated to Utah in October, 1927.

Johan A. Dalsbo of LeGrande, Oregon, who had come to Norway to gather genealogy, was called into the missionary field, March 15, 1925, and, after laboring in the Larvik, Drammen and Arendal branches, was appointed to preside over the Bergen Conference, which position he held until released, Aug. 26, 1926.

Harold H. Erickson, of Murray, Utah, arrived July 17, 1925, and was appointed to labor in the Trondhjem Conference. He later became president of said conference.

John T. B. Johnson of Salt Lake City, Utah, arrived Sept. 24, 1925, and was appointed presiding Elder at Arendal.

With the beginning of 1925, the name of Christiania, the capital of Norway, was changed to Oslo; hence the conference hitherto known as the Christiania Conference was, after that, called the Oslo Conference.

The following missionaries from Zion arrived in the Norwegian Mission during the year 1926: Martin Christoffersen of Salt Lake City,

Utah, arrived Jan. 20th. Hyrum L. Jensen of Preston, Idaho, and Hyrum Domgaard of Manti, Utah, arrived Jan. 29th. Elias John Ellefsen of

JAMES ERICKSON

Was born Jan. 10, 1861, near Frederikstad, Norway, the son of Erik Jorgensen and Oliana Larsen. He was baptized March 11, 1870, at Frederikstad and emigrated to Utah in 1881, making his home in Ogden, where he took an active part in Church affairs and acted as a counselor in the presidency of the Scandinavian meetings. He was later ordained a High Priest and acted as a member of the High Council of the North Weber Stake. Brother Erickson filled a mission to Norway in 1891-1893, laboring mostly in the Frederikstad and Bergen branches. He filled a second mission to Norway in 1904-1906, again laboring in the Christiania Conference, and in 1926 he was called on a third mission to Norway and is now (1927) laboring in the Christiania (Oslo) Conference.

Salt Lake City, Utah, arrived Feb. 9th. Howard John Engh of Salt Lake City, Utah, arrived April 24th. Harold S. Sörensen of Sugar City, Idaho, arrived from Sweden (where he had labored six months) April 29th. John

Wilhelm Olsen of Salt Lake City, Utah, arrived July 12th. Marius Anthon Jensen of Salt Lake City, Utah, arrived August 1st, and Thomas Olaf Short of Salt Lake City, Utah, arrived Sept. 12th. Hyrum Elof Straaberg of Salt Lake City, Utah, arrived Oct. 12th. Ole Anderson of Pleasant Grove, Utah, arrived Oct. 17th. James Erickson of Ogden and Lorenzo W. Andersen of Brigham City, Utah, arrived Oct. 25th, and Alonzo Anderson of Brigham City, Utah, arrived Dec. 19th.

Martin Christoffersen succeeded Albert Richard Peterson as president of the Norwegian Mission in January, 1926. Hyrum L. Jensen and Harold S. Sörensen were appointed to labor in the Trondhjem Conference, Elias John Ellefsen, Thomas O. Short and Ole Andersen in the Bergen Conference, and Hyrum Domgaard, Howard John Engh, John Wilhelm Olsen, Marius Anthon Jensen Hall, Hyrum E. Straaberg, James Erickson, Lorenzo W. Andersen and Alonzo Anderson in the Oslo (Christiania) Conference.

At the close of the year 1926, the Norwegian Mission consisted (as it had since 1899) of three conferences, namely, the Oslo (formerly Christiania), the Bergen and the Trondhjem Conference. Fourteen Elders from Zion and five local Elders labored as missionaries in Norway, and the total local membership in the mission according to the statistical report of Dec. 31, 1926, was 1,648.

The Norwegian Mission was created in 1920, when Norway was separated from Denmark, as a Latterday Saint missionary field. Originally Norway belonged to the Scandinavian Mission, which from 1850 to 1905 embraced Denmark, Sweden and Norway. From 1905 to 1920, Norway, together with Denmark, was still known by the old name (the

Scandinavian Mission), but in this volume it is called the Danish-Norwegian Mission. Since 1920, the Norwegian Mission has embraced Norway only.

Following are the names of the presidents of the Norwegian Mission since its separation from Denmark in 1920:

1. August S. Schou, from 1920 to 1923.
2. Albert Richard Peterson, 1923-1926.
3. Martin Christoffersen, 1926-1927.
4. Lorenzo W. Andersen, 1927.

CHRISTIANIA CONFERENCE

Christiania (originally Brevig) Conference was organized at a general conference of the Scandinavian Mission held in Copenhagen, Denmark, Aug. 14, 1852. In 1862 its name was changed to the Christiania Conference. From 1852 to 1899 the Christiania Conference included all of Norway, but in 1899 the Bergen and the Trondhjem conferences were organized out of the western and northern parts of the country, since which the Christiania Conference has consisted of the southeastern part of Norway only.

Following is a complete list of the Elders who have presided over the Brevig or Christiania Conference since the beginning:

1. Christian J. Larsen, from 1852-1853.
2. Erik G. M. Hogan, 1853-1854.
3. Canute Peterson, 1854-1855.
4. Carl C. A. Christensen, 1855-1857.
5. Hans Peter Lund, 1857-1858.
6. Saamund Gudmundsen, 1858-1860.
7. Carl C. N. Dorius, 1860-1863.
8. Johan P. R. Johansen, 1863-1864.
9. George M. Brown, 1864-1866.
10. Carl C. A. Christensen (2nd term), 1866-1868.
11. Saamund Gudmundsen (2nd term), 1868-1869.
12. Christian D. Fjeldsted, 1869-1870.
13. Mons Andersen (pro tem.), 1870.
14. Peter A. Brown, 1870-1871.
15. Jens C. A. Weibye, 1871-1873.
16. Lars S. Andersen, 1873-1875.
17. Sören Petersen, 1875-1876.
18. Niels Mortensen (Petersen), 1876-1877.
19. John F. F. Dorius, 1877-1878.
20. Jacob Rolfsen, 1878-1879.
21. Jonas Halvorsen, 1879-1880.
22. Christian Hogensen, 1880-1882.
23. Hans A. Hansen, 1882-1883.
24. Niels C. Schougaard, 1883-1884.
25. Martin Christoffersen, 1884-1885.
26. Hans J. Christiansen, 1885-1888.
27. Anthon L. Skanchy, 1888-1889.
28. Ole H. Berg, 1889-1891.
29. John Johnson, 1891-1892.
30. Adolph Madsen, 1892-1893.
31. Andrew M. Israelsen, 1893.
32. Hans J. Christiansen (2nd term), 1893-1895.
33. Peter Andersen, 1895-1897.
34. Daniel K. Brown, 1897-1898.
35. Canute W. Peterson, 1898-1899.
36. Hans Andreas Pedersen, 1899-1901.
37. Hans O. Young (pro tem.), 1901.
38. Willard A. Chirstopherson, 1901-1903.
39. John A. Hendrickson, 1903-1904.
40. Gilbert Torgesen, 1904-1906.
41. Sören Rasmussen, 1906-1907.
42. Edward C. Ekman, 1907-1908.
43. Alma B. Larsen, 1908-1909.
44. John H. Berg, 1909-1910.
45. Sören Andersen, 1910.
46. Peter C. Rasmussen, 1910-1912.
47. John Halvorsen, 1912.
48. Iver Carl M. Nielsen, 1912-1914.
49. Andrew Amundsen, 1914-1915.
50. Nephi L. Williams, 1915.
51. James F. Petersen, 1915-1916.
52. Adolph M. Nielsen, 1916-1917.
53. John J. Plowman, 1917-1919.
54. Hyrum P. Nökleby, 1919-1920.

55. Aug. S. Schow, 1920-1923.
56. A. Richards Peterson, 1923-1926.
57. Martin Christoffersen, 1926-1927.

BERGEN CONFERENCE

The Bergen Conference was organized at a Priesthood meeting held in Christiania, Norway, May 8, 1899, when the Christiania Conference which, up to that time, had included all of Norway, was divided into three conferences, namely, the Christiania, the Bergen and the Trondhjem conferences. At the time of its organization, the Bergen Conference consisted of five branches, namely, Bergen, Stavanger, Egersund, Aalesund and Hardanger.

Following is a complete list of the presidents of the Bergen Conference since its first organization:

1. Hyrum Jensen, from 1899 to 1900.
2. Peter N. Garff, 1900-1901.
3. Peter Jensen, 1901-1903.
4. Niels C. Mortensen, 1903-1904.
5. Erik Christian Henricksen, 1904-1905.
6. Adolph M. Nielsen, 1905-1907.
7. Peter Borup, 1907-1908.
8. James M. Keller, 1908-1909.
9. Enoch Elijah Christoffersen, 1909.
10. Ole Sitterud, 1909-1910.
11. Erastus Johnsen, 1910-1911.
12. Christen M. Jensen, 1911-1912.
13. Hyrum D. Jensen, 1912-1913.
14. Ole Anderson, 1913-1914.
15. Nephi L. Williams, 1914-1915.
16. James F. Petersen, 1915.
17. Adolph M. Nielsen (2nd term), 1915-1916.
18. Andrew Dahlsrud, 1916-1917.
19. Robert J. Bishoff, 1917-1918.
20. Cephus E. Andersen, 1918-1919.

21. Oluf K. Karlsen*, 1919-1926.
22. James Leland Andersen, 1926.

TRONDHJEM CONFERENCE

The Trondhjem Conference was organized in May, 1899, at a conference held in Christiania, Norway. The new conference included the northern part of Norway with headquarters at Trondhjem, the northernmost cathedral city in the world.

Following is a list of the presidents of the Trondhjem Conference since its organization:

1. Niels P. Nielsen, 1899-1900.
2. Charles C. Rönnow, 1900-1901.
3. Enoch C. Lybbert, 1901-1902.
4. Charles J. Olsen, 1902.
5. James Monson, 1902-1903.
6. Albert Hagen, 1903-1904.
7. Niels Evensen, 1904-1906.
8. Ephraim Petersen, 1906.
9. Mathias J. Benson, 1906-1908.
10. Andrew H. Andersen, 1908-1909.
11. Sören Andersen, 1909-1910.
12. Heber J. Hansen, 1910.
13. James A. Stevenson, 1910-1911.
14. Jacob W. Olsen, 1911.
15. Fred C. Michelsen, 1911-1912.
16. Jesse H. Nielsen, 1912-1913.
17. James C. Bolander, 1913-1914.
18. Abel M. Poulsen, 1914.
19. Lawrence Hansen, 1914-1915.
20. Alma M. Andreasen, 1915-1916.
21. Mikkael A. Faldmo, 1916-1917.
22. Erastus L. Otteson, 1917.
23. Hyrum Parley Nökleby, 1917-1919.
24. Eyolf R. Larsen*, 1919-1921.
25. Erastus Johnsen, 1921-1922.
26. George A. Widsten, 1922-1923.
27. Carl Jensen (Carl Gustaf Johanson*), 1923-1926.
28. Harold H. Eriksen, 1926-1927.

———————
*Local Elders.

Biographical Notes

Some of the following biographical notes came to hand too late to be inserted in the body of the work, while others are placed at the end of the volume because they could not very well be grouped elsewhere.

ANDERS ANDERSEN

An active Elder in the Church, was born at Östre Torsley, Randers amt, Jutland, Denmark, was baptized in May, 1905, and emigrated to America in 1910, arriving in Salt Lake City, Utah, Aug. 10, 1910. He was called to perform a mission to Denmark in

1917, but was prevented from so doing because of the war. Instead, he labored in the Eastern States sixteen months, mostly in Jamestown, New York, and was later transferred to the Northern States Mission and labored in Chicago about ten months. Being honorably released he returned home in May, 1919. Brother Andersen is a tailor by trade.

NIELS P. ANDERSON

Born Dec. 12, 1853, at Killebäckstorp, Kristianstad län, Sweden, the son of Andreas Anderson and Johanne Olsdotter; moved to Copenhagen in 1864 with his parents; was baptized Nov. 15, 1865; ordained a Deacon in 1872, a Priest in 1873, an Elder in 1878, a Seventy in 1906 and a High Priest in 1920. He emigrated to Utah in 1874, arriving in Salt Lake City, July 22nd; went to Brigham City; married Betty Liljenström Nov. 1, 1876; she died May 22, 1888, after bearing 7 children. He married Hansine Nielson the same year, who, after bearing 7 children, died March 24, 1909. He next married Frida Hodell who had three children and died Nov. 3, 1918.

He next married Johanna Maria Anderson, Sept. 3, 1919. Of his 17 children, 13 are still living. Bro. Anderson moved to Salt Lake City in 1917. He has been a ward

teacher for thirty years. Two of his sons have filled missions, one to Norway and one to Denmark.

AXEL J. ANDRESEN

A convert to the Church from Norway, was born July 1, 1896, at Trondhjem, Norway,

son of Gerhardt, M. Andresen and Julie Nielsen. He emigrated to Utah in November, 1912, and in 1920 (July 7th) he married Asta Gustava Kristiansen of Christiania, Norway. He was called to fill a mission to the Eastern States soon after his marriage and labored in the Brooklyn, West Virginia and East Pennsylvania conferences, acting as president in the latter. He is now a member of the Grant Stake Y. M. M. I. A. Board.

NIELS PETER ANDERSEN

Was born July 18, 1864, at Ulsted, Aalborg amt, Jutland, Denmark, the son of Andreas Anders Glad and Anne Marie Jensdatter. Becoming converts to the restored gospel. Niels Peter Andersen and his wife Nielsine Petrine Olsen, whom he had married July 21, 1884,

were baptized Feb. 10, 1887, and emigrated to Utah the same year. They located in Salt Lake City, where they and the children who were born to them are faithful members of the Church. Bro. Andersen kept three of his sons in the mission field and four of his sons served in the World war. Bro. Andersen has also held many responsible positions in the Church. Bishop A. P Anderson Glad of the 28th Ward, Salt Lake City, is one of Bro. Andersen's sons.

OSCAR FRITHIOF BERGSTRÖM

Missionary in Sweden, was born Aug. 15, 1895, in Christiania, Norway, the son of Andreas Oscar Bergström and Anna Mathilda Uppsall. In 1902 the family moved to Stockholm, Sweden, where they later joined the Church. Oscar F. was baptized Feb. 21, 1905, by John Felt and confirmed by Axel B. C. Ohlson, was ordained a Deacon April 3, 1911, by Carl A. Carlquist, a Priest Jan. 2, 1912, by Andreas Peterson, and an Elder Jan. 7, 1913, by A. Theodore Johnson. In January, 1912, he was called to labor as a local missionary in Sweden, his principal field of labor being the Morgongåva, Eskilstuna, Vesterås, Örebro and Gefle branches, until released in March, 1914, when he emigrated to Utah and located in Salt Lake City, where he has been active in Church affairs in the different Wards where he has resided. He has also been con-

nected with the Swedish organization of Ensign Stake, acting as president of the young people's organization from 1917 to 1923. In

1918 (May 29th) he married Eva Theresia Lundborg from Eskilstuna, Sweden. They have two children.

OSCAR HELMER BJÖRKLUND

A convert to the Church from Sweden, was born Sept. 11, 1887, at Valbo, Gefleborg län, Sweden, son of Olof Björklund and Erika Wahlun. He was baptized and confirmed Jan.

15, 1917, by John Johnson and ordained an Elder, July 3, 1921, by Mathias Erickson. In 1916 (March 25th) he married Elsie Wilhelmine Stjernborg, and two children have been born to them: Curt Elmer and Blensch Elsie Viola. Brother Björklund emigrated from Sweden to Utah, arriving in Salt Lake City, Aug. 31, 1921; his wife arrived one year later. Since their arrival in this country, they have performed much Temple work in the Salt Lake Temple, and on June 25, 1924, they were sealed for eternity.

WILLIAM (WILHELM) BJÖRK

Born April 6, 1837, at Hjo, Sweden, the son of John and Catherine Erickson Björk, came to Utah, Aug. 19, 1868, in John R. Murdock company; Dec. 29, 1868, he married Augusta Gustava Anderson, daughter of Anders and Anna Maja Anderson Nielson; their only child, was Whilhelmina, born Sept. 9, 1869; Aug. 12, 1885, he married Eva C. Anderson of

Logan; children, Velma, born Jan. 5, 1890; Beatrice, born Oct. 18, 1892; performed missionary work in Sweden for six years; is a High Priest. Brother Björk was one of the first presiding Elders in the Hjo branch. He is still alive, residing on the Provo bench, Utah Co., and enjoys good health, notwithstanding his high age.

AUGUST JOHANSON BORG

Son of Johannes Anderson and Kristina Andersdotter, was born Nov. 2, 1853, at Lidköping, Skaraborg län, Sweden. He married Johanna Charlotta Erickson Oct. 21, 1883, and to them were born four sons and six daughters. Brother Borg and his wife were baptized Aug. 15, 1890. A few years later some of the children emigrated to Salt Lake City, Utah, but the father and mother, together with the rest of the children, did not emigrate from Sweden until 1911; they arrived in Salt Lake City, Utah, Aug. 3, 1911, and settled at Sandy, where they engaged in farming. Since Brother Borg arrived in Utah, he together with

his wife has performed considerable work in the Temple for their ancestors, and they have also taken active part in other Church ac-

tivities, both in Sweden and the Stakes of Zion. The youngest son, Tidion, is in Sweden filling a mission at the present time. Brother Borg died Sept. 28, 1915.

HULDA A. N. CARLQUIST

Wife of Bishop Carl A. Carlquist, was born July 2, 1857, at Jönköping, Sweden, was baptized by Laurentius Dahlquist in 1874 and emigrated to Utah in 1875. She became the

wife of Carl A. Carlquist Sept. 3, 1877, and later the mother of nine children, five of whom are still living. Sister Carlquist has been an active worker in the Fifth Ward Relief Society for more than twenty-five years and has also been a faithful Temple worker.

ARNT ENGH

An able and energetic Elder of the Church, was born Aug. 22, 1877, in Christiania, Norway, son of Johannes Engh, master of the Royal Norwegian Arsenal, and his wife, Marie H. Engh. He graduated from Sörensen's "Middelskole," and attended the Christiania Technological Evening School and the Royal Art and Trade School. Becoming a convert to "Mormonism," he was baptized Dec. 11, 1897, and became identified with the Christiania Branch Sunday school and Y. M. M. I. A., and also in missionary work, taking

an active part in the organizations named as an officer. Emigrating to Utah, he arrived in Salt Lake City, Aug. 28, 1901. After his arrival in Utah, he has followed mechanical pursuits, and is, at the present time, foreman of the Oregon Short Line machine shops in Salt Lake City. Elder Engh has been active in Church capacities wherever he has resided. For a number of years he acted as a counselor in the Granite Stake Scandinavian presidency, and from 1925 to 1927 he was first counselor in the presidency of the Norwegian meetings held in the 14th Ward, Salt Lake City. He is also one of the presidents of the 137th Quorum of Seventy.

JOHAN JOEL ERIKSON

A convert to the Church from Sweden, was born April 4, 1884, at Elfkarleby, Upsala, Sweden. He was baptized Aug. 18, 1917, by Elder A. Lind; confirmed by Elder John Johnson; ordained an Elder in April, 1919, by Anders P. Anderson and called to preside over the Gefle Branch, which position he held for about two years. Emigrating with his family to America, he arrived in Salt Lake City, April 2, 1923. Concerning his conversion, Elder Erikson says that he received a testimony of the existence of God through the study of the stars and planets and of the truth of the Bible through the prophecies of

Daniel. Then, when he read the tract "Främlingen från Vestern," written by Ben

E. Rich, he received a testimony of the divine calling of the Prophet Joseph Smith.

JOHN ERICKSON

Who came to Utah in 1880, is the son of Eric Madson and Catharine Pearson, and was

born Aug. 26, 1854, in Harg socken, Uppland, Sweden; was baptized by C. P. Larson Aug. 24, 1878. In July, 1880, he emigrated to

Utah, first locating in Salina, Sevier County. Since 1882 he has been a resident of Sandy, Salt Lake County, where he has been a successful farmer for 43 years. He has held the following offices in the Priesthood: Priest, Elder, Seventy and High Priest. Brother Erickson has taken an active part in Church activities ever since he was baptized, and has acted as president of the Scandinavian meetings in Sandy for about twenty years. He is now acting as ward teacher, home missionary and member of the Genealogical Society. Brother Erickson married Anna Amelia Johnson Dec. 6, 1879, from which marriage were born nine children, five of whom are living. Their son, John Oliver, filled an honorable mission to Sweden in 1908-1911.

JOHAN EVENSEN,

Who came to Utah in 1881, is the son of Even Jacobsen (Strömness) and was born in Aker,

bravely to rear her family until April, **1893,** when she married Niels Olson.

CHARLES E. FORSBERG

Was born Jan. 4, 1871, at Horndal, Sweden, son of John E. Forsberg and Gustava E. Hed-

Norway, March 27, 1841. He was baptized Sept. 4, 1879, at Christiania, and labored as a teacher in the Christiania Branch prior to emigrating to America, in 1881. He married Oline Amundsen in the Logan Temple Nov. 13, 1884. Elder Evensen died in Salt Lake City, Nov. 1, 1889.

MRS. OLINE AMUNDSEN EVENSEN (OLSON),

Wife of Johan Evensen, was born July 21, 1852, in Romedalen, Hedemarken, Norway, was baptized in January, 1874, by Elder Oluf Olsen and imprisoned two days for this act. She moved to Christiania the following summer, where she acted first as a counselor in the Christiania Branch Relief Society and later as president of the Y. L. M. I. A. She emigrated to Utah in September, 1884, and was married to Johan Evensen in the Logan Temple Nov. 13, 1884. After being left a widow with three small children Nov. 1, 1889, she struggled
33

ström; emigrated to America in 1888, arriving in Minneapolis May 5, 1888, and in Salt Lake City March 16, 1890. Bro. Forsberg was baptized March 29, 1893, by Elder Nathaniel V. Jones. On March 18, 1896, he married Anna H. Olson. He left for a mission to Sweden April 10, 1898, labored in the Norrköping Branch, and then presided over the Göteborg Conference till released, July 6, 1900. He is employed as superintendent of buildings and grounds at the University of Utah, has labored in the Y. M. M. I. A., presided over the Scandinavian organization in Liberty Stake for three years; was ordained a High Priest March 21, 1909, and married Sophronia Nielsen June 21, 1917, the first wife having passed away Nov. 30, 1915, and was ordained Bishop of the Thirty-third Ward March 15, 1919. On June 22, 1925, Bishop Forsberg left Utah in company with his wife, daughter and one son for Europe, and especially Sweden, to do missionary work and gather genealogical data.

SOPHRONIA N. FORSBERG

Wife of Bishop Charles E. Forsberg, was born April 22, 1880, at Draper, Salt Lake Co., Utah, daughter of Peter A. and Olivia J. Nielsen. She acted as assistant postmaster at Draper for nine years, was teacher in the Sunday school for ten years, and also labored as a teacher in the Draper Ward Primary

Association and Y. L. M. I. A. In 1905 (August 8th) she married George H. Cottrell, who died July 14, 1911. Sister Sophronia then moved to Salt Lake City with her parents and located in the 33rd Ward in 1911. There she became principal of the Religion Class in 1913, filling this position four years, and was then appointed president of the 33rd Ward Relief Society in 1917. She married Bishop Charles E. Forsberg, June 21, 1917, and accompanied her husband on a trip to Scandinavia and other countries in Europe in June, 1925.

FERDINAND FRIIS HINTZE

Was born May 13, 1854, at Roskilde, Denmark, the son of Anders and Karen Hintze. He

was baptized May 13, 1862, emigrated with his parents to Utah in 1864, located in Big Cottonwood, Salt Lake County, and passed through the hardships of pioneer life. He has performed three missions to the United States (1877-1878, 1879-1880 and 1904-1905), one to Scandinavia (1884-1886),and two to Turkey and Palestine (1886-1890 and 1897-1900). While in

the Orient he traveled through Asia Minor and established several branches of the Church; accompanying Pres. Anthon H. Lund in 1897 he looked for a place of gathering for the Oriental Saints, and published 29,000 tracts in the Turkish and Armenian languages. Later he published the Book of Mormon in Turkish. He has served as a member of the High Council and president of the High Priests' quorum in the Granite Stake. Brother Hintze has been married four times and is the father of 32 children, of whom 22 are living.

FERDINAND FRIIS HINTZE, JUN.

A.B., A.M., Ph.D.

A son of Ferdinand Friis Hintze, was born Dec 8, 1881, at Big Cottonwood, Salt Lake County, Utah, and became an earnest student from his early youth. Thus he took a college course leading to a bachelor's degree at the University of Utah in 1908, took a post graduate course in geology at the University of Utah in 1909-1911, leading to a Master of Arts degree, took a post graduate course in geology in Columbia University in New York in 1911-1913, leading to the degree of Doctor of Philosophy; acted as Professor of Physical Sciences in the Weber Academy at Ogden, Utah, 1908-1909; Instructor in Mineralogy Laboratory, University of Utah, 1909-1911; Assistant in Paleontology at Columbia University, 1911-1913; Lecturer in Geology, Columbia Extension School, 1912-1913; Professor of Geology, at Lehigh University, South Bethlehem, Penn., 1913-1918; Geologist, Wyoming State Geological Survey, 1914; Geologist, United States Geological Survey, 1915; Geologist for the Texas Company, summer of 1917;

Chief Geologist for Producers & Refiners Corporation, Denver, Colo., 1918-1924, and Consulting Geologist, Denver, Colo., 1924-1927. He is also a Fellow of the Geological Society of America,

Fellow of the American Association of Petroleum Geologists and Member Sigma Xi Fraternity (Columbia Chapter). Dr. Hintze is a married man and has five children.

AUGUST JOEL HÖGLUND

Born in Fundbo, Upsala län, Sweden, Sept. 14, 1855, was baptized Sept. 14, 1873, by Elder

Knut W. Karlgren, ordained an Elder April 25, 1874, and called to labor as a missionary. His field of labor was Nerike, Södermanland and Norrland of the Stockholm Conference, until 1876, when he was called to the Göteborg Conference, where he labored in the branches of Norrköping and Vestervik. After four years in the missionary field, he emigrated to Utah, where he married Anna Mathilda Svenson, April 10, 1889. In 1893-1895 he again labored as a missionary in Sweden, presiding over the Göteborg Conference. While on that mission he visited Finland and Russia, and in St. Petersburg (now Leningrad) he baptized Jeweler Lindelöf and his family. Elder Höglund was one of the first Elders who visited Russia, and the baptisms mentioned were the first performed with divine authority in Russia during the present dispensation. Brother Höglund was a miner and machinist, but he spent much of his time in the interest of the Church. He presided several years over the 29th Ward Sunday school, Salt Lake City, and was later an active member of the High Priests' quorum in Bountiful, where he died Dec. 12, 1926.

CHRISTIAN VALDEMAR HANSEN,

One of the Saints emigrating to Zion in 1883, crossed the Atlantic in the steamship "Nevada." sailing from Liverpool June 20, 1883.

He was born May 23, 1870, at Svendstrup, Sjælland, Denmark, the son of Hans J. Hansen and Marie Nielsen was baptized Sept. 1 1879, and emigrated to Utah with his parents, arriving in Logan, Cache County, July 8, 1883. In 1908 he moved to Idaho and in July, 1920, to Provo, Utah. He has filled important positions in the Church, performed two home missions, one in Cache Stake in 1894 and another in Fremont Stake (Idaho) in 1913. In

1917 he was ordained a High Priest by James .E. Talmage. From his earliest youth Bro. Hansen has taken an active part in Church affairs, teaching in Sunday schools and in the Seventies' and High Priests' quorums, and also been active in genealogical work. In 1893 he married Olivia Nelson in the Logan Temple and is the father of eleven children, five of whom have passed away. His wife died July 1, 1926, leaving him with six children and eight grandchildren.

AXEL HERMAN HOLMGREN

Son of Anders G. Holmgren and Anna Augusta Anderson, was born Feb. 21, 1890, at Hagstugan, Svarta, Södermanland, Sweden, was baptized in 1903, by Elder Emanuel M. Ohlson, and confirmed at the same time. Emigrating to Utah he arrived in Salt Lake City, May 21, 1909; located in the Taylor Ward, Weber County, Utah; moved to Midvale, Utah, where he remained for four years;

married Anna D. Carlson, June 1, 1910, in the Salt Lake Temple, President Anthon H. Lund officiating. The following children have been born to them: Lilly Dorothy, Arthur Herman, Carl Melvin, Esther Mary and Evelyn Lucile Clarissa. Brother Holmgren has held offices in the Priesthood as Priest, Elder, and Seventy; has acted as chorister, secretary and treasurer of the Scandinavian organization in the Grant Ward, Cottonwood Stake, and been a member of the finance committee of the Grant Ward. Being a musician, Brother Holmgren is often called upon to take part in entertainments in different Wards.

ANDERS GUSTAV HOLMGREN

An active Church worker, was born Sept. 21, 1856, at Svarta, Nyköping län, Sweden, the son of Anders Petter Holmgren and Christina Carlson. He was baptized July 22, 1900, by Elder Joseph Felt and confirmed by Elder John Johnson. In 1881 (November 6th) he married Anna Augusta Anderson, and

the family, consisting of four boys and two girls, emigrated to America, arriving in Salt Lake City, Utah, Aug. 3, 1911, and settled in Midvale, Salt Lake County, where the Holm-

gren family is well known for their faithful activities in the Church. Brother Holmgren has taken a most active part in all Church affairs, both in Sweden and Utah.

JOHN P. HOLMGREN

A convert to the Church from Sweden, was born Jan. 31, 1871, at Nyvik, Alnö, Sundsvall, Sweden. Being converted to "Mormonism,"

he and his wife were baptized Sept. 13, 1911, by Elder Fred. Anderson, and he was ordained an Elder Sept. 28, 1912, by Andreas Peterson. In October, 1912, the American Elders were driven out of Sundsvall, and Brother Holmgren was appointed to take charge of the Sundsvall Branch and the conference office until Dec. 26, 1912, when Elder John W. Anderson of Grantsville, Utah, took charge as conference president. Brother Holmgren's wife died Sept. 6, 1913, after which he emigrated to Utah with his two children, arriving in Logan, Utah, July 3rd. In 1919 (March 12th) he married Emma Sonne; he kept his son Eric on a mission in Sweden from 1923 to 1925.

JOHAN HULTERSTRÖM

Was born in Vestra Ny socken, Östergötland, Sweden, Jan. 2, 1855, of godfearing parents. He first joined the Baptist church

and fifteen years later came in touch with missionaries from the Church of Jesus Christ of Latter-day Saints, and receiving a testimony that the so-called "Mormonism" was true, he was baptized by Elder Gustave Johanson, May 6, 1894. Emigrating to America he arrived in Utah in December, 1904. He has held the offices of Priest, Elder and Seventy and was ordained a High Priest, March 30, 1919, by Elder Andrew Jenson; married Sophia K. Peterson, who died in August, 1882. The following children were born in that marriage: Ester, Hannah, Einar, Elias and Enock. Later he married Adla Sophia Widestrand, who died Oct. 7, 1886. A son, Gideon, was born in that marriage, who is now filling his third mission to Sweden. He also married Karin Augusta Erickson, in which marriage five children were born, namely: Walter Rolf, Alfhild, Gote and Elva. His third wife died Feb. 16, 1922.

JENS SEVERIN JENSEN

Born in Aasrode, near Grenaa, Denmark, April 3, 1852; baptized Jan. 1, 1872, by Elder Sören Madsen; emigrated to Utah in 1873 and located in Salt Lake City, where he engaged in the watchmaker and jewelry busi-

ness, with considerable success. He was ordained a Seventy Feb. 7, 1876, and acted as trustee of the Eighteenth Ward Latter-day Saints' Seminary for four years and served with fidelity in other Church capacities. March

20, 1898, he was set apart as second counselor to J. M Sjödahl, president of the Scandinavian meetings in Salt Lake City. Elder Jensen died in Salt Lake City, Dec. 3, 1926.

OSCAR VALENTINE JOHANSON

A convert to the Church from Sweden, was born Dec. 1, 1884, in Svedevi, Vestmanland, Sweden, the son of Adolf R. Johanson and

Christina Elizabeth Läckström. In 1907 (Nov. 9th) he married Brita Brändström, and together with his wife was baptized Nov. 21, 1909. In 1915-1919, he labored in Vesterås, and was one of the presiding brethren of the branch. Being called into the mission field in August, 1919, he labored as a traveling Elder in the Stockholm Conference, and also presided over the Eskilstuna Branch. On Aug. 17, 1921, he was called to act as assistant editor of "Nordstjernan," ,which position he held until July 17, 1922, when he emigrated to Utah, arriving in Salt Lake City,. Aug. 5, 1922. He is at this writing a resident of the 27th Ward, Salt Lake City, and acts as first counselor in the presidency of the Swedish Y. M. M. I. A.

EPHRAIM JOHANSSON,

a local missionary in Sweden, was born Feb. 19, 1848, at Solberg, Skaraborg län, Sweden. He joined the Church April 30, 1873, was ordained an Elder in 1874 and labored first as a missionary in Jämtland, where the power of God was manifested in the healing of the sick under his hands and in the preaching of the gospel. In 1875 he was transferred to Uppland, where the sick were again healed under his administrations, and where he baptized sev-

eral families. In 1876 he went to Vermland, where he labored six months, and was then sent to Sundsvall, where several were baptized. In 1877 he was again sent to Jämtland and while laboring there he was prompted to administer to a sick man who had been given up by the physicians; the man recovered. In 1877 he was transferred to Uppland, where he labored with success, and in 1878 he labored in Södermanland. In 1879 he was appointed to labor in the Stockholm Conference. In 1882 he emigrated to America and located in Murray, Salt Lake County, Utah. During his mission before emigrating from Sweden he baptized 450 persons.

ALGOT JOHNSON

An active Elder in the Church, was born Nov. 7, 1888, at Ousby, Christiantad län, Skåne, Sweden. He was raised as a farmer, and first heard the gospel through a .friend, Nils Jönsson, in the summer of 1918. After attending a conference at Malmö, Oct. 20, 1918, he was converted to "Mormonism" and was

baptized by Elder John Johnson and confirmed by Pres. Anders P. Anderson. He at once began to testify of the restored gospel to relatives and friends, was ordained a Priest by A. P. Anderson May 29, 1919, and an Elder by Theodore Tobiason Nov. 7, 1919. In August, 1921, he was called by Isaac P. Thunell to labor as a missionary in the Skåne Conference, and acted as president of said conference from April, 1923, to April, 1924. Emigrating to Zion, he arrived in Salt Lake City, Sept. 26, 1925.

JOHAN WILHELM JOHNSON

A convert to the Church from Sweden, was born Dec. 29, 1855, at Vardinge, Södermanland, Sweden, son of Johan Fredrick Johnson and Christina Charlotta Anderson. In 1881 (November 5th) he married Ulrika Vilhelmina Gustafson, who was born April 10, 1860. Two sons and three daughters were born to them. His wife was the first of her kindred to embrace the gospel, being baptized April 13, 1889. Brother Johnson was baptized Nov. 22, 1898, by Carl C. Garff. In Sweden, the family resided at Sparreholm, Södermanland, 38 years. The Elders always had a home with the family and meetings were frequently held in their house. With wife and daughter (Edith) Brother Johnson emigrated to Utah, arriving in Salt Lake City, Aug. 15, 1919. Two children had previously emigrated, and two others died in Sweden. On their arrival in Utah, the family located in Sandy, where they have resided ever since. Brother Johnson has been a very diligent Temple worker and has taken

CHRISTIAN JÖRGENSEN
A convert to the Church from Denmark, was born Dec. 26, 1873, in Kolding, Denmark. In 1900 (April 3rd) he married Elsie M. Mortensen of Brorup, Denmark, was baptized Aug. 31, 1905, in Randers by Elder Niels Mikkelsen Thorup, emigrated to Utah in 1910, and later located at Preston, Idaho,

an active part in Church affairs from the beginning.

AUGUST JOHNSON

Was born Dec. 13, 1856, at Stora Vånga församling, Skaraborg län, Sweden, the son of John Erickson and Anna Greta Svenson, was baptized Oct. 1, 1880, ordained an Elder Nov. 25, 1882, and called by Pres. Nils C. Flygare in 1885 to labor as a missionary in the city of Stockholm. During his mission he baptized 28 persons, and subsequently emigrated to Utah. In 1904 (March 26th) he was ordained a

where he is still living. There are five boys in the family. Brother Jörgensen and wife have always been faithful as active members of the Church, and he is now (1926) president of the Scandinavian meetings in Preston.

NILS M. JOHNSON

Born June 8, 1854, at Himmelstorp, Malmö-

High Priest. He married Emily Samuelson of Salt Lake City, Aug. 15, 1917. Brother Johnson has always been a faithful Church worker.

hus län, Sweden, was baptized July 15, 1876, by Nils Bengtson at Malmö; labored as a missionary in the Lund, Hessleholm and Christianstad branches. Emigrating to Utah, he arrived in Salt Lake City July 15, 1881, and located in Provo, Utah County. He married Ellen Persson in the Endowment House, Salt Lake City, and by her became the father of six children, including two pairs of twins (who lived only a short time), a daughter (Ellen Dori) born August 30, 1885, and a son (Alma Nils) born March 18, 1888. Bro. Johnson presided five years over the Scandinavian meetings at Provo, moved to Salt Lake City, where he lived twelve years, and then built a home in Sandy, Salt Lake County. He has been a High Priest for 18 years and filled several other positions of honor and responsibility.

ELLEN PERSSON JOHNSON,

Wife of Nils M. Johnson, was born Dec. 18, 1847, at Vidtsköfle, Sweden, was baptized by Karl H. P. Nordberg in Everöd, Jan. 9, 1879,

and, emigrating to Utah, arrived in Salt Lake City July 28, 1880. She was the mother of six children and died at Sandy, Utah County, Jan. 25, 1925, loved and respected by all who knew her.

GUSTAV OSCAR JOHANNES KLEVEN

A convert to the Church from Norway, was born Sept. 2, 1882, in Ulstein, Norway, the second son of Knut Eliasen Kleven and Kornelia Iversen Hatlo; received a good education in the grade schools, a junior high school and a business college. Becoming a convert to the restored gospel, he was baptized March 22, 1909, by Elder Carl Kjær in Bergen, Norway. Emigrating to the United States, he arrived in Minneapolis, Minnesota, April 20, 1909. Here he resided a few months, and then migrated to Utah, arriving in Salt Lake City, Sept. 4, 1909, and located in the 14th Ward.

He was ordained an Elder April 25, 1910, by M. O. Fröisland, and in 1910 (May 19th) he married Anna Gundine Hjörnevik in the Salt

Lake Temple. The following children were born to them: Gustave, Irene, Birger Lorenzo, Edna Margaret, and Adaline Naomi.

CARL JOHAN LARSON

A faithful Elder in the Church, was born Feb. 26, 1845, at Lindesberg, Örebro, Sweden,

the son of Lars Larson and Anna Christina Segerstedt. He married Johanna Erickson and they were both baptized Jan. 30, 1891, by Elder Söderlund. Three sons were born to them, namely: Carl E. Gideon (Segerstedt), Gustave Arvid (Thornwall) and John August (Segerstedt), all living in Salt Lake City, Utah, and taking active parts in Church work. Brother

Larson died March 22, 1925, as a faithful member of the Church, 80 years old. For a number of years he presided over the Bred district of the Vesterås Branch, Stockholm Conference, and his wife was president of the Relief Society in the same district. Brother Larson and wife were the first of their kindred to join the Church.

CHARLES A. LARSON

A faithful Elder in the Church, was born March 20, 1871, in Tjule parish, Nyköping län, Sweden, was baptized April 5, 1891 by Elder Joseph B. Olson, and called into the missionary field in October, 1891. After laboring one year in the Sundsvall Branch and six months in Solfvarbo, Borlänge, Dalarne, he emigrated

ters are still (1927) living. Brother Larsen's wife and one son died several years ago.

PER GUSTAVE LUNDELL,

Who came to Utah from Sweden in 1886, was born Oct. 26, 1847, at Närlunda, Badelunda parish, Vestmanland län, Sweden, the son of Anders Gustaf and Carolina Lundell. He was

to Utah in June, 1893, and located at Logan. In 1896 he moved to Preston, Idaho, where he still resides, and now acts as secretary of the High Priests' Quorum of the Oneida Stake. In 1898 he married Abbie Lundgren; the issue of this marriage is seven children, six boys and one girl. One son is now (1926) filling a mission in Canada.

CHRISTEN RAAHAUGE LARSEN

Who came to Utah in 1880, was born at Nakskov, Lolland, Denmark, Dec. 23, 1856, the son of Rasmus Larsen Kaare and Marie Magdeline Raahauge; becoming a convert to the gospel he was baptized Jan. 3, 1877, at Aarhus, Jutland, Denmark, by Christen Simonsen and confirmed by Jens P. Olsen; was called on a local mission in the fall of 1877 and labored in that capacity until the spring of 1880, when he was released and left Copenhagen July 4, 1880, to emigrate to Utah, arriving in Salt Lake City the latter part of July. He began work as a moulder in the old Salt Lake Foundry while the late Thomas Pierpont was manager; moved to Spanish Fork in 1880, where he established the Spanish Fork Foundry, of which he is still the proprietor. In 1927 he filled a short mission to the Northern States. December 15, 1881, he married Karen Stine Henriksen in the Endowment House; eight children were born, of whom four sons and three daugh-

baptized Jan. 27, 1886, by Charles J. A. Lindquist and ordained an Elder by Anders Olson June 13, 1886. Emigrating to Utah in June, 1886, he first located in Fountain Green, Sanpete County, later in Salt Lake City, and still later in Benjamin, Utah County. In 1905 he changed his residence to Sandy, lived in Salt Lake City from 1908-1920, resides at present at Herriman, Salt Lake County. He was ordained a High Priest in April, 1914, by Edward T. Ashton, and has taken an active part in Church affairs generally.

ELISE CHRISTINE MADSEN

Wife of Peter W. Madsen, was born at Eiby, near Odense, Fyen, Denmark, April 12, 1855; joined the Church in 1874, and emigrated to Utah in 1875, where she married Peter W. Madsen. She was an active Church member all her life, and was especially prominent in benevolent and charitable undertakings, especially so in matters pertaining to the Scandinavian people, always being ready to assist them in every way possible. In social gatherings. Brother and Sister Madsen always took leading parts, and enjoyable social affairs, to which friends of the family were invited, were frequent happenings in the Madsen home. Sister Madsen died Feb. 21, 1927, in Los Angeles, Cal. Her remains were shipped to Salt Lake City for interment.

PETER WILHELM MADSEN

A distinguished business man of Salt Lake City, Utah, was born Nov. 4, 1852, in Fredericia, Jutland, Denmark, was baptized when nine years of age, and emigrated to Utah in 1875, locating in Salt Lake City, where he at once engaged in business and was successful in a number of enterprises, until he became proprietor of the P. W. Madsen Furniture Company, president and manager of the Utah Stove and Hardware Company, president and manager of the Salt Lake Livery and Transfer Company, president of the Western Loan and Building Company, vice-president of the Utah Commercial and Savings Bank, and a director in the banks at Lehi and Springville. In 1875 (August 2nd) he married Elise Christine Larsen, who bore him eight children, namely, Richard W., Emil W., Viggo R., H. Harry, Peter W., Louise, Laura and Florence. In a Church capacity Brother Madsen always took an active and prominent part in affairs

pertaining to the welfare of the Scandinavians in Salt Lake City, assisting by advice and means. He died as a High Priest, Feb. 23,

1922, in Stockton, California, and was buried in Salt Lake City Utah.

THEODOR ALFRED MADSEN

A faithful Church member, was born Sept. 4, 1881, at Rönnebjerg, Vreilev parish, Denmark; married Anna Martine Andersen, daugh-

ter of Niels Andersen of Hjorup, Denmark; was baptized Oct. 8, 1908, by Jens C. Christensen, at Aalborg, Denmark; emigrated to Provo, Utah, in 1912. Brother Madsen and

wife have had 12 children, eleven of whom
are now living; one son has filled a mission
to Denmark. Brother Madsen is a tailor by
trade and runs a fine establishment at Provo.

EMIL A. F. MALMBERG

A convert to the Church from Sweden, was
born Nov. 5, 1886, at Malmö, Sweden, the
son of Lars Pettersson Malmberg and Kersti
Olson. Emigrating to Utah, he arrived in Salt
Lake City in August, 1906. One year later
he returned to his father the means he had
borrowed, with which the father then emigrated

to Utah. The following year (1908) his father
died at Sandy, and the responsibility of assisting his father's family to emigrate to
Utah now rested upon him. The family (five
souls), arrived in Utah, Oct. 20, 1909.
Brother Malmberg's residence at that time was
at Sandy. He married Hilda Louise Ohlson,
April 10, 1918, and two hours after the marriage he was drafted into the U. S. army,
to take part in the World war; he left almost
immediately for France, where he took part
in four battles and went through many hardships. After one year's service, he returned to
Salt Lake City, April 26, 1919, and is now an
active Church worker in the Sandy Second
Ward.

LARS PETTERSSON MALMBERG

A faithful Church worker, was born May
24, 1860, in Skabersjö, Malmöhus län, Sweden,
the son of Petter Mårtenson and Kersti Hylle-
ström. He became a member of the Church
in 1895, being baptized by Elder Peter Magnuson. Soon after his baptism, he commenced
local missionary work. His home was always
open to the missionaries, and meetings were
frequently held in his house. Together with
other local Saints and the missionaries, he
underwent considerable persecution, but was
always happy when he had an opportunity to
defend the gospel. He married Kersti Olson,
which union was blessed with fourteen children, of whom six are still living. Emigrating
to Utah, he arrived in Salt Lake City, Sept.
28, 1907, and made his home in Sandy, Salt

Lake County, where his oldest son was already living. He continued active in Church

matters until his death, which occurred at
Sandy, Sept. 8, 1908.

BROR JULIUS LEOPOLD MÖRCK

An energetic Church worker, was born Feb.
7, 1880, in Malmö, Sweden, the son of Wilhelm Alfred Julius Mörck and Elida Lindquist. He was baptized May 19, 1898, by

Elder John D. Hagman and confirmed by
Charles Olson. In 1903 (January 18th) he
married Ellen Bernhardina Nilsson of Malmö,
Sweden. This marriage was blessed with
one daughter. In 1900 Brother and Sister
Mörck moved to Copenhagen, Denmark, where
they resided until 1909, when they emigrated
to Utah and located at Pleasant Grove, Utah

County, where they still reside. Brother and
Sister Mörck are both blessed with musical
talent, and have in Denmark and Utah exercised their talents for the benefit of the
Saints. Elder Mörck is acting as agent for
the History of the Scandinavian Mission and
Associated Newspapers.

JÖNS MONSON

Was born Oct. 30, 1850, at Yngsjö, Åhus
socken, Kristianstad län, Sweden, son of
Måns Jönsson and Bothilda Larsdotter; was
baptized Dec. 26, 1871, by Nils Lundberg, labored as a local missionary in 1873-1875, in
Kristianstad Branch; emigrated to Utah in
1875; married Hanna Svensdotter Aug. 18,
1875. To them were born five children, 3 boys

and 2 girls. Elder Monson has always been a
faithful member and worker in the Church.
His wife died in 1885. The following year
he married Kjersti Kristofferson; they had
three children. She died in 1913. In 1915
he married Maria Swenson. Brother Monson
has resided in Pleasant Grove, Utah Co., Utah,
since 1880.

MONS MONSON,

Who came to Utah in 1877, is the son of
Mons Johnson and Botilda Lundgren and was
born July 22, 1862, at Olseröd, Skåne, Sweden;
was baptized Sept. 12, 1877. Emigrating to
Utah, he arrived in Salt Lake City Oct. 3, 1877.
He lived successively in Sandy, Pleasant Grove
and Provo, engaged in making homes, farms,
orchards, gardens, and also in building roads,
bridges, canals and ditches, and changing the
country into the flourishing conditions that
exist today. For three years he was engaged
in railroad building in Utah and Colorado.
He attended the B. Y. Academy at Provo in
1880-1881, studying under Dr. Karl G. Maeser
and Dr. James E. Talmage. In 1886 (Nov.
11th) he married Lydia S. Broberg, who bore
him eleven children (8 sons and 3 daughters),
ten of whom are still (1927) living. Brother
Monson has been active in Y. M. M. I. A.,
Sunday school, as a home missionary and sec-

retary of the 44th quorum of Seventy; he has
also labored as ward clerk for twenty years.

CARL HAROLD NELSON

A convert to the Church from Sweden, was
born Feb. 7, 1891, at Lund, Malmöhus län,
Sweden, the son of Anders Nilsson and Jo-
hanna Person. He became a member of the
Church Oct. 2, 1899, being baptized by Elder
Alfred Hanson. Emigrating to Utah with his

parents, he arrived in Salt Lake City, June
4, 1903. After residing two years in Murray,
the family made their permanent home at
Sandy, where Brother Nelson has filled the
offices of Deacon, Teacher, Priest, Elder and
Seventy, and takes an active part in Church
affairs. At present he is laboring in the
Sandy First Ward as a home missionary and
Ward teacher. In 1915 (October 7th) he
married Martha Elizabeth Skoglund, which

marriage has been blessed with one boy and one girl.

THORA L. M. PFEIFFER NICOLAYSEN

Wife of Morten A. C. Nicolaysen, was born July 4, 1878, at Skovshoved, near Copenhagen, Denmark. Becoming a convert to "Mormonism" she was baptized April 30, 1898, and became a living witness of several remarkable manifestations of the power of God, including visits from the world of immortality, with personal messages of comfort. She is a firm believer in Jesus of Nazareth, as the true

er for "Skandinaviens Stjerne" about three years. In 1905 (July 4th) he married Thora L. M. Pfeiffer in Copenhagen, and emigrated to Utah the same year. In Salt Lake City, he labored as associate editor of "Bikuben" seven years, and was ordained a Seventy, Jan.

15, 1912. For a number of years he has been engaged also in typographical labors. (See L. D. S. Bio. Ency. Vol. 3: 802.)

ANDERS OTTO NILSON

A faithful member of the Church, was born May 18, 1862, at Igellösa, Malmöhus län, Sweden, son of Nils Anderson and Marna Bengtson. In 1888 (May 18th) he married Johanna Person. Believing the gospel, he was

and living Christ, and the promised Messiah, in the restoration of the gospel and the divine authority of the Prophet Joseph Smith. In 1905, she emigrated to Utah with her husband, and she has become the happy mother of seven children, namely, Mack, Edward, Carl, Irmeline, Lily, John and Johanne. Sister Nicolaysen has always taken an active part in Church work, and before leaving Denmark she presided over the Copenhagen Branch Y. L. M. I. A. and also labored as a Sunday School teacher.

MORTEN A. C. NICOLAYSEN

Typographer, missionary and translator, was born April 22, 1876, at Skive, Jutland, Denmark. He first heard of the restored gospel while setting type for "Skandinaviens Stjerne" at Copenhagen; studied the Book of Mormon; was converted and received baptism Dec. 14, 1897. He obtained a testimony of the truth of the gospel with peace and joy, and the sweet influence of the Holy Spirit. Soon after his baptism, he acted as president of the Copenhagen Branch, Y. M. M. I. A. and Sunday school, and labored as translator and writ-

baptized by Elder P. G. Hansen, June 17,
1897; his wife was baptized May 6, 1897, by
Elder Norman Lee. Brother Nilson emigrated
with his family to Utah, arriving in Salt Lake
City, June 5, 1903, and after residing fifteen
months at Murray, he settled permanently at
Sandy, where he leased a farm from Postmaster W. W. Wilson for ten years. The family
then moved to Union, where they bought a
twenty-acre farm, Brother Nilson being a successful farmer. From the beginning, Brother
Nilson was a faithful Church worker and
was ordained successively to the offices of
Teacher, Elder, Seventy and High Priest. At
present he is acting as a Ward teacher. He
has done considerable work in the Temple,
and his children are also taking an active part
in Church affairs.

SVEN NILSSON

Born Aug. 11, 1836, in Gustafva parish,
Malmöhus län, Sweden, was baptized by Pol
Åkesson, March 30, 1860; labored as a mis-
sionary in the Skåne Conference, Sweden,
about four years, first as president of the
Helsingborg Branch, later as traveling Elder

in three branches and still later as traveling
Elder in the whole conference; finally he became president of the Skåne Conference. He
emigrated to Utah in 1865. In filling his
mission to Sweden (1875-1877) he labored
first as a traveling Elder in and later as
president of the Skåne Conference. After
returning from his mission, he acted as a
member of the High Council of the Tooele
Stake and died in Tooele.

ERIK ERIKSON ÖSTLUND

Born 19 April, 1829, at Östervåle, Westmanland, Sweden. Later he located at Karlshamn,
where he married Mrs. Hanna Ohlson Danielson and soon afterwards embraced the gospel.
He suffered much persecution and at one
time nearly lost his life at the hands of a mob.
He emigrated to Utah in June, 1873, locating

in Sandy, where for many years he acted as
president of the Scandinavian meetings, and held
the office of a High Priest. Brother Östlund

died Oct. 24, 1905, his wife having preceded
him about a year before. His daughter, Mrs.
John A. Larson of Sandy, was in the Stake
presidency of Relief Society in the Jordan
Stake for 22 years.

AXEL BOGISLAUS CONRAD OHLSON

An active Elder in the Church, was born
Feb. 18, 1880, at Össjö, Christianstad län,
Sweden, the son of Pehr Olof Ohlsson and

Karna Larsson. At the age of 15 he was
employed in a steamship agency office in
Helsingborg; held responsible positions in the
Helsingborg India Rubber Company, where
he met Elin Bengtson, who told him of "Mor-

monism." He was baptized May 18, 1901, by Elder Swen J. Nilson; ordained an Elder Feb. 10, 1902, by John B. Bunderson; appointed secretary of the Helsingborg Branch and set apart Feb. 11, 1904, to do missionary work. He labored eleven months in Gefle and fourteen months in Stockholm, where he presided over the Branch eight months. Emigrating to Utah, he arrived in Salt Lake City April 27, 1906. In Ogden, he acted as a Ward clerk, and during his residence in Brigham City in 1907-1909, he acted as Stake Sunday School chorister. He was ordained a Seventy Feb. 28, 1909, by Seymour B. Young, moved to Salt Lake City in 1909, and has been affiliated with the Beneficial Life Insurance Company since 1909. In 1915 (June 6th) he was ordained a High Priest and set apart as first counselor to Bishop Hyrum G. Olson of the Liberty Ward. From 1916 to 1922, he presided over the Swedish meetings in Salt Lake City, and on Feb. 12, 1922, he was chosen as first counselor to Bishop Joel Richards in the 27th Ward. Being musically gifted, he has been a prominent figure in that line of Church service. In 1907 (June 28th) he married Esther Amalia Elizabeth Anderson, who died Feb. 7, 1920. In 1922 (June 30th) he married Anna Gertrud Jacobson. He is the father of six sons and two daughters. Two of the sons have passed away.

NILS GUNNAR RASMUSSON

A convert to the Church from Sweden, was born June 10, 1889, at Ystad, Sweden, the son of Nils Rasmusson and Kerstin Mattson. He was baptized in May, 1905, emigrated

to Utah the same year and settled in Pleasant Grove, where he graduated from the High School in 1912. He filled a mission to the Northern States in 1912-1914. In 1915 (June 10th) he married Leona West of Pleasant Grove. He taught school in the Alpine and Nebo districts for six years; served as a minute clerk in the House of Representatives of the Utah Legislature in 1919; acted as judge of the Juvenile Court in Utah, Wasatch and Juab counties for two years; studied at the Brigham Young University at Provo; became news reporter for the Provo "Herald" and

city editor in 1924; in September, 1926, he became editor and manager. For three years he has acted as Stake secretary of the Utah Stake Sunday School Board.

JENS FREDERIK ROSENKILDE

A faithful Elder of the Church, was born July 27, 1849, in Jutland, Denmark, and be-

coming a convert to "Mormonism," he was baptized in 1880. His wife died in Aalborg in 1900, after which he emigrated to Utah in 1903, and located in Eden, Weber Co., where he died May 27, 1927, leaving five children and many grandchildren. His remains were interred in Huntsville, Weber Co.

CARL J. SANDERS

An active Elder in the Church, was born Dec. 27, 1878, at Skuttunge parish, Upsala

län, Sweden, the son of Jöns and Augusta Carolina Anderson, who were among the first to join the Church in that neighborhood. Carl served in the Swedish army for three years and was engaged in railroad work at Tomteboda station, Stockholm, sixteen years. In 1901, he married Johanna Maria Sandberg, who was born Feb. 16, 1878, in Tofta parish, Upsala län, Sweden. Together with his wife, Brother Sanders joined the Church May 19, 1903. In the spring of 1914 he was called by Pres. Theodore Tobiason to do missionary work. He baptized six persons, and, emigrating to Utah, he arrived at Ogden, Sept. 1, 1916. Two years later he located in Salt Lake City. His marriage has been blessed with two girls and one boy.

FREDERICK REINHOLD OLSON SANDBERG

Was born May 5, 1855, in Uppland, Sweden, the son of Reinhold Olson and Johanna C.

Sandberg. He was baptized April 17, 1881, by P. G. Peterson, ordained an Elder by Carl A. Ek Sept. 8, 1884, and appointed to labor as a missionary at Upsala. One year later he was transferred to Sundsvall, where he labored six months, after which he was sent to Finland. He arrived in Åbo, Finland, June 18, 1886, and returned to Stockholm three months later. Emigrating to Utah, he arrived in Salt Lake City Nov. 1, 1886. In 1888 (Feb. 8th) he married Hanna Höglund, who bore him four children (Fred, Laura, Irene and Elmer). His wife died Feb. 6, 1912, and in 1916 (March 15th) he married Ellen M. Larson, by whom he had four more children (Wayne, Helen, Robert and Donald). His daughter Laura has filled a mission to the Northwestern States.

ANDERS A. SCHEBY

A convert to the Church from Denmark, was born in 1877, baptized in Randers in 1906, and, emigrating to Utah with his wife, his son Henry and his daughter Vera, arrived in Salt Lake City in June, 1907. After residing there four years he moved to Logan in 1911, where he still resides. In 1914, he was called on a mission to Denmark, but as all

the American Elders had been called away from that country, he filled his mission in the **Northwestern States, in 1915 and 1916.**

Elder Scheby served as a counselor in the Scandinavian organization of Logan, and since 1924 he has presided over said organization. His son Henry filled a mission to Holland, and before returning home he visited Denmark, where he held successful meetings with relatives and friends.

JOHN A. L. SEGERSTEDT

A faithful Elder in the Church, was born Jan. 5, 1882, at Seglingsberg, Ramnäs parish, Vestmanland, Sweden. His parents moved to

Broby, Björksta parish, when he was six years old, and there they became acquainted with "Mormonism" and joined the Church, Brother Segerstedt being baptized by Matts

Anderson May 10, 1896. He had many opportunities of defending the gospel. At the age of 22, he married Emma M. Larson, who bore him four children, of whom two, Dagmar and Greger, are now living. His wife and children joined the Church Feb. 5, 1918, and the family emigrated to Utah in August of that year. Brother Segerstedt has been a counselor in the Elders' quorum and is an active Church worker in the 27th Ward of Salt Lake City.

OTTO A. SPJUT

An active Church worker, was born Aug. 20, 1861, in Risinge parish, Östergötland, Sweden, son of Johan Malmstedt and Amalia Karolina Hellström. His sister, Rosina, and her husband (Pettersson) joined the Church and became active in the same. Brother Spjut left home at the age of seventeen, and served twenty-three years in the Swedish army. In

when he emigrated to Utah and located in Salt Lake City. From April 2, 1925, to

October, 1927, he acted as second counselor in the presidency of the Norwegian meetings held in the 14th Ward, Salt Lake City.

HYRUM A. STRAABERG

An active Elder in the Church, was born Dec. 21, 1873, in Christiania, Norway. His parents were among the early members of the

1882, he married Sofia Carolina Stenberg from Östergötland, who has borne him ten children, one of which died in infancy. He emigrated to Utah and located in Salt Lake City in 1910, having been preceded by three of his children. He joined the Church and was baptized July 28, 1923, by Elder C. O. Johnson. His wife and all the children except three were already members of the Church.

RUDOLPH MARTINIUS JENSEN STOCKSETH

A convert to the Church from Norway, was born Feb. 5, 1881, at Christiania, Norway, the son of Fredrik Waldemar Jensen and Josefine Birgitte Nielsen. He learned typography at a printing office in Christiania, and attended the Technological evening school. He learned the principles of the restored gospel from Brother Nordli, an employe of the same establishment, and was baptized Aug. 12, 1901, by Elder Lorenzo Anderson. After laboring as a teacher in the Christiania Branch and taking an active part in the Y. M. M. I. A., he was called into the missionary field June 10, 1904. He labored in Tönsberg, Frederikstad, Larvik and Skien until October, 1906,

34

Church in that country. He labored as a local Elder in 1896-1897, mostly in Arendal and Risör, where the restored gospel was preached as early as 1851. He found friends and baptized some in Arendal, where he organized a branch of the Church. In 1899-1901, he performed missionary work in Guldbrandsdalen, Hedemarken, Solar and Odalen, and also visited Sweden. Since his arrival in Utah, he has been engaged in business, and is at present connected with the Modern Furniture Company, Salt Lake City.

ANDREW SWENSON

Was born July 22, 1860, at Sönnarslöf, Christianstad län, Sweden, the son of Sven Abrahamson and Hanna Torkelson. In 1881 he married Elsa Person of Huaröd. Having become converts to the gospel, Brother Swenson and his family were baptized in 1894 by

Elder Nils Monson, and emigrated to Utah two years later, locating in Pleasant Grove, Utah. Brother Swenson's wife died in 1897, leaving four children, and in 1901 he married Emma Anderberg of Provo; five children were born to them. They are faithful members of the Church.

ALBERT WALLIN

A faithful member of the Church, was born March 31, 1879, in Vallby parish, Södermanland, Sweden, the son of Erick A. Wallin and Clara A. Sundquist. He was baptized June 3, 1892, and, emigrating to Utah, arrived in Salt Lake City, May 21, 1898. In 1901 (April 18th) he married Hilda Anderson in the Salt Lake Temple. This marriage has been blessed with four children, three of whom are still living. Brother Wallin has held several positions in the Church, having acted as block teacher, and parent class leader in the 26th Ward and the Waterloo Ward of Salt Lake City. He has also acted as assistant Sunday school superintendent and later as superintendent of the 26th Ward Sunday school. He resides at present in the Second Ward.

Salt Lake City, and presides over the Ward missionaries.

GUSTAV ARVID THORNWALL

A convert to "Mormonism" from Sweden, was born July 5, 1874, the son of Carl Johan Larson. In 1915, he attended a Latter-day Saint meeting in Stockholm, and became a convert. After being baptized he joined the

Stockholm Branch choir and soon became an active member of the branch. He enjoyed singing the songs of Zion. Emigrating to Utah in 1919, he was followed by his family the following year. Brother Thornwall is a strong believer in the divine mission of Joseph Smith and is using his talents and ability in the interests of the Church.

ANNE MARIE WILSTED

Wife of Hans Peter Wilsted (nee Sörensen), was born Aug. 9, 1862, in Aarhus, Denmark. She was left a widow Sept. 20, 1906, 44 years old, with seven children, far from

parish, Hanherred, Aalborg amt, Denmark, the son of Peter Wilsted and Christine Wilsted. Having been educated as an architect and builder, and served his term in the army, Hans Peter moved to Aarhus, where he married Anna Marie Sörensen, who, after the

her relatives and friends. In 1908 (Nov. 6th) she married Henry Gray Robinson in the Salt Lake Temple, where he was engaged as a Temple worker, and where he is still (1927) employed.

THE WILSTED FAMILY

Hans Peter Wilsted, his wife Anne Marie and four of their children (Harold, Louis, Peter and Alvilda).

HANS PETER WILSTED

A faithful member of the Church, was born Oct. 4, 1861, at the Kokkedal estate, Torslev

death of her mother, worked for Carl Berthelsen, a wholesale merchant, at whose home the ceremony was performed. Harold, their oldest son, was born Nov. 28, 1886, and the second son, Louis, March 16, 1888. One son, Peter, was born at Varde, March 26, 1889, and died as an infant. Another son, Viggo, was born in Aarhus, Feb. 29, 1890, and died the next day. Another son, Peter, was born Jan. 1, 1891, and Alvilda Marie, Jan. 8, 1892. Hans Peter Wilsted, emigrating to America, left Aarhus March 24, 1892, and crossed the Atlantic on the steamship "Thingvalla," but he returned to Denmark in July, following. Shortly afterwards the family met Elders from Utah and joined the Church March 26, 1893. A daughter, Mary Abigail, was born June 20, 1894, and died in Pennsylvania May 28, 1895. In 1895, the family emigrated to America and located temporarily in Erie, Pennsylvania, where relatives were living. During the following ten years three other children, Theodore, William and Louisa Abigail, were born. The family left Pennsylvania for Utah, where they arrived Oct. 1, 1904, and where Hans Peter Wilsted died Sept. 20, 1906.

AMANDA WESSMAN

A faithful Temple worker, was born April 7, 1848, at Tanum parish, near Strömstad, Bohus län, Sweden. She was baptized March 26, 1878, by Elder Ingwald C. Thoresen, and on March 25, 1898, she married Johan Bengtson Wessman in Göteborg. Emigrating to Utah, she arrived in Salt Lake City in October, 1893. Her husband died May 15, 1896, leaving the widow and five children, two having preceded him beyond the vail. Sister Wessman was miraculously healed from a severe sickness in the House of the Lord, and since 1898 she has been laboring in the Salt Lake Temple. At the time of this writing, she has been baptized for 130,000 women, and

(the first convert to "Mormonism" in that city); labored as a missionary about two years and composed a number of hymns which are still contained in the Danish Latter-day Saint hymn book; emigrated to Utah in 1853-1854; became widely known as an artist (painter), and died March 14, 1900, in South Cottonwood, Salt Lake Co., Utah.

OLE A. WINTER

A convert to the Church from Norway, was born April 24, 1879, at Svelvig, Norway, was baptized April 4, 1899, emigrated to Utah and

has been endowed for four thousand. Her son, Herbert, is a druggist at Yukon, Idaho.

JACOB JOHANNES MARTINUS BOHN

Born April 27, 1823, in Aalborg, Denmark; baptized Oct. 28, 1851, at Randers, Denmark.

located in Ogden, in August, 1901. In December, 1901, he married Laura Schou, which union has been blessed with ten children, five sons and five daughters. The family moved to Salt Lake City, in 1911. From 1915 to 1925, Brother Winter acted as second counselor to Ole Gulbrandsen in the presidency of the Scandinavian meetings in Salt Lake City, and from March, 1925, to October, 1927, he acted as second counselor to Frederik F. Samuelsen in the presidency of said meetings.

Year	Conferences	Branches	Elders fr. Zion	Miss. Sisters	Elders	Priests	Teachers	Deacons	Lay Members	Total	Baptized	Received	Emigrated	Removed	Died	Excommunicated
1850	..	2	4	..	...	4	4	5	126	139	160	....	17	....	....	4
1851	3	...	3	..	17	20	22	8	488	555	479	8	....	4	2	65
1852	7	3	1	..	35	42	41	11	863	992	723	35	220	52	6	43
1853	8	57	..	..	80	76	71	32	793	2,052	1,657	8	423	....	25	157
1854	9	59	2	..	105	95	93	53	2,137	2,483	1,291	3	337	191	30	305
1855	10	79	2	..	158	98	89	83	2,264	2,692	897	49	311	45	27	354
1856	10	94	1	..	311	118	118	73	2368	2,988	1,059	....	113	278	30	342
1857	13	142	3	..	403	159	140	73	2,578	3,353	1,621	10	603	87	47	529
1858	14	125	..	..	492	184	167	88	2,778	3,709	1,038	69	70	71	55	555
1859	15	145	2	..	554	191	165	86	2,938	3,934	929	59	263	....	40	460
1860	15	145	12	..	587	185	180	85	3,379	4,416	1,107	49	240	17	67	350
1861	15	166	14	..	240	209	211	105	4 420	5,585	1,954	27	455	8	44	305
1862	15	155	14	..	595	216	215	97	4,677	5,800	1,977	39	1,177	65	56	503
1863	15	132	10	..	499	198	210	100	4,639	5,646	1,587	44	1,061	41	57	626
1864	12	93	7	..	453	175	188	99	4,539	5,454	1,213	13	601	133	95	589
1865	11	84	25	..	483	164	190	106	4 445	5,388	1,010	35	454	22	55	580
1866	11	83	18	..	458	180	98	87	4,036	4,959	1,269	27	831	212	74	608
1867	11	78	19	..	490	165	183	81	4022	4,941	881	....	248	113	68	470
1868	9	70	12	..	448	163	178	83	3,936	4,808	1,017	29	622	26	52	479
1869	9	70	16	..	404	148	152	82	3 866	4,652	872	7	463	89	56	427
1870	7	65	15	..	408	148	167	61	4,005	4,789	853	....	275	19	63	359
1871	8	63	13	..	391	154	146	65	4,151	4,907	1,021	21	467	52	73	332
1872	7	58	11	..	400	149	151	69	4,049	4,817	929	20	605	20	77	337
1873	7	56	22	..	371	143	166	73	3,896	4,649	980	48	793	2	61	340
1874	7	45	18	..	364	143	146	65	3,812	4,530	935	24	674	24	81	299
1875	7	47	23	..	374	140	153	69	3,732	4,468	818	16	583	....	72	241
1876	7	44	24	..	385	162	157	63	3,770	4,537	832	....	402	73	52	236
1877	7	45	30	..	419	182	160	72	4,029	4,762	1,056	71	584	28	50	240
1878	7	46	35	..	458	184	196	73	4,158	5,069	1,255	36	589	50	48	297
1879	7	44	47	..	456	178	198	92	4,283	5,207	886	5	368	69	57	259
1880	7	45	56	..	468	183	209	99	4 404	5,363	1,160	7	549	34	92	336
1881	7	46	61	..	376	175	219	87	4 390	5,247	1,088	....	656	218	62	268
1882	7	45	83	..	331	183	183	76	4 183	4,956	990	....	794	125	77	285
1883	7	44	83	..	284	114	196	71	3 868	4,563	851	6	711	224	76	239
1884	7	43	63	..	262	131	192	57	3 768	4,410	767	12	531	78	66	257
1885	7	44	73	..	239	127	180	58	3,604	4,208	567	71	477	146	38	179
1886	7	43	67	..	243	135	177	49	3,309	3,913	576	4	408	250	45	172
1887	7	43	61	..	249	138	166	51	3 304	3,908	658	12	408	82	48	137
1888	7	44	60	..	253	131	160	57	3,333	3,934	644	6	386	69	45	124
1889	7	43	53	..	265	127	149	52	3 367	3,960	572	5	344	45	35	127
1890	7	45	67	..	272	137	148	45	3 299	3,901	557	44	404	71	72	113
1891	7	45	75	..	262	129	131	55	3 221	3,798	576	5	409	125	50	100
1892	7	46	103	..	269	134	135	66	3 182	3,786	464	53	275	77	59	118
1893	7	48	90	..	273	126	135	74	3 094	3,702	395	9	264	61	53	110
1894	7	51	98	..	279	118	133	78	3 060	3,668	437	17	205	143	49	91
1895	7	49	99	..	285	119	139	85	3 101	3,729	424	36	150	111	56	82
1896	7	48	107	..	282	140	142	82	3 282	3,928	496	31	137	64	65	62
1897	7	52	136	..	270	142	141	85	3,419	4,057	502	10	160	119	50	54
1898	7	53	162	..	261	147	152	72	3,589	4,221	590	2	214	87	60	67
1899	9	58	158	..	267	152	146	59	3,820	4,444	433	115	184	29	62	50
1900	9	60	165	..	268	163	143	71	3,890	4,535	471	65	228	78	84	55
1901	9	63	154	..	279	157	134	87	3 867	4,524	434	....	196	113	69	67
1902	10	71	172	..	264	148	155	78	3,673	4,318	529	17	273	326	74	79
1903	10	71	198	3	245	132	159	63	3,822	4,421	478	13	177	56	77	78
1904	10	69	196	3	245	127	160	55	3,811	4,398	396	2	187	91	88	55
1905	11	63	190	4	232	132	149	64	3,829	4,406	415	90	295	61	77	64
1906	11	67	199	4	224	137	151	68	3,723	4,306	345	....	234	97	53	64
1907	11	67	210	1	200	140	129	70	3 530	4,069	383	13	248	282	55	45
1908	11	63	213	1	202	152	123	90	3,472	4,039	403	46	189	195	66	29
1909	11	64	200	2	198	148	112	79	3,671	4,208	508	20	229	39	65	26
1910	11	60	216	1	197	144	135	94	3,863	4,433	627	2	286	25	64	29
1911	11	57	192	2	196	155	153	82	4,043	4,629	485	46	198	26	54	57
1912	11	56	161	3	208	153	164	87	3,897	4,509	347	6	143	215	76	39
1913	11	53	145	3	218	164	153	98	3,878	4,511	318	2	184	39	56	39
1914	11	54	99	2	233	140	154	88	3,825	4,440	286	....	193	55	67	42
1915	11	54	37	..	238	129	148	88	3,775	4,378	157	6	126	7	73	19
1916	11	55	41	..	241	130	153	89	3,775	4,388	177	93	150	2	74	34
1917	11	53	41	..	231	145	159	95	3,799	4,429	209	2	92	2	56	20
1918	11	52	15	..	244	140	160	96	3,790	4,430	164	31	100	3	70	21
1919	11	52	10	..	245	139	156	101	3,758	4,399	162	46	154	....	75	10
1920	11	54	14	..	238	117	145	104	3,689	4,293	95	11	92	65	45	10
1921	11	48	22	1	225	136	144	115	3 702	4,322	176	1	56	40	49	3
1922	11	50	19	4	273	145	128	120	3,617	4,283	180	78	56	154	67	20
1923	11	50	22	2	285	134	148	118	3 645	4,330	229	3	60	47	57	21
1924	11	50	42	2	259	116	113	105	3,984	4,577	193	343	73	114	78	24
1925	11	50	67	4	285	114	106	99	3,894	4,498	216	127	75	252	77	18
1926	11	50	75	3	281	121	112	94	3,899	4,507	165	6	46	40	70	6
											53,601	2,266	25,855	6,373	4,496	14,636

Year	Conferences	Branches	Elders fr. Zion	Miss. Sisters	Elders	Priests	Teachers	Deacons	Lay Members	Total	Baptized	Received	Emigrated	Removed	Died	Excommunicated
1850		2	4	..	...	4	4	5	122	135	139	....	....	....	....	4
1851	3	...	3	..	17	20	22	8	480	547	476	7	....	4	2	65
1852	6	...	1	..	29	37	39	10	780	895	664	....	218	52	4	42
1853	6	45	...	..	61	59	59	26	1 498	1,703	1,314	....	384	....	19	103
1854	6	43	1	..	78	80	78	48	1 785	2,069	916	....	255	20	17	258
1855	7	60	2	..	122	72	66	65	1 829	2,154	656	38	262	36	24	287
1856	7	66	1	..	242	88	82	51	1 741	2,204	700	....	113	269	25	243
1857	9	106	3	..	296	95	90	43	1 793	2,317	1,117	....	500	77	35	389
1858	9	102	...	..	357	93	96	49	1,897	2,492	619	22	62	....	37	367
1859	9	97	2	..	364	80	88	49	1 931	2,512	541	3	186	....	23	315
1860	9	95	8	..	376	74	88	43	2,138	2,719	668	....	158	11	54	238
1861	9	102	11	..	404	97	109	64	2 795	3,469	1,297	....	328	7	33	179
1862	9	80	9	..	360	96	103	45	2 751	3,355	1,142	....	865	65	26	300
1863	9	56	5	..	280	85	102	42	2,605	3,114	789	....	602	41	32	355
1864	6	35	3	..	244	79	74	49	2,426	2,872	525	....	349	96	57	265
1865	6	31	15	..	266	88	71	54	2 372	2,851	533	35	236	....	36	317
1866	6	30	12	..	238	84	74	43	2,124	2,563	692	....	521	68	43	348
1867	6	28	10	..	250	66	67	40	2 036	2,459	457	....	208	87	34	232
1868	4	23	7	..	227	64	63	37	1 967	2,358	521	29	417	....	29	205
1869	4	24	8	..	196	62	54	34	1 885	2,231	401	....	218	67	29	214
1870	3	22	8	..	204	66	60	21	1,843	2,194	299	....	150	13	28	145
1871	4	20	7	..	202	63	56	29	1,889	2,239	435	21	235	....	48	128
1872	4	16	6	..	197	79	69	31	1,843	2,210	418	1	296	....	41	111
1873	3	16	13	..	175	59	72	24	1,755	2,085	456	41	472	....	24	126
1874	3	17	10	..	154	55	64	21	1,754	2,048	446	22	363	....	34	108
1875	3	17	15	..	167	50	71	25	1,707	2,020	358	15	280	....	34	87
1876	3	14	13	..	170	63	82	33	1 775	2,123	462	....	212	24	24	99
1877	3	16	12	..	171	93	81	33	1 886	2,264	636	30	389	....	18	118
1878	3	17	13	..	186	82	101	30	1,842	2,241	597	....	389	42	31	158
1879	3	17	26	..	185	69	83	38	1,807	2,182	343	....	210	53	25	114
1880	3	17	28	..	186	65	80	41	1 842	2,214	500	7	279	....	37	159
1881	3	16	31	..	125	57	88	36	1 841	2,147	470	....	329	59	18	131
1882	3	16	45	..	108	61	77	28	1 660	1,934	413	....	348	107	24	147
1883	3	15	41	..	88	36	83	34	1 490	1,731	354	6	399	38	28	98
1884	3	15	30	..	75	37	71	22	1 391	1,596	279	....	244	55	12	103
1885	3	15	33	..	75	33	67	24	1 165.	1,264	224	....	233	146	6	71
1886	3	14	31	..	78	32	67	12	852	1,041	204	....	186	250	19	72
1887	3	14	27	..	80	30	52	13	842	1,017	221	7	187	7	14	44
1888	3	14	30	..	79	26	49	13	821	988	202	....	158	16	14	43
1889	3	13	19	..	79	29	36	10	863	1,017	223	....	132	5	6	51
1890	3	14	29	..	92	22	33	7	865	1,019	193	41	172	4	15	41
1891	3	14	36	..	86	27	38	18	906	1,075	240	5	122	21	21	25
1892	3	14	41	..	91	29	39	18	908	1,085	187	50	111	42	21	53
1893	3	14	38	..	90	30	40	17	855	1,032	143	5	115	31	9	46
1894	3	16	44	..	89	27	33	24	837	1,010	141	....	74	53	2	34
1895	3	15	39	..	75	30	45	29	838	1,017	139	6	65	47	11	15
1896	3	14	43	..	78	31	43	20	833	1,005	127	....	48	52	19	20
1897	3	18	52	..	73	39	43	18	896	1,069	162	....	64	15	6	13
1898	3	17	62	..	59	37	47	13	976	1,132	177	....	72	6	14	22
1899	3	17	58	..	55	36	33	8	1 059.	1,191	148	2	68	....	8	15
1900	3	18	58	..	57	41	33	12	1 084	1,227	169	....	66	29	17	21
1901	3	22	53	..	69	37	26	16	1 072	1,220	145	....	78	29	15	30
1902	3	24	59	..	63	34	29	19	924	1,069	182	....	103	172	24	34
1903	3	18	67	1	66	24	40	16	978	1,124	194	....	66	33	18	22
1904	3	17	66	1	59	32	39	15	944	1,089	123	....	56	59	22	21
1905	3	17	67	2	53	27	35	18	1 002	1,135	173	52	137	....	19	23
1906	3	17	65	2	48	28	37	22	1 002	1,137	150	....	112	10	6	20
1907	3	17	75	1	38	35	28	19	1 009	1,129	94	....	74	1	16	11
1908	3	17	80	0	47	41	30	23	909	1,050	157	....	66	162	6	2
1909	3	18	73	1	42	47	24	25	1 039	1,177	214	19	86	....	19	1
1910	3	17	68	..	36	43	35	32	1 121	1,267	245	....	119	13	14	9
1911	3	17	65	1	39	43	52	29	1 253	1,416	239	5	59	....	12	24
1912	3	16	49	2	43	50	64	26	1 290	1,473	144	6	67	....	21	5
1913	3	16	44	1	53	57	52	33	1 289	1,484	154	....	99	22	15	7
1914	3	16	39	..	52	55	53	25	1 237	1,422	98	....	110	27	15	8
1915	3	16	13	..	63	51	51	25	1,185	1,375	37	....	55	5	16	8
1916	3	15	11	..	66	49	50	27	1 170	1,362	56	14	50	....	18	15
1917	3	13	13	..	64	48	51	35	1,193	1,391	59	....	14	....	11	5
1918	3	13	4	..	65	51	51	35	1 190	1,392	41	....	17	3	13	7
1919	3	13	4	..	73	49	47	45	1.186	1.400	62	40	44	....	40	10
1920	3	13	4	..	74	45	48	45	1.137	1.379	15	....	27	....	6	3
1921	3	9	8	..	74	49	44	48	1 173	1 388	31	1	11	....	10	2
1922	3	10	6	..	75	53	37	44	1 165	1.374	38	....	21	11	13	7
1923	3	10	15	1	75	49	42	43	1.177	1.386	49	....	10	3	12	12
1924	3	10	23	..	70	50	44	44	1 135	1,343	37	6	48	....	31	7
1925	3	10	23	1	77	31	37	28	1,336	1.509	73	127	19	....	10	5
1926	3	10	30	2	74	35	42	20	1.362	1.533	46	5	12	....	13	3
											26,389	668	13,910	2,565	1,605	7,444

STATISTICS OF THE SWEDISH MISSION

Year	Conferences	Branches	Elders fr. Zion	Miss. Sisters	Elders	Priests	Teachers	Deacons	Lay Members	Total	Baptized	Received	Emigrated	Removed	Died	Excommunicated
1850									4	4	21		17			
1851									5	5		1				
1852					2	2			21	25	13	9	2			
1853	1	8			10	8	5	2	155	180	198	5	16		1	31
1854	2	10			15	12	9	3	186	225	260	3	43	155	10	10
1855	2	13			21	19	15	11	274	340	163	11	22		2	35
1856	2	20			43	21	22	16	402	504	238			9	3	62
1857	3	25			73	52	36	24	541	726	367	10	64		6	85
1858	4	10			86	71	43	30	526	756	235		6	71	13	115
1859	5	35			128	70	45	23	594	860	235	26	61		13	83
1860	5	36	1		141	63	51	25	722	1,002	283		53	6	5	77
1861	5	47	1		154	70	58	28	978	1,288	462		73	1	4	98
1862	5	58	3		153	75	71	36	1,02	1,537	640	37	276		21	131
1863	5	60	3		139	73	80	44	1,289	1,625	621	44	361		16	200
1864	5	42	2		127	64	77	41	1,296	1,605	509		224	37	24	244
1865	4	39	5	10	129	49	80	40	1 258	1,556	331		164	13	15	188
1866	4	38	3		143	68	84	33	1,220	1,548	390	27	210		22	193
1867	4	39	6		162	69	76	32	1 305	1,644	320		18	16	17	173
1868	4	38	3		146	71	71	35	1 324	1,647	397		144	14	11	225
1869	4	39	5		144	53	55	38	1 320	1,610	371		201	22	21	164
1870	3	36	4		136	52	58	31	1 488	1,765	438		93	6	30	154
1871	3	36	4		125	68	55	23	1 535	1,811	464		181	46	19	172
1872	3	35	4		120	59	58	25	1 510	1,772	389	19	257		22	168
1874	3	21	5		116	62	49	30	1 470	1,731	399	7	260		26	161
1873	3	32	6		110	64	58	29	1 329	1,586	307		230	24	39	159
1875	3	23	7		128	62	49	27	1 357	1,623	322	1	151		23	112
1876	3	23	8		128	76	41	19	1 317	1,581	270		128	48	21	115
1877	3	23	14		154	58	44	22	1 328	1,606	315		139	28	25	98
1878	3	22	15		158	66	65	26	1553	1,868	571		160	8	14	127
1879	3	20	15		158	75	75	34	1 722	2,064	462	5	128		24	119
1880	3	20	22		167	73	91	40	1 818	2,189	540		229	25	35	126
1881	3	21	21		142	71	87	35	1,807	2,142	479		266	124	33	103
1882	3	21	25		136	75	72	34	1 788	2,105	455		343	8	37	104
1883	3	21	30		120	74	75	32	1 744	2,045	370		222	68	37	103
1884	3	20	25		116	65	78	28	1 735	2,022	368		204	23	37	127
1885	3	21	26		105	65	89	27	1 775	2,061	259	47	167		27	73
1886	3	21	23		110	74	75	30	1 781	2,070	276	2	175		17	77
1887	3	21	24		114	77	88	29	1 845	2,153	366		167	19	27	70
1888	3	21	23		121	78	87	33	1 881	2,200	347		161	51	25	63
1889	3	21	21		129	78	87	35	1 899	2,228	282	5	171	12	22	54
1890	3	21	27		130	96	89	31	1 837	2,183	298		172	67	47	57
1891	3	21	28		128	87	68	32	1 789	2,104	293		212	79	28	53
1892	3	22	46		129	88	74	38	1 786	2,115	248		130	25	29	53
1893	3	23	38		132	79	72	46	1,735	2,064	192		122	25	36	60
1894	3	24	36		141	78	68	47	1 692	2,026	211		119	38	42	50
1895	3	23	41		151	76	71	46	1 704	2,048	191		62	14	33	60
1896	3	23	41		147	88	79	50	1,761	2,125	214		66	1	42	28
1897	3	23	57		144	85	74	50	1 806	2,159	244		57	87	33	33
1898	3	23	64		157	97	82	49	1 844	2,229	307		95	80	32	30
1899	3	22	60		163	93	80	41	1 911	2,288	183	61	97	25	38	25
1900	3	24	61		160	95	78	46	1 912	2,291	175	47	118	29	50	22
1901	3	24	57		156	85	71	51	1 872	2,235	150		74	61	42	29
1902	4	28	62		149	82	73	40	1 866	2,210	157	17	113	41	35	10
1903	4	28	70		139	79	82	35	1,892	2,227	134	13	69		39	22
1904	4	26	65		143	67	73	30	1 868	2,181	123		74	32	42	21
1905	5	28	64		138	65	71	30	1 754	2,058	110		96	61	49	27
1906	5	28	66		139	70	73	32	1 680	1,994	91		76	21	30	28
1907	5	27	64		131	67	62	37	1 674	1,971	124	13	104		29	27
1908	5	25	68	1	123	67	62	40	1 638	1,930	121		70	33	38	21
1909	5	25	69	1	130	61	52	32	1 629	1,904	140		80	39	28	19
1910	5	25	84	1	132	63	51	40	1 659	1,945	194		92	12	38	13
1911	5	25	68		128	66	54	35	1 656	1,939	140		79	26	27	14
1912	5	25	60		127	61	57	42	1 510	1,797	86		35	151	38	4
1913	5	25	60	1	127	62	61	38	1,484	1,772	53	2	41		28	11
1914	5	26	15	2	138	49	62	38	1,456	1,743	86		51	23	40	1
1915	5	26	15		135	50	60	38	1,460	1,743	67	6	40		27	6
1916	5	26	20		135	50	63	34	1,478	1,760	85		42	2	22	2
1917	5	26	18		127	56	65	32	1,468	1,748	83	2	60		28	9
1918	5	25	7		128	55	53	30	1,437	1,703	50	4	66		19	
1919	5	25	5		120	53	63	34	1,397	1,627	48		31	65	27	1
1920	5	25	8		104	41	51	34	1,405	1,647	70		15	3	32	
1921	5	23	8		90	56	54	42	1,405	1,647	70		17	143	39	9
1922	5	23	9	3	118	60	46	39	1,263	1,526	87		24	44	31	6
1923	5	23	12	3	126	52	55	37	1,266	1,536	115		12		33	12
1924	5	23	20	2	111	39	30	28	1,662	1,870	54	337	12		33	12
1925	5	23	33	1	129	49	35	35	1,368	1,616	63		45	216	49	7
1926	5	23	31	1	122	50	33	33	1,336	1,674						
											18,839	772	8,508	2,317	2,039	5,173

STATISTICS OF THE NORWEGIAN MISSION

Year	Conferences	Branches	Elders fr. Zion	Miss. Sisters	Elders	Priests	Teachers	Deacons	Lay Members	Total	Baptized	Received	Emigrated	Removed	Died	Excommunicated
1851									3	3	3					
1852	1	3			4	3	2	1	62	72	46	26			2	1
1853	1	4			9	9	7	4	140	169	145	3	23		5	23
1854	1	6	1		12	3	6	2	166	189	115		39	16	3	37
1855	1	6			15	7	8	7	161	198	78		27	9	1	32
1856	1	8			26	9	14	6	225	280	121				2	37
1857	1	11			34	12	14	6	244	310	137		39	10	3	55
1858	1	13			49	20	28	9	355	461	184	47	2		5	73
1859	1	13			62	41	32	14	413	562	153	30	16		4	62
1860	1	14	3		70	48	41	17	519	695	156	49	29		8	35
1861	1	17	2		82	42	44	13	647	828	195	27	54		7	28
1862	1	17	2		82	45	41	16	724	908	195	2	36		9	72
1863	1	16	2		80	40	28	14	745	907	177		98		9	71
1864	1	16	2		82	32	37	9	817	977	179	13	28		14	80
1865	1	14	5		88	27	39	12	815	981	146		54	9	4	75
1866	1	15	3		77	28	40	11	692	848	187		100	144	9	67
1867	1	11	3		78	30	40	9	681	838	104		22	10	17	65
1868	1	9	2		75	28	44	11	645	803	99		61	12	12	49
1869	1	7	3		64	33	43	10	661	811	100	7	44		6	49
1870	1	7	3		68	30	49	9	674	830	116		32		5	60
1871	1	7	2		64	23	35	8	727	857	122		51	6	6	32
1872	1	7	1		83	20	24	12	696	835	122		52	20	14	58
1873	1	8	3		86	20	36	20	671	833	125		61	2	11	53
1874	1	7	3		94	26	33	14	729	896	182	2	81		8	32
1875	1	7	1		79	28	33	17	668	825	138		152		15	42
1876	1	7	3		87	23	34	11	678	833	100		62	1	7	22
1877	1	6	4		94	31	35	17	715	892	105	41	56		7	24
1878	1	7	7		114	36	30	17	763	960	87	36	40		3	12
1879	1	7	6		113	34	40	20	754	961	81		30	16	8	26
1880	1	8	6		115	45	38	18	744	960	120		41	9	20	51
1881	1	9	9		109	47	44	16	742	958	139		61	35	11	34
1882	1	8	13		87	47	34	14	735	917	122		103	10	16	34
1883	1	8	12		76	34	38	5	634	787	127		90	118	11	38
1884	1	8	8		71	29	43	7	642	792	120	12	83		17	27
1885	1	8	14		59	29	24	7	664	783	84	24	77		5	35
1886	1	8	13		55	29	35	7	676	802	96	2	47		9	23
1887	1	8	10		55	31	26	9	617	738	71	5	54	56	7	23
1888	1	9	7		53	27	24	11	631	746	95	6	67	2	6	18
1889	1	9	13		57	20	26	7	605	715	67		41	28	7	22
1890	1	10	11		50	19	26	7	597	699	66	3	60		10	15
1891	1	10	11		48	15	25	5	526	619	43		75	25	1	22
1892	1	10	16		49	17	22	10	488	586	29	3	34	10	9	12
1893	1	11	14		51	17	23	11	504	606	60	4	27	5	8	4
1894	1	11	18		49	13	32	7	531	632	85	17	12	52	5	7
1895	1	11	19		59	13	23	10	559	664	94	30	23	50	12	7
1896	1	11	23		57	21	20	12	688	798	155	31	23	11	4	14
1897	1	11	27		53	18	24	17	717	829	96	10	39	17	11	8
1898	1	13	36		45	13	23	10	769	860	106	2	47	1	14	15
1899	3	19	40		49	23	33	10	850	965	102	52	19	4	16	10
1900	3	18	46		51	27	32	13	894	1,017	127	18	44	20	17	12
1901	3	17	44		54	35	37	20	923	1,069	139		44	23	12	8
1902	3	19	51		52	32	53	19	883	1,039	190		57	113	15	35
1903	3	25	61	2	40	29	37	12	952	1,070	150		42	23	20	34
1904	3	26	65	2	43	28	48	10	999	1,128	150	2	57		24	13
1905	3	18	59	2	41	40	43	16	1,073	1,213	132	38	62		9	14
1906	3	22	68	2	37	39	41	14	1,041	1,172	104		46	66	17	16
1907	3	23	71		31	38	39	14	847	969	165		70	281	10	7
1908	3	21	65		32	44	31	27	925	1,059	125	46	53		22	6
1909	3	21	58		26	40	36	22	1 003	1,127	154	1	63		18	6
1910	3	18	64		29	38	49	22	1,003	1,221	188	2	75		12	9
1911	3	15	59	1	29	46	47	18	1,134	1,274	106	41	60		15	19
1912	3	15	40	1	38	42	43	19	1,097	1,239	117		41	64	17	30
1913	3	12	41	1	38	45	40	27	1,105	1,255	111		44	17	13	21
1914	3	12	45	1	43	36	39	25	1,132	1,275	102		32	5	12	33
1915	3	12	9	1	40	28	37	25	1,130	1,260	53		31	2	30	5
1916	3	14	10		40	31	40	28	1,127	1,266	36	79	58		34	17
1917	3	14	10		40	41	43	28	1,138	1,290	67		18	2	17	6
1918	3	14	4		51	34	47	29	1,143	1,304	66	20	39		24	9
1919	3	14	1		52	37	46	26	1,135	1,296	50	2	44		16	
1920	3	16	3		60	31	46	25	1,125	1,287	32	11	34		12	6
1921	3	16	6	1	61	31	46	25	1 124	1,287	75		30	37	7	1
1922	3	17	6	1	80	32	45	37	1,189	1,383	55	78	18		15	4
1923	3	17	5	2	84	33	51	38	1,202	1,408	65	3	26		14	3
1924	3	17	7	4	78	27	39	33	1,187	1,364	102		13	114	14	5
1925	3	17	8	2	78	34	34	36	1 190	1,373	80		11	36	18	6
1926	3	17	15		84	36	37	41	1,201	1,400	57	1	13		15	3
											8.373	826	3,437	1,491	852	2,019

INDEX

The * denotes portraits and other illustrations.

35

ERRATA

Page	Line	
156	14	Strike out "grants".
183	33	Chapter 45, not 44.
184	6	B. S. Kimball, not B. L. Kimball.
187	45	(Second column) Chapter 46, not 45.
223	12	Should read: "Larsen in the Aalborg Conference," and not "president of the Skåne Conference".
238	10	(Second column) Should read: "River City, and Peder Nielsen of," and not "Salt Lake City, Ole N. Stohl of".
415	7	Nilsson, and not Nielson.

SCANDINAVIANS IN AMERICA

An Arno Press Collection

Ander, O. Fritiof. **The Cultural Heritage of the Swedish Immigrant:** Selected References. [1956]

Ander, Oscar Fritiof. **T.N. Hasselquist:** The Career and Influence of a Swedish American Clergyman, Journalist and Editor. 1931

Barton, H. Arnold, editor. **Clipper Ship and Covered Wagon:** Essays From the *Swedish Pioneer Historical Quarterly.* 1979

Blegen, Theodore C. and Martin B. Ruud, editors and translators. **Norwegian Emigrant Songs and Ballads.** Songs harmonized by Gunnar J. Maimin. 1936

Christensen, Thomas Peter. **A History of the Danes in Iowa.** 1952

Duus, Olaus Fredrik. **Frontier Parsonage:** The Letters of Olaus Fredrik Duus, Norwegian Pastor in Wisconsin, 1855-1858. Translated by the Verdandi Study Club of Minneapolis. Edited by Theodore C. Blegen. 1947

Erickson, E. Walfred. **Swedish-American Periodicals:** A Selective Bibliography. 1979

Gjerset, Knut. **Norwegian Sailors in American Waters:** A Study in the History of Maritime Activity on the Eastern Seaboard. 1933

Gjerset, Knut. **Norwegian Sailors on the Great Lakes:** A Study in the History of American Inland Transportation. 1928

Hale, Frederick. **Trans-Atlantic Conservative Protestantism in the Evangelical Free and Mission Covenant Traditions** (Doctoral Thesis, The Johns Hopkins University, 1976, Revised Edition). 1979

Hogland, A. William. **Finnish Immigrants in America:** 1880-1920. 1960

Hokanson, Nels. **Swedish Immigrants in Lincoln's Time.** With a Foreword by Carl Sandberg. 1942

Hummasti, Paul George. **Finnish Radicals in Astoria, Oregon, 1904-1940:** A Study in Immigrant Socialism (Doctoral Dissertation, University of Oregon, 1975, Revised Edition). 1979

Hustvedt, Lloyd. **Rasmus Bjørn Anderson:** Pioneer Scholar. 1966

Jenson, Andrew. **History of the Scandinavian Mission.** 1927

Kolehmainen, John I. **Sow the Golden Seed:** A History of the Fitchburg (Massachusetts) Finnish American Newspaper, Raivaaja, (The Pioneer), 1905-1955. 1955

Kolehmainen, John I. and George W. Hill. **Haven in the Woods:** The Story of the Finns in Wisconsin. 1965

Koren, Elisabeth. **The Diary of Elisabeth Koren:** 1853-1855. Translated and Edited by David T. Nelson. 1955

Larson, Esther Elisabeth. **Swedish Commentators on America, 1638-1865:** An Annotated List of Selected Manuscript and Printed Materials. 1963

Lindeström, Peter. **Geographia Americae With An Account of the Delaware Indians.** 1925

Marzolf, Marion Tuttle. **The Danish Language Press in America** (Doctoral Dissertation, the University of Michigan, 1972). 1979

McKnight, Roger. **Moberg's Emigrant Novels and the *Journals* of Andrew Peterson:** A Study of Influences and Parallels (Doctoral Thesis, the University of Minnesota, 1974). 1979

Mattson, Hans. **Reminiscences:** The Story of an Immigrant. 1891

Mortenson, Enok. **Danish-American Life and Letters:** A Bibliography. 1945

Nelson, Helge. **The Swedes and the Swedish Settlements in North America.** 1943. 2 vols. in 1

Nielson, Alfred C. **Life in an American Denmark.** 1962

Olson, Ernst W., Anders Schon and Martin J. Engberg, editors. **History of the Swedes of Illinois.** 1908. 2 vols.

Puotinen, Arthur Edwin. **Finnish Radicals and Religion in Midwestern Mining Towns,** 1865-1914 (Doctoral Dissertation, the University of Chicago, 1973). 1979

Raaen, Aagot. **Grass of the Earth:** Immigrant Life in the Dakota Country. 1950

Scott, Franklin D. **Trans-Atlantica:** Essays on Scandinavian Migration and Culture. 1979

Strombeck, Rita. **Leonard Strömberg—A Swedish-American Writer** (Doctoral Thesis, the University of Chicago, 1975, Revised Edition). 1979

Svendsen, Gro. **Frontier Mother:** The Letters of Gro Svendsen. Translated and edited by Pauline Farseth and Theodore C. Blegen. 1950

Vogel-Jorgensen, T[homas]. **Peter Lassen Af California.** 1937

Waerenskjold, Elise. **The Lady with the Pen:** Elise Waerenskjold in Texas. Edited by C.A. Clausen with a foreword by Theodore C. Blegen. 1961

Weintraub, Hyman. **Andrew Furuseth:** Emancipator of the Seamen. 1959

Winther, Sophus Keith. **Mortgage Your Heart.** 1937